JESUITS
A MULTIBIOGRAPHY

De Gaulle: The Rebel 1890–1944
De Gaulle: The Ruler 1945–1970
Pierre Mendès-France
François Mauriac
Léon Blum
André Malraux
Nasser
The Demigods: Charismatic Leadership in the Third World
Ho Chi Minh

JESUITS

A MULTIBIOGRAPHY

Jean Lacouture

TRANSLATED BY JEREMY LEGGATT

COUNTERPOINT

WASHINGTON, D.C.

English translation by Jeremy Leggatt and editing
copyright © 1995 by Counterpoint

First published in French in 1991 and 1992 by Éditions du Seuil
under the title *Jésuites: Une Multibiographie*
Copyright © October 1991 and October 1992, Éditions du Seuil

We gratefully acknowledge permission to reprint from *A Pilgrim's
Journey: The Autobiography of Ignatius of Loyola*, translated by Joseph N.
Tylenda, S.J., copyright © 1991 by The Order of St. Benedict, Inc.
Published by The Liturgical Press, Collegeville, Minnesota.

Library of Congress Cataloging-in-Publication Data
Lacouture, Jean.
[Jésuites. English]
Jesuits: a multibiography / Jean Lacouture;
translated from the French by Jeremy Leggatt.
"A Cornelia and Michael Bessie book."
Includes bibliographical references.
1. Jesuits—History. 2. Jesuits—Biography. I. Title.
BX3706.2.L33   1995
271'.53—dc20   95-34002
ISBN 1-887178-05-8 (alk. paper)

FIRST PRINTING
Printed in the United States of America
on acid-free paper that meets the
American National Standards Institute
Z39-48 Standard

Editorial Consultant: Norman MacAfee
Designer: David Bullen

🕭 A CORNELIA AND MICHAEL BESSIE BOOK

COUNTERPOINT
P.O. Box 65793
Washington, D.C. 20035-5793

Distributed by Publishers Group West

CONTENTS

PREFACE

This book, condensed from the two-volume work published in France in 1991 and 1992 under the collective title *Jésuites: Une Multibiographie* (the first volume was called *Les Conquérants* [The Conquerors] and the second *Les Revenants* [The Return]), makes no attempt to present a history of the Company of Jesus; it aims instead to tell the story of certain individual Jesuits, arbitrarily chosen by the author. Since some chapters were relevant only to the French experience, the American publisher (my friend Michael Bessie) and I agreed that some excisions and a certain amount of reshuffling would better meet the expectations of English-speaking readers.

Having reached this decision, we realized that readers of this leaner version might regret the absence of certain developments explored in the French original—in particular, the significant role played in French history by the Jesuit confessors of France's kings. Hearing the confession of an all-powerful monarch was a terrifying task. It was France's Henry IV—a Protestant converted for political reasons to Catholicism (his adherence to the Reformed faith had disqualified him from the throne) who became an ardent Catholic (although not a champion of virtue or conjugal fidelity)—who first requested a Jesuit as spiritual director. Because he knew a Jesuit would turn a deaf ear to his escapades? No. His confessor was lavish with reproaches, but the royal contrition was invariably short-lived.

Equally fleeting was the remorse of Henry's great-grandson Louis XIV, as pious as he was addicted to extra-conjugal liaisons. This raised a problem every year when Easter Communion came around: for the King (like his subjects) could not receive the Host unless unburdened of his sins by confession. Therefore, the King would send his current favorite "to the country," swearing never to see her again; then, his religious duty done, he bid the fair one to return. A cynical strategy, which three successive Jesuit fathers winked at, believing that excommunicating the Sun King would have provoked a schism along English lines. Indeed it poses a tantalizing historical enigma: In what ways would European history have changed if Louis XIV had followed Henry VIII's example?

Given the private lives led by the various kings who bore the name Louis, we must acknowledge that the conduct of their Jesuit confessors between 1603 and 1776 was of a reprehensible opportunism. But from a political point of view we cannot accept the charges that have given birth to the "Black Legend" of a calculating, Machiavellian Jesuitry. It is fairly clear, for example, that Père de La Chaize, the best known of Louis XIV's confessors, was not involved in plotting that huge crime against the French state, the revocation in 1695 of the Edict of Nantes (which had extended protection of French law to Protestants). Revocation was foolish—stripping France of many of her best scientists, sailors, and soldiers. In fact, Père de La Chaize advised against the step. And if the Jesuits have been more or less linked to the physical liquidation of the Jansenist faction (friends of the austere Blaise Pascal and foes of the "soft" faith of the Jesuits), it was not their influence that led to the royal repression: It was Louis XIV's conviction that these severe, intractable men were in spirit "Republican," the French equivalent of Oliver Cromwell's Puritans.

Many French historians, influenced by Protestantism or Jansenism, or swayed by the anti-Jesuit writings of the great nineteenth-century historian Jules Michelet, attribute to the Jesuits—whether as confessors of kings or as teachers of Europe's ruling classes—all the misdeeds of conservatism and counterrevolution. As we shall see, the charge has been fed more by legend than by fact.

But twists of fate, rather than deliberate strategy, have often tied the Company to the most reactionary policies and the most conservative social groups in every country in Europe. The Jesuits thus betrayed the calling of a Society whose objective, set by its founder, had been to amass learning and discover the world "for the greater Glory of God." In other words, to further the Enlightenment.

They saw themselves as pioneers, as trailblazers; and in the sixteenth and seventeenth centuries (and again in the twentieth) they often were these things. But circumstances beyond their control, thirst for power, and attacks showered on them by "liberals" (who might have been their natural allies) sometimes made of them not the engines but the brakes of history, particularly in nineteenth-century Europe.

The four-hundred-year evolution of the Society of Jesus, which with 25,000 members scattered around the world is now Christendom's most powerful religious order, teaches us that in the order of human events (the only order we are concerned with here), intentions do not always shape the acts they engender or the results that ensue—but that in God's eyes man himself is responsible for what Christians call salvation. Because, in the final analysis, he is free.

Why did the author spend so many months resurrecting this extraordinary company of priests? Because he saw in them discoverers of worlds, of peoples, of diverse civilizations. Because he saw them as culture-gobblers, passionate enough about the human animal in all its contradictions to make of themselves "all things to all men." Because he saw in them defeated conquerors caught in the net of a dialogue without an end, if not without finality. Man—seen in a certain light—is perhaps more than the sum of his acts. But whoever attempts, for better or worse, to harvest the most significant characteristics of the history of this Company must acknowledge the overpowering part played by initiative and striving in an enterprise that the Jesuits—*ad majorem Dei gloriam*—stamped upon the raw, intractable clay of life.

As for the relevance of those labors to our own day, the author has observed that they update themselves spontaneously. If we agree that two of the most urgent problems facing the world today are rooted first in relations between a wealthy "North" and a "South" apparently doomed to famine and anarchy; and second in the linkage of politics to religion, in the growing dominance of human affairs by priestly hierarchies, then we can safely say that the Company Ignatius of Loyola founded in 1540 still has much to tell us. For it has often raised its voice in both areas, justly and unjustly, at the right and the wrong times. And it has paid dearly, in Japan, China, Paraguay, Rome, Paris, and San Salvador, for monumental mistakes or for transformative acts of daring.

The purpose of this book is not to seek lessons for our time from the passing centuries, from the Japan of the *daimyos* to the dissensions arising from rigid Jesuit obedience to the Vatican. Nevertheless, lessons have surfaced in the course of the author's research, lessons of benefit to himself, if not necessarily to his readers. Lessons about the contribution of the Jesuits—perennially ready to acknowledge the manifold validity of diverse cultures (if not faiths)—to the art of human relations. Lessons springing from the part they played not only in the extension of spiritual freedom but also in the liquidation of that most totalitarian of Catholic axioms: "No salvation outside the Church."

The author will rightly be faulted for not addressing certain themes, people, and events central to the Jesuit story—such as Roberto de Nobili's work in India, that of the Fathers in Quebec, and of Jacques Marquette on the Mississippi. Or their contribution to the blossoming of baroque art, their part in our acknowledgment of Muslim spirituality, their actions in the Slavic world after 1820, their participation in attempts at reform in the Philippines, and above all their contribution to the great adventure of the worker-priests following the

Second World War. The author's only excuse for these failings is the dispropor-
tion between his means and the vastness of his task.

As for the thanks traditionally offered at such times, the author believes he
owes too much to men sworn to humility to differentiate between one and another, between the novice in Avignon and the "General" in Rome. Along the way
he will have confirmed that, while the Jesuits do not shrink from ostentation, as
the proud façades of their churches and most of their colleges proclaim, their
concern to serve the greater glory of God does not allow them to hide the darker
side of their history—any more than it impels them to veil that history's luminous passages.

JEAN LACOUTURE

JESUITS

A MULTIBIOGRAPHY

·1·

THE VAGABOND
AND THE INQUISITOR

*A World Bursting Its Seams • In the Cannon's Mouth • A Mule
Points the Way • A Cave in Manresa • The Spiritual Exercises •
Expulsion from Jerusalem • Burning to Study • The Alumbrado of
Alcalá • Paris, Cradle of the Arts*

A LAME MAN PULLED himself along the banks of the Llobregat River, on the *camino real* from Manresa to Barcelona in northeastern Spain. He was alone. Behind him loomed the jagged organ-pipe formations of the Montserrat range, their sandstone columns rising toward heaven like so many severed stumps.

Small and horribly thin, he wore a skimpy sackcloth tunic as rough as a hairshirt. One of his frail hands gripped a weighty staff. Across his shoulder hung a leather satchel. On his right foot was a rope-soled sandal. His left was bare and bloody.

A strange face. A ship's prow of a nose, sharp cheekbones, a broad forehead fringed with fiery red curls.* The eyes burned as fiercely as a forge in their deep sockets. The face, bony, lopsided, scorched-looking, was framed in a russet beard—a flint giving off wild sparks.

John the Baptist splashing through the shallows of the Jordan must have aroused the same astonishment in the Hebrews as this vagabond stirred in the good folk of Catalonia whose path he crossed—much as the startled citizens of Arles, centuries later, must have watched Van Gogh shamble sun-struck and

---

*Traditional iconography gives him dark brown hair, but descriptions of the young Loyola at the court of Castile speak of his "fair locks."

crazed toward Saint-Rémy. Was this wild redheaded man possessed? It was a time when the wanderer, the vagabond, and the solitary wayfarer could still be taken for the Devil.

Iñigo López de Loyola, lame Iñigo, was hobbling to Jerusalem. In his cast-off habit, his manner borrowed from the Christianity of the Crusades, he was embarked on the most uncertain of journeys, bound for the Holy Sepulcher in Jerusalem. But his true rendezvous lay far beyond, with a humankind from which no man was excluded and in which no man was cursed, with a boundless world, and with a created being that would no longer see itself as the Creator's mistake but as a daring project whose fulfillment would also be his own lifework—man. In short, as he limped toward what we now know as humanism, our gaunt sackcloth-clad pilgrim was leaving the Middle Ages and entering the new world of the Renaissance.

Nothing is more futile than attempting to draw a frontier between two ages. The fourteenth century had crackled with pre-Renaissance signals. The sixteenth would ring with echoes of medieval civilization. And the last decade of the fifteenth century, with almost everything either in exuberant flux or coming hesitantly into bloom, could credibly be said to mark a threshold between the two ages.

In those ten years the world grew vast, and humanity stepped to center stage. For more than ten centuries that world had been identified with Christianity, with European Christendom. Beyond were infidels, barbarians, Turks, wild beasts. Suddenly frontiers faded, swept away by the winds that drove the Spanish caravels westward and the Portuguese galleons south and east. Nor was it only Columbus, Vasco da Gama, and Magellan who opened up space for the denizens of the planet—Copernicus was already revealing to them that they were but passengers aboard one vessel in a numberless armada.

When Iñigo de Loyola came into the world in 1491, Erasmus was twenty-five, Machiavelli twenty-two, Copernicus eighteen, Michelangelo sixteen, Thomas More eleven, and Luther had just turned seven. The very next year, along with the gold and limitless prospects of America, Columbus presented the keys of the world to the Catholic sovereigns of Spain. And perhaps the clearest signal that an era was over went up in Florence: There, the medieval execution of Savonarola at the stake closed one century but opened the way for the New Man, second chancery secretary Niccolò Machiavelli—while Erasmus, casting off his monk's habit, settled in a Paris where Guillaume Budé was struggling to introduce the teaching of Greek. The inventors of the future were now in place.

It was against this shifting backcloth that the son of the lords of Loyola now entered the lists. Throughout Loyola's life, the forces of modernity would sporadically but steadily push back medieval tradition. Everything binding him to the Middle Ages—aristocratic truculence, feudal tribalism, belief based on fear—would gradually give way before the thrust of inner and outer forces, the quest for knowledge, the awareness of freedom. The urge to seize the world in both hands. And at the end of it all (but not without reservations and setbacks) the worldwide triumph of humanism.

Seen in that light, this seminal life falls into exactly equal halves. The break does not coincide with the 1521 "conversion" of squire-courtier Iñigo, shattered by a war that first of all saw him limping in the footsteps of his Basque forebears and the Crusaders, launching himself into the frenzied asceticism of Catalonia and pilgrimage to Palestine. No, the break occurs on his return in 1524 from the Holy Land, when he decided, near Venice, to "study." It was then that the unkempt wanderer was transformed into the student who would soon be accused of Erasmianism. It was then that the extreme acts of mortification of the visionary of Manresa turned into long nights of study, into the systematic conquest of learning. It was then that God's beggar became first a man in search of human structures and then a master of the art of the possible.

Thus it was that in 1524 "his" Middle Ages were receding before the combined forces of knowledge and of new social norms. Fascinated by humanism, in which he thought he had found a way of reaching "souls," Iñigo López de Oñaz y Loyola became, perhaps despite himself, a precursor of modern times.

He was thirty-three. Europe was in a fever, as if unhinged by the realization that it was no longer alone in the world but was surrounded by infinite space, by half-glimpsed empires. In this dizzying perspective it looked vainly for guidance. For the Habsburg kings, through inheritance, marriage, musket-play, and colonial conquest, now saw themselves in a position to restore the Holy Roman Empire—and to their own advantage. This was of course unacceptable to the Tudors, the Valois, and the Pope (not to mention the German Protestant princes and the Turks). Once Charles V, Henry VIII, Francis I, and Julius II were all enthroned, permanent warfare ensued. It would lay the whole of Europe waste.

All except for Spain, where a golden age (both figuratively and literally) now dawned. Isabella and Ferdinand presided (at least in Castile) over an order unrivaled in the rest of Europe. Their powerful state machinery was underwritten by the "gold of the Indies," which filled the chests of the sovereign at Valladolid, paid his armies, manned his fleets. Victors over the Moors, conquerors of America, masters of the Low Countries, with firm footholds in Italy and Central Europe, Their Most Catholic Majesties were on the verge of consolidating world hegemony.

But however powerful, however wealthy, Spain* in the early sixteenth century had its problems. Castile's population was dwindling, and the surrounding provinces or kingdoms, Aragon, Catalonia, and Galicia, were turbulent, unsafe, and plagued by *bandoleros,* gangs of pillagers against whom pilgrims and traveling merchants were virtually defenseless.

As for Navarre and Guipúzcoa—the womb that produced the first two Jesuit saints, Loyola and Francis Xavier—they were crippled by violent inter-clan rivalries, while externally they were pawns in intractable feuds between the kings north and south of the Pyrenees. In those quarrels the Loyolas and the Xaviers asserted their rights and sometimes clashed by sword, with legal writ, and through seizure of Church property.

Throughout this period the Catholic Church—ruled successively by a Borgia (Alexander VI), a Medici (Leo X), and a Farnese (Paul III)—was a morass of iniquity. No one knew this better than the Medici Lorenzo the Magnificent of Florence, who arranged his son's marriage to the Pope's daughter and who (a notable expert on the matter) saw Rome as the "den of all vices." From his journey there in 1510, Martin Luther had drawn his own well-known conclusions. And from the palaces of Rome the ecclesiastical free-for-all had radiated out to the poorest parishes of Navarre, where church positions were up for grabs, and people would kill to get one.

But Spain was spared this leprosy, or at least sought its cure: not that those "Catholic" sovereigns Isabella and Ferdinand crowned their administrative achievements with an overarching sanctity. Far from it . . . But Spanish Catholicism possessed a dignity that could not be wholly tarnished by the horrors of an Inquisition at that time bent on hunting down converts from Judaism.

It might seem surprising that Spain, all innovation and native reform, did not remain the seat and springboard of the purifying mission that this youngest of the lords of Loyola was contemplating. But no! It was the Roman institution—shamelessly manipulated by simoniac pontiffs festooned with quarrelsome bastards, greedy mistresses, and twelve-year-old cardinals—that catalyzed the energy and faith of the dozen or so adventurers who were to found the Society of Jesus. An enigma that "men of little faith" are still trying to unravel.

To dedicate yourself to the magnification of Christ's glory was doubtless a noble endeavor. But to do so in a Rome teeming with the bullyboys and procuresses of the Borgias and the Medicis, and—in a sort of explosion of papalist exaltation—to place "the honor of God" in the hands of the purveyors of vice, to do this was to set a mysterious, baroque, almost defiant seal on the origins of this vast undertaking.

*A term of convenience. "The Two Spains"—Aragon in the east, Castile in the west—would be more accurate.

But paradox has been seen time and again to lie at the very heart of the Jesuit enterprise. And Ignatius and his first companions—men ablaze like torches—sought freedom through the most provocative kind of obedience, at a time when the Protestants were placing their own rebellion at the service of predestination.

The *Autobiography*, dictated by the founder thirty years later to Luis Gonçalvez da Câmara and written in the third person, is regally terse on the subject of his stormy youth: "Up to his twenty-sixth year* he was a man given to worldly vanities, and having a vain and overpowering desire to gain renown, he found special delight in the exercise of arms."[1] Since then, historians, storytellers, and biographers have elaborated on the childhood, teens, and early manhood of the young lord of Loyola, before he became the vagabond in sackcloth limping toward Jerusalem.

At the end of the fifteenth century, Azpeitia—five or six leagues from Donostia (San Sebastián) and the Bidassoa River—was just a hamlet huddled at the foot of a Basque mountain, Izarraïtz, overlooking the Urola Valley, a swollen stream lined with walnut, apple, and chestnut trees. A backwater, but a charming one.

Here the Loyolas (whether they went by that name or the clan name of Oñaz) ruled over a small peasant population. Petty squires? No. Rather, lords of the manor, *parientes mayores* who—particularly since the thirteenth century—had brilliantly and not unprofitably served the crown of Castile, weaving strong ties between Valladolid, the seat of power, and this region of Guipúzcoa, already a byword for turbulence, if not outright dissidence. The clan's culture was Basque, its ways were unruly, its traditions violent—and its collective piety most bountiful.

The last male heir and thirteenth child of Beltrán and Marina de Loyola† was given the Basque name Eneko, which translates into Spanish as Iñigo.‡ It was only forty-three years later, in Paris, when he was about to be named bachelor of arts, that the youngest Loyola chose the Christian name Ignatius. His birth date has given rise to endless argument, since there were no Azpeitia parish registers before 1537. In his *Autobiography*, he situates his "conversion"—which occurred, beyond any possible doubt, in 1521—in his twenty-sixth year. Which would indicate that he was born in 1495. But the youngest Loyola's nurse gave the date of 1491 to emissaries of the Company, who questioned her after the founder's death. That date is confirmed by the fact that Iñigo was able to sign

*For more on this figure, see below.

†There were also apparently two or three illegitimate offspring, who were raised with their half-brothers and sisters.

‡The Basque language does not use the tilde, which, in Castilian, caps the *n* in Inigo.

legal documents at the time of his father's death in 1507—which would have been forbidden if he had been under sixteen.

By faithfully serving the crown of Castile (four of Beltrán's sons had fought for Catholic monarchs under far-flung skies, from the Lowlands to Naples—where two of them died—to the Americas), the Loyolas had also served Ignatius well. Their self-sacrifice and loyalty earned them the royal favor. On his father's death, Iñigo was summoned by a person of considerable substance, the Contado Mayor, or Finance Minister, of Queen Isabella. He was Don Juan Velázquez de Cuéllar, who resided in Arévalo, a small Castilian city between Valladolid, the political capital, and Salamanca, the cultural metropolis. The Velázquez family was, in fact, related on the female side to the Loyolas.

By taking Iñigo under his wing, Don Juan offered an unhoped-for opportunity, in the innermost corridors of power (he was the executor of Queen Isabella's will), to a youngest son penned in by the mists of his remote native mountains. As a small child, Iñigo had been tonsured, and thereby promised to a life in the Church—like his brother Pedro, the family ne'er-do-well, who had been assured the parish of Azpeitia. The best ecclesiastical place being thus spoken for and the youngest son's vocation being highly uncertain, his mother had decided to "give" him to Velázquez, in other words to the government. A boundless future!

Iñigo was sixteen. He was slender and short and walked with chest thrust forward. His fair locks tumbled to his shoulders. A bold gaze, a firm waist, and muscular Basque calves hardened by stalking the Pyrenean chamois. All in all, a young man destined for a great career, sword in hand, in the service of the man who controlled the regime's exchequer. Was he already a D'Artagnan? Was he a page, as is widely believed? Sixteen was precisely the age when youthful courtiers were dubbed "page," a subordinate rank calling for decidedly assiduous pursuit of the ladies of the court. Could he have been a squire? It was perhaps more likely that he served as a secretary, at least during the second phase of his ten-year stay at Arévalo. And it was probably the performance of these functions that gave him the calligraphic talents he would boast of to his dying day, and which would play a part in his spiritual life.

Page, squire, or secretary—in any case, he was what used to be called a gay blade. Two of his closest confidants, his successor Diego Laínez and his secretary Juan de Polanco, have left us an eloquent glimpse of those early days. "Although attached to his faith," wrote Polanco, "he did not live his life in conformity with it, nor did he avoid sin; he was particularly given to gambling and to female matters, as well as to brawling and the exercise of arms." And Laínez, more forthright, said: "He was tempted and overcome by the pitfalls of the flesh."

Swashbuckler, gambler, skirt-chaser? This russet-locked Iñigo certainly seems to have been a most disreputable character. Whenever he returned to his birth-place from Arévalo, he "scandalized the good folk of Azpeitia with his unruly ways." Ways that at least once took criminal form: In 1515 (when he was twenty-four), Iñigo de Loyola was charged with crimes pronounced "muy enormes . . . cometido . . . de noche y de proposito . . . sobre asechanza y alevosamente" (most monstrous crimes, committed by night and by premeditation, through ambush and treachery).

From the few documents available to historians, it does not seem that the court sought Iñigo's death. Was it a moral scandal, perhaps an abduction? The offense occurred during carnival. Was it a brawl over the Azpeitia position, from which his brother Pedro was impatient to expel the incumbent, a certain Juan de Anchieta? The abduction of an ecclesiastic for blackmail purposes? In any case, a "muy enorme" crime.

Having received the tonsure at an early age, and confident in the multiple safeguards the feudal system afforded the well-born, Iñigo de Loyola fled to Pamplona, escaping the civil courts and giving himself up to Church justice—which, despite the protests of the royal authorities, released him after a short prison term. Few men have undergone such intense self-mortification as Saint Ignatius. But many others would have paid much more dearly than he did for that obscure misdeed in Azpeitia.

At that point, our Iñigo may have been far from heaven, but he was close in spirit to the heroes of chivalry. In one of his confidential footnotes, the man who took down Loyola's dictated *Autobiography* shows us Iñigo dreaming of the exploits he might accomplish "in the service of a certain lady [who] was by no means of the lesser nobility: neither countess nor duchess, but of even higher estate."[2]

But despite what has often been written, perhaps under the influence of the Romantic movement, we must abandon the notion that the Queen herself was the object of this passion. Germaine de Foix, King Ferdinand's second wife, was (says the chronicle) "obese and given to drink." Iñigo's fair lady was more probably Princess Catalina, or Catherine, sister of Charles V, whom their mother Joan the Mad (Juana la Loca) kept sequestered with her at Tordesillas. King Ferdinand, accompanied by Juan Velázquez and his household (to which the Loyola boy belonged), often called on her. How could Iñigo not have dreamed of the captive Infanta, her charms the more moving for being so rarely glimpsed?

And Doña Catalina was to play a more substantial part in the life of the youngest Loyola: From the very beginning, as wife of King John III of Portugal, she would be one of the staunchest supporters of the Company of Jesus. Further proof that the ways of the Lord are inscrutable, and that worldly vanities may also serve the ends of the founders of orders.

* * *

But everything suddenly collapsed in 1516, when Ferdinand's death stripped the all-powerful Contado Mayor of royal favor. Ferdinand's grandson Charles, the future Emperor Charles V, did not simply replace the grand treasurer—he also planned to remove his Arévalo fief and give it to the late king's widow. Refusing to bend, his great vassal made an angry but futile attempt at rebellion. In 1517 Don Juan died, leaving his followers destitute. But his widow, Doña Maria, offered one last proof of her attachment to Iñigo, entrusting him to her cousin Don Antonio Manrique de Lara, Duke of Najéra, Viceroy of Navarre, and acknowledged suzerain of the Oñaz clan.

This sudden reversal of fortune must have made the strongest of impressions on the young man who, at twenty-six, was now obliged to leave Arévalo. But Iñigo apparently kept happy memories of those ten years in Castile, where he had acquired a taste for music that never faded and where he had dabbled in verse. It was also in Castile that this son of Azpeitia bumpkins had acquired "manners"—which, when he was Padre Maestro Ignacio in Rome, led a visitor to remember him as "the most courteous and the politest of men" and which gave him "a dignity eminently worthy of the court."[3]

So here he was, secretary-turned-squire, in Pamplona, capital of Navarre. The refinements of courtly love, of the viola da gamba, of silk doublet and hose, were gone. Blessed or cursed with unruly subjects, the Viceroy of Navarre first and foremost required swordsmanship from his followers.

Navarre had been attached to Castile only nine years earlier, and perhaps it longed for the freedom it had once enjoyed as an overlooked corner of France's sphere of influence. In this particular year its new status suddenly came under threat. Scarcely was the future Emperor Charles V crowned King of Castile than the citizens, jealous of their local prerogatives, rose against him. Francis I of France needed no further excuse to try to undermine his Spanish rival.

On May 12, 1521, thirteen thousand Franco-Navarrese troops marched up from Bidassoa and pitched camp under the battlements of Pamplona. Ordered by the Viceroy to hold the city, the garrison commander had scarcely a thousand fighting men, among them Iñigo. Deciding he could not hold off his attackers, he left the stronghold, followed by the eldest Loyola, Martín, who had meanwhile arrived from his village. Iñigo, ashamed at "appearing to run away,"[4] took refuge in the citadel beside its commander, the *alcaide* (governor) Miguel de Herrera—while the townsfolk, reluctant to be caught in the crossfire between besiegers and besieged, were swearing fealty to the invading side. Herrera then proposed parleying with the French. But Iñigo de Loyola pointed out that the Viceroy might soon send reinforcements and that in any case the conditions imposed by the attackers—surrender followed by the garrison's disciplined withdrawal—were demeaning: His advice was to fight.

So the courtier-secretary-diplomat now played the role of diehard defender, a man resolved not to give an inch. He was fully aware that the struggle was hopeless: The attackers enjoyed overwhelming superiority in men and in artillery pieces. But we could not mention this crucial episode in Iñigo's life without quoting his own vivid version of the event:

> Thus he was in a fortress under attack by the French, and while everyone else clearly saw that they could not defend themselves and thought that they should surrender to save their lives, he offered so many reasons to the fortress's commander that he talked them into defending it. Though this was contrary to the opinion of all the other knights, still each drew encouragement from his firmness and fearlessness. When the day of the expected assault came he made his confession to one of his comrades in arms and after the attack had lasted a good while,* a cannonball hit him in a leg, shattering it completely, and since the ball passed between both legs, the other one was likewise severely wounded.[5]

With his right tibia splintered and his left calf carried away, Iñigo de Loyola was supine on the battlements when the attackers entered the fortress. Perhaps because of his birth, he was shown "courtesy and kindness" by the victors. Having cared for him on the spot as best they could for two weeks, "they transported him on a litter to his home country."[6]

It is something like thirty miles from Pamplona to Azpeitia. The litter bearers took more than ten days to cover the distance, moving from pathway to pathway on steep mountainsides. Iñigo must have died a thousand deaths,† but his agony was only just beginning. When they reached the Casa y Solar he was put to bed in a big corner room on the third floor,‡ where he was visited by every surgeon in the district, including his fellow Azpeitian, Martín de Iztiola. The latter was forced to conclude that despite their "courtesy," the victors had not operated very skillfully on the wounded man—unless the hardships of the trek had spoiled their handiwork. It was "agreed that the leg should be broken again and the bones reset," Iñigo recalled, and the "butchery was repeated."[7] The word he used was *carnicería*, the crudest term he could find to describe the operation at a time when anesthesia was unknown. And proud of his stoicism, he added, "As in other such operations that he had undergone before and would later undergo, he never uttered a word nor did he show any sign of pain other than clenching his fists."[8]

A few days later he was at death's door. After the last rites were administered on the feast of Saint Peter, he prayed for the founding apostle's intervention—

*Six hours, it is believed.
†There is a statue commemorating the episode, and a copy outside the Casa y Solar in Azpeitia.
‡Now carefully restored.

and then attributed to the saint his sudden recovery. But all heaven's saints were unable to dissuade him from a further ordeal in which their role was slight indeed: Once his bones were reset, he realized that one of them overlapped the other so obviously "that it made an unsightly bump. Because he was determined to make a way for himself in the world he could not tolerate such ugliness and thought it marred his appearance."

Unable to accept that he had been rendered thus "unsightly," unable to wear a "close-fitting and elegant boot" (as his first biographer Pedro de Ribadeneira reported), he asked his surgeons if they could not "remove it, if possible."

> They told him that it could certainly be sawn away, but the pain would be greater than any he had suffered up to now, since the leg had healed and it would take some time to remove the bump. Nevertheless, he was determined to endure this martyrdom to satisfy his personal taste. His older brother was horrified and said that he himself would not dare undergo such pain, but the wounded man suffered it with his accustomed patience.[9]

The grisly operation was a success,* but his right leg remained inches shorter than the left. He would limp until the day when, in Rome, he began to wear a higher right heel.

The convalescent was ordered to stay in bed. What to do? He asked his stepsister Magdalena to find him chivalrous tales like the ones he used to read at Arévalo, such as the popular romance *Amadís de Gaula*. But the lords of Loyola had little taste for literature: All that could be unearthed were edifying books, a *Life of Christ* written by a Carthusian father, Ludolph of Saxony, and the *Flos Sanctorum*, or *Anthology of the Saints*, also known as the *Golden Legend*, by Jacopo da Voragine.

These works were not too far distant from the knightly extravaganzas the courtier of Arévalo had delighted in. Through the eyes of Ludolph the monk or the Italian bishop, Christ and Saint Francis, Pilate and the hermits of Sinai became vivid heroes of romance embodying good and evil—the ancestors of today's comic-book heroes. Iñigo found what he sought. Cripple that he was (or as he now saw himself), what chance had he of emulating Amadís or approaching Catherine?

Not that he had given up dreaming of the little Castilian Infanta. The passage of the *Autobiography* devoted to this episode suggests that "a certain lady" continued to haunt the stricken knight, who was still so "enraptured with these thoughts of his that he never considered how impossible it was for him to accomplish them."

But at this point a psychic and affective shift took place—a change that his-

*Martín de Iztiola's fee was thirteen ducats; but Iñigo's eldest brother refused to pay him more than ten.

torian Alain Guillermou has very rightly called a *metanoia,* or spiritual conversion. It opened the way to the crucial Ignatian notion of "discernment of spirits." From that "certain lady," from his reading about Amadís and the apostles and Saint Dominic, a new direction, a turnabout, came over Iñigo. But heroism, prowess, spirit, growth (here of glory or honor), the wellspring of his life, remained at the core of this intense interior fusion. Was this progress? Transformation? We must leave the description of this decisive journey to Iñigo himself:

> Thus in his thoughts he dwelt on many good deeds, always suggesting to himself great and difficult ones, but as soon as he considered doing them, they all appeared easy of performance. Throughout these thoughts he used to say to himself: "Saint Dominic did this, so I have to do it too. Saint Francis did this, so I have to do it too." These thoughts lasted a long time, but [then] worldly ones returned to him and he dwelt on them for quite some length. This succession of such diverse thoughts—of worldly exploits that he desired to accomplish, or those of God that came to his imagination—stayed with him for a long time as he turned them over in his mind, and when he grew weary of them he set them aside to think of other matters.
>
> There was this difference, however. When he thought of worldly matters he found much delight, but after growing weary and dismissing them he found that he was dry and unhappy. But when he thought of going barefoot to Jerusalem and of eating nothing but vegetables and of imitating the saints in all the austerities they performed, he not only found consolation in these thoughts but even after they had left him he remained happy and joyful. He did not consider nor did he stop to examine this difference until one day his eyes were partially opened and he began to wonder at this difference and to reflect upon it. From experience he knew that some thoughts left him sad while others made him happy, and little by little he came to perceive the different spirits that were moving him; one coming from the devil, the other coming from God.[10]

It all seems to be there, and said with stunning simplicity: If among these "spirits" he discerned on the one hand those born of Satan, and on the other those born of God, it was because his musings on the *hazañas mundanas* left him "weary," "dry," "unhappy," while thoughts of the *hazañas de Dios* left him "joyful" and "happy." Whence it seems that Iñigo de Loyola, the future barefoot pilgrim, the future beggar of God, the future author of *The Spiritual Exercises,* turned toward the *hazañas de Dios* because he felt more at ease in them, more "joyful" (and the Castilian for joy, *alegría,* is a powerful word!) than when he let himself dream about Princess Catherine.

And thus we slip from the theme of pleasure in God to that of giving pleasure to God, to penance, to pain—and here the episode of the leg operation comes again to mind: "he was determined to endure this martyrdom to satisfy his personal taste." Was this masochism or hedonism? We must be circumspect in our handling of such terms and such ideas.

The sick man in the Casa y Solar now reached a decision around which his whole life would be built: He would journey to Jerusalem, forcing himself to "observe the fasts and to practice the discipline as any generous soul on fire with God is accustomed to do."

On fire with God? How could he any longer doubt it, now that he saw himself granted a "spiritual visitation" of decisive consequences:

> One night, as he lay sleepless, he clearly saw the likeness of Our Lady with the Holy Child Jesus, and because of this vision he enjoyed an excess of consolation for a remarkably long time. He felt so great a loathesomeness for all his past life, especially for the deeds of the flesh [*cosas de carne*], that it seemed to him that all the images that had been previously imprinted on his mind were now erased. Thus from that hour until August 1553, when this is being written, he never again consented, not even in the least matter, to the motions of the flesh.[11]

Is this a vision to be viewed with suspicion, exacerbating as it does the hatred of self he had conceived? This is certainly not the last time we will be asking this kind of question, although we should note that—in describing a "spiritual visitation" that kindled an "excess of consolation" in him—Iñigo himself had healthy doubts about the origin of the phenomenon. Was it "God's doing"? One might think so, he soberly adds, given the "effect in him." But he refrained from proclaiming a miracle. Simply an "interior change."

He longed to leave, to decamp for Jerusalem. But he was still too weak, his leg still too badly scarred. He therefore spent several months, proud of his calligrapher's talents, copying out fragments of his readings—in which, according to Ludolph and Voragine, Christ or the Virgin spoke—covering great quarto parchment sheets with his beautiful hand: three hundred pages, he tells us, with Jesus' words written in red and Mary's in blue. At nightfall he contemplated sky and stars, from which he drew his "greatest consolation."

A consolation so powerful that it finally spurred him to depart, his right leg still heavily bandaged. When his brother Martín tried to prevent him from leaving, to deter his younger brother from his obvious obsession with worldly renunciation, he was able, as he recalls, "without departing from the truth, for he was by now very scrupulous about that, [to answer] in a way that enabled him to slip away from his brother." Thus, as February 1522 came to an end, Iñigo said farewell to the Casa y Solar where he had so cruelly suffered and where, for strong but still equivocal reasons, he had elected to exchange one order of chivalry for another, to exchange courtly love for love of God, to exchange the ample benefits of the feudal condition for poverty on the road to Jerusalem.

A convert, no two ways about it. But from what to what? The courtier of Arévalo was no longer either the roustabout fleeing justice or the Infanta's knight-errant or the lord of Najera's squire or the indomitable defender of Pamplona. He was about to proclaim himself a pilgrim, to become first a vagabond and then a hermit visionary. He had slipped his moorings and was heading toward an elsewhere that he situated among "las cosas de Dios" and summed up in the single obsessive, haunting word: Jerusalem.

As he rode his mule from Rioja toward Aragón he was overtaken by a Moor, also on muleback, one of those Moors who had chosen to convert in order to escape the proscriptions of 1492. He was enough of a convert to fall into conversation and hold his own on the burning question of Mary's virginity. This "New Christian" was of an accommodating bent. He was perfectly willing to admit that the Virgin had conceived without the aid of man or the stain of sin. What stuck in his throat was the notion that having given birth she remained a virgin.

You did not have to be a Moor and a brand-new Christian to find the idea puzzling. But Iñigo saw deliberate ill-will. He argued with growing vehemence, so much so that the dark-skinned skeptic took fright: Could this skeletal rider with the burning gaze, harsh voice, and imperious tones be somehow connected to the Inquisition? The Moor abruptly spurred his mule forward, anxious to put a healthy distance between this stormy believer and his own doubts.

Iñigo was left alone to mull darkly over the dispute as his mule plodded onward. He became "disturbed in soul." How could he have allowed this infidel to doubt Our Lady's virtue? How could he, a knight of Loyola, have permitted Mary's honor to be thus questioned? He would have to fight for that "honor," he decided, smite the unbeliever "with his dagger." And he was in a position to do so, for the Moor had immediately confided his destination—a township close to the *camino real*, the main road that led away from the route he was taking. But could he thus—as in the past—surrender to violence?

> Tired of trying to figure out what would be the good thing to do, and
> unable to come to any definite decision, he determined on the following, namely, to give the mule free rein and to let it go by itself to the
> point where the roads met. If the mule took the road to the village,
> he would then search out the Moor and use his dagger on him; if the
> mule took the highway and not the village road, he would then let
> the Moor go scot-free. And he did just as he decided. Our Lord
> brought it about that though the village was little more than twenty

or thirty paces away and the road leading to it was quite wide and in good condition, the mule chose the highway and disregarded the village road.[12]

That admirable mule, its wisdom the instrument of divine wisdom, thus saved the life of a poor Moor as inept at perceiving the virginity of Our Lord's Mother as any run-of-the-mill Archbishop of Canterbury or rabble of Lutheran divines. And what a strange convert—to throw himself upon his mount's judgment (just as good in its way as the Holy Office's ordeal by fire)! Iñigo had merely exchanged one Lady for another, taking up arms for the Virgin Mary rather than the little Infanta: He was still the Basque younger son, elder brother of Cyrano's Gascon cadets, burning with "vain and overpowering desire to gain renown."

But what strikes so deep is not so much what this story tells us about the pilgrim of 1522. It is what it reveals of the grizzled leader who—thirty-two years later, in all his glory as confessor to the world, as "General" of both hemispheres of the planet, as the "Black Pope"—was able to tell this barbaric and delectable fable, tell of the spluttering fury of the future pilgrim, tell of the mule's consecration as God's interpreter. If the knight of Pedrola was still a strange Christian, the General of 1555 was still a simple man.

It was now, before reaching Montserrat, that he pulled on his sackcloth tunic. "It was," he said, "of a loose weave and bristly to the touch." Da Câmara adds that he then purchased rope-soled shoes, "of which he took just one; and this not for style but because he had one leg all tied up with a bandage and somewhat neglected." Remounting his mule, he scaled the heights of Montserrat to the Benedictine monastery where the Virgen Morena, the Black Madonna, was venerated.

There, shut in a cell for three days, he drew up his general confession, delivered in the strictest secrecy (as regarded his name and origins) to a French monk, Jean de Chanon, to whom he then confided his plans: abstinence, absolute poverty, vow of chastity, pilgrimage to the Holy Land.

And then, on March 24, 1552, came the ceremony most closely attuned to the ethical and esthetic spirit of the day—the act of solemn rupture between the knight and the "vainglory" he had already denounced but continued to pursue. It was an act not of investiture but of divestiture, performed at the altar of the Black Virgin, a ceremony in which he stripped himself of all his feudal attributes, hanging his remaining weapons on the chapel railings, drawing on his sackcloth tunic, and kneeling down to pray all night long, a new man.

A splendid poem by Bartolomé Leonardo, "A colgar San Ignacio las armas en Montserrat," evokes the grandeur of his gesture:

> Like a trophy in the temple Ignatius hung his arms
> Beseeching the One who so fired his blood
> To replace them with weapons of His own.

Even so did the young Hebrew shepherd
Set aside his royal trappings—for which act of loyalty
He was granted the pristine stones to cast
At the Philistine's haughty brow.[13]

Here then he stood in his primitive garb, ready for the great journey. He had intended to stop first at Barcelona. But it was not to be. Iñigo's halting steps took him not to the port where Columbus's caravel now slumbers but to "a town called Manresa." There "he decided he would remain for several days in a hospital," in order to restore vigor to his exhausted body and to care for the leg that had swollen continuously over the 190 miles he had covered between Azpeitia and Montserrat. He also wanted to "jot down a few items in the book that he guardedly carried with him and that offered him much consolation."

Strange, his sudden reference to this book. Could he have meant a notebook containing *The Spiritual Exercises* in embryonic form? Or a book Jean de Chanon might have given him, the *Exercitario de la Vida Spiritual* by the abbey's prior, García de Cisneros? This last possibility is an attractive hypothesis. Of course, it calls into question the "revolutionary" originality of the founder of the Jesuits. But what inventor does not draw inspiration from some genius who has gone before?

The fact is that what Iñigo had originally foreseen as a simple halt in Manresa would turn into ten long months, months that would represent an incandescent high point in his spiritual adventure, his inner revolution. Manresa was a psychic upheaval for him, a journey through the flames, the womb of "Ignatianism." He called Manresa his "Early Church."

So far we have focused consistently on Iñigo's beginnings in the Basque squirearchy, on his ten years of subsequent growth at the court of Castile, and his later cultivation of the knightly virtues in Navarre.

So far, through youthful escapades, favors received, and his own self-imposed ordeals, Iñigo has been merely an inheritor more or less visited by grace. But at Manresa he plunged into another world, one of fury, blinding light, turmoil. There was no escape from it except in sanctity or in madness. He would be either freed from or captive of a power that called clearly to him—but from where? From now on—until the final reconquest of self—immoderation, excess, even the "suprarational" would be his daily diet.

Here is his own description of the life he now led, the life of a street dweller assailed by hallucinations:

> He begged alms every day. He ate no meat, nor did he drink wine,
> though both were offered him. On Sundays he did not fast, and if
> someone gave him wine, he drank it. And because he had been quite
> meticulous in caring for his hair, which was according to the fashion

of the day—and he had a good crop of hair—he decided to let it grow naturally without combing, cutting, or covering it with anything either during the day or night. For the same reason he let the nails of his feet and hands grow since he had also been overly neat with regard to them.

His first shelter was a cave on the banks of the Cardoner, a stream that flows through Manresa. His confessor, a Dominican, wanted him to lodge in the Dominican monastery or else sleep at the dingy hospital in Santa Lucia. But neither there nor elsewhere did he feel at peace:

> While living in this hospital it many times happened that in full daylight he saw a form in the air near him and this form gave him much consolation because it was exceedingly beautiful. He did not understand what it really was, but it somehow seemed to have the shape of a serpent and had many things that shone like eyes, but were not eyes. He received much delight and consolation from gazing upon this object . . . but when the object vanished he became disconsolate.

It would be several months before he detected in this "exceedingly beautiful" thing, in this alluring many-eyed serpent, a manifestation of the "evil spirit," which he drove away with his pilgrim's staff "as a mark of his disdain."

In Manresa at that time was an old woman whose reputation for piety was so great that King Ferdinand had once summoned her to visit him. During his stay, Iñigo met her. "May it please my Lord Jesus Christ to appear one day before you!" she said to him. "And why should Jesus Christ appear to me?" he asked in alarm.

For the ten months of his stay in Manresa, he lived through a hurricane of moral doubt, of thirst for confession, of hunger for mortification. He spent his nights in uninterrupted prayer, almost killing himself in the process. He was visited by suicidal urges which tempted him to "throw himself into a deep hole in his room which was near the place where he used to pray." Then he would go for a whole week without eating or drinking, even though his confessor warned him against such follies.

"During this time," he later recalled, "God was dealing with him in the same way a schoolteacher deals with a child while instructing him." A violent teacher, a harsh school, a mad child! But of these drastic times, when his mind almost foundered and his health was permanently ruined, he was willing only to retain the moments of illumination. In later years he discouraged those of his disciples bent on following him along the path of systematic mortification.

The author of the *Autobiography* has left us full descriptions of the phenomena that now assailed him from all sides. In examining those phenomena, skeptics will not be the only ones to ask whether they might be hallucinations brought on by self-inflicted pain and starvation.

One day, as he was saying the hours of Our Lady on the monastery's steps, his understanding was raised on high, so as to see the Most Holy Trinity under the aspect of three keys of a musical instrument, and as a result he shed many tears and sobbed so strongly that he could not control himself. . . . One day it was granted him to understand, with great spiritual joy, the way in which God had created the world. He seemed to see a bright object with rays stemming from it, from which God made light. He neither knew how to explain these things nor did he fully remember the spiritual lights that God had then imprinted on his soul.

During prayer he often, and for an extended period of time, saw with inward eyes the humanity of Christ, whose form appeared to him as a white body, neither very large nor very small; nor did he see any differentiation of members. He often saw this in Manresa; and if he were to say twenty times or forty times, he would not presume to say that he was lying. . . . He also saw Our Lady in similar form, without differentiation of members. These things that he saw at that time fortified him and gave such great support to his faith that many times he thought to himself: if there were no Scriptures to teach us these matters of faith, he would still resolve to die for them on the basis of what he had seen.[14]

To die on the basis of what he had seen . . . *Seen?* That last word of course raises many questions. Was it internal vision or external projection? And do such questions make the slightest sense? What else could these vague, shapeless, almost routine "visions" have been if not the "great support to his faith" vouchsafed to him in his cave, a support that was then more decisive for him than the Scriptures?

It was to yet another experience—this one wholly internalized—that Iñigo would attach the greatest importance: the one his biographers know as "the Cardoner revelation," for it was on banks of this stream that the pilgrim experienced his most blinding "illumination" so far.

That day at the beginning of 1523—it was near the end of his time at Manresa and he had adopted a more moderate way of life, no longer wearing his sackcloth but "two brown-colored jackets, made of very coarse cloth, and a beret of the same material as a cap"—he decided to go and pray in the church of Saint Paul, which overlooked the Cardoner:

The road followed the path of the river and he was taken up with his devotions; he sat down for a while facing the river flowing far below him. As he sat there the eyes of his understanding were opened and though he saw no vision [*no que viese alguna visión*] he understood and perceived many things, numerous spiritual things as well as matters touching on faith and learning, and this was an elucidation so bright that all these things seemed new to him. He cannot expound in detail what he then understood, for they were many things, but he can state that he received such a lucidity in understanding that during the course of his entire life—now having passed his sixty-second year—if he were to gather all the helps he received from God and everything he knew, and add them together, he does not think they would add up to all that he received on that one occasion.[15]

Here, as we have seen, the word "lucidity" takes on strictly intellectual coloring. Not only because this enlightenment was tied to "no vision" but because it was as much involved with secular "learning" as with things spiritual. We are dealing here with the "intellect"—Newton watching the apple fall, Champollion deciphering the hieroglyphs on the Rosetta stone for the first time. And the footnote later tacked on in the *Autobiography* by Gonçalves da Câmara is even more explicit: "Ignatius now understood these truths with such a clarity that even though he had reflected on them in the past they were as totally new to him."

Who could fail to see here a key to the future conduct of the founder of the Company, given that this decisive moment was not simply one of "spiritual ecstasy" but of "intellectual understanding," and that it fused the sacred with the profane? "Everything he knew." The old man in Rome, near death, who indeed "knew" many things—about the century and men and God—gave most of the credit to this illumination of his "intellect." Knowledge first—then "understanding."

From the storm of moral doubts, of "scruples," to that exquisite dawn on the banks of the Cardoner, Iñigo had lived for several months more or less alone in spiritual turmoil, jostled, harried, provoked by quasi-psychiatric "shocks" and "stimuli," prey to "motions" amounting to violent creative impulses. The fruit of this journey through the flames was *The Spiritual Exercises*, his central work, the work through which, for four and a half centuries, he has participated in the lives of countless people seeking asceticism and contact with the divine.

The *Exercises*, first written in rough Latin—the kind of Latin a minor Basque nobleman lightly brushed with the manners of the Castilian court at the turn of the sixteenth century might essay—were not the fruit of a single season. Perhaps sketched in note form at the end of his stay at the Casa y Solar and written out in full in the last six months of the pilgrim's pitiful sojourn in Manresa, they would be continually revised and augmented by the Padre Maestro of Rome until the end of the 1540s. The most reliable authority on the subject, Loyola's first successor, Diego Laínez, would stress that the "substance" of the *Exercises* dated from Manresa.

Iñigo's relationship to the *Exercises* was not that of an author to "his" work. He saw them as revealed, handed down by the Lord, as a prophet would. And above all, he would never propose them for "reading" but for "performing." Neither were they a book or a "diary" or a treatise on spirituality like Thomas à Kempis's *Imitation of Christ* or the rule of an order, but a practical manual.

Once again, the wording is all-important. A term like "exercise"* explains a lot, as does "perform." Everything is dedicated to action, to disciplining both behavior and intellect, and is aimed at great numbers of "exercisers." We should note too that while in practice the founder of the Society of Jesus offered his *Exercises* to strangers, since he considered the manual to be self-contained, he also judged it healthier for an adviser to act as intermediary between exerciser and manual, an adviser concerned with adapting the method to individual temperament and spirituality. This again was a typical way of going about things: adaptation, adjustment, the case-by-case approach.

If the hermit of the Cardoner believed that his method had been inspired to him, dictated by a higher will, he also knew that it was part and parcel of himself, of his flesh, the reflection of his own harrowing experience. There was nothing in it that had not been first lived through, that had not first been exercised upon himself. The four-week action retreat that he urged upon his neighbor was something he himself had lived for nearly eleven months, and those first months had been a long and painful hallucination.

There has been interminable speculation about the influences that inspired Iñigo's method. Two are obvious: *The Imitation* (at that time attributed not to Thomas à Kempis but to Jean Gerson, Chancellor of the University of Paris) and above all the *Exercitario* of García de Cisneros. But the latter was intended for a specific community, the Benedictines at Montserrat, and the former did not aspire to such concrete results. Nevertheless, both works underlay the thinking of our scruffy pilgrim preparing, perhaps unconsciously, to turn into the highly judicious maestro of Rome.

Yes, Rome already . . . What is striking, among the thousand facets of this strange instrument of power that contributed so much to Loyola's image as a "dictator of souls"—a view shared by one of his best biographers, Léon Marcuse[16]—was the docility, or at least the loyalty, he professed for the visible Church. Not even the cynical bacchanalia of Rome (of which he would one day be a most alert witness) could induce him to challenge the papacy—which for him remained the landmark reference, the intangible pole around which "the service of God in the vast world" must revolve.

* * *

*The Spanish word for "exercise" is *ejercicio*, and for "army," *ejército*.

But Jerusalem remained his primary goal. In March 1523, having survived a painful illness that gave proof of the attachment certain residents of Manresa (such as the Ferraras and several ladies "of the first rank") felt for him, he left the banks of the Cardoner and headed for Barcelona. There he sought sea passage, first of all for Italy, to seek the Pope's permission and blessing in Rome.

He spoke no Italian, hardly any Latin, no Arabic. He knew two things only: that he would leave alone, and that he would embark *sin blanca,* without a penny, even when offered as alms, in order "to have only God as his refuge." At length he found a captain willing to take him on board for nothing, but on condition that he bring his own supply of biscuits, for otherwise the crew might fear that he would beg provisions from them. He initially refused ("so much for trust in God!"), but his confessor urged him to accept. He yielded, but only after leaving his few remaining donated coins on a bench by the sea; then he said farewell to the friends he had made during his brief stop in the great Catalan port, Inès Pascual, Isabel Rosell, and their families (we shall meet them all again), and on March 20, 1523, set sail for Gaeta.

We will pass rapidly over his Italian tribulations, the risks of plague, and the attempted rape (foiled by Iñigo's lusty shouts of alarm) of two traveling companions that marked his visit to Rome—a visit that drew from him only a terse mention of the blessing bestowed by Pope Adrian VI—his overland trek, village by village, to Venice, sleeping in doorways, begging ducats, and shortly thereafter giving them away. He spent one night in a field in Padua (where "Christ appeared to him in the way that He usually appeared to him," as he noted with an entirely new brand of nonchalance), and finally arrived in Venice, where he was accosted and taken home by a rich Spaniard who, not content with sheltering this visionary vagabond, introduced him to the doge, Andrea Gritti. The master of the Most Serene Republic may have been surprised at the sight of the wanderer, but he obtained passage for Iñigo aboard the *Negrona,* the "governor's ship," which plied the waters between the city of the Doges and Cyprus, then a Venetian colony.

The day before embarking, the pilgrim fell ill. They purged him. He struggled to get back on his feet. Could he leave for the Holy Land? Yes, answered the physician—"to be buried there." But, once hauled aboard, he recovered his spirits, enough in any case to observe that "openly lewd and obscene behavior" took place on board: He condemned it so vehemently that the crew "considered depositing him on some island or another." Nevertheless he arrived in Cyprus, where the "pilgrim ship" was waiting at dockside; once again he took aboard with him nothing "except his confidence in God." That confidence was repaid in the course of the crossing by new apparitions, including "a large round object, as though it were of gold."

In Jaffa, the inwardly absorbed Iñigo had not a word to say about the cultural shock he must assuredly have felt. Nor had he much to say about his first sight of Jerusalem: "When the Pilgrim did see the city, he experienced great consolation, and . . . a joy that did not seem natural." Once again, only abstract words, "consolation," "joy." Did he possess eyes for seeing these overwhelming wonders? Did his "external" eyes really see nothing of the city's honey-colored crenelated battlements, seemingly designed less for war than for framing and tempering the light of Jerusalem? Nothing of the lovely Romanesque façade of Saint Anne's, nothing of Mount Carmel?

Nor was he more forthcoming about the Turkish masters of Palestine—rapacious and menacing, indeed unbearably so, according to the other pilgrims with whom he first sought lodging at Saint John's Hospital, virtually under siege by the Pasha's janissaries. But not to the point of deterring them from visiting Calvary, Bethlehem, Gethsemane, Jericho . . .

If Iñigo had in mind a protracted stay in Jerusalem, it was in order to visit, to be immersed in, the Holy Places, and to "help souls," as he put it—which clearly implied some kind of apostolic mission. But he revealed only the first of these intentions to the local Franciscans, in order to avoid alarming them (a freelance rival in their midst?). Even his proposed sightseeing was too much: the brothers answered that they were already living in such poverty that they planned to send some of their number back to Europe with Iñigo's pilgrim group.

Iñigo appealed to the provincial of the order, to whom he presented his letters of accreditation from Rome. He was cordially received, but his request was rejected. Many, the Franciscan told him, had voiced the same desire. But some had died and some had fallen into captivity—in which case the order was obliged to ransom them. He therefore begged Iñigo to leave on the morrow with his fellow pilgrims. But Iñigo was stubborn:

> He replied that his decision to remain was fixed and that nothing
> could prevent him from carrying it out. . . . Though the provincial
> did not agree with him, he would not renounce his plans out of fear.
> In answer to this the provincial said that they had authority from the
> Holy See to expel or to keep anyone they chose, and to excommuni-
> cate anyone who refused to obey.

Excommunication was too much, and Iñigo had no choice but to obey. But before leaving the Holy Places he wished to see the Mount of Olives again, and above all else the

> stone from which Our Lord ascended into heaven, and his footprints
> are still visible there. . . . Thus, without saying anything, and without
> taking a guide (and those who go about without a Turk as guide run
> great risks), he slipped away from the others and went by himself to

the Mount of Olives. The guards there did not want to let him enter but he gave them a penknife that he had with him. After he had said his prayers with heartfelt consolation, he got the desire to go to Bethpage. While there he remembered that he had not taken full note of the direction in which the right foot was pointing and which the left. On his return there he gave his scissors, I think, to the guards so that they would let him enter.

Back at the monastery the Franciscans were in an uproar: What if this mad-man took it into his head to make for the desert like a second Saint Anthony! They sent out a man armed with a cudgel to look for him. When he found Iñigo he threatened him with a drubbing, seized him by the collar, and marched him back to St. John's Hospital in time to reembark with his fellow pilgrims. Unde-terred by this treatment, Iñigo later noted that, "held tightly by the Christian, Our Lord granted him great consolation and it seemed to him that he saw Christ above him the whole way. This consolation remained with him in great measure until he arrived at the monastery."[17]

Three weeks in the Holy Land (September 3 to 23, 1523): It sounds almost like a travel agent's brochure. But this was a time when pilgrims were in danger of losing more than their lives, and it needed little imagination to relive Christ's passion in the Holy Sepulcher. In any case, Iñigo drank it in—apparently "with-out differentiating in his mind" between truth and fable. Had he already under-stood that his mission did not lie in this Jerusalem so firmly in the clutches of the Unbeliever? Apparently not. Twelve years later, standing before the Pope with his first *compañeros* at his side, it was again to Jerusalem that he proposed dispatching his newborn Company's emissaries.

The homeward run was even livelier than the outbound leg. On the Mediter-ranean, clashes with the Turks were more or less constant; and in Italy itself French armies—first under Charles VIII, then under Francis I—were perma-nently on the prowl. In freezing winter temperatures, done up like some ragged jester in puffed hose that left his legs bare below the knee, in a tattered jerkin and short threadbare doublet, Iñigo wandered across war-ravaged landscapes.

In Lombardy he was arrested by Spanish soldiers who took him for a French spy. Hauled in chains before their captain, "the Pilgrim had a representation of how Christ was led away, but this was not a vision as the others were." Should he address the captain as "My Lord," and thus perhaps escape torture at the sol-diers' hands (the veteran of the Pamplona siege had a shrewd idea of the psy-chology of a captain in His Most Catholic Majesty's forces)? No! Recognizing that this idea "was a temptation" (discernment of spirits!), he decided not to "show him any mark of respect, nor . . . take my cap off to him." The discon-certed captain took him for a madman and ordered his men to throw him out.

No sooner was he free of the Spanish than he fell into French hands. He was dragged before a lieutenant who asked him where he came from. From Guipúzcoa? But the French lieutenant was also a Basque, from the Bayonne region! Francis I's soldiers were ordered to feed Iñigo and treat him well. Thus did our mystic vagabond, our heaven-blest innocent, make his way across a warring world.

Yet it was not on the battlefield but on the outskirts of worldly, pleasure-loving Venice that he experienced the decisive moment of this mad pilgrimage. There, at the home of the Spanish friend who had given him refuge on the outward journey, he mulled over his pilgrimage, his expulsion from the Holy Land, and his future course. And it was there, as the *Autobiography* tells us, that he was first "inclined toward spending . . . time in study."[18]

Naturally, it would be "in order to help souls." But this sudden thirst for learning for the sake of teaching—like the *metanoia* of the Casa y Solar or the visions of Manresa—was a turning point in this epic destiny—perhaps even the decisive threshold of his own life and his Jesuit lifework. The knight had turned hermit. The hermit, pilgrim. The pilgrim burned to turn doctor. And the doctor would send his disciples to inform the world and seek knowledge of the world.

He was done with martial "vainglory," with gallantry, with courtly ways. He had disciplined himself, buried himself like an animal in a cave, journeyed on mule and horseback, limped on foot, taken ship, trembled in the grip of the infidel, begged alms on all the roads, slept with chattering teeth in doorways and against city walls, feigned madness to wriggle from the soldiers' grasp. But now, however harsh the ordeal he inflicted upon his body, however intense the "motions" of his soul, however imperious the demands of his faith, however urgent the goals of his charity, it was his intellect that this ragged vagabond, spewed out by the Holy Land, would henceforth nourish.

His goal now was Barcelona. To the heir of the Loyolas, the great Catalan city was first and foremost a seat of art and learning. And he had friends there—those same Pascuals, Ferrers, and Rosells who had lodged, helped, and understood him, despite his wild appearance. It was there he would embark on his new mission—study.

Barcelona at the beginning of the sixteenth century was not quite the intellectual center Iñigo had imagined. Until 1533 it had no university, merely a handful of schools. But the humanist movement there boasted a famous champion, Miguel Mai, as well as a few good Latinists grouped around the Basque Martín de Ibarra. And at that time the pilgrim from Palestine was looking not so much for renowned thinkers as for a master capable of inculcating in him the fundamental means of expression—grammar and Latin.

Jerónimo Ardévol was that man. Under the guidance of this close collaborator of Ibarra's and friend of the Ferrers and Rosells, the vagabond in search of knowledge was transformed—at more than thirty-three years of age—into a docile scholar. In lieu of a contract, Iñigo assured Ardévol that he would continue to follow his lessons for as long as he could "find bread and water in Barcelona to support myself." (In fact Ardévol asked no compensation, and Iñigo's hosts, the Pascuals, provided him with the basic necessities.)

Iñigo now faced a strange ordeal. As he tells us in his *Autobiography*, when he settled down to study under Ardévol he was overcome by "new understandings of spiritual things and new delights" strong enough to disturb him. Convinced they were inspired by the Evil One, he confided in his master. Clearly these "spiritual things" might threaten his thoroughly worldly campaign to acquire knowledge. In this baffling dilemma we have a foretaste of the kind of problems the founder would be obliged to solve twenty years later.

He set about sharpening the "discernment" that set his genius apart, the art he already possessed of distinguishing the essential from the incidental, the urgent from the everyday, of recognizing the primacy of rendering unto Caesar what is Caesar's. But committed though he was to the acquisition of wisdom, Iñigo remained a glutton for ostentatious acts of self-mortification. Although he finally agreed to put on footwear (to combat "stomach pain," he cheerfully explains), he also contrived to "make holes in the soles of his shoes and kept enlarging them little by little, so that when winter's cold came there was nothing there but the upper part of the shoes."

The pilgrim had not yet tamed the vagabond within. Inevitably, he attracted the attention of others, in particular a handful of men who would be his first disciples: Calixto de Sá, Lope de Cáceres, Juan de Artéaga, and a young Frenchman, Jean Raynald, known as "Juanico." Although drawn to him because of his eccentric behavior, it was perhaps because of it too that they would not long be loyal to the *home del sac,* now better known as the man with holes in his shoes and, more seriously, as the man of *The Spiritual Exercises*. But we shall follow them with him as far as Castile.

Jerónimo Ardévol kept the aging schoolboy under his guidance for two whole years before declaring him ready to study "the arts" and "philosophy" at the university. But at which one? Ardévol decided to direct his pupil to Alcalá de Henares, which for the past twenty-five years had been the most brilliant cultural center—after Salamanca—on the Peninsula. And so, at the age of thirty-five (and armed with the favorable opinion of a Catalan theologian who had examined him and declared him equal to the enterprise), he left for the little Catalan city where Miguel de Cervantes would be born twenty years later, and where Erasmus's glory still glittered.

The historian Lucien Febvre makes an eloquent comment on Marcel Bataillon's fine book, *Érasme et l'Espagne.*[19] Without actually naming him, he refers to Erasmus's role in a Castile "aflame with all-consuming ardor, the ardor of the Cisneros, of the Valdés, and in the background, of the Loyolas—the Spain of the *alumbrados,* which was also that of the *conversos,* and which honored among its spiritual fathers and its prayer-leaders the sickly thin-blooded little man whose smile third-rate detractors have compared, and still compare, to Voltaire's."[20]

The names of the alumbrados and the conversos so often haunt this story that we must examine their meaning. The alumbrados (the Illuminated) sprang up more or less everywhere—but particularly in Castile—from fertile popular soil, soil in which the expectations of the faithful had been disappointed by the teachings and behavior of an inadequate and corrupt clergy.

They represented a movement that brought together projects for monastic reform (emanating most particularly from the Franciscans) and a spontaneous spirituality fanned in lay circles by the *beati,* the "blissful ones," who would play an active part at Iñigo's side. There were also the *dejados,* those who had abandoned themselves to God's will (*no hacer nada*—do nothing but lean upon His love), the forerunners of quietism.

As for the conversos, they were "New Christians," Jews converted willingly or by force;* some of these were *Marranos,* who concealed behind their formal adherence to Christianity a dogged (and dangerous) loyalty to their original faith. Others had been genuinely won over to Catholicism and would play a crucial role in the history of the Jesuits and of Spain. Several observers, including the Venetian ambassador, calculated that by 1530 a third of Spanish Christianity was of Jewish origin.[21] Given the attitude of a clergy suspicious or contemptuous of them, many conversos preferred to live their neo-Christianity on the margins of its sway, in the sphere of the alumbrados. Whence an immense spiritual ferment between these diverse moving currents of outsiders, fertile ground for sowers of disorder and inventors of order.

Erasmianists, crazed visionaries, converts: It was through this bubbling cauldron of mingled waters and crashing waves that naïve, stammering Iñigo, athirst for "philosophy," navigated in the little Castilian city he reached in March 1527. He at once became a target of suspicion and surveillance by the guardians of the faith. For the Inquisition† was on the prowl, aroused by all this temerity and innovation. It reserved most of its thunder for the conversos but was suspicious of anything that might not fit the rigorous framework of the Roman system.

*In 1492 a decree of the Catholic sovereigns forced Jews and Muslims to choose between conversion and exile.
†Restored a half century previously.

Still begging, preaching to the common people, sometimes the butt of gibes and insults from passersby, particularly priests, Iñigo abandoned his vagrant's rags and—like his companions, who had all followed him from Barcelona—was dressed in a long tunic of *pardillo,* a grayish fabric worn by the poor. And he was again barefoot. But he had been given decent lodging in a hospice—bread, bed, a candle. And above all, he had made important contacts, Diego and Miguel de Eguía from Navarre. Miguel, a prosperous printer, was the publisher in Castilian of Erasmus's *Enchiridion Militis Christiani (Manual of the Christian Knight).*

Should we assume, given this association, that he was already won over to humanism? No. Curiously enough, in fact, when his Portuguese confessor urged him to read the works of the great man of Rotterdam (as the lettered folk of Barcelona had already done before him), this seeker of knowledge refused. Why? Because, according to his confidant Luis Gonçalves da Câmara, "certain authorities disapproved of him."

So it was not as an Erasmian that Iñigo would undergo so many trials and find himself the butt of priestly resentment; nor was it even as a suspected Lutheran that he was brushed by the Inquisition's flames. It was because people identified his street-corner perorations with the activities of the alumbrados. But let us listen to his own incomparably flavored words:

> . . . rumors began flying throughout that region about the things happening in Alcalá; some individuals said one thing while others said something else. This matter reached the Inquisition in Toledo and when the Inquisitors came to Alcalá the Pilgrim was warned by their host, who told him that they were calling them "sack wearers," and "enlightened ones" I believe, and that they were going to make mincemeat of them [*hacer carnicería en ellos*]. . . .

A *carnicería?* God's body! But were Iñigo and his followers in gray really alumbrados? In his *Érasme et l'Espagne,*[22] Marcel Bataillon points out that in any case—whether or not he had "deserved this appellation"—Loyola was "at that time seen as a visionary . . . and was apparently a supporter of the religious revolution" that was then more or less everywhere assuming forms threatening to the Church establishment.

Admittedly, both alumbrados and dejados had long been tolerated, since their zeal and spirituality seemed linked to the Franciscan reforms of which Cardinal de Cisneros was a promoter. But around 1525, Grand Inquisitor Manrique, favorable toward Erasmianism and various forms of spontaneous evangelism, had detected signs of Lutheran penetration of the Iberian Peninsula through the ideas of visionary anticlericalism. These suspicions deepened when he realized that some of the most renowned alumbrados, such as Pedro de

Alcaraz, were conversos, New Christians of Jewish origin. Veiled Lutheranism, creeping Judaism:* It was a lot for an Inquisitor—even one sensitive to the message of Erasmus—to swallow. Under such circumstances, passing for an alumbrado could easily mean you were tarred with the brush of heresy: whence the promised carnicería.

The Inquisition turned up many witnesses. The magistrate Alonso Mejías, delegated by the bishops' tribunal, first called in a Franciscan priest, then a "blissful one," a disciple of Iñigo's, then his janitor, and then several fanatically religious ladies from whom he hoped to extract damaging testimony. When the janitor stated that two of the men in gray sometimes slept in Iñigo's room or that veiled women called on him early in the morning or that the preachers received gifts in return for their teachings, the magistrate pricked up his ears. "What gifts?" "Bunches of grapes or pieces of lard."

But he received more promising ammunition when he heard from Iñigo's most fervent female disciples, Doña Leonor, Doña María, and Doña Beatriz, who were unable to conceal the degree of hysteria underlying their zeal: One fell senseless, another sometimes rolled about on the ground, another had been seen in the grip of convulsions or shuddering and sweating in anguish. These disorders had taken place while the Basque pilgrim and his companions were preaching. Don Alonso knew such signs well; they were by no means confined to Iñigo's listeners. However, when he questioned witnesses about the substance of the sermons, he was forced to agree that the teachings of the men in gray hewed to the orthodox line.

When Mejias's inquiry was over, Iñigo and his disciples were summoned by the grand vicar, Figueroa, who announced that the investigator had "found no error in their doctrine or in their way of life." But since they belonged to no religious order, it was improper "that they went about clad as they were."

> It would be better . . . if two of them, here he pointed to the Pilgrim and to Artéaga, were to dye their habits black, and the other two, Calixto and Cáceres, to dye theirs a light brown. Juanico, who was a Frenchman, could remain as he was. The Pilgrim said, "I do not know how beneficial such investigations are. . . . We would like to know whether they have found any heresy in us." Figueroa answered: "No; if they had, they would have burned you." "They would likewise have burned you," the Pilgrim retorted, "if they found heresy in you."

Bull's-eye! Just like Joan of Arc facing Bishop Cauchon: And why not a stake for the Inquisitor too? Bravo, Iñigo! But the investigation was to spring back to

---

*As we shall see, the imputation here would be very direct.

life, and for an apparently serious reason that Iñigo serenely sets out for us: "A married woman of some prominence, who had a special interest in the Pilgrim, came to the hospital one morning, at dawn, and in order not to be recognized wore a veil, as is the custom in Alcalá de Henares. When she entered . . . she removed her veil and went to the Pilgrim's room."

Now this could be a hanging matter, even if you believed the haggard vagabond to be above suspicion. But these same Inquisitors, to whom the color of a habit was as a red rag to a bull, quickly closed the case on this titillating affair. Only later did the situation turn threatening: "A policeman came one day to his door and . . . put him in jail." Admittedly, he was not closely confined and received many visits, doing, as he tells us, "the same there as when he was free." But he remained imprisoned for seventeen days without being informed of the charge, before Figueroa came "and questioned him about many matters, even asking him if he encouraged others to observe Saturday. . . . "

Saturday? The Sabbath? Perhaps the student-preacher was no longer suspected only of Illuminism or of Erasmianism, but of something much more serious in the Inquisition's eyes—crypto-Judaism. But no—Figueroa at last revealed the real motive for his arrest: Two ladies of the town, a mother and daughter, both widows ("The daughter was very young and beautiful," Iñigo tells us helpfully), had set out on foot and alone for Saint Veronica's shrine in Jaén* and were begging alms: conduct so outrageous that the barefoot vagabond was suspected of inspiring it. And by what witcheries or evil spells?

Iñigo had little difficulty proving that he had in fact attempted to dissuade the pious couple from venturing out on the highway, pointing out to them that if they wished to succor the poor, there was no lack of opportunity in Alcalá. But he had to await the errant ladies' return to their homes before he was set free—with a stern warning: He was to refrain from speaking "on matters of faith for the next four years until" he had pursued further studies.

The whole business demonstrates that Iñigo was no longer the delirious hermit of the Catalan grotto, that he had conquered the temptations of destitution, that he had acquired authority, even that he possessed a charisma to which neither Inquisitors nor the ladies were immune, that he was now a past master of argument, and that he could call on influential friendships and sponsors. But— as he acknowledged when he was asked—he spoke and acted "without solid foundation . . . since . . . he had no formal studies."

Although he had left Barcelona for Alcalá de Henares with the precise goal of formal study, he had not achieved it. Instead, he had devoted himself to preaching, indoctrinating, disseminating his *Spiritual Exercises.* Clearly he had gone off

---

*In Andalusia, more than a hundred leagues from Alcalá.

course, and he realized it. To get back on track, this penitent suspected of being a visionary (if not a Lutheran or a Jew) needed advice. He accordingly sought out no less a person than the Primate of Spain, Alonso de Fonseca, in Valladolid:* "The archbishop listened attentively and, realizing that [Iñigo] wanted to go to Salamanca, said that he had friends in Salamanca as well as a college, and offered all this to him. As he was leaving, the archbishop gave him four escudos."

Was it from reading his beloved Erasmus that Alonso de Fonseca had acquired such a discerning spirit? Or because he sensed in Iñigo (or thought he sensed it) a kindred would-be Erasmianist? Whatever the reason, here were four escudos for the cause.

In short, it was under the indirect patronage of the humanist of Rotterdam that Iñigo de Loyola, on the instructions of the all-powerful Primate of Spain, entered Salamanca-the-Magnificent, whither his four early companions had preceded him in July 1527.

We must not picture him strolling beneath the peerless arcades of the Plaza Mayor, gazing upon the marvelous Casa de las Conchas, climbing, neck craned, the numberless steps of the city's many cathedrals—for he would not rest until he had found a confessor. Chance (perhaps) decreed that this confessor would be a Dominican. Iñigo's instincts (particularly now that he had been bitten by the learning bug) inclined him more to the Carthusians or the Franciscans. But the Preaching Brothers, as the Dominicans were known, were the masters of San Estéban, the most majestic of the city's monasteries and the first one to meet a visitor's gaze. So—although Iñigo was not without qualms—it was to be the Dominican.

He had been in Salamanca less than a fortnight when this confessor unmasked his batteries: "The Fathers here in the house would like to speak with you. . . . Come and dine with us on Sunday, but I want to tell you in advance that they will want to know many things about you."

With Calixto by his side, Iñigo was received and fed, then led to a chapel where the interrogation began. Asked what they had studied, the pilgrim confessed how limited their training had been.

"Then, about what do you preach?" And the Pilgrim said: "We do not preach. We speak to a few in a friendly manner about the things of God. . . . " "But," the friar asked, "of what godly things do you speak?" . . . "Sometimes we speak about one virtue, then another, always with praise; sometimes we speak about one vice, then another, always condemning it." "You have had no education . . . and you speak out about virtue and vice? No one can speak of these

*Where Fonseca, Archbishop of Toledo, had been summoned by the Emperor Charles V to baptize his son Philip.

except . . . because of having been educated, or by the Holy Spirit.

Since you have had no education, then it is by the Holy Spirit."

Here, the *Autobiography* goes on to tell us, "the Pilgrim was now on his guard, for this way of arguing did not seem good to him." And he was right! He had at once scented the danger. The friars had put him on trial, and with possibly far-reaching consequences, for to claim inspiration from the Holy Spirit was to declare oneself an alumbrado, a visionary, a luminary, perhaps even possessed. "After a bit of silence he said there was no further need to discuss these matters. The friar pressed on: 'With so many errors now deceiving the world, as those of Erasmus and of many others, you are unwilling to explain what you mean?' "

So that was it! At Alcalá they had asked him if he observed the Sabbath on Saturday. Here they were questioning him about Erasmus. Why not Luther as well? He would have to possess solid virtue—or extreme prudence—to appeal beyond his interrogators to Rome and its followers, to the vast papal machinery and its agents. Meanwhile he chose silence, and clearly told the Dominicans (the order most closely linked to the Inquisition) that he would not utter another word unless required to do so by his superiors. But he was now in the utmost danger, as his hosts' reply indicated: "Remain here; we will easily get you to tell all."

In 1527—and spoken in Castilian—these were words calculated to strike terror in the heart of a man being interrogated by the friars of San Estéban. What followed seemed to confirm the threat implicit in the words: "The friars then locked all the doors and went . . . to discuss the matter with the judges. [Iñigo and Calixto] stayed at the monastery for three days . . . without anything being said to them about a trial. Their room was almost always full of friars who came to see them [and] many showed that their sympathy was with them."

Which was scarcely surprising: They seemed truly deserving of sympathy. But a strange event now transformed pity into admiration. One day, profiting from a lapse in their warders' attention, all the prisoners flew the coop. All, that is, except two. "When they were found the next morning, all alone with the doors wide open, everyone was deeply edified, and this caused much talk in the city. Because of this they put all of them in a nearby mansion as their prison."

Summoned to hear their sentence after twenty-two days' confinement, they were released and told they could continue to teach the catechism and speak "about the things of God"—on condition that they not seek to distinguish between venial and mortal sins until they had completed four years of serious study.

Apprentice-preacher Iñigo's reaction was strange indeed. He had had a narrow escape, yet he seemed no more troubled by the danger than he had been concerned to break out of prison a few days earlier. Not only that, but he looked decidedly gloomy as he left San Estéban, for his strange vocation had been called into question. They were "forcing his mouth closed." He did "not agree with the sentence," but would do as ordered "as long as he remained within the jurisdiction of Salamanca." A mental reservation of the clearest kind, its implications crystallized by the fact that he had already decided to leave this town where—from interrogations and trials to harassment and prison—he had been so shamefully treated. It would be rash indeed to claim that this supreme advocate of obedience always practiced it himself.

But he had taken stock of the precariousness of his position. He, the self-educated wanderer, the seer of Manresa, was behaving like an alumbrado. Everything about him singled him out as an outsider (worse, the leader of a small band of outsiders!): his spontaneous utterances on the most sacred matters, his acquaintances, his bizarre disciples, his remarkably untrammeled relations with women who were neither Magdalens nor Samaritans but who still made tongues wag, the almost Lutheran nature of his aclericalism, his eccentric appearance, the exotic roughness of his accent (Basque when he spoke Spanish and Spanish when he attempted to speak Latin).

At this stage in his story, the author of the *Autobiography* (perhaps thinking back to an earlier period, and speaking somewhat elliptically) suggests that he contemplated entering a religious order. In 1521, at the time of his "conversion," he had already considered joining the Carthusians in Seville. His thoughts on this score now take on singular coloring: "With the thought of entering religion, he also thought of entering a congregation that was lax and unreformed* so that he could suffer the more in it."

Stranger and stranger . . . Still proud enough to think that in these circumstances, and covered as he was with "insults and hurts," it was he who (with God's help, as he points out) would reform the order, rather than be dragged down into laxity by it. But why embark on such a perilous course? Why should he not himself lay utterly new foundations and—with a view to "studying" in order to "help souls"—gather about him a handful of companions inspired with the same goal?

It is impossible to say whether the idea of founding a new institution came to him at this point. What is certain is that the key word to emerge from all this threatening upheaval was "study." It was not just because he behaved like an anarchist that, like Christ, he had clashed with judges and police. It was because he had not "studied." And "thus," says the *Autobiography,* "he decided on going to Paris."

Why Paris, so distant, so exotic, so "Babylonian"? Iñigo felt alienated from the clerical establishment in Spain, which in those years was inseparable from the

---

*He would have had an embarrassment of choices. Could he (in view of his perilous adventure) have been thinking of the Dominicans? The Franciscans were largely reformed, and he could hardly have called the Carthusians "lax." Of course, he was dictating all this thirty years later.

academic. If he had to leave his native land, Paris beckoned more convincingly than Bologna or Tübingen. The theological faculty at Paris, a towering beacon of learning in the Christian West, was already disseminating its famous method—the *modus parisiensis*—across the world.

Since the twelfth century, scores of voices had been raised throughout Christendom to celebrate the learning of the city of Abelard and Gerson. Thus John of Salisbury in a letter to Thomas à Becket: "In Paris I looked with wonder upon the diversity of philosophical interests, recalling Jacob's ladder whose topmost rungs reached Heaven. . . . I was obliged to admit that 'God is in this place and I did not know it' (Genesis, XXVIII, 16). I also recalled the verse: 'Blessed is the exile who shall inherit this place.'"

We may also surmise that in choosing to immerse himself in a society whose vernacular and social behavior were unknown to him, Iñigo had made a choice (which he was unable to exercise either in Alcalá or Salamanca) between acquiring knowledge and propagating his faith. No question here of lecturing to crowds. What would Parisians make of his ecstatic but hybrid Basque-Latin-Spanish homilies? Farewell (for now) to his mission, and hail to the "learning" he must somehow acquire.

And finally let us turn to his own words: "Twenty days after leaving prison he set out by himself, carrying some books on a donkey. When he came to Barcelona, all who knew him tried to dissuade him from going into France because of the violent battles going on there* . . . even telling him that they skewered Spaniards on spits."[23]

But "never did he have any fear." In early January of 1528 he crossed the Pyrenees and continued toward Paris, convinced it was in this city that he, the barefoot vagabond, would slake his *libido sciendi,* far from the wrath of the Inquisition.

One detail, perhaps unimportant: If he limped his way for two months (January–February 1528) up the roads of France, all the way from the Pyrenees to Paris in the depths of winter, it was because he had elected not to straddle the little donkey that friends had given the still-infirm pilgrim, but to load it with books.

---

*Broken off after the battle of Pavia and the Treaty of Madrid in 1526, war flared again the next year between the King of Spain (who would be anointed Emperor in 1530) and Francis I, then the ally of Henry VIII.

· 11 ·

The Scholars
from Montmartre

"Idlers and Buffoons of Paris" · *Horrors of Montaigu, Heights of*
Sainte-Barbe · *A Shepherd Boy and a Spanish Blueblood* ·
"Molder of Men" · *The Shame of Rome* · *Beautiful Giulia's*
Brother on the Throne · *Their New Jerusalem* ·
From Adventure to Organization

T HERE IS A PERSISTENT legend of a Company of Jesus drawn up
along the lines of some pious roughneck militia, a papal commando
assailing the armies of the Reformation, subduing them, if not routing
them, under the command of a militant Loyola. The legend is so persistent and
resurfaces so regularly that a conflicting theory seems called for. This would
make of the original band of "Iñiguists" a brotherhood of students, enlightened
by the great minds who had turned Francis I's Paris into the intellectual center
of the West. They then transformed themselves into a "Society of Jesus" by virtually spontaneous fertilization, in an environment already prodigiously fertile
and energized by unprecedented levels of spiritual and intellectual ferment.

For we should at once make it clear that the six men who on August 15, 1534,
joined the lord of Loyola in a solemn oath in a small rustic church on the slope
of a hill named Montmartre were what we would now call "intellectuals." Over
the past ten years they had been tempered in the crucible of humanism—of the
many humanisms—that was the Paris of Francis I. There they had received an
education that was "above all else philosophical and literary."[1] And this momentous gathering of Castilians, Navarrese, Savoyards, Basques, and Portuguese in

35

the intellectual capital of the West did not take place primarily at the bidding of faith, but of learning.

It would of course be wrong to reduce that pious oath on Montmartre to a mere secretion of the Parisian humanism that had exploded during this prodigious decade. Starting in 1525, the year of the decisive debate between Erasmus (*De libero arbitrio*) and Luther (*De servo arbitrio*) on the liberty of a mankind torn between nature and grace, it encompassed the creation in 1530 of the Collège de France and the 1532 publication of Rabelais's *Pantagruel*, and closed in 1536, the year John Calvin's *Institutes of the Christian Religion* was published.

No, it was the Renaissance, blossoming later (and all the more lustily for being late) in France than in Italy, England, the Rhineland, and the Low Countries, that framed and shaped the Iñiguists' enterprise. The Renaissance, that movement which exhorted Christian Europe to rediscover and resurrect pre-Christian cultures (as sources of knowledge for some, as alternative avenues for others) and to challenge the texts underpinning Church teaching.

Why did Iñigo and his companions leap into this furnace? To temper their weapons, to forge a breastplate against "error" through ordeal by fire? Or because they realized that "discernment" (that hallmark Ignatian term) would come only from plurality? After all, it was knowledge they had come to find in Paris—and at the feet of masters whose teachings did not always reflect those of Thomas Aquinas or Jean Gerson.

The masters of Iñigo de Loyola and those he gathered around him were among the most renowned propagators of humanism in the fields of ancient languages, philosophy, and mathematics. How could these young people not have been marked by such teaching—just as François Rabelais and John Calvin had been influenced (although in different ways) before them?

The Paris of the people initially known as Iñiguists was thus characterized by a mighty effervescence, in which scholarly debate alternated with the crackle of flames at the foot of the stake. The air was dense with colliding ideas, clashing methods, prosecuted opinions, doctrinal confrontation. A tidal wave of change on whose crest—in a city in the full throes of demographic, architectural, and commercial growth, and inflamed by the more or less permanent war between the French King and the Spanish Emperor—the Middle Ages, in a series of convulsions, breathed its last. It would give way to a newborn society, novel more for the complexity of its learning and the breadth of its appetites than for its way of life.

Those seeing Paris for the first time toward the middle of the reign of Francis I were entering a lush and dangerous jungle. Its thickets teemed with innovations and furies and acts of daring, with discoveries and assassinations. And in it, although challenged, wounded, and provoked, Catholicism remained (by means of the most devious methods) master of a battlefield whose contenders were king, merchants, clergy, and university.

In the seventeenth chapter of his *Gargantua,* Rabelais, inspired by his sympathy for the Reformation, recalls it all in acid tones: "The people of Paris are so sottish, so *badot,* so foolish and fond by nature, that a juggler, a carrier of indulgences, a sumpter-horse, or mule with cymbals or tinkling bells . . . shall draw a greater confluence of people together, than an Evangelical preacher.*"

It was this Paris of the 1530s that our heroes sought out. It was a city that was—as Emmanuel Le Roy Ladurie noted in his introduction to volume II of the *Histoire de la France urbaine*²—with its "idlers, its buffoons, its hurdy-gurdy players," a sort of "archipelago of warmhearted and often Catholic social ease."

As we have seen, it was not astride a mule but walking behind a small donkey (and one, *pace* Rabelais, laden not with relics or cymbals but with books) that Iñigo de Loyola entered Paris on February 2, 1528.

We do not know what route he took from Barcelona to Paris across a France at war with his sovereign, the Emperor Charles. The donkey and the lame traveler, crossing Languedoc, the Auvergne, Berry, and Beauce in the heart of winter—and comparing them to their own Basque or Catalan countryside—must have reflected that the Kingdom of France was much impoverished by war.

Two precursors—Pierre Favre and Francis Xavier—had entered Paris through the Porte Saint-Jacques thirty months before. One was from Savoy, the other from Navarre; both were eager to conquer the Golden Fleece of learning and win badges of merit from the city's universities. Well before Iñigo, they had seen from afar the somewhat battered ramparts crowning the Montagne Sainte-Geneviève, had threaded their way around the mill of the Gobelins, had seen the Vaugirard Charterhouse silhouetted against the southern suburbs of the capital, and had glimpsed through the trees the slope of the Contrescarpe.

Once inside the city gates, Iñigo found himself on the Rue Saint-Jacques, the ancient Roman road from Orléans to Lutetia, and later the pilgrim road to Compostela. It was now the central artery of the Latin Quarter, which fanned out to the east and west of it. Within a few steps he was in the heart of this teeming university warren where (if we exclude a handful of excursions to northern Europe) he would spend the next seven years of his life, years that would give birth to the grand design still buried within him.

Looming majestically to the right was the Abbey of Sainte-Geneviève, next

---

*In other words, a preacher favoring Reform.

to the parish church of Saint-Étienne-du-Mont. On his left, the imposing mon-astery of the Jacobins (the Parisian name for the Dominicans), and a little far-ther on, the whole complex of university buildings, the church of Saint-Benoît, and the Hôtel de Cluny. But first he headed to the right, branching off into the Rue Saint-Étienne and plunging down a dark alleyway known then as the Rue Saint-Symphorien and later called the Rue des Chiens: On this same Street of Dogs stood the Collège de Montaigu, the most austere, daunting, malodorous, insalubrious, and inhospitable of Paris's fifty colleges. It was on this institution that our lover of mortification, fresh from the cave at Manresa and prison in Alcalá, had set his heart.

But what exactly was the Paris that this man and his book-laden donkey had just entered? The city's demarcation lines were clearly drawn between the Uni-versity, where knowledge was purveyed; the City, seat of administrative power; and the Town, center of trade. The University was of course in the "Latin Quarter"—so called for the predominance of that language* which, although challenged by the humanists, was still the undisputed vehicle of learning as well as the lingua franca of the various communities jostling one another in the streets of the quarter.

From the heights of Sainte-Geneviève to the Seine, between the Cistercian monastery on the east and the Augustinians on the west, this Latin Quarter in the sixteenth century covered an area slightly different from its present extent. This was not just because its main axis was then the Rue Saint-Jacques and not the Boulevard Saint-Michel (which did not yet exist) but because out of its three component sub-neighborhoods—Sainte-Geneviève with its still rustic parish church; Saint-Séverin; and Saint-André-des-Arts—only the first two truly served a university function. To the west of the Sorbonne, where the Rue Haute-feuille begins, the republic of learning blended into a residential quarter where royal mistresses, high officers of the law, noblemen, and foreign diplomats were lodged.

From the Collège du Cardinal-Lemoine on the east to the Porte Saint-Germain on the west, from the Porte Saint-Jacques to the Petit-Châtelet, it was a formidable labyrinth of alleyways, lanes, and slum backyards, strewn with filth and overrun by rodents, wastrels, and thieves (who were often laymen or clerics existing on the fringes of university life). Schools, churches, taverns, col-leges, convents, shops, bawdy houses, palaces, print shops, tutors, and cram-mers formed a nameless, odoriferous pile, a world at once God-fearing and doubting, a marketplace of learning where superstition and science rubbed shoulders, a vast thunderous bonfire of the vanities where knowledge was

*Not until 1539 would French be decreed the official language of law and education.

bought, sold, and bartered in a chaos of dispute, insult, and metaphor—a glorious hubbub from which there somehow emerged whatever a denizen of this ingenious century needed to know in order to be a little more human.

Let us picture our itinerant Basque, lost in the bowels of this maze, of this Babel, finally mastering his great astonishment and finding a stable for his donkey. Breaking into the twenty-five escudos provided by his Barcelona friends the Rosells, he spends a few days in an inn where "there were Spaniards,"[3] before hastening to enroll in the Collège de Montaigu.

The University of Paris, which then mustered about 12,000 students,* half of them foreigners, was a republic of professors made up of four faculties—theology; medicine; law; and the arts (today we would say the humanities)—a detail that speaks worlds for the changes wrought by triumphant humanism, for the latter group now ruled the roost, with the University Rector elected from among its masters in the Church of Saint-Julien-le-Pauvre and thereafter obeyed by the whole teaching and student body.

The students in the arts faculty were divided by place of origin into four "nations": the nation of Normandy for "Normans and natives of Le Mans," the nation of Picardy for "Picards, men of Artois, and Walloons," the nation of Germany for "Germans, Flemings, Englishmen, and Scots," and the nation of France for Parisians, Southern Frenchmen, Italians, Spaniards, Portuguese, Turks, and Egyptians.

But scholars were not differentiated solely by their "nation"; they were also in effect set apart by their social background, determined by the contribution they paid to the principal of one or the other of the fifty or so Paris colleges where the majority of the student body were enrolled.

At the top of the heap, rich and envied, were the *caméristes,* who boasted separate bedchambers, who often had private tutors, and who ate at their own expense. Lower down the ladder came the *convicteurs* or *portionistes* (what we would call boarders), entrusted to the principal and the regent for "nourishment, discipline, and instruction." The *martinets* (or day students) were bound to the regent only by a payment negotiated at the start of the year, and to the principal at the time they sat their bachelor's exam: It was he who—upon payment of a fee—certified that they had duly attended classes. Even lower were the *galoches,* who derived their name from the clogs that protected them from neighborhood mud and who, as "superannuated students," were usually taking courses for want of anything better to do.

And finally, lowest of all, the *domestiques,* for "almost all those who swept or scrubbed in the colleges were poor boys who performed these tasks for the

---

*Different authors quote figures ranging from 5,000 to 30,000.

chance it gave them to pick up bits and pieces of Latin and philosophy. They were assigned to the whole house, to the *caméristes*, or to the regents. And each necessarily obeyed his own masters."[4]

While most of the future founders of the Company were portionistes, Iñigo de Loyola wandered—it was his lot—from one category to the next, although never venturing as high as the proud caméristes. If he never belonged to the lowest group, it was not—as we shall see—for want of trying. But he was briefly a galoche, a martinet for a longer spell, and finally spent years as a portioniste alongside Favre and Xavier.

As for teaching, let us confine ourselves to "the arts," since it was in that faculty that all our heroes independently chose to enroll. Like everything else in those days, the faculty was undergoing radical change, both in form and substance. That substance had been transformed, as we know, by the eruption of humanism into the closed academic world. Worth noting in that context is a vivid page by Jules Quicherat, a good enough pedagogue to have sensed, three centuries after the event, the state of mind of his predecessors:

> When . . . in order to slake their thirsts at Antiquity's crystal
> spring . . . the first works were brought to them from Italy . . . the
> practitioners of the "-*us*," the dignitaries of the Latin people . . . were
> obliged to admit that they knew nothing of Latin. Most preferred to
> brandish their diplomas, which asserted the contrary. Only a few possessed the modesty and the good sense to acknowledge their inadequacy, and the courage to unlearn in order to instruct themselves
> anew. It was through these few that the sacred fire was rekindled upon
> the learned mountain. And in short order it set the young aflame.[5]

No doubt. But as we shall see, many masters perceived that fire as calamitous—unless it actually consumed the bodies of heretics. We shall be returning often, and on several counts, to one of these—the eminent "Sorbonnogre," Noël Beda, a "theologulper," sworn foe of Erasmus and of everything that seemed to put medieval teaching—not just its content but its form—in question.

The bell rang at four a.m., and the first lesson began an hour later. Only after Mass, held at seven, was bread distributed, fresh from the ovens. From eight to ten, "main lessons" were followed by "exercises" and then, at eleven, dinner. Public announcements and punishments followed the meal. Supper at six p.m.; a session of questions; vespers in chapel; lights out at nine.

"Recreation" took place only twice a week, following afternoon class on Tuesday and Thursday. On those days the young people were led out to the Pré-aux-Clercs (Priests' Meadow), or to the Île Notre-Dame, today's Île Saint-Louis, which was then uninhabited and given over to games and physical exertions. Holy days were frequent, and devoted to religious ceremonies. As for vacations, they were often called *vendanges*, or "grape harvests," from the time of year they occurred—late August to late October—and tied to parliamentary recess so that the gentlemen involved might be free to take care of their vineyards.

And the classrooms? "Apart from the master's pulpit, they had no chairs or benches of any kind; they were strewn with straw in winter and fresh grass in summer. The pupils had to roll in this litter 'as an act of humility.' Their uniform, a long robe cinched at the waist by a strap, was designed to sweep up the filth as well as to cover it."[6]

As for the communication of knowledge, it was more or less confined to reading one of the few books in the college's possession. This monotonous one-way process was interrupted only for examinations, which were always oral and, until around 1530, still marked by the spirit of scholasticism. Witness this beguiling report by the great humanist Luis Vivés, a friend of Erasmus, visiting the Collège de Sainte-Barbe (considered at that time to be the most "advanced" in the university):

"Tell me, child, in what month did Virgil die?"

"In September, Master."

"And in what place?"

"At Brindisi."

"On which day of September?"

"On the ninth of the calends."

"Wretch, will you dishonor me before these gentlemen? Hand me my rod, roll up your sleeve, and stretch out your hand for saying the ninth instead of the tenth. Take care to respond better in the future. As you shall see, gentlemen, this is a child of considerable learning. At the beginning of his *Catalina*, did Sallust write *omneis homines* or *omnis homines?*"

"The general belief is that he wrote *omnis*, but I am of the belief that he may have written *omneis* and that we should spell it with an *eis*, unlike the printers who spell it only with *is*."

"What was the name of Remus's brother, and how did he wear his beard?"

"Some say that he was called Romulus, Master, and others Romus, whence the name of Roma, but that as a mark of affection people used the diminutive Romulus in speaking of him. When he went to war he wore no beard; but in time of peace he wore it long. That is how he is pictured, in color, in the works of Livy printed in Venice."

"How did Alexander pick himself up after falling when he first set foot on Asian soil?"

"By raising himself with both hands and gazing upward."[7]

We have just mentioned corporal punishment. Since the end of the Middle Ages it had lost some of its barbarity. But in Chapter XXV of his *Essays*, written in mid-century, Montaigne still spoke of the "screams of tortured children and of masters intoxicated by their own rage." Even with the spread of humanism, schoolmasters still mounted the dais rod in hand. Every "serious error"—speaking French instead of Latin, for example—was punished by a whipping in the refectory. One teacher lamented the "growing indulgence" of the times, and warned that youth was doomed unless its arrogance was tamed with blows. Du Boulay himself summarized the current belief: "Bruise the flesh, the better to brand learning into the mind and heart."[8]

This barbaric principle was not everywhere applied with equal harshness. Iñigo de Loyola would first experience teaching of the harshest kind at the Collège de Montaigu, followed by the relatively modernist or humanist version practiced at Sainte-Barbe—which would inspire his own teaching methods.

Everything—history, topography, and the cast of characters inhabiting them—seems to conspire to confront not Montagues and Capulets but the Collège de Montaigu and the Collège de Sainte-Barbe, the two most dissimilar and the most antinomic of institutions Epistemon or Pangloss could have dreamed up. Philosophy, theology, discipline, principles of health and education, everything opposed them just as surely as scholasticism opposed humanism, with a virulence aggravated by the fact that they were neighbors, joined by brick and mortar across the wretched Street of Dogs.

Virtually every sneer and barb the century of Luther and Rabelais could devise has already been rained on the Collège de Montaigu. The soft-spoken Erasmus, who spent the year 1495 there, had horrified memories of this "vinegar institution." In his *Colloquies*, he relates this exchange:

"So you come from Montaigu, your head full of laurels?"

"No, of lice."

Rabelais was there too; he remembers the "college of squalor" and portrays the rector, Pierre Tempête *(horride tempestas)*, as an outstanding flogger of children.

But instruction at Montaigu was more modern than its discipline. It was embodied in one man, Jan Standonck, who had arrived as a beggar from Malines in Belgium a half century earlier and who died in an odor of near-sanctity (he was known to convert heretics at the foot of the stake). His only rule seemed to be to make his adolescent charges pay for the ordeals and privations of his own youth. This "saint" had set about regenerating the young through mortification and "poor" students through particular humiliations. Their heads shaved, their bodies clad in a hooded robe that earned them the derisive nickname *capettes*, or "hoodlets," condemned to every kind of drudgery, they were obliged to keep their eyes constantly lowered at the back of the classroom and to live in a separate enclosure under a "father" other than the college principal.

But however demeaning these practices, the zeal and numbers of the poorer students finally won them equal status (in mortification but also in knowledge) during the last years of Jan Standonck's life. Shortly after the arrival of Iñigo de Loyola, when Noël Beda took Montaigu in hand, the institution was almost as noted for the quality of its teaching, particularly in Latin grammar, as for its "squalor."

Beda! We have already met this zealous purveyor of candidates for the stake. As if his role of syndic in the faculty of theology were not enough to inspire terror, he had been named principal of Montaigu: "Physically ill-favored (he was potbellied and a hunchback), and morally equally ugly, but a skilled dialectician, upright in his ways, an upholder of orthodoxy the more zealous for having himself been censured for the boldness of his views, impervious to attacks, indifferent as to means, and always ready to bare his teeth at colleagues and enemies alike."[9]

He seemed to come out of the pages of some grim cautionary tale from the past. Among the thousand barbs his intolerance inspired, Erasmus in his *Colloquies* infallibly called Beda "bêta" (roughly, "doltish"). And this at the risk of tempting the flames to which the theologulper dreamed of consigning him, as he and his potbelly and his hump jogged on muleback from the Sorbonne to the Street of Dogs.

It was into the clutches of this Quasimodo of scholastic fundamentalism that Iñigo fell in late February 1528. Why had he chosen the squalor of Montaigu rather than the college across the street, Sainte-Barbe, where Pierre Favre and Francis Xavier (with whom he would join forces a few years later) had been studying for more than two years? His own explanation is that "he was without a good foundation. He went to class with young lads and made progress according to the prescribed curriculum of Paris." The "young lads" being of course the "poor students" admitted by Jan Standonck's college at the price of the abovementioned humiliations—capettes and galochards grubbing in the straw at the back of the class. And alongside them Iñigo, lame and almost forty, under the rod of a heavyhanded rector.

No doubt that under such a regime he made swift progress in Latin grammar. But fresh trials interrupted his studies. He had thought it prudent to deposit his twenty-five escudos—a sum that should have kept him until the end of the year—with one of the Spaniards living at the inn where he lodged. The nest egg melted like water in its guardian's hands.

Destitute (his habitual condition), he was forced to resume begging and to seek shelter in the hospice of Saint-Jacques, built to house pilgrims leaving for

Compostela. But this refuge was far from Montaigu, on the right bank and in "town," not far from the Porte Saint-Denis. Nearly an hour's walk.* Since the hospice closed its doors from nightfall to sunrise, Iñigo missed the first and last classes at Montaigu. And begging for alms was a time-consuming chore. "Living for some time in this way, at the hospital and by begging, and seeing that he was making little progress in his studies, he started to think about what he should do. He knew that there were some who served the regents in the colleges and had time for their studies, so he decided to look for someone to employ him."[10]

Whether it was his clothes, his exotic look, or the incoherent Spanish-Latin he was reduced to speaking, he found no employer. Then a Spanish monk advised him to make his way to Flanders,† to ask help from the wealthy Spanish merchants of Antwerp and Bruges. It proved to be a way to make ends meet. "Once he even went to England, and brought back more alms than he usually did."[11]

The Latin Quarter now witnessed an astonishing episode. A merry trio of Spanish students from the Collège de Sainte-Barbe—a Basque named Amador de Elduayén and two Castilians, Juan de Castro and Miguel Peralta—had acquired great prestige with their master and their schoolfellows. But in early 1529 it became clear that these budding geniuses, apparently destined for the most glittering prizes, had changed their ways. They had abandoned themselves to piety, desisting from study, giving away their possessions. One day the three young men disappeared. The Spanish student community quickly found that they had taken up residence at the hospice of Saint-Jacques.

Heading there en masse, and "with weapons in their hands," they demanded the release of their comrades. When the latter sent word that they had renounced the world and chosen a life of charity, the mob broke down the doors, seized the recluses, and hauled them back to Sainte-Barbe. There Amador confessed to his questioners. The man responsible was a Spaniard known as "the Pilgrim," a student called Iñigo.

Whereupon the aging Montaigu student found "not only his countrymen but almost the whole University in full cry against him. Children shied away from him as if from a dangerous beast. . . . He was even denounced to the Inquisition by Pedro Ortiz, then regent at Montaigu."[12] His own recollection of the event confirms the historians' versions: "In Paris, a slander campaign began against the Pilgrim, especially among the Spaniards. . . . Gouvea [the principal of Sainte-Barbe] said that he had turned Amador . . . into a madman."[13]

As we have seen, Iñigo had been sufficiently master of himself in Venice in

*Nowadays between thirty and forty minutes (I checked). But road surfaces have improved, the Petit-Châtelet no longer exists, and I was not wounded at Pamplona.
†Then under Spanish rule.

1523 to opt for a life of study. Having made this decision, why had he suddenly embarked on this dangerous campaign of spiritual seduction? Whatever the answer, he had now apparently forced himself to flee Paris, as he had already fled Alcalá and Salamanca.

Alerted by Pedro Ortiz, the Inquisitor sought his whereabouts. He learned that Iñigo had left for Rouen, his criminal flight seeming only to aggravate the case. But the truth suddenly came out, once again raising Iñigo up in men's minds: He had left for Normandy only to give succor to the countryman who had relieved him of his twenty-five escudos the previous year, and who was now dying or at death's door. In three days our lame hero reached the hospital in Rouen, where he cared for the sick man, offered him money for his return to Spain, and gave him the addresses of his Salamanca friends, Calixto, Artéaga, and Cáceres.* On his return to Paris, Iñigo learned that the Inquisitor sought him and duly called on the man.

We should note here that the significance of such a summons in Paris was quite different from what it had been in Salamanca. Here there was no need for apprehension of a physical nature. In France at that time neither political leaders nor society would have tolerated a "hard" Inquisition.

Mathieu Ory was prior of the great Dominican monastery on the Rue Saint-Jacques, the street that had earned the Dominicans their French name, Jacobins.† Ory was an august personage, and perhaps himself an Inquisitor at this time. Because of the ties that bound the Dominicans to the Inquisition, it is possible that he played the part Iñigo attributes to him in his account.

In any case, the Jacobin prior was better natured than his colleagues of Alcalá and Salamanca. There seems no reason to question Iñigo when he assures us that Mathieu Ory "only told him that it was true that they had spoken about his activities, and so on." (That "and so on" does not sound like the dreaded Inquisition!) And "the Inquisitor never called him again," he concludes tersely[14]— although, as we shall see, the Jacobin would not be the last of his kind to enter Iñigo's life.

Our vagabond, relegated for the past eighteen months to the ignominy of capette and galochard status at Montaigu, could now at last devote himself to his Parisian project: study. And he resolved to give his studies priority over any other activity, since he was now temporarily freed from the shackles of beggary (if not of preaching), and hungry above all else for knowledge. This same hunger inspired his decision to cross the Street of Dogs and move from Montaigu to Sainte-Barbe, from the college of mortification to that of illumination. As one

*Cáceres would become a secret agent of Francis I in Spain.
†By extension, the Dominicans are also known as Jacobins in other French cities even when their houses are not located on a Rue Saint-Jacques.

might have chosen twenty centuries before to leave Sparta for Athens, which, to a Spartan, was no foregone decision. . . .

Particularly since Iñigo's own odious reputation as a fanatic had preceded him to Sainte-Barbe. He must have known that the complaint lodged against him with the Inquisition had come from this college, where he was moreover considered responsible for the "corruption" of the three Spanish students. Here we are doubly surprised: first, that he should put his head in the lion's mouth (although with Iñigo, nothing can surprise us anymore), and second, that the Sainte-Barbe regents agreed to accept him.

In any case, the move represents yet another turning point, a defining moment in Iñigo's life, and thus in the prenatal life of the Company. It was as decisive as his "conversion" of 1521, as his visions at Manresa, as the impulse "to study" that overcame him in Venice in 1525. It is tempting to say that by crossing the Street of Dogs, by moving from Montaigu to Sainte-Barbe, the "college of the arts," the youngest of the Loyolas was opting for the Renaissance over the Middle Ages.

But the idea is perhaps a little pat. There were other reasons for the transfer. Montaigu had impressed the student from Salamanca as an institution in which to "catch up" scholastically, as a factory for churning out Latinists and grammarians at a level that might correspond to today's eighth to eleventh graders. But Sainte-Barbe beckoned from the margins of a more ambitious cycle of learning, at the midpoint between humanities and philosophy. It was in a sense like embarking on higher education today.

And there was a qualitative gap between the two institutions. Montaigu lagged in intellectual inquiry and the exchange of ideas. If Iñigo elected to take the plunge, it was almost certainly because he was aware of his need to climb the ladder of knowledge.

There was another important aspect to this decision, of direct benefit to millions of young people in the centuries since: By leaving the "college of lice" (where he had undoubtedly experienced the holy joys of physical penance offered up in the name of the Almighty) for the more human regime of Sainte-Barbe, Iñigo de Loyola chose a direction that still bears its fruits today. The awful law that consisted, as we have seen, of "bruising the flesh the better to brand mind and heart" was repudiated. The "liberal" teaching method of the Jesuits (no matter how harsh it may have seemed to countless schoolchildren down the centuries) was now born, a rejection of the brutal experience Iñigo had suffered behind the walls of the college where Erasmus and Rabelais had felt the sting of Standonck's or Beda's rod.

But let us not oversimplify: If Sainte-Barbe differed from its neighbor both in disciplinary approach and in intellectual ambition, its masters, and more particularly its regent, Diego de Gouvea, made no claims of turning it into a citadel of militant humanism—still less of Reform—in the teeth of the Sorbonnogre Beda. Indeed, as we shall see, this same Gouvea (more circumspect than his nephew André and several teachers in his own college) sometimes closed ranks with the conservatives. He was a remarkable administrator, a consummate diplomat, rather than a thinker. Today we would call him a manager of genius—and the best fund-raiser of his time.

Nor did his colleagues claim to dispense an education in keeping with Montaigne's ideals; Gouvea's students called him "mustard eater," which cannot mean that they considered him angelic, and corporal punishment was not unknown in his college. Witness the adventure that christened, or almost christened, Loyola's Sainte-Barbe career.

The author of the *Autobiography* assures us that he entered the "college of the liberal arts" determined not to "go about looking to add other [companions] so that he could comfortably give himself to his studies."[15] He entered Sainte-Barbe in possession of alms that allowed him to enroll there as a portioniste, which meant paying rent and sharing a room with three companions. The regent who placed him in the corner turret overlooking the Street of Dogs had no idea that he would be turning this circular room into the first cell of the Society of Jesus: All he had intended was to keep a sharp eye on this firebrand preacher.

The turret room was in fact already occupied by three people: two advanced students, Pierre Favre and Francisco de Iassu de Azpilcueta y Xavier, and a teacher of philosophy, Juan de la Peña. It was hoped that Amador's seducer, living under the teacher's nose and flanked by these two worthy students, would keep the peace. In any case, such was the advice he received from Juan de la Peña.

They might as well have ordered a nightingale not to sing. However free he might have been of missionary aims when he entered Sainte-Barbe, Iñigo could not altogether curb his nature; and that Sunday, at the hour when students were summoned to philosophical debate, he called together a goodly number to incite them to pray for their salvation. But let us turn here to one of his earliest French biographers, a certain Hercule Rasiel, the author, in 1736, of an *Histoire de l'admirable Dom Iñigo de Guipuzcoa, fondateur de la monarchie des Iñiguistes* (History of the Admirable Dom Iñigo de Guipuzcoa, Founder of the Iñiguist Monarchy), a picturesque title that should not deter us from reading it, for his sources are reliable* and his accents highly flavored:

> The teacher of philosophy, Juan de la Peña, highly displeased that
> Iñigo should thus corrupt his disciples, made him most bloody reproaches and warned him that if he continued to turn them from

*The most obvious being Ribadeneira, one of Loyola's first companions in Rome.

their studies he would have him chastised without mercy. But, seeing that he persisted upon his course and so infatuated them with who can say what Fanatical Devotion that several had quite abandoned their philosophy lessons in order to take the habit, he represented to Doctor Gouvea, principal of Sainte-Barbe, the urgent necessity to inflict exemplary punishment upon a pupil who caused such disorders: "If we do not reestablish order, he will make so many Monks of our pupils, and we shall soon see our College deserted." Gouvea, already irritated at Iñigo because of the affair of the three Spanish students, finally decided to chastise him publicly.

It was the custom in those days, in punishing those who disturbed Studies, to summon the whole college to the refectory with the bell. Rods in hand, the Regents one after another would strike the guilty one in the presence of his schoolmates. This punishment, known as "Refectory," was the one to be visited upon Iñigo. . . . His friends advised him not to venture into Sainte-Barbe, and even to absent himself from the college forever. But instead of following this counsel, he resolved to present himself, delighted at this opportunity of exercising his patience.

"I am ready," he said, "to undergo the punishment to which you have condemned me. The rods of your college, of the whole universe, even the gallows strike no fear in me. On the contrary, I can conceive of no greater delight in this world than to suffer in a good cause. I fear but one thing: that a scholar of my age [almost 40] be dishonored by an ignoble punishment; that these children to whom I have revealed the religious life may abandon it on seeing their spiritual Father defamed as a corrupter of youth. Dear Sir, think well on it: I free my conscience of it, and burden your own. Do now with me as you will. Here I am, prepared to suffer all."

Moved by Iñigo's fanatic utterance, Gouvea threw himself at his feet and implored his pardon for having given credence to false report. Then he rose and said aloud: "This is a Saint, who would eagerly suffer the most hideous torments."[16]

Jules Quicherat has been held up to the worst kinds of obloquy by pious historians of the Company* for casting doubt on that final touch—Diego de Gouvea throwing himself, before his assembled college, at the feet of a firebrand who stubbornly flouted the rules and upset the smooth running of the institution. Let us nevertheless hear Quicherat's version: "All he found to say was that

---

*Although not by Father Ravier, who sensibly (and fervently) agrees with him.

Ignatius of Loyola was a man of holy ways who had let himself be carried away by excessive zeal; that he had given his word that he would henceforward behave with greater discretion; that he himself, before the whole college, now renewed that promise in his name; and that in consequence he excused him the punishment pronounced against him."[17]

Whatever either man may have said, it is time now to direct our gaze at three characters from among this audience of "Barbists" denied the spectacle of Iñigo's humiliation. We have already met them: Juan de la Peña, the frustrated master; Pierre Favre,* and Francisco de Iassu de Azpilcueta y Xavier.†

There is not too much to be said of Juan de la Peña, who, once the "refectory" incident was over, seems to have enjoyed good relations with Iñigo. He was Iñigo's first philosophy teacher, as he had been for Favre and Xavier. We must focus instead on Iñigo's two other chambermates rather than on this master logician.

The author of *The Spiritual Exercises* had so far been unlucky in his attempts, conscious or unconscious, to recruit disciples. But this time, what some would call fate and others providence was to forge quite different alliances.

Pierre Favre was born in Savoy in 1506, in a village tucked away in the bottom of the Grand-Bornand Valley. His parents were pious, well-to-do peasants. His *Memoirs,* wonderfully edited and prefaced by Michel de Certeau, give us the basic facts: How when he was about ten, "herding sheep," he was seized with the urge to study. "I wept," Pierre writes, "for I wished with all my heart to go to school; so much so that my parents were obliged, most reluctantly, to send me." A Carthusian uncle took him in hand and entrusted him to the humanist Pierre Veillard, who succeeded in turning the little shepherd lad into a student worthy of Paris.

When Iñigo entered Sainte-Barbe, Pierre—described by all who knew him as the most likable, even-tempered, pleasant, and stable of people—was about to take the exam for master of arts. It was only natural that Juan de la Peña should charge him with watching over the unruly Basque (even though Favre was fifteen years Iñigo's junior). The new arrival seemed finally to be sticking to his virtuous resolution to confine himself to study. His mentor, bound by directives from Peña (who had good reason to be wary of Iñigo's evangelical outbursts), confined their exchanges to Aristotle's *Logic* and *Grammar.* Moreover Favre, who dreamed of becoming a physician, was uncertain of his own religious vocation. Only in 1531, two years after they began to live together, did Favre receive the *Exercises* from Loyola. That was just a few months before he was ordained—the first of the founders of the Society to become a priest.

*Sometimes also called Fabre or Lefèvre by seventeenth- and eighteenth-century historians. But writings in his own hand are always signed Favre.
†Hereafter referred to as Francis Xavier.

In a lonely shack on the Rue Saint-Jacques, in the neighborhood of what is today the Val-de-Grâce military hospital, the graduate student from Savoy shut himself away in February 1534. It was a dreadful winter, with wagons rumbling across a frozen Seine. To heighten his sufferings, Pierre made a bed of the logs people had brought him to warm himself. He went for a week without food, refusing to swallow the wine Iñigo put before him; he even spent several nights on his knees in the snow. At last even the shaggy hermit of Manresa was alarmed enough to put an end to such acts of madness.

Favre's *Memoirs,* written ten years later, make no mention of these excesses. Serenely and subtly, he describes the evolving relationship between Pierre and Iñigo: "Peña having ordered me to instruct this holy man, I first enjoyed his more public discourse, and later his more intimate conversation. We lived together in the same room, at a common table, and with a common purse. He was my master in spiritual things and he showed me the path to growth in knowledge of God's will. And thus at last we became one and the same being."[18]

Iñigo's experience with the fourth portioniste of the Sainte-Barbe turret room—Francis Xavier—would not be so serene a coming together as with the studious, modest, affectionate shepherd boy from Savoy. The gentleman of Navarre was all sharp edges, bravado, hauteur: What a musketeer he would have made a few decades later with his countryman Henry of Navarre!

He was a sturdy noble in the service of the little kingdom of Pamplona. His father was both Don Juan de Iassu and Jean III d'Albret. His mother's family, the Azpilcuetas, were of even nobler origin. Everything seemed to mark their son (born, like Pierre Favre, in 1506) for a brilliant future. But Francis's father died on the eve of his tenth birthday. His brothers—who had been on the French side when Iñigo de Loyola fought in the ranks of the Spanish party at Pamplona—were first condemned to death and then pardoned by Charles V.

Those reversals did not entirely shatter the plans of the Xaviers. In September 1525, shortly after his mother's death, Francis left for Paris, where diligent studying was bound to assure him an important ecclesiastical benefice in the diocese of Pamplona. He was by now a Parisian. Handsome, energetic, hot-blooded, he was active in every field—eloquent in disputation, passionate in debate, he was also high-jump champion of the Île Notre-Dame.

Was he a playboy? Francis appears to have held himself constantly aloof from women. According to his latest biographer, Georg Schurhammer, S.J., it was for very precise reasons: "His comrades led him on their nocturnal escapades, with one of their teachers. But God protected him from the gravest of errors. Seeing the hideous pustules on the faces of certain classmates and of a corrupt master—who later lost his life—he conceived a terror of the abyss that kept him forever from it, and lived chaste amid all the pitfalls of university life."[19]

And, on a racier note, the excellent Hercule Rasiel: "He was of lively mind, pleasant humor, lofty soul, and high heart, but he was proud, vain, and ambitious. At first he sneered at Iñigo, at his sayings, at his behavior, at his fanatical utterances; and far from listening to him, he mocked the beggarly life which Iñigo led and tried to persuade others to lead."[20] Indeed, in Francis's eyes this Iñigo—this limping graybeard, scruffy and sermonizing, this "Basque madman" (as any good Navarrese would have thought him)—was "the simpleton of the Street of Dogs."

Need we add that Loyola could not have cared less? Nobody has better described the relationship that developed between them than Juan de Polanco, the founder's secretary, pouring out his heart twenty years later to the French Jesuit Edmond Auger: "I heard it said by our great molder of men* Ignatius that the roughest clay he ever had to knead was this young Francis Xavier in the early years. . . . He was a sturdy, well-born man of Biscay;† having studied philosophy assiduously enough, he had little consideration for Ignatius who at that time kept himself alive by the charity of others. . . . He could scarcely set eyes on him without making sport of his plans."[21]

"Our great molder of men Ignatius . . . " In 1550 that was the most obvious thing in the world. But it was already a fact in 1532 at the time our small lame man, already a most formidable "Jesuit," laid siege to this Navarrese, a man jealous enough of his honor to have had his letters of nobility solemnly confirmed in 1531. Having been appointed professor of philosophy at the Collège de Beauvais, Xavier was as proud of his master status as of his blue trans-Pyrenean blood.

Loyola played on this vanity like a virtuoso, singlemindedly drumming up enthusiastic audiences for Xavier's classes, surrounding him with fervor and praise. This merry-go-round (to a lover of bullfighting the term *faena* seems quite appropriate) went on for two whole years. Not until early in 1533 did Iñigo deliver the coup de grâce. According to legend, his weapon was the biblical question, which he put to Xavier: "How shall it profit a man to gain the whole world if he loses his soul?" Many biographers have passed the story on. Schurhammer questions its authenticity, but reminds us that Francis himself would quote those momentous words up to his dying day.[22]

It was at Alcalá, where they were studying, that Diego Laínez and Alfonso Salmerón first heard about Iñigo de Loyola. Born in 1512 at Almazán in Old Castile, Laínez came from a family of "New Christians"—that is, of Jewish converts

---

*A phrase worthy of Montaigne.
†Biscay is one of the seven provinces of the Basque-Navarre country. It is here used to denote the whole territory.

to Catholicism. Salmerón, born in 1515, was from Toledo. We cannot claim that they decided to go to Paris to join the man of the *Exercises*. In fact, they went there to round out their philosophical studies. But there is evidence that by the summer of 1533 they were seeking the Basque preacher in the Latin Quarter. According to Rasiel: "Even though they had never before laid eyes on him, they recognized him, simply from people's descriptions, in the first lame man to cross their path. His haggard countenance, his pious air, and his Spanish visage left no doubt that this was the man they sought."[23]

And splendid recruits they turned out to be.

Iñigo may already have been acquainted with Simón Rodrigues and Nicolás Alonso, known as Bobadilla after his native village near Palencia. In his historical notes on the Company, Rodrigues writes that the founder's fourth companion, after Favre and Xavier, but before Laínez and Salmerón, was "a Portuguese who, being unworthy, is not even deserving of mention." This anonymous and unworthy Portuguese was the writer himself, Rodrigues de Azevedo, one of the fifty young noblemen to whom King John III had awarded scholarships to attend Sainte-Barbe. There, Rodrigues naturally met the three other "conspirators."

Bobadilla, on the other hand, was extremely poor, even though he had acquired and then himself taught some rudiments of philosophy at Valladolid. He had come to Paris to follow classes in the Collège des Trois Langues, later to become the Collège de France. Perhaps it was there that he met Iñigo—who told him that the Collège's teaching was "dangerous" and took him under his wing. Irascible, tireless, outspoken, Nicolás would be the enfant terrible of the "Iñiguists" for the next thirty years.

So much for the seven founding fathers. They would soon be joined by three French recruits: Claude Le Jay from Savoy, Paschase (or Pasquier) Broët from Picardy, and the Provençal Jean Codure. A little later a very young Spaniard, Diego Hocés, joined their number; he would soon be carried off by illness. But before they could take the decisive step several of them, and Iñigo in particular, had first to complete the studies that had brought them to Paris.

It is hard to identify the teachers of Iñigo, Pierre, and Francis at the "College of the Arts." We know all about the masters who brought glory upon it: Mathurin Cordier, Jacques-Louis d'Estrebay, George Buchanan, Gelida and Guillaume Postel, Jean Fernel, and André de Gouvea. (De Gouvea was the principal's nephew, who, suspected of harboring Lutheran sympathies, had to go underground before emerging as director of the Collège de Guyenne in Bordeaux. There he won the admiration of the student Michel de Montaigne.)

There is nothing to confirm that any of these humanists played a direct part in educating our scholars at Sainte-Barbe. But we do know that, like Pierre

Favre, Iñigo de Loyola followed the classes of the Franciscan Pierre de Cornibus and of François Picart (the former being open to humanism, the latter less so). Picart, a populist preacher, was close to Noël Beda and "ardently opposed to the innovators."[24]

We need to linger for a moment in contemplation of these troubled waters in which the "Iñiguists" swam. The founding fathers lived those Latin Quarter years in the midst of fundamental debate, debate that inevitably brought them to fruition in a spiritually bellicose and somber climate, in which many of them staked their lives and more than their lives. But what is remarkable is that these men—who twenty years later, after the Council of Trent, would be considered the champions of the Counter-Reformation—scarcely mentioned the fact of Lutheranism in their writings of the time (and Calvinism of course would make its appearance only after their Paris sojourn).

A reading of contemporary chroniclers, of diarists such as the "Burgher of Paris," suggests that Paris was a battlefield in which the Lutheran offensive constantly threatened Catholic supremacy, from the Court[*] to the bishoprics of Paris and Meaux, from the nobility to the Latin Quarter. Do we find an echo of all this in Iñigo and his friends? None at all—apart from the briefest of allusions in Francis Xavier's correspondence and shreds of recollections in the later writings of Rodrigues or Bobadilla.

Men like Pierre Favre and Loyola never doubted the legitimacy of the Catholic Church or its sacramental apparatus. But their every act led toward active personalization of a spiritual life based as much on affectivity as on intellect, on fundamental, militant poverty, on a passionate quest for knowledge. Quite enough to keep the cowled policemen on their toes.

Favre, Francis, and Iñigo did not journey hand in hand toward the "master of arts," or doctorate, offered by the University of Paris:[†] The first two had a three-year start on their elder, and as we know, Xavier had been teaching with great success since 1530 at the Collège de Dormans-Beauvais.

It was in March 1532, after three years and a few months of study at Sainte-Barbe, that Iñigo de Loyola, now a little over forty-one, a member of the *veneranda natio Gallicana* (as we have seen, Spanish students, like all others from southern Europe, were subsumed into the "nation of France"), sat down before four examiners (one for each "nation") to take the examination known as *déterminance:* the aim being to *determinare quaestionem,* to sustain an argument.

---

*Where the King's mistress joined forces with his sister and his confessor Pierre Duchatel to encourage the sovereign to tolerance.

†Laínez, Salmerón, Rodrigues, and Bobadilla had already won their diplomas in Spain and Portugal.

It is easy to picture him, a small, limping, shabbily dressed forty-one-year-old, tense and stiff as he faced the four doctors and held forth in a Latin that (to judge from his own writings) was probably as sketchy as his mongrel brand of Castilian, Basque, and French. We do not know the theme of his argument. We know only that he passed thirtieth out of a hundred candidates. This was no mean achievement, in view of the handicaps he had overcome (and perhaps in view of the legend of Iñigo the footloose visionary—which could not have found unanimous favor among his robed judges).

It took him another year to progress to his master's degree. The final hurdle consisted of two examinations. One was a private (or *in cameris*) test known as the *quodlibetarius,* which might bear upon absolutely any subject, selected at random by the examiner; it was held in the church of Saint-Julien-le-Pauvre. The other was a public hearing at Sainte-Geneviève before a jury presided over by the university chancellor. Then, at a date set by the rector, graduates were assembled in ceremonial costume and led before the same chancellor who delivered their "licenses" and his apostolic blessing.

The Company's archives in Rome have preserved the diploma conferred on the grizzled graduate a year and two months after he sat the examination during Lent of 1533:

> We . . . desirous by these presents of bearing witness to the truth, by whomsoever it may be possessed, let it be known that our well-beloved and discreet Master Ignatius of Loyola, of the diocese of Pamplona, Master of Arts, has honorably and laudably achieved the status of Master in the illustrious Faculty of Arts at Paris after rigorous examinations concluded in the Year of Our Lord one thousand five hundred and thirty-four after Easter, in accordance with the statutes and customs of the said faculty and with all the solemnity associated with the occasion. In witness whereof we affix our great seal. Given at Paris, at our general assembly solemnly convened in the Church of the Mathurins, in the abovementioned Year of Our Lord 1534 on the fourteenth day of May. Signed, Le Roux.

The reader will of course have noted the name given the recipient: Ignatius of Loyola. This is the first time Iñigo was so named, but not the last. Why? Was it because the *reverenda natio Gallicana* or the University did not recognize as sufficiently Christian a name borne a few centuries earlier by a Spanish abbot unknown to the Parisian authorities? We do not know whether the person concerned was consulted; whether, being requested to choose a better-known patron, he himself plumped for Saint Ignatius* of Antioch, a disciple of Saint

---

*After *Ignis,* or "fire."

John, martyred under Trajan and a Father of the Church. From now on "the graduate Iñigo" would be "Master Ignatius." The "Iñiguists" would have to cast about for another name.

The new Master of Arts could consider his Parisian goals achieved: No Castilian or Roman inquisitor could now avoid taking his Master's gown and biretta or his Parisian honors into consideration. But Ignatius himself was fully aware that although he had acquitted himself well at the University of Paris, he remained virtually unacquainted with theology—which was after all his chief concern. He knew nothing of Duns Scotus, of William of Occam, even of Thomas Aquinas.

As his new masters he chose the Dominicans, or "Jacobins," of the Rue Saint-Jacques. By no means an obvious choice. He had after all little reason to look fondly on the order: From Alcalá to Salamanca to Paris, the Inquisition had always addressed him (admittedly in relatively benign terms) through the voice of the preaching friars. If Master Ignatius elected to knock at the gate of the Jacobins, where he knew he would be at the mercy of "his own" inquisitor, Mathieu Ory, it was probably because they purveyed the teachings of Thomas Aquinas—who had received his degree in theology there three centuries earlier—better than anyone else. If the masters both at Sainte-Barbe and at Montaigu considered Aristotle the beginning and end of all knowledge, for Iñigo the "angelic doctor" Aquinas remained the supreme authority in matters theological. It was thus an education saturated in Saint Thomas* that the author of the *Exercises* imbibed for the next eighteen months.

Although a fearless tactician, a bold strategist, and an unpredictable guerrilla fighter on so many battlefields, Iñigo was no ideological revolutionary. Why look beyond what the author of the *Summa* had proposed to the world for the reconciliation, once and for all, of faith and reason, science and religion? Clearly we have moved some distance away from those visionary ecstasies, not far removed from irrationality, to which the author of the *Exercises* had once been suspected of surrendering himself.

Was our doctor, newly dignified by his biretta, now thoroughly pacified? Subdued? Ready to carry out the great politico-spiritual commandments? Already of Rome, already a "General," already master of casuistry and moderation? No. A few swift strokes will suffice to remind us of our hero's baroque side, of the explosions of missionary exhibitionism that still recall the man of Manresa.

No chronicler, except for the Loyola of the *Autobiography,* brings more flavor to these Parisian *Fioretti* than our good Hercule Rasiel. Let us once again give him the floor:

*The only scholastic author the humanists respected.

A man of his acquaintance enjoyed gallant relations with a woman living in a village hard by Paris. What did Iñigo do in order to extract him from this commerce? He walked out into a lake beside the road this man would be taking. Then, with its near-freezing waters up to his chin, he cried out to the man: "Wretch! Whither are you bound? Do you not hear the roar of thunder? Do you not see the sword of Divine Justice readied to strike you? Well then," he went on in a terrible voice, "go and slake your brutish passion: I shall suffer here for you until the Wrath of Heaven is appeased." Struck by such an extraordinary act, the swain turned about in his tracks, and began a changed life. . . . Iñigo, proud of the success of this extravagant method, told those who disapproved of him that in order to win souls he would willingly wander the streets barefoot, his head festooned with horns, clad in the most ridiculous and even the most demeaning of costumes.

Meanwhile, and despite the fact that he was now "Master" Iñigo, he had reverted to his old habit of self-mortification. He would retire, says Rasiel, "to a dark and deep quarry of Montmartre, and there again inflicted on his body the pious cruelties he had practiced in the cave at Manresa, which this quarry recalled to him." In consequence, as he himself admitted, his stomach pains returned* with such unbearable insistence that this stoic was reduced to consulting doctors—who enjoined him, as the price of survival, from practicing any further self-mortification.

Survival? The project steadily ripening in his heart made it mandatory. The cohort of companions he had so long failed to assemble was now gathered around him. His university goals were attained. And his adventures in the quarries of Montmartre had revealed to him the appropriate site for a ritual that increasingly obsessed him: a chapel built into the side of the hill overlooking the northern walls of the capital. That was the spot where he would bring his companions together, where the vows that would forever bind them would be pronounced.

Let Pierre Favre's *Memoirs* take up the story, as he describes—in terms so fastidiously evangelical they approach parody—the fateful day when the foundations of the Society of Jesus were laid:

> On Saint Mary's day in the month of August, in this year of 1534, already united by a like determination and all (with the exception of Master Francis [Xavier] who had not yet performed them but shared in our designs) well versed in the *Exercises*, we betook us to Our Lady

*Or as Father Fouqueray unforgettably said, "It pleased God to visit His servant with a cruel illness" (Fouqueray, *Histoire*, p. 51).

of Montmartre near Paris, where each one of us swore the vow to leave for Jerusalem at the appointed date and to place ourselves upon our return under the authority of the Pontiff of Rome, and also, at the appropriate hour, "to leave our families and our nets*".[25]

The little chapel then called Notre-Dame (and later the Chapelle des Martyres) clung to the slopes of Montmartre (Mount of Martyrs), half an hour on foot from the ramparts of Saint-Denis. A semicrypt, virtually a catacomb. You stooped beneath the low entrance vault to reach the partly buried altar inside. There was another chapel on the floor above, but the companions assembled on this lower level.

Did Ignatius choose this distant hermitage, cared for by the Benedictines, because it recalled the perilous existence of the early Christians—or even, as Pierre Favre's words suggest, the labors of the Apostles? We can perhaps glimpse the reasons that made this site attractive to Loyola's fevered imagination: In it he found both the wildness of Manresa (his own "Early Church") and the Catholic order with which he wished to remain involved, that blend of spontaneity and discipline which by turns inflamed and curbed his anguished temperament. On that bucolic hill, in sight of the city where he had just conquered the rudiments of learning, he was at the crossroads of the natural and the man-made, looking out over the broadest of horizons, in a place at once free and consecrated. And "so much apart" already, already "so very Jesuit" . . .

We can dream. We can picture the seven companions—the lame man with the sparse gray hair and the absorbed gaze and the six cheerful students, walking together on this summer dawn toward the gypsum cliffs dug out of the hillside. An almost rustic landscape dotted with small garden plots, with here and there a barn or an inn, a scattering of windmills among the vineyards on the upper slopes, and higher still the Benedictine abbey that crowns the Mount of Martyrs with groups of local peasants climbing, and perhaps singing, toward it. A fifteenth day of August.

And on the same path our band from the Latin Quarter. The big ones, muscular Francis, the short ones, the fragile ones like Laínez. There are the extroverts, like hot-tempered Bobadilla, and the intense ones, like Salmerón. Even the one who believed himself driven by the most personal of inspirations, Simón Rodrigues. But all—even though they had not all "done" *The Spiritual Exercises*—shared an intense spiritual familiarity with Ignatius of Loyola. All burned for departure, to the Holy Land, to martyrdom. In short, they were adventurers, in quest of something immense: men of their time.

Jerusalem, the earthly Jerusalem, was their overriding goal. Such was their

---

*Which were of course the working instruments of Christ's Apostles.

shared desire to incarnate their faith, to live it in their flesh and their blood, that the site of Christ's Passion counted for more with them than any dangers that might lurk there. But they had weighed their chances: War, epidemic, and Islamic rule might well put Palestine beyond their reach. In which case they would travel as far as Venice, and wait there a year. If it turned out that the enterprise was doomed, then they would "help souls" in Rome under the aegis of the Pope.

This subproject, envisaged within the framework of the first, is already strikingly "Jesuit" in nature. The law of possibilities . . . However intoxicated they might be by their vast Eastern project, they were careful to build another just downstream from it, so that failure to achieve the first goal would not mean overall failure. It was a question of striking a balance between dream and hope.

And poverty? They did of course vow to observe it, and to make it radical, evangelical. They decided it would enter into force three years later, when they expected to have completed the theological studies that several of them (including Loyola) had not yet finished. They even specified a ban on receiving anything at all in exchange for celebrating Mass or hearing confession.

But one issue in the discussion, which was "long,"[26] remained unresolved: Some of them wanted to emphasize that the group's goals consisted of "carrying the truth to the Infidel," and very specifically to the Holy Land, mirroring the spirit, if not the methods, of the Crusades. Others, while not opposing the pilgrimage to Jerusalem, framed the question in more universal terms, already arguing from a perspective that was to be the Company's in the centuries ahead —the perspective of the planet itself.*

After Pierre Favre, ordained three months earlier (the only one of them so far), had said Mass and administered Communion, the companions decided to indulge themselves in a picnic around a spring their guide had discovered. Despite his determination to seem fully in control of himself, Ignatius could not conceal his exhilaration. At last he had them, this band of devout rebels, of hardheads and hotheads, of intellectuals and builders, of vagabond theologians. Give me seven determined men and I will change the face of the world!

That such a moment of grace and exaltation should find no echo in Ignatius's *Autobiography* (even though it was dictated twenty years later) is incomprehensible. The equivalent of reducing the story of Christ's Passion to a police report mentioning Pilate, the Cross, the tomb . . .

Normally so concerned with setting the stage, with the importance of sight, of the visual, Ignatius unaccountably neglected to recreate that scene, that landscape, those "rich hours" so spontaneously etched in the memory of every par-

*For additional matter on this score, see Chapter III.

ticipant, just as he "forgot" to evoke Jerusalem rising up out of the Holy Land before his eyes ten years earlier. Here we are in a zone of enigmas, of the still-unresolved shadows swathing this inscrutable figure.

A few of his later disciples, more ingenuous perhaps than the founder, took it upon themselves to lay a plaque (which was later removed) on the spot. It read:

Societas Jesu
Qui sanctum Ignatium Loyolam
Patrem agnoscit, Lutetiam matrem
(The Society of Jesus which recognizes Saint Ignatius as
father and Lutetia [Paris] as mother)[7]

The ringleader of the August 15 conspirators now made ready to leave for Spain: He finally agreed with the doctors who had urged him to restore his ruined health in his native land. There were other reasons for his going, in particular his concern to persuade the families of Xavier, Laínez, and Salmerón not to oppose their vocation (their vow of poverty being not without consequences for the family fortunes).

But on the eve of departure he was advised that the Inquisition sought him. This time he was not reproached with the evangelical excess he had demonstrated at Alcalá or in the "Amador affair." This time it was the contrary offense of excessive secretiveness, the underground conspiracy that had brought the seven doctors together in the crypt of a distant suburb. The bogeymen of the Black Legend of Jesuitry were already astir!

True to his established method, he hastened to call on the Inquisitor, who was no longer Mathieu Ory but another Dominican, Valentin Liévin—who demanded to see the *Exercises.* In them the preaching brother found no harm, but on the contrary much to admire, and he asked for a copy. But Ignatius was not to be put off with kind words in such dangerous territory. He felt entitled to insist on a solemn acquittal (*quitus*), and received it. The document has not been preserved, but in Rome, Father Fouqueray unearthed a message addressed to Loyola in 1537, doubtless on his renewed insistence:

> We, Brother Thomas Laurent, of the Order of Preaching Friars, lecturer in theology and Inquisitor General of heretical error and of the Catholic Faith in the Kingdom of France, do here certify and make known to all . . . that our predecessor Brother Valentin Liévin . . . , Inquisitor General for the whole Kingdom of France, at a past date conducted an inquiry touching the life and the doctrine of Ignatius of Loyola, and that we who were his secretary have never heard it said that there was in him anything unfitting in a Catholic and Christian man. We have furthermore known the said Loyola and Master Pierre

Le Fèvre,* as also several other of his familiars; and we have always seen them leading a Catholic and virtuous life without ever discerning in them anything not fitting perfectly Christian men. Moreover the *Exercises* purveyed by the said Ignatius appeared to us Catholic insofar as we were able, after examination, to determine.

Ignatius could go in peace. Until the next scare. He took his leave in February 1535, exactly seven years after reaching Paris. But first he had arranged to meet his six companions again, in the spring of 1537, in Venice. The first stage of the great adventure was under way.

Reaching Venice—jumping-off point for the Orient—a few months before his companions, Loyola was reunited with his Spanish friends from Alcalá, Diego and Estéban de Eguía, and recruited a young graduate named Diego Hocés. In January 1537 Favre, Xavier, Laínez, and the others joined him in the City of the doges, intending to leave for Rome and ask the Pope's blessing for the journey to the Holy Land.

But it soon became clear to them that the Turkish thrust into the eastern Mediterranean and the Adriatic made nonsense of the Palestinian dream. For how long? Perhaps forever. While they waited, they nursed the sick and volunteered their services in the Venetian hospitals where incurables, particularly lepers, were housed. After that they dispersed through the cities of northern Italy, from Venice to Ravenna and from Verona to Padua. (In Padua the first of Ignatius's disciples, and the newest of his recruits, Diego Hocés, died of exhaustion.)

Ordained a priest (along with most of his companions) in Venice in June 1537, Loyola now resigned himself to a radical redirection of the group's energies. He describes this crucial decision in the following words: "They decided that after a year† had passed, and if they still found no passage, they would go to Rome."

It was October 1537. Ignatius decided to travel with Favre and Laínez. With Favre on one side and Laínez on the other, the master of the *Exercises* was only four leagues from the Eternal City when he called a halt at a place called La Storta, where a small chapel now stands.‡ There he buried himself in prayer. For what subsequently occurred we must first turn to the Pilgrim's own brief version of events, however terse and naive, before fleshing it out with other accounts:

. . . he felt a great change in his soul and so clearly did he see God the

<hr />

*Favre.
†The year 1537, spent in Venice.
‡The chapel is still visited today. Bombed in 1944, it has been restored.

Father place him with Christ, His Son, that he had no doubts that
God the Father did place him with His Son.*

As we know, the *Autobiography* was dictated to Gonçalves da Câmara, who,
as a close associate of the founders, had already heard several of them describe
this decisive episode. As the old "General" reawakened this memory, Gonçalves
da Câmara broke in to remind him that Laínez, who witnessed the incident,†
had expanded on it considerably. "You may well be right!" was Ignatius's retort,
"but I have no recollection of it." It is pointless to wonder at this memory lapse:
Ignatius's character is full of surprises, and saints are not reporters. But what
does Laínez have to say about the matter?

That the Eternal Father told Loyola: " 'I will be favorable to you in Rome.'
And then, turning to where Jesus His Son stood by His side, the Cross upon His
shoulder: 'I wish You to take him as Your servant.' Jesus then directed these
words to Ignatius: 'I wish you to be Our servant.' "[28]

Favorable to Ignatius in Rome . . . Did that mean He would stand surety for
the undertaking dreamed up in Montmartre and modified in Venice? Laínez reported nothing of the kind, but said that in trying to explain that word "favorable" Ignatius confided: "Perhaps we will be crucified in Rome." In other words,
what might sound to the uninitiated like an astonishing burst of pride was in
fact the Roman version of the Palestinian plan—martyrdom on Golgotha . . .
Christ's fate replaced by Saint Peter's . . . We are in strange waters indeed.

But what the narrator has to stress here is the supreme confirmation of the
Roman option, the Roman "expedient." As Pedro de Leturia wrote, the seer of
La Storta heard exactly the words he hoped for. They were words that conferred
a mystic, imaginary, "affective" dimension on a choice that had been more or
less forced on him, the same dimension he had "so often felt in the pull exerted
on him by Jerusalem and Palestine."[29] The effect of the La Storta experience was
to turn Rome (most opportunely) into another Jerusalem.

By the time Ignatius and his companions reached it, Rome was not just the most
corrupt city in the Christian West: It was also a humiliated, wounded city,
brooding over its shame, binding its oozing sores.

Ten years earlier, the Constable of Bourbon's German pikemen, carelessly
tossed into the city by Charles V, had joined the hordes raised by Italian princelings at odds with the Holy See to sack the Eternal City. Barricaded for more
than a week behind the formidable ramparts of the Castel Sant'Angelo, trem-
bling and sobbing, Pope Clement VII had witnessed the methodical destruction
of his capital, which Erasmus considered "not the end of a city but the end of

---

Lo metteva con suo Figliolo, extremely down-to-earth wording—almost his "little one," his "lad."
†As did Pierre Favre.

the world." A week of rape and pillaging, of murder and defilement, the altars strewn with filth and turned over to black masses, the confessional booths transformed into bordellos, donkeys parading on the Pincio draped in priestly habits.

For the head of the Catholic Church the harshest blow was the conclusion by the people of Rome that the disaster was a punishment, like that visited upon Sodom and Gomorrah, of a city that had for too long tried God's patience. The shock to the papacy was all the harder because Luther was at that very moment wresting a third of Europe from Roman sway; the Turk, scimitar in hand, was laying siege to Balkan and Danubian Christendom; and the giddy rise of Charles V's empire was outshining the Vatican's.

In 1534, ten years after the earthquake that swept Clement VII aside, old Alessandro Farnese was elected Pope under the name of Paul III. The Society conceived in Montmartre as he was being elected would be born under his aegis.

What a curious sponsor for these vagabonds of God! Less extraordinary, perhaps, than an Alexander VI whose whole reign was one long sacrilege, a bloody-handed Julius II, or a cheerfully cynical Leo X. But the brother of Giulia Farnese, the Borgia Pope's favorite mistress, was at first sight scarcely different from this gallery of pontiffs who had turned Savonarola into a martyr and Luther into the widely heeded spokesman of a vast anger.

Alessandro sprang from one of those tribes, as rapacious as it was fabulously wealthy—the Medici, the Colonnas, the d'Estes, the delle Roveres*—who filled the conclaves, ran the Curia, pandered to the pleasures of the princes of the Church, and provided the pontifical armies with war leaders. It was because he was the brother of Giulia la Bella, Lucrezia's rival for the Borgia Pope's favors, that Alessandro Farnese had at twenty donned his Cardinal's hat. Far too young for the purple to cool his blood: Bastards clustered about him like apples around a tree. It was now his great age and particularly his unimpeachable neutrality in the quarrel between Charles V and Francis I—rather than his talents—that opened for him the succession to the unfortunate Clement. And at first nothing indicated that he might be the reformer on whom the salvation of the Catholic Church depended. Indeed, the first two cardinals he designated were his nephews, one fourteen, the other seventeen.

But a few months later the Pope the Romans called "our good old man" announced a series of decisions that made of him the initiator of a Catholic reform that the "doctors of Paris" would soon stamp with their own ferocious energy. In the space of a few months two groups of cardinals were promoted, re-

*The Borgias were Spanish.

shaping the Sacred College: Jean du Bellay, John Fisher, Gasparro Contarini, Reginald Pole, Otto von Truchsess, and Marcello Cervini, the leading intellects of a Catholicism at bay.

But Paul III was not content simply to refashion the Curia: He named an episcopal committee to address the state of the Church and offer proposals for its reformation. The report of these "wise men" is an indictment more terrible than Luther's railings:

Like the horse of Troy, O Most Holy Father, such a host of evils and abuses dwells within God's Church as to lead us to despair of its salvation. This state of affairs is known even to the Infidel, whence the derision in which they hold our religion and the dishonor they heap upon Christ. . . .

Blessed Father, foreigners are scandalized on entering the Church of Saint Peter to find Mass celebrated by certain ignorant priests clothed in filthy vestments. . . . That is true for the other Churches as well. Courtesans move about the city with the ease of matrons, traveling in mule-drawn carriages, escorted in broad daylight by members of the nobility, by the close acquaintances of cardinals, by priests. In no other city is such disorder to be seen.

The report concludes with this wistful exhortation to Paul III: "You have chosen the name of Paul. . . . We hope that you have been elected to restore in our hearts and in our works the name of Christ, forgotten by the people and by us the priests, in order to cure our ills . . . and to turn away from us the wrath of Christ and the deserved vengeance already hanging above our heads."[30]

Such was Rome and such Rome's state of mind—made up of disgust, bitterness, and a vague hankering for cleansing if not for reform—as Ignatius of Loyola and his companions made their way there in small groups and following different paths.

But why Rome? Why did God's most recent Fools choose to settle in a city threatened by the "wrath of a forgotten and dishonored Christ"? Why throw themselves on the mercy of a Pontiff whose faults were better known to them than his very recent efforts at reform? And why did these ascetic vagabonds grasp that tottering discredited throne so firmly that they became forever known as *papistissimi* ("most papalist of all")—as those who at the Council of Trent would "hamstring" so many reform-minded candidates the better to assure papal supremacy?

It is tempting to attribute this Roman fixation of the founders to an overriding need to cauterize the tumor at its most advanced spot. But this explanation will not stand. Themselves reformed, and most exactingly so, the gypsies of

Montmartre had no intention of storming the pulpits of Rome in order to rant there against the corruption of others. It was elsewhere, or in other ways, that they meant to carry word and example.

Nor is it any more judicious to see Counter-Reformation as their principal objective (not at any rate until the Council of Trent, which lay ten years ahead), or to see their action as a strategic deployment in a citadel under heretic bombardment. To advance this theory would be to feed the obsessive "military" myth of the Jesuits, a myth we have already disposed of.

Admittedly, one of the original texts by the founding fathers indicates that they proposed not only to convert the Turk but to bring the Lutherans back to the fold. But that was not their raison d'être or their modus operandi: According to one of the best historians of the Company's beginnings, the Spanish Jesuit Pedro de Leturia, their goal was not primarily "polemical," nor was their behavior inspired by "reaction" or their concern "focused on counter-reform."

In a penetrating article in the Jesuit magazine *Civiltà Cattolica*, Leturia opposes the notion that the founding fathers' "Roman" choice stemmed from a grand Vatican strategy, sprung fully armed from the military mind of the lord of Loyola. It is of course easy to imagine Loyola contemplating the universe from the academic heights of Paris and perceiving Rome as the strategic center, first of the struggle against Protestantism, and then of the future conquests and dominion of a giant and soon-to-be-united Christendom. But according to de Leturia, who bases his arguments on the contemporary testimony of Pierre Favre, Simón Rodrigues, Laínez, and the punctilious Polanco, as well as on Ignatius's *Autobiography* and correspondence, the Society's choice of Rome was not the fulfillment of a "primary ideal" but a matter of second-rank expediency.

For they had to accept the obvious. Jerusalem was beyond reach, the Holy Land forbidden. Dangerous in 1523, when Iñigo went there, the pilgrimage was now suicidal. It was this inability to enter or remain in the Holy Land, writes Pierre Favre, that decided them to submit "to the will and judgment of the Supreme Pontiff, for we knew that he possessed greater knowledge of what was most meet for all Christendom."

Rather than a sponsor or a father, they sought a guide, a direction finder. And what makes this movement to Rome so important for the rest of the story is that it stamped the Company with a brand-new seal, that of realism, if not of modernity. From their very first steps, Ignatius and his companions had to defer to realities, adapt their actions to what was feasible, redirect their thirst for the absolute into humble service. Soon—heading for the East and West Indies—they would again take wing. But that radical turnaround of 1538, those Roman moorings, would impose upon Loyola and his comrades a kind of doctrine, a philosophy of action—the replacement of a symbolic site, Jerusalem, by a center of operations, Rome, the substitution of an expedient for an ideal.

And what of Pope Paul III in all this? If the companions' decision to take root in Rome seems disconcerting, the welcome that old Farnese extended to these dervishes of virtue is even more so. He had already set the machinery of reformation in motion, calling into its service the least orthodox of the leaders of humanistic Catholicism. But that did not explain the spectacle of the brother of Giulia la Bella joining forces with these exalted puritans, these tatterdemalion rabble-rousers.

There were two reasons for his reaction. The Church was in such great danger that any support seemed helpful to this politically acute Pontiff (much as the feeble Charles VII of France had earlier seized the chance of recruiting the shepherd girl from Lorraine to his cause). There was more: The cynical Paul III, wise in all his century's machinations, was nevertheless astounded (and very soon moved) to be approached by these threadbare cobweb-spinners who (could it even be possible?) asked nothing but to put themselves at his service! Nothing, really nothing? It was enough to throw any Farnese or Medici right off his stride.

"It was at that time unimaginable," observed the Jesuit historian Charles O'Neill recently. "Because he was a man with heart, and with a mind already committed to reform, Paul III was overwhelmed."[31]

Thus the person about to enter Rome was still very far from the hard-edged realist historians have tried to make of him (even though he would later provide a host of arguments in favor of such a reading).

Whether or not "crucifixion" awaited them, it took the companions only a few days to find shelter in Rome, in a small house sitting among the vines close to the church of Trinità dei Monti, on the present Piazza di Spagna, made over to them by a certain Guarzoni. Two of them would soon be teaching at the Collegio della Sapienza, while Ignatius who (although boasting a Paris doctorate) could preach only in Spanish, would do so at Santa Maria di Monserrat.

Their Roman welcome surpassed all their hopes. In particular, they enjoyed the open support of Cardinal Contarini and of Don Pedro Ortiz. The latter, who had once denounced Loyola for "corrupting" the Spanish students of Sainte-Barbe, was now the Emperor Charles V's highly influential ambassador to the Holy See. In this capacity he favored them with every possible mark of esteem. Indeed the highest possible mark, for under Ignatius's direction, he himself performed *The Spiritual Exercises* at the monastery of Monte Cassino.

Admittedly, there had been the Mainardi affair. It is difficult for us today to determine how seriously the "Parisian doctors" were threatened by the strife that arose around this man. Yet Iñigo—who had undergone incarceration in Alcalá, flight from Salamanca, the hardships of Montaigu, and the attentions of half a dozen inquisitors—later pronounced this set-to with a fire-and-brimstone preacher and his supporters "the most severe" persecution "that he had ever undergone." Or, as Leturia expressed it, "the cross awaiting him in the Eternal City."

A Piedmontese preacher named Agostino Mainardi (like Luther, an Augustinian monk) was drawing crowds to the Church of the Augustinians. Favre and Laínez went inside, and emerged astonished: Luther himself was speaking through Mainardi's mouth, if not on the morals of the papacy, at least on the crucial question of justification through grace. They warned the Augustinian, who sneered at them; and from then on they devoted their own sermons to a refutation of his theses.

Mainardi had ardent supporters. They included a group of Spanish dignitaries who, to hit back at the "Parisian doctors," whispered that they were scoundrels, charlatans, fugitives from justice who had been hounded from Alcalá to Paris to Venice by every arm of secular and ecclesiastical law—and who were on top of all else ill-disguised Lutherans. Provoked beyond endurance, Ignatius gave full vent to his genius for litigation. He insisted on seeing Paul III, making his case before him, obtaining his protection. For a holy man hungering after martyrdom, he certainly showed great fire in debate and great skill in presenting a brief! Was he already a Jesuit General? Or still in the cannon's mouth on the ramparts at Pamplona?

Paul III was at Nice, striving to effect a reconciliation of Charles V and Francis I—no mean agenda! Nevertheless, he invited the leader of the "Iñiguists" to call on him at the delightful Palazzo Frascati, his summer residence.

It was a happy man Ignatius went to meet. Paul III had just arranged an armistice—albeit fleeting—between the two most powerful sovereigns in Europe, and had married his grandson Ottavio to Charles V's natural daughter. Such felicities could not fail to put him in a golden mood. And now old Farnese, heir of the princes of Orvieto (it required a certain boldness to say that he was Pope by God's grace), stood face-to-face with the scion of the lords of Loyola, who had beggared himself and assumed command of a beggarly crew in order to exalt the Almighty.

It was Ignatius's first real encounter with a Supreme Pontiff. On the eve of departure for Jerusalem in 1524 he had stood among a group of pilgrims and received the papal blessing (from Adrian VI); but Paul III himself, who for several months had been inviting Favre and Laínez to his table for theological discussions, had not yet opened his doors to this savage and passionately controversial figure.

Had the old man been given a favorable report by his astrologers, who classi-fied visitors according to the signs of the zodiac? To examine the small gaunt man before him, Paul thrust out a very pale face, lengthened by the beard worn by popes since the sack of Rome, in token, or so it was said, of mourning. His gaze was sharp, his movements still lively. He spoke in a low voice and in a highly refined Latin that contrasted with the rudimentary variety spoken by the author of the *Exercises*. Ignatius's plea—studded with painful memories in which the Inquisition played a leading part (he knew that this humanist Pope set small store by the institution, even though he knew how to exploit it)—seemed to touch Paul. But Ignatius did not seek kind words. He wanted a real trial, a written, irrefutable judgment. Paul III wanted to see justice done. But where were the witnesses, the plaintiffs, the lawyers?

Whether or not we see here the hand of God, Ignatius would owe the acquit-tal he sought to an extraordinary convergence of circumstances: Three of the men who for ten years had hounded him (before finally exonerating him) across the face of Europe—the Inquisitor of Alcalá, Figueroa; the Paris Inquisi-tor, Mathieu Ory; and Venice's episcopal judge, Gasparro de Dotti—chanced to be passing through Rome, where Pedro Ortiz also happened to reside. It re-mained only to garner their testimony and their references for the Basque plain-tiff to obtain his certificate of good faith and good conduct.

Was this moral and technical success just a formality? No. For the "Master of Arts" made this settlement with the Church establishment a precondition for the process that would flow from the Montmartre covenant, in order to give its meaning and its "line"—even its itinerary—to that project. Once the Palestin-ian dream waned, the "Parisian doctors" were forced back onto the decisive choices: Should they then and there put themselves under the Pope's direct or-ders? Should they found an order? Or should they fan out as missionaries to all points of the compass?

Less than a year after putting down roots in Rome, the founders had thus forged personal ties to Paul III—good in Ignatius's case, excellent in the case of Favre and Laínez. But they were still just a small band of reform-minded priests, regarded by the ecclesiastical powers with a blend of curiosity and admiration. Genuinely poor, and exuding zeal, altruism, and conviction: most unusual in the Rome of 1538 . . .

In November they finally succeeded in accomplishing what they called their "oblation" to the Pope. Paul III ordered them to "work in Rome," which would, he said, be their "Jerusalem." They were already resigned to accepting this ap-parently lackluster mission. But not in order to bend to just any task. They had not yet reached the *perinde ac cadaver* stage of Jesuit obedience (see Chapter III), as these words, written to Isabel Rosell in December 1538, indicate:

"We have been importuned [*infestados*] by a great quantity of prelates to bring forth fruit in their vineyards. But let us await better opportunities."[32] Most haughty vagabonds! (They would be more receptive to the King of Portugal or the Emperor Charles.)

It was from March to June of 1539, at their second Roman residence (presented by a Signor Frangipani and known as "the haunted house"), that they held the crucial deliberations which would give birth to a Society of Jesus ready to take immediate action. It is worth lingering a while over these debates, which went on for a hundred days. The minutes,[33] drawn up in Latin by (perhaps) Pierre Favre's hand, have been preserved. In their disorder, intensity, and contradictions, in their astounding human wealth, they were to the Company and its imperious Constitutions what the deliberations of the Estates-General would later be to France's First Republic.

One word stands out as starkly as a title page: *"scindebamur!"* ("We were divided!") It is followed by this first explanation: "We were Frenchmen, Spaniards, Savoyards, Cantabrians.* . . . Holy personages differed, too, and even resisted." They agreed on only one point: "To offer ourselves in holocaust for the glory of God, in Whom all that is ours shall be made nothing."

The first question: Should they keep the group together? Did not their commitment to the Pope guarantee that the missions Rome assigned them would splinter the Montmartre band (which had since increased in number)? Their decision was clear: The diversity of their assignments and duties must not in any way provoke the dissolution of the original group, "each one caring for and remaining informed of everyone else."

The second debate hinged on the need to choose a leader. Should they add to their vows of poverty and chastity a vow of obedience to one of their own number? It is striking (considering that we are talking about the future Jesuits) that they struggled long over this particular point. One objected that mention of obedience was "hateful to the people of Christ because of our sins," another that having to vow obedience to one member of the group "would drive away recruits."

But concern to avoid anarchy, to guarantee cohesion, and to curb individual pride drove the ten founders o conclude (after forty days' deliberation) that "it was better† for the group . . . to promise obedience to one among us." Readers will not be surprised to hear that we will be returning to this subject.

Before the deliberations were over, a quarrel broke out over a question then apparently only of secondary importance but one that would become central to the Company's existence: education. Should they pledge to "instruct children for forty days, each day for one hour, on pain of mortal sin"? One voice arose

*From the Cantabrian Gulf, and by extension Navarrese and Basques.
†The comparative, not the absolute.

(most violently) against this provision—that of Nicolás Alonso, Bobadilla, for whom this would be neither the first nor the last *casus belli*. This obliged them to drop their rule of unanimity in decision making. They also pushed the rule aside in rejecting Laínez's proposal to establish university "colleges" on the Paris model:* a negative decision imposed by the risks such institutions would pose to the rule of poverty.

What is surprising here is that their discussions of group cohesion and the duty of obedience did not immediately and explicitly raise the question of founding an order. That project—their consolation for the aborted grand pilgrimage—ripened only slowly. Denied movement and epic adventure, they would in the meantime work to assure the unity and the strength of their organization. But, just like their decision to settle in Rome, this would be only a substitute plan. For want of adventure, organization. (And until better things came along . . .)

Then Ignatius, Favre, and Codure set to work. In July and August of 1539 they hammered out a document to be submitted to the Pope—whose signature could alone give official life to the organization. It was the "First Formula of the Institute of the Society of Jesus" (*Prima Societatis Jesu Instituti Summa*). Two of those words merit special attention.

First, *Societatis*. Why has this peaceable word been so often translated as the misleadingly warlike "Company"? For more than four centuries its members have added the two letters S.J. to their signatures, the S referring to "Society." Is it because the majority of the founders were Spanish, and were thinking of the word *compañía* (which has no Latin equivalent), that they adopted *societas*?† If they had wanted to sound martial, the word *legio* would probably have been closer to the mark. And then perhaps this "hermaphrodite" formulation, more civilian in Latin, more warlike in Spanish, was already a masterpiece of the Jesuit mind.

As for the direct reference to Jesus, it had strongly suggested itself to Ignatius very early on, and had apparently been confirmed by his La Storta vision. Nevertheless, it was a potent factor in rousing public opinion against the new institution, and in giving the word that designates Society members a connotation of jealousy and scorn. But it does seem surprising that the Pope and the Curia, where many protectors of rival orders were on permanent alert, allowed the newcomers to appropriate to themselves the name of Christ. After all, predecessor orders had mustered under the names of their founders—Benedict,

*And in the medieval sense of the word: funded establishments offering support and educational asistance to students following university curricula.
†This is how the current Superior General, Father Kolvenbach, an expert on the subject, explained this semantic leap to me in Rome in April 1990.

Francis, Dominic—or else the site of their foundation—Cîteaux (home of the Cistercians), or Carmel.

In this 1539 *Summa,* which would serve as the basis both for the papal bull authorizing the order and for its final *Constitutions,* three essential points particularly struck contemporaries and most historians: the extremely subtle definition of the obedience due the Superior General of the Society; the exaltation of poverty as a human ideal; and renunciation of all forms of monastic ceremonial, particularly communal prayer.

Most interesting of these is the commentary accompanying the definition of the leader's functions. It specifies that the "Superior" must exercise authority "in council"; that he is required to heed "the opinion of his friends"; and that his decisions are to be arrived at "by majority vote." From which it emerges that the "Superior," elected for life (a provision that would trigger later debates), wielded executive power but that his legislative power was tempered by the council.

On the vow of poverty, the *Summa* is inexhaustible—but is not without a major reservation. In explicit reference to their own experience, Loyola and his companions wrote, "[There is] no purer or more joyful life . . . than that most sheltered from the pestilence which is love of money. . . . Let each and every one be happy to receive nothing but alms." But in order to "attract highly gifted students to their group and there train them . . . they may acquire from lay sources revenues and property . . . for the upkeep of such scholars." (We will be seeing what agonies these few words inflicted on the author of *The Spiritual Exercises.*)

No less remarkable are the provisions laid down by the composers of this preliminary draft of the *Constitutions* concerning ritual or disciplinary rules: Prayer is "by each person in private." Neither choir, nor plainsong, nor organs: Energy was better spent on the poor and the sick. Nor would there be debilitating fasts, special vestments, hairshirts, or other corporal mortifications: The service accepted by Ignatius's companions was too hard to warrant dissipating their energy or health for other ends.

It is easy to imagine the criticisms such provisions could elicit in that day and age: This stress on "private" devotion inevitably raised cries of Protestantism. And was not this refusal of ritual penances (proposed by the emaciated visionary of Manresa!) certain to attract protests, to raise the ghost of Erasmus? Was this not a repudiation of the long history of monasticism in favor of a utilitarianism of unblushingly secular inspiration—along the lines of "We have better things to do with our time than worry about such monkish goings-on . . . "?

Of a different order, but almost equally scandalous, was their repudiation of all ecclesiastical dignity, whether bishop's miter or cardinal's hat—except at the Pope's express command. Such pride-wrapped-in-humility was bound to make the Curia's prebendaries gnash their teeth.

The astonishing thing is that Paul III (although this is perhaps proof of the humanist Pope's title to full membership in his time) at first found nothing to object to in this text with its powerful whiff of Reform. It is even claimed that as he read it, old Farnese muttered, "This is indeed the Hand of God!"

Had Loyola thus won his first victory? Not quite. For his order to see the light of day, he needed the Pope's blessing: in other words, the approval of the Roman Curia. Which shifted the debate: From a confrontation between a fanatic for God wise enough to take men's needs into account and a Supreme Pontiff intelligent enough to see great wisdom in the sublime folly of some men, it degenerated into a series of intrigues and deals involving hoary ecclesiastics, royal courtiers, Roman noblemen, and highborn ladies.

The ecclesiastics could be boiled down to three: Cardinal Contarini was in favor, Cardinal Ghinucci sought amendments, and Cardinal Giudiccioni based his firm opposition upon one conviction—that the disorders within the Church stemmed from the proliferation of religious orders. Powerful as he was, however, Giudiccioni was forced to capitulate before the intervention of a sovereign (John III of Portugal), pressure from a great feudal lord (Ercole d'Este), and the urgings of an influential figure (Margaret of Austria).

Did one have to be "an enemy of the Company," as André Ravier writes,[34] to suggest that Loyola obtained papal support "thanks to the role played by a handful of great ladies close to Paul III—in particular Margaret of Parma, bastard daughter of the Emperor Charles and wife of the Pope's nephew, Ottavio Farnese"?* This excellent Jesuit historian felt it would be useful to refute this "rumor" by quoting Ignatius himself: "We were indeed in contact with Madame's† household, but her support was never solicited" (letter to Bartolomé de Torres, May 1556). But did the Farneses wait to be "solicited" before beginning to pull strings? When you are the Pope's granddaughter and you consider a cause worth defending, you do not wait for a holy man's pleas to start campaigning for that cause within the bosom of your own family.

But such of course was not the issue. Once the Supreme Pontiff had seen "the Hand of God" in the Company's formation, and foreseen both advantage and security in the mustering of this legion burning to serve him, Ghinucci and Giudiccioni could do no more than delay its birth.

When he signed the bull *Regimini Militantis Ecclesiae* on September 27, 1540, Paul III gave canonical life to the Company, or Society, of Jesus. Ecclesiastical clerks and scriveners had inflicted a minimum of amendments to the text— tactfully erasing its repudiation of monastic practices, while the number of

---

*Ravier is too delicate. Ottavio was not his "nephew" but his grandson.
†The name they used when discussing Margaret.

"professed," or full-fledged, members who had pronounced all vows was limited to sixty (although you could be sure that these pious militants would interpret this rule* liberally and on a case-by-case basis).

Now arose the question of the appointment-for-life of the Company's Superior General. Ignatius had the authority. Should that authority be transformed into power, and for life? He clearly signified that his election was not desirable, given his scandalous (and in Spain stormy) past and his misadventures with the Inquisition. But even if official sanction of his authority was not a foregone conclusion, his ascendancy over his youthful companions was such, his seniority so binding, his dominance so obvious, and his charisma so powerful, that removing him would have been even harder than electing him.

The election took place on April 8, 1541. It took typically Jesuit form: In other words, it was strongly personalized, its form well ordered, its conclusions logical, its content dramatic. There was no need to be a Schiller to extract the stuff of a third act of tragedy from the Company's *Narrative Sources:*

IGNATIUS: Jesus! I disqualify myself, and cast my vote with him who receives the greatest number. I have designated nobody, but should all of you wish it, I am ready to do so.

XAVIER: I, Francisco, insist that the man we must elect is our old leader and our true father, Don Ignatius, who gathered us together at the cost of so much labor and who best knows each one of us, and that after his death his successor shall be Pierre Favre. . . .

FAVRE: I give my vote to Ignatius and, in case of his death (which God forfend), to Master Francis Xavier.

LAÍNEZ: I, Diego Laínez, driven by zeal for God's glory and for my soul's salvation, I choose Father Ignatius Loyola as my superior and the Company's Superior.

SALMERÓN: I, Alfonso Salmerón, unworthiest of all this Company, I choose as Superior Ignatius of Loyola who engendered us all in Christ and suckled us when we were small and will lead us to the green pastures of Paradise. . . .

RODRIGUES: By the best light available to me, Ignatius is the only one we can choose. If by ill-luck this choice is denied us, Pierre Favre must be elected.†

LE JAY: I desire that Ignatius, whom God has given us for our father these past years, be elected Superior, and to him, after God and the Saints, I submit my whole will, body and soul.

BROËT: I, Paschase Broët, choose Father Ignatius as Superior General.

CODURE: The one I have always known as the most zealous advocate of God's glory and the salvation of souls must be raised above the others because

*Abrogated ten years later by Pope Julius III.
†The votes for Favre and Francis Xavier were in writing.

he himself has taken the lowest place by serving the whole world. I mean Father Ignatius. And I would vote likewise were I at the very hour of death.[35]

Since Pierre Favre, Francis Xavier, and Rodrigues had departed on mission, Favre for Germany, the other two for Asia, they had to send in their votes. The group waited in vain for the ever-unpredictable Bobadilla's vote; in his *Autobiography*, not published until 1589, he assures us that he voted for Loyola.

Ignatius protested that he was incapable of governing even himself, let alone others, and that his former sins, as well as the wretched state of his health, argued against his assuming such a task. In any case, he begged his companions to take time—several days—to seek someone better qualified. It can be pointed out, of course, that this psychologist, this "great molder of men" as we know him to be, could have had no doubt of his election. No need to be deeply cynical to detect something Machiavellian here. What better way of proving yourself indispensable, of making your supremacy stick?

Four days later, the six companions who were present confirmed their vote. When Loyola again refused, the most substantial of his electors, Diego Laínez (who would be the first to succeed Ignatius), flared up in anger. Drawing himself up on his chair, he addressed the man they had elected in a tone unusual in him, particularly in dealings with his elders. If "Father Ignatius" persisted in ignoring his companions' choice—a choice so clearly inspired by the Lord—he, Laínez, would withdraw from the Company, for he refused to obey any other than the elect of God.

Shaken, Loyola went on trying to sidestep, declaring that he would leave the issue to his confessor, the Franciscan Fra Theodosio, who could only enjoin him to bow to the majority of the group. Nevertheless, it took further days of prayer, lasting through Holy Week, before he resigned himself (on April 22, 1541) to formal acceptance of his responsibilities.

It would have been too much to hope that the new Superior's proofs of humility should stop at these electoral maneuvers. Here is the worldly Hercule Rasiel's description of his first steps as Father General:

> The General broached his new functions by embracing the lowliest of tasks. The office of cook seeming too grand to him, he chose that of scullion. He drew water, he carried wood, he lit the fire, he keeled pots, he turned the spit, he scoured the pans, washed the dishes, and swept the kitchen.
>
> After leaving this rare example of humility for his successors, he set about taking the smaller children through their Catechism in the Church of Santa Maria de Strada, which Pietro Codacio, Officer of the Pope and a man of influence in Rome, had given the Iñighistes when they still possessed nothing but a rented house.

... Although Iñigo, bound by his vow, truly directed his teachings at the children, nevertheless all manner of persons attended, even men and women of rank, theologians and canonists. He explained the Mysteries of the Faith in not-too-learned terms and in very broken Italian; yet he spoke so powerfully with face, hands, and eyes that, according to witnesses . . . , his zeal made up for his deficiencies of learning and the barbarity of his utterances.[36]

· III ·

"PERINDE
AC CADAVER"

All Things to All Men • *Pierre Favre and the "Heretics"* • *Flies on
the Wall at Trent* • *Kingdom of the Iñiguists* • *"Holy Obedience"* •
Polanco's Pen • *The Gift of Tears* • *"Be Always Ready to Move"* •
A Most Ordinary Death • *The Stigmata of "Politics"*

J UST TEN MEN, assembled in Rome but ready at a moment's notice to
leave for the farthest corners of the earth, from Lisbon to Goa, from
Ratisbon to Yamaguchi.

Ten men bound by solemn vows. And owing eternal obedience to the man
who had devised those vows—and who had himself pledged obedience to a
Pope whose diplomatic skills barely masked his native authoritarianism.

Ten men squeezed into a shack adjoining the dilapidated church of Santa
Maria della Strada*—but about to raise a clamor through Christendom more
uproarious than any crusade or schism.

Such, in the spring and summer of 1541, was the tiny embryo of the mighty
Company of Jesus.

You can still visit that tumbledown Roman dwelling, now backed against the
Jesuit church at the foot of the Capitol known simply as the Gesù. It was long the
Company's control center, with its baroque chapel and the three *camerette* where
Ignatius of Loyola lived, worked, and died, daily giving clearer shape to the curi-
ous institution whose worldwide deployment he was cautiously planning.

*Now gone, it was close to the present-day Gesú.

At the back of a storeroom there,* ridiculous and sublime, is Loyola's life-size effigy, looking like a wax-museum exhibit. What friend (or foe) could fail to be touched by this wax doll? Tiny (a shade over five feet), wiry, bilious-hued, with a scraggly beard, the body encased in a country priest's soutane, the head topped with the biretta of a Master of Arts of the University of Paris, the expression strained—our padre maestro, the little lame beggar of Azpeitia, seems frozen on an eternal vagabond journey. With what goal in mind? Does this puny, tear-streaked, pain-wracked man even guess that he is building an empire bigger and longer-lasting than that of the Emperor Charles V?

By its own primary vocation, the community grouped around Ignatius was doomed to disintegration. Chapter II of the draft *Constitutions,* written in 1539, is clear:

> All that His Holiness will command us for the good of souls or the propagation of the faith, we are bound to carry out with neither procrastination nor excuse, at once and to the fullest extent of our power, whether he send us among the Turks, to the New Worlds, to the Lutherans† or any other manner of believers or unbelievers. . . . This vow may scatter us to distant parts of the world.

The Company's initial vocation was not educational but apostolic. True, its statutes very soon included provisions for the instruction of children. But at first this involved only instruction in the Christian religion—what might be called short-range missionary work. The initial intention had been shaped by the Palestinian dream—the march against the unbeliever, the chance of a martyr's crown.

Created by a vagabond, the order was necessarily vagabond in nature. Its earliest sanctuaries, Manresa, Montmartre, La Storta, lay by roadsides. Its first parish church in Rome was Santa Maria *della Strada*—"of the road." Even later, when it planted its colleges in the heart of predominantly industrial civilizations, it would never cease to seek fortune and misfortune far afield, from the Philippines to Peru.

The first stroke in the great Jesuit diaspora was a dramatic one: Francis Xavier's departure for India. Even before the official foundation of the order and Ignatius's election as its Superior General, Xavier the Navarrese was off on the long journey to Asia.

Asked by his former principal at Sainte-Barbe, Diego de Gouvea, to dispatch missionaries to Portugal's new East Indian colonies, Loyola replied that the decision awaited only a word from the Pope. Under skillful pressure from the Por-

---

*This was written in 1990.

†Father Ravier notes that this provision was, "if not unique, then at least very rare in the writings of the first fathers."

tuguese king, Paul III asked Loyola to send six of his La Strada companions to the Indies. "What will I have left for the rest of the world?" cried Ignatius. It was finally agreed to send two missionaries, the Portuguese Rodrigues and intrepid Bobadilla. But when the latter was injured, Ignatius turned to Xavier:

"Esta es vuestra empresa!" (This is your undertaking!)

"Pues! Sus! Heme acqui!" (Very well then! Here I am!)

An irreproachably knightly response.

The very next day, after ironing hose and cassock, Francis was on his way to Portugal. The two Sainte-Barbe students, the athlete and the cripple, would never meet again.

At Lisbon, where the King tried to heap the voyager with gifts, Francis accepted "only the few books needed in the Indies and a cloak for the Cape of Good Hope." And when the Count of Castañeda insisted on providing him with a servant to wash his clothes, as his gentleman's dignity required, he retorted: "It is this dignity which has brought the Church of God to its present condition. . . . True dignity lies in washing one's own laundry and boiling one's own pot." We will meet the man of Navarre again (complete with shabby laundry and ill-garnished pot) at the other end of the world.

It was not to Xavier but to another pair of companions (Broët and Salmerón, who were leaving to proselytize among the Irish) that Loyola addressed the instructions which follow. In a few sentences, a blend of boldness and prudence, they sum up both Ignatius's and the Company's pioneering phase in terms that France's King Henry, counseled by Machiavelli and tempered by Montaigne, might have used to his ambassadors:

> In dealing with people and above all with equals or inferiors, speak little but listen long and willingly, according to their rank. Let greetings and farewells be merry and courteous. If you speak with persons of influence consider first (to win their affection and snare them in your toils for the greater service to God) what their character is, and adapt yours to it.
>
> If a man be passionate and lively of speech, speak in the same manner, avoiding grave or melancholy expressions. With those who are by nature circumspect, reticent, and slow of speech, model your delivery accordingly, for this is what pleases them. With those who are sad or tempted, you will be affable, showing great joy to struggle against their low spirits.
>
> Be all things to all men. . . .
>
> Have neither mule* nor horse. . . . On board ship or at inns, strive

*In fact, the *primi patres* often made use of mules: The historian Fernand Braudel has some savory comments about "the victory of the mule in the sixteenth century."

always for simplicity, confining yourself at most to half or a third of normal expenditures. . . . Accept no alms or remuneration. . . . If for the Glory of God and the good of souls it is necessary to risk your lives you must be willing to do so, but without rashness, without tempting God. . . . And deploy all your skills to avoid being captured by the agents of the king.[1]

Equipped with such a code of conduct—Loyola's *Missionary* is every bit as good as Machiavelli's *Prince*—is it any wonder that the Jesuits made their mark on the world? Basques are said to be impulsive, and this particular Basque was certainly not driven by reason alone. But how many "pious deceptions" there are in these precepts, how much social navigation, how judicious a dose of abnegation! Many fat books, some of them good ones, have been written on the secret of Jesuit power. But here it is, for better or for worse, in just a few lines.

While his first Sainte-Barbe chambermate voyaged from ocean to ocean, Pierre Favre plodded, sometimes on foot (as Ignatius recommended) and sometimes on muleback, from Rome to Worms, from Coïmbra to Ratisbon, and from Louvain to Cologne. Francis was immersed in the world of Asia's "unbelievers." Favre was in the steadily expanding "heretic" world of Teutonic Europe. And while it is true that after the Council of Trent the writings and decisions of Loyola, Laínez, and Canisius did much to confirm the image of a Company transformed into a war machine against Lutheranism and Calvinism, we must pause for a moment to consider Favre's actions and ideas.

First the man. His personal charm, his capacity for empathy, and his charisma are universally recognized. "His relations with others were of rare and delectable sweetness," wrote Simón Rodrigues. His conduct, like his spiritual life, was marked by an overflowing human warmth, which often prevailed over the promptings of his intellect—even though the man possessed the liveliest of intelligences and an academic baggage sturdier than that of any of his companions except Laínez.

What strikes the reader in Favre's *Memoirs**** is the use he makes of the word "reformation." He says—using the word always in a positive sense—that he has been sent *para la reformación.* And for him it was less a question of reforming others than of reforming oneself, "in order to rebuild the ruins of Catholicism." Throughout his wanderings in Germany between 1540 and 1546, and above all in the Rhineland, where he lived the final months of his life, Favre met few of the founding fathers of Lutheranism, even though he had planned to meet Melanchton: He encountered chiefly Catholics who had crossed over or were

*We refer variously to the text or to Michel de Certeau's penetrating commentary (Paris: Desclée de Brouwer, 1960).

crossing over into Protestantism, not by force or compulsion but as a result of internal disintegration stemming from the pervasive corruption of their own Church.

His diagnosis of Catholic decadence was not on an intellectual level. He believed in example based on actual experience. There must be a return to the sources of early Christianity, a conscious attempt to find the way back—beyond moral shortcomings, which could always be justified by later argument—to every person's "heart." "There lies the beginning," he wrote. "If the heart stops being truly Catholic, the behavior quickly stops as well."

He declared to his friend Kalkbrenner, Prior of Cologne: "It hurts me that the earthly Powers have no other activity, no other concern, no other thought, than to extirpate notorious Lutherans. . . . Why do we not return to the ways of the first Christians?"[2] Whence the method he suggests for dealing with "heretics," whether recent or "notorious." They must not be "confounded" by argument but induced to change their life, and thus call into question their commitment to heresy. For "evil is not first and foremost in the intelligence, but in the feet and hands of the body and the soul." It was by "awakening worthy feelings" that a return to the "wholeness of faith" could be effected.* Was such evangelical zeal naïve? In any case, it clearly inspired the advice he gave Diego Laínez, who had asked him how the Protestants should be handled:

> Whoever wishes to be of use to the heretics of this day must first of all love them all with real love, shutting out from his mind all that might cool his respect for them. He must then conquer their minds that they may love us in their turn, and keep a place for us in their hearts. This we can achieve by chatting familiarly with them, discussing points, avoiding any confrontation.[3]

By the time Favre died, exhausted, at the founder's side in Rome on August 1, 1546, the cause of the Reformation had triumphed virtually throughout Germany. His successors, from Cologne to Munich, would have recourse to other methods. Methods that would stamp Peter Canisius, for example, as the "hammer of the heretics," and would give the name "Jesuit" a sinister connotation all the way from the Rhine to the Danube.

When, at the Pope's request, Ignatius dispatched a handful of his companions to the Council of Trent, he may already have decided to turn the little Alpine city into another Pamplona, a fortress against the forward march of heresy. It is possible too that in thus offering a sharp check to the enemy he was deliberately

---

*Favre had lived in Mainz with a priest who cohabited with a woman. His disciple Canisius wrote, "Of this servant of concubinage he made a Carthusian."

conferring on "his" Company an aggressiveness that would soon become its hallmark. But as so often in the history of the "Iñiguists," everything flowed from the workings of a series of chances.

At the opening of the Council, convened by Pope Paul III in 1545 to demonstrate the vitality of Catholicism in the face of the Reformation, only Claude Le Jay represented the Society of Jesus. And even he had simply been placed at the disposition of the Cardinal-Archbishop of Augsburg, Otto von Truchsess, one of the reform-minded prelates the Pope had summoned to the Curia with Church reform in mind.

But Paul III made a direct request to Ignatius for three of his disciples to serve in the capacity of "Pope's theologians" (a quite staggering development, since the companions of La Strada had won a reputation for action rather than contemplation). We have to conclude that the title of "Doctor of Paris" still struck sparks. And let us not forget that old Pope Farnese had once been in the habit of inviting Laínez and Favre to his table for "theological discussions."

Laínez, Salmerón, and Favre were designated: The latter, hastily recalled from Spain, returned to Rome only to die there. The other two, the Spaniards, joined Le Jay at Trent where they were reinforced by Canisius, a Netherlander with a fluent command of German—and therefore a man most useful in the event of clashes with the Lutherans. Thus, fewer than six years after the foundation of their order, the "Iñiguists" entered the lists with four of their champions (almost half their entire strength) in a debate intended to decide the future of Catholicism.

A letter from the "General" served as their charter. Let us pause over this astonishing text, in which Ignatius outlined the conduct he expected of his companions:

> I would be slow and amiable of speech. . . . I would listen closely, the better to understand the speaker's point of view. . . . In advancing a subject I would also give the countervailing reasons in order not to appear partial or to inconvenience anyone. . . . If the answer were so obvious that it could not be silenced, I would offer my opinion modestly, concluding deferentially in the sense of the best judgment. . . . In the pulpit,* I would make no reference to the differences† between Protestants and Catholics.

(Not all the fathers attending the Council followed these precepts: It is said that one day the debate took such an evil turn that the Bishop of La Cava attacked the Bishop of Crete's beard, which earned him a prison sentence.)

And although Diego Laínez was supposed to respect Loyola's advice, it would be wrong to suggest that he invariably assumed the angelic mildness recom-

---

*Not being official delegates to the Council, the Jesuits could preach on the outskirts of the debates.
†A fine example of understatement: "differences" rather than "quarrels."

mended by the "General." On October 8, 1546, a certain Father Seripando, of reputedly peerless knowledge and unimpeachable orthodoxy (and acting in the clear intention of humoring the reform-minded adversary), pronounced an apology for justification through grace in which our four Paris doctors discerned the accents of Lutheranism.

Whereupon a small man rose to his feet, his face white, tense, and momentarily without the smile that usually warmed it. With his great hooked arrogant nose pointed like a scimitar at the "Lutheran," his glittering gaze already suffused with triumph, Diego Laínez, "Pope's theologian," proceeded to harpoon the said Seripando with such gusto that the Council fathers requested the inclusion of this outsider's remarks in the record of the proceedings. (Yet had not Ignatius written, "I would give my opinion with modesty"?)

Advocate of moderation though he was, the Padre Maestro was not the man to take offense at such triumphs. There is nothing to suggest that he called the furious Laínez—whose controversial arguments would do so much to modify the Company's path—to order. Apparently indifferent to the essential points at issue, he was eager for personal news of his "doctors": their life at Trent, their sermons, their reception at the Council, their food and housing conditions. Gonçalves da Câmara records that the General once exclaimed in his presence: "*Cierto!* How I would like to know how many fleas feed on them at night!"

In 1547 a plague epidemic forced the adjournment of the Council, after a brief session in Bologna. In 1551 sessions began again in Trent. Here one of the fiercest clashes ever to pit Jesuits against Dominicans took place. The duelists were two towering champions: Diego Laínez, already being compared to Augustine of Hippo, and Fray Melchor Cano, most famous of the preaching brothers. (In Salamanca, Cano had been a ruthless pursuer of the "Iñiguists," who in his eyes reincarnated the "cursed sect of the Illuminati.")

Did this silver-tongued Dominican's arrival in Trent send a shudder through Laínez and his acolytes? Hardly. They even requested an audience with him before the debates opened, to clarify their differences and points of agreement. They were icily received by a Fray Melchor seemingly impervious to Jesuit arguments. Particularly from such an accursed source!

After two hours of sterile debate with this monolith of contempt, Loyola's spokesman rebelled:

LAÍNEZ: By what right do you set yourself above the judgment of the bishops and of Christ's Vicar by condemning this Company, which they have approved?

CANO: Would Your Honor have the dogs* refrain from barking when the shepherds nod?

*His name was Cano—and although the Spanish for "dog" is in fact *perro*, this was a traditional play on words among the Domini*cano*s.

LAÍNEZ: Let them bark—but at wolves, not at other dogs.

Ribadeneira, who has told the story thus far, dares not bring it to its conclusion. But the bolder Geronimo Nadal reports that an exchange of insults cut the confrontation short. So much so that, "upon a fresh insult by Cano, Laínez responded with an epithet not used in society and banished from the dictionaries," and left the room. As soon as he was out on the street he regretted this license, and returned to fling himself at Cano's feet (the Dominican was twenty years his senior) to ask forgiveness. But Fray Melchor judged the offense so foul that he forever refused to divulge its exact nature.[4]

The reprimand from Loyola was scathing. So scathing that Laínez the firebrand submitted himself, both figuratively and literally, to discipline. He wrote to the General: "I ask you, Father, to punish me as often as need be. . . . Deprive me of the guidance of others, put an end to my preaching and my studies, set me to serve in kitchen and garden and in the most elementary of grammar classes until my dying day!"

Which brings us to the real heart of the matter— "obedience."

If we should remember only one basic rule from the *Constitutions* Ignatius had been working on for fifteen years (they were unfinished when he died), it is the one relating to discipline.

As the Benedictine defined himself in the world's eyes by his intellectual zeal, the Franciscan by his humility, and the Carthusian by his terseness, so the Jesuit readily summed himself up with the word "obedience." This leitmotif— "Loyolaesque" if anything ever was—the founder strove ceaselessly to clarify, refining and hammering away at it by turns, not just in the sixth chapter of the *Constitutions*, but also in the famous *Letter to the Portuguese Jesuits* of March 23, 1553, in which he wrote: "We may agree to being surpassed by other religious orders in terms of fasts, vigils, and other austerities. . . . But in purity and perfection of obedience . . . and abnegation of judgment, dearest brothers, I hope most earnestly that those who follow God within this Company may be singled out."

In the minds of ordinary people, this precept is embodied in the notion of obedience *perinde ac cadaver* (like a cadaver). For such would be the conduct demanded of a Jesuit by the rule of his order: abolition of will, perfect meekness, "indifference" to his own thoughts and impulses, total annihilation at the hands of the General and, through him, of the Pope of Rome.

Those three Latin words have done as much as the order's generic title (primevally arrogant, deceptively meek) and its association with "casuistry" to discredit the Company in the world's eyes. It is easy to understand why Loyola's advocates and followers feel their hackles rise as soon as the *perinde* is mentioned. There is not a single Jesuit writer who has not tried to exonerate his companions of it, or to prove that Ignatius did not invent the phrase.

Thus the great German theologian Karl Rahner roundly denounces the formula as "idiotic."[5] And to underline his disagreement Rahner, invoking Loyola's protective signature, even asserts that the Jesuits of Paraguay* were wrong to obey the Vatican order to dissolve and abandon their missions there.

No doubt. But in the final analysis we must turn for enlightenment to the founder's own words. Again at the end of his life, at a time when all his sharp corners seemed to be softening, he dictated these "instructions on obedience" to Jean-Philippe Vito, injunctions that sought "mortification" only of the recalcitrant:

> I must belong not to myself but to Him who made me and to His representative, and let myself be ruled and led as a wax ball is led on a string . . . putting all my zeal into what is commanded of me. I must behave: first, like a cadaver possessing neither will nor understanding; second, like a small crucifix that can easily be moved from one place to another; and third, I must consider myself and conduct myself as a staff in the hand of an old man who will place me where he wishes and where I serve him best. In such a way must I stand ready to serve the Order and be used by it in all that may be commanded of me.

It is certainly true that others before Ignatius had invoked equally gloomy images. The following precept occurs in the Rule of the Benedictine Order: "If by chance a brother is given a command that is *too onerous* or *impossible,* let him nevertheless receive that order from his superior with meekness and obedience." Elsewhere, Saint Bonaventure insists that Francis of Assisi "used the example of a corpse in enjoining obedience." And centuries before him the author of the *Monastic Constitutions* (Saint Basil?) had suggested as a model "the tool that lets itself be handled as the workman sees fit."

On these points, as we shall see, the Ignatian rule is less rigid. But the fact remains that halfway through the century of humanism, at a time when Christianity was reinventing itself in conformity with the Renaissance (which was essentially a rebirth of the individual human being with his rights and his freedom of action), Ignatius of Loyola inserted into the sixth part of the *Constitutions* of his order (under the blazing title "De lo que toca a la obedancia"—"Concerning Obedience") these iron precepts:

> All our strength must be bent to the acquisition of that virtue we call obedience, due first to the Pope and next to the Superior of the Order. For every matter to which obedience in love may be applied, every-

*See Chapter VIII.

one, at a single word from the leader (as if that word issued from the mouth of Christ Himself), will at once be ready, renouncing every other activity, even the completion of an unfinished letter of the alphabet. All our thoughts and all our efforts in the Lord must tend toward the goal of making the holy virtue of obedience ever more perfect within us, as much in its execution as in our will and in our intelligence, while with perseverance and inner joy we most willingly accomplish everything with which we are charged.

Every order must be acceptable. For our part we will deny all other ways of seeing and all other opinions in a kind of blind obedience, and this in everything which is not sin. Each of us must be convinced that whosoever lives in obedience must let himself be guided and directed by divine Providence, through the intermediary of his superiors, as if he were a dead body (*perinde ac cadaver*) that can be carried anywhere and treated in any fashion, like the old man's staff that serves all ends in all places.

We have already seen that it would be absurd to relate this disciplinary rigor to the military world, to the "soldier" or "warrior" Iñigo of whom—simply because he was wounded one day on a rampart in Navarre—we hear so much. Moreover, as Alain Guillermou notes, nothing was less disciplined than sixteenth-century armies: The sack of Rome had been the caricature—but by no means an out-of-the-ordinary one—of a military code dominated by an anarchy that neither the Emperor's nor the French King's captains could curb.

What underpins the hyperbolic obedience that Ignatius sought to make the distinguishing mark of his order is the very special vocation to which he had committed it: its "worldliness," its total involvement in public and private affairs, its "presence in the world" (in all worlds) of which the Jesuits were so proud, but which inevitably went hand in hand with conflict, distractions, dispersion of energy, and the emergence of centrifugal forces.

Would twenty men gathered in an Alpine monastery for the purposes of study, contemplation, and choral song accept such imperious authority on the part of their prior? But with the same twenty men scattered amid tempests and worldly temptations, from Valparaiso to Gdansk to Shanghai, one confronting the origins of matter in a Siberian laboratory, another wrestling with the guerrilla movement in Peru? Here a quite different kind of tie becomes necessary, a blend of coercion and collective decision making within the bosom of an "order."

Of course, every totalitarian organization has made similar claims. Is this the case with the Jesuits? Two notorious examples suggest that it might be. One is of the Jesuit founders of the Republic of the Paraguayan Guaranís, who (although defending a cause sufficiently just to have been championed by no less a thinker than Montesquieu) bowed to the darkest injunctions of European imperialism, addressed to them through the intermediary of their order and the Papacy.* The second example is that of Pierre Teilhard de Chardin, shattering his career and his educational work to kneel before the imperatives of the Holy Office.†

For we must keep in mind that the "holy obedience" of the Jesuits was a two-phase process. We should remember too that the formidable authority of the Superior General was overlaid by the even more imposing power of the Roman Curia, whose writ, as we have seen, was acknowledged to supersede that of the Jesuit General. The Jesuit on trial has no choice of judges, but those judges have historically tended to join forces and multiply more often than they have contended with one another. And constraint, if not repression, almost always wins.

In this context, then, it is no wonder that Ignatius of Loyola—alongside Savonarola and Calvin, Cromwell and Robespierre—has been presented as an inventor of modern totalitarianism. This being so, we should lend an ear to the defense, which tells us that the Jesuit rule of obedience is not so depersonalizing, not such a grinder of the individual's bones as the texts and a few unfortunately famous examples suggest.

The Protestant historian Van Dyke makes this plea: "Ignatius's conception of his order was personal, not mechanical. It was to be made up of men, not of formulae. He saw the Company's unity as spiritual, not based on rule. He did not see his rules as an iron breastplate. He made provision for exceptions, and those he mentioned were clearly aimed at saving the spirit at the expense of the letter."[6]

As he drew up the *Constitutions* and his *Letter on Obedience*, written in 1553, Ignatius could not forget his own story, his rebellions, his struggles, his clashes with the Inquisition as well as with the Holy See and Curia. The great proponent of the "virtue of obedience" had himself been a rebel, and the embers still glowed beneath the ashes. The historian Gaétan Bernoville describes him in those years as "a soul by turns showered with blessings, saturated with sweetness, and then tumbling into a mystical night in which he could advance only gropingly, dazzled, hesitating, convinced, sobbing, and then once again serene."[7]

How could this virtuoso of the human heart, this tested psychologist, this great prober of the depths have failed to see that there was no such thing as an unbreakable rule (unless you wanted to trigger an explosion), that you had to give "slack," provide safety valves? The discipline Loyola devised was full of escape hatches designed to mitigate the disgrace of being seen as the mere mechanical executant of orders from above which—military-style—could be rescinded only by a counterorder.

*See Chapter VIII.
†See Chapter XIII.

It was specifically stipulated that if he disapproved of an order the "subordinate" might or perhaps should frame "respectful objections" to his superior. But it was no less true that if his remonstrances failed he had to bow to the command, even to show what the Company called "obedience of judgment." To the point where offenders were considered *membra putrida* of the *corpus Societatis* ... Terrifying!

But let us listen to Father André Ravier, himself a practitioner:

Authority* has strict and rigorous obligations: the obligation fully to divulge; the obligation to consult and discuss not only with the usual advisers but with every person competent in the matter to be decided; the obligation to confer in depth; the obligation of spiritual conversation—of conscience-to-conscience exchange—with the subject in question in order to adapt the order as closely as possible to his own temperament and his capacity for grace; the obligation to give the widest possible place, as if to an important sign from God, to the opinion of the majority; and finally the obligation of prayer and of choice when faced with one's conscience and with God. Only if he observes such obligations may the Superior legitimately decide and command. Exercising authority as laid down in the *Constitutions* is an act as highly spiritual as it is one of extreme human prudence.[8]

But how did the first Father General in his tiny Roman *retiro* behave toward those around him, toward his "sons" scattered from Trent to Kagoshima? In his presence there reigned what Company historians call "blind obedience"; we see it particularly in the memoirs of Luis Gonçalves da Câmara, Ignatius's closest daily companion: "Our Father . . . punished lack of obedience not only in its essential aspects but . . . in every other particular." But he added: "Our Father is accustomed . . . in all he may accomplish with gentleness . . . not to call upon obedience; when he is able to have someone do such and such a thing without having received a command."

Across the board, in fact, Loyola's behavior was unpredictable. André Ravier lists a whole series of cases in which his finicky authoritarianism gives way to intelligent liberalism: "In 1545 he conveyed to the uncontrollable Simón Rodrigues his wish to see him in Rome, but added: 'For myself, I appeal to your conscience.' Let his old companion judge for himself." In 1548, Ribadeneira was to study philosophy: Let him choose "*en su election*" (as he saw fit) between Spain and Italy. In 1549 he suggested three missions to the turbulent Bobadilla—"*que hager a su plazer*" (Do as you please)—because he knew Bobadilla would do only what suited himself. And when Guzmán and Loarte entered the

---

*Which he himself wielded at the highest levels as Provincial of Lyon and of Southern France.

Company he allowed them their choice of theater, either Rome or Spain.

In short, he would leave the final decision to the "election" of subjects with whose level of obedience he was familiar. Which did not deter him from giving orders *ex virtute obedientiae* to men he knew to be devoted body and soul, men won over to what he called the state of "indifference," in which desires, drives, tastes, and interests were forgotten.

As we have seen, that stout chronicler Hercule Rasiel da Silva dubbed Dom Iñigo de Guipúzcoa founder of the "Kingdom of the Iniguists." And why not? But the Company constantly renewed itself, operated with an eye to electoral dynamics, and on broad foundations. Counsel and debate had their place in it, which did nothing to alter the fact that no Catholic institution, the Vatican aside, was so tightly pinioned within the principle of personal, centralized authority.

What Ignatius of Loyola created was not "the most despotic monarchy that ever there was,"[9] but a muscular constitutional monarchy, which in terms of discipline outstripped all its rivals in the Catholic world. For with all the checks and balances devised at various stages of the decision-making process in order to channel the power of the Superior General and his various subordinates (assistants, provincials, superiors, prefects), the Company remained stamped with the seal set upon it in Rome at the middle of the sixteenth century, a seal that can be summed up in the word "discipline." That was what the frail sixty-year-old inside the walls of Santa Maria della Strada wanted, and what he got. Once the *corpus* (whether Company or *Societas*) was established, this "molder of men" made sure that the chief fruit of "order" would be effectiveness.

We know, or think we know, many things about Jesuit discipline, but perhaps not the following: Early in the 1980s, both Dominicans and Jesuits happened to hold almost simultaneous elections for their new superiors, whose prerogatives were at times much closer than people realized. But one essential characteristic distinguished them: Once elected, the Dominican superior declared that he had better things to do than wield authority, and returned to his beloved studies. Was the new Jesuit General, Father Peter Hans Kolvenbach, himself a renowned intellectual and prestigious linguist, tempted to follow suit? Jesuit rule forbade it. Had he refused to bow to the rule and exercise authority, he would have been one of those *membra putrida* that the Society of Jesus (the Merciful) would have been obliged to cast out.

Insofar as the "Iñiguists" (particularly after the Council of Trent) defined themselves by the primacy of action over predestination, of accomplished works over the arbitrary workings of grace, it is on their "works" that we are inclined to judge them now, on their public or private initiatives, on their journey through the century and the mark they made on it.

We have seen them "missionizing" from the Danube to the Tagus and the North Atlantic to the Indian Ocean. That primary vocation would steadily expand. But another, less predictable enterprise would soon assume such importance that it would tend to be confused with the overall mission: teaching.

This was not an early concern, as we know. We have seen Iñigo of Loyola teaching the catechism to children and ladies, to onlookers in Alcalá and scholars at Sainte-Barbe, then to the sick of Venice and the merchants on the Piazza dei Fiori. But that had been merely a primary brand of preaching, which had little to do with the systematic shaping of minds.

The origins of this change of direction are hard to find. The impulse probably came from Diego Laínez, and as we have seen, no one could stand up to the inspired jouster of the Council of Trent. Not even Loyola. And indeed how could this society of "Doctors of Paris," diplomas and birettas at the ready, have failed to inherit a calling to teach?

If Loyola agreed, it was probably because he at once saw that this educational work would constitute the finest "school for managers" imaginable. He was thinking less of teaching as such than of teaching teachers—teaching the first hundred, the first thousand Jesuits. A profound and ultimately fruitful insight.

Thus did the Company (which from its earliest days had served notice of a superior opportunism by bartering martyrdom in Jerusalem for Roman roots) give fresh proof of its flexibility by agreeing ten years or so after its birth to let the exception conceded by Loyola become the rule: to let the words "Jesuit" and "teacher" become synonymous, massively synonymous.

The first of the colleges that soon sprang up everywhere, first for the training of young Jesuits and later—free of charge—for teaching young people in general, were not in Rome but Messina, then Barcelona, Padua, Lisbon, Naples, and Louvain. The first Roman college did not open its doors until 1551, at the foot of the Capitol, under the direction of a French priest, Jean Pelletier, who was presumed to possess the secret of that *modus parisiensis* to which the founder had remained attached. But it would take years, and untold maneuvering, disputes, and battles for Paris itself to admit the teachers dispatched from Rome.

Ignatius and his little group had devoted themselves to more conventional, more "charitable" efforts—dissociated from preaching, caring for the sick, and the other good works envisaged since the Montmartre vows. Two are worth recalling: the attempt to convert and admit Jews (for want of the distant Muslims) and the redemption of "women of ill repute."

Hercule Rasiel observes those "good works" with unblinking eye and in colorful language:

> Undertaking to convert the Jews, Iñigo began with the most destitute among them, feeding them in the House of his Order so as to per-

suade them to accept baptism. Then he put his admirable Talents for Begging to work & collected enough to found a House for the Upkeep of all poor Jews who would in the future embrace the Catholic Faith.

At his urging, Paul III issued a Decree* ordaining that all of that Nation who converted would keep all their Goods: that Children who became Catholic despite their Parents would inherit from them as if they had remained Jewish; and that Goods acquired through usury, whose true Master was unknown, would be given to the new Converts.

The chronicler's comments are scarcely less interesting than Loyola's actions:
These Establishments & these Decrees from time to time caused the passage from the Synagogue to the Catholic Church of a very small number of Wretches who were dying of Hunger, some ill-handled Children who sought to escape Parental Authority, & almost never Folk sincerely persuaded of the Truth of Christ. But, dubious as these Conversions might be, the Church trumpeted them without stay, because for the Church only Outer things counted.

Rasiel is just as judicious on the salvation of female sinners:
Iñigo's Zeal drove him with equal ardor to the conversion of Women of ill Repute. Rome the Holy teemed with a prodigious number of Harlots. The Convent of the Little Magdalenes received those who wished to renounce their vile Profession: but first they had to promise themselves to lifelong Seclusion & to all the Vows of that House of Penitence. This Condition was harsh for married Women, for Girls, & for young Widows, who wanted most sincerely to withdraw from Corruption but not to lead so austere a Life.

The eternal law of possibilities . . . And just as he had considered it absurd to ask men both to ruin themselves and change religions, Iñigo decided in the same spirit not to inflict penitential virtue on women:
Iñigo, entering into these different needs, & desiring to remove from these three sorts of Female Sinner any Pretext for continuing their Debauches, hatched the plan for another House where Lay Girls & married Women would be admitted without distinction, without pronouncing any Vow. He was the first to contribute to the Building of this House. Spurred by his Example, quantity of Lords & Ladies of the highest Distinction came forward with large Sums so that in a short time they raised a big Building where they settled this kind of Repentant Women.† . . . He himself sought out Ladies of the Night to

---

* *Cupientes judeos* of March 1542.
†Known as Saint Martha's House, to which Saint Catherine's House (for the daughters of prostitutes) was later added.

take them there, not blushing to be seen in the Town with a Troop of these Creatures. Some told him he but wasted his Time, & that these Wretches were too inured to Sin to be able to abandon it for good. "If I stay them from offending God for one night," he gave answer, "I would hold my Efforts well spent, & I should not regret it even if I were assured that they would return on the morrow to their infamous Commerce."

The vagabond of the 1530s, increasingly tormented by liver ailments and stomach pains contracted during his violent early acts of penance, now ventured less and less often from his retreat in Santa Maria della Strada. He remained most often shut away in the three *camerette* where he lived bedridden—and pen in hand.

Would that pen have been so fluent if he had not been joined in 1547 by Juan Alfonso de Polanco? This was yet another Spaniard, and one of stature. Born in Burgos of a prosperous family whose ancestors were probably converted Jews, like those of Diego Laínez, and like him educated at the University of Paris (but a few years after the founders), he had become a high papal official at a very tender age. In 1541 he performed *The Spiritual Exercises,* despite pressures and threats from his family, who already saw him as a cardinal. He then joined the "Iñiguists."

Loyola's sharp eye soon saw in him the ideal collaborator, of an education infinitely wider and suppler than his own, of admirable loyalty, and possessing the kind of obedience that preceded directives and then went out to meet them. From 1547 till the founder's death nine years later, only the handwriting tells us which of the texts (whether the correspondence, the final drafts of the *Constitutions,* or even *The Spiritual Exercises*) are pure Loyola and which are the documents they increasingly worked on together.

It was Polanco, after Favre and Salmerón, who put the finishing touches to the Latin version of *The Spiritual Exercises,* originally written in Spanish. Yet it would be wrong to call him the fifth author of a work in which Roland Barthes detected (in a "flash of genius," as present Superior General Kolvenbach has put it) four texts: the *literal,* from Ignatius to the director of the *Exercises;* the *semantic,* from the director to the practitioner; the *allegoric,* from the practitioner to God; and the *anagogic,* from God to the practitioner.[10]

But it was from the date of its Latinization, completed in 1548, that Ignatius considered the work and its revolutionary freight accomplished. It is again Barthes who has pointed out an "overthrow of the hierarchy of the senses" in the *Exercises.* Whereas the Christian Middle Ages had enthroned the primacy of hearing, of the word, of song (*auditum verbi Dei, id est fidem*)—a primacy accentuated by Luther for whom the ear alone was the organ for the Christian (while great temptations entered him through the eye), the author of the *Exercises* stressed "site and physical arrangement" (*composicion viendo al lugar*) and image, which is the "constant matter of the *Exercises*." Let us not forget that Iñigo, a great lover of music, was the first founder of an order to prohibit plainsong, and the first to link his operations and his history to a visual, plastic esthetic, good or bad.*

Ignatius of Loyola's correspondence, which after 1547 was very often dictated to Polanco, but sometimes written directly by Polanco and then reread without indulgence by the signer, is monumental: 6,800 letters, some of them extremely long, detailed, closely reasoned, visibly pondered or discussed beforehand, and sometimes springing from one of those endless prayers the little dark-faced man would drown in.

Popes, kings, cardinals, grandees of Spain and elsewhere, princesses, confessors, university chancellors—even Charles V and Philip II—there was hardly a notable of his day, within the Catholic Church and from America to Japan, with whom Loyola did not exchange advice, precepts, demands, or arguments. And these were not hasty notes scattered to the four winds by a hard-pressed manager. In a letter to Pierre Favre in 1542, the founder has left us some very curious clues about the way his letters took shape:

> I write the principal letter once. In it I say edifying things and then, scrutinizing and correcting, bearing in mind that it will be seen by all eyes, I return to writing it or I have it written a second time, for what one writes should be much nearer fruition than what one says. . . . As for me, I force myself to write a principal letter twice, in order that a certain order should reign in it . . . for the written endures; it forever bears witness, and it is neither corrected nor explained with so much facility as the spoken word.

We have quoted and we shall continue to quote from this or that letter by Ignatius of Loyola on specific themes. But from the great mass of his writings it might be useful at this point to extract one typical example of government by the pen—a pen without art, of stunted eloquence, of rough style, but a pen that conveyed something of the muted charisma that founded an empire. The lines are from the "rules of our Father Ignatius," copied at an unspecified date by an unknown Jesuit, the vehicle of a message perhaps more Stoic than Christian:

> Never train your gaze on the defects of others, but be forever prompt to excuse them; on the contrary be quick to accuse yourself. More than that, seek to be known to all, as much within as without.

---

*On the other hand, we shall later observe the part played in the spirituality of the aging Ignatius by *loquelas*, "heavenly" words or melodies. It is worth noting too that the Franciscans are closely associated with the history of painting. And that Fra Angelico was a Dominican.

. . . Do not speak, do not reply, do not meditate, do not go abroad, indeed do nothing without first asking yourself: Does this please God, is this an example that will edify my neighbor?

. . . Maintain at all times freedom of the mind and, before whomsoever you stand, make distinction of no one; but even in the most contrary circumstances remain always in an equal freedom of spirit; let no kind of obstacle make you lose it. Never fail on this point.

. . . Do not be equally free of speech and easy of access with all you encounter; but think to whom the spirit would most readily wing. Forget not, however, to examine the order and nature of the impulses which incline you toward this one or that.

. . . Exercise continually, in your acts, in your mind; be willing to pass for foolish or deranged in the eyes of men in order to be acknowledged faithful and wise by your Lord Jesus Christ: in this way, in contempt of all else you will gain Him. Amen.[11]

As the little man limped up and down a few short months before his death, dictating his "Pilgrim's memoirs," Gonçalves da Câmara tells us that Ignatius showed him a "great bundle of manuscripts" of which he read "a goodly part." They dealt with the "visions he had seen in confirmation of some clause adopted in the *Constitutions*. . . . I wished to look more closely upon the papers he showed me . . . and I begged him to let me keep them for a while. But he would not."[12]

What were these papers the founder refused to pass along to the man to whom he had just boldly told his life story? We know today that only some fifty pages of that "great bundle" (partly consumed by fire) have survived. They contain a kind of intimate journal, a confidential memorandum on the events of the years 1544 and 1545, a time when Loyola was (painfully) striving to perfect the *Constitutions* of his order.

The term "journal," even if we give it the label "spiritual," as did those who published parts of it in 1892,* is in fact inappropriate. It would seem wiser, as the writer of its most recent preface, Maurice Giuliani, suggests, to retain the term written by an unknown hand in the flyleaf of the original manuscript: *interna mentis sensa* (which might be rendered as "movements of the soul"†). For it is not an account of intimate happenings or even of reflections, impressions, observations, but of what Father Giuliani calls "the fragile and almost elusive thread that strives, through words, to pinpoint the movements that the Mind of God stamps in a soul, the marks of His passage, as mysterious and baffling as the wind."

*Reverend Father de la Torre.
†A recent French edition is entitled *Journal des motions intérieures* (Journal of Inner Movements).

These fragments of his "journal" send us back an echo of the violent inner conflicts tormenting Ignatius, particularly over what forms of poverty to impose on members of the Society in the event that they were obliged to undertake intense "worldly" activities involving expenditures and the movement of funds.

Deciphered with great difficulty by his first publishers, then by later commentators, it is a breathless confession—to call it prayer would be unintelligible to anyone ignorant of what a "movement," a surge of the soul, meant to Loyola. And to an even greater extent it is a *loquela*, that word no exegetist has ever ventured to translate, and which Ignatius himself defined as "heavenly music." This "confession," this *loquela*, seems to be the counterpart, in the domain of the senses, of what "vision" conveys in the world of images. Perhaps we are touching here on a purely inner phenomenon, as we have already (quoting Iñigo) done with reference to the Manresa "visions." Yet we should add that Loyola occasionally speaks of "inner *loquelas*," which seems to imply that he had encountered other kinds.*

This disturbing text is not just a transcription of muted ecstasy. It is also a record of trances shot through with recollections of the composition of the *Constitutions:* the questions of relative or of utter poverty (*tener, tener poco, non tener nada . . .*), the portion to be earmarked for far-flung missions, the prohibition of dignities (*contra ambitum*). It is as much to the inner conflicts shaking him, to the distress he strove to master, to the visible and audible visitations the little man experienced, that we must attribute the flood of tears that drowned him—a blinding gift that exhausted him, transported him, revealed him to himself.

Here are some brief fragments, in Father Giuliani's version, from this peerless piece of evidence:

> Thursday May 22 [1544]. Ascension. Before Mass, in my chamber and in chapel, many tears. Through most of Mass, tearless and intense *loquela*. Yet doubts assailed me as to the taste or the sweetness of the *loquela*, fearing that it might be the bad spirit because the spiritual visitation of tears then ceased. Going forward a little farther, it seemed to me that I took too great pleasure in the tone of the *loquela*, as to its sound, without paying attention enough to the meaning of the words and of the *loquela* itself. And something was imparted to me of the conduct I must observe, while still waiting for more instruction for the future.
>
> Friday [May 23]. Tears.
> Saturday [May 24]. Without tears.

*Perhaps we might say it a question of two dimensions of the same phenomenon rather than two phenomena.

Wednesday May 28. Before and after Mass, tears.

Friday May 30. Without tears.

Wednesday June 4. Many and unceasing tears.

And then, as if this reckoning up of "movements," of "tears," and of *loquelas* irritated him, eating up his time without restoring his freedom from them, he devised a shorthand system: "o" for *oficias* (services), "c" for *camera* (chamber), "é" or "y" for *yglesia* (church) "a" for *antes* (before Mass), "l" for *lagrimas* (tears), "d" for *despues* (after Mass). But also three dots above the "a" if he shed tears through all three Masses, or two or just one if he had received two or one acts of grace:

a l d, Monday December 1. Before, o c y, and during, many, and so too for the evening.

a l d, Tuesday. Before, o, é; and during great abundance, and also after.

a, Wednesday. Before, o.

a l d, Thursday. Before, o, é; and during, many, and after.

This mystical stenography ends on a somewhat inconclusive note:

"OCY. En misa mucha, abundancia y continuadas. Despuès."*

Such was this Jesuit "General," manipulating worlds from his command post at La Strada. Hard to imagine Caesar or Bonaparte in similar states. Hysteria of course comes to mind. We can content ourselves—as Father François Lhermitte has already done for us—with detecting in those states an anguish unmasked and confirmed by his own striving to regulate, channel, and defeat it.

When the padre maestro—with the same wariness he had directed at himself—studied the case of a French Jesuit, Father Onfroy, who claimed to be visited by visions, he warned him against habits ruinous to the health and therefore to "judgment and reflection." A "materialist" consideration, suggests his biographer Léon Marcuse. Or simply rational, modern?

Thus (from those majestic *Constitutions* that form the background fabric of this long spiritual trance; to that peremptory discipline, aiming at "indifference," which was to become the hallmark of the Society; to the Company's worldwide deployment) the whole powerful apparatus would be the active response to the kind of agony in which extreme torments, crosses, stigmata, would be replaced by this exquisite and dolorous flow that would bring the founder to the edge of blindness, and those *loquelas* that might have been (who knows?) the intrusion of some "bad spirit."

Strange trials indeed for our industrious and all-powerful "General."

---

*During Mass many, copious and unceasing. After.

He grew older, his physical sufferings unending and often unbearable. Gall-stones, stomach ulcer. He had to lie down for long periods, and left the *camerette* less and less frequently. One of his biographers has written that "this regnant monk created a desert around himself."[13] How could he reach such a conclusion? Around the padre maestro were Polanco, Nadal, Gonçalves da Câmara, Ribadeneira, Madrid, Des Freux, Ponce Cogordan, often Laínez, and (between missions) Salmerón, Broët, or Bobadilla, all mounting turbulent guard, tireless, unquenchable, full of the world's clamor. And the guard was constantly changing, for the legion of men he had levied had to be (as he himself had said) "always on the move."

Did he himself, between his torrents of tears, live in growing bliss? No. From the failure of his mission to Ireland, the foundering of his attempt to revive the kingdom of "Prester John" in Ethiopia, Simón Rodrigues's worrying intrigues in Portugal, the indiscretions periodically attributed to mulish Bobadilla, the obstacles facing the fathers attempting to implant the Company in France, the tussles with the Emperor, the sudden deterioration of relations between Papacy and Company following the election (as Paul IV) of Cardinal Caraffa, bitter enemy of Spaniards—no, we could not say that these last days of the founder were in any way serene.

Did the climate of victory nevertheless envelop him? Was it his age, the unsubservient veneration that surrounded him? Was it the approach of hoped-for death? The hothead of Manresa no longer seemed closed to all earthly happiness.

"A Spaniard of small stature, rather lame, with joyful eyes." Thus a visitor from Padua described him. Could those glaring eyes show joy? At all events, he allowed no one to look directly at him—any more than he allowed himself to stare at others. Even within the Company, it was a rule of which he often had to remind his confidant, Gonçalves da Câmara, when dictating his *Autobiography*. Whenever Gonçalves, strolling beside his master, stole a glance at the pilgrim, he heard the terse reminder: "The rule!"*

Let us (unbound by discipline) observe him venturing from La Strada to visit Margaret of Parma, bastard daughter of the Emperor Charles V, or to visit a community of the poor in Trastevere. Head protected by a flat hat tied around the chin with a dark ribbon, eyes half-closed, the right hem of his short black cape slung under his left arm, in his right hand a crude staff doing service as a cane, he trots across the uneven pavingstones beside the Tiber. . . . Let us watch this "fragile" little man who moves worlds.

And how can we resist the pleasure of quoting the admirable portrait of him by André Suarès:

*Which was also an accepted part of the general code of conduct of the time.

Here he is in the Prado, in the portrait painted by Morales.* . . .
Ageless, when all is said and done . . . Nothing remains of the old
man save the patrician air, a kind of veiled light in which the already
disregarded fires of command still glow. Not the smallest trace of
hauteur or of smugness, nor of harshness, nor of self-indulgence. The
perfect simplicity of the great absorbed soul. He wears black, a dull
flat black unrelieved by anything except a small white collar with two
sharp points, in flawless taste.

A narrow face, a big nose, a broad bare forehead with vertically
sculpted temples. The flesh has fallen away—the emaciation of
chronic gastric pain. A spare mustache flowing into a sparse short
beard, shading mouth and chin between them. The lips richly drawn,
the upper slender, the lower full and meaty, fiery and eloquent, with
an almost tender curve. But all else fades before the deep, exhausted,
morbidly gentle eyes. They are large and unextinguished—embers
beneath the ashes. A big musician's ear, set well back in the shadows
behind the cheek.

Everything in this haggard face is subdued light, a flame lodged
deep in the heart of the sepulcher which is life in this world. Neither
glory nor even conquest has any more sense for this countenance. . . .
He is sovereign here, where he imposes his will upon all; but face to
face he makes nothing of his sovereignty. What does life matter to
him? Or the world? He has the blissful pain and the unspeakable happiness of being no longer of it."[14]

After 1550, Ignatius of Loyola merely survived. One time they pronounced
him on his deathbed—which made him so happy that he forbade himself to
think too often about death (as we read in the *Autobiography*), "for fear it might
give him too much consolation."

Early in 1556 he became so weak that for more than a month he stopped celebrating Mass (although he still said it in one of the two chambers next to his
own). His old friend from Alcalá days, Diego de Eguía, kept informed by his
physician, reports that "his life hung on a miracle." On July 2 they carried him to
the farm on the grounds of the Jesuit college in Rome, in the pure air among the
grapevines. But they brought him back to La Strada on the 27th. He had survived so many alarms that no one realized the seriousness of his condition. It
was Ignatius, the stoic, who sent for Reverend Father Torres, physician and
priest of the Company.

On July 30, he asked Polanco to warn the Pope that he had "reached the very

*After Ignatius's death.

end," and to "ask His Holiness to give him his blessing as also to Master Laínez, for he too was in danger." Polanco pointed out to him that the physician had detected no worsening of his condition, and that before he went to the papal palace he had important letters to write for the Company. Ignatius insisted: "I am near indeed to giving up the ghost, but I put myself in your hands." Strangely, Polanco went on sending out his letters.*

In the course of the night, the infirmary brother heard him murmur, "My God . . . My God . . . " At first light Polanco, Madrid, and Des Freux found him expiring, too late for them to administer the last rites or to reach Paul IV, who demonstrated a sorrow for the dead man as lively as the antipathy he had expressed for the living Ignatius.

As the judicious Polanco summed it up: "He departed this world in the most ordinary way."

He had marked that world with his stamp. Strongly enough to have remained there, nailed, committed, even secularized? *Ad majorem Dei gloriam . . .* , not *maximam* (the greatest), but *majorem* (the greater). More a political than a mystical watchword, encompassing only what was possible. "Cut your coat according to your cloth." The concern to magnify God's glory opens so many doors, so many trails, and leads to such detours . . .

Was he then the prisoner of an earth to which, despite everything, his psychological and political genius had bound him? A prisoner of his genius for power, the virtuosity he displayed in the area Dominique Bertrand calls "sociodoxy,"† the science of human society, of the governance of men?

So here we have him forever stamped with the stigmata of "politics," of everything the management of public affairs and of power relationships offers that is disturbing, sticky, cumbersome, uncertain.

The courtier of Arévalo had turned himself into a hirsute clairvoyant hermit. The crazed wanderer of Italy changed into the architect of a planet-straddling organization. There the image has stuck. The little tear-stained limping man endures in men's imaginations as the ultimate model of the social engineer. Planted in cruel ground.

"Be all things to all men," he had told his missionaries. We will see where this opening would lead, this flexibility, this malleability, however harsh the abnegation that inspired them.

Yet it was not an opportunistic or a soothing message he bequeathed to his disciples: "*Ite et inflammate!*"—"Go, and set the world ablaze!"

*Typically Jesuit behavior: "Give yourself wholly to your task."
†In a masterly work significantly entitled *La politique de saint Ignace* (The Politics of Saint Ignatius).

· IV ·

FRANCIS XAVIER,
ORIENTALIST

Barefoot into Japan • *"Fleeing the Indies"* • *A People Gifted with
Reason* • *Searching for Tenjiku* • *From Daimyo to Daimyo* •
Resentment of the Bonzes • *Ruins of Myako* • *Silk or Cotton?* •
Revolutionary Mission • *Prophet of Crossculturalism*

O
N THE TWENTY-SEVENTH day of the seventh month of the
Tenbun era (August 15, 1549), a Chinese junk nosed into the little
port of Kagoshima in southern Kyushu, itself the most southerly
major island of the Japanese archipelago.

An unimpressive vessel of 250 tons, thirty-five feet long and carrying two
bamboo masts. Its owner, sole master on board after God, was a man named
Avan, known simply as *o Ladrao* (the Thief, or—at its kindest—the Pirate) to
his Portuguese clients.

Apart from that detail, there was nothing about the small junk to draw the
attention of the Japanese sentinels strolling, swords at their sides, along the
Kagoshima wharfside. Nothing, that is, save the strange cargo the Pirate had
brought safely to these rarely frequented waters through a half dozen storms,
from the Macao shipyards where the junk was built, down the Cochin Chinese
coast and north into the China Sea. Aboard the junk were three Spanish priests
(discreetly calling themselves Portuguese), Francis Xavier, Cosme de Torres,
and Juan Fernández. Then there was Anjiro, a Japanese converted to Catholi-

Note: This chapter owes much to Father Georg Schurhammer's monumental biography and to the
excellent edition of Xavier's correspondence published in 1987 by Hugues Didier.

cism at Goa, where he had taken the name Paulo de Santa Fé; two other Japanese, baptized Antonio and Joane; Manuel, a Chinese; and a Malabar Indian named Amador.

We last saw Francis Xavier nine years earlier in Lisbon, entrusted by Loyola—at the request of John III, King of Portugal and the Company's eminent protector—with carrying the Gospel to Asia ("Esta es vuestra empresa. . . . Heme aquí!"). While his companions finished building the Company, made Ignatius their formal leader, disputed at Trent, and founded their first colleges, Francis Xavier had become a Flying Dutchman of the faith, braving the seas from the Cape of Good Hope to Mozambique, from the Pirate Coast of Goa to the Moluccas.

Bearing the title—more show than substance, as it happened—of apostolic nuncio, the Pope's special envoy for Asia, but wearing a worn, patched cassock, he had crisscrossed Southeast Asia for nine long years, "treating the oceans as others treat Lake Geneva," wrote André Bellessort. He had converted the illiterate masses of India and Malaysia, blessing them with rhythmically sweeping gestures ("There are days when my arms ache with weariness," he wrote), preaching in a pidgin made up of his own bizarre Portuguese and of one or another of the numberless languages spoken across India's provinces and Indonesia's islands, dedicated to a solitude too often broken by the compromising protection of King John's men-at-arms. Baptism in the shadow of the sword . . .

For more than seven years his mission, as far as we can decipher it from his correspondence and the accounts of his first biographers and historians, was marked first and foremost by his unbelievable insensitivity to nature, to these prodigious worlds his vocation had thrown him into, to the vastnesses laid at Europe's feet by Vasco da Gama (of that whole universe, wrote one of his biographers, "he beheld only the stars"), and an equal ignorance of the peoples whose salvation he had undertaken. But was it ignorance, or lack of interest?

He had left for Asia as if for an overpopulated wasteland, one of those expanses that contemporary cartographers marked *Hic Sunt Leones* (Here Be Fierce Beastes), carrying with him, it was said, "only his prayerbook and his crucifix." The latter assertion is, incidentally, questioned by Henri Bernard-Maître, who reports that the nuncio had received books "to the value of one hundred cruzados" (a large sum for the time) from King John. But what is certain is that they had barely served him: In the Indies he used only a grammar and a "collection of edifying tales" by Marulus. He simply did away with his past as a humanist intellectual "Master of Arts" of the University of Paris, making no effort to discern the greatness that Indian and Brahman civilizations concealed beneath the wretchedness of appearances.

And if in January 1549 he launched an appeal to his former teachers at the Sorbonne to come and take part in his missionary venture, if he urged his companions in Rome to persuade Pierre de Cornibus or François Picart to abandon their prestigious Paris chairs to fight alongside him for the spiritual conquest of Asia, it was both with penitence in mind (let these haughty university figures shoulder their share of sacrifice!) and in the spirit of a cassocked conquistador, intent only on converting—the way others have machine-gunned crowds or decimated forests.

Of the Indians, of the unreckonable Indian peoples, from Goa to Cochin, from Travancore to Ceylon, he seems to have noticed nothing beyond their material destitution, their ignorance, their fundamental lack of direction. Neither their spirituality nor their capacity for feeling nor what they inevitably reflected of ancient metaphysics-haunted cultures seemed to touch him. His sense of charity, but not his intelligence, was moved by these faceless brown-skinned masses, a hotchpotch of pearlfishers known as Paravers, of peasants, of dirt-poor Singhalese craftsmen. All he saw was idolatry, the absence of God, cynical exploitation by a hypocritical Christianity.

Furthermore, Southern India was at that time particularly ill-suited to what might be called the Jesuit system: There was no central power to lean on or to fight against. A sprinkling of principalities, a small galaxy of half-colonized petty kings, and a Portuguese colonial system confined to trading counters—authority that was either inaccessible or accessible only through abuse . . . If only one could be faced here with a Charles V or a Cortéz!

Even more puzzling were the methods the holy man resorted to. For more than seven years he was apparently concerned only with "bringing forth fruit," that phrase learned from Loyola in which concern for effectiveness and success is expressed in such raw terms, casting upon Ignatian spirituality a most disturbing aura of victory at all costs. For a long time, he thought only of "conquering the Gentiles"—that "rabble they call the Brahmans." Faced with such people, "the most perverse in the world," he thought only in terms of coercion, of division, of separating convert groups from the mass of "idolaters": Indeed one might almost see in his approach (expressed for example in his letter of January 15, 1544, from Cochin) a strategist of apartheid, a paratrooper colonel imbued with the principles of "psychological warfare."

For years, apparently uncomplainingly, he operated within a system of relationships of which a contemporary witness, describing the corporal punishment known as the bastinado, said (in a touch worthy of Chateaubriand), "They counted out the blows on a rosary."

We do not know every step of the journey Francis Xavier's conscience took, nor exactly when the horrible ambiguity of his situation became clear to him.

But we have several letters in which his indignation explodes as he realizes that he is being used as a respected and acquiescent accomplice in the fearful piracy that was Portuguese colonization at that time. And, going deeper still, the utter incompatibility between the Gospel and European conquest.

From among the dozens of documents that throw light on this overwhelming realization, we will quote two letters addressed to King John III, faithful protector of the Ignatian Company, the same monarch who had furnished him with the means for his departure from Lisbon. In the first, dated April 19, 1549, there is an undertone of anger—and of menace:

> Experience has taught me that Your Highness does not wield power in India only for the increase of faith in Christ, but also in order to seize the temporal wealth of India. . . . Let Your Majesty make full and exact reckoning of all the fruit and all the temporal riches he gathers from the Indies by God's good doing. . . . May Our Lord make plain, to the bottom of Your Highness's soul, His most holy will, and may He give Your Highness grace to accomplish it in such a way that Your Highness will have cause to rejoice at the hour of death when he gives God an account of his life; and that hour will come sooner than Your Highness thinks. His kingdoms and possessions have an end. . . . It will be a thing unheard-of, a thing Your Highness has never experienced, to find himself stripped of them.

And next day the scandalized priest returned gloomily to the attack: "Your Highness [must act] in such a way as to face God's judgment in all confidence. . . . Let Your Highness not wait until the hour of his death, for death's pains are so great that they leave not the slightest place to think of all those things which we now reserve for that moment."

No warning could have been more brutal.

Although belatedly aware, after these first ten years of mass conversions, of the incompatibility of the Gospel message and the colonial enterprise, Xavier had not yet fully grasped the terrifying nature of the conviction underlying missionary strategy. A conviction that might be summed up in the following terms: However crude the combined colonialist-Christian approach, however dismissive it might seem of the exercise of free will and of human nature, it was inevitable, and in any case preferable to any other behavior, since it alone snatched from hellfire those multitudes heretofore deprived of the Church's succor.

Francis Xavier, whose every act proclaimed courage and virtue in the accomplishment of his mission and in the face of the powers on which he depended, and who was to demonstrate in so many fields a clearsightedness far in advance of his times, remained a prisoner of the appalling certainty that, from millennium to millennium, his supposedly compassionate God had peopled the earth with beings, His own creatures, almost all of whom were doomed to everlasting hellfire—until such a time as a Francis Xavier would dare brave headland and gale to come and baptize them with his weary arms, thus saving them from inevitable mass damnation.

He would retain that barbaric conviction to the very end, as the letters he wrote throughout his years in Japan testify. When Captain Avan—the Pirate—died at Kagoshima a few months after bringing him to safe haven there, he noted that the dead man had been "good" to him—but that since he had not received baptism, "he is this night in Hell." Worse was to come: When tearful Japanese converts asked him whether their poor parents, dead before his coming, could not now be snatched from the jaws of Hell, the holy man answered, "Never!"

It can be argued that such were the certainties of the day. That theologians had not yet managed to discredit this notion of exclusion, formulated (on the basis of Saint Paul's teachings?) by Saint Augustine, and suggest instead the profound workings of a pre-Christian salvation. And that it would take another four centuries for Karl Rahner, Schillebeekx, and Domenico Grasso* to absolve God of the mass damnation of those who had never heard the Gospel message.

Nevertheless, such an implacable position is especially strange, even shocking, in a man to whom one of his first biographers, João de Lucena, attributed a "prayer for the unfaithful" (but unfaithful to what? To be unfaithful you must first have been offered a faith and then have broken with it) of revolutionary ambiguity:

> Eternal God, Creator of all things, remember that Thou alone hast created the souls of the Unfaithful, whom Thou hast created in Thine own image and likeness. Behold, Lord, that in Thy reproach they now fill the halls of Hell. Remember, Lord, that Thy Son Jesus Christ suffered for them in generously shedding His blood.†

One day in January 1549, Xavier had the courage to act upon his anger. Unable to go on, he wrote the following words to the King of Portugal. They would seal his own destiny and change that of millions of human beings—as if Columbus, perceiving his mistake as he approached the Caribbean islands, had changed course to reach the true East. "For myself, My Lord, I know what happens here. I have therefore no hope that the orders and prescriptions Your Majesty may

---

*Although it is true that they had an eighteenth-century precursor in Bergier.

†This prayer, which leaves nothing unsaid, may have been the work of Father Lucena, Xavier's biographer (Lisbon, 1600) rather than the nuncio himself. Hugues Didier, who published and annotated Xavier's correspondence, suggests the possibility. But not without the pertinent remark that "in any case, this text is certainly more Xavier's than the Epistle to the Hebrews is Saint Paul's."

send for the benefit of Christianity will be obeyed in India. It is for this that I now leave for Japan, almost fleeing, so as not to lose any more time."[1]

"Fleeing . . . " Why this "flight" to Japan? Why this sense of hopelessness? Why this confession of time lost by the apostle already hailed from continent to continent as a saint, a planetary hero haloed in a glory attested by a hundred witnesses, credited with "miracles" that have not all been counterfeited over the centuries by pious biographers? All of a sudden our gentleman of Navarre seems ashamed of "Saint Francis Xavier," just as Oppenheimer and Sakharov would four centuries later be shattered by the implications of their discoveries.

First of all, there was the disgust he would henceforth feel for the whole colonial enterprise. Or rather for the nauseating symbiosis between his own apostolic mission and the most cynical aspects of European imperialism, whether these took the form of organized pillage, of naked greed, or even, as in Ceylon, of the protection extended by the Portuguese proconsul to King Buvanekha, who harassed his Christian subjects because they had dared hope that their "conversion" would earn them rights and protection from the "colonizer." For there was this painful question to which he had no answer (even to ask it would have seemed impious to him): Why did these wretched populations convert to this mysterious foreign religion in the first place?

Was it in hope of favors or at least protection from the conquerors (a hope often swiftly disappointed)? The attraction exerted by the obvious and sometimes heroic dedication of preachers who could also nurse the sick and bring social succor? Or convenience? In a film shown on French television about a valley in South China, a peasant explained his conversion to Protestantism in the following terms: "Witchcraft costs too much. With the Christian priest we are freed from such problems." Too cynical, perhaps?

In the letters Francis wrote from 1548 onward to his companions in Rome and to the King of Portugal, we begin to glimpse his rejection of the one-way relationship between the administrator of blessings and a passive flock delivered from Gehenna by an ill-defined ritual, his rejection of the role of automatic dispenser of tickets to heaven. He had finally disavowed a machinery whose holy ends did not redeem its discriminatory—not to say contemptuous—means. The pride of faith . . . What he finally awaited was the intervention—the double intervention—of human intelligence in his mission.

If we have chosen to isolate the two-year-long Japanese episode from the rest of the apostolic epic of this Christian Ulysses, it is because it represented his repudiation of a mission too long poisoned by the spirit of Crusade, of holy war, and of mass exclusion—and his acceptance of its opposite: the discovery of a humankind whose civilization was no longer to be denied but to be explored, through active exchange and mutual fertilization. It was a first glimpse of the anthropological approach that would become the Jesuits' glory, from Ricci and Nobili in China and India to the Latin American trailblazers and to Pierre Charles in Africa.

The "manifesto" of this radical transformation is the letter Francis Xavier wrote on January 20, 1548 to his "companions living in Rome" and foremost to the man he called "my true father in the bowels of Christ," Ignatius of Loyola. In it, the spirit of learning finally dislodges the ethos of conquest, and a new human being emerges: "Portuguese merchants* in this city of Malacca have provided me with ample information on large, recently discovered islands, known as the 'isles of Japan.' In their view there is much fruit to be garnered there; we would extend our Holy Faith there much more than in any part of India, for they are folk extraordinarily eager to learn, unlike the Gentiles of India."

Anjiro now makes a first appearance in Francis Xavier's letter. He had come to confess himself to the missionary of "certain sins committed in his youth."† Of him Francis said, "If all Japanese are as hungry for learning as this Anjiro, then it seems to me that they are the most eager for knowledge of all the countries we have discovered." He rounded off the description with a decisive stroke:

> I asked Anjiro whether, in the event that I went to his country with
> him, the people of Japan would become Christian. He replied that the
> people there would not at once become Christian. He said that they
> would first ask many questions of me, that they would see what I re-
> plied, and above all whether I lived according to what I said. If I did
> those two things well, speaking well and answering their questions in
> satisfactory manner, as well as living in such a way as to furnish no
> cause for reproach, it would want but half a year after having this ex-
> perience of me for the king, the nobility, and others capable of dis-
> cernment to become Christians. He told me that they are indeed
> people governed only by reason.[2]

Reason: the key word of this radical and all-inclusive manifesto. Here, in a few lines, is the philosophy that would henceforth fire the Navarrese Jesuit: from critical aloofness to a spirit of inquiry and experimentation, from initial dialogue to a willingness for exchange, from a spirit of scrutiny to a concern for equity and truth.

Should we attribute so wrenching a revision of his sense of mission to the tales of Anjiro, a Japanese wanderer in search of forgiveness, of shelter, and of redemption—and perhaps seeking credit by making up stories? Xavier is careful to back his own remarks with those of Jorge Alvares, the Portuguese captain who, after making landfall in several Japanese ports, had taken in the fugitive

---

*First of the Western navigators, the Portuguese landed on the Ryuku Islands in 1543. Their successors, from Spain, christened the archipelago *islas platerías* (the silver islands).
†This youthful transgression was a murder.

Anjiro: Yes, yes, said Alvares, the Japanese were astonishingly curious, highly reasonable, very brave, conscious of their culture and individual personality: "They are proud and sensitive. Not greedy but generous, and hospitable to strangers. Curious, forever asking questions. They hate theft, which they punish with death. Not given to drunkenness, they are discreet and soft-spoken, despising foreigners who raise their voices. They are a religious people."[3]

Such were the beginnings of Xavier's inquiry into the prospects for a mission to Japan. The inquiry continued for more than a year, while Xavier's relations with the Portuguese authorities steadily soured. At one point, he even asked the King to "make his mind up finally to punish a Governor." His encounter with Anjiro and Alvares had redirected the passion, energy, and imagination of the sublime adventurer toward those "new islands" where men gifted with reason awaited him.

And soon, from letter to letter (whether his correspondent was the Jesuit General or the Portuguese King), Francis hinted at intentions that slowly ripened into an increasingly precise and obsessive plan: He would undertake, "in a year or eighteen months," a "pilgrimage" to the mysterious archipelago. After a year of study and preparation, he at last informed Ignatius of Loyola that he had "made his decision"—based on the "manifold pieces of information" he had gathered—to journey to this "island situated close to China [where] folk are most curious-minded."

Referring again to information supplied by Anjiro, whom he now called Paulo de Santa Fé, or Paul of the Holy Faith, and his countrymen Antonio and Joane (baptized in Goa like Anjiro), Francis unveiled the plan to his leader. It is immediately clear how different his new role would be after years spent converting illiterate masses in the shadow of the conquerors' guns:

> I leave with the intention first of going to the place of residence of the king, and thence to the universities where they study. . . . As for the Law observed there, Paul has told me that it was brought from a country called Tenjiku,* which according to Paul lies beyond China and Tartan.† . . . Once in Japan I will write to Your Charity . . . about what is taught in the great university of Tenjiku. . . . When I have seen the Scriptures of Japan and have conferred with the people of the universities, . . . I will make it my duty to write to the University of Paris so that, through its good offices, all the other universities of Europe may be informed."[4]

*Which others spell Chenjiko, and in Chinese is Chen-Djou-Kouo.
†Francis Xavier is as far astray as Christopher Columbus was a half century earlier. For him (situated on the west coast of India), Tenjiku was not "on the other side of" China and "Tartan," but on his own side—for Tenjiku was northern India, where Buddhism was born.

Everything had changed. His was now a true cultural mission. Suddenly the Paris "intellectual" had been brought back to life within the wandering priest in his threadbare cassock. We might be reading a letter by Champollion before his departure for Egypt in 1828, a "European" scholar at the head of his exotic "literary expedition." Information, knowledge. And that way of referring—capitalized—to the "Scriptures of Japan"! In a letter to his friend Simón Rodrigues, he even mentioned the books of these Japanese sages, "which they say come from God." Staggering, after what he had said about the Brahmin "rabble" . . .

Soon the "apostolic nuncio for Asia" went further. Referring to the Japanese alphabet, he came out wholeheartedly in favor of reciprocity, of the equivalence of cultures, and against the prevalent Eurocentrism. According to a letter to Loyola, dated January 14, 1549: "They write in a manner very different from ours, from the top to the bottom. I asked Paul why they did not write as we do, and he answered: Why should we not write as they do? And for a reason he said that just as a man has his head in the air and his feet below, so when he writes that man should [do it] from top to bottom."

Why indeed should we have expected these recently "discovered" peoples to bend to our customs, above all when they had such sagacious reasons for acting otherwise? The fathers of La Strada must have found it hard to conceal their surprise: Could their Xavier be "Asianized" so soon? Their successors would encounter more of the same with Ricci and Nobili. But the decisive break had already been made.

Had Xavier been prepared for such an opening by his humanist studies in Paris? Had his exploration of classical culture, that vast journey across the dead centuries, destined him for the exploration of geographical space?

Henri Bernard-Maître points out that a student and laureate of the Collège de Sainte-Barbe, a protégé of the Portuguese Diego de Gouvea, a man blessed with multiple worldwide contacts, a close friend of the Lisbon king, would inevitably have known about the expeditions of Jacques Cartier or of Verrazano in America; that the orientalist dreams of Guillaume de Postel must surely have seduced him; that the teachings of Guillaume Budé (even though Francis later turned his back on them) must have led him to hope for a transposition or an expansion of humanism into universalism. Did the passion for learning not have to develop in space as well as through time?

While it is true that a historic conjunction between Erasmian humanism and the multiplication of worlds by the great explorers did occasionally take place, it is difficult to discern a relationship of cause and effect, of concerted deployment, between them. In a 1953 publication of the Guillaume Budé Association, the Indian specialist Jean Filliozat argued that "Renaissance humanism did not predispose men to the spiritual discovery of the East. It did not open onto all humankind. It was Greco-Roman, not universal. While study of the humanities opened endless perspectives on the rediscovered treasures of Antiquity . . . it was aimed at measuring man—not at paving the way for a study of all men."

It might be objected that the itinerary of Guillaume Postel, a fiery orientalist hatched in the Jesuit cradle in Rome, had made it possible from the very first to think in terms of worlds. And the whole Jesuit enterprise in Asia was to consist of throwing a bridge between the man of the Renaissance, defined by Erasmus, and these different men, who wrote from top to bottom and had such good "reasons" for doing so.

It was the quest for reason, the quest for man truly as man, in all his fullness, living in a permanent exchange of questions and answers, the quest for an encounter on the scale of all humankind, which led Francis Xavier, the infidel-hunter, the amasser of Indian souls, into Far Eastern waters. At the end of the voyage there would of course be his evangelical duties. But henceforth on a basis of mutual knowledge, of intellectual exchange.

We can of course sneer at the state of the "knowledge" he then possessed of Japan. It boiled down to three ideas. First, that this island "next door to China" was inhabited by people both "reasonable" and filled with curiosity. Second, that a king ruled over it at the head of a central government. Third, that universities comparable to those of Europe dispensed teachings that came from Tenjiku. Naïve, perhaps. But who at that time knew much more about those "large recently discovered islands"?

All he knew he had learned from a Kyushu fugitive, a man almost illiterate but nonetheless involved with the economic and social life of Japan's most southerly province, and through it the China trade. Anjiro was ignorant of Chinese characters and of almost everything outside his own province of Satzuma, in southern Kyushu: It was as if a native of sixteenth-century rural Europe had attempted to explain the kingdom of France and its government to Nipponese monks. As for Captain Jorge Alvares, Xavier's other informant, he had seen only the ports of southwestern Japan—Kagoshima, Hirado, and the fledgling Nagasaki, far from "imperial" cities and centers of learning.

This "ideal" Japan for which Xavier was bound is strikingly different from the one described by modern historians of sixteenth-century Japan. Of the three basic conclusions he had drawn from the accounts of Anjiro and Alvares, only the first would be confirmed, and then only with many subtle differences: the rational nature of the Japanese people, allied to its courage, its curiosity about the outside world, and its courteous hospitality. Whereas the "King" (with whom the missionary hoped to have an immediate audience in order to obtain permission to teach the Gospels to his people) and the universities he dreamed of visiting were ideas he was quickly forced to abandon.

But before considering the nature and the distribution of power in post-feudal Japan, we should note that—once the gloomy parenthesis of collaboration with colonialism in India and Southeast Asia was closed—Francis Xavier would still be left with the Jesuit method created and defined ten years earlier in the European theater by Loyola: that of close cooperation with principalities and powers. A cooperation founded on recognition of Caesar's rights,* but also on the need to give God His due. Ignatius saw nothing wrong in associating the power he wielded in symbiosis with the papacy with that of the Habsburgs or the Bourbons, but always in a spirit of mutual equality and freedom. You operated "with" this or that sovereign, not "for" or "under" him. Cooperation, not feudal duty or service.

In principle, at least. As we shall see, and have already seen, the Company could on the one hand slip into dependency, compromise, and action on behalf of authority, as with Father Antonio Araoz at the Spanish court, or it could veer toward more or less open conflict with authority—as in eighteenth-century Paraguay.† Nothing of the sort happened in Japan. Not because Francis Xavier was too conciliatory or obsequious or cowardly or insolent, but quite simply because there was no "king."

At mid-sixteenth century, that is to say before the attempts undertaken by Oda Nobunaga and later Toyotomi Hideyoshi and Tokugawa Ieyasu to unite the empire, during the vacuum that existed between the feudal system and the rise of the central State, Japan was both politically and geographically an archipelago. Authority, enfeebled and long divided at its summit, was wielded by a multitude of local lords comparable to the princes of sixteenth-century Italy and Germany, rulers who no longer acknowledged the slightest bond of vassalage to the central power.

At the top were two focal points of power. One was symbolic, dynastic, the repository of sovereignty, of "the mandate of heaven"; this had traditionally been the *tenno*, very roughly translated as Emperor. But the real power was that supposedly exercised by the *shoguns* (commanders in chief), a blend of palace mayor and high constable. They would later become absolute masters of Japan, particularly under the Tokugawas, a veritable dynasty of shoguns founded by Ieyasu at the beginning of the seventeenth century.

By the time Francis Xavier prepared to visit Japan, the tenno was no more than the ghostly heir of a vanished power. The ruling family, the Fujiwaras, ruined by the rise to power of local potentates who had appropriated all tax revenues to themselves, was reduced to working for its survival. Here, says

*If those rights were unquestioned. When they were challenged, the Jesuits could go very far indeed, as we shall see.
†See Chapter VIII.

American historian Edwin O. Reischauer, was "an Emperor reduced to doing calligraphic work, obliged to copy, by hand and for a modest fee, a handful of poems . . . commissioned by a client. . . . Three times in the course of the sixteenth century, the hard-pressed royal family had to abandon the installation of successors for lack of the means to pay for the deceased emperor's funeral and his successor's coronation!"[5]

The Japanese people must have been truly attached to the dynastic principle (but also, we must admit, to the virtues of work) for the imperial system to have survived such hardship. Is it conceivable that a Valois or a Tudor could have maintained his prestige in such circumstances?

Curiously, though, the tenno's decline did not at that time work to the advantage of the parallel ruling power, the shoguns. The deeper the Fujiwaras slid into destitution, the more the masters of military power, the Ashikagas, allowed their proverbial might to be nibbled away by peripheral potentates. As in certain cases of drowning, tenno and shogun (who, equally curiously, shared the same capital, Miyako, the future Kyoto) seemed to cling desperately to one another as both went under.

Those years thus saw the apogee of centrifugal forces, forces embodied in the person of local lords, the daimyos, whose feudal ties to the shogun steadily weakened. Indeed it was from one of these local cells that the reunification of the empire began, under the aegis of Nobunaga, daimyo of the central province of Nagoya. And we should note here that Francis Xavier, lacking an imperial interlocutor, would adapt most intelligently to this splintering of power and would improvise—from daimyo to daimyo—a version of the "render unto Caesar" relationship he had planned to enjoy with the king.

But as we have seen, he had not contented himself with merely political objectives in shaping his mission. He also sought those "universities" aglow with the principles imported from Tenjiku, places of learning where he might compare the lessons of his own faith with those that surely lay in the "Books" the Japanese believed "came from God." And it was true that large Buddhist monasteries of Zen inspiration then dominated spiritual and cultural life, launching works of graphic art that would be the glory of Japan—until Chinese Confucianism came to serve as a model for conduct and as a corrective to the supreme rule of Japanese noble and military tradition, the *bushido,* or the Way of the Warrior.

Encountering this political-military chaos, this trampling of central authority, a foreign observer, and particularly a Spaniard coming from the most highly organized state system of the day, would readily have delivered a gloomy diagnosis of mid-sixteenth-century Japan. Where was the King? Where was the army? Where, even, was religion?

But we have seen that even peripheral visitors, like the skipper Jorge Alvares, had been able to glimpse the profound vitality and the appetite for exchange bubbling beneath all these disorders. According to Reischauer:

> During the dark years of political anarchy, Japanese craftsmen had developed their art to the point of eclipsing the masters of Chinese industry [and] succeeded in developing a solid commercial system. Thanks to the dynamism of their "merchant-knights," they made themselves masters of the East Asian seas. . . . Paradoxically, the Japanese emerged stronger from their long period of feudal anarchy and could henceforth deal on equal terms with European traders and even with the Chinese.[6]

In other words, the Japan for which Francis Xavier now set sail was by no means a decadent one. However different it might be from the kingdom of his dreams—and the enormous attraction of his adventure lies precisely in the confrontation of those dreams with reality—he was heading for a nation passionately eager to make its mark, and convinced that knowledge was the only sure means of doing so. Knowledge that yesterday came from Tenjiku. And what of tomorrow?

Yet the voyage began badly. It almost never took place at all. It was all very well for Francis Xavier to write to Ignatius or John III announcing his intention to take ship, but first he had to find a ship. Few people at that time were eager to set sail, through stormy pirate-infested waters, with no guarantee of profit, for those "large islands in the North" where their welcome was uncertain, no matter what men like Jorge Alvares might say of the destination.

Who, even in Malacca, would take on these new-style adventurers from whom almost nothing could be expected in return? Finally the Governor of Malacca, Don Pedro da Silva, stepped in. He knew (as an inmate of the harbor prison?) the Chinese trader Avan "the Pirate," whom we have already met. He ordered Avan to set a course for Japan. But unwilling to voyage farther than China, Avan hinted that even if the official goal was the archipelago, he might decide in Canton to call a halt to the risky voyage. The Captain-Governor replied that if Avan did not take the missionary and if he did not bring back to Malacca a letter from the holy man attesting that he had been brought safe to Japan, the Pirate would never again see his wife and children.[7] It was thus through a mixture of blackmail and hostage taking that the mission—*ad majorem Dei gloriam*—began.*

The apostolic nuncio for Asia, the former high-jump champion from Paris's Pré-aux-Clercs, was now forty-three. He had only three more years to live, but

---

*Historians fail to say whether Xavier ever knew about this blackmail.

he was still a powerful personality and possessed a charm that conquered everyone. According to Father Bouhours, "His stature was a little above average, his constitution robust, his looks equally agreeable and majestic. He had fine coloring, a broad forehead, a well-shaped nose, lively and piercing blue eyes, and hair and beard of dark chestnut. His continual labors soon turned his hair gray, and in the last year of his life it was almost totally white."[8]

Xavier left the Indies haloed in a kind of glory: In nine years of preaching, teaching, caring for the sick, negotiating with the authorities, traveling from Goa to Malacca and from the Fisher Coast to Morotai in the northern Moluccas, he had built for himself a legend founded on his magnetic and truly charismatic personality, and on a love for his fellow man so powerful and so obvious that his companions had no difficulty convincing their Japanese hosts of his sanctity.

But his radiant personality was all that Francis brought with him to the great rendezvous. He possessed no serious information, and had only the vaguest notions of the Japanese language; in fact, he would never speak it except to parrot a few roughly translated prayers, learned by heart and delivered amid perplexity or general hilarity. And we know that, apart from two episodes, his actions in Japan never involved weapons or coercion. This latter was, in fact, probably his greatest asset, for he came almost barehanded to meet this intensely military people who, proud to a fault, would never have tolerated anything resembling constraint.

Not quite barehanded, however. He had stowed aboard Avan's junk thirty barrels of powder, furnished by the Governor of Malacca to do service as a passport. The Japanese were greedy for it, and no other gift could better have earned their friendship. He also brought a clock and several holy images. And he was not truly alone. He had persuaded Anjiro and the other two Japanese novices from Goa to accompany him; as we shall see, their presence was extremely useful, at least at the start. As for his other two companions, Father Cosme de Torres and Brother Juan Fernández Oviedo, they were volunteers for the mission. The former saw chiefly spiritual promise in their quest, while the latter appears from the outset to have glimpsed its cultural possibilities.

Father Torres was a Jesuit from Valencia. Historians differ as to his intellectual gifts and his cultural baggage. Let us concede, along with the majority, that he was "lettered." His correspondence from Yamaguchi after Xavier's departure in 1552 speaks in his favor: It is the work of a zealous disciple. Like Xavier, he never learned Japanese. But Francis Xavier gave him countless proofs of confidence, and there is no indication that these were carelessly accorded.

It was Brother Oviedo's gift for languages that made him the group's real interpreter once Anjiro left them.* Almost all accounts indicate that he managed

*See p. 118.

to understand his counterparts and make himself understood by them. They found in his Japanese an exotic charm they called *muxaree.*[9] The missionaries' lengthy debates with the monks of Yamaguchi, which he took down in writing and to which we shall be returning,* could not have been reported except by a man with a good command of the local language and culture.

Nevertheless, the essential link in the chain between Francis Xavier and Japan was Anjiro, disturbed and disturbing Anjiro. Fleeing a murder charge in 1547, he had sought refuge on a Portuguese vessel bound for the Indies and would end his life as a pirate—himself killed by pirates on the China coast. Even more disconcertingly, this Anjiro was not a penniless adventurer, a *ronin,* as one historian claimed, but a man with a stable family, children, and two servants. A curious customer! But Francis Xavier, deeply in Anjiro's debt, never questioned the basic sincerity of his repentance or his conversion, although he sometimes had to admit that the information Anjiro supplied could be hazardous. It did not matter: It was to this adventurer that he owed the essential—his instant love for Japan.

We know much less about Francis Xavier's other companions. In a letter to John III he describes them almost wholly from the spiritual perspective, and without naming them: We know only from other sources that they had been christened Antonio and Joane. "The three men from Japan are excellent Christians . . . instructed at the College of the Holy Faith in Goa. All three can read and write, and all three are pious. All three have done *The Spiritual Exercises* with much benefit, . . . confessing and communicating often, and moved by a great desire to make Christians of their countrymen."

None of the three was a member of the Company, but their leader treated them as if they were. From the moment of departure, Xavier carefully solicited their opinions, reporting for example that, according to them, "the priests of the Japanese would be shocked if they saw [us] eating fish and meat"—and concluding that they too would have to go without such things.

The apostolic nuncio took in stride the following information, emanating from the same source: that in Japanese monasteries they performed meditative exercises.† He also described to his companions in Rome "Hell," "Purgatory," and the "Devil" as Zen Buddhism (according to Anjiro) conceived them. A "Christocentric" view of Japan, to put it mildly.

In short, Francis Xavier, who had just spent nine years in and around the Indian subcontinent in total ignorance of the vast civilization that had given Buddhism to the world, was now preparing to broach Japan in a radically altered

*See pp. 126–31.
†With a capital E.

spirit—full of reverence and admiration for the culture of his hosts, and convinced that this people so hungry for knowledge was capable in its turn of transmitting enormous human, cultural, and spiritual wealth. He set off not with a view to conquest but to exchange in his encounter with a nation for which, in prospect, he felt great respect.

But this radical transformation, which led him from pity to respect, from a spirit of crusade among vaguely defined "infidels" to a hope for dialogue with another culture whose fertility he had already perceived, was not all that stood between the Xavier of India and the Francis of Japan. There was also this major difference: He would land on the archipelago weaponless, free of the colonial, imperial, military, and commercial trappings that had tainted his message in India, forcing him "almost to flee." Here he was no longer a cog in a vast machine for exploiting and destroying civilizations: He was a man, the center of a tiny group, bearing nothing but a word.

And yet, despite the purity of his intentions, Francis noted that if those in power gave him a warm welcome it was partly because they realized that European navigators—dealers, among other things, in firearms—preferred the coasts of Kyushu and Honshu because Christian priests had been warmly received there. In a letter to Don Pedro da Silva, the Jesuit nuncio was at pains to say that if "we reap much fruit in souls" it was because others reaped much fruit in other fields. There is no human undertaking too noble not to be shadowed by self-interest—but should we then conclude that such shadows were dishonoring?

Anjiro's overriding importance in this encounter between our argonauts and Japan was further enhanced by the fact that destiny, in the shape of Pacific winds (although it may have been nudged by a secret pact between Anjiro and the Pirate), refused to blow Avan's vessel toward a port in Honshu, the central island, where Xavier hoped to head straight for Miyako, the royal capital. Instead it carried them to Kyushu and to Anjiro's native city, Kagoshima—whence the "family-style" welcome the voyagers enjoyed.

But why not listen to Xavier himself? The account he sent his companions in Goa (in a rambling letter written on November 15, 1549, three months after Avan's junk had landed) is a document of great beauty, with all its contradictions, repetitions, and digressions, clearly sincere, enriched by a thousand details garnered during those first weeks of discoveries, of wonders, and of disappointments as well. For the real Japan turned out to be different from the land described to him by Paulo de Santa Fé, and even different from the one he saw and described—apparently unaware that these likable Japanese privately called the new arrivals *nambandjin,* "southern barbarians":

On Our Lady's Day in August 1549, . . . we reached Kagoshima, the home of Paulo de Santa Fé [where] everyone greeted us with much love, his family just as warmly as those unrelated to him. . . . The Captain of that country [the *iodai*, or military leader] and the Mayor of the place [the *bugio*, or civil governor], as well as all the people, welcomed us, for all marveled to see priests come from the land of the Portuguese: They are in no way shocked that Paulo has become a Christian, on the contrary, [and they esteem him] for having been in India and having there seen things which the people here never saw.

Once again, the Japanese appetite for knowledge! But while they were delighted by this openness of mind, the voyagers were also astonished that nobody seemed ready to hold Anjiro-Paulo accountable for the crime that had sent him fleeing to India thirty months earlier: On the contrary, the authorities heaped him "with great honors." So much the better. And now they were lavishly entertained in Anjiro-Paulo's house, where the convert's mother and sister would soon themselves convert to Christianity.

Francis's letter goes on:

I will now relate to you what we have learned of Japan. First, the people with whom we have until now conversed are the best we have yet discovered. It seems to me that, of all infidel* peoples, the Japanese are the finest. They are a people of most agreeable intercourse, setting honor above all other things. No Christian country can boast, as they can, of treating a very poor gentleman with as much honor as if he were rich. . . . They thus count honor higher than riches. They are a most courteous people. . . . They value weapons and set great reliance on them: at the age of fourteen they already carry swords and daggers. . . . They tolerate no insult nor any word uttered in contempt. . . . Although frugal eaters, they are inclined to drink. . . . They never gamble. . . . Never have I encountered people as irreproachable in their attitude to theft. . . . A goodly part of the population can read and write. . . . They have but one wife . . .

This fine description, which more than one competent anthropologist would happily have penned, would be incomplete unless Xavier also mentioned the relation between people and religion:

They take great pleasure in hearing about the things of God, above all when they understand them.† . . . They worship no idols with human faces‡ [but] many worship the sun and moon. Most of them believe in men of past times who, according to my understanding of the mat-

*That term again!

†Which was not a foregone conclusion: Christian doctrine explained in bad Japanese to Buddhists with a dash of Shintoism . . .

‡A Hindu failing that horrified Francis.

ter, were men who lived like philosophers. . . . They delight in hearing things consonant with reason. . . . Give thanks to the Lord: This isle of Japan seems most propitious for the extension of our Holy Faith. If we could speak its language, I have no hesitation in believing that many would become Christian.[10]

Francis Xavier was a good psychologist but an ineffective reporter, and through him we fail to "see" Japan. Only recourse to other witnesses, first- or secondhand, and to his earliest biographers, gives us a glimpse of this world in ferment, which could not have failed to disconcert these newly landed Iberians, whatever the "courtesy" and warmth of their welcome. Were they really so little shaken by this new world of powerfully exotic style and color? By the fragile graceful dwellings, by the kimonos, by the topknots worn by both men and women, the sculptured faces, the abrupt gestures, the vigorous gaits, in such glaring contradiction to brown and somnolent India?

But the sober Xavier does give us a few comments on diet: "The people here neither kill nor eat any of their livestock; sometimes they eat small quantities of fish with their rice and wheat. The country has many herbs which they consume, as well as some fruit. . . . Their health is amazingly good, and there are many old people. It seems clear from a study of the Japanese that, although nothing satisfies human nature, very little is needed here to maintain it."[11]

Francis Xavier would not have been a Jesuit had he not at once evoked the question of relations with authority—as we have seen from the very first lines he wrote about Japan, a nation he believed possessed of a king, a clergy, and great universities. But the reality was less simple, as we have seen. Real power was woefully fragmented and in the hands of provincial feudal leaders—the daimyos—who were independent of the tenno in Myako and even of the shogun.

Kagoshima was the capital of Satzuma, a southern province of Kyushu. It was then a poor region; its chief export was fighting men. Historian André Bellesort compares it to Sparta—which suggests that there was an Athens in that particular Japan, and that Satzuma held a strong position in the empire. But no. The provincial daimyo, although all-powerful on his own lands, was a lord of the second rank.

Shimahu Takahisa was then twenty-six. The young shogun, held to be a devout Buddhist, a member of the strict Shingon sect, and protector of the great Zen temple of Fukusho-ji in Kagoshima, preferred to live in his small fortified manor in Ijuin, the cradle of his family. It was there he first welcomed Anjiro, who had already been received with honor, as we have seen, by the civil and military authorities of the port, despite his past and his conversion. The daimyo was eager to learn everything about India, the foreigners who had just landed in Satzuma, and the religion they would be preaching.

If we can believe the report Anjiro-Paulo brought back to his Spanish companions, that first interview augured well: Takahisa, fascinated by the information he received from the convert (was it as imaginative as that which Xavier had received from the same mouth in Goa?), said he was deeply moved by a picture given to the missionaries by Don Pedro da Silva as they went aboard at Malacca. It depicted the Virgin and Child, and was one of the gifts intended to soften the "king of Japan." Was it not the goddess of compassion, Kannu? The daimyo prostrated himself before the effigy, asking his courtiers to emulate him, while his mother assailed Anjiro with questions about this religion that produced such beautiful pictures, begging him to set its fundamental beliefs down in writing—which the visitor eagerly did.

A month later, Francis Xavier himself was received with great pomp by Takahisa. His account is sober and unadorned: "On Saint Michael's Day [September 29, 1549] we conversed with the duke of this country; he showed us great honor and said he carefully guarded the books wherein is written the Law of the Christians, adding that if the Law of Jesus Christ was true and good, the Devil would be much vexed by it. A few days later, he gave permission to his vassals to become Christians, if they so desired."

Ever the good practitioner, Francis added: "This winter, we shall draw up the articles of the Faith in the language of Japan. . . . Our very dear brother Paulo will translate faithfully into his language all that is needful for the salvation of their souls."[12]

Which was done. Between October and December 1549 a full accounting of Christian doctrine in two volumes, the first relative to the Old Testament, the second to the New, was written by Xavier and Torres and translated (but how well?) by Anjiro. The fruit of his improvised labors appeared to have no more direct effect on Japanese populations than the promised sermons—their texts learned by heart—that the apostolic nuncio briefly delivered (until Juan Fernández Oviedo took over the preaching role a little more successfully). We shall be returning to the subject.

We have seen Francis Xavier inclined to admire this religion imported from Tenjiku with its "Book," which, according to its devotees, "came from God." There was nothing contemptuous or ironic in this. (Of course, there were also those, the Shintoists, who worshipped the sun.) But even when he spoke of this Japanese faith "in men of past times who . . . lived like philosophers"—and in whom we discern not only Buddha but Confucius—it is clear that he felt genuine respect for it.

Every religion sins first and foremost through its ministers. And however well disposed he was at the outset, Francis was very soon interspersing his generally benevolent reflections on the Japanese religion with increasingly virulent attacks on the *bonzes,* the monks who served the diverse sects of Japan—the most important one in Satzuma being the Shingon, into which Anjiro had been initiated and to which the daimyo Takahisa still belonged.

He would never direct at these monks the same contempt he had leveled at India's "rabble" of Brahmans, but he scarcely troubled to ascertain whether charges against them—of which he became a willing echo—were true. From his very first letter to his companions, dated November 5, 1549, he condemned one by one all those who, "robed in gray like monks,* both heads and chins shaved, live together with nuns of the same order as themselves, who, when they are pregnant, swallow a drug in order to abort—for which reason the people hold them in the lowest esteem."

He is even more outspoken in his denunciation of those bonzes who "in their monasteries have many young boys, the sons of gentlemen, whom they teach to read and write and with whom they commit turpitudes . . . which they do not deny. The matter is known to all. Those who are not bonzes take great pleasure in hearing us inveigh against this abominable sin, . . . but the bonzes themselves find us amusing, they care not a fig and feel no shame at hearing us criticize them."[13]

Historians of the period also note that pederasty was widespread in Buddhist monasteries, particularly Zen institutions, where they were apparently as closely integrated into the educational system as in the Athens of Alcibiades. Although it is of course true that if a Buddhist missionary had surveyed European monasteries of the day he would have unearthed equal "turpitudes"—just as Iñigo de Loyola had unearthed them in Barcelona.

Was there, then, corruption everywhere? Just as in the Roman clergy that had disgusted Luther forty years earlier? No. The Pope's envoy found at least one just man in Sodom:

> I often converse with a bonze respected by everyone for his knowl-
> edge, his way of life, his dignity, and his great age. He is called Ninxit.†
> He is as a bishop among them. During our many conversations‡ I felt
> that he was full of doubts and unable to determine whether our soul is
> immortal. . . . Many times he has said yes and at other times no. I fear
> it is the same with the other clerics.** This Ninxit is now so much my
> friend that it is a great wonder. Everyone here, lay people as well as

---

*Others, called *hokke,* wore a white robe covered with a black tunic.
†Xavier's spelling. His name was Ninjitsu.
‡Probably with Anjiro interpreting.
**Of the five principle Japanese Buddhist sects, four professed the soul's immortality.

bonzes, takes great pleasure in our company: They are surprised that we have come from a country as far from Japan as Portugal . . . and only in order to speak of things of God.

How far we are from those Indian throngs "converted" and blessed by Xavier's weary arms! It is tempting to imagine the exchanges between this old Japanese, brimming over with questions and with doubts, and this Jesuit come from afar "only in order to speak of things of God"—the two of them surrounded by an audience that marveled at their joust as it crouched on the floor of the Fukusho-ji monastery.

But Xavier was a realist. He saw that these "very numerous" monks were "swiftly obeyed" and "much esteemed" despite their "sins" because of the "great abstinence in which they live," and also because they could "spin fables touching on what they believed." As he shrewdly concluded: "Given that on this point we have very contrary opinions on how to feel God and on the road that people must follow to gain salvation, it will not be surprising that we should be persecuted by them, and with more than words."

For how many Ninxits were there for him to converse with? There was the agonizing language problem. Anjiro-Paulo was increasingly absorbed by his family—he had already converted his mother, wife, and daughter—and although Fernandez was strenuously trying to absorb Japanese characters it would be a year before he could serve as interpreter. Yet here were the first converts, and foremost among them a certain Bernardo, who two short years later would be hailed as a saint in Europe.

The blossoming of Bernardo's character would by itself justify Francis Xavier's long journey, for everything said about him is worthy of his spiritual master. The son of an outcast samurai, and perhaps reduced to the state of a ronin—that blend of knight errant and bandit that Akira Kurosawa and Kenji Mizoguchi have elevated to cinematographic myth—Bernardo was a semi-invalid, and so ugly that he frightened children. We do not know whether he was the first Japanese converted to Catholicism by the Navarrese missionary, but he proved the most faithful of Xavier's disciples. When he went to Europe in 1552, he touched everyone he met. He died at Coimbra in 1559.

We can imagine him huddled close to Xavier as the nuncio twice daily took his seat before one of the pillars at the gate entrance to Fukusho-ji monastery, and attempted to recite the catechism (or rather a truncated version of it, hastily rearranged after his arrival in Japan in a translation improvised by the semi-literate Anjiro-Paulo).

Bernardo, who did not speak Portuguese, could not interpret for Xavier. But he was too accustomed to the sneers his own pathetic appearance drew not to understand the mockery that greeted his master's perorations as he strove to explain the Christian mysteries set forth in his outlandish jargon. For who was this ecstatic orator with the blazing eyes and forked tongue: a madman, a magician, a village idiot? He left his Japanese listeners both baffled and derisive.

But it was not to escape their jeers that Xavier decided after a year in Satzuma to continue his northward progress. After all, the "fruit" harvested in Anjiro's home province had not been negligible: a hundred conversions, obtained not by the imposition of a foreign order but by a sort of persuasion, of closely reasoned seduction. Considering the rough-hewn character of the people of Satzuma, the "new Xavier," the one who had chosen to respect the beliefs of the alien, the "Other," had every reason to be optimistic.

When he moved (fully intending to return), leaving Anjiro behind to continue his mission, it was to pursue what had always been his goal: to reach the capital of Japan and there meet the "King"—at that time the tenno Go-nara—whom he hoped to convert together with his people. His decision to leave was reinforced by the fact that the ties he had initially formed with the daimyo Takahisa had loosened and then snapped under pressure from the bonzes, particularly those of the Shingon sect. As the Jesuit nuncio explained to his Roman companions:

> The bonzes told the lord of the country . . . that if he consented to his vassals' adoption of the Law of God, the country would be undone, its pagodas destroyed and desecrated. . . . The Law of God, they said, was indeed contrary to their own Laws, and those who embraced the Law of God would lose their devotion for the Saints who had established those Laws. The bonzes thus prevailed on the Duke, lord of the country, to issue an edict forbidding conversion to Christianity on pain of death.[14]

The Shingon monks thus injected their own instincts for exclusion and monopoly into the initially welcoming spirit of the daimyo and the benevolent curiosity of the venerable Ninjitsu. Was this only for religious reasons, or was it because of the concern they shared with the daimyo for maintaining a mutually supportive system of established powers? It may also have been because Takahisa was disappointed at the failure of Portuguese traders to follow in Xavier's footsteps.

Francis Xavier decided to make his second stop in Hirado, an island off the west coast of Kyushu. There he would again meet Portuguese, not only their military apparatus this time, but their energetic trading presence as well. Which meant that his mission remained tainted. More or less driven from Satzuma, was he now seeking refuge under the guns of the Portuguese man-of-war moored off Hirado?

In the long report he wrote in January 1552 to his companions in Rome, the passage dealing with his stay in Hirado is astonishingly naïve—almost, one might say, hypocritical. Conversions there, he wrote, were quicker than at Kagoshima "thanks to the book we had translated into Japanese and the discussions we held there." And the presence of the Portuguese? And the respect inspired by the guns mounted on their ship? And the greed its cargo inspired, the desire to please these powerful foreigners? Apparently our holy man, ever mindful of the need to "gather fruit in souls," had not yet fully grasped the transition from the means to the end.

Father Bouhours says it all with disarming simplicity:

> The Portuguese did all in their power to receive Father Xavier with honor. When he arrived they loosed off all their cannon and flew all their banners and sounded all their trumpets, and finally every ship gave a great shout of happiness at sight of the man of God. He was led with the same pomp to the King's palace; and all this magnificence played no small part in gaining the respect of a pagan court. . . . The Portuguese indicated to the King how important the man they brought was in the eyes of their master. . . . All the populace flocked to hear the bonzes from Europe . . . and in fewer than three weeks he baptized more infidels [in Hirado] than he had managed in a year at Kagoshima.

The tone is unmistakably that of a subject of the Sun King. The passage clearly hints at the risks Francis now ran of repeating his Indian mistakes. But while his description of events was disastrously naïve, his actions remained firmly on track. Although well received by the local daimyo, Francis quickly realized that Hirado must be an abbreviated stay: The Portuguese presence was certainly a comfort, but it was also an obstacle to the kind of mission he was slowly conceiving. Before two months had passed, he decided to journey to a much more important center, Yamaguchi, one of the wealthiest in Japan because of the silver mines surrounding it. Its ruler, Yoshikata, was one of the most powerful lords in the empire.

He left behind him Cosme de Torres, entrusting him with the little Christian island he had brought into being. He took with him Juan Fernández Oviedo (who by now could express himself in rough and ready Japanese), Bernardo, and another convert, Matteo. At the end of January 1551, after crossing from Hakata to Shimonoseki, they trudged for three weeks toward Yamaguchi in terrible cold and dense snow, in search of the mighty Yoshikata—the last intermediary, or so the missionary thought, between him and the "King" of Japan.

Here we must give Xavier the floor, so precise-seeming is the account he wrote for his companions in Rome on January 29, 1552, so faithfully does his style reflect the spirit of this undertaking once it was unburdened of the artillery, banners, and trumpets of European power:

> Yamaguchi is a town of more than 10,000 inhabitants, whose houses are all of wood. There were in this town numerous gentlemen and others who greatly desired to know what was the Law we preached. We therefore decided to preach for long days in the streets, and twice daily: We read the book we had brought and we held discussions in conformity with the book we read. Many were the people who hastened to our preachings.* We were summoned to the homes of great gentlemen to be asked what the Law we preached might be, and we were told that if it were better than their own, they would accept it. Many showed great joy at hearing the Law of God so proclaimed, others mocked it, and still others found it displeasing.

> When we walked in the street, children and others followed, mocking us and saying, "These are the men who say we must worship God to be saved and that no one can save us except the Creator of all things." Others said, "These are the men who preach that a man may have only one wife." Others said, "These are the men who forbid the sin of sodomy" (for the latter blemish is widespread among them). In this way they recited the other commandments of our Law, in order to make sport of us.

But although now innocent of the brutal arguments of imperialism, Xavier's mission still looked for the sources of local power:

> We were summoned by the Duke of Yamaguchi, for he was in the city itself. . . . When he asked us who we were and why we had come to Japan, we answered that we had been sent there to preach the Law of God, since no one can be saved unless he worship God and believe in Jesus Christ, Savior of all mankind. He then asked us to explain the Law of God to him, and thus we read him a great part of the book. He was very attentive throughout our reading, which lasted perhaps an hour, then he dismissed us.

Here Francis fails to make clear what was nevertheless to his credit: He was "dismissed" principally because he had reproached the all-powerful daimyo for his dissolute life and his numberless concubines. In short, he had angered the prince and, according to Fernando, expected to be killed.

This would not augur well for the future harvesting of "fruit." Yet the missionary relates that when he recounted the life of Christ in the streets, "people wept at the story of His Passion." But he had no great illusions: "Very few were

---

*"Our"? Only Fernández was comprehensible to listeners.

those who became Christian. Given the scanty fruit we were gathering, we decided to leave for a city, the biggest in all Japan, which is called . . . Miyako."[15]

Among the reasons for the failure of this first mission to Yamaguchi, Bouhours proposes the following explanation: "Since vice always went hand in hand with wealth, it was a corrupt city, replete with the most monstrous debaucheries. . . . This strange corruption of spirit filled Francis at once with horror and with pity."[16]

After this half-failure at Yamaguchi, we find Francis on the road to Miyako: "We were two days on the road; we had to face many dangers . . . by reason of the numerous wars going on in the regions we crossed. I say nothing of the great cold that prevails in this country of Miyako or of the many bandits who beset this roadway."

But let us for once allow Francis to appear in all his human freshness, through the recollections of his poor companion Bernardo. Three years after Xavier's death, the samurai's son was welcomed at the Jesuits' college in Rome on the Villa Balbino. One evening—in the company of Polanco, Frusio, and Palmio—he recalled his master's (and his own) trek to Miyako. Edmond Auger, then a student at the college, gives us a delightful echo of that journey as he heard it from Polanco:

> What his proselyte Bernard the Japanese, who is still with us, revealed
> to us after dinner one evening of his gaiety and kindness surpasses the
> humor of every other man of his sort. He had on him only his black
> cloth robe with a small bonnet on his head, such as is worn by the Si-
> amese, also of cloth, his feet and legs bare, his little parcel [made up]
> of his Bible and his breviary, and a surplice on his back. Trotting
> through the snows and hard-frozen forests, in the guise of a lackey* in
> order not to lose the company of certain barbarians on horseback,†
> he sometimes hopped, he laughed and tossed an apple in the air,
> catching it again and again in his hand, his face bathed in joyful tears,
> with the profoundest words on the goodness and mercy of God Who
> had chosen him to sow His heavenly doctrine in provinces that
> seemed so distant, so cut off from the world.[17]

Almost a portrait of the other Francis, the one from Assisi, as an imitator of Joinville might have described him.

But let us return to Xavier's account: "We reached Miyako and remained several days there, seeking to speak with the King and crave his permission to preach the Law of God in his kingdom. But we were unable to do so. As we later heard that he is not obeyed even by his own people, we stopped insisting that we be permitted to preach in his kingdom."

*As a lackey would have done.
†Samurai bound for Miyako.

Thus a terrible disappointment marked their arrival in the imperial capital. The "King"—at least for the moment—was but a myth. Since his first contacts with Anjiro and Alvares in India, Francis had constantly been told by daimyos, monks, and men of letters that Japan had no "King" in the European sense. Rather, it recognized two principles of sovereignty: a dynastically descended ruler, the tenno,* and an all-powerful military leader, the shogun. Moreover, the dynastic heir, the tenno Go-nara, was merely a crowned indigent—not that this meant greater power for the shogun Ashikaga. A whole cornerstone of the Jesuit system had thus collapsed: There was no main negotiator, no Pope, no King. Francis would have to continue to deal with the marginal feudal authorities, the daimyos.

Not only the imperial throne was in ruins. The capital itself was in wretched condition: "This city of Miyako is very big: It is at present, on account of the wars, very much in ruins. Many people say it once had more than four hundred thousand houses, and the area it covers is so vast that it seems this must be true. It is now much demolished and burned, although it still seems to me to boast more than a hundred thousand dwellings. . . . This region was not sufficiently at peace for the Law of God to be made manifest there."

A curious statement. But Jesuits liked neither disorder nor ruins nor a power vacuum. The rationalism that inspired—or solaced—his spirituality, and that had brought Francis to this "people gifted with reason," now faltered and acknowledged its helplessness. His kind of energy needed something to lean on. The lyrical spirit that had hovered over the long march to Miyako collapsed into rueful frustration. Just like Caillé, three centuries later, reaching the fabled Timbuktu to find it only a huddle of misshapen mud huts . . .

There was no question of being received by the tenno, perhaps because the Emperor was reluctant to reveal his abasement to foreigners, perhaps because the monks around him wished to protect what remained of the imperial majesty from such a taint. Nor would they be seen by the shogun Yoshiteru Ashikaga (himself scarcely more respected than the Emperor), even though Xavier tried to track him to Sakamoto, two days' walk from the capital.

It was a journey triply disappointing. First, Xavier and his companions were refused an audience. Second, they were subjected to what a Portuguese traveler called *muitas injurias* (many insults) and what others called persecutions (even, according to Father Bouhours, an attempt at stoning), and were everywhere harassed by swarms of children sneeringly imitating the missionaries' chants—"Deos, Deos . . ." Third, the doors of the most famous monasteries were slammed in their faces, particularly those of Hiei-zan, which, more than any

*What Westerners once called the Mikado.

other, deserved to be considered as one of those "great universities" that the barefoot nuncio had sought ever since leaving Goa.

The great dream he had lived since his first meetings with Anjiro and Alvares was collapsing. But not the new knowledge he had acquired, that of human relations, of respect for the Other, of reciprocity, of exchange and dialogue with "infidels," with "idolaters." Having learned all this, how could he fail to understand that in the eyes of his often unwelcoming hosts he too was a "barbarian," the propagator of a message that threatened their own beliefs and was incomprehensible to boot?

He decided to return to Yamaguchi. Not that he had achieved great success in that city or obtained any great promises, but he knew that he could have at least a valid dialogue there. His moralizing lectures had certainly irritated the daimyo Yoshikata, who had sent him away but not without being heard, listened to, not without arousing obvious interest. It was with this man that he would pick up the dialogue and the enterprise once more, and on a new footing.

And indeed, Francis Xavier's second stay in Yamaguchi was an episode as decisive for the propagation of Christianity in Asia as was his discovery of the greatness of Buddhist civilization. Then he had realized that the key to conversion was in discovery of and respect for the Other. Now he would realize that conversion was also self-conversion, or at least self-adaptation. It meant shaping and reshaping oneself to fit the contours of another culture: The whole of Ricci* and of Nobili is in this prodigious experience in the domains of the daimyo Yoshikata.

For this time Francis came neither empty-handed nor in beggar's clothes. He had made a point of returning through Hirado, where he had stored gifts from the Viceroy of the Indies and the Governor of Malacca. He brought with him, wrote Father Bonhours, "a small ringing clock, a most harmonious musical instrument, and divers works of art whose whole value lay in their rarity." Even better: "He had a new—and even quite clean—habit made for him from the alms the Portuguese had given him." Whereupon the good father offers this maxim, which in twenty-three words sums up five centuries of Jesuit history: "An apostle must be all things to all men† and, to win over people of the world, must bend somewhat to their weaknesses."[18]

A crucial question, of course, which would for decades stamp missionary action and has at times been summed up in the formula "silk or cotton?" The "silk or cotton?" controversy would still be bubbling nearly thirty years later, when Father João Cabral had become Superior of the Jesuit mission to Japan: Rejecting the appeals of Japanese novices hailing from the ruling classes, he forced

*See Chapter VII.
†The formula Loyola had adapted from Saint Paul, 1 Corinthians 9:22.

them, out of respect for the virtue of poverty, to wear cotton. Which rubbed feelings raw. According to Henri Bernard-Maitre: "In Japan the use of silk was not a luxury but a requirement. Only beggars wore cotton clothes, and it was not suitable, the Japanese Christians thought, that because of their clothing the missionaries should be associated with them, thus discrediting the faith they had come to announce to a particularly receptive people."

In 1579 the controversy generated tensions felt as far afield as Rome. An inspector of missions was sent to Japan, Father Alessandro Valignano, an intelligent Neapolitan who would prove to be the historic link between Xavier and Ricci. After three years of inquiry and reflection, he decided against Cabral and voted for the silk. It generated a fresh wave of controversies, from Goa all the way to the Holy See, but Valignano prevailed. He did so by referring among other things to Francis Xavier's second passage through Yamaguchi.

But let us listen to Xavier, now swathed in silk, and received by the daimyo this time not simply as the Pope's ambassador but as the envoy of the Viceroy of the Indies: "At Yamaguchi we gave the Duke letters from the Governor [Viceroy] and Bishop [of Goa] which we were carrying, as well as a gift he had sent him as a token of friendship. The Duke took great pleasure both in this gift and the letter. He offered us many things but we were unable to accept anything although he offered us much gold and silver."

In fact, as we have seen, the "gift" the nuncio brought was a collection of gifts. According to the Yoshitaka-ki, the daimyo's appointments calendar, Francis gave him "a box exactly designating, in twelve regular intervals, the hours of the day and night," in other words, a clock (for which no Japanese word yet existed), "a thirteen-stringed musical instrument" (a zither?), and "a smoothed surface whereon, without the slightest tarnishing, the face is reflected . . . every object a marvel of its kind."*

How could this powerful man not have been swayed in favor of such munificent, magnificent visitors? Exploitation of the "riches of iniquity" for a good end is recommended in the Gospel, and Christ's raiment was apparently finer than that of the Apostles' (in addition to being seamless). In short, it was time to gather "fruit" from such seed:

> We then asked him if he would grant us one favor, for we would be asking no other of him, to wit, that he give us license to preach the Law of God on his lands, and freedom to accept it for whosoever wished it.
>
> He gave us this permission with much love and . . . ordered that a text be posted in the streets of the city, in his name, giving his permis-

*Quoted in Schurhammer, *Francis Xavier, His Life, His Times,* vol. IV, p. 217.

sion to whosoever wished to adopt it. At the same time, he gave us a monastery for a college so that we might take up residence there.

When we were in this monastery, many persons came there to hear us preach the Word of God, which we generally did twice a day. At the end of the sermon a disputation* took place and lasted a good while.

Now the great dialogue opened, the dialogue the barefoot nuncio had dreamed of since the birth of his Japanese project two years earlier in Goa. The great dialogue of cultures and beliefs, on which point he is both admirable and unquenchable:

> We were constantly occupied in answering questions and preaching. Many were the Japanese priests, nuns, and gentlemen, as well as other folk who attended. . . . I strove mightily to ascertain whether, at some past time, there had been knowledge of God and of Christ in Japan. According to their Scriptures† and to what the people themselves say, I determined that they had never possessed this knowledge. . . . They asked us so many questions, and we gave them so many answers, that they acknowledged that the Laws of the saints in whom they had believed were false, and that the Law of God is true.

It is difficult not to go on quoting the correspondence of this anthropologically minded missionary, a correspondence replete with humanity's most basic questions, an echo of every great spiritual debate in the history of thought and faith. Was Xavier fully aware of the power of the objections he so faithfully reflects? We must in any case agree that these "idolaters" fully justified their reputation for sagacity.

> The Japanese possess . . . no knowledge of the world's creation, sun, moon, stars, sky, earth, and sea, or of any other thing. It seems to them that it was all without beginning. What has struck them most is to hear us say that souls have a Creator. . . .
>
> Since there is no mention of the Creator in the stories of their saints, there could be no Creator of All Things. They say moreover that if all things in the world had a beginning, the people of China would have known it. For it is from China that they have the Laws that are in their possession. They deem the Chinese to be informed both of the things of the other world and of the Government of the State.
>
> They asked us many things about this Principle which created all things, whether it be good or evil and whether there is a Principle of all good things and another of all bad things. We told them there is but one Principle and that it is good, free of the slightest taint of evil.

*Public debate. An essential component of Jesuit teaching, also known as "concertation."
†Remarkable terminology in a text on "idolaters."

It seemed to them that this could not be, because they believe that demons exist, that these are evil and enemies of the human species and that, if God is good, He would not have created such wicked things.

To which we gave reply that God had created them good but that they themselves had chosen evil, and for that reason God had punished them and that punishment would be without end. To this they said that God was not compassionate since he punished so cruelly. They added that if it was true (as we said) that God had created humankind, and if He was good, God would not have created men with so many weaknesses and so wholly given to sin; He would have created them utterly without wickedness. Therefore, they said, this Principle cannot be good, for it created Hell, the worst imaginable thing, and has no pity for those who journey there, since they must remain there for eternity (according to what we had told them).

. . . It seemed to them very, very ill of God to have provided no redemption for those who go to Hell; they say their own Laws are more firmly based on pity than the Law of God. . . . They felt great doubts as to God's supreme goodness, and said He could not be compassionate since He had not shown himself to them earlier, before we ourselves came there. If it was true (as we said) that those who do not worship God go to Hell, God, they said, has shown no mercy to their ancestors for He has left them in Hell without vouchsafing the slightest knowledge of Himself to them.

Lord, how shrewd these Japanese of the "decadent period" could be! Almost as shrewd as Montesquieu's Persians—and in their own homeland! But we have to admire the pious missionary's honesty in quoting his opponents rather than praising the force of his own arguments, which so often seem to backfire on him. As in the following, which could have come from the pen of a Voltaire in full cry against the Catholic Church, against the Catholic archenemy:

We gave them the reason which proved to them that the Law of God is the first of all laws, by saying: Before the Laws of China came to Japan, the Japanese knew that killing, stealing, bearing false witness, and flouting the Ten Commandments was evil; they already felt remorse for the ills they committed, for eschewing evil and doing good were things inscribed in the hearts of men. People therefore knew the commandments of God without teaching by anybody else, if it was not the Creator of all people.

If they had doubts on this score, they could make this experiment: Take a man who had grown up in the forest, with no knowledge of the Laws that came from China and none of reading and writing. Let them ask of this man who had grown up in the wilds whether killing, stealing, or flouting the Ten Commandments were or were not sins, whether it were good or not to observe them. From the reply of this man, however savage he might be and despite the fact that no one had instructed him, they would clearly see that he knew the Law of God. Who then had taught him of good and evil, if not the God Who created him? And if such knowledge exists among savages, what must it not be among folk imbued with wisdom? Thus, even before a written Law came into being, the Law of God was written in the hearts of men. This reasoning pleased them all so much that they were content with it. By thus relieving them of this doubt we greatly helped them to become Christian.

What charm Francis must have possessed, what power of conviction and fiery speech, for such "reasoning" not to have led to his discomfiture. But if he often prevailed in "disputations," it was by virtue of other arguments, which had little to do with divine mercy, or revelation. "They did not know that the world is round* and they were equally ignorant of the sun's course: They asked questions about these and other things, such as comets, lightning, snows, and similar matters. We answered them, and gave them explanations, with which they were most contented and most satisfied, considering us as learned men, which helped them no little toward according great credit to our words."[19]

Here again, we are swept right to the center of the Jesuit system, with the candid Francis Xavier establishing himself as the precursor of Christophonus Clavius and Matteo Ricci. For if his words gained "credit," it was through the very human paths of science. It was not (or not only) because he believed more (or better) than his interlocutors, it was because he knew more (or better). It was not the power of his metaphysical or religious arguments that prevailed, it was his alliance with a science that he and his companions had acknowledged and validated. The former professor of the Collège de Beauvais was once again playing the part of the pioneer.

Having resolved to abandon everything, to leave behind him all bookish impedimenta, keeping only (but was this really true?) his crucifix and his breviary, our nuncio was now dangling all the discoveries of European science before dazzled Japanese eyes. In two years, he had moved on from mass conversions in India to exchange with the Other, from cultural rejection to the dissemination of knowledge. It had been a twofold revolution.

---

*"The world is round . . . " Galileo's trial did not take place until 1633, but Copernicus (in 1543) had already posited the bases of the system—which Rome officially contested. Although the debate bore less on the "world's" roundness than on what lay at its center, Xavier's expression proves that on this point too the Jesuits were ahead of the Curia.

But however detailed the debate that now ensued, however rich in extensions if not in convergences, it posed a basic problem of definition. First of all because in Xavier's group only Juan Fernández was (more or less) bilingual, unlike the leader and Bernardo. Yet had all three been equally conversant with Japanese and Portuguese they could not have overcome every obstacle, for "few languages lend themselves less than Japanese to the discussion of theological texts. There is a lack of adequate terms . . . and it is unlikely that any foreigner has ever achieved a mastery of the language sufficient to open the way to such dissertations."[20]

Worse still, if linguistic equivalencies were lacking, what was to be said of the simple difficulty of giving God a name? At first, in Kagoshima, Xavier and his companions had followed Anjiro's advice and used the word Daimichi, utilized by Zen monks to name the vital principle. Daimichi was represented with three heads, and another divinity named Cogi was so closely associated with him that they were as one. The temptation to see some resemblance here with the Christian Trinity must have been powerful indeed.

But others had pointed out that to the Shintoists, Daimichi meant the "great sun": Was it appropriate to borrow from the deepest-rooted beliefs of paganism? They then considered Hotoké, one of the Buddha's manifestations. But they decided that although this did indeed express the notion of "principle," it lacked the other attributes of the Christian God.

Next Xavier decided to revert to the European formulation, and to speak of Deus or Deos. Alas, Japanese pronunciation changed the word to Deusu, and the barefoot nuncio soon learned (as he wrote to his Roman companions) that his listeners happily turned "Deusu" into "Dauso," which in their language meant "great lie."[21]

Naturally the Buddhist monks manipulated and aggravated these linguistic pitfalls. It had been a long time since the monasteries of Kagoshima or Hirado had displayed curiosity rather than hostility to the newcomers. The sporadic progress registered by the European missionaries—due more to the benevolence of two or three daimyos seduced by the Jesuits' theories and by Xavier's personality than to their preaching—inevitably stirred the jealousy of the native priesthood and filled them with very natural anxiety. For, said Francis,

> if they did not preach they would have nothing to eat and nothing wherewith to clothe themselves. As time went by, alms from their devotees dwindled and they began to suffer from want and from discredit. . . . Many are they who return to lay life and expose the turpitudes of those who live in the monasteries. It is because of this that the monks and nuns of Yamaguchi are gradually losing much of their reputation. The Christians have told me that of the hundred monas-

teries of monks and nuns this place once boasted, many will be deserted for lack of alms before many years have passed.

The missionaries had thus assailed the bonzes' credibility, performing more conversions in Yamaguchi than in all the rest of Japan. But the victory of Christianity over "idolatry" was by no means sealed. Francis Xavier would soon be forced to recognize that his pious objectives depended on the powers and vicissitudes of princes—whether he came empty-handed or bearing gifts, unarmed or flanked by the representatives of Portuguese power, garbed in cotton or arrayed in silk.

It was under the protection of local authority that the little group of missionaries busied itself (not without "fruit") in disputations, preaching, and disputes with the monks of Yamaguchi. But the nuncio and his followers failed in their fundamental aim of converting the most influential feudal leaders. Including the daimyo, because Xavier had told him that as a convert he would have to give up his many concubines. And the daimyo's chief minister because, having donated heavily to the Buddhist "divinities" Shaka and Amida, he feared he would lose his investment if he turned Christian.

Such calculations—but what, after all, was Pascal's wager?—did not stand in the way of every conversion. Indeed many came about as a result of the princes' favor. And many others resulted from Xavier's personal charisma, which inevitably became the stuff of legend: When the process of his canonization was launched a few years later, Father Quadros told his superiors that unlike the other missionaries, who were able to answer only "one idolater at a time, Father Xavier dealt with ten or a dozen questions in a single reply, as if addressing each adversary in person." It was this that had most astounded the Japanese. There is in any case no doubt that the Navarrese exercised an extraordinary ascendancy over his numberless listeners in Yamaguchi.

And of course he knew it. However detached he was from "vainglory," Francis Xavier could not be unaware of his own; and inasmuch as it tended to "the greater glory of God," he relished it. As he told his friends: "Although I am now entirely white-haired, I am more vigorous and robust than ever [eighteen months before his death]. For the labors one endures, in order to cultivate a reasonable nation which loves truth and desires its own salvation, bring much joy. Never in all my life have I known such joy as in Yamaguchi."[22]

His joy was short-lived. At the end of the fourth month of this fruitful sojourn in Yamaguchi, he received notice from the *yakata** of Bungo, named Yoshishige, that a Portuguese vessel had just moored in Funai (today's Oita), the capital of that northeastern province of Kyushu. Better still, the ship was com-

---

*A military title. Direct delegate of the shogun, unlike the daimyo whose power was independent.

manded by Duarte da Gama, a son of the great Vasco and an old friend of Xavier's from Goa days. Da Gama had also sent Xavier a message. He advised him to depart for Bungo, adding that the yakata Yoshishige was a powerful ally, with strong links to the Portuguese, a man from whom he could expect "great fruit," and one he might even hope to convert.

Organized aboard ship by Duarte da Gama, the welcome prepared for nuncio Xavier, who had walked for five days (September 15 to 20, 1551) from Yamaguchi, was as sumptuous as his earlier reception at Hirado had been: banners and drums and red carpets. The captain was eager to show his Japanese hosts that this saintly priest bore on his shoulders all power and glory, and indeed the whole empire, from beyond the seas. We have no reason to believe that the missionary was shocked by this, except that he refused to mount a horse for the journey from the port to the palace of Funai. What we do know is that the young yakata of Bungo (he was twenty-two) was so stirred by the visitor's arrival that Francis quickly had hopes of an early conversion. But as it turned out, Xavier's preaching produced strictly limited results. According to Father Bouhours, "Father Francis's chief concern in meeting the prince was to inspire in him a horror of the infamous vice the bonzes had taught him. . . . [Soon] Yoshishige dismissed from his chamber and his palace a most handsome boy who was his favorite."[23]

Could Francis Xavier now begin to lay the foundations of what could become his mission's fairest bridgehead in Funai? Alas, no. The holy virtue of obedience and the frantic ups and downs of Japanese politics deflected him. While he was wondering whether the religious convictions of the young yakata of Bungo would prove more resistant to his charms than his way of life had been,* the nuncio heard from his friend Duarte da Gama first that Goa (and then Rome) had urgently recalled him, and second that his ship would be sailing within two weeks. He was therefore obliged to return to India, perhaps to Rome, though not without hopes of coming back.

But his distress at the news was soon aggravated by information from Yamaguchi, where a revolt had broken out. Yoshikata had fallen, and the missionaries themselves had barely escaped with their lives from a mob goaded by the bonzes.

The rebellion, led by the most important of Yoshikata's vassals, Sue Takafasa, had taken the daimyo by surprise, forcing him to seek refuge in the Hosen-ji monastery. Then, seeing that those loyal to him were scattering and that his enemies' forces were growing, he fled west to the mountains, hoping to reach Kyushu by sea. But he was trapped, along with his six-year-old son and a few

*Yoshishige later converted to Christianity.

loyal diehards, and he decided to make an end of it. After stabbing the child, he committed seppuku (known for mysterious reasons in the West as hara-kiri).

Although it is doubtful that the revolt was brought on by the daimyo's benevolence toward the foreign priests, the lives of Torres and Fernández were so obviously threatened by the rebels that a great lady found them shelter in a monastery, and later took them into her own house—until Yoshikata's successor assured them of his official protection. In losing Yoshikata, Xavier and his companions had lost a very valuable friend, but as it turned out, their cause was not damaged.

With the safety of Torres and Fernández assured, it was time for Xavier to leave for India. He had decided to take with him four of the Japanese converts, Bernardo, Matteo, Joane, and Antonio, the first two in order to deepen their knowledge of Christianity in Europe, the others to teach the rudiments of Japanese in Goa to future missionaries. As for the lord of Bungo, he sent along an ambassador to the Portuguese court to tell King John that he would continue to protect those who came to Japan in Francis Xavier's name.

On November 19, 1552, twenty-seven months and four days after landing at Kagoshima on "the Pirate's" junk, Francis Xavier watched the coasts of Japan fade away. He was almost sure he would soon be returning—unless he obtained permission to breach the even more tightly sealed coastline of China. There, he felt, he would be at the headwaters of the Japanese civilization that had just transformed him: a mass converter of the heathen himself converted into a spiritual partner.

However, he could not leave his beloved Japan without passing on a few precepts to his friends in Goa and Rome. But it would be wrong to look on these precepts as a kind of last will and testament. It was in his own interests—as the man responsible for the Company's future in Asia, as an intellectual, and as a Christian, not just for his friends—that he set down the principles and the proposals arising from his mission, as well as the spiritual upheaval it had caused within him.

When he was back in Cochin, on January 29, 1552, he composed for his Roman friends the famous letter we have already quoted from.* In a sense, it is his ethnographical treatise on Japan. But it is also a chart for future action:

> In this country of Japan there is a very great university named
> Kwanto; it is there that the bonzes gather to learn the teachings of
> their sects. The latter, as I have already said, come from China and are
> written in Chinese characters. . . . China is a vast country, peaceful

---

*One of only four extant handwritten originals.

and untroubled by war . . . where great justice reigns. According to the writings of the Portuguese who live there, there is more justice in China than in any country of Christendom.*

The people of China I have so far seen are of penetrating intelligence and lofty mind, more so than the Japanese, and they are people much given to study. The country is blessed with all manner of goods, most populous, full of large cities with houses of finely worked stone and, as everyone proclaims, very rich in all manner of silks. Through information given me by Chinese, I know that there are in China great numbers of people who follow divers Laws; according to what I have been told, these must be Moors or Jews.† They are unable to tell me whether there are any Christians there.‡

I think that in this year of 1552 I shall leave for the place where the King of China dwells. It is in fact a country where we may hope greatly to extend the Law of Our Lord Jesus Christ; and if the people there accepted it, that would greatly help the people of Japan lose confidence in the sects they believe in.

. . . At present, if it please the Lord our God, Fathers of the Company will leave every year for Japan; we shall found a Company house in Yamaguchi, and they will there learn the language; they will furthermore gain knowledge of the stories each sect possesses; in this way, when persons worthy of great trust arrive from Europe to attend these universities, they will find in Yamaguchi Fathers and Brothers of the Company speaking the language fluently and conversant with the errors of the sects.

Three months later, on April 9, 1552, Xavier wrote to the Superior General in Rome, suggesting criteria for those "Fathers who will attend the universities of Japan," as if he were a schools inspector tallying available teachers and instructors for his superiors:

They must possess knowledge so as to be able to reply to the many questions asked by the Japanese. It would be good if they were worthy Masters of Arts and would do no hurt if they were dialecticians also. . . . And that they know somewhat of the celestial sphere, for the Japanese take extreme pleasure in learning the movements of the heavens, solar eclipses, the waxing and waning of the moon, and knowing what produces water and rain, snow and hail, as well as

*Written to Christians and by a Christian.
†The former were an important minority, the latter less numerous.
‡Nestorian Christians had in fact gained a foothold in China in the seventh century.

thunder, lightning, comets, and other things of like nature. . . . It is most profitable to explain these things in order to gain the goodwill of the people.

We could of course choose to ignore all but that last sentence, with its hint at what was perhaps the ulterior motivation of future Jesuit strategy in China. Honey for flies, houses of cards for unwary gawkers . . . But everything that had gone before, and everything that followed it, indicates that, consciously or not, Xavier and his followers had progressed beyond such simple tactics. Or rather that those tactics had evolved into a strategy and the strategy into an ideology— and that the ideology was none other than Christian humanism. Thunder and lightning, rains and "movements of the heavens," were not snares for the unwary, machines for the seduction of fools. In the minds of Xavier and his followers, they were the work of God, and as such deserved to be illumined by the gaze of all humankind.

That this hope henceforth inspired Xavier (although he was perhaps not yet fully aware of it) is further demonstrated in an article by Henri Bernard-Maître, "Saint Francis Xavier, Orientalist."

In the last months of Xavier's life, well before a Portuguese caravel left Europe bearing a letter of recall from Ignatius of Loyola,* he made feverish preparations for his "China campaign," for a spiritual conquest that he foresaw would be momentous, enormous, and that would, he hoped, decide the future of Christianity in Asia. Among the books he considered it "necessary to take to China" (this from the man who, on leaving Europe for the Indies, had decided to take "only his prayerbook and his crucifix"), one mentioned by Bernard-Maître speaks worlds: *Suma de doctrina christiana en que se contiene todo lo principal y necessario que el hombre christiano deve saber y obra* (Summary of Christian Doctrine, Containing All It Is Fitting That a Christian Man Know and Do)." The author, a canon of Seville named Constantino Ponce de la Fuente, had been condemned by the Inquisition in 1543 for "Lutheranism." The Inquisition had taken issue with his "disturbing silences" on the question of obedience to the Pope, of intercession by the Virgin Mary. It had been concerned too by his insistence on stressing the inner life rather than ritual obligations—all good reasons for alarming the champions of Counter-Reformation and of a Spanish Church wary of alumbrados and other popular mystics. But in the case of Asia,

---

*Not, apparently, because Rome feared that his intellectual evolution vis-à-vis "paganism" had gone too far; nor because the General wanted to bring back to his side a possible successor; but simply because the Company "needed him." *Perinde ac cadaver.* And in case Xavier—intelligently interpreting the rule of obedience—should point out that the immensity of his task in Asia took precedence over all other usefulness he might have, Ignatius let him know that "if you consider that your presence there is important for governing, you could as easily govern, and even better, from Portugal as from Japan or China. You have often had to accept longer absences."

such discordant notes seemed unlikely to cause trouble.

By his recourse to this work, considered by some to be inflammatory, says Bernard-Maître, "Xavier showed his awareness of the needs of those coming to Christianity from an atmosphere dominated by the spirit of Buddhism; he showed thereby a broadmindedness not shared by all those who carried on his apostolate."

Francis Xavier the evangelist of Japan? It is tempting to suggest instead that Japan evangelized Francis Xavier. It was this first encounter, between a generous man and a great culture, that would inspire future Jesuit strategy. It was a strategy with illustrious precedents: We have only to recall Alexander the Great astounding his rough-hewn Greek lieutenants by adopting the customs of the Persian foe. It was a strategy that today's Jesuits call "inculturation." But would it not be better to speak of "acculturation"? What had occurred, after all, was not simply immersion in the culture of the Other: It was a dialogue, exchange, cultural symbiosis. And, well before Ricci and Nobili, it was launched by Xavier.

Moreover, "acculturation" better defines the limits inherent in this kind of enterprise, no matter how noble. Convergence rather than fusion, and sometimes even collision and conflict. By the end of the seventeenth century, Japan counted 300,000 Christians. But as distrust of the powerful foreigners mounted, a price of 500 pieces of silver would soon be placed on every Jesuit's head.

· V ·

NO WOMEN
NEED APPLY

"All of Them Snares for Men" • *Madeleine's Sweet Face* • *For the*
Infanta of Castile • *The Good Deeds of "Madama"* • *"God Preserve*
Me, Roser!" • *The Only (and Most Secret) Woman Jesuit*

LL THE GREAT orders—Benedictines, Dominicans, Carthusians,
Franciscans—have their female counterparts, some wielding greater
influence than the original institutions. All, that is, but the Jesuits.
There have been a score of attempts at transplanting, some of which have
nearly borne fruit. Indeed the Jesuit order, with its strict but simple rules, the
flexibility of its practice, and its professed concern for the traditions of the outsider, the "Other," seems likelier than other Catholic orders to inspire adaptation or imitation. Yet it has no sister branch. Except for one famous and roundly
denounced exception, there have never been, nor are there now, "Lady Jesuits."
Why?

Historians have blamed the misogyny of the founders, particularly of Ignatius. And certain texts undeniably support this explanation of an exclusion that
has survived the centuries, an irreversible veto bleakly enshrined in the Jesuits'
Constitutions. The antifemale prejudices that leap from some of Loyola's utterances seem to go far beyond Catholic tradition, which itself excludes half the
human race from the priesthood.

"Consuming flame or blackening smoke"—thus did the founding father in
his last days describe relations (no matter how pure) with women. A few years
earlier he had said, "From head to foot they are all of them snares for men." Or
else: "They return tirelessly to faith, as soon as flesh or lassitude makes them de-

sire it." There was worse—the equation of Woman with the Devil in Loyola's *Spiritual Exercises*—incriminating words if any ever were:

Twelfth rule: the enemy [the Devil] conducts himself as a woman in his blending of feeble physical strength and strident insolence. Indeed, just as it is the way of woman when she quarrels with a man to lose heart, fleeing when the man resolutely confronts her; and on the contrary, if the man begins to lose heart and give way, the anger, the vengefulness, the ferocity of the woman waxes beyond all measure.

Sinister? Yes. Even for those dark times. But we shall see that the history of relations between the padre maestro and women cannot simply be rendered down to these barbaric sentiments. The admirable *Ignace de Loyola et les femmes de son temps* (Ignatius of Loyola and the Women of His Day), by Hugo Rahner,[1] based on the Pilgrim's (and later the General's) correspondence with the greatest ladies and the humblest female penitents of his period reveals an exchange of surprising wealth, diversity, and subtlety.

It emerges from these exchanges that if Loyola fought tooth and nail to evade the responsibilities implicit in institutional ties to the female world, it was not simply because he was baffled by the contradictions to which (as he thought) his women penitents and other female contacts were addicted. It was also because the fascination he exerted over the opposite sex invariably elicited an outpouring of possessive demands, insistence on "rights" he considered premature or unjustified (women "getting their claws" into him). It all seemed most threatening to the total freedom of action he wanted for his "skirmishers," his "snipers," who were by definition male.

A strategy of evasion—not to say a headlong retreat—which might seem amusing if it did not reflect what Father Rahmer has called a "truly dramatic spiritual struggle." Whence the highly colored language of the "plea" Ignatius sent Paul III in the hope of persuading the Supreme Pontiff to drop plans to found a female order modeled on the Jesuits. In effect, argued Ignatius, the order had to "remain free," its "breastplates buckled," and "ready to move at a moment's notice."

Yet had not this same Loyola spent years framing rules that (while they did indeed enjoin buckled breastplates and readiness to move at a moment's notice) most assuredly did not seek to foster total freedom of movement to everyone everywhere? His language does seem to imply a hierarchy of values (which is understandable) and of the sexes (which perhaps is not). If the Jesuit had to remain "without encumberment," was it to serve the "essential needs" of a God before whom woman was condemned to marginal or supplicant status (while the most ostentatious devotion was simultaneously professed for Our Lady)? Did the famous goal of "helping souls," proclaimed by the Pilgrim, the hermit, the student, and the General, imply a form of segregation? Did souls have a sex—with one less worthy of help than the other? To be helped by joint action, or by its own efforts?

When he discussed women, Loyola spoke with authority. Francis Xavier confided to one of his last companions that he had never known a woman. The same could probably be said for Pierre Favre (although Favre had seriously contemplated marriage) and for several others of the founder's companions. But, as we have seen, the briefest of glances at the *Autobiography* reveals that Iñigo had been "a man given to worldly vanities."

He was not yet seven when his mother, Doña Marina, died. His nurse, María Guerin, who called him Txikiye (Little One), probably made no attempt to hide the origins of the two bastard brothers who grew up with him. Very early on, in a life intimately bound up with livestock breeding and meals eaten out in the fields, Iñigo must have been well informed about relations between the sexes. And very soon after his mother's death a woman was to appear in his life— Madeleine, his eldest brother's wife. It was natural that this sister-in-law should play a major emotional and spiritual role in his life.

Madeleine de Araoz, a lady-in-waiting of Isabella the Catholic, stood so high in the Queen's favor that Isabella gave her an image of the Virgin as a wedding present. She placed it in the family chapel where (according to Pedro de Leturia, the best of the chroniclers of Iñigo's childhood[2]) it was the first object of the youngest Loyola's fervor. Thus we slide almost seamlessly—and leapfrogging the 1521 conversion—to the other side of Madeleine's influence over Iñigo.

It is a beautiful and somewhat disturbing story. Saint Ignatius one day told a Belgian novice that a particular image of the Holy Virgin possessed a beauty so powerfully evocative of his sister-in-law Madeleine that it troubled him during his prayers. To put an end to this, he had stuck a strip of paper across the face of the image.[3]

This gives us one of the keys to the riddle. How could this Fool of God have permitted these too-beautiful faces to distract him from his conversation with the Creator? Yet by the time of this incident, the fire and pursuit of passion had long since immunized Ignatius, and his swift decision to face down the overpowering attractions of the effigy was born of repeated storms and bitter lessons.

Perhaps Iñigo took the image of that fair sister-mother with him when, at the age of sixteen, he left Azpeitia for Arévalo. And there is no doubt that at the court of the Contado Mayor of Castile, Don Juan Velásquez, the "vanities of the age" available to the diminutive fair-haired secretary were not all linked to arms, arts, and laws.

Exactly when did the little Infanta of Castile, youngest daughter of Joan the Mad and sister of the Emperor Charles V, locked away with her mother in the fortress of Tordesillas, enter the life (or at least the thoughts) of the Txikiye from Azpeitia? During a visit to the demented queen by her father Ferdinand of Aragon, accompanied by Don Juan Velásquez and a retinue that must have included Iñigo? Or in the course of a mission sent by the future Charles V to his mother to plead for the release of his sister, then aged thirteen, a mission supported by the Duke of Najera and the gentlemen of his household, Loyola (then eighteen to twenty) included?

A young courtier of that period was honor-bound to dream, even to go into ecstasies, about a faraway princess. But there would have been real-life escapades as well. And we have seen that the young Loyola was properly addicted to such escapades, even to the point of being charged in the public courts with "muy enormes" crimes. But what can we say about the wounded, pain-racked man lying by his window in Azpeitia, dreaming for "three or four hours at a stretch . . . of the exploits he would accomplish in the service of a certain lady" and of ways "to reach the place where she dwelled"?[4] And since the rebellious *communeros* were then besieging the royal fortress of Tordesillas, where Joan and Catherine were sequestered, those dreams must have been doubly poignant.

How could the wounded man not have dreamed of hurling himself into the fray? And how could he then fail to establish a link between the princess's destiny and his own? For if the royal forces finally broke the siege, it was because they had abandoned Pamplona's defenders, themselves under Franco-Navarrese siege, to their fate. In a sense, Iñigo's wounds and suffering had paid for Catherine's freedom.

All the heroic romanticism of the age is there, a fable in the manner of Ariosto. It is, in fact, astonishing that the sufferer was not swallowed up by this heartrending dream,* that he did not become its singer—as another of war's victims, Miguel de Cervantes, was soon to be.

But it was once again Madeleine, the fair sister with the sweet face, who would lead him from this epic of courtly (and pain-racked) love. To distract him, she put into his hands the only two books to be found in this noble manor house of rustic and virtually unlettered lords. They were there because she herself had brought them. The two books, as we have seen, were a *Life of Christ* and an *Anthology of the Saints*. Reading them, the bedridden Iñigo found decisive inspiration in the sublime acts of Francis of Assisi, Dominic-the-Castilian, and Ignatius of Antioch.

And it was shortly thereafter that the "visitation" took place, recorded in these words in the *Autobiography:*

> He clearly saw an image of Our Lady with the Holy Infant
> Jesus, . . . an extraordinary inner motion [that gave him] such ex-

*But we shall meet Catherine again, this time serving Iñigo's cause.

traordinary revulsion at his whole past life and especially the things of the flesh, that it was as if someone had removed from his soul every kind of picture painted there.* Thus, from that hour to August of 1553 when these lines are being written, he never again in any way admitted the things of the flesh.[5]

Such is Loyola's power to convince that we accept it when he says that his relations with women took on entirely new meaning from the moment of this "motion" in Azpeitia. We believe it even though we know that he was later disturbed by the excessive charms of a Madonna, and gave serious thought to "slitting the throat" of a Moorish New Christian simply because he had cast doubts on Mary's virginity.

The zealot of Azpeitia did not now sever all his ties to women. But those who henceforward entered his life bore little resemblance to the ladies of the house of Loyola, to the dowagers and ladies-in-waiting of Arévalo, or to the Infanta in Tordesillas. They would be mostly simple, pious women, whether poor or from the more prosperous classes, who were moved by the poverty (and snared by the charisma) of the vagabond from the banks of the Cardoner.

We shall content ourselves here with considering just one of those encounters, the first of them: Inès Pascual, widow of a Barcelona merchant. Traveling from Montserrat to Manresa one day in 1522, she met a haggard redheaded limping pilgrim on the road, whose "modesty" and "dignity" so struck her that "looking more closely at him . . . she felt herself impelled to piety and devotion."[6]

Those few words say it all: Pity was an infallible path to piety, for the women who met the frail Catalonian wanderer, for those who encountered the "gray man" of Alcalá, the beggar-orderly of Venice, and even the General in Rome, tiny beneath his biretta. A look of gloomy distinction, a very male air of resolution, an all-pervading fragility—and that fire, smoldering within and occasionally flaring outward. What woman of feeling and intelligence could resist such charisma?

We cannot list all the women of all walks of life who from then on laid siege to the little man, some offering hospitality, one telling him that Christ would appear to him one day, others courting fame by visiting him and favoring him with alms. As Iñigo soberly summed it up: "From that time, many distinguished women felt great admiration for him." He even referred to the "devotion" professed for him by "numerous ladies of the first rank" or by "women in positions of leadership."[7] It was the time when, by a thousand paths, the eternally fevered women not unmaliciously known as *iñiguas* or *iñiguistas* flocked out to greet the Jerusalem pilgrim on his return to Barcelona.

---

*A telling allusion, placed as it is between two references to "the flesh."

The fever would assume more alarming form at Alcalá, verging on mystical (or erotico-mystical?) effusion, on an offering, an abandonment, of self: Indeed people at this time spoke of the *dejadas,* or "consecrated ones." We have touched on the murky matters* dragged into the three ecclesiastical trials to which the Inquisition subjected the man in gray homespun. We have mentioned fragments of the exhibitionist confessions of these "orantes" and "beatae," whose extreme piety did not necessarily lead to virtue. Some writers have had the courage to call them "hysterics." And it was this "little world of everyday life, a mixture of sin and of piety," as Father Rahmer deftly puts it, that Iñigo navigated. But was it as "everyday" as all that, Father?

It was a time when, according to the Pilgrim, "at first light a married woman of quality [who] felt [for him] a special devotion" came to visit him in his chamber. And a time too when he was charged with bewitching two widows, a mother and daughter (the latter, he said, beautiful enough to "attract many looks") into leaving on barefoot pilgrimage for distant Andalusia. How, after all that, could the itinerant preacher with the burning message have failed to become the target of pitiless campaigns? Did you have to be an Inquisitor to catch the whiff of sulphur swirling about this fanatic and his swooning entourage?

Iñigo of Loyola was perhaps the *only* man ever to go to Paris to escape from women. Here at least was a city where he would be able to converse only in Latin. It can be argued of course that at Montaigu, as at Sainte-Barbe, you had no need to be able to quote Ovid in the original or speak "Biscayan" in order to catch the "Neapolitan disease"† (like Francis Xavier's "master gone astray"). Xavier would preserve his own virtue less by studying the holy books than by remembering the horrible pustules on the sinner's face. The fact is that in the story of Ignatius, Paris was perhaps the only period when the issue of the other sex never arose.

But the question reared its head again in 1535, during the months "Master Ignatius" spent with his family in Azpeitia. There we find him intervening, Calvin-style, to regulate morals, and naturally it was matters sexual he had in mind. As the *Autobiography* tells us: "In that country girls always go bareheaded, never covering themselves until the day of their marriage. But many of them become priests' concubines . . . and are as true to them as to husbands. It is so widespread a custom that concubines feel not the slightest shame in saying that they have covered their heads for this or that man."[8]

Master Ignatius tells us blithely how he persuaded the governor "to pass a law whereby any woman who covered her head for someone without being his spouse would be brought to justice." Strange, when all is said and done, this re-

*See Chapter I.
†Which Neapolitans (and many others) call the "French disease."

former who chose to prosecute the woman who "covered her head" rather than the erring priest!

Nor have we forgotten that in 1538, as he rode into Rome-of-the-thousand-bordellos, "encrusted with the filth of prostitution" (as Ribadeneira put it), he muttered to his two companions, Laínez and Favre, that they should be on their guard and "hold no commerce with women unless they were of high rank." That tells us a lot, not only about relations between the sexes depending on whether the interlocutor was a harlot or a lady but also about the relative yield the Iñiguists—*ad majorem Dei gloriam*—might expect to reap.

Of course, the founder did not cultivate connections exclusively with the grand. The early establishment of foundations like the convents of Saint Martha and Saint Catherine* is proof of that. But such nods in the direction of evangelical charity were not unaccompanied by links of another kind, operating in what we might call a virtuous circle, since succor of the poor most often involved an appeal to the wealthy. Every "repentant" harlot meant a call on a marquise.

That such contacts might have horrified the former vagabond was no more obvious in Rome than it had been in Barcelona. We must not underestimate either Loyola's reserve or his candor, which are both apparent in his correspondence. But let us first scan the list of "benefactresses" and then (since you collect more doubloons from princes than from shoemakers) admire the mastery of this "vagabond in God's kingdom," who also called himself a "retainer in the Court of Heaven."

We find Joan of Aragon, wife of the Duke of Colonna, and Margaret of Parma, known to the Romans as "Madama," illegitimate daughter of Charles V. We find the daughter of Constantius, the reigning Pope, Countess of Santa Fiore. And also Vittoria Colonna, Marquise of Pescara, and Countess Carpi, Countess Orsini, and Countess Salviati. And the wife of the imperial ambassador Juan de Vega, and finally (and perhaps especially: we shall be dwelling at length on this lady), the Infanta Joan, Charles V's legitimate daughter—the one who would, as if by chance, become the world's only "Jesuitess."

One woman would offer Iñigo her influence, another her lands, another a few hundred ducats. And how to value the support of the lady Eleonora de Mascarenhas, who had earlier met Iñigo in Castile, and who married Juan de Vega, the Spanish King's ambassador in Rome, thanks to which the Company saw so many doors opened to it—and one or two slammed shut?

But a favor is never entirely free. There are two kinds of price. One was the jealousy such favors incurred, if only among rival benefactresses. The other was insistence on a return, on a tit-for-tat, on some kind of "exchange." There is no

*See Chapter III, pp. 89–90.

great lady who does not hide deep within herself a courtesan: What will you give me, holy man, in exchange? A dangerous commerce, in which the Company's veneer of glory would inevitably be chipped away.

Jealousy struck first, and the tales that were its symptoms quickly did the rounds. The founder himself tells us that shortly after the "Doctors of Paris" settled in Rome, "Master Francis Xavier was confessing a lady and visited her from time to time to converse with her of spiritual things. Later she was found to be pregnant, but the Lord decreed that the one who committed the fault was discovered."[9]

In 1547 the Dominicans judged it necessary to take matters in hand. In the footsteps of Fray Melchor Cano, sworn enemy of the Company, who thundered from the pulpit against "these men who take pleasure in lax relations with women and go to them on pretext of converting them," a certain Fra Theophilus submitted a complaint to the Inquisition—controlled by his own order— against "priests who take the name of 'Company of Jesus' and who are also called the 'reformed, illuminati and Ignatians.'" They had, he said, "inflicted public shame upon the ladies Giovanna and Costanza Conti by broadcasting through their chatter the secrets of the confessional."[10] It took all Master Ignatius's negotiating skills to persuade the illustrious Contis to withdraw their complaint.

There was another clash over his Convent of Saint Martha, created to shelter "repentant harlots." Particularly those of the kind known as *onorate cortegiane*, or "honored courtesans," who were often well-to-do married women in search of other sensations or trying to feather their nests by publicly dispensing their favors to the Roman nobility and others.

This time it was the Franciscans who put a hot iron into their neighbor's wound. Fra Barbarán alerted not the Inquisition but the Pope, warning him of the Jesuit plan to "banish all adulterous women from Rome" (a tall order . . .), which was a free and somewhat uncharitable interpretation of the Ignatian project. Should we believe Ignatius when he reports that, according to this Fra Barbarán, "Every Jesuit from Perpignan to Seville deserves the stake"?[11]

The stake! That was not what the next critic, one Matteo di Cassiano, a high pontifical dignitary and lover of an *onorata cortegiana*, demanded. That woman, suddenly remorseful or tired of the man, sought refuge at Saint Martha's. Drunk with rage, Matteo told the Pope that the convent was nothing but "the Jesuits' harem." The stock reaction of a rejected lover. It met with papal skepticism but triggered one of those counter-assaults Ignatius loved so much—inquiry, witnesses, trial, acquittal . . .

To conclude from all this that the less the man of God involved himself in women's affairs, the better he felt, is but a short step. It is an equally short step to conclude that chastity, or at least celibacy, had not been imposed upon hermits, monks, and priests for nothing, that it was the mark of a higher wisdom, and that "every woman is more or less a Delilah."

Faced with this wave of suspicion, the Iñiguists implemented a counter-feminist defense strategy, whose description we shall entrust to Hercule Rasiel. Here he excels himself:

> Seeing that they were not Esteemed in the World for the frequent conversations that his Companions practiced with the Women they directed and fearing lest a perilous Commerce prove fatal to their Chastity and give rise to some Scandalous adventure that might be Seized upon to denigrate the Company, . . . Loyola would not rest until he hit upon a sure Means of preventing such an evil. He therefore made a Rule whereby anyone going to see Women in their Houses, whether to confess them or for any other cause, would take with him a Companion who would be present for the whole time the Confession or Conversation endured; and if the physical arrangements of the Place permitted, the Companion would remain in a spot whence he could see everything that transpired yet without in any way hearing what must be secret. If the Disposition of the Place did not allow of this, the Chamber must at all events be well lit and its door always open.*

The founder is still more explicit on certain other points, recommending "reserve" in relations with women "even if they seem devout or really are so, and above all if they are young or beautiful, or of lowly condition or of low reputation." And in a directive sent in July 1553 to all Jesuit confessors on the proper way to confess women, he urges the fathers to "send women swiftly away, particularly if they are devout."[12] But he voiced disapproval of the Venetian prefect who proposed to forbid the confession of women to any priest under the age of thirty-six.

And we find him rather understanding on the use of paint and rouge—in which many of his companions saw the mark of Satan. For him, the intention counted for everything: If a wife wanted nothing more than to please her husband, one should hesitate at seeing true evil in the practice, but rather an "imperfection" it was proper to warn the penitent against.

Indeed it was on this very question that Ignatius of Loyola, first Superior General of the Society of Jesus, uttered the following aphorism. It could be the preface to a history of the Company, alongside *ad majorem Dei gloriam* and *perinde ac cadaver:*

---

*Rules common to every Catholic religious order.

"In these matters we must never seek to establish a rule so rigid as to leave no room for exceptions." Thus—a century before its time—he threw down the gauntlet to Blaise Pascal.

By turns, "rules" and "exceptions" would govern relations between women and the Company. Particularly relations, epistolary or otherwise, between the padre maestro and a handful of ladies who were among the most remarkable in a century that, from Margaret of Navarre to Catherine de Médicis, was extraordinarily rich in such women.

The first of these exchanges, and the most moving of all, sends us back to the beginnings of our story, and the woman who linked the Company's expansion to that of the Portuguese crown. Its heroine is Queen Catherine, wife of John III —that same Catherine who, as a small Infanta of Castile immured in Tordesillas with the mad queen her mother, made the cripple of Pamplona, Iñigo, youngest of the Loyolas, dream so ardently and so long.

To attempt to make this story live again in the manner of Paul Claudel's *The Satin Slipper* (Rodrigo's brother was a Jesuit and silver-tongued) would be to take the noble paths of fiction. And indeed, who could fail to dream of an epistolary novel in which, from Lisbon to Rome, in the tones of a Portuguese nun, Queen Catherine tries to rekindle the flame in the former knight, turned general of the most active of the religious orders and the most reserved in matters of sex?

But we shall approach this theme, so worthy of a romance, through the prism of cold reality. And the reality was vast if we consider the service the Portuguese court rendered the fledgling order, opening the doors of Asia to it, and giving it the means to go and maintain itself there. Needless to say, Queen Catherine knew nothing of the feelings the founder had once nursed toward her, even though the text of the *Autobiography* was eloquent on the issue, or at least decipherable to Loyola's companions. And even though the story circulated under the title *Hechos del Padre Ignacio* (*Acts of Father Ignatius*) shortly after his death, and its author, Luis Gonçalves da Câmara, a Portuguese, returned to Lisbon before Queen Catherine's long life ended. If the aging sovereign did indeed read it, it could only have been well after the disappearance of the padre maestro, and well after the services she performed for his Company.

At the age of eighteen, the daughter of Joanna the Mad had married John of Portugal—at the time when Iñigo, avoiding by a hair the abyss of suicidal madness, was starting out on the adventure of sanctity. The foundation and aims of the order were very soon (by 1540, in fact) made known to the young queen, first by the Portuguese Simón Rodrigues, then by Francis Xavier.

We have already spoken of the birth of Francis's Indian mission, and the enthusiastic welcome he received from the Portuguese sovereigns. And it is clear that the Company owed its official sanction to the intercession of a handful of great Roman ladies (especially those belonging to the Pope's family). It is even clearer that the greatest of the Jesuits' missionary ventures began in this Portuguese court where—haunted by the terrors of hereditary madness and of the vices associated with tragic inbreeding—the woman who had inhabited the dreams of the wounded man in Azpeitia now reigned.

We have several clues to the closeness of the ties between the Portuguese sovereigns and the founding fathers, and to what Father Rahner has called "the Queen's unwavering faith in the Company of Jesus."[13] One such piece of testimony is Ignatius's letter to "My Lady in Our Lord" about some relics requested by the sovereign and obtained from the Pope through the intervention of the Superior General. Announcing the success of his campaign, Loyola adds: "I will not again offer my own person and all the members of our smallest of Companies to the continued service of Your Highnesses in Our Lord, since for many years now we have rightly considered ourselves, and Your Highnesses too, I believe, so consider us, as belonging wholly to them in Our Lord."*

When we take into account the style of the period and the mandatory courtly manner, the words constitute a kind of oblation that the fathers would certainly not have offered the Emperor, and still less—for reasons that will become clear—the King of France. Did such oaths of allegiance really sit well with the cherished freedom of men "ready to move at a moment's notice" with their "breastplates buckled" and firmly committed to the exclusion of women—of women, that is, less elevated than Catherine of Portugal?

Utterly different ties (provided, it is true, that the founder desisted from frequenting the destitute of La Strada) would link Loyola to a woman scarcely less elevated than Queen Catherine. This was Joan, or Joanna, or Juana, of Aragon, the woman whom Renaissance Europe, after Ariosto, called la diva signoria, whose unearthly beauty was forever captured by Raphael.

The divine Joan was a potent instrument of Charles V's Italian policy—directed sometimes against the Pope and always against Francis I of France. At Charles's urging, she had married the most powerful lord in southern Italy, Ascanio Colonna, Duke of Tagliocazzo, brother of the poet Vittoria Colonna, the cherished friend of Michelangelo and, to a lesser degree, of Ignatius. It was a dreadful marriage, however useful it may have been to the Spanish cause. Ascanio was a rapacious brute who had taken part in the sack of Rome: While la diva signoria surrounded herself at Ischia with poets and philosophers, the Duke squandered his wealth in the bordellos of Naples.

*Moreover, Ignatius's aunt, María de Velásquez, who had welcomed him to Arévalo, was a lady-in-waiting to the Queen.

Yet it was not Ascanio's misconduct that alerted the Jesuits and focused their gaze on the troubled Italian South. It was rather the Duchess's support of the humanist Juan de Valdés, who was received with honors at Ischia and soon became the oracle of Joan's little court. It was only a small step away from the path of orthodoxy, but Loyola deemed it serious enough to send two of his companions to Ischia. Their task there was to counter Valdés's teachings and, but only incidentally, to reconcile the divine beauty and her brutal beast. On the second point, to no avail.

A setback for the Company? After years of patience, when the wreckage of the Colonna marriage was the talk of Europe, the vagabond who had not left Rome or its immediate surroundings for twelve years (and who had twenty years earlier been at death's door), climbed onto a mule. With Polanco at his side, he began the long journey south to achieve (at least formally) what neither Pope nor Emperor had managed: the reconciliation of the quarrelsome couple.

It is hard for us today to understand such behavior, the prodigious care the little man invested in this marriage between the Spanish diva (a little long in the tooth for the period: she was then forty-five) and the Neapolitan ruffian. But an institution (marriage) and a strategy (Charles V's) were at stake. And so the Superior General, "ready to move at a moment's notice," "breastplate buckled," departed on his matrimonial crusade.

Together with her charms, the lady had lost some of her equable nature. She did not altogether welcome Ignatius, despite her admiration for him and her appreciation of his attentions. She had no intention of falling back into the clutches of Ascanio, from whom, she said, she feared assault and battery, and who was now greedily gobbling up their daughters' dowry while simultaneously negotiating a reversal of alliances against Charles V with the King of France.

Once again Ignatius took up his pen. At his little desk in La Strada, he wrote Joan a long letter, which we may consider a kind of Ignatian marriage manual. He found no fewer than twenty-six arguments, if not for reconciliation of the spouses, then at least for a resumption of cohabitation (just one option would suffice if the cause were good). A glimpse of a half dozen of these arguments will give us a strong sense of his beliefs about conjugal duty and the hierarchy of the sexes:

Madame,

All things considered, the best solution is for you to shore up your heart in trust in the Lord and return to the Lord Ascagne [Ascanio], putting yourself entirely in his hands, neither seeking new assurances nor making new agreements, like a woman who is and should be in her husband's power. The reasons that dictate my conclusion are as follows:

First. If harmony is to be wholly and perfectly achieved, there is no other way but by winning over Lord Ascagne's heart and love. This will not be obtained by agreements or by guarantees, as between enemies, but by clear demonstration of the love, humility, and trust owed to a husband. . . .

Second. Truth to tell, if one of the parties does not bend and show humility, peace will remain elusive and hearts' wounds will continue to gape. But if one of the two bends and is humble, and since it is reasonable that it be the wife rather than the husband who demonstrates humility, how much guiltier would she be before God and men if her lack of humility prevented establishment of the union which must exist between them!

Third. Such a step would bespeak considerable strength and greatness of soul, worthy of your lineage and your generous heart. For by taking it you would show that you do not even fear the mortal danger which others than you might apprehend.* That is the touchstone of great hearts. . . .

Fourth. The more arduous this manner of proceeding, the greater the heroism. You would thereby conquer yourself and subdue passions you might have nurtured and may still nurture toward the Lord Ascagne. It would therefore be most meritorious in the eyes of the Lord Our God so to do. . . .

Sixth. It would harmonize more closely with the laws His Heavenly Majesty has imposed on holy wedlock, as the Scriptures tell us in so many passages, saying that the husband is the wife's leader, that wives must be subject to their husbands, and holding up for example Sarah who called her husband her lord . . .

Tenth. In like manner, it would be a great kindness to him not only to relieve him of domestic cares by administering his household, but also to provide him peace, joy, and a happy old age. Being now sixty, he indeed approaches the twilight. He might thus end his days in union, in the lap of the love of his wife and his sons. . . .

Sixteenth. If it seems meet, as justice ordains, that you throw your reputation and honor into the scales, I am certain that you would assure them more remarkably in this fashion. Honor is itself the reward virtue merits. This being so, to the degree that . . . your situation is public and known in the world, to the same degree the fame of your greatness of soul will be widely broadcast. Your glory will be the greater on earth as in Heaven. . . .

*Including Joan—and Ignatius knew she had good reasons for her fear.

Eighteenth. If you wish to take into account the temporal advantage you will thus enjoy, it is certain that the way proposed is the right one. Thereby the Lord Ascagne will become, so to speak, your war booty and your slave. He will pay his debts and in future defray your expenses. You will be mistress and steward of all his goods.[14]

These extraordinary lines, in which virtually everything is stated or suggested, from the "humility" proper to women to the "heroism" to be expected of a great heart (even a female one), from the cult of "honor," the just reward of "virtue" (particularly Spanish virtue), to the not negligible question of "temporal advantage," are almost a concentrate of Jesuit strategy, and all the more surprising for being applied to an apparently minor battle.

But Ignatius and his realist's genius failed. A few months later, Ascanio drew up a will disinheriting his son Marcantonio for (among other crimes) "entertaining impure relations with the testator's spouse." Loyola's intervention was thus aborted—and in a way likely to sharpen the mediator's prejudices against all temptresses: for when a couple was sundered, was it not the woman who had failed to humble herself in time?

With "Madama," as the Romans called Margaret of Parma, bastard daughter of Charles V (and of a Flemish serving woman), the padre maestro moved on from marital affairs to affairs of state, at the very highest levels.

Not that Madama's conjugal life was much calmer than that of *la diva signoria:* Married at fourteen to the unspeakable Alessandro de' Medici (and freed of him by Lorenzaccio's dagger), she remained a widow for a year before marrying the Pope's grandson, Ottavio Farnese, a depraved youth, younger than she, who led her a life as hellish as his Florentine predecessor had done.

To prevent the worst between his grandson and the Emperor's daughter (there was more at stake here than marital harmony!), Paul III appealed to his Jesuit friends. First Jean Codure, then Diego Laínez, then Ignatius himself became Margaret's "directors of conscience" (thereby inaugurating the famous Jesuit tradition of confessing kings).

The part played by the woman Loyola called "nuestra Madama" in the foundation and expansion of the Company of Jesus has sometimes been exaggerated. It has been claimed that it was chiefly her intervention with Paul III that had won papal approval of the Jesuits in the teeth of opposition by Cardinals Ghinucci and Giudiccioni. This would make her a kind of cofounder of the Company. Ignatius vigorously rejected the story, insisting that her support had not been "solicited." Which does not mean that it was not spontaneously offered.

Others have chosen to see in Margaret the "first accomplished pupil" of the Jesuits, which would be enough on its own to make her a key character. Indeed, given Margaret's ties to Ignatius and his companions, given the development over time of her character, the authority of her views on the management of power (particularly in the governance of the Low Countries), and of course her services to the Company, this princess was the very model of what Jesuit "direction" could accomplish in the handling of public affairs.

Very near the Piazza Navona, on the Corso Rinascimento, stands an elegant if somewhat austere building known as the Palazzo Madama: Today it houses the Italian Senate. It was here that the padre maestro hurried to confess Margaret of Parma and here one day in 1545 that he baptized the princess's surviving twin son. Here too, funds were handed over for several of the Company's undertakings, particularly the Convent of Saint Martha and the seminary for novice Jewish converts, projects the Emperor's daughter occasionally sponsored.

Among all the services *nuestra Madama* performed for her Jesuit friends (and independently of the gifts she showered on them), we should mention at least two: In the 1540s, her moderation of the dislike her father the Emperor felt for the "Doctors of Paris"; and in the 1560s, the support she provided for the Company in Flanders when she was Regent there.

Charles V's attitude toward Ignatius and his followers has never been satisfactorily explained. Did he see them as clandestine propagators of French influence? Enemies of the Dominicans and Franciscans, whom he trusted? Or simply (as French monarchs were long to believe) an anti-State organism incompatible with his own absolutist notions?

Whatever the answer, his daughter Margaret (she was never diminished in his eyes by the conditions of her birth, and her loyalty to him was unswerving) worked patiently to erode his formidable suspicion of the order she so passionately supported. Above all, she was able to make the Emperor see how much her Jesuit "directors of conscience" had contributed to the survival (shaky, but much desired by the Pope) of her marriage to Ottavio Farnese.

As for her masterful regency in Flanders, which she exercised on behalf of her half-brother Philip II from 1559 to 1567, it opened as many avenues for the Company in that crucial region as the Portuguese sovereigns had opened for them in Asia. Among others, the University of Louvain was to enjoy unrivaled importance in the great northern European debate between the two main branches of Protestantism.

A lesser personage crystallized the Company's doctrine regarding female participation in the cause, and particularly the question of a "sister order." We have mentioned Isabel Roser,* the Barcelona matron who had been Iñigo's hostess,

---

*Variously spelled Rosell (more Catalan), Rosés, Rozés. See Chapter I.

fervent disciple, and benefactress. Isabel was wealthy; her husband was a prosperous merchant who had gone blind. The hermit of Manresa had met Señora Roser before leaving for Jerusalem. But it was when he returned to Barcelona that his debt to her began, since it was she who paid for his studies. It was she again, during Iñigo's long stay in Paris, who sent him (and sometimes Francis Xavier as well) a monthly stipend, so that in 1533 the "Master of Arts" wrote to her: "I am more deeply obliged to you than to anyone else in the world."

A sustained correspondence then followed between Iñigo (now Ignatius and living in Rome) and the good lady of Barcelona. Her protégé kept her informed of the ups and downs of his project, in which she rightly considered herself an initiator, even a participant. Letters from the founder to his benefactress read like a report sent to a distant fellow worker, a representative, or an associate. Such as the interminable letter he sent to her from Rome on December 19, 1538: Not a single detail of the ordeals, trials, persecutions, or progress of the group (shortly to become the *Societas Jesu*) is omitted. How could Doña Isabel, thus constantly reminded of the benefits she had showered upon Ignatius, have failed to conclude that his immense enterprise was also her own?

Less than half a year after Loyola's election as Superior General of the brand-new Company, Isabel became a widow. With her friend Teresa Rejadella, another of Loyola's confidantes, she considered taking the veil at the Franciscan convent of Saint Claire. But conditions in the convents of Catalonia were so uncertain that she changed her mind. And the following year, Isabel conceived the daring plan of joining the band on Santa Maria della Strada and placing herself under the rule of her spiritual master.

Immediately scenting danger, Ignatius wrote to the enterprising widow to ask whether such a project had been whispered into her ear "by a good or an evil spirit." Señora Roser was not discouraged. On November 6, 1542, she sent a letter to her "very dear father Messire Ignatius," in which reminders and appeals ring out like warning bells: "I trust in God our Lord that you will remember that we are all of us your neighbor.* . . . For the love of God, help us then rather than hinder us, and remember Barcelona.† . . . [I am] resolved to journey to Rome to see you before I die."[15]

Five months later, she landed at Ostia with a vast train of companions, serving women, and baggage.

Her reunion with the "General" was reported in the following terms during Loyola's official beatification:

*Ah yes, even women . . .
†Meaning, "the many gifts I gave you."

"When Father Ignatius saw Isabel he was extremely surprised. Taking his head in his hands, he said, 'God preserve me, Roser! You in this place? Who brings you here?'

"She answered: 'God and you, my Father!'"[16]

God preserve me, Roser . . . It might have been the title of one of the romances then popular, in which picturesque extremes jostled constantly with spiritual tragedy.

The first problem to be solved, of course, was what to do with this benefactress, whose demands and protestations of devotion—or of spite—would soon ring more clamorously than her prayers.

One solution suggested itself. Why not entrust her with the care of repentant—or potentially repentant—fallen women at Saint Martha's and Saint Catherine's? Doña Isabel needed little urging to devote herself to this task in which, treated like the Mother Superior of a convent, she was associated at a certain remove with two illustrious fellow workers, Vittoria Colonna and Margaret of Parma.

But the lady from Barcelona, mindful of her past services, aimed higher: to be the first woman admitted to the Company and tied by the vow of obedience to dear "Messire Ignatius." In short, to be the first "Jesuitess," just as he had been the first Jesuit. To forestall this ambition, which seemed to him absurd, Loyola engaged in a masterful series of twists and turns and delaying tactics. For nearly two years he played deaf—perhaps less hostile to the principle than unsure of the consequences: They were already saying in Barcelona that the lady Roser had as good as won, which meant that Loyola might soon be engulfed by a wave of jealous women.

Since the General refused to listen, she appealed directly to the Pope, asking that he "order Master Ignatius to receive into his hands this solemn vow" so that she might "be one with the Congregation." Old Paul III yielded. On Christmas Day 1543, Isabel Roser and her two "followers," Francesca Cruyllas and Lucretia de Bradina, pronounced before Ignatius the vows that bound them to the Company. The path to a sister Jesuit order now lay open.

With great speed the padre maestro stopped behaving like a staff in the hands of the Pope. He retrenched and returned to the attack, his resolution heightened by the fact that the good lady, flushed with her newfound glory, had summoned two of her nephews from Catalonia with the intention of finding them good marriages. Was the Company of Jesus now a matrimonial agency? Even worse! For the nephews now raised retroactive objections to the gifts their wealthy aunt had made to the fathers—and the aunt herself began to go over her accounts and demand her due.

From that moment on, the General thought only of ejecting the nephew-encumbered intruder on the Company. The opportunity came when Isabel called on him, in a scene worthy of Molière, to restate her claims, listing all the gifts she had lavished on the Jesuits: laces, napkins, mattresses—"at least four hundred and sixty-five ducats' worth!" The General retorted that if they began reckoning up accounts, the lady was in for a surprise. A true Basque lawyer. Sensing trouble, the benefactress tried to turn the situation around: What if she offered an additional 200 ducats? "Two hundred ducats," replied the inimitable Messire Ignatius, "would not in any way modify the decision I have made for the greater glory of God!"

And on October 1, 1546, the lady Isabel received a letter from the Superior General. It was a verdict.

> By my conscience, it is not fitting that the Company especially preoc-
> cupy itself with women bound by the vow of obedience, as I amply
> explained six months ago to His Holiness. . . . I must therefore dis-
> charge myself of the care of having you as a spiritual daughter in obe-
> dience to me. But you shall be the good and pious mother that you
> have so long been for me. . . . I entrust you, to the extent of my
> power, to the most prudent judgment, guidance, and decision of His
> Holiness.

Needless to say, the good lady did not immediately give up the fight. She allowed her nephew Ferrer to shout to the rooftops that the Company was a "band of scoundrels" and Ignatius "a brigand [who] purposed to steal my aunt's fortune" (in which she was anticipating the Black Legend of the Jesuits that in later centuries would attract so many believers).

But Isabel Roser was honest. As soon as she was free of the itch to become a female Jesuit—comparable to the itch any honest bourgeois might feel to become a gentleman—she begged the padre maestro to forgive her excessive demands. She resumed (by correspondence) the most trusting of relations with him, unprotestingly entered the Franciscan convent in Barcelona, which Ignatius had recommended, and there piously met her end.

But the clash had taught its lesson. In May 1547, less than eighteen months after Isabel Roser and her two companions had pronounced their vows, he sent Paul III a plea intended to free the Company forever of the burden of women bent on swearing obedience to him:

> Most Holy Father,
>
> Humbly soliciting Your Holiness, the Superior General and the Fa-
> thers of the Company of Jesus . . . are pressed in divers cities and
> countries to accept the vows and the charge of novices and women
> who wish devoutly to serve God. . . .
>
> Most Holy Father, we who solicit your grace have seen in this a

great obstacle to the primordial functions and ministries to which, for the service of God and by Your Holiness's basic provision, their vocation has called them. And since that task is but now beginning, we fear that what is an initial stumbling block may in time become something much more intractable.

For this reason, we who solicit Your Holiness's grace most humbly beg the following of you after you have considered what has been said: that—in order that we may move forward more freely according to the terms of our vocation and the provision approving the foundation of this Company—it be decided and forever ordained that we be henceforth exonerated from accepting from any convent or house of female novices or Nuns, or from any other women living in common and desirous of serving the Lord of Virtues into our Company; that we be dispensed from the charge of receiving into our obedience, as set forth above, the said women; that we be and remain perpetually exempted and relieved of such a charge.

This is the basic text. The papal bull it inspired as well as Chapter VI of the *Constitutions* (which deals with the same problem) merely paraphrase it. It says everything. It goes well beyond a simple refusal to create a sister branch of the order to frame a kind of inverted image of the *perinde ac cadaver* principle: It is not obedience that is postulated here, but on the contrary refusal to exercise authority—the authority to envisage any kind of community of women.

Nevertheless, however discouraging the "Roser affair" might have been (we have confined ourselves to her, but there were others), we must pronounce this exclusion of women sinister. For it raised the strangest of barriers (and for the strangest of motives!) around the principle of brotherly love.

But in Loyola's eyes, as we know, there could be no "rule so rigid as to leave no room for exceptions." Which we are about to see—although we should not be too surprised at the fact that this particular "exception" was tailored for a very great lady, indeed more exalted and more powerful than any other. A woman through whom the glory of the Company—and at the same time the glory of God—would be raised to the heavens.

The Infanta Joan was the second daughter of Charles V and Isabel of Portugal. She was four when her mother died. For maternal guidance she would turn to Eleonora de Mascarenhas, a woman whose name recurs in the life of Ignatius of Loyola and his Company, and who inevitably prejudiced her in favor of the newborn order. A fleeting marriage to a ghostly Portuguese prince left her, at twenty, a widow and mother of a sickly child. Then, before he retired to die in the monastery of Yuste, her father the Emperor made her Regent of Spain (her brother Philip II being detained in England by his marriage to Mary Tudor).

Charles V's daughter handled that five-year interregnum with truly sovereign authority, although in the strangest of circumstances. In a letter written in 1556 to Ignatius of Loyola, a sober observer of the Castilian court reported that "the Regent's palace has the look of a nunnery." We can almost see the faint smile on the lips of the founder, naturally well aware of the reasons for this singular phenomenon: For in spite of every ban, decision, supplication, and veto, in spite of the *Constitutions,* in spite of the papal bull *Licet debitum,* in spite of the lady Roser and her excesses, in spite of Ignatius's prejudices, of his deepest-laid plans, of his proverbial energy, and even perhaps in spite of God, the Regent had become a member of the Company of Jesus—history's only undeniable "Jesuitess."

The Regent had not entered the Company, of course, under her illustrious name or sovereign title, but as the masculine and utterly commonplace Matteo Sánchez. The abundant correspondence of the founding fathers, first about the project itself, then about the status of Joan of Spain, never mentions any but that obscure name, which might as easily have been that of a Toledo water carrier or a bull breeder of Jerez.* But male, of course . . .

After her husband's death the Emperor's daughter had at first agreed to retire among the Franciscans, even pronouncing her preliminary vows. But no sooner had she been appointed Regent (her power was limited only by the frontiers of Spain) in the summer of 1554 than she conveyed to her Jesuit familiars in Valladolid her intention of taking the vows of obedience.

What must old Ignatius have felt when he learned of the Regent's decision! Perhaps a fervent "Madre de Dios!" crossed his lips. He at once organized a "congress" in Rome to hear the opinion of his best counselors, Polanco, Nadal, and Gonçalves da Câmara. This was a will stronger than his own!

Hugo Rahner asserted that it was "simply impossible to reject the explicit request of Her Spanish Highness."[17] But in the light of what we know about the frail and indomitable General, all kinds of other objections come to mind. Was it wise, for example, to impose the vows of poverty and chastity on this twenty-year-old widow, a major player in a game of matrimonial politics as important for the balance of power in Europe and the world as that of the Habsburgs? In any event, the decision the "congress" of fathers reached in October 1554 is a fine politico-spiritual balancing act:

> Considering on the one hand our *Constitutions* which forbid admissions of this kind and the prerogative mentioned in our bulls of not being forced to accept such a charge; and knowing on the other hand

---

*After Loyola's death, the princess's pseudonym was changed to Montoya, with no first name.

that three persons* of this sort† were in the beginning admitted, and having taken note of the above-mentioned bull, we have decided as follows:

This person may be admitted and it is fitting that it be done in the same manner in which scholastics of the Company are admitted, on a trial basis for two years (and more if the Superior so decides). . . .

Moreover, it has seemed right to convey to this person that these vows remain in vigor and in force as long as the Superior wishes to maintain in the Company the person who has made them, and no longer. . . .

Likewise again the above-named Fathers have decided that this person, whosoever she be, since she alone enjoys such special privilege of being admitted into the Company, must keep her admission under the seal of secrecy as if in confession. If the fact should become known, it must not become a precedent lest another person of this kind embarrass the Company by soliciting admission.

For the rest, this person shall have to change neither habit nor dwelling, nor give any kind of evidence of what it must suffice her to guard between her soul and God our Lord. The Company or one of its members will have the obligation of caring for her soul, as much as is needful for the service of God and for her personal consolation, for the glory of God our Lord.

Understatement, containment, suture . . . The introduction by both parties of a subtle freedom at the very heart of the most implacable system of obedience and discipline. Thus the padre maestro, having consulted his followers, agreed to admit into the bosom of this male Company the greatest and most powerful woman of her day, the absolute mistress of a Spain supreme in this Golden Century of Europe—but merely "on a trial basis" and for a period of two years, and under the seal of secrecy as absolute as that obtaining "in confession." Which signified worlds.

And above all else, Father Ignatius agreed to let the Regent commit herself body and soul by the strictest of vows (farewell Habsburg matrimonial strategy!). He, however, remained free. He reserved for himself the discretionary right to cast out the illustrious adherent before or after her final vows. She was in the Company only for so long as the Superior General consented to "maintain" her there . . . *Perinde ac cadaver*—but for her, not for him!

Loyola was still too closely linked to the Spanish feudal order not to mitigate this hammerblow verdict with a series of courtly grace notes. Four months later,

*Isabel Roser and her two followers.
†Not to say sex . . .

he sent the probationary "Jesuit" Regent these friendly lines: "I have learned by a letter from Father Francisco Borgia* how happy Your Highness would be if we found a formula permitting the fulfillment of a person's pious and holy desires. Although this matter is fraught with considerable difficulty, all has been made subordinate to the desire we should have and do have to serve Your Highness in Our Lord. . . . I shall say no more, save humbly to beg Your Highness to consider us as being wholly hers."

Would it have been better to write "to consider herself as wholly ours"? No. For although this Company was already powerful enough to admit the Regent of Spain on a very conditional basis, power relations persisted. The lady of Valladolid was stronger than the little man in black. The Spanish crown still weighed more heavily than the order, as the French crown had earlier outweighed the Templars, and later would outweigh the Jesuits themselves.

Of course, the Regent Joan was lavish with deeds and interventions in the Company's favor. She defended it against Dominican attack and the assaults of a nobility that was irritated by so many favors and that condemned the "Jesuit regime of Valladolid" and the "empire of the Ignatians." And she supported the Order's implantation in Flanders and Catalonia. Observing that Ignatius had most decidedly "taken seriously the vocation of the Emperor's daughter," Father Rahner sheds light on "this so characteristic ability of the Saint to demand much of the women he had won over to the Kingdom of God, from each according to her station."[18]

Whence the letters leaving Rome for Castile, all pleas and requests for favors (or, those favors once received, requesting new services). People knew, and it provoked mutterings, jealousy, gossip, slander—even talk of the relations between Joan and her confessors. Let us again quote the shrewd and farsighted Father Rahner: "Perhaps court gossip was not entirely wrong in calling the Queen's residence a Jesuit enterprise, and her palace a nunnery." Later on, however, more than one Jesuit complained that the Jesuit "college at Valladolid was a state chancery rather than a house of religion."

A tangled double game of religion and politics, a bewildering confusion (or fusion). A court serving cassocks, cassocks serving the court: The machinery rolled cumbersomely into place, and long remained there. We shall be encountering it again.

The extraordinary affair of the Jesuit Regent taught Ignatius and his companions a valuable lesson in that it reminded them of the implicit—or explicit—supremacy of royal power. If they had needed only one proof, they found it in this almost toothless letter from the Regent to her "General" in Feb-

*Himself Duke of Gandía and a future General of the order, long a secret Jesuit, like the Regent—whose confessor he was.

ruary 1556 to dissuade him from recalling Fathers Araoz and Borgia (from whom she could not bear to be separated) to Rome: "In order that these two fathers may not move without my authorization, you would be kind indeed to grant me power over them so that I may command them in the name of obedience. You will thus be occasioning me very great pleasure."

When we recall the vows she had sworn, the conditions she had accepted, the theoretical relations between the only woman Jesuit and the founder who could at any moment expel her, it is clear that every word of this extraordinary "plea" must be remembered and weighed if we are to understand the relationship of God to Caesar—whether or not the latter had made his obeisance to the former: "Grant me power over them," "command them in the name of obedience," "you will be occasioning me very great pleasure." Particularly that last word, thrown out with stunning nonchalance. We have often attempted to imagine Ignatius's reactions—but here they are beyond imagining.

"Matteo Sánchez," later called "Montoya," her true name Joan of Spain, daughter of Charles V, died at thirty-eight. She had not once swerved from her vow of chastity, despite the numberless marriage plans concocted around her—the strangest of them being the attempt to unite her to her nephew Don Carlos, the visionary hero of Schiller and Verdi.

As for poverty, Joan had demonstrated toward it a very special concern, founding the Convent of the Descalzadas (Barefoot Women) in Madrid, and drawing its recruits—for want of women Jesuits—from the order of the Little Sisters of Claire. She often stayed there, like Teresa of Avila, tolerant of the fact that the convent's very real austerity was tempered by a taste for fine paintings, which visitors can still admire today in their original setting (perhaps reflecting that it would be easier to tolerate fasting and going barefoot under a Zurbarán's gaze).

By the time she expired, her "pious Father Ignatius" had been dead for years. We have no idea what the founder made of this flamboyant modification of his *Constitutions*. But there are many reasons for believing that "Matteo Sánchez's" ideas about discipline, like Isabel Roser's extravagant behavior, would not have made him rescind his original ban on the formation of an order peopled by "this sort."

Nevertheless, from century to century, that iron exclusion of women would continue to raise obstacles and prompt transgression. Every new generation would give birth to a new female candidate for election, a heroine eager to grasp the bitter laurels of the little cripple from Azpeitia, impatient to remind the world that in the Creator's eyes neither sex nor race exist and that, with or without fire and brimstone, woman is not unworthy of magnifying God's glory.

A remark by the Reverend Father Kolvenbach, the present Superior General of the Company, reflects this perennial female urge to join the Jesuits despite all snubs, disappointments, vetoes, and rejections. In the spring of 1990 he told the author that throughout his mission as Far Eastern Provincial he had been under pressure from the "ladies of the Holy Heart"* (known to young French Jesuits, playing on the similar sounds of Saint-Coeur and *cinq heures,* as the "five o'clock ladies") who, although unimpeachably devout,† wanted to be considered auxiliaries of the Company of Jesus. He had been obliged to confront them with the vetoes enshrined in the *Constitutions,* he told me.

It is a controversy that has endured since Isabel Roser. Its most famous Amazon was the Englishwoman Mary Ward, the founder in 1609 of the Institute of the Blessed Virgin Mary at Saint-Omer in western France. Adopting most of the Company's rule (worldly activity outside the convent walls, rejection of all outward signs in clothing, abandonment of choral chant), Miss Ward also dispensed teaching of a quality comparable to that with which the fathers are credited. But her attempts to create a parallel (not to say a twin) order with the Ignatians were deemed too aggressive, and in 1630 the Jesuits obtained a papal bull that put an end to this presumption.

Under the aegis of Jesuit directors with heaven-sent names—Father Medaglia, Father Estasi—there arose in Auvergne in the mid-seventeenth century a congregation known as the Sisters of Saint Joseph. They too hoped to place themselves within the sphere of the Roman Company, whose vitality in central France was linked to the renowned Collège de Billom, near Clermont-Ferrand —under the sarcastic gaze of a neighbor named Blaise Pascal. This "hermaphrodite Jesuitry" (masculine initiative, female piety) was to wield a steady and effective influence that extended as far as the United States. So much so that— quantitatively at least—it rivaled the masculine order: At the beginning of the 1980s there were some 25,000 Sisters of Saint Joseph, about as many as there were Jesuits.[19]

But if Loyola's regiment really had a female sibling, it was the Sisters of the Sacred Heart. At least in France, and in the sociology of education. With its revolutionary variants, like the Ladies of the Fawn in Lyons, its early nineteenth-century‡ boarding schools, it reflected a most intelligently adapted *ratio studiorum* inspired by Madeleine-Sophie Barat, a woman who was intellectually on a par with Favre or Laínez.

---

*Not to be confused with the "Sacred Heart."
†Distinguishing themselves particularly in the East and in Africa.
‡At that time the Company—suppressed in 1773—was surviving in semisecret in France under the name of the Congregation of the Sacred Heart or Fathers of the Faith, under the guidance of Fathers Clorivière and Varin.

Although the Republic that arose from the French Revolution deprived them of their mother house,* the next-door neighbor (as was fitting) of the Church of Saint Francis Xavier, the Ladies of the Sacred Heart offered the daughters of well-to-do French Catholic families a teaching method based faithfully on the system Loyola had developed from his own acquaintance with the *modus parisiensis:* balanced fields of knowledge, disciplined thought, clarity of expression, ease of deportment, chaste piety . . .

Was there as much Fénélon as Loyola in this art of teaching young women? If the little man of La Strada was in any sense dispossessed of his quasi-monopoly on education by any rival at all, we can boldly say that—where women were concerned—he got what was coming to him.

*To turn it some time later into the Maison Rodin, where General de Gaulle briefly thought of taking up official residence, finally deciding against it because of the treatment visited on the Ladies of the Sacred Heart by the Third Republic.

· VI ·

ThE JEWS
ANd ThE JESUITS

Fatal Decree · Limpieza de sangre · *Ignatius, Christ's "Jewish
Origins," and Spain's "error nacional"* · *Ancestry and Diego Laínez*
· *Angry Men of Toledo* · *1593 and 1608: Capitulations* ·
Jesuitry and Jewry

N O M A T T E R H O W vital the formative Parisian intellectual period
nor how constraining the Company's geographical ties to Rome, it
was the sixteenth-century Spanish world that gave birth to the
Company of Jesus. But this world was, from the religious standpoint, complex
and tragic.

A fateful date marks its historical beginnings: 1492, the year Their Most
Catholic Majesties* imposed upon Jews and "Moors" the infamous choice:
"bautismo o expulsión," baptism or expulsion. Such a measure would have
shaken many a society to its foundations, but none so thoroughly as Spain,
"Semitized" for long centuries as a result of a Judeo-Arabic penetration that,
from the eighth century to the reconquest of Granada, had engendered the glittering prosperity of the Andalusian kingdoms.

The Spanish Jesuit historian Eusebio Rey has suggested that "the surgical act
of 1492, after every kind of medicinal therapy had failed, was the ultimate possible remedy against the imminent Jewish peril."[1] Whatever we make of his theory, it is a fact that Spain's situation at that time was quite extraordinary, quite
exceptional.

---

*A somewhat anachronistic usage, since the papal bull conferring this title on them was issued only
in 1496.

It was not a question of attack, of external pressure, of an attempt at penetration (this had already happened). Marcel Bataillon, in *Érasme et l'Espagne* (1937), calculated that by the end of the fourteenth century, the Spanish Church was peopled with conversos who had contributed to the reshaping of Spanish Christendom.* The decree of 1492 sought to put an end to this insemination, but only intensified it, for the sudden incorporation of some 50,000 converts† could only internalize rather than solve the problem.

And how truly assimilated were these conversos? Whether they and their descendants embraced and professed Catholicism with total sincerity is what Lucien Febvre has called "an insoluble question, like all questions of sincerity." But he suggests that the converts might, "from before the Middle Ages, from before the origins of Christianity, have held on to some tendency to reach back to the Hebrew tradition of psalms and prophecy. . . . Living on in the recesses of their minds and hearts, might not the moral and religious inspiration of the prophets have prolonged itself in them in a kind of Messianic anxiety?"[2]

Having asked this question—which is really in itself a reply—Febvre goes on to propose a systematic (and instructive) comparison of the "capital texts of Judaism [available] in medieval Spain with the feelings, opinions, and attitudes of reform-minded Spanish Christians at the dawn of the sixteenth century."[3]

The fact is that the Jewish limb grafted onto Spanish Christianity had taken well and remained sturdy a quarter century after Their Most Catholic Majesties' edict. So much so that Erasmus, a man not given to fanaticism or prejudice, made it his excuse for refusing an invitation to Spain in 1517. Erasmus, a humanist who moved about so effortlessly in a northern Europe penetrated by Lutheranism, was reluctant to tread Spanish soil, which was too "Semitized" (both Arabian and Jewish) for his taste. That is to say (for a man like Erasmus, who was incapable of what we now call racism), a soil permeated by the irrational.

We have already spoken‡ of the role played by the "New Christians" in the Illuminati movement, which shook the Spanish Catholic world before Erasmianism conferred upon it a fleeting rationality. The part they played in such a movement—verging on anarchy, impervious to hierarchy and ritual—is readily understandable, and the prophetic genius of Judaism contributed powerfully to it, as did the natural mistrust these conversos must have felt for the rough-and-ready cassock-wearing instruments of conversion.

Eusebio Rey further draws attention to an inverse brand of militancy practiced inside the religious orders and the Church hierarchy, even within the Inquisition, by these New Christians. Authors like Marcel Bataillon and Americo

*Conversos from Islam were more numerous than those from Judaism.
†Estimate suggested by L. Loeb in *Revue des études juives*, 1887.
‡See pp. 27–29.

Castro also point to the zeal and inflexibility of the conversos in those areas, although this phenomenon could of course be seen as a manifestation of the kind of extremism traditional with neophytes. But according to Father Rey, there is another reason, social in origin, behind the converts' eagerness to "join the party." As they infiltrated the religious orders and the Catholic hierarchy, he says, the newcomers discovered "a way of life that represented a defense against the humiliations inflicted upon them by a society excessively sensitive to the question of purity of blood."

For this problem of *limpieza de sangre* had obviously not been solved by Their Most Catholic Majesties' edict. Indeed, by shifting the debate from the religious to the racial plane, the decree of 1492 ushered in the implementation of a thoroughgoing ethnic-cleansing program. The hammerblow of 1492, which claimed to unite religion and society, had in fact divided Spaniards into two castes,* the "pure" and the "impure," formally set apart from one another by a Statute on Purity of Blood published in 1547 by Monsignor Martínez Siliceo, Archbishop of Toledo.

It was to be a three-phase operation: "differentiation," "isolation" (through quarantining of the "impure"), and "elimination" (through banishment or death). Whence the frightful triage carried out under the aegis of Siliceo and the Inquisition, which turned Spanish social life into a permanent open season on false converts and into a never-ending kangaroo court in a climate of pervasive suspicion.

Such was the poison eating at the most glorious and puissant Spain of the Golden Age, as it does in all societies that seek to base law and order on discrimination of groups and inequality of races. For who would have dared stand up against this blood law and proclaim (in full awareness of the consequences) that in the eyes of God there is no master race and no accursed people? And that if a chosen people did exist . . .

Íñigo of Loyola, son of Beltrán the rustic Basque nobleman, courtier of Arévalo, diehard of Pamplona, had challenged none of the anti-Semitic prejudices infecting the society of his day. Indeed, scholars have unearthed one of his Spanish brothers in Murcia, in the heart of "Semitized" Andalusia, who shouted to the rooftops that—like all native-born Guipúzcoans—he "descended from old Christians unsullied by the evil race [*limpios de mala raza*]."

Better still, we have seen Íñigo,† many months after his "conversion," appearing before Juan Rodríguez de Figueroa in Alcalá and coming face to face with the problem. When the Inquisitor asked whether he and his disciples observed

*In Spain the word "caste" is preferred to "race." Which in no way changes the root of the problem.
†See Chapter I.

the Sabbath he retorted, "On Saturdays I urge upon my listeners a special devotion to the Virgin. As for other rules governing Saturdays I know them not, since my native land never knew Jews." Words through which, two years after Iñigo's "conversion" and months after his return from Jerusalem, the winds of a generalized anti-Semitism undoubtedly blew, even in this far northwest corner of the Peninsula where the Jewish presence was weaker than elsewhere.

But obviously there was a presence of sorts. From Bilbao to Bayonne in southwestern France,* where Jews were numerous in the seventeenth century, small Jewish colonies engaged in local trade. Were the Loyolas linked to them, perhaps by marriage? In his 1916 *Historia Crítica de San Ignacio*[4] Pey Ordeix actually suggests that Loyola may have been Jewish. Another biographer, the German Georg Lomer, describes him simply as "half-Jewish." But these are risky assertions, and inadequate in any case to explain the attitude of the Company's founder to the Children of Israel.

And if we have seen him thus touchy and defensive on the question in Alcalá days, we shall later find him more than welcoming to the *hebreos,* constantly alert for attempts at exclusion of Jews by the Spanish Church, constantly ready to recall Christianity's Jewish origins.

Here we must mention two or three classic anecdotes whose authenticity is attested by the character of the teller, Pedro de Ribadeneira,[5] a confidant of the founder if ever there was one. (Ribadeneira, himself born into the Spanish nobility at a time when love of Jews was rare, was a man whom we shall later find embroiled in the struggle over the question of admitting conversos into the Society of Jesus.)

> One day as we dined together in a numerous company, the padre maestro declared that he would have deemed it a special grace of Our Lord and the glorious Virgin Mary to have been born of Jewish blood, which would make him of the same family as Christ and His Mother. And it was said with such great feeling that tears flowed down his face in such floods that all present were struck. But one of his assistants, Pedro de Sarte, a Biscayan close to Loyola and a Knight of Jerusalem, cried out: "Jewish! I despise that word." To which Ignatius gave answer: "Very well, Don Pedro, let us debate the matter. And when you have heard my reasons, you too will wish you were of Jewish descent."

Long years later, when it was said in the presence of Superior General Mercurian (Loyola's third successor) that Jewish ancestry brought with it a degree of infamy, the father intervened. "Nothing," he said, "flies more in the face

*A branch of French Socialist leader Pierre Mendès-France's family settled and prospered there.

of the teachings of Father Ignatius, who always repeated to us that he would have been grateful to God for allowing him to be one of that lineage."

It would be wrong to interpret those words of the founder as pious and inconsequential sentimentality. Loyola was not the man to restrict such confidences to himself and his close associates. He never failed to reveal his feelings over the "injustice" of the measures initiated against the Jews by those responsible for the 1492 edict and by the royal courts of Valladolid and Lisbon. Most important, he took two distinct practical steps: He founded an organization to facilitate "conversion" of Jews; and he insisted on routine admission of "New Christians" into the Company, no matter what the reaction of this or that of his companions, of this or that Pope (such as the anti-Semitic Paul IV), of the Spanish court and the Spanish Church hierarchy.

The question of "conversion" of Jews to Christianity is not one to be broached lightly. And this is not the place to judge whether (as many Jews saw it) there was both insult and injury in the Christian desire to make of them—first among the children of Abraham—members of a Church they considered heretical and at whose hands they had cruelly suffered.

Many Christians learn with surprise or disappointment that what they consider to be demonstrations of warm and active sympathy for the people of Israel are condemned by their Jewish counterparts as aggressive or insulting attempts at conversion. A classic example of the cultural gap between two ways of belonging, one founded in the Alliance, the other in the will. One rejecting the notion of conversion and cultivating loyalty, the other living only in dissemination of the Gospel and deriving glory from its own missionary zeal.

But if we put a positive interpretation on Loyola's attitude to the Jews it is because—unlike the great *auto da fé* of 1492—it was based on a grandiose (if not quite accurate) vision of Judeo-Christian continuity, of Christianity's Jewish roots. It was not apostasy that Loyola proposed to the Jews, but a new stage on a road opened and signposted by the message of Abraham.

Whatever we may think of the principles involved in such a project, it is obvious that, in the case of the little recluse of Santa Maria della Strada, the motive was love. And equally clearly, the founder often clashed with his own closest associates in order to achieve these ends.

Was it a legitimate goal or a subtle extension of Christianity's conquistador spirit? Loyola's Judeophilia is perhaps best illustrated by the controversy over the admission of "New Christians" into the Company. Loyola flatly dismissed all discrimination based on a person's origins as a product of what he called the *humor español* and of the *humor del corte e del Rey de España* (we can translate *humor* here as "temperament" or "peculiarity"), or else of *error nacional* (national error). He publicly expressed regret at not being born Jewish. And he stipulated—as a fundamental rule for admission into the Company—that no obstacle be raised with respect to a postulant's origins. The *Constitutions* say that the question must be asked, but only for the purpose of information, to allow for a more precise "direction" of the newcomer.

Had he known ever since Montmartre about the Jewish origins of Diego Laínez (who would be his successor)? Did he wonder about the ancestry of the man, Juan de Polanco, who was to become his secretary, his shadow? There is no doubt that he knew of the Jewish roots of Juan de Avila, Francisco de Toledo, Juan Bautista Romano, and many others whose names—designating birthplace or baptismal site—proclaimed to the world that they were "recent" Christians.

Today, the founder's position seems merely unexceptionable. But at the time it was revolutionary, and occasionally heroic. It was the position of a man totally dedicated to the fostering and expansion of his fledgling Company (and consequently obliged to handle principalities and powers with kid gloves), a man fully aware of the risks such an attitude entailed in dealings with the Church hierarchy and the Castilian and Portuguese courts.

The fiercest critic of Loyola's Judeophilia was Martínez Siliceo, Cardinal-Archbishop of Toledo, author of the Statute on Purity of Blood. For years this all-powerful prelate, the Primate of Spain, pressed Loyola to exclude Jews from the Company, dangling many privileges before his eyes (including the foundation of a major Jesuit school in Alcalá) if the founder would observe the terms of the Toledo statute. All in vain.

Equally fruitless were similar pressures from the Spanish court, such as the reproof addressed to Ignatius by the second most powerful man in the kingdom, Don Ruy Gómez da Silva, Count of Eboli.* The founder's reply, according to Eusebio Rey, was the "testament in which Saint Ignatius expressed his irrevocable will" on this vexed question: "I am told that Your Lordship is displeased that we admit so many 'New Christians' to our Company. The Company may and must not exclude anyone. . . . It may refuse no talent, nor any man of quality, whether he be 'New Christian' or noble knight or another, if his religious comportment is useful and conforms to the universal good." One could hardly be more tactful in telling a favorite of Philip II that a good Christian should not look to a person's origins, only to his merits.

But Ignatius faced opposition much closer to home. Antonio Araoz, his cousin (or rather the cousin of his beloved stepsister Madeleine), was a ferocious antagonist of the Jews and an opponent of the admission of "New Christians" to the Company. A typical product of Biscayan anti-Semitism, Araoz

---

*Whose wife (if we are to believe Schiller and Verdi) was the mistress of Philip II and sent the Infante Don Carlos, whom she loved, to his death.

stirred up what Ribadeneira called *grandes turbulencias* in the Company's bosom, repeatedly criticizing Laínez and Polanco, Loyola's two most visible fellow workers of Jewish origin.

When he became Spain's first Jesuit Provincial, Araoz sent repeated pleas and warnings on the question to Rome, arguing that his considerable personal credit at the Spanish court was at serious risk. He received only rebuffs from Ignatius. Or this kind of reply by Polanco: "If in consequence of the attitude of Court and King you deem it impossible to admit converts in Spain, send them here as long as they be of good character: In Rome we do not trouble ourselves as to the origins of a man, only his qualities."

It was not just Spain's principalities and powers (even the ones he himself had created) who rose in opposition to the welcome, past and present, Ignatius extended to the Jews. Yet even in Rome he was not always obeyed on this point. The papacy usually showed Jewish communities an elementary humanitarian concern and—in Rome as in Avignon—extended a welcome to exiles. However, we should bear in mind that Pope Alexander VI (a Borgia, and therefore Spanish) had hailed the fatal decree of 1492 as a triumph, conferring on its authors, Isabella and Ferdinand (who had recently retaken Granada from the Moors), the style of "Most Catholic" monarchs.

And Paul IV, who was not Spanish but Neapolitan—and virulently anti-Spanish—could find no crueler insult for his enemies on the Iberian peninsula than calling them a "pile of Moors and Jews." At the top of his endless list of grievances against Loyola was the exasperation engendered in an anti-Semite of his stripe by the Jesuit's acknowledgment of Jewish greatness. And this Jew-lover was a Spaniard to boot!

The founder knew how to handle a Pope, even a brutal and vengeful one. What he could not do was turn the minds of his own countrymen upside down. And it was on this battlefield, that of the *humor español*, of the *error nacional*, that Ignatius, defying prejudices and great fears, was to suffer most cruelly.

"New Christians" lived in great numbers at Córdoba. A powerful family, the Counts of Priego, ruled the city. The Countess, who had made many bequests to the Company, felt entitled to demand that her protégés henceforth refuse to admit the conversos, whose "ignominy" was inevitably reflected on them. Araoz, Provincial of the Company in Spain, needed no further urging. He issued the requested ban—which the Superior General immediately rescinded.

But twenty years later Ignatius was no longer there to gauge the costs of his principled stand. The Father of the Jesuit school at Córdoba wrote to Loyola's second successor, Francesco Borgia, that although his school boasted more than 600 students, all of them noble, not one displayed the slightest intention of becoming a Jesuit: "Those possessing the vocation enter the Dominican monastery of San Pablo which, they say, is a community of *caballeros,* whereas in our school only Jews turn Jesuit. Prejudice on this point is so strong that whenever anyone is bold enough to join us, he is looked upon as one who has received the *san-benito.**"

Over the door of one of the three plain rooms at 5 Borgo San Spirito, in the shadow of the Vatican, occupied by the current Superior General of the Jesuits (who, in 1990, was Father Hans Peter Kolvenbach), hangs the tiny portrait of a man of striking features: Beneath the doctor's biretta and pale forehead, flaming eyes glitter over an aggressive, aquiline nose and an imperious mouth. A mood of meditative ardor, of focused ambition.

It is not the effigy of the founder but (and the tribute is meaningful) the portrait of his successor, Diego Laínez, the man whose task it was, for nine terrible years (1556 to 1565), to prove that Loyola's death was not also the Company's.

We have already caught glimpses of him, crisscrossing France and Italy, supporting Ignatius, preaching to the Venetians, indoctrinating the Romans, and intervening with well-schooled fury at the Council of Trent. Everything about him recalls Saint Paul, the man whose intensity, boldness, communicative talents, and ability to captivate turned the Gospel into a rule, and turned that rule into a law sometimes more constraining than the founder had apparently intended. A fighter and leader of fighters, a man indisputably great, worthy of his leader, and most assuredly regarded by Loyola (although the founder felt greater personal love for his first fellow disciples Favre and Xavier) as his greatest follower.

Why has the Catholic Church, which canonized the founder and his companion Francis, and beatified Pierre Favre, failed to single out Laínez for similar distinction? The answer probably lies in Diego's Jewish origins. There had of course been precedents, beginning with the Twelve Apostles. But they had not added insult to injury by being Jesuits into the bargain.

The origins of Loyola's first successor have given rise to the most heated argument among historians of the Company. Bearing in mind the racial passions that shook sixteenth-century Spain, it is obvious that doubts as to the *limpieza de sangre* of the direct successor to the founder of the order most closely tied to the Papacy was bound to whip up storms.

The family's Jewish origins are no longer questioned by serious historians, who differ only on their importance. One of his more recent biographers, the Spaniard Feliciano Cereceda,[6] still felt it necessary to refer to Laínez's *quasi cierta* ("almost certain") *ascendencia semita.* A pointlessly mealy-mouthed evasion.†

---

*A yellow tunic struck in front and back with a Saint Andrew's cross. It was worn by false converts sniffed out and punished by the Inquisition.
†Though admittedly made during the Franco regime.

The clearest evidence of Laínez's Jewishness is in his file in Rome's *Monumenta historica.*[7] It contains a letter from Father Rodríguez, censor for material about the second Superior General. The letter, which invokes Laínez's ancestry, warns of the "ignominy that could flow therefrom onto the Superior General and the Company."

Diego's parents, Juan Laínez and Isabel Gómez de León, were solid citizens of Almazán, a small town near Soria in Old Castile. Were they noble, or merely well-to-do burghers? Historians are undecided, some arguing that they were indeed members of the nobility and therefore certified members of the *limpieza de sangre* elite. Which is nonsense: As Cereceda himself wrote, such an argument cannot be applied to a period "when fusion of Jewish and blue blood amounted to a veritable invasion." He added that according to Cardinal de Mendoza's *Tizón de la nobleza española*, "There is scarcely a noble house in Spain untainted by such blood."[8]

Practicing the Catholic faith was no more effective than flaunting a family escutcheon, no matter how glorious, in erasing one's origins. But it is a fact that the Laínez family made a show of edifying piety. Diego's brothers and sisters included three priests and a cloistered nun, and his own behavior in Alcalá and Paris would be inexplicable had he not enjoyed a very sound religious training. All of which highlights the extraordinary complexity of the Judeo-Catholic question in sixteenth-century Spain, decades after Their Most Catholic Majesties' decree.

Some historians have actually attempted what Cereceda calls the "rehabilitation" of Laínez as a Christian. In 1908, for example, one Jesuit chronicler, Father Palacin, added his voice to those who argued that the family's noble status and links to certain "Spanish grandees" proved that the Laínezes were "Old Christians." (In fact, according to the best sources, particularly Father Antonio Astrain, author of the official history of the Jesuits in Spain, the "conversion of Diego Laínez's forebears reached back four generations.")

The silence observed on this point by Pedro de Ribadeneira, an intimate both of the first and the second General, and the biographer of both, is disturbing. Perhaps he makes a veiled reference to Laínez's Jewish origins when he alludes to his *nariz larga y aquilina* (large aquiline nose). His reticence has been on all other points invoked by those who deny the Jewishness of the Pope's delegate at the Council of Trent. A well-known Italian historian, Tacchi Venturi, sees in this silence a very Spanish sense of "propriety" over the question—and faults Ribadeneira as a historian.

Spanish chroniclers have reacted badly to this criticism. Eusebio Rey sees in it a mark of "Hispanophobia": In the name of what historical law, he asks, "must we reproach an author for not pointing out that Laínez's great-grandfather was a converted Jew?" Father Rey does not go so far as to say that Laínez's Jew-ishness was a mere detail, but almost. Which amounts to taking his readers for fools—as if the fact that the second Jesuit General, the bearer of Ignatius's torch, was of Jewish descent was not worthy of mention! As if it was not to the Company's honor to have surmounted the pressures of a dominant, not to say regnant, anti-Semitism and elected the best of its number without looking to his origins.

For if there is one hard proof of Laínez's Jewish origins, it is the fury of the Spanish court and the Archbishop of Toledo at his election to the position of Superior General. Countless historians have mentioned it, including Philip II's biographer William Thomas Walsh, who reminds his readers that the King, like his father the Emperor, employed considerable numbers of "New Christians" at court and in high public positions.

Truth exists only for those who believe in it. Everyone knew about Laínez's origins, or was in a position to find out. Yet the revelation of those origins, in a text destined almost half a century after his death for wide readership, ignited an enormous scandal. It generated such shock waves in the Church of Spain that the Company's Roman superiors were forced into humiliating surrender—proof positive that it had been Loyola's iron hand that bent his order to virtue on this point.

In 1614 and 1622 the first two volumes of *The History of the Jesuits* appeared. The task had been entrusted twenty years earlier to Reverend Father Orlandini. When Orlandini died it was taken over and completed by Father Paolo Sacchini, who is credited with its authorship. Given the controversies and "secrets" inevi-tably brought to light in any history of the Company's foundation and expan-sion, the undertaking was not entirely risk-free. And obviously, one of those risks lay in the secret of the origins of Loyola's successor and most influential fellow worker.

Paolo Sacchini published the story as he had received it from the mouths of companions of the second Superior General (he himself had entered the Com-pany only in 1570, five years after Laínez's death), particularly from Ribadeneira, who was freer with the spoken word on this subject than he was with the writ-ten. He had, moreover, inherited a very serene approach to the Judeo-Christian question from Loyola. Sure of his sources—and as a good Tuscan unfamiliar with the *humor español*—Sacchini was staggered by the denunciatory fury that greeted his book in Spain, particularly in Andalusia and Toledo (Cardinal Siliceo's city). Such as the following collective protest from the Jesuits of Toledo:

> The Province of Toledo, gathered in congregation, request with one
> voice of our Superior General [Mutius Vitelleschi, Loyola's fifth suc-
> cessor] that he order the erasure of what is said in the second volume

of the History of the Jesuits on the origins of Father Laínez. We request the withdrawal of such a great stain on the memory of such a Father.

Our Province insists that there be no more mention of it in the second edition, and that the Superior General immediately order the suppression of the page containing this insane filth, which sullies the whole Company, and replace it with a page attesting to the purity and nobility of the Father's lineage. We add some reasons that may incite His Fatherhood to consent to this request. Primo: What the History avers on the birth of this great man is in the first place false, as is confirmed by witnesses of unimpeachable honesty who have examined the question. Secundo: Even if this proved true, to set such a stamp of infamy on one who was among the founders of the Company would serve no purpose, but would cause great ill and would be certain sin. Tertio: This vile assertion affects not only Father Laínez but falls on all his family. . . . Among others the Marquis of Almazan, who does not blush to number the Father among his family, has been deeply offended.

Meaning that you could be a Jesuit and still be ignorant or unappreciative of Ignatius of Loyola . . .

Paolo Sacchini delivered an elegant response. On the first point raised by the good fathers of Toledo, he has no trouble producing the historical proofs of Laínez's Jewish origins, including those quoted above. On the second and third points, he reveals himself as a model of honesty, or rather of historical intelligence:

In the case of Laínez . . . history must respect facts, and not indulge itself through the satisfaction of its prejudices; it must reflect good and evil, commingled as in life itself; a historian who hides a fact susceptible of strife renders all the rest suspect and saps the authority of his work. And a Jesuit historian may thus indulge himself even less than others, given the astounding collection of phantasmagoria published on the matter of his Order.

Sacchini's conclusion lives up to his professional principles:

We are proud of our Laínez, whose so-called stain is ignominious only to minds both vulgar and stuffed with prejudices. It is our duty to make war on such prejudices and destroy them. Is it also ignominious to encounter Our Lord only at day's end? What possible stain survives in a man become the temple of God, the son of God, an heir of God, and a fellow inheritor of Christ?

Must we blush at thinking like the Apostle to the Gentiles? It is he who forbids the wild olive tree to look with disdain upon the broken branches of the domestic olive tree on which—through no merit of their own—the foreign branches have been grafted. How may a man who loves Christ be offended at seeing one of His own race approach Him?

. . . But I have not to plead the New Christians' cause. I wish only to make clear that I in no way repent what I have written about Laínez. As a Christian, his Jewish origin did not stamp him with ignominy but instead conferred upon him nobility, for he was not, like every one of us, a wild bough but a branch fallen from the original olive tree, and gently set back in place on the paternal trunk.

This model sermon failed to deter a certain school of Spanish historians from blowing mists of obfuscation around the "Laínez question" and around the whole subject of Jewish-Jesuit relations in sixteenth-century Spain. Consider the tone in which Father Feliciano Cereceda strives to gloss over the "painful behavior" of the framers of those Toledo protests of 1692. He links them all to the "disgust" voiced by Philip II's court at the election of the Company's second Superior General. For Cereceda, these objections stemmed from "a collective anti-Jewish psychosis then all-powerful in Spain"—which he admits "today may seem excessive." He then invokes anti-Semitic passages from Lope de Vega, Cervantes, and Quevedo, thus blithely equating such sallies (examples of which are scattered throughout literary works born of the imagination, with no need to open their accounts to the Church) with the solemn proclamation issued by an order founded by the man who never tired of proclaiming the original Jewishness of Christianity.

Cereceda goes still further. Having dug up these disparate signs of anti-Semitism (not difficult in the Europe of that day—France, for instance, gave asylum to just 3,000 of the 150,000 Jews driven from Spain at the end of the fifteenth century), he sees fit to quote this remark by the historian Gabriel Maura (not a Jesuit), author of the *Vida y Reinado de Carlos II:* "The phenomenon that (in a barbarous neologism imported from other idioms) has been called the race problem never existed in Spain . . . for these were groups of immigrants who, once converted and assimilated, aspired only to acquire patents of nobility, which were moreover sold to them at exorbitant prices."[9]

Having thus (with the help of a complaisant lay historian) exonerated the Toledo prelates of racial prejudice, Cereceda is nevertheless forced to acknowledge that Archbishop Siliceo's "Institute for Purity of Blood" somewhat skewed the factors in the equation. The name alone foreshadows the most murderous writings of the Frenchman Vacher de Lapouge and the Englishman Houston Stewart Chamberlain. And the anti-Semitic rage it invoked was echoed at the other end of sixteenth-century Europe in the sermons of the famous Polish Jesuit preacher Skarza, the man responsible for pogroms that sent waves of blood over the kingdom recently inherited by a French prince, the future Henry III. Even some of Luther's writings are not blameless on the question.

The Toledo operation did not remain confined to its native country. It bore other fruit. Although perfectly aware of the truth—he had personally asked Sacchini to shed full light on Laínez's origins—the sixth General, the Italian Mutius Vitelleschi, finally stooped to appease the angry men of Toledo in view of the "racial difficulties and the animosities then vexing Spain." He expunged from the official history all mention of the origins of Ignatius's first successor. Inevitably, such actions have fed the Black Legend of Jesuitry.

Was this a momentary slip? A political and locally contained act of appeasement? No. Worse was to come—the sorry (and consequence-laden) adoption by the Sixth General Congregation of the Company in 1593 of the so-called pure blood decree.

It is easy to argue that such acts were part and parcel of the "spirit of the times," that you must be totally without a sense of history to judge them by twentieth-century standards, and that other orders and other faiths (including the Reformed variety) acted no differently. But what damns the Jesuit fathers of 1593 is the fact that the founder himself had challenged the "spirit of the times" and Spain's *error nacional* in order to push through the breach and open the way. Courageously, clearly, Loyola had told them a truth ahead of its time—and his successors, despite their vow of obedience, blind to the light he shone on them, proved unworthy.

"For more than half a century," writes Eusebio Rey, "the Company of Jesus had resisted the Spanish national psychosis, but in the end the myth of *limpieza de sangre* prevailed within its bosom, just as it had done earlier in the other religious orders." But having made this honest admission, this Jesuit of Spain cannot resist pointing out that it was from Portugal that the virus of exclusion came—or returned—to Spain. Indeed in 1573 the court at Lisbon had notified Pope Gregory XIII that it intended to speak with the greatest anxiety of the probable election to the head of the Company of Father Polanco, "himself a New Christian or favorable to that cause." It added that if the promotion of "persons of this race" were countenanced, it would lead to the Company's downfall.[10] Threat, blackmail, or prophecy?

And so we move from the "Laínez case" to the "Polanco case." The secretary, the shadow (dare we say the Man Friday?) of Ignatius of Loyola, was in fact the second of the Company's "great Jews." True, his origins are more obscure than those of Laínez, and even more so than those of Juan de Avila or Francisco de Toledo, both first-generation converts. Nevertheless the Polancos, a Burgos family that had long been Catholic, were held to descend from New Christians. And the least that can be said is that Polanco, who wrote so many letters in the founding father's name, never questioned Loyola's determination to admit Jewish converts to the Company.

Thus the possibility of Polanco's accession to the Generalate after Francesco Borgia (who had not yielded an inch of ground on the Jewish question, and had spurned the constant pressures from Madrid with all the hauteur of a Spanish grandee) inevitably spread alarm among the New Christians' enemies in Portugal and Spain. And so, following a report by Father Alonso Sánchez on the converts' plans to "undermine" the Company from within—a document that received the formal support of the Inquisition and Philip II—the Jesuits took a step heavy with consequences. At their Fifth General Congregation, on December 23, 1593, they adopted a decree ordaining the expulsion of descendants of Jews and Muslims from the Company.

Some of the participants at the Congregation had asked that the Superior General (the Italian Claudio Acquaviva) be allowed to name exceptions to this exclusion, but they were in a minority. Thus, says Eusebio Rey, in 1593 "the Company of Jesus, or more accurately the Spanish and Portuguese Companies . . . was made finally subject to a statute of rigid *limpieza*, and one that granted no exceptions." Ignatius of Loyola's defeat at the hands of his "sons" was total.

Or would have been, had the voice of Pedro de Ribadeneira not been raised against this treason. However reluctant he had been to expand on the origins of Diego Laínez, Loyola's old comrade-in-arms now had the courage to invoke the Company's highest principles of moderation and loyalty. He delivered a twelve-point memorandum to General Acquaviva, enumerating "the reasons for leaving intact the rules of admission to the Company." It has the simplicity, the power, and the lucid stubbornness of Loyola's best writings.

The first reason is that such a step is contrary to our *Constitutions*. . . .

The second reason is that it is disloyal to the heart and spirit of Father Ignatius. . . .

The third, fourth, and fifth reasons are that it contradicts our Fathers General Laínez, Borgia, and Acquaviva* himself.

The sixth reason is that contrary to what is here alleged, people of this lineage have done no wrong to the Company.

The seventh reason is that this step runs contrary to the honor of the Company and of the whole Spanish nation.

*To whom the memorandum is addressed.

We shall spare the reader Ribadeneira's last five points. Those we have just quoted (above all the last one) should suffice. Thus, as the century came to an end, the man who could rightly claim to have been the closest and most constant companion of the founders declared the decision to expel Jewish converts was contrary to Company rules, to the spirit of the founders, and to honor. To which Superior General Acquaviva, who cannot have studied the decree without shame, or read Ribadeneira's words without remorse, added a letter to his Toledo colleagues telling them that their text was also contrary to "brotherly love."

Gradually, as its negative effects became apparent, reactions to the decree of exclusion took shape. Numerous observers, particularly in Aragón, reported that "many good vocations" had indeed been lost as a result of the ban. But when Ribadeneira, then in his eighties, appealed to Acquaviva to rescind the edict, the Superior General (a leader who had been more happily inspired on other occasions) replied: "Rather than rescind it, we would be wiser, with Christian prudence, to moderate it."

Which led in 1608* to a second major decree. While holding the line on across-the-board exclusion of "moros e judios qui son considerados como infames," the new decision provided for latitude toward those who were of "honest family" or who enjoyed an "honorable reputation" by allowing them to prove Christian ancestry going back five generations, on condition that matters be handled "con prudencia y exactitud."[11]

However sly and hypocritical this text (would the founder have read it with any less revulsion than its predecessor?), it helped normalize the situation by leaving the Company's door ajar for conversos. There were indeed many Jesuits who could show that their ancestors had converted at the time of Their Most Catholic Majesties' decree. But although its fangs had been drawn somewhat, the question of Judeo-Christian relations loomed over Spain for further long years. "The religious problem," said Eusebio Rey, "had been transmuted into a caste problem . . . , an exaggerated form of Spanish honor in the time of Philip IV."†

Was it then just a question of local folklore, a period curiosity? We should after all remember that the members of the Company of Jesus were not and are not just any group of *caballeros* and courtiers, merchants and pikemen, but men called to a supernatural mission by a man whose greatness lay precisely in his ability to discern what had to be condemned in the *humor español*. A man who, with a boldness staggering for his day, had denounced what Father Rey calls its "anti-evangelical nature." So much so that we could summarize the present chapter by calling it the battle of the Spanish Jesuits against Loyola.

*Fourteen years before the Toledo Jesuits protested against Sacchini's book.
†A famous sitter for Velásquez, and Louis XIV's father-in-law.

We shall see that relations between Jew and Jesuit were to take still stranger form elsewhere, with first conciliation and then persecution making of them an ambiguous, even tragic couple. It was at all events in France, in Paris, that Étienne Pasquier would soon write that "Jesuitry and Jewry had many things in common."

·VII·

LI MATEOU, THE CLOCK, AND THE MASTER OF HEAVEN

"A Land Peopled with Numberless Wise Men" • *Writing with a Paintbrush* • *Robed as a Bonze* • *The Whims of Wang Pan* • *"Speak Truth on This . . . and We Will Believe You on Religion"* • *The "Sage of the West" and Qu Rukuei* • *Confucian Man of Letters in Scarlet Silk* • *Emperor Wanli's Eunuchs* • *Confucianism and Christianity* • *A Tomb Near the Forbidden City*

UCH AS MICHELANGELO's benevolent God reaches a hand across the sky of the Sistine Chapel ceiling to bring Man to life, so did Francis Xavier, dying in December 1552 on the island of Sancian (today's Sangzhun) off the South China coast, designate his successor— or at least his successor's mission and the path he would have to follow.

Eight months earlier, telling his master Ignatius of Loyola of his decision to go to China, "which lies near Japan" and "from where one can travel to Jerusalem," he had presented his project in the following way: "China is an immense country, peopled with highly intelligent folk and numberless wise men. . . . They are so devoted to knowledge that the most learned among them is the noblest. . . . If God so wills, we shall describe in detail the affairs of China, how we have been received, and what opportunities this country offers for the propagation of our Holy Faith."[1]

Apart from that last point (which is of course fundamental), it is the work plan of a scientific expedition, an anthropological investigation, or a major news-gathering project: The accent is on information, intelligence gathering, and understanding as conditions for the progress of the faith. The Navarrese has left far behind him the spirit of the conquistador, of the harvester of souls of his Indian days. He simply puts the question, pregnant with his new respect for the Other, as to what kind of "opportunities this country offers."

Thus, by the time the forerunner's hand fell, exhausted, the mission had been defined: to go among this people of "wise men" in order to "describe in detail the affairs of China." The man brought to life by these words, like Man in the Sistine Chapel called into being by the Eternal One, would not be born until a few months after that decisive letter from Sancian, and only a few weeks before Xavier's death. His name was Matteo Ricci. Rarely had an arrow so faithfully obeyed the bow that sped it on its way.

Ricci would make of that faith his glory when he wrote in his *History of the Christian Expedition to the Kingdom of China* that he would never have tackled the project without crediting "the man who first undertook it, and who by dying and leaving his remains there took possession, as it were, of this conquest."[2]

But however fine it had been to foresee the greatness of the venture and to knock at the gates of China, it was even more admirable to enter. And more praiseworthy still to remain there, at the close of a sixteenth century in which all Europe was repeating the words uttered in 1579 by the Franciscan Francisco de Alfaro: "With or without soldiers, attempting to go to China is like trying to seize the moon."

It is common to hear of Chinese xenophobia. And in the case of South China during the Ming era, particularly Guangdong province, the word is not too strong. But before attempting to find a more appropriate term for the denizens of the Middle Empire, we might briefly survey the political-military climate on the empire's fringes as the century drew to a close—a century stunned by the audacious moves of an epic, voracious West that was bursting at the seams.

For nearly the whole of that century, tremendous waves had battered the Chinese fortress. Since Alfonso de Albuquerque reached it in 1511, the China Sea and its surrounding archipelagoes, from the Moluccas to Japan, had been crisscrossed by ships laden both with menace and with a greed that was all the more virulent for being fanned by implacable rivalry.

The Portuguese had blazed the trail. But the Castilians would never have dreamed of tolerating Portuguese hegemony. Between the people known as the "Spice Crusaders" and the "Cinnamon Hajji," commercial competition quickly deteriorated, as in South America, into territorial struggles. And, just as it had failed to smooth matters between Mexico and the Azores, the unification of the two Iberian crowns under Philip II in 1580 did nothing to stop the quarreling. The Portuguese held Goa and Malacca. The Spanish held Manila—where an atrocious massacre would shortly remind the people of Asia that the conquest of markets is never innocent, and would foreshadow other, similar acts.

Nor did these enterprises cool the blood of the Japanese* pirates in the China Sea, more dangerous than ever for the fact that as the century waned the Japanese islands came under the sway of increasingly enterprising leaders, such as Hideyoshi, who in 1595 carried war to Korea—with a further eye to China. To the West, it was true, the Great Wall held back Tartars and Mongols of every stripe. But eastward an ill wind blew, for the shores of the great Empire were powerless to stop the "Barbarians."

Its ineffectiveness was compounded by the fact that after two centuries of power the Ming dynasty was showing every sign of exhaustion. The decline seemed as irreversible as the monstrous obesity of the Emperor Wanli, condemned to an immobility that intensified year by year. As the Ming Empire awaited the collapse that would occur a half century later under the hammerblows of the Manchus, it lived corseted by mistrust and mesmerized by the swarms of "Barbarians" buzzing around it. What could they do except bolt all their doors to fend off Western cupidity?

Not that the Empire was or ever had been tight-sealed. Non-Chinese communities scratched a living here and there. They were Muslims and Jews, and were collectively known as *huihui*. The former, of whom there were many ("These Saracens are everywhere," wrote Ricci), came from Persia or India, or had arrived in the baggage trains of the Tartar dynasty. The second group, "the *huihui* who refuse violence," lived in very small communities huddled around a handful of synagogues, particularly in the Nanking region. As long as they obeyed the law they were apparently permitted to live undisturbed.

There were even Christians, almost all of them Syrian Nestorians, who had been condemned by the Council of Ephesus in 431 for proclaiming that Christ's dual nature implied opposition of the human and the divine. Patriarch Nestorius's banished supporters had then fled eastward, some to Persia, some beyond. The latter had been given asylum in Han China, and from the seventh century onward, under the Tang, had been allowed to build churches. A stele uncovered at Sin Ngan Fou in 1925 confirmed that Nestorianism flourished in the Han Empire. Since most of them were merchants, the Nestorians had settled mainly along the Silk Road. Marco Polo met some of them in the vicinity of Kashgar.

But these tiny islands posed no challenge to the powerful homogeneity of the

*So-called, although they were often Chinese.

Chinese citadel, any more than did the bold handful from the steppes of Central Asia or from the open sea who had briefly put down roots in the Middle Empire.

Since Marco Polo late in the thirteenth century, merchants and monks had crossed the Wall or landed on the south coast. A Portuguese ambassador named Pires had been received at Canton in 1517, but quickly expelled. Half a century later, emissaries from Lisbon had tried to outdo him and gain a foothold in Canton: They ended up in prison.

Nor had churchmen fared much better. Whether they came from Goa, New Spain (Mexico), or the Philippines, whether they were Portuguese, Spanish, or Italian, whether Franciscan, Dominican, or Jesuit, their Chinese career was quickly cut short. Nevertheless in 1554 the Dominican Gaspar de la Cruz, and later on the Portuguese Jesuit Nunez Barreto, had been able to assemble a few facts about the Empire. Even more successful was the Augustinian de Rada, coming from Manila, who in the wake of incidents provoked by a pirate named Limahong was permitted to spend a month in Fukien, whence he "brought back a Chinese library of some hundred volumes, with whose help he [had] drawn up a report on China."[3]

Yet the most interesting of these pioneers was a Jesuit, Francisco Perez, who around 1565 addressed a verbal plea to the Canton authorities:

> I am a master of learning, and travel the world teaching God's religion. . . . And since I have heard that the Kingdom of China is vast and contains many Masters and wise men, I come to ask of Your Lordships license and permission to converse with them that we may mutually communicate to one another our teachings; furthermore, I request leave to live on land, in a small house, for as long as you may judge fitting. . . . Moreover I am already advanced in years [fifty-seven by Chinese reckoning] and wearied by sickness, and the sharp cold at sea would surely bring on a new infirmity: In this you would be granting me great charity.[4]

When the Cantonese mandarins asked to be told the faculty in which he was master, he told them through the interpreter that he was master of the things of God and the manner in which men might save themselves. . . . Which satisfied them so completely that they at once ordered a servitor to give the father "a piece of pink damask to wear around his neck as a sign that he was a Master and a man of God. . . . Then they asked whether he brought books with him: He replied that he had only the Breviary: They all stared. One asked whether he spoke the Chinese tongue. When he said no, the mandarin told him that for this reason he would not be able to travel in China because he would need an interpreter, but if he did speak it, he would encounter no obstacle."

A promising start, and not the slightest hint of xenophobia. Only one condition was imposed on his preaching: that he learn Chinese. A condition that Ricci would bear in mind as he prepared to enter through the door Perez* had opened.

Already, cracks were appearing in the wall of interdictions raised by Beijing, First the Portuguese—who offered such tantalizing goods!—had received permission to take part in Canton's annual spring fair. Then, in return for services rendered to the Cantonese authorities in their struggle against the Chinese-Japanese pirates, they were permitted to settle permanently on a tiny peninsula ("an islet," wrote Ricci) called Amacao, from the name of the goddess Ama (*cao* means "strait"). It was simplified to Macao. This small trading post would be the springboard for European expansion into China. But for a long time the "islet" seemed to be cut off from China by an impassable moat. The Chinese residents of Macao were seen as uprooted people, reduced to the role of interpreters and go-betweens, despised by the mainlanders. To say someone was "from Macao" was the supreme insult, and meant he could only be a Japanese agent or European spy.

The Manila Franciscans were the first to reside there, followed by the Jesuit Sánchez. In 1587, at the urging of Alessandro Valignano, Jesuits planted firmer roots there, in the "House of Saint Martin." During his stay of nearly a year in Macao, from 1578 to 1579, Valignano at once saw the extraordinary advantages of this window into mainland China and the possibilities it offered, on condition that the House of Saint Martin were converted into a linguistic and ethnographic institute. For everyone was saying that converting the Middle Empire would be harder than "whitening an Ethiop" *(lavare Aethiopem)*.

It would be inconceivable to attempt to describe Christian penetration of China without mentioning the decisive part played by the Neapolitan giant, Alessandro Valignano, the man who passed the torch from Francis Xavier to Matteo Ricci. It was on the basis of the Navarrese missionary's correspondence, and on observations apparently gathered by Francisco Perez, that Father Valignano, the Company's "visitor" for Asia, drew the broad lines of the future mission, and chose its themes and actors. He had realized during his stay in Macao that its two basic features should be a solid linguistic framework—in other words mastery not only of the South Cantonese dialect but of Mandarin, the language of power—and deep assimilation into Chinese culture.

But let us listen to Ricci:

> Alexander Valignanus, visitor for all the Indies, took ship to go and
> see those beyond the Ganges; and, having finally made land at
> Amacao . . . and having more diligently considered the matter of

---

*Who died twenty years later in India, without being able to take advantage of the proffered hospitality.

China, he rekindled the zealous desires and the extinguished ardor of this voyage. . . . From the extent of the empire, the nobility of its people, the widespread state of peace already several centuries old, the prudence of the magistrates and administrators of the Republic, he calculated, and not vainly, that the Chinese, ingenious and given to the study of all good arts and sciences, might well be persuaded to let live in their kingdom a few persons excelling in virtue and in letters, and particularly those now able to speak the natural language of their country and possessing knowledge of their letters. And more than that, he also entertained fair hope that one day the statutes of our Most Holy Faith might prove agreeable to this people, since not only do these statutes not disturb the political administration of the republic, but on the contrary render it good service.[5]

The Neapolitan Jesuit's biography of Francis Xavier reveals the part he believed China should play in the propagation of Christianity in Asia: Three chapters are devoted to the Middle Empire. The book is a panegyric that falls far short of true ethnography; but it proves that the Company's pioneers were now even farther than Marco Polo from the contempt or sarcasm that apparently marked first contacts between Europeans and Chinese.

The subject will arise again when we examine Matteo's first reports in Macao: Far from seeming backward or worm-eaten, late Ming China is seen, or glimpsed, by these candidates for the great journey as a universe of order and peace, a vast empire of the intelligence. And it was this promised land that Matteo Ricci proposed, by his intelligence alone, to conquer.

He was an Italian born on the Adriatic coast in the little city of Macerata, near Ancona, an enclave of the Papal States, on October 6, 1552, two months before the death of Francis Xavier. His family was well-off (his father was a pharmacist) and of strong Catholic tradition. Matteo was not yet ten when the Jesuits opened their college in Macerata. There he did his pre-university studies before going to Rome, whose wounded majesty hurt him to the core. He would remain forever marked by its vestiges of Greco-Roman culture, and by its synthesis in the waning sixteenth century of Catholic spirituality and the civilization rediscovered by the Renaissance. At nineteen, he entered the Jesuit novitiate in Rome.

At the Roman college, which Montaigne called "Christianity's finest seminary," he was taught by Claudio Acquaviva, who would become "his" Superior General, the fourth in line after Loyola. He would later say he "was born there." His letters bear witness to his basic concern to make life easier for his non-Italian fellow novices who were somewhat lost in these surroundings. Already a passion for the Other.

The Spiritual Exercises *dictated to Ignatius. The allusion to the Virgin Mary is eloquent, as is the style.*

Archives of the Province of France, Society of Jesus, Vanves.

The Casa y Solar, where Ignatius of Loyola was born, near Azpeítia.
Private collection.

Pierre Favre, first of Loyola's companions, master of philosophy and Greek.
Archives of the Province of France, Society of Jesus, Vanves.

Pope Paul III accepting the oath of the "Ignatians."

Lauros-Giraudon Archives. Bibliothèque Nationale, Paris.

The Gesù, Roman seat of the Company. A prototype of the style commonly—and wrongly—called "Jesuit."

Archives of the Province of France, Society of Jesus, Vanves.

*This portrait of Ignatius, painted in 1543, is the only one executed
during his lifetime.*

Private collection, Sondrio Museum, Valtelina.

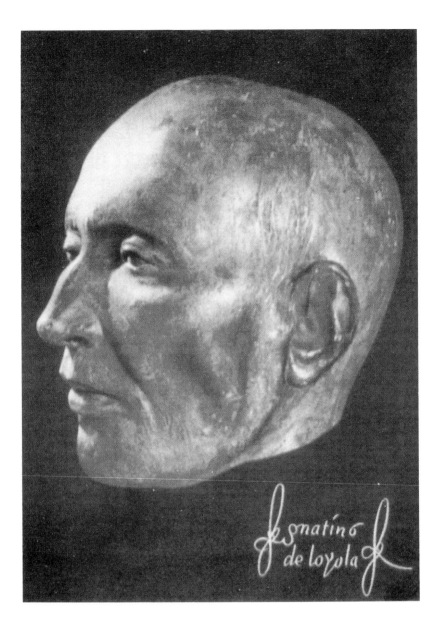

Death mask of Ignatius.
Brother Gebhardt Fröhlich collection.

Brushed with fable, the Jesuits arrive in Japan.
Archives of the Province of France, Society of Jesus, Vanves.

*Francis Xavier, emissary of the "molder of men," as sketched by
Gidinho de Eredia at Goa in 1542.*
Private collection.

Queen Catherine of Portugal, the "Little Infanta" who became the
Company's most fervent sponsor.

Archives of the Province of France, Society of Jesus, Vanves.

Joan of Aragon—Raphael's model, Loyola's friend, unhappy wife.
Giraudon Archives. Louvre, Paris.

Margaret of Parma, bastard daughter of the Emperor Charles V, in a portrait by Antonio Moro. A powerful advocate of the fledgling Company's cause.

Gemäldegalerie, Berlin.

Joan of Spain, history's only "Jesuitess," in a portrait by Antonio Moro.
Prado, Madrid.

Diego Laínez, the intellectual giant among Loyola's disciples.
"*Les Fontaines*" *library, Society of Jesus, Chantilly.*

REPUBLIC OF CHINA

18 1583–1983

念紀年週百四華來竇瑪利

Matteo Ricci commemorative stamp, People's Republic of China. Li Mateou as august mandarin, with towering headgear and flowing beard.
Archives of the Province of France, Society of Jesus, Vanves.

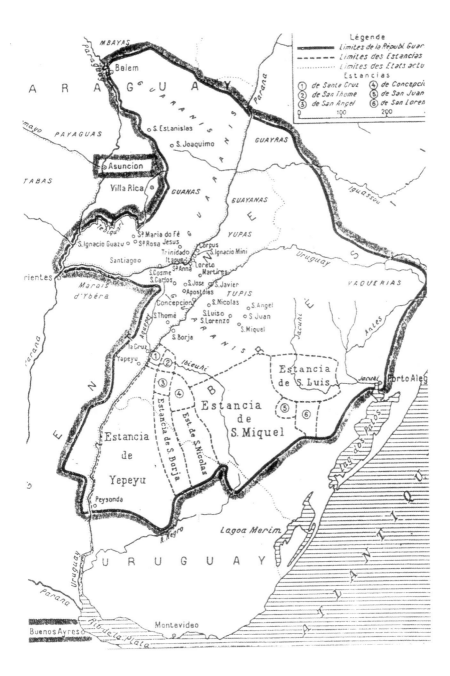

Map of central South America, showing the extent of the Guaraní reductions.
Archives of the Province of France, Society of Jesus, Vanves.

Plan of a reduction (the Candelaria Mission in Paraguay), with the accent on the "ideal" or utopian aspect of the enterprise.
Lauros-Giraudon Archives. Bibliothèque Nationale, Paris.

Two teachers of genius inspired his education and remained his models: the German mathematician Christophonus Clavius, whose name will come up again, and the Italian theologian Roberto Bellarmino, peerless advocate of an enlightened Christianity, of tolerance and joy ("my saint," Goethe later called him). What better guru for a man nurtured on Roman humanism and about to go out and meet Confucian wisdom?

But this school of pluralistic benevolence was no hedonistic academy preparing its pupils for an undemanding apostolate. At the very first opportunity to leave (the visit to Rome of the procurator of the Eastern missions, who sought volunteers), Ricci put his name down. Then, refusing even the comforts of a last visit to his family in Macerata, he hastened to Portugal, where the college in Coïmbra trained missionaries for the Far East. It was May 1577, and he was twenty-five.

In Portugal, during the last days of the reign of Don Sebastião, who would soon leave to shatter his dreams and Portuguese power in Morocco, he followed the lectures of one of the high priests of Jesuit thinking, Luis de Molina. He also met three of his future companions in Asia, Rodolfo Acquaviva, Francesco Pasio, and the man whose lieutenant he would become, Michele Ruggieri. With them and ten other Jesuits, Matteo Ricci took ship for Goa on March 29, 1578. Six months on the high seas, rounding the Cape of Good Hope and leaving Mozambique to westward, haunted by scurvy, typhus, and storms, and shut into coffin-like "cabins" in which they could neither sit nor stand . . .

Ricci would spend more than three years in India, from 1578 to 1582, from Goa to Cochin and back to Goa. There he taught Greek and then grammar, while completing his own theological studies preparatory to taking Holy Orders. It would be tempting (since he seems to have seen India as merely a stepping stone to the Chinese civilization for which he thirsted) to think that, like Francis Xavier, he "sidestepped" the Indian world. But the truth is that, assigned by one of his superiors to write a history of the Portuguese Indies, he examined and wrote many reports on the customs of the Malabars and the conversions that took place along the Fisher Coast—and much more on the brief mission of his friend Rodolfo Acquaviva to the court of Akbar, the "Great Mogul."

But nothing says more about Ricci's intellectual qualities than the critical care with which he handled the facts that emerged from his research, in which (true to the spirit of his times) half-belief in the miraculous blends with the most adventurous apologetics. Witness this letter to his superior, Father Mattei:

> Your Reverence doubtless knows all things better than I. But I am *in situ*, and observe matters with my own eyes. . . . It is better to say nothing of the Indian kings than to hazard a conjecture. . . . Given my desire to see your writings truly flawless, I urge Your Reverence to

decide nothing without obtaining our opinion. . . . If you will agree, I shall draw up a map and a description of all these countries. . . . I can assure you that because of the charts we have drawn up . . . the account I write for Your Reverence will be much more accurate than anything published heretofore. . . . For Your Reverence should be aware that the commentaries and correspondence from India and Japan abound in obvious mistakes.

Just by writing that letter, Matteo Ricci justified his long stay in India, where he was at least able to sharpen his sense of observation and his critical spirit.

But India was already far behind, and China beckoned: His traveling companion Michele Ruggieri, who had stayed less than a year in India and had been living in Macao for thirty months, had requested the presence at his side of this excellent mathematician. Father Valignano, based in Japan, approved the idea, and in April 1582 Ricci set sail for Malacca and then Macao, where he landed, in poor health, on August 7.

In the gloomy, dilapidated building that is still the Casa de São Martinho, and that Valignano had decided to turn into the focal point of his experiment in dialogue with China, Matteo Ricci found Ruggieri deeply discouraged. He was sapped by his isolation (he did not get on with the two Portuguese fathers who shared the house with him) and wearied by the pitfalls of the Chinese language, which he still scarcely spoke. He was exasperated at the obstacles raised by the imperial administration to his plans to take up residence on the mainland—where he was allowed to make only the most fleeting of appearances. Whence the cry of alarm Ricci transmitted to Valignano: "These three years in Macao have been a semi-martyrdom for Father Ruggieri."[6]

But the newcomer threw himself passionately into the study of Chinese and, at the request of Alessandro Valignano (who had stopped in Macao on his way from Japan to Goa) into preparation of a broad account of China intended for inclusion in the book the visiting Jesuit was writing about Francis Xavier. Then, in December, a strange message reached Macao. It was signed by the Viceroy of Guangdong, resident in Zhaoqing (which Ricci spelled Sciauquin). Hearing that Matteo Ricci had brought from Goa a clock intended for presentation to an imperial dignitary, he invited Father Ruggieri to bring it to him, at the same time forwarding "letters patent" entitling him to settle in his own city and to build two houses there, one for worship, one for living in. Ruggieri responded right off the bat. Accompanied by Pasio and a Portuguese brother named Mendes, he landed at Zhaoqing in early December, leaving Ricci to run the House of Saint Martin, to sweat over his Chinese lessons, and to work on his description of China.

Their hopes were quickly dashed. A few weeks after the Jesuit settled in

Zhaoqing the Viceroy was stripped of his functions. Was it for admitting these "foreign bonzes" into China? At any event, his enemies must have used this argument against him. But the fact is that the newcomers' expulsion was ordered, and they returned hangdog to Macao.

Was this a manifestation of truly Chinese sectarianism, intolerance, fanaticism? Let us try to imagine the reception a Buddhist monk—bent on preaching his holy beliefs—might have received from the governor of Marseille under the Most Christian Louis XIV! Or simply a Jesuit harboring the same ambitions in Amsterdam! A Lutheran pastor in Padua!

In short, the first attempt at permanent implantation on Chinese soil did not last four months. But it opened up channels, and established Michele Ruggieri as the pioneer in China of the "inculturation" that Francis Xavier had first essayed in Japan—"silk rather than cotton!"—and which Valignano hoped to make the golden rule of Jesuit action in Asia.

For in fact, a month after his fleeting sojourn in Shiuhing had begun, Ruggieri sent his companion Mendes back to Macao to report on the mission's happy beginnings. Ricci and his associates at the House of Saint Martin looked on in amazement as the messenger came ashore: The Portuguese brother had exchanged his European garb for a long Chinese gown. The explanation for this surprising transformation was provided in a letter in which Ruggieri described initial contacts to his assistant in Macao. The visitor had first told the viceroy the reasons for his presence:

> Having learned in his own country how good were the Chinese, how gentle and peaceful their temper, with so many excellent rites and customs, so much learning, so many books inspired by reason and so many centers of virtuous living . . . he had greatly desired to come there and learn and know the greatness of this kingdom by living in the midst of so virtuous a nation. Such was the motive that had led him to leave his country and journey here, the voyage lasting three years and passing through many seas and dangers; but since he could not do it in Macao, he requested leave to live on the mainland, there to live and die. In which the Viceroy beheld great honor for the Chinese, judging moreover that to welcome such persons would make civilized and reasonable beings of them, who were now but wild and akin to beasts.[7]

Then Ruggieri and Paolo called on the general commanding the Guangdong garrison and discussed the kind of life they should adopt: "As we were speaking of raiment, he himself drew a bonnet for us, saying that the Viceroy and [all the] mandarins wished us to wear the clothing of their 'padres' in Beijing . . . who are most respected and esteemed."

Imitate Buddhist monks? Ruggieri at once decided that it was the best way of gaining local status in this empire he dreamed of settling in. He and his companions had their heads and faces shaved and put on the long brown robe, tied in the front, of Buddhist monks—"to make themselves all things to all men, *ut Christo Sinas lucrifacerem* (to gain profit for Christ in China)."

Thus, even before his leader returned from China, Matteo Ricci received from him a lesson in "inculturation" which would have decisive influence on his contacts with Chinese civilization—although he would add first refinements and then wholesale revision to such rules of conduct.

Matteo had also moved boldly ahead with his initiation into Chinese culture. With the help of two Portuguese of mixed blood named Manuel and Antonio, he launched into his apprenticeship in Chinese, whose pitfalls he described in a letter to his teacher in Rome, Father Fornari:

> I have applied myself to the Chinese language and can assure Your Reverence that it is a different thing from Greek or German. . . . The spoken tongue is prey to so many ambiguities that many sounds mean more than a thousand things, and sometimes there is no more difference between the one and the other than in pronouncing the sound with the voice raised or lowered in four kinds of tone. Which is why, when speaking among themselves, they write down what they are saying in order for their meaning to be understood, for in writing things are distinct from one another.
>
> As to the alphabet, it is a thing one would not believe in had one not seen and tried it as I have. There are as many letters as there are words or things, so that their numbers appear to exceed sixty thousand.*
>
> Their manner of writing more closely resembles painting, which is why they write with a brush in the manner of our painters. The advantage of this is that all nations possessing this writing may understand one another through letters and books even though their languages greatly differ.[8]

But the contribution he made during these years went well beyond his linguistic achievements: It rested more on his mission (entrusted to him by Valignano) to collate, assess, and use the information acquired with a view to the "Chinese chapters" of his biography of Saint Francis Xavier. Sometimes published separately under the title *Treatise on the Wonders of China*, beneath the signature of Alessandro Valignano, who was the editor of the whole book, it is in a sense a "State of the Chinese Nation" and a mirror of the state of mind of these would-be missionaries.

*He would later pull back from this figure: With only ten thousand characters at your command, you were a great man of letters.

Was this an idyllic, uncritical vision? Of course. But its picture of hope reveals, not only in its title but in its content, that a man like Ricci (no matter how much he admired Greco-Roman culture and its Catholic variant) undertook his mission in a spirit of respect and esteem for the civilization of Asia, convinced that "nothing in the world is greater" than this empire still closed to the world.

Ricci's description of China, written for Valignano in 1582 with Ruggieri's help, opened with an unambiguous declaration: "China is the most important and the wealthiest thing in the East, all other of whose kingdoms it surpasses. In many points it resembles the wealth and perfection of our Europe, and in many it outshines it."[9]

The pioneer Sinologist then demonstrated his claim by listing "seven points of excellence" and "five points of disorder." It would be difficult to be more Jesuit in exposition. First, excellence:

One. It is the greatest state whose obedience any single king ever commanded. . . . [Oh, that Jesuit yearning for a centralizing crown in India and Japan!]

Two. It is the most populous . . . with more than sixty million folk paying taxes. . . .

Three. There is no kingdom more fertile and better provisioned. Although the Chinese are bigger eaters than Europeans, they have enough to satisfy them all . . . at very good prices. . . .

Four. Public wealth is equaled by that of no other kingdom: Silver and gold mines abound. . . . The Emperor's revenues are greater for him alone than for all the kings and lords of Europe, and perhaps Africa, combined. . . .

Five. No region appears to equal it for coolness and peace, so much so that it seems a thing painted rather than a product of nature. . . .

Six. The inhabitants are the most industrious in the world; even the halt and the blind earn their bread, and one sees few beggars. . . .

Seven. It is the most peaceful and best governed of discovered countries.[10]

This latter point in particular drew the Jesuits' attention. They ascribed it to the fact that employment and power were linked to education: whence the number and standard of schools and universities, the fact that the Chinese "possess more books than we in Europe do, all printed, and treating of all the Sciences, astronomy, mathematics, medicine, and others."

Could this then be an earthly Paradise?

No, answer Valignano, Ricci, and Ruggieri,

. . . because they lack the principal bounty, which is knowledge of God and of His holy religion. That is why the order and prudence that they maintain in the matter of governance are not enough to prevent all manner of grave disorders. These are:

One. The many injustices and tyrannies perpetrated by the mandarins. . . .

Two. Mistrust of the profession of arms, which induces cowardice. . . .

Three. Their distance from all that is foreign, which means that from this point of view the populace is the end of the world. . . .

Four. The multitude of brigands and of pirates, even though the squadrons patrolling the coasts could cause even more harm than they. . . .

Five. Monstrous vices, such as that against nature and the sin of gluttony, to such a degree that as gifted as they are for prudence and discretion in government, so are they crude and blinded toward God, the welfare of their souls, and the things of the next world.[11]

(That pederasty and gluttony unfitted a man for metaphysics is a claim seemingly contradicted at countless points in the history of the world's philosophies.)

From this passage, most toothsome and auguring well for the great endeavor contemplated by the Macao fathers, it emerges that the admiration they felt for the empire (of which only Ruggieri had the smallest experience) was based not on antiquity or exoticism, nor on morals, nor on the supposed wealth of this nation, but on the organization of its cities, its social harmony, the maintenance of peace (*pax Sinica*), and on the observation they initially made and later discarded, but which was their starting hypothesis: that it was the realization of what Plato had only been able to imagine, a "republic of philosophers." What more hopeful point of view, what more humanistic predispositions ever inspired a "missionary" enterprise?

It would be satisfying to think that this exemplary frame of mind now led Ricci and Ruggieri to benefit from a surprising and hopeful turn of events. After such a declaration of love, how could the country to which it was addressed fail to open itself to them? Matteo Ricci preferred to see in it the "finger of the Almighty."[12] But whether by merit or miracle, it was indeed astonishing when, a few weeks after the crestfallen return of the missionaries, the Macao fathers received a call from a mere palace guard of the same Viceroy who had just expelled them. He bore an authorization for them to take up residence in Zhaoqing.

This scarcely conformed to that admirable philosophical order with which the father's report had credited China. Could this "halbardier" be merely scrounging a tip? Such was the start of the vast "Christian expedition" to the kingdom of China! But as we have seen, blackmail had lain at the heart of Francis Xavier's entry into Japan.

In short order (and this time with Ricci jumping the gun on Ruggieri), they were off to Zhaoqing, and straightaway received not by the Viceroy but by Governor Wang Pan. Kneeling in their monks' robes, they begged him to grant them, as "religious men, drawn by the Empire's fame to journey three or four years from the farthest corners of the West, the right to build there two small houses, and to worship God in one of them until their dying day."[13]

The august official replied that "he doubted not of their virtue" and that "his first sight of them inspired him to take them under his protection." Which was done. They were given a field by the stream that watered the town. On it a tower, known as the "flowering tower," had recently been erected, and there they built their tiny house and the church they called the Temple of the Holy Saints' Flowers. They had their foothold in China; the great adventure could begin. What disaster or what triumph lay ahead?

Matteo Ricci had just turned thirty. Tall and thin, but of robust constitution, he had overcome painful "colonial" maladies in India and at the start of his sojourn in Macao. Henceforth he would be free of them. He was a glutton for work and indefatigably cheerful, surrounding himself with a surfeit of acquaintances and gifted with a memory that would have seemed monstrous had it not been medicated and strengthened by his own methods, to which we shall be referring later on.

All eyewitnesses and all who spoke with him confirm that he projected intense dignity, an aura of simple greatness, what the sages of ancient Rome called *auctoritas*. Indeed the sages seem to have designated Ricci to display to the Middle Empire the image of a West reshaped by Christianity but recalled by the Renaissance to its intellectual and esthetic origins.

Matteo Ricci was the perfect man of culture, a polymath versed in all things, mathematics and literature, philosophy and poetry, mechanics and astronomy. Not for nothing was he the pupil of Christophonus Clavius, Roberto Bellarmino, and Luis de Molina. But he denied that he was a theologian, although others say he was. And as we shall see, in his hands the exact sciences as well as morals and logic would be turned into the weapons of apologetics.

Was he eaten up from the very start by a "hunger for the East," by a fevered expectation of the China Francis Xavier had known in his last months? Apparently not. It was rather a huge appetite for knowledge and ideas, a tireless reaching out to the Other—if not Indian (for we have seen him disconcerted rather than attracted by that first encounter), at least to the Chinese, and thereafter bewitched, inspired. Knowledge first and foremost, with his apostolate apparently only the crown.

So here they were in China. Here they were, grappling barehanded with the biggest empire in the world, an empire bristling with prohibitions. Here they were in this promised and long inaccessible land—Michele Ruggieri, who had already made a few brief calls, and Matteo Ricci, who had so far known only the tumbledown outskirts of Macao.

Like his master, the newcomer wore a gown "reaching to his heels and with very long sleeves" and had shaved his head and face, like the bonzes. Both of them kowtowed in triple prostration before Governor Wang Pan, knocking their foreheads on the ground. When the governor led them to the field where they were to build their house, and they asked him for a little more land on which to construct their church, he was astonished to find that God could be worshipped in any but the Chinese way. But he said good-naturedly to his mandarins, "We shall build them a temple and they can set there the images of whatever god they desire."[14]

Curiously enough, Ricci's *History* gives us no description or evaluation of the importance of Zhaoqing, the capital of Guangdong. We learn only that the town was watered by a "large stream," and that from his capital the Viceroy imposed taxes on eleven towns. But nothing about population size, trade, or customs: timid beginnings indeed for a master anthropologist!

But a very interesting note on their reception: "The people here never having seen foreigners, we stir derision and astonishment. . . . When we walk in the street, we must do so in haste lest our way be obstructed by the multitude of onlookers. We are given a thousand names, of which the commonest is 'foreign devils.' But distinguished people honor us greatly and come with great politeness to our house and our chapel."

But one anecdote makes us pause to reflect on the "innate viciousness" of the people of Guangdong, a southern province "numbered ignominiously by the others as being among the barbarians," who—already so wary of the foreigners at their doorstep—convinced themselves that the Portuguese "made off with children so as to eat them." Father Ruggieri having returned to Macao to collect alms for completion of their house, neighborhood urchins got into the habit of showering the fathers' hermitage with stones. A servant of Ricci's grabbed one of the boldest and locked him up. A crowd at once gathered to condemn the kidnapping . . . and perhaps worse. Matteo Ricci was hauled before the magistrate and charged with being not only a barbarian but a cannibal.

Would he be "interrogated" by means of a public flogging—a common custom here—and thenceforth dishonored, his mission universally disavowed? His grasp of Chinese was still uncertain: Unnerved, he botched his story and lost face. But one of the servants hit on the idea of presenting as evidence a handful of the stones the children had rained on the house. And three old men working in surrounding fields came to testify in favor of the accused. Whose only duty now, as he knelt with his forehead in the dust, was to beg the judge not to inflict more than thirty strokes of the cane on his slanderers.

Could he now begin to preach Christian doctrine? On the altar of their little church, they had placed a charming picture of Mary with the Infant Jesus in her arms. The picture enchanted visitors. But was it not perhaps misleading? The Chinese soon spread the word that "these long-robed barbarians have a woman for a God." They had to substitute an effigy of Christ for the excessively charming picture of Mary, although as we shall see this too had its disadvantages. Meanwhile, Matteo Ricci launched into a translation of the Decalogue and an abbreviated catechism into "the Mandarin tongue." Until now, Christian texts had been translated only in Latin characters. So hard did he work that within a year he was able to propose a reading to Governor Wang Pan, a widely read man, who said he was most tempted.

However, their first convert was not someone from the governor's world of letters (to which Ricci would tie his and Christianity's destiny in the empire). In his words:

> The pride of the Chinese had not yet lowered itself to the point
> at which they might seem ready to receive a foreign religion that
> none of their fellow citizens had ever embraced. Thus the first to
> profess the Christian faith in the kingdom of China was of the lowest
> orders. . . .
>
> This man, racked by an incurable illness, and for whom the physi-
> cians had no hope, had been ejected from his house by his own par-
> ents and left to lie on the ground in public, because his parents could
> scarcely feed themselves. Having learned of this, our fathers sought
> him out and asked him whether he wished to receive a law that—his
> body being already despaired of—would guide his soul to the safe ha-
> ven of eternal felicity. Whereupon he answered courageously that this
> law seemed most pleasant to him if it occasioned in his own kind
> such acts of compassion. The Fathers therefore had their servants
> erect for him a rustic but tidy cabin where they took care of all his
> needs, and together they taught him the chief points of the Christian
> faith. And as soon as he appeared sufficiently instructed, he received
> the first baptism in the kingdom of China, and then, to lose none of
> the innocence he had received in becoming the first fruits of the Chi-
> nese kingdom to be offered to God, he flew up to Heaven, as we have
> good reason to hope, a few days later!

With its strong overtones of Saint Francis, the story is beautiful as it stands. But there was better still to come, spiced with local color:

So that His servants should not chance to lose even the smallest merit accruing to them from so pious an act, the Lord granted that the deed be attacked by evil tongues. Some therefore declared that these foreigners had perceived from the visage of this man that he had a most precious stone hidden inside his head, which was why they had offered such kindness to the living man, in order that his corpse should be in their power so that they could extract from it this jewel of great price.[15]

But by now Ricci and Wang Pan had formed a personal relationship founded on their common love of books: Every visitor to the house asked to be shown their "gilt-bound" books of canon law, judging that so fine an outward appearance could not but harbor a noble science. For, notes Ricci, "the Chinese are veritable gobblers of books," which meant that "the chief points of our faith can be more properly explained through writing than words."[16] A whole strategy was thus evolved between "peoples of the book." But it was on different ground—cartography—that Matteo made his first conceptual breakthrough.

There hung in the hallway of the house a cosmographic description in European characters. Chinese men of letters studied it with pleasure, and when they learned that the disposition of the whole world could be seen and understood in this description, they greatly desired to be able to read it in Chinese characters. For the Chinese, who had practically no commerce with foreign peoples, were grossly ignorant of the parts of the world. Their own cosmographic tables bore the title of universal description of the whole world [but] reduced the extent of the earth to their own fifteen provinces; and on the seas painted around they set a few small islands, adding the names of the few kingdoms of which they might have heard, all of which kingdoms taken together would scarcely equal the smallest province of the Chinese Empire, which is why they have not hesitated to adorn their empire with the same name as the whole universe, calling it Dianha, which is to say everything under the heavens.

Thus, hearing and seeing that their China was confined to a corner of the East, they wondered at this description of the universe as something unheard of by them, and desired to read what was written on it to judge the truth thereof. So the governor advised Father Matteo Ricci to arrange with his connivance to have the table speak Chinese. . . .

[Ricci] applied his intelligence to this description, which was not at variance with his design of preaching the Gospel, knowing full well that one has not always made use of the same means in order—according to divine disposition—to draw a people to the faith of Jesus Christ. And in truth, by this first spark, several among the Chinese were drawn into the Church's net.*

Neither will I forget what he hit upon to win the good graces of the Chinese. They believe that the sky is round yet hold that the earth is square, at the center of which they readily believe their Empire to be set. They accordingly bore it ill that their China should be thrust by the geographers into a remote extremity of the Orient. And although they were not yet able to understand the mathematical proofs whereby it could easily be demonstrated that the earth and the sea form a globe, and that by the nature of circular forms that globe could have neither beginning nor end, he somewhat altered our project, relegating to the right and left margins of his geographic description the first meridian on the Fortunate Isles, in such manner that the kingdom of China, to their great pleasure and satisfaction, appeared at the center of the description. One could not at that time have found a more appropriate device for disposing this people to receive the mysteries of our religion.[17]

To the innocent telling of this masterpiece of Jesuit strategy (was it not the perfect "pious fraud"?), Ricci adds a most penetrating observation: that this chart, showing the immensity of the lands and seas separating China and Europe, had the effect of mitigating whatever fear they might have of possible invaders, and for that very reason of strengthening chances of winning the Chinese to Christianity, "for we are hindered by nothing so much as these shadows of suspicion."

The prestige of Matteo Ricci—whose mission was daily acquiring a more personal character, owing to the attractiveness of his personality and to Ruggieri's increasingly frequent absences —was not founded only on his books and maps and his growing mastery of Mandarin Chinese. It was based too on what he called his *cosette* (bits and pieces): With the help of an industrious Indian brother from Goa, he busied himself making metallic spheres, sundials, prisms, and clocks, modeled on those he had brought with him in 1583. Governor Wang Pan had said of them that "no gift could more greatly please the Emperor." And nothing did more to nourish Ricci's legend, leading some to see him as a magician of clockwork and others as the prince of astrologers or as a wizard of alchemy.

But if his glory was spreading in the still confined framework of Guangdong, the fruits of his evangelism were meager: forty conversions in three years, in-

*"If you speak truth on this point," said his learned friends, "we will believe you on religion."

cluding that of the aged father of the governor (whose prestige was now waning for reasons apparently unconnected with his parent's fall into the "Church's nets"). Why so meager a harvest? Let us for the moment ignore the basic incompatibilities between Christian vision and Chinese thought,* and study instead a letter from Ricci to his former rector at the Roman college, Father Maselli. It draws up a gloomy balance of three years of proselytizing in the Empire, and stresses what was a crucial stumbling-block: their adopted status as Buddhist monks: "Until now, we have failed to make a Christian of any except the Governor's father. . . . We hope that in regions where folk are more greatly concerned over the soul's salvation, such as Zhejiang, there will be a turnabout among the great of the land. But it will be only at the cost of weariness and sweat."

Were they giving up? The temptation to do so was fleeting. Their explanation speaks worlds: "The bonzes are so base and held in such low esteem that, despite all the honor shown us, we remain to this day the butt of all slanders, and the insults visited on us are such that we may not set them down in a letter."

That was the heart of the matter: It was less as Christians that they† suffered such persecution than as Chinese monks, wearers of a cloth that betokened not virtue but a way of life held in contempt by the people. It consisted of begging, petty crime, and bawdiness of the kind the leaders of the Reformation in Europe had for nearly a century ascribed to the wearers of monastic robes.

Valignano, on a short visit to Zhaoqing, leaves us a telling picture of Ricci's life: "He could never sit in the presence of the mandarins and, during audiences, had perforce to remain on his knees. He was suspected of spying for the Portuguese of Macao. His residence was considered as a pagoda where the mandarins held their banquets. . . . In spite of what he endured and the slender hopes of these first years, never did he write to tell me he wished to return or that to stay in China was to waste his time, as many people were saying."

Yet it became necessary to relax his grip and take leave of Zhaoqing. On one occasion, the council of elders accused the Jesuits of accepting 5,000 escudos from the Portuguese for the building of their pagoda, "in order to sow dissension among the people." Another time, it was whispered to the Viceroy that the foreigners had built their temple near the water in order to have swifter communication with Macao, where the Portuguese were watching the Empire. Finally the Viceroy himself removed his mask: Recently appointed to Guangdong, he had set his heart on turning the house built by the "Western sacrificers" into his residence. He offered Ricci sixty escudos to go as far away as possible, out of his province and preferably outside China.

*See pp. 221–23.
†A Portuguese priest, Father Almeida, had now joined Ricci.

Ricci, loath to appear to be agreeing to an injustice, refused the sum and fled to Canton. Overtaken by a viceregal junk, he was ordered to return to Zhaoqing. There, following a pitiful scene, he finally accepted the mandarin's escudos in exchange for the right to live at Shaozhou in northern Guangdong.

Thus ended in discord an encounter in which (permanently prostrated though he was) he had insisted upon his rights through six years of a thankless initiation into China in the Empire's sourest, most backward, and least enlightened province. He had tested his command of Chinese, published (in 1584) a revised and more critical edition of the *Treatise on the Wonders of China,* and gauged his master Ruggieri's mistake in choosing the way of life and the status of Buddhist monk. He had acquired a kind of glory as clock-maker, cartographer, and virtuoso manipulator of mechanical things—his *cosette.* He had forged an initial alliance with the world of letters, and understood that Chinese civilization was of the book, of the written, of ideograms.

His first Chinese admirers had adorned him, in his status as a Buddhist monk, with a noble nickname: Si-Taï (Sage of the West), which had won him entry into the Chinese community. But it was among the people that he would be remembered, under the name Li Mateou (a Chinese version of Ricci Matteo, the letter *r* being nonexistent in China, where names never exceeded three syllables). Soon he would cease to be known as Si-Taï. Li Mateou had arrived.

We shall not follow Li Mateou every step of the way on his "long march" from Zhaoqing to Beijing. They were twelve years of wandering from muddy and quarrelsome Guangdong to the imperial city of Emperor Wanli. Long years that saw the forging of the legend of the great Western man of letters—while his own perception of the Chinese grew more refined. But we must not overlook the all-important acquaintances he made, first at Shaozhou, then at Nanchang and Nanxiong, nor the discoveries and the convergences that flowed from them and that gave birth not so much to Chinese Christianity as to the beginnings of Sinology.

The six years (1589 to 1595) Ricci spent in northern Guangdong would have been the darkest of his life had he not met the first true friend China offered him, the man who may have had the most decisive influence on his direction, his ideas, and above all his decisions.

Qu Rukuei (also written as Kiu Taïsou or Ch'u Taïsu) was a mandarin's son, renowned for his success at examinations, for his books, and for his honesty as President of the Nanxiong Court of Justice. Uninterested in repeating such exploits, which presented no challenge to his talents, he had for some time "thrown himself into the precipice of divers vices."[18] Then, wearying of them, he had adopted the style of a wit, a gourmet, a dabbler, the typical "go-between" of Chinese tradition without whose intervention nothing could be done, skillful at "procuring" (procuring what? Ricci wrote), men who recall certain lordlings of Molière's France, learned libertines furiously striving to conceal their genius behind a mask of cynical frivolity.

To Ricci, bogged down in his dealings with self-important mandarins and jealous Buddhist monks, Qu Rukuei at one stroke revealed a brilliant China, nimble, open, curious about the world, and utterly dedicated to the cult of knowledge. Was he more representative of the Chinese world than the greedy Viceroy of Shiu-hing? Impossible to answer the question—but here he was, offering himself like a brother (a cousin?) of the spirit, such as Matteo Ricci might have encountered in Florence, Salamanca, or Paris, eager to engage in intellectual dispute with Montaigne or Bellarmino.

The first visit the cultured wit paid to the Jesuit had a surprising motive, but one that carries its own somewhat Renaissance overtones. Fascinated by alchemy, Qu had heard of the reputation of these fathers, "able to turn cinnabar into silver," and now declared himself the great magician's disciple. We know that there were few methods Ricci overlooked in the interests of drawing a soul "into the net." But he drew the line at magic!

Since Qu had introduced himself with the splendid ceremony expected of one asking a master to accept him as a disciple, the Jesuit could refuse neither his three ritual prostrations nor the solemn banquet held in Qu's apartments nor the lengths of silk and other precious articles he brought. However, forced to bring everything into the open, he did it in words which—far from discouraging his superb postulant—bound the two men forever.

At first it was the Chinese who seemed to benefit from their exchanges:

> Enchanted by the novelty, he seemed wholly unable to drink his fill of learning: first arithmetic, Father Clavius's "Sphere" and the first book of Euclid's Elements. Night and day, Ricci reports, he went over what had been taught him, or "adorned his commentaries with figures so beautiful that they yielded not a whit to those of our Europe," himself "elegantly and skillfully" building, in wood, copper, and even in silver, all kinds of instruments, sextants, spheres, astrolabes, quarter-circles and "magnet-boxes."[19]

Then he wanted to have Christian doctrine explained. Was Li Mateou getting warm?

> He insisted that they set aside the rest, and for three or four days exposed the whole catechism to him. The Chinese disciple listened attentively and took notes. Then he indicated his difficulties in writing, leaving blank spaces so that the Father could write the answer on the side. To Ricci's surprise, these were the greatest difficulties and most

knotty problems dealt with in theology, and the man of letters was no less surprised to see all the knots loosened. . . . When he was shown examples of saints who had given up everything for God he replied, "That is neither painful nor difficult, above all for people who hope for happiness in the next life as your religion promises; until now we Chinese have not exercised ourselves upon such matters because no religion of ours ever assured us of such a reward!"[20]

Whatever "revelation" Qu may have received (he converted ten years later under the name Ignatius), his "master" profited no less from these interchanges. In these exchanges between the spokesman of the humanist and Christian Renaissance West and the representative of a China suddenly opened to the world, it is the words of the latter that weigh more heavily as our story continues.

A letter written to his colleague Duarte de Sanda tells us what Matteo Ricci then knew of the religion (he prudently writes "wisdom") of the Chinese of his day:

The people of China . . . while at the same time most ingenious, gifted with high and extraordinary abilities, have ever lived in ignorance of the faith, letting themselves be led into divers errors and following varied sects. . . .

The first is that of Confucius, a notable philosopher, . . . the most eminent and incorruptible of men. . . . His doctrine would have men follow the light of nature as their guide, strive worthily to acquire the virtues, and take care to govern their families and their community in ordered fashion. All that, beyond a doubt, would merit praise if Confucius had made mention of Almighty God and of the life to come. . . . Despite this, we must admit that no other doctrine among the Chinese comes so near to the truth as his.

The second sect is that of the Sacas.* . . . The "Seng," who are their bonzes, have some inkling of the life to come, of reward for good people and retribution for the wicked; nevertheless, all their declarations are mingled with errors.

In third place come the Taos, who emulate a certain man† who must be worshipped, they believe, for his sanctity. The priests of these two last sects lead the vilest and most servile of lives.

That last stroke betrays the disgust Matteo Ricci felt toward the monkish condition to which he had been submitted for the last twelve years—and by the same token toward Buddhism. We cannot know whether he could have moved away from it without Qu's intervention. But the latter had no trouble convinc-

*For Sakyamuni, or Buddha.
†Lao Tzu.

ing him of the absurdity, not of the Buddha's teachings, but of the choice that had reduced him to a humiliated position, to a diminished status, which in the eyes of the Chinese permanently darkened both his character and the doctrine he brought them. Garbed in this fashion, what hope did he have?

But Qu Rukuei, man of letters, son of a man of letters, could open all the doors of that Chinese world. No intermediary could have been so ready and effective as he was along the high road to knowledge and to those who held its keys in China. The disciple had turned pathfinder. You would have to have been less steeped than Li Mateou in concern for the effectiveness of *ad majorem Dei gloriam* not to open your eyes to the obvious: In a world governed by reason, why not follow the road taken by reasonable, learned men? You would have to have had a guide other than Ruggieri not to have seen that "everything in China springs from the subordination they observe according to their rank, up to the king himself." And you would have had to have been less well informed than this disciple of Valignano's on the very brief history of evangelism in Japan not to have known of the choice Francis Xavier made at Yamaguchi: silk, not cotton.

Before examining the possible intellectual and *realpolitik* justifications for this revolution in lifestyles—from Buddhist to Confucian—which naturally also implied a degree of spiritual adaptation, let us study appearances (which are never innocent, particularly in China).

From his crucial exchanges with disciple turned master Qu Rukuei, a new Matteo Ricci emerged. Just as the first act of Goethe's *Faust* shows us an old scholar transformed into a rakish gentleman, so a monk's robes tossed into the nettles turned the humiliated bonze of Guangdong into a Renaissance lord, a different man. The same Ricci, whom we have seen wrapped in his long brown robe, shaved from skull to chin, on his knees before the least of village mandarins, his forehead in the dust of the law courts, now wore

> a habit of dark red silk, its lapels, hem, cuffs, and collar lined with a band of silk of lightest blue the breadth of a man's hand. The sleeves are very wide and loose, somewhat like those of Venice. The belt is of the same red hue, it too bordered in blue, stitched to the gown and divided into two ribbons reaching to the ground, like those worn by widows in Italy. The shoes are of embroidered silk; the headgear is of extraordinary configuration, not very different from that worn by Spanish priests but a little taller, pointed like a bishop's miter and fitted with two wings of equal size that fall off as soon as the wearer makes a careless move. This hat is covered with a black veil, and is called *sutumpo*. When he goes abroad to pay a visit, he is borne on a palanquin and accompanied by a scribe and one or two servants. . . .

He has let his hair grow down to his ears, no longer clipped as the

French once practiced, but as with women curled into ringlets, with a small lock protruding from a hole. All this under a hat. . . . By the end of one year, his beard has grown down to his belt—a great wonder for the Chinese, who never have more than four, eight, or ten sparse hairs on their chins.[21]

Glory, reverend father Li Mateou? What about your vow of poverty,* of the humility which Ignatius held so dear? Ricci's answer is touchingly mischievous:

True, it is not part of our calling to seek honors [but] in this country where the religion of Our Lord is unknown and where the fame of that Holy Law so depends on the reputation and the credit of its preachers, it is necessary for us to adapt ourselves outwardly to the customs and the ways of the Chinese. . . . This honor and credit we begin to enjoy will not harm our souls; for twelve whole years, Our Lord first made us pass through such humiliation, abasement, and injury, and so many persecutions, as to serve as a sound basis for virtue; on all occasions we were treated and considered as the dregs of humankind. Which is why Our Lord, having granted us strength to persevere among so many travails, will, I hope, also lend us the grace not to puff up with pride among all these honors. And the more so because, always needing to make progress, we shall not fail to meet many occasions on which we shall suffer greatly for Our Lord.[22]

Since the habit makes—or unmakes—the monk, Li Mateou was not content with clothing himself in silk: He also chose to follow the social paths his new clothing, and very soon his new way of life, opened up for him. Living and dressing as a Confucian scholar from 1595 onward, he would soon conduct himself as one, and then even think like one. For he had not turned Confucian in order to wear fine clothes or grow long nails. He demonstrated his right to membership in the club in the most unarguable terms possible—by publishing his first book in Chinese. Ricci's *Treatise on Friendship* (1595) not only gave him high status among scholars, but better still among those who respected him most of all, the moralists. He thus nobly paid his dues for admission to the Association of Sages, and in the least controversial of ways, for if there was a single point on which the Western priest and Confucian masters could agree, it was morals. Misunderstanding and incompatibility arose in other areas.

The change of course suggested by his friend Qu Rukuei radically changed Ricci's perspective, his methods, and his strategy. He was in China: He made himself Chinese. He had been the butt of petty irritations and of persecutions: Henceforth he would live among those who wielded authority. In these few

*Consulted in 1592 through the intermediary Cattaneo, the all-powerful Valignano had authorized Ricci to go ahead with this bold transformation, in 1595, twelve years after his entry into China.

months he followed the same path as the one it had taken Ignatius of Loyola twenty years to complete, from La Storta to the corridors of pontifical power. Was he simply telescoping previous Jesuit experience? This conclusion is tempting. But a closer study of Ricci's motives permits a subtler analysis.

His diatribes against Buddhism, for example, call for an explanation. This rejection is often expressed angrily, almost contemptuously—most uncharacteristic of this noble mind—in Ricci's *History*. Of course, the ordeals he had endured when in monks' habit had not disposed him to a lofty view of the religion. It is true, of course, that a monk's robes scarcely attracted automatic respect in Europe at that time (see Chapter II)—to say nothing of Erasmus's jeers and Luther's thunderbolts. A Capuchin wandering from one Paris neighborhood to the next received more brickbats than bounty. But this contempt and ill-treatment did not disqualify Catholicism in everyone's eyes. In firing off his frequent shafts at Buddhism the condemnation he so often expressed (although his tones became more generous toward the end of his life), Ricci seems to have ignored the many factors arguing in favor of China's Buddhists.

Was he unimpressed by Marco Polo's *Description of the World*, which so appealingly speaks of the Saga Moni (Sakyamuni, the Buddha), justly praising the moral qualities of this "saint who lacked only baptism" and who was worthy of being one of "Christ's companions"?[23] And had he not read the astounding Guillaume Postel, only an ephemeral Jesuit but a bold enough humanist to have hailed Buddhism as the "most wonderful religion in the world"?

Most surprising of all, our faithful Ricci, taught by the faithful Valignano, seems to have inherited none of the interest that Francis Xavier (at first badly informed by Anjiro) showed toward the Buddhist sect called Shingon (which he wrote as Xingoufou), with its aspirations toward the beauty and even the immortality of the soul. It is true that Xavier had condemned the mediocrity and the "turpitude" of the bonzes (or the plots they wove against him) well before Ricci. But his approach to Buddhism was nevertheless marked by greater esteem and respect than Ricci's.

It was apparently Valignano's rectification of Francis Xavier's ideas about Buddhism, particularly when he was writing the saint's biography, that fatally distorted relations between Matteo Ricci and the religion imported from northern India. And this transpired well before Ricci's humiliating experience of the monastic life in Guangdong. Let us not forget, either, that in Japan the shogun Ieyasu actually confused Buddhism with Catholicism, banning in the same edict "Christianity, the Hiden sect, and Fujufuze, three branches of the same sect all of which worship the god Godzu-Kirisaitan-Teidzu-Butzu."[24]

Yet Ricci, already snared in his dream of reconciling Pythagoras with Buddha, was irrevocably deflected from Buddhism by his master Valignano (who equated Amidist Buddhism with the teachings of Luther "since," as he pointed out, "the Evil One even gave both of them their doctrine, unchanged save for the name of the person in whom they believe and hope"). It was this curious assimilation of the gentle doctrine of Amida, the universal interceder, to the Protestant thesis of "salvation through faith" that blinded Ricci to Buddhism's "soul of faith"—to what theologians were already starting to call a "providential preparation" for Christianity.

What the first Jesuits thus found in China was not a national adaptation of Buddhism but an amalgam of religious systems that had borrowed over the centuries from very diverse sources. According to Henri Bernard-Maître,

> Popular syncretism was neither Confucianism nor Taoism nor Buddhism, but a highly malleable and flexible religion with wide variations from region to region and family to family: ancient native divinities, great men from India, historic heroes recently deified, and Taoist figures, all thrown together pell-mell. In the absence of an authority capable of codifying the evolution of this folklore, doctrine and mythology had been lumped formlessly together in an association of ideas and characters that had seized the popular imagination in different periods and that remained a hodgepodge of contradictions and overlapping functions.[25]

It was not surprising that Ruggieri and Ricci were discouraged by this baffling blend, so infinitely remote from the Olympic simplicities of their beloved Greco-Roman Antiquity. Whence this rather disgusted remark by Ricci in September 1584, two years after arriving in Guangdong: "There is no religion, and what little worship there is has such complex form that even its priests are unable to explain it."

But what then of Confucianism, to which Ricci turned in 1592, and whose three outward manifestations he would so gloriously flaunt? If instead of a religion the Chinese people had adapted an indecipherable syncretism, what is to be said about the version henceforth professed by Li Mateou, a.k.a. Matteo Ricci? At least three well-known specialists have asked the question. Jacques Gernet in *Chine et Christianisme*,[26] René Étiemble in *L'Europe chinoise*,[27] and the Australian philosopher Paul Rule in *Kung Tsu or Confucius: The Jesuit Interpretation of Confucianism,* all agree on the futility of Li Mateou's efforts (in the book he called *The True Doctrine of the Master of Heaven*) to bring about a convergence of Confucianism and Christianity.

But let us retrace his steps, which in ten years brought him from curiosity about Confucianism (a system of wisdom and social morals with echoes of Epictetus and Seneca) to sympathy, and finally to admiration, sending him on a passionate search for traces of a spirituality and even a metaphysics harmonizing with Christianity. In the words of Paul Rule: "That this alliance and then this assimilation with Confucianism was originally tactical is difficult to deny. Ricci assumed his position for outward advantage, but it did not remain a tactic. His successive letters show that his favorable judgment progressively turned into a sincere intellectual bond, born of the conviction that these steps corresponded to a need, and that Confucianism was his destiny."

His destiny, beyond a doubt. But mere use of the word points to the risks inherent in the venture. It was his desire to reconcile the Confucianism he lived in with the Christianity he lived for. And what if China needed not to be converted but revealed to herself? And what if this bottomless moral bequest from that timeless sage, that Master Kung in whom Socrates, Plato, and Epictetus converged, was a prefiguration of Judeo-Christianity, a proto-Christian doctrine—*naturaliter Christiana,* to use Saint Augustine's formula?

We must keep in mind that Matteo Ricci, shaped in Rome at the height of the Renaissance and under the influence of Bellarmino and Francis de Sales, was a humanist. A man for whom the Gospel was a supernatural burgeoning of the natural genius and virtues of Antiquity. How intoxicating it must have been for him to encounter in China—where his mission was to open the Empire to the lessons Christ taught of the wisdom and moral lore of the Ancients—this Confucian prefiguration of the immense heritage that nourished Christian teaching.

In an address to the International Sinology Symposium held at Chantilly, near Paris, in September 1974, Jean Sainsaulieu quoted passages in Ricci's correspondence that assimilated Confucius first to Plato and then to Aristotle, assuring his listeners that "many passages on God, the soul, and the saints are propitious for the teaching of our faith." Sainsaulieu then proposed this bold thesis: "The 'China' Jesuits suddenly found themselves once again in the role of Masters of Arts and scholars of the University of Paris, the golden age* of the Company. Their Confucian adventure was to them a pilgrimage to their sources, well beyond the demarcation lines of lay or secular clergy that had been imposed upon them in Europe. China restored them to themselves."

It was saying a lot—but it perhaps suggested the essence of Ricci's intentions. Was it in this spirit of deep loyalty to an idea that he sought a syncretism, an "accommodation," an "encounter," as Paul Rule suggests, or better still perhaps a convergence of natural illumination and of revelation? Sainsaulieu seems reckless indeed to link such an approach to that of the Company's founders, intent as they were on hewing to the orthodox line. But it would be much less bold to equate Li Mateou's efforts with those of his contemporaries in Rome who were

*But none the less embryonic.

striving to impose retroactive Christian baptism on the Stoics and make of them Fathers of the Church.

Thus Saint Jerome had ranked Seneca in a list of "Saints," while Saint Cyril had included Plato. Why not accord the same treatment to the most virtuous Confucius, despite the intervening cultural gap? Ricci's reasoning is clear to see. But the fact is, this wasn't a gap: It was a chasm. And here we must give the floor to the prosecution—to those who, while admiring Ricci's generosity, his bold immersion in the Chinese world, his truly pioneering role in this exalted exchange among civilizations, nevertheless condemn the absurdity of his attempt at "accommodation," at seeking some sort of parental link.

Confucius's fundamental precept, to "respect Heaven," was naturally seductive to the erudite Li Mateou and his followers. They were fascinated by the idea of a "natural religion"—an idea as fertile in China as in Europe, whether or not it had been energized by a biblical message sprung from ancient preachings. Father Bernard-Maître quotes[28] a letter in which Ricci speaks of the "adoration" the Chinese of antiquity professed for a supreme being they called the "Master of Heaven" (Dianzhu), and maintains that the "canonical works" of Confucianism are inferior to none of "our natural philosophers." So much so that "we may hope that many of these ancient [sages] found salvation in observing natural law with the aid that God in His goodness showed them." (And we might note in passing how far the philosophical mind had progressed since the time, less than a half century earlier, when Francis Xavier held that all those who had not received the word of Christ were doomed to eternal hellfire.)

Moved though he is by the Jesuit's endearing efforts to reach out toward Master Kung, Étiemble cannot resist pointing out how desperate that effort was: "Confucius expressly states that the man who knows nothing or next to nothing about life would be impertinent to claim to speak . . . of what might happen to him at the point of death." According to Confucius, Étiemble recalls, "Heaven remains silent." And he concludes: "Ricci is willing to admire Confucius and Confucianism—on the understanding that this modest, flawed doctrine lacks God, the immortal soul, and any kind of dogma. He simply forgets this: If burdened with an immortal soul, hung about with dogmas and mysteries, and obliged to believe in a Divine Creator, the philosopher Confucius would have been anything we wish except a Confucian. Perhaps he would have been a Christian humanist."[29]

Jacques Gernet is even terser: "In attempting to fuse the Heaven and the Sovereign on High of the Chinese with the God of the Bible, the Jesuits were trying to assimilate irreconcilable notions." This Sovereign on High (Shangdi) was not "an only God, an almighty creator of heaven and earth, but an expression of submission to destiny, of the religious observance of ritual, of seriousness and sincerity of conduct; [he] was indissociable from a ritualistic and polytheistic context whose spirit was radically different from that of Judaism."[30]

Gernet also notes that the mandarins were indignant at the deification of "Yesu, a criminal from a Western kingdom of the Han era." They were "shocked," he adds, "by an egalitarianism in opposition to the hierarchies (familial or feudal) crucial to Confucianism—but [believed] that once rid of their false ideas, such as belief in a creator God, the missionaries might have made tolerable Confucians."[31]

And even when he sought God not in Shangdi but in Dianzhu (Master of Heaven), as he did in his most theoretical treatise, *The True Meaning of the Lord of Heaven,* or as other Jesuits did, in the organizing principle of Li, Matteo Ricci obviously had no hope of extracting even a hybrid Christianity from the womb of a society tightly closed to the distinction between matter and spirit, between the body and the soul, between eternity and nothingness—and stubbornly dismissive of the notion of sin.

But let us listen again to Henri Bernard-Maître, who suggests a parallel between the movement begun in China by Ricci and the antithetical, "philosophical" movement of which Montaigne was then the most diligent promoter in Christian Europe: Whereas the French thinker attempted to secularize morality by assimilating it to a penetrating analysis of the human heart, Ricci on the contrary proposed as a guideline for men (Chinese or European) not just a "natural awareness" of duty but an inextricable linkage to a mandatory belief in an afterlife.

To Li Mateou and his companions, this was not "just" a question of religion. It was also one of policy—which in the final analysis led right back again to religion. For, in working at this accommodation between Christianity and Confucianism, the missionaries also (or especially?) strove to locate their mission within a framework in which everything emanated from and ended in a Sovereign. The smaller the hiatus between the two visions of the world and the two kinds of conduct, the smoother would be the road that led the Christian emissaries to the Emperor.

As good Jesuits, as good disciples of Ignatius of Loyola and Francis Xavier, they believed that the future of their religion depended at the local level on a decision by the supreme wielder of authority. Witness this excerpt from a letter by Michele Ruggieri, written in Macao in 1581, before Ricci's arrival: "The whole thing is for the King to be visited with the desire and wish to summon the fathers to him, for I doubt not that he would give them leave to preach and to teach their doctrine."[32]

From the beginning, then, Matteo Ricci had been taught that his long march as the apostle of China would first of all be a long march toward the Emperor.

Neither Ruggieri nor he had foreseen that this progress would take them through a kind of "conversion to a hybrid form of Confucianism." It was their humiliating experience as "Chinese monks," followed by the eye-opening encounter with Qu Rukuei, that determined this development.

In any case, there could not have been a more propitious start to their expedition to the Forbidden City than Ricci's almost alchemical transmutation into a lofty Confucian man of letters and author of a *Treatise on Friendship*. Henceforth, the silk-clad sage would be introduced standing on a carpet of red, the color of grandeur and beauty in China.

It was in the sphere of one of the Chinese gods (to whom he would later be assimilated in Chinese minds) that Ricci took the first of his "great leaps forward," to Nanchang, in the spring of 1595. It took him to the very steps of the imperial throne. The "god" in question was Si Ye, a retired Viceroy recalled by the Emperor to the very highest responsibilities in Peking, where the threat of a Japanese invasion hung in the air. This renowned mandarin, who had heard Ricci's praises sung, invited the missionary to accompany him to the north, where he would place in his care a son driven mad by failure in his triennial exams. A worthy mission indeed for the "Great Sage of the West."

And so we find our newborn mandarin in a noble waterborne progress up the Ganjiang River aboard the illustrious Si Ye's sumptuous junk. He naturally asked the Emperor's minister to help him get as far as Beijing. "Beijing is impossible. I can offer you Nanxiong," replied Si Ye. But while he was preparing the ground for his new friend to settle in China's southern capital, the great mandarin advised Ricci to take up residence in Nanchang, a city of lettered folk that would be the ideal setting in which to polish his new status as Confucian master, with a view to cutting the appropriate figure in Beijing.

To his great surprise, Ricci learned on arriving in Nanchang that many scholars there had heard of him, possibly through one of Qu Rukuei's daughters, who had married a young cousin of the Emperor. A foreigner, they were saying, gifted with unimaginable knowledge and virtue, had just arrived from Guangdong. He had scarcely settled down (very unpretentiously, in a house on the city's outskirts) when the Viceroy's guards came to summon him.

> I hastened to the audience, in no way certain of what awaited
> me. . . . When I entered the room, the Viceroy was seated; he rose,
> greeting me with his hands and forbidding me to kneel, a most signal
> favor. . . . I offered him explanations of the life and the doctrines we
> professed, as also of mathematics and the art of building sundials. He
> broke in with frequent expressions of praise which covered me with
> confusion: "It is enough to see your face and person to sense that you

are a worthy man. . . . Everyone knows that you are in China only to care for men's salvation and that you know all the Chinese books." I was beside myself, believing that in this happening, which so far exceeded all my hopes, I was witnessing a miracle. . . .

At this juncture the physician entered on his daily visit: He spoke of my sundials, of my memory exercises, of the triangular prism, and so forth. The Viceroy desired to see the prism, and after contemplating the iridescent play of light he sent it to be shown to his wives. He himself desired a sundial and an astrolabe. He also desired me to write a treatise on mnemonics for his three sons, who were restrained by propriety from leaving the palace. He concluded by saying: "Why then do you not remain in our noble city?"

And so Li Mateou was made a citizen of Nanchang. Thenceforth the number of his friends miraculously grew. People spoke of the "fragrance of the scholar of the West." His door was so often under siege and "the cards of his visitors piled up in such numbers," he wrote, "that I had not the time to eat my meal before noon and could recite my breviary only at nightfall."

Here it was more the moralist who was in demand than the mathematician, the geographer, the clockmaker, or the "alchemist." In this city of scholars there was a fad for "academies," restricted literary circles where "preachers of virtue" held forth. Li Mateou proved a virtuoso of the breed, and deployed all the virtuous and discreet charms of Christian humanism. Here he is, free of all false modesty, recalling one of those harmonious moments:

I speak from dawn till dusk. . . . Although at present I do not discourse on all the mysteries of our Holy Faith, yet I make progress in laying the first foundations: There is a God Who created Heaven and earth, the soul is undying, . . . all things utterly unknown to them [as Confucians] and which until now have never been believed. Many hearing this doctrine feel such contentment that they let their tears fall, as if it were I myself who had made this discovery. In these first steps, it seems preferable to begin with explanations founded on reason.

How right he was! From now on, moving from one "academy" to the next, his utterances were so successful that his admirers had them printed (at first without his knowledge) in a volume that, he wrote, "brought upon me and upon our Europe more credit than anything we had theretofore done, for the other objects had won us renown as men expert at manufacturing instruments and mechanical devices, but by means of this treatise we acquired the reputation of scholars, allies of the mind and of virtue."

His best-known admirer was Kien-ngan, the man called "King" in Nanchang because he was a member of the Emperor's family and wore a kind of royal crown. From their first meeting they were like old friends, exchanging learned thoughts and their perceptions of the "other life." This intimacy grew apace; Kien-ngan offered Ricci the hospitality of his home, and barely a week passed without their exchanging gifts. His lofty position made it impossible for the "King" to declare himself the Jesuit's "disciple"; he therefore announced that he was Ricci's "companion." "He is not far removed from the kingdom of God," wrote Ricci, "and had I come here for him alone, all my labors would seem well rewarded."

Inevitably, echoes of his fame reached the ears of Qu Rukuei in Beijing, who eagerly broadcast it throughout the Empire. Thus the disciple, proud of his master's success, wrote to him in 1596: "The *Pimpu* [military mandarin in Nanxiong] makes much of Your Reverence . . . and last year loudly insisted that I bring you with me to Beijing . . . but at that time I was not free to part for the South. . . . Other mandarins, themselves advisers to the court in Beijing, and most learned . . . wish to invite you. . . . Let me know if you can accept."

Accept? Had Li Mateou ever wanted anything more fiercely? Particularly as the motives spurring him to Beijing had multiplied. During a visit to Macao in 1579, the Jesuit "Visitor" Valignano had decided to appoint Ricci Superior of the China mission, an operation that he had embodied since Ruggieri's retirement and on which he had conferred astonishing personal luster. Along with the news of this promotion, Ricci received a crate of presents for the Emperor, accompanied by an exhortation from his superiors to visit the imperial court without delay: a statue each of the Madonna and Christ bought in Spain, two bronze clocks, a large map of the world, musical instruments made of fine strips of inlaid wood, and two trigonal glasses.

However, it was not his beloved Qu Rukuei but another admirer who now took the silk-robed missionary in hand. While Ricci was still in Guangdong, Wangzuo (also written Wang Chong Minh), president of the Tribunal of Rites, had earlier asked the Jesuit to accompany him to Beijing in order to reform the official imperial calendar. Wangzuo was now returning through Nanchang on the road to Beijing where, it was said, he might be appointed *gelao*, or Prime Minister.

This illustrious traveler, whom Ricci invariably addressed as the President, offered without ado to take him to the capital for the Emperor's birthday, to be celebrated on September 17, 1598. Suddenly all doors seemed to be opening before the man who ten years earlier—skull shaven, shivering in his mud-colored robe—had bumped his forehead on Zhaoqing soil to beg a petty southern king not to expel him contemptuously from Macao.

From Nanchang to Nanxiong, from Nanxiong to Beijing: For seven or eight weeks he journeyed aboard a magnificent junk, by canal or along the Yangzi-

Gan and the Grand Canal, under the "President's" protection. His arrival in the capital inspired the wandering Jesuit to write a page worthy of Marco Polo:

> This royal city is situated at the kingdom's northern end, and is but one hundred miles distant from those renowned great walls raised against the Tartar. In size, configuration of streets, volume of houses and munitions, it is in truth inferior to Nanxiong; but it surpasses it on the contrary for the multitude of its inhabitants and the number of its magistrates and soldiers.

> To the south, it is ringed by two high strong walls so wide that twelve horses may easily run abreast upon them. . . . In height, they far surpass those of our towns in Europe. . . . To the north, it is shielded by only one wall. Bands of soldiers watch from these walls as closely as if the country were inflamed by war. By day, eunuchs guard the gates, or say they do; for in fact they demand taxes, which is not the custom in other towns.

> There are few streets in the city of Beijing paved with bricks or gravel, leading one to wonder at which season the going is least bad. For in winter mud, in summer dust, both most troublesome, alike impede the walker. And since it does not rain often in this province, all the ground is reduced to dust, which being raised aloft by the smallest wind, there is no house which it does not penetrate, spoiling everything . . . so much so that nobody, of whatsoever rank, walks or rides a horse in the street without a veil, which hangs from the head-gear to the breast, so that he himself can easily see and the dust cannot pass through.

> There is an added advantage to this veil, for it permits you to be known only when you please. Whence, unburdened of an infinity of greetings, and each walking with whatever following or pomp he pleases, suffers less irritation and expense; for the Chinese, thinking it not magnificent enough to go abroad on horseback and the cost of a litter in this country being high, can thus without shame reduce their expenses.[33]

But this would not be a long visit to the capital. The "President" did indeed settle our budding anthropologist into his house, and presented him, among other things, with a highly influential eunuch. The latter had heard that the visitor could change quicksilver (or cinnabar) into refined silver. When would he display his talents? Nothing would please the Emperor more. "And thus we see," reflected a downcast Li Mateou, "that no wealth can sate human avarice, even when such wealth is virtually infinite, as is that of the kings of China." And when the Jesuit guest admitted that in spite of the legend he was no alchemist, the eunuch's face darkened.

But it was not this that doomed the great Western scholar's first embassy to Beijing. It was the political situation. As Ricci reported, "Every day brought news from the kingdom of Coria [Korea] that several thousand men had died in battle and that the Japons had firmly resolved to enter the kingdom of China. And since the Chinese make no distinction, or barely make distinction, among foreigners, whom they lump together under one name, holding them to be all the same or more or less alike, on this occasion they took our people for Nippons."[34]

Which is why his sworn protector, the "President," soon deemed it imprudent to burden himself with such a compromising figure. Li Mateou was politely asked to turn back to the South, where the threat of war was less clamorous and he ran less chance of being mistaken for a "Nippon." And so, with his lieutenant Cattaneo at his side, the man in the silk gown beat a retreat to Nanxiong.

He was back again in the capital of the South—recently toppled by Beijing from its position as the imperial city, but still considered by the Chinese to be "the greatest and fairest city of the world, as much for the splendor of its public buildings, towers, and numberless bridges over the Yangzi as for the fertility of its countryside, its favorable climate, the civility of its manners, the elegance of its language, and finally for its multitude of inhabitants."

What better measure of the stature acquired by the "Great Sage of the West" in Chinese society than the interest he inspired in this illustrious city, teeming with scholars, where no great mandarin's glory went unchallenged? A letter written by one of these, Li Zhi, a philosopher known for his independence of mind, gives us the finest description of the Italian Jesuit who—in this final flickering of the sixteenth century in Nanxiong—had become the focus of all gazes:

> I have received your questions concerning Li Xitai.* He is a man from the regions of the distant West who traveled more than 100,000 li to reach China. He first stopped in South India, where he learned of the existence of Buddhism, after a voyage of more than 40,000 li. Only on reaching the Southern Seas, near Canton, did he learn that our kingdom of the Great Ming had first had Yao and Shun, and then Duke Zhou and Confucius.† He then lived some twenty years‡ at Zhaoqing and there is none of our books he has not read. He asked an aged man

*The first mandarin name bestowed on Ricci, before Li Mateou.
†The "patron saints," according to Gernet, of Confucianism.
‡In fact, as we have seen, only twelve years.

to set down for him the sounds and meanings of written characters; he asked someone skilled in the philosophy of the four books to explain their general meaning to him; he asked someone knowledgeable about the commentaries of the six Classics to provide him with the necessary clarifications. Now, he is perfectly able to speak our language, to write our characters and to conform to our sense of propriety.

He is a wholly remarkable man. Himself extremely refined, he is externally of great simplicity. In a noisy and disorderly assembly of several score persons, with questions and answers flying in every direction, the disputations he attends pass quite without strife. Among all the people I have seen, he has not his equal. [Indeed], others sin through excess of rigidity or through an excess of complaisance, or they flaunt their intelligence or they are of narrow mind. All are his inferiors. But I am not certain what he is come here to do. I have already met him three times, yet still I do not know his purpose here. I think that if he wishes to replace the teachings of Duke Zhou and Confucius with his own, that would be indeed too foolish. It therefore cannot be that.[35]

"Too foolish" for this man who "has not his equal" to replace the teachings of Confucius with his own? The noble Li Zhi was not far off the mark in putting the question in those terms. For as we know, Ricci's idea was less "replacement" than a flowering, a grafting, a revelation—distinctly less "foolish" but perhaps equally rash.

What is obvious is that Li Mateou had made an overwhelming impression on the denizens of a world overflowing with cultural (and national, if the term may here be applied) pride. His height, his long thin face and piercing eyes, the vast beard flowing down the splendid red gown, the elegance of his spoken and written Chinese, his knowledge of the Four Books underpinning Confucianism, the lofty tenor of his treatises on morals, the sparkle of his conversation, his extreme courtesy, his mathematical talents, everything conspired to make of him the *Jiren*, the "wholly remarkable" man hailed by Li Zhi.

Nor was this compleat Jesuit a man to squander such assets. Witness this observation, relayed by Nicolas Trigault, which prefaces the chapter of his *History* dealing with his stay in Nanxiong: "Across so many succeeding centuries God has not always deployed the same means for drawing men to Him. Thus we must not be surprised that our people have offered this bait to draw fish into the net."[36]

But why, in expressing this glorious maxim, did he use the singular from among all the means he had accumulated for the fulfillment of his precious objectives—why "this bait"? As if answering the question, Li Mateou explains that "with no other device had he so astounded the whole troop of Chinese philosophers than with the novelty of the sciences of Europe [and] principally of mathematics."

He was admittedly more likely to astound in that field than in many others. Knowing him to be averse to contempt for the Chinese, indeed inclined to admiration for them, we can safely conjecture from his writings that Chinese science in these waning years of the Ming dynasty—a science which considerably predated that of Europe—had fallen into the strangest of slumbers. After a visit to the Nanxiong College of Mathematics, Ricci's judgment was terse: "Large buildings, small science." One teacher had told him that the moon was pale because it envied the splendor of the sun.

Yet he had visited a splendidly equipped astronomical observatory on a mountain near the city. Its spheres, dials, glasses, diopters, and astrolabes excelled those of Europe. But no one there could operate these machines, which, he was told, were two hundred years old and which seemed to have come from a distant planet.

Under such circumstances, this pupil of Clavius could easily proceed (still without the approval of the Company of Jesus, but no longer formally forbidden) to shed a brilliant light—*ad majorem Dei gloriam*—on a European science that Copernicus, Kepler, and Galileo were raising to the summits.

But Beijing—seat of power, capital of that "King" he was enjoined to seek out by the Company's monarch-fixated traditions and at Valignano's express command—remained his goal. Through the banquets, honors, and debates of Nanxiong, all his energies remained focused on Beijing. He even spoke outright of a "second offensive." Gifts intended for the sovereign flowed in from Macao — clocks, oil paintings, looking glasses, hourglasses, ostrich plumes, and a copy of Ortelius's *Theatrum Mundi,** all things he wryly called "oil for the wheels of commerce."

While Qu Rukuei continued to besiege the Nanxiong authorities for passports to Beijing for Li Mateou, a young assistant, the Spanish father Diego de Pantoja, arrived from Macao to be his traveling companion,† and was soon learning to play the spinet for the future edification of the imperial court. At last an imperial eunuch appeared, with a ship to take them to the capital. On March 18, 1600, Li Mateou floated out onto the Imperial Canal aboard a junk laden with a gigantic bronze clock (telling the hours in Chinese characters), its hand a "sunbird."

---

*Theater of the World, a seventy-plate atlas published in 1570 by the Flemish cosmographer and republished in 1595.
†The last of Ricci's fellow travelers; Ruggieri, Almeida, De Petris were exhausted, dead, or in retirement in Macao.

Thus began the final stage of a journey of nearly twenty years across the Middle Empire. But one last ordeal awaited him. It would be the "Christian Expedition's" final initiation.

On the route to Beijing stood Tianjin. And at the approaches to Tianjin towered a terrifying character, the eunuch Ma Tang, "toll-keeper" to the capital, a man so ferociously dedicated to fiscal depredation that the people, goaded beyond endurance, had set fire to his palace and attempted to slit his throat. Learning that the renowned Li Mateou proposed to enter Tianjin on his way to Beijing, he announced that he wished to see the gifts intended for the Emperor. The senior oarsman at once warned Li Mateou: "Do not hope to escape him. For nowadays the eunuchs rule . . . and the greatest magistrates cannot resist their injuries!"

At this point we must briefly examine this curious corporation of eunuchs and the power they wielded, which was exactly as the oarsman had described it. In Imperial China, the mandarin caste traditionally monopolized public offices, which they acquired through the examination system but which were constantly subjected to reevaluation, to multifarious checks and balances, and in which promotions were matched by demotions and dismissals. Against this apparently Platonic meritocracy stood its leering counterpart, the corps of eunuchs, condemned by Ming historians as "the cancer of China" and more especially of the institution of the Emperor that was its center and its apex. For while the Emperor's harem, dominated by the Queen Mother, formed the inner circle of power, it was itself hemmed around by the "protective" swarm of the eunuchs, well placed to manipulate, intrigue, and arbitrate conflicts among the Emperor's favorite concubines.

A minor matter, one that would scarcely have surprised the favorite-plagued courts of Europe? No. For these eunuchs were men of sometimes astonishing influence. From the very beginning they had been held in contempt, since the foundation of Chinese society was the family—in other words, fatherhood. And even more so because castration in China was not merely a deliberate and radical security measure tailored for the harem (or an operation undertaken for musical ends, as in Italy) but a punishment enshrined in criminal law. Gradually, though, the eunuchs had emerged from the harem to become secretaries, drawing up edicts (in violation of the ancient law banning convicted persons from this task) that were tainted ever afterward. "They were entrusted with coups d'état," according to Henri Bernard-Maître. Soon their sponsorship was essential to any candidate for office; via enormous bribes, they secured promotion. Flouting all principles, the Ming Emperors bestowed titles of nobility upon them, permitting those who had not fathered children before castration to adopt descendants who could inherit their property and rank. In conformity with Chinese tradition, which makes a starved and wandering ghost of a child-less old man, they were thus assured of traditional care in old age and given the power to create lasting clans.

They too had to undergo an "exam" to determine who from among their to-tal number of more than 10,000 would become the privileged 2,000 or so enti-tled to practice their profession—but the only qualifications required were good looks and glibness.

Such obvious contempt for Confucian principles, which linked the exercise of power to merit and proven ability, did not go unopposed by its victims: Em-peror Wanli's reign—which concerns us here—was one long, bitter, and merci-less struggle between the essentially Beijing-based power of the eunuchs and the peripheral sway of the mandarins. Some scholars wielded a power acknowl-edged in the capital; some eunuchs exercised authority in distant provinces—above all as tax collectors.* But it is safe to say that the closer you came to Beijing, the more the scales of power tipped in favor of the castrati.†

Whence the violence of the clash between Li Mateou and Ma Tang. For the latter saw in Ricci not only a rival (the Emperor had heard of the talents of this fabulous man from afar—and what could be more tempting for a bored poten-tate?) but also a man who had opted to become a scholar, to join the loathed mandarin caste and thus reinforce the enemy camp. In short, there was no vex-ation and no obstacle the "great mandarin from the West" could not expect to suffer from Ma Tang, who would soon also shatter the career of the great man-darin Wangzuo.

First, the eunuch insisted that the gifts destined for the Emperor be brought to his palace. Ricci refused. To lull him, Ma Tang gave a banquet in his honor. To no avail. He then summoned him to give him the Emperor's message,

> costumed as was habitual for criminals, in a cotton garment and
> round common bonnet. [Then] he ordered him to listen on his
> knees, according to the custom with the king's commands; then again
> commanded him in the hearing of all present to set down in his own
> hand the presents he had brought for the king, and then taking them
> into his possession he had them borne to his palace. . . . Having laid
> hands upon the goods, Ma Tang then had his visitors shut into a tem-
> ple of idols . . . and burst in with two hundred men who were no
> more than brigands. . . . Then opening all the coffers and cases, he
> looked through everything at leisure, making the insult more unbear-
> able still by his fury. . . .

*Bernard-Maître draws a parallel between the mandarins and the Pharisees of Jewish tradition: a comparison it is tempting to complete by coupling eunuchs with publicans.
†Although apparently not all eunuchs were castrated.

At each object not yet viewed by the enraged eunuch, he complained that all this had been stolen from him, taking everything that pleased him and setting it aside. But finally, seeing that there was nothing at all there of what he had imagined, and finding himself more ashamed than rage-filled, decided to augment his injustice precisely where he should have diminished it. But of all he had seen, nothing so angered him as the sight of Our Savior hanging from the Cross; he charged that this ghost had doubtless been devised to kill the king through wizardry.[37]

The foreign "wizards" remained in their temple-prison for months. When they finally managed to dispatch one of their number, Brother Sebastian, to seek information, they received this reply: "Yours is a hopeless case. Ma Tang has accused you of witchcraft. Hasten back to Canton even if it means losing all your baggage. Crush your crucifixes into dust!"

Ricci concluded that there was no more to hope "from men's succor or his own efforts, whereupon he turned all his thoughts to God, readying himself with great steadfastness and joy to suffer death in a cause that brought Ma Tang's persecution upon him."

God heard and helped them. Through the unhoped-for intercession of the Emperor Wanli, who one day cried out in the depths of his palace: "Where is that bell* that they said rang of its own accord, and that I was told foreigners had brought for me?" At once all obstacles fell: Ma Tang was forced to release his prisoners, restore the presents and baggage, including the mathematics texts, which were supposedly forbidden and which he had in consequence confiscated. And since the canals were frozen over, he was obliged to "lease for them at public expense horses and carriage to bear them to Beijing."

Who exactly was this Emperor Wanli, on whom everything depended—in particular the future of Li Mateou and the conversion of China? Everything written about him is highly problematic, since nobody set eyes on him during his forty-seven years on the throne except his wives and his eunuchs—many of whom paid with their lives for the irritation their master felt at their excessive power.

Wanli was his "throne name." Before his coronation in 1573, at the age of ten, he was called Chen Song. Everything about him seemed to augur a good sovereign, starting with the twelve honorable principles posted on his orders in the Purple Room of the Forbidden City:

Obey Heaven's injunctions, entrust office only to the Wise, have only righteous ministers, set aside flatterers and sycophants, reward and

*The chiming clock, of course.

punish with justice, balance the budget, conduct yourself well, be so-ber at meat and at drink, govern your heart wisely, act according to conscience, willingly accept sincere advice, be moderate in the use of material goods.

But alas! Twenty years later Wanli had so fully implemented these principles that an incorruptible judge named Lao Jen felt obliged to reproach him with his excesses: "drunkenness, lechery, greed, anger"—without suffering impalement for his rashness. Indeed this glutton, lost in total idleness in the depths of his vast palace, among a hundred women and thousands of eunuchs, had become so monstrously obese that, "impeded by overflowing flesh, his voice was inau-dible at two paces."*

Apparently impervious to the threat of Japanese invasion in 1595, and seem-ingly unconcerned at the rise of the Manchu ambitions, which were soon to cut his dynasty short, he seemed to interest himself only in palace intrigues, in du-els for the succession among his legitimate and bastard offspring, and (passion-ately) in ceramics and rare and precious objects. It has been confirmed that in a single year he had his craftsmen deliver "twenty-seven thousand teacups, sixty-five hundred wine goblets, six thousand pitchers, and seven hundred goldfish bowls."

This extravagant taste for the rare and the unexpected plays a very substan-tial part in our story. Had the corpulent Emperor not been possessed of a curi-ous mind, he might never have taken any interest in Li Mateou, in his clocks and his prisms, in his images and his astrolabes, or in his person. And we should note that, sunk as he was in terrifying idleness, and surprised by the gifts he re-ceived from the visitors from the West, it never occurred to Wanli, in ten years, to admit the great scholar with the flowing beard to the foot of the throne.

Yet Ricci's supplication was eloquent:

Your servant from the distant West respectfully craves leave to offer you these articles from his country. . . . Despite great distance, the fame of the magnificent institutions that the imperial court has be-stowed on all its peoples has reached me. Myself desiring to share in these bounties, and to number myself my whole life long among your subjects: trusting besides that I shall not myself prove wholly useless . . . I have acquired a fair knowledge of the doctrine and of the ancient Sages of China, I have read and learned by heart something of the classical books and other works, and understood some little of their meaning. . . . The extreme benevolence with which the present glorious dynasty invites and treats all visitors has fired me with the

*This portrait is a composite of the (secondhand) notations of Fathers Pantoja, Bartoli, Weegner, and Bernard-Maître.

courage to come straight to the imperial palace, bearing with me objects that have traveled with me from my country. . . . They have no great value but, coming from the farthest reaches of the West, they may appear rare and curious. . . .

Since my childhood, I have striven to cultivate virtue. Never having married, I am free of all embarrassments* and hope for no favors. In offering you holy images, my only desire is that they serve to beseech for you long life, unmixed prosperity, and Heaven's protection for the kingdom and the people's peace. I humbly beg the Emperor to have pity on me, who am come to submit wholeheartedly to his law.

In his own country long ago, your servant has known preferment; he has acquired office and honors. He knows perfectly the celestial sphere, geography, geometry, and calculus. With the aid of instruments, he observes the heavenly bodies and makes use of the *gnomon;* his methods are wholly in keeping with those of the ancient Chinese. If the Emperor will not spurn an ignorant and incapable man, if he permits me to exercise my feeble talents, my most burning wish is to employ them in the service of so great a prince. But I should never dare promise anything, given my limited abilities.

Your servant awaits your command.

How many days or weeks did it take for this plea and these presents to journey from eunuch to eunuch and finally to the Emperor? We have no way of knowing. But we have an idea, from the account some of them gave Ricci, of the sovereign's reaction to the pious images he was offered:

Seeing these pictures, the King was stupefied, saying: "This is a living Buddha!" (all the other gods he worships are dead gods). That name has continued to be attached to our pictures and they call [us] "those who offered the living God." But the King was so afraid of this living God that he sent the pictures of the Madonna to his mother who was a great worshipper of idols,† who was also frightened by such a life-like impression; she therefore sent them to be kept with her treasures, where they remain to this day, and many mandarins go to see them by the grace of the eunuchs who guard this treasure.[38]

While the Emperor was most certainly struck by these images, it is hard to tell whether his reaction was favorable or not. What is certain is that he horrifiedly thrust a reliquary away from him: Nothing was more repellent to a Chinese, whether prince or commoner, than old bones. Even more certain, he was enchanted and conquered by Ricci's great clock, and since no ceiling in the pal-

*This, to a man besieged by a hundred wives and not a few "embarrassments"!
†In other words, a fervent Buddhist.

ace was high enough to accommodate its system of weights and counter-weights, he had a small wooden tower built in the garden next to his private apartments, where he spent long hours in the company of the "bells which rang of themselves." Nothing did more than that clock to "cement the position" of Li Mateou, wrote one of his companions, Father Díaz—not only because Wanli was charmed by the gift but because he insisted for months that only its donor could make it keep time.

Although he refused to see the missionaries, Wanli was so fascinated by them that he sent his best painter to execute their portraits. When he saw them in likeness he exclaimed, "But they are Muslims [*huihui*]!"—whereupon the eunuch present said that these particular barbarians ate pork. Still through the secondhand intermediary of the eunuchs, the Emperor asked the fathers about the way of life of Europe's sovereigns. Nothing made him laugh harder than hearing that at the Escorial or the Louvre they lived in many-storied houses: What could be more dangerous or uncomfortable!

However well disposed toward Ricci (had he not reprimanded Ma Tang for the injuries inflicted on the missionary?), the Emperor asked one of his mandarins for a report on the barbarian clockmaker and on the attitude to adopt toward him. The report attests most eloquently to the fragility of the position of the "Great Sage of the West":

> Li Mateou appears to be a beggar. He claims to come from Ta Si Yang: according to the Code of Laws, there is indeed a country named Si Yang So-li, but no one has heard of Ta Si Yang. This country has no relations with us and does not acknowledge our laws. This man did not come to the capital until he had lived twenty years in China, and he sought to give his presents to the King through the intermediary of the eunuch Ma Tang, contrary to Chinese law which ordains that foreigners first inform the Viceroy of the province through which they enter, and the Viceroy then informs the King before suffering them to go farther. But since they are foreigners with little knowledge of our customs, we should forgive them. All they bring in tribute to the King are objects of curiosity, in no wise comparable to the rare and costly gifts ordinarily offered by the envoys of foreign countries: for example the likenesses of the Lord of Heaven and his mother! They bring also the bones of Immortals—as if whosoever rises to Heaven does not take his bones with him! On a similar occasion (concerning the Buddha's tooth), Han Yu warned that it was unwise to introduce such novelties into the palace for fear of attracting misfortune.
>
> We therefore consider that these presents should not be accepted and that Li Mateou should not be permitted to stay in Beijing, but

that he should be sent back to Guangdong whence the mandarins shall ship him back to his country if they think it advisable. And that Ricci be given a hat and a belt by the bounty of the King, and that the price of his gifts be reimbursed according to their estimated value.[39]

The ensuing intrigues among eunuchs and mandarins, among mandarins of the court and the Tribunal of Rites, among all of them and the Queen Mother, were indescribable. But the outcome was that the Emperor would not tolerate the departure of Ricci and Diego de Pantoja—if only because they would now be able to divulge to their fellow barbarians the secrets of China and were the only ones able to keep "the bells that rang of themselves" in working order. As soon as the imperial wish became clear, Li Mateou found himself not only accepted but feasted, flattered, received in private audience by the *gelao* (Prime Minister), and raised higher than all the other scholars of the capital. Henceforth he was the Emperor's protégé, a protégé determined to use his privileged position as a springboard for the accomplishment of his mission, which was—as he unblinkingly replied in answer to questions from the Tribunal of Rites—"preaching God's Law."

But there are so many ways of preaching God's Law, even when one held that there was but one God and one Law. And who better than Ricci had demonstrated through twenty years of life in China that proselytizing could take many forms—whether you emulated the Francis of the Indian phase, "turning out Christians" en masse, or drew inspiration from the Xavier of the Japanese period by seeking to convince rather than convert, caring less about mass baptisms than about agreement on substance?

Li Mateou had long since chosen his own direction. It was qualitative rather than quantitative, rational rather than inspired, comparative rather than conquering. "More fruit is to be reaped from conversations than from sermons," he said. Rather than force a people away from its beliefs, could one not demonstrate that its beliefs led it to a more imperious faith, its culture and wisdom to a more inspired wisdom—and that through virtue one could progress to charity?

But what made the "Ricci method" so original, compared to moves in a similar direction by his models Francis Xavier and Valignano (adaptation, immersion, inculturation), was the role he assigned to science and technology. "If you speak truth about geography, we will believe you about the rest," as his first friends in Guangdong had told him as far back as 1585.

Ricci never forgot that it was science above all else, Western science, that would impress the Chinese, rehabilitate the mission of the "foreign devils," and thence (who could tell?) implant the idea of conversion.[40]

"Ricci's goal," says Jonathan Spence, "was to draw the Chinese into his scientific labors so that they would become more receptive to the Christian faith. . . . It can be said with certainty that his hopes of bringing important Chinese scholars to the Christian faith through elevated scientific discussion proved justified."[41]

For his day, Ricci's scientific baggage was exceptional. We have seen* that in Rome he was the pupil of Clavius, the "modern Euclid," who became Galileo's friend (although not a supporter of his ideas) and lifelong correspondent. A good mathematician and well-informed geographer, Ricci was also a knowledgeable enough astronomer to realize that in this field his Chinese friends were not necessarily less advanced than he was.

Here are three examples of the apostolic effectiveness of science. While it is true that his first friend, Qu Rukuei, did not approach him for authentically scientific reasons but because of his reputation as an alchemist, he was persuaded by Ricci to study Clavius's *Sphere,* and labored to translate it before his conversion to Christianity. The same approach was adopted by the most renowned and influential of the Chinese converts, Xu Guangqi, who became "Paul"—except that their shared work resulted in the best translation of Euclid into Chinese. And it was again the Euclidean angle that brought the great mandarin Li Zhizao (Ricci's fellow author of a mathematical treatise) to turn to Christianity in the twilight of Li Mateou's life.

Jonathan Spence gives us a timely reminder that in these areas "China had a long and rich past, even though the Jesuits rarely spoke of it." But it is no less true that this past had been more or less murdered by the Emperor Qinshi who, toward the end of the third century B.C., had every scientific work destroyed; and that what the great scholars hoped for from Ricci was the means of resurrecting this banished knowledge.

Among the most promising of these fields was astronomy. Ricci saw this so clearly that in 1605 he wrote to his European superiors asking them to send him "a good astronomer" who could help him "translate our tables into Chinese" and undertake the "rectification of their calendar, which would secure us high reputation and give us wider access to China." Although this project was carried out not by Ricci but by his successors, Fathers Schall and Verbiest, it could not have been a more spectacular success. Of all the Company's contributions to the Empire, this would be the most lasting.

But another branch of knowledge also buttressed Li Mateou's prestige: mnemonics. That Ricci possessed an extraordinary natural memory is beyond any doubt. He assures us that after reading through four or five hundred randomly selected Chinese ideograms he could recite the list backwards and his friends reported that he could recite whole volumes of classical authors after reading

*See above, page 183.

them just once. But circumstances had led him to sharpen these exceptional faculties still further, if only because he could not carry with him the books that were the basis of his teachings.

And so, resuscitating the ancient and medieval methods taught in rhetoric courses at the Jesuit College in Rome, he had constructed his *Memory Palace,* a mnemonic technique involving the situation of ideas, words, and characters in a spatial or architectural framework. Utterly faithful to the essentially Ignatian notion of "composition of place," it rested on the exaltation of image and form within the memory as within spirituality.

Of this treatise on mnemonics, which he wrote for his Chinese friends and pupils, Li Mateou makes this particular point:

> Once your places are all fixed in order, then you can walk through the door and make your start. Turn to the right and proceed from there. As with the practice of calligraphy, in which you move from the beginning to the end, as with fish who swim along in ordered schools, so is everything arranged in your brain, and all the images are ready for whatever you seek to remember.[42]

Well, yes . . . But you still have to keep clearly in mind the technique, the images, and all the tricks implicit in the process—as Li Mateou's Chinese pupils regularly protested. Particularly since some of the images Ricci chose to illustrate his manual and his technique, such as Christ crossing the Sea of Galilee or talking with his disciples of Emmaus, were not so compelling to a young Confucian as to a Jesuit student in Rome. Nevertheless, Ricci's method brought him fame and opened doors, and helped make of him the prodigious walking library that for a quarter century was a major focal point of scientific activity in China.

But had Ricci penetrated China simply to extol and promote Western science? However attractive his humanist approach may seem, with its respect for the culture of the Other, and its concern to substitute a kind of spiritual synthesis for "conquest" (why convert if you could instead converge?), it was not his ultimate goal. He had come to Beijing, and was prepared to die there, to proclaim the Gospel. And although he very often did proclaim it, recall it, and recapitulate it for his Chinese friends, he sometimes seemed to have forgotten it so completely that the question has to be asked. Particularly as Li Mateou himself has supplied the answer.

When his old friend Father Costa wrote from Rome in 1599 to tell him that they were disappointed at the small number of conversions reported by the China mission, Ricci retorted:

> Day and night our thoughts are on nothing else. It is with this object that we have come here, leaving behind us our countries and most

dear friends, garbed and shod Chinese-fashion, neither speaking nor eating nor drinking nor lodging in any but Chinese fashion, but God has willed that our labors have not yet borne such great fruit. Yet I believe that the results of our efforts bear comparison with those of other missions that, it seems, work wonders, and may even be said to surpass them; for at this moment we are not in China to reap or even sow, but simply to clear the forest. . . . The most suspicious tactic it would be possible to pursue in China would be to surround ourselves with a great number of Christians. Ever since China has been China, none can recall a foreigner achieving a position akin to ours. . . . We live here with our religion held in great esteem by all, and some consider us the greatest saints who ever lived in China, miraculously come from the extremities of the world. And the Chinese are not so wanting in intelligence that a single one of them is misled as to our final intentions.

True. And no less true that the apostle Ricci's "prey" was of high caliber. We have mentioned the three scientists who embraced Christianity through the good graces of Euclid. But we must linger on the case of Paul, the great mandarin Xu (or Siu or Ciú or Xú or Zhou) Guangqi (or Kwang-chi), known to the missionaries as "our Paul"—so brilliantly did he represent and buttress Chinese Christianity for thirty years after his conversion and his elevation to the highest rank in the Empire—*gelao*, or Prime Minister.

Born into a family of scholars in the Yangzi Valley, he had dedicated his youth to a long intellectual pilgrimage through the various streams of Confucianism and the multiple Buddhist sects. Passing the most prestigious exams, he had met Ricci in Nanxiong in 1600 and been struck—but not overcome—by the idea of a single creator God. The *History* written by Ricci and Trigault reports that it was a dream, in which a temple divided into three chapels appeared to him, that revealed the essence of Christianity to Paul. He became a convert in 1603—without the slightest harm or impediment to his glittering career . . . which again calls into question Chinese xenophobia.

Let us try to imagine how a minister of Louis XIV, already converted to Confucianism, would have progressed at the court of Versailles. The attempt leads us to consider the nature of the upheaval Christian preaching would have wrought in a Chinese mind, and the kind of tremors and quakes implicit in the word "conversion." If we are still unconvinced, we have only to look at comments made by contemporary Chinese scholars who, attempting to understand the content of the missionaries' message, were forced to admit their horror.

"In China they set small store by the things of salvation," Ricci sadly noted when he was still living as a monk in Guangdong. What is surprising is that he modified this viewpoint in relation to Confucianism, which stood even further from the Christian idea of personal "salvation" than did Buddhism.

We have already seen, through the words of Étiemble, Gernet, and many others, the apparent incompatibility between the two opposing visions of the world, the two conceptions of "Heaven," the two kinds of relation to matter—monism and dualism. The Chinese were repelled by the idea of redemption through suffering, a revulsion embodied in the virtually universal horror they felt at the image of Christ. However loathsome (and loathed) the eunuch Ma Tang might have been, he was clearly behaving like any Chinese when he condemned the crucifix offered to the Emperor as a work of black magic. Even though the image of the Virgin and Child enchanted them ("They have a woman for [a] God . . . "), the "nailed man," that "criminal of the Han period," seemed worthy of execration.

But beyond all metaphysical or symbolic obstacles, the major obstacle, defending Chinese society like a Great Wall against Christian penetration or lodgement, was perhaps a political one—in the sense that religion in the Empire was an affair of state.* A cult, even a God, had no residential rights unless the Emperor decreed them. In this, Ricci had been right. But it turned out that the notion of "rendering unto Caesar," however sensible in Europe, was quite intolerable to the Chinese.

The following extract from a contemporary Chinese commentary, selected and translated by Jacques Gernet, says everything:

> They acknowledge two sovereigns in their country. One is the political sovereign, the other the doctrinal. The first has in his hands the governance of but one kingdom, the other a power that extends to all the world's kingdoms. The first reigns by right of succession and passes on his task to his heirs. Nevertheless, he depends on the doctrinal sovereign to whom he must furnish gifts and tribute. To appoint a successor to the doctrinal sovereign a man skilled in the doctrine of the Master of Heaven is chosen. All this is like having two suns in the same sky, two masters in the same kingdom. Might this mean that . . . even our own Emperor would have to submit to this doctrinal sovereign and send him tribute? What audacity on the part of these calamitous barbarians who would thus disturb the morality (both political and moral) of China by introducing this barbarous usage of two sovereigns.[43]

More straightforward still, Huang Zhen does not even discuss the texts. To refute them, he has merely to point out their foreign origins: "Ricci himself may

---

*Which was still largely the case in Europe ("cujus regio, ejus religio"), but on a less monumental scale.

have lived for twenty years in China, but his Shangdi [Lord on High] was born to a barbarian woman. They would compare their great country of the West to our peerless China, as if there could be two Empires in the world." Spoken, as Sainsaulieu has remarked, like an emperor. In *The True Meaning of the Lord of Heaven*, Ricci had bravely tried to overcome these contradictions (the kind that in the Mao era were called "warring") by giving the cosmic foundations of Confucianism and by playing on the moral and social convergences and the theme of "holiness," more or less reduced to respect for an ethic. But even in the field of morality, in which Li Mateou had shed light on so many and such rich similarities, the divergences were basic: while Confucianism aimed only at perfection of self, Christianity transferred the same effort to the "Master of Heaven." Which was why, says Gernet, "Christian charity and the Chinese virtue of humanity *(ren)*, although linked by the missionaries, could not have the same content."[44]

Yet Li Mateou so heroically pursued his attempt at "accommodation" between the two mental and spiritual worlds that most of the Empire's scholars considered him a sage and respected him as such. And however reserved he might have been on the principle of accelerated conversions, he brought into being* through his example and his works, from Guangdong to Beijing, a Christian community of some 2,000 persons whose adhesion to the Western religion owed nothing to intimidation, pandering, or conformism.

As the year 1610 began in Beijing, the Great Sage of the West was at the peak of his fame. The Emperor had just decreed that his "description of the world" would be printed in the palace. Rome had sent Li Mateou the requested astronomer, Father Sabattino de Ursis, whose work fascinated the capital's scholars. Li Mateou took part in the deliberations of the jury that had to elect 300 laureates from among a doctoral candidate list of 5,000; he was writing his "Commentary," which, translated into Latin by Trigault, would become the *History* we have so often referred to; he was giving mathematics lessons to several people close to the palace; discoursing on science and philosophy before audiences of famous scholars; and entertaining a countless stream of guests at the Jesuit residence he had built five years earlier.

The death of his master, Alessandro Valignano, in 1606 had hit him hard. But that spring, he recorded the conversion of his most renowned disciple after Paul, the great mandarin Li Zhizao. Did he now feel that he had achieved his boldest goals? His companions reported him saying, "The best thing that could happen for China now would be my death."

He grew old. Racked by frequent cruel headaches, he began to worry and felt

*With the help of his "rival" and later his successor, Longobardi.

with growing discomfort the results of a wound suffered in his left leg during an attack on one of his dwellings in Guangdong, twenty years earlier. His beard was snow-white and more majestic than ever, and his presence remained magnificent. Whether making one of his four prescribed annual visits to the Forbidden City (where he prostrated himself before a throne that was always empty), or entertaining his illustrious friends Xu (now Paul) or Li (now Leo), or presiding over a physics experiment at the College of Mathematics, he always seemed to tower above his surroundings. His Chinese had grown more refined than ever, and the mother-of-pearl buttons on his silken tunic shone with a thousand lights. He was Li Mateou, and also Li Sitaï, the Sage of the West.

But in early May 1610 he had to take to his bed, suffering from what is assumed to have been pulmonary congestion. The most famous doctors in the capital came to see him. In vain. "So powerful was his illness that his mind wandered." He was heard to mutter, "I leave you a door opened onto great merits, but not without many perils and travails." Then he quoted with great reverence a famous Jesuit whom he had never met, Father Coton, confessor to the French King Henry IV, and "slept very gently in the Lord, in his fifty-eighth year."[45]

Next day, his assistant Diego de Pantoja appealed to the Emperor (who had "never ordered burial for any foreigner") for the grant of a "piece of ground to cover in this great kingdom [this man] who wedded himself to the virtues that your books enjoin."

Ricci's companions knew that Wanli could grant him no higher honor. They obtained it only after the most tangled and Chinese of negotiations: The story of their various approaches, of pleas dispatched, returned, submitted, revised, transmitted from mandarins to eunuchs and from the Jesuits to the Queen Mother, reads like something out of *Gulliver's Travels*—and often reveals, in its deepest and most refined forms, the nature of Chinese hospitality.

The Jesuits' request for Ricci's remains elicited a most moving plea to the Emperor by the President of the Tribunal of Rites: "Who would not feel compassion for the dead body of a foreigner come from the most distant regions? . . . I entreat Your Majesty that some deserted and uninhabited temple be found for his sepulcher." Wanli annotated the plea with a single word in his own hand: "Xi" (Let it so be done). Armed with the request, the Governor of Beijing unearthed a temple on the outskirts of the city, adorned with the name Temple of Discipline, which had been confiscated by a eunuch who had since been condemned to death. The solution seemed a happy one. But no one had reckoned with the fury of the Queen Mother, "a little old woman much devoted to idols"—and unwilling to have them broken, thrown away, and burned in order to bury a Jesuit. But in spite of his respect for his mother, the corpulent Emperor refused to have his will opposed.

And so, after waiting a whole year in its coffin "smeared with gleaming pitch," Li Mateou's body was finally buried on November 1, 1611, in the "cemetery" at Zhala, "with the usual pomp of the Chinese, whose magnificence more closely resembles a triumph than an occasion for mourning,"[46] beneath a stone with this four-character inscription: "Mo y lien wén" ("To the man from the distant West, renowned judge, author of famous books").

Was this posthumous tribute Ricci's true victory? The crowning of the Jesuit's Long March? Could this burial on Chinese soil, not far from the Forbidden City and decreed by the Emperor himself, be taken as official recognition of Christianity in China? The Company's Fathers at once proclaimed it so. Too loudly—and provoking indignant replies from many scholars. For a gesture of compassion was not to be interpreted as a concession.

In assessing the spiritual (politico-spiritual?) epic of Li Mateou, we are tempted to observe first of all, like Jean Sainsaulieu, that the fate of the Great Sage of the West recalls that of Confucius—who, though greatly admired, was held at arm's length by the wielders of power. One should not, writes Sainsaulieu, "try to be more Confucian than Confucius, nor insist on recognition because one deserves recognition." But he adds that "after his death there emerged an identification of Jesuits and scholars; by becoming disciples of Master Kung, the missionaries had acquired a kind of Chinese citizenship."

Beyond question, Matteo Ricci and his companions opened up new intellectual prospects for the Empire. Particularly as concerned the critical mind and knowledge of the world—at once geographical and historical—and scientific logic, revealing to their hosts what one writer has called a "quasi-Martian learning." But did the sown seed ripen?

The Australian scholar Paul Rule questions the influence exercised on Ming China by these ambassadors of Renaissance Europe who also happened to be Jesuits. According to Rule, Ricci and his companions, having deliberately embraced Chinese ways, were "absorbed" by the redoubtable Chinese universe much more than they transformed it. Rule only just avoids stating that the thousand or so Jesuit fathers dispatched to China between 1580 and 1760, from Ruggieri to Father Amyot, harvested "fruit" there that was greatly outweighed by the corresponding impoverishment of a Europe deprived of their genius. In short, the most ambitious scientific expedition of modern times succeeded only in plowing the heavens.

But what cannot be denied is the great light bequeathed to Europe by the labors of the Great Sage of the West. Those twenty-eight years of experiment, stumbling, inquiry, and communion did at the very least produce Ricci's and Trigault's *History,* which remained the most beautiful and most faithful introduction to China available to men until the blossoming of contemporary Sinology.

Apostle, reformer, pioneer of the experimental method, inventor of impossible syntheses, Matteo Ricci may be challenged on all counts save one: After Marco Polo, but working as a student of civilizations, he had revealed China to the world.

We have no intention of dealing here with the "quarrel of the rites"* which erupted in the eighteenth century. As a fascinated Europe looked on, Ricci's young disciples (bent on accommodating the gestures and vestments of Catholic ritual to a vaguely Confucian ceremonial) found themselves confronted by a monolithic Roman Curia, always seeking blind obedience, and egged on against this laxity by outraged Dominicans and Franciscans (and by Pascal). It was a quarrel that ended with the condemnation of Loyola's Company.

A behavior suicidal for Christianity in Asia? It has often been so claimed. If it was, it speaks worlds for the chances for success of the "accommodation" so heroically attempted by Li Mateou between the tragic and metaphysical Heaven of Christians and the harmonious and reassuring *dian* of Confucius.†

---

*On which subject we direct readers to Étiemble's masterly book of the same title.
†To quote one last time from Gernet: "During the quarrel of the rites, around 1700, Europe passionately debated the question of whether Chinese Confucianism was superstitious and incompatible with the Christian faith, or purely civil and political and thus compatible with it. This represented a summary reduction to a single detail (which was meaningless outside the mental confines of the West) of a question of a very general nature: whether Christianity might be reconciled with a mental and sociopolitical system fundamentally different from the one in which it had evolved, and from which it was inseparable. It is a question unanswered by individual conversions."

· VIII ·

UTOPIA AND THE
GUARANÍ REPUBLIC

Harmonious Space, Authentic Art • *The Golden Legend, from
Voltaire to Chateaubriand* • *The Semi-Nomadic Tupi-Guaraní* •
Reducti Sunt • *A Spanish Bastion Against the Portuguese* •
The Mameloucos • *Maté Empire?* • *The Guaraní War* •
Hunting Indians . . . and Jesuits • *Two Films, Two Views*

IRST THE FOREST, the *selva*.
On either side of the line that cuts straight as a conquistador's sword from Fos de Iguazúin, Brazil, to Posadas in Argentina, across the province named Misiones, stretches a thick forest of dark-leafed auracaria and eucalyptus, undeniably thick, but much less dense than when the Guaranís roamed five centuries ago and when the first Jesuits, machetes in hand, hacked their way through.

About a hundred miles south of the miraculous Iguazú Falls, San Ignacio seems at first just an ordinary village, like so many others: houses of brick and wood, stores, a church. But it has a shaky little sign pointing to "Ruinas Jesuiticas." What traces can have remained of the great plunder of 1767 and of the fire of 1817, lit by the Paraguayan dictator Rodríguez de Francia?

At first masked by branches, then crouching inside its clearing like a decapitated Angkor, a battle of lianas and red basalt or sandstone at the heart of a silence striated by birdcalls. Here it is, the "reduction"* of San Ignacio Mini, where a large stone covers the remains of the two pioneers of the so-called Guaraní Republic, Giuseppe Cataldino and Simone Maceta.

---

*For more on this word, see p. 237 ff.

You walk upon scarlet tiles between walls overgrown with bushes—*laurel negro, cocú,* and *yerba,* the bush from which maté is made—gazing at baroque capitals that speak of the descriptive and visionary genius of the "savages" who for nearly a century, under the guidance of the good fathers, made of this papal kibbutz a crucible of cultural redefinition. For better and worse . . .

And at once the meaning of the project swims imperiously into view: a reinvention of landscape and of space, subjected to the dictates of line and stone, to the decree of an intellect dominated, as in Beijing, Versailles, or Saint Petersburg, by the laws of reason. What was built here (in what is now Argentina) in the heart of the forest, although perhaps not Tommaso Campanella's City of the Sun, was a city of "civilizing" order, rational, productive, and aspiring to such perfection that it could not have been conceived and constructed by any except a one and almighty God.

Of all the enigmas—spiritual, political, cultural, linguistic, historical—raised by the ambiguous saga of the Jesuit reductions in Paraguay, there is one that is dispelled by the simple act of beholding: the one linked to the nature of the enterprise—or the enterprise as it was after its late seventeenth-century evolution through successes and failures, tragedies and victories.

It was clearly an autocratic reordering, first of a landscape and through it of a people. In short, a vision of the world such as the great European monasteries, the Benedictines in particular, sought to create during the Middle Ages, rooting and organizing the barbaric forest tribes. Three centuries later, it is said, the great town planner Lúcio Costa drew his inspiration from these models to design and build Brasilia.

But it is not the original San Mini (1610) whose ruins you visit in the 1990s: This is the third version of the reduction founded by the Italian fathers Cataldino and Maceta. However vital it had been from the start to settle, sedentarize, and group the Guaranís (who had in any case been only seminomadic), the first communities had been doomed to instability by the convulsions that then shook what was called Paraguay, triggered by the greed of slave hunters and by Spanish-Portuguese rivalries.

Fleeing their native Guairá, which had been stripped bare by the raids of Portuguese-led slave dealers, San Ignacio's parishioners were forced, twenty years after their first settlement, to trek southward beyond the giant Iguazú Falls to the "fertile triangle" framed by the Paraná and Uruguay rivers. That second settlement was also destroyed. It was then, in 1696, that two Italian Jesuit architects, first Father Angelo Paragressa and then Brother Giuseppe Brasanelli (apparently known as "the little Michelangelo") built the third San Ignacio, known as Mini (small) in opposition to the first one (in present-day Paraguay), known as Guazú (big).

If the geometrical layout of the reduction spoke worlds for the didactic spirit of the project—rationalization of space, the fostering of a small, closely supervised, productive, and monotheistic community—the plastic details of the buildings tell us something quite different: true cultural synthesis, or at the very least a hybridization. The planning was authoritarian and reductive and drew on foreign concepts. The carving was free, "native," pregnant with authenticity. What could have been more eloquent than the portico leading to the cloisters of San Ignacio, which art historian Enrique Busaniche has called "the jewel of American art" (Why didn't he say "Amerindian"?).

Departing radically from Brasanelli's neoclassical buildings, the bas relief that decorates this portico and many other decorative details display a luxuriance of imagination, of form, of themes whose symbolism speaks powerfully of a tropical culture—so much so that a Roman "visitor," no matter how inured to rococo exuberance, might have discerned a barbaric deviltry in it. For this Guaraní baroque was not simply a Roman grafting. It had its own flavor.

Colonized, their vision of the world and their traffic with that world "reduced," the Guaranís thus recalled to their masters the vitality of their native genius* and turned the reductions into a celebration of cultural cross-breeding. It was admittedly an unequal marriage. But the vigorous forest is not the only factor here to remind us that the reductions designed for the Guaraní were not exclusively a triumph of imported culture over yielding nature.

Was this cultural fertilization? Violation of a natural equilibrium? The debate on the meaning and spirit of the Jesuit missions to the Guaraní remains wide open, and is lively even within the Company. Soon after my visit to San Ignacio Mini I went to the 5,000-student Jesuit School in Rio de Janeiro and met two remarkable people: the rector, and a sister of the Sacred Heart clearly invested with an authority that would have surprised the founder.

I asked each of them how they saw the multi-visaged epic of the Guaraní reductions. The rector replied that the "Jesuit republic" saved a people and a language: "By leading the Guaraní beyond the Iguazú rapids they protected them from the *Paulistas*.† By insisting that only Guaraní be spoken in the missions, they allowed it to remain a written language."

To which Sister Mariana calmly riposted: "Yes. But a culture is not just a people and a language. Sociologists specializing in Indian studies now present a more subtly shaded picture—even a negative one—of the experience the Jesuits brought to the Guaraní. We know what was won. But not what was lost. What values, what beliefs, what balances were destroyed: We have to look at it all over again."

*We shall see the same phenomenon in music.
†São Paulo (hence, *Paulista*) slave raiders.

A process that is already under way, led by a Spanish Jesuit, Father Bartolomeu Melia. Living among the Indians, this sociologist has attempted in his *El Guaraní Conquistado y Reducido* (The Guaraní Conquered and Reduced) to reconstruct that sixteenth-century cultural shock and to evaluate its positive and negative consequences for the people indoctrinated by the men who founded the reductions.

It is thus in the very heart of the Company that the problems we shall now examine are being debated. It would perhaps be too brutal to reduce them to a double-edged question: In attempting to prevent genocide, were the founders of the so-called Guaraní Republic guilty of "ethnocide"? Or else, to avoid ethnocide, did they not simply replace slavery with a devout form of colonialism, or even a fatherly (and we should not recoil from the word) apartheid? Such questions are not the sum of the author's opinions on the subject. But they are a good starting point for an inquiry.

You cannot examine the case of the Guaraní Republic without referring to the Golden Legend that enveloped it from the start, sometimes the work of sworn enemies of the Company like Voltaire or d'Alembert. The current of malicious rumor that, particularly in France, so often followed the Jesuits' moves—from their attempts to rival the Sorbonne to the quarrel over "Chinese rites" to the arguments over Gallicanism or Jansenism—here seems to have been reversed. For the century of the *philosophes* now witnessed a gathering wave of praise for the men of Loyola, so recently attacked by the likes of Pasquier and Pascal.

The man initially responsible for this sustained eulogy was the Italian philosopher Antonio Muratori, a native of Modena who never once left his birthplace: His information was largely based on the letters of a fellow countryman, Father Cattaneo, who had "missionized" in Paraguay. Muratori's book, published in 1743 under the title *Il Cristianesimo felice nelle missioni della Compagnia di Gesù* (Happy Christianity in the Jesuit Missions), had been an enormous success.

Charles-Louis Montesquieu owed much to him, and conferred the authority of his more scientific and "secular" outlook on the apologia of Muratori, a most fervent Catholic who saw the missions as a reincarnation of the Early Church. Comparing their Jesuit lawmakers to Lycurgus and Plato, Montesquieu saluted them as founders of the ideal city, where they had managed to "govern men by making them happy" and glimpsed in this "model republic" a finally realized Utopia.

Denis Diderot attempted in vain to put his readers on their guard against the "curious mania" of these individuals who traveled to the far corners of the earth, leaving behind them "the commodities of life," to devote themselves to "the painful and unhappy function of missionary" under the spur of "that terrible impulsion that is religious enthusiasm." In vain did he castigate the Paraguayan Jesuits as "harsh Spartans and blackjackets": He was submerged by the wave of admiration felt by the Europe of the Enlightenment for this ideal city the good fathers had built for the Guaraní.

The author of the *Supplément au voyage de Bougainville*, having praised the great French navigator's farsightedness and "philosophical" mind and a vision that "seized at once the essence of things," could hardly object to Bougainville's verdict on the Jesuit achievement: "Of a barbarous nation without customs or religion, they created a gentle, disciplined people . . . charmed by these men they saw sacrificing themselves to their happiness."

In *Candide,* Voltaire was pleased to convey his hero through Paraguay, where he saw Jesuits eating "a luncheon in golden bowls . . . in a verdant room adorned with parrots, hummingbirds, and flycatchers," while Indians ate "maize in wooden gourds in their fields by the heat of the sun," and where the head of the mission, a German colonel, helmet on head and sword in hand, proclaimed: "We shall give a vigorous welcome to the King of Spain's men. I tell you they will be excommunicated and beaten." But in his *Essai sur les moeurs,* the same Voltaire almost fervently hails this Society, in which everything undertaken was in the name of "reason" and by the paths of "persuasion" and which on many counts was a "triumph of mankind." Buffon, the Abbé Raynal (he had been a member of the Company), shared this enthusiasm, which was to be tempered by pity when the fathers fell victim to the terrible repression unleashed by Europe's kings after the Guaraní War.

Later still, Chateaubriand—normally reserved on the subject of the Jesuits, whose relations with the Bourbons seemed suspect to him—and Auguste Comte, who so admired them that he proposed to forge an alliance with the Company to found the Positivist State he dreamed of, became heralds of the Jesuit-Guaraní myth.

It is through these clouds of incense that we must try to discern the truth about one of the boldest enterprises in the history of society, culture, and belief, about this peaceful (but can we say nonviolent?) intrusion of reason into the world of myth, of order into the world of the forest, of the state into a society without a state, and of Utopia into history.

The Jesuits had not been the first Christians here, as they had been in Japan or China. If only by reason of the date of their founding (1540), they had been preceded at the beginning of the century by the Franciscans, as well as the Dominicans and Fray Bartolomé de las Casas and Fray Montesinos, who had bravely condemned the European massacre of the Indians.

Yet since mid-century, Fathers Manuel de Nobrega and José de Anchieta, the founder of São Paulo, had been laying the first Jesuit foundations from Bahia toward Peru, the River Plate, and Paraguay, where Asuncíon was the center of the adventures to come. A Jesuit school was founded there in 1595. And it was there, in 1603, that a synod convened at the instigation of a cousin of Ignatius of Loyola, Martín, decided to send Jesuits to Guairá, the land of the Guaraní, on the Paraná River.

Franciscan missionaries had already tried to evangelize the "savages" and herd them into communities. But their efforts were overshadowed by struggles between rival Spanish and Portuguese imperialist forces and by the worst kinds of colonial excesses, and the conversions they obtained not only were meaningless but failed to achieve even a modicum of regional peace. Which was why Francisco de Victoria, the Bishop of Tucumán, a Dominican impressed by the experimental communities founded in Brazil by Father de Nobrega, had resigned himself to calling on the Jesuits, whose fifth Superior General, Claudio Acquaviva, was already preparing the move in Rome.

But to understand the methods and strategies involved in the creation and expansion of the Paraguayan reductions, we must briefly examine the tensions then plaguing the South American continent, the interpower conflicts, and the condition of the tribes who would become first the stakes and then the central players in the game.

Immediately after Christopher Columbus had claimed the continent in the name of the Spanish sovereigns (those of Portugal and France having refused their help), Pope Alexander VI—a Borgia, and therefore Spanish—had persuaded the courts of Lisbon and Madrid to sign the Treaty of Tordesillas of 1594, demarcating their two empires: The Castilians were assigned all lands west, and the Lusitanians all those east, of the 50th meridian, some 350 miles from the Azores, not far from modern São Paulo. Despite the theoretical union of the Spanish and Portuguese crowns in 1580, this totally arbitrary line became the source of permanent clashes, which would shape the history of the Jesuit reductions in Paraguay.

Bitter as it was, Spanish-Portuguese rivalry was not simply a matter of diplomacy and state, of frontiers and territories. It was also cultural and practical. It cannot be said that Spanish colonization of the Amerindian continent was sweet or reasonable. Slaughter was its initial mode of expression. But following the stern warnings issued by las Casas and Cortéz's Franciscans, Spanish power attempted to "civilize" its approach, to proceed less through plunder and extermination than by influence and persuasion, challenging the practice of slavery, which was increasingly condemned for practical rather than moral reasons.

Many learned men evoked Aristotle and his justification of the enslavement of barbarians, but it was clear that the tribes would rather resist than submit.

The ideas of las Casas made inroads in the Spanish colonies: In 1543, "new laws" for the prohibition of slavery were being prepared—at the same time maintaining the *encomienda* system, which put the native at the disposal of the settler, who was master no longer of the native's body but (on condition the settler brought him "to the Christian faith") of his capacity for work. Nothing was less likely to rally the Indians to the Gospel than this form of servitude, whether practiced in its most radical or in its milder (*mita*) form. The encomienda could assume such ferocious forms—in the Potosí silver mines, for example—that the wretched Indians sent to work there were obliged to hear the Service for the Dead before their caravans headed out.

Terrible though it was, the Spanish yoke was at least mitigated by rules, admittedly based more on physical yield than on human need, but which the Governors in Lima, Buenos Aires, and Asuncíon strove to apply. In Portuguese territory, the harshest kind of jungle law held sway. The settler was king or god. Despite the exhortations of a great Jesuit missionary, Antonio Vieyra, the Indian was regarded as livestock, raw strength, something to be hunted down like game. Worse, the most powerful São Paulo families had raised bands of Indo-Portuguese so ferocious that they were called *mameloucos* (in memory of the Moorish Mamluks' occupation of the Iberian Peninsula), whose only function was to capture "savages."

As soon as the Spanish began their attempt at self-improvement, entrusting innovative missionaries with the transformation of relations between the Indian world and European order, the brutal energies unleashed from São Paulo by the feebler Portuguese administration inevitably clashed with them: two powers, two world views, even two centuries—that of pure rapine in the Portuguese East, of colonization in the Spanish West—now fought with no quarter asked or given. Against this background, between 1610 and 1767, the adventure of the Guaraní Republic unfolded.

The territory where our story took place must not be confused with what we now call Paraguay. It was from that region that the movement started, with Asunción more or less its starting point. But the cradle of the enterprise was the province called Guairá, the land of the Guaraní, which now extends across two provinces in Brazil (Paraná and Río Grande Do Sul) and northern Argentina (Misiones and Corrientes).

In fact, the history of the Guaraní Republic is one of physical movement. It looked like an extended voyage up three rivers—the Paraguay, Paraná, and Uruguay—with the Paraná as its main axis. The first cities were born on the west bank of the upper Paraná, and the great exodus of 1630 began on the Paranapanema, its tributary. It was in Entre-Ríos, between the Paraná and the Uruguay rivers, that the confederation that astonished the world for a century and a half was established.

If we look at today's frontiers we see that of the thirty-eight reductions which for decades survived* looters, killers, and *mamelouco* slave-catchers, fifteen were in Argentina, eight in Paraguay, seven in Brazil†—in total, an area of about 500 by 210 miles (over 100,000 square miles), an area half as big as Texas. They involved the destiny of about 200,000 Guaraní Indians and a little more than 200 Jesuit fathers (of whom some thirty were slaughtered for one reason or another).

But who were these Guaraní? The most important and probably most numerous of the tribes, or confederations of tribes, were between Peru, Amazonia, and the Río de la Plata. No connection, of course, with peoples as advanced as the Incas, Mayas, or Aztecs, who had built urban civilizations and developed a sumptuous artistic heritage. And very different from the wandering throngs of Late Stone Age hunters, like their neighbors the Guaycurú or Charrúa.

The Guaraní—anthropologists prefer the name Tupi-Guaraní—were semi-nomads practicing simple slash-and-burn farming techniques. Possessing only wooden digging implements, they moved from site to site, depending on crop and season. Great hunters, sporadic livestock-raisers, they lived in small groups made up of twenty or so nuclear families. They were polygamous and practiced cannibalism, above all on prisoners of war.

Peaceable but brave, they had at first welcomed the Europeans, seeing in them (as the Incas and Aztecs had done before them) demigods possessed of supernatural powers—whereas their neighbors the Guaycurú, much more warlike, always resisted European penetration. It had taken the excesses of the conquerors, then the encomiendas, and then the Paulista slave raids to make them rise up against the newcomers. During Holy Week in 1539, they attempted to seize Asunción, bringing terrible repression down on their heads. But when the Jesuits approached them with intelligence and understanding, their just anger gave way to curiosity, often to welcome, sometimes even to conversion.

It is true that the Fathers very soon made it a practice to learn the Guaraní language, with the most eminent of them, Antonio Ruiz de Montoya, drawing up a Guaraní grammar and lexicon. From 1615 on, no Jesuit was sent among the Guaraní unless he could speak the language. It is also true that the Jesuits brought with them gifts much preferable to the usual trinkets, glass beads, mir-

*Forty-eight were founded.
†Within their present frontiers.

rors, and musical instruments:* iron tools, particularly the axe, whose introduction revolutionized agricultural productivity and constituted, in Alfred Métraux's words, "a true cultural revolution." In fact it is unanimously agreed that the Jesuits derived much of their prestige from their position as suppliers of harpoons for fishing, of hooks, and of plowshares. No gift was more appreciated by their pupils.

The basic fact of Guaraní society, as Pierre Clastres, among others, described it (in his *L'Esprit des lois sauvages*), was the total absence of central authority, or rather of any coercive institutionalized authority, since the *caciques,* or chiefs, exercised a merely provisional authority, tempered by that of the shamans, wizards possessing indefinable powers (the most famous of them being known as *karaï*).

In this kind of society, both sources of authority—caciques and shamans—had more duties toward the community than means of swaying that community: Indeed, the chief was beholden to the group rather than the other way around. For better or worse, the Guaraní community, which was in any case highly individualistic outside the framework of the nuclear family, was quite simply a society without a state and even without any form of higher authority.

Roger Lacombe remarks that the Jesuits were well placed to understand such a state of affairs. They had of course woven many alliances with state powers in the course of their history, particularly with the most powerful of them in Europe, the court of Castile—not to mention the Holy See. But they were by nature prone to distrusting established powers, which had, after all, crucified Jesus, persecuted Christians, reduced the Pope to a vassal of the Holy Roman Empire, made Lutheranism the official religion of half Germany, and forbidden the Jesuits to turn the Sorbonne into a second Gregorian Institute.

Religion itself did not in any case constitute an impassable barrier between Guaraní and Jesuit. The beliefs of the Guairá Indians—which varied from tribe to tribe—of course had little in common with those the newcomers brought with them. But there was a bit of common ground.

Some Tupi-Guaraní tribes were animists: One of the first historians of the "Jesuit Republic," Father de Charlevoix, reports that two missionaries came across a village that revered a giant snake endowed with an altar on the same scale. Underlying such cults was the need for protection against the demons who controlled forest and storms. It was against these implacable forces that the help of the shamans was invoked. The most feared of these deities was Tupan, lord of the thunder.

But other tribes believed in a higher Being, master of the Land without Evil, where the just would one day be led by a "civilizing hero," something not unlike

*To which we shall of course be returning.

the Christian Paradise. They revered a certain Païe-Sumé, in whom the Jesuits claimed to have found a Saint Thomas who apparently evangelized not only the East Indies* but also the West: quite an accomplishment for a saint of notoriously little faith!

Speaking of the Tupi-Guaraní, Roger Lacombe points to "a certain messianism, a fairly common characteristic among nomad peoples," adding that they believed in a promised land and that it "lay before them": whence the myth of El Dorado, so named by the conquerors for the supposedly abundant gold there—a gold that meant nothing either to the "savages" or the missionaries. This shared absence of greed was possibly the strongest link between them.

The plan to make of the Guaraní—given their gentler customs and their "higher" beliefs—a sort of model community, after rescuing them from the permanent depredations of raiders seeking women and slaves, from the servitude of the encomienda and from seminomadism, was not born in the brain of just one Jesuit or colonial administrator. Under the aegis of Governor Hernandarias, and inspired by a great Jesuit, Diego de Torres-Bollo, it grew on the spot and step by step in the very first years of the sixteenth century, from the Synod of Asunción in 1603 to the so-called Alfaro Decrees of 1611. Sometimes, too, Jesuits impatient for action jumped the gun on the process (the first reduction, Loreto, was founded as early as 1609).

The decrees issued by the magistrate Francisco de Alfaro and inspired by the inventive genius of Torres—who was already aware of a similar project encouraged by Bartolomé de las Casas and the sporadic efforts of the Franciscans—can be summarized as follows:

One. Prohibition of all forms of slavery and encomiendas† for converted Indians.

Two. Gathering of the tribes into settled villages with a cacique and an independent town council, or *cabildo*.

Three. These communities to be off-limits to Spanish, Portuguese, Negroes, and half-breeds.

Those were the principles underpinning the "basic law" of the great venture: rejection of slavery, settlement, enclosure . . . which might also be called segregation. Spanish civil power played a decisive role through the intelligence of officials who were convinced of the harmfulness of uncontrolled exploitation; they were inclined to believe that a lightening of the colonial yoke, in the hands

---

*See Chapter IV.

†The abolition of the encomiendas was compensated by a tribute paid to the Spanish crown, a payment made through the intermediary of the Jesuits at the request of the Indians. Whence a surplus of power for the Company, which became a subject of furious debate, particularly in the eighteenth century.

of these Jesuit specialists in social engineering and spiritual persuasion, would better serve the interests of the Crown (particularly against the ambitions of the Portuguese, now dishonored by the Paulista slave raiders) than the ferocity of those who emulated Pizarro and the settlers. In the beginning, therefore, there was common ground between the objectives of the King and those of the Company. In the beginning . . .

It is now time to define the "reductions"—both the word and the phenomenon, which would in any case evolve profoundly between 1610 and 1760 through experiments, trials, successes, failures, and outside pressures.

We should first note that the Guaraní communities gathered together by the Jesuits from 1609 were not at first known as "reductions." They were at times called *doctrinas* or parishes, sometimes *pueblos* or villages (*aldeas* in Brazil). Nevertheless, they have come down in history under this curious name.

There are three standard definitions of the word: the one that comes from the Latin charter texts of the Jesuits; the one given by one of the heroes of the adventure, the great Ruiz de Montoya; and the one which Muratori, a century later, borrowed from Cicero.

First the charter declaration: "Ad vitam civilam et ad ecclesiam reducti sunt" (They have been reduced to civic life and the Church). Here the stress is on the authoritarian nature of the operation, imposed from above, on the transition to urban culture and conversion to Catholicism. We shall return to these points.

Ruiz de Montoya is more precise, defining the reduction as "a village of Indians who, from living according to their ancient customs, were reduced by the diligence of the Fathers to living in large centers, to living a human life there and clothing themselves." A most interesting observation as far as ancient customs were concerned, but recalling only nakedness and making no reference to cannibalism or polygamy, nor—and it is to this point in particular that we shall be returning—to idleness.

The third description of the reduction is by Muratori: He praises "the first man able to assemble and unite in one place men previously scattered in the countryside or in lairs in the rocks. . . . From being ferocious and cruel, he made them human and peaceable." Here the meaning of the Latin and Spanish words *reducere* and *reducir* becomes striking: It amounts to the grouping together of beings earlier doomed to being "scattered," that is, people thought, to savagery. Bring them together, and they will become men . . . *civilized, policed:** We return constantly to this idea of the city, of the group, of settled cohabitation.

But another of the givens implicit in this word must be taken into account: It

---

Civitas, polis.

is strategic. We shall be returning to the intentions of the founders, anxious to protect "their" Indians from the Paulista slave hunters. Caesar was known to be skilled in the art of *reducere,* of concentrating his lines of defense the better to repel attackers. And the first Jesuit maps designated the future reductions as *oppida Christianorum*—Christian fortresses—singularly military terminology.

The word is thus complex and pregnant with questions. Only one of the many interpretations suggested by historians seems wrong: the one that sees in the word the notion of "bringing back" the Indians to the true religion. Of course the evangelical intention was obvious, even basic. But that *reducti sunt* has an essentially sociological and cultural meaning. If it had been primarily a question of religion, the founders would have written *ducti sunt*—not "led back" but simply "led." Unless they considered them the disciples of Paï-Sumé, of Saint Thomas . . .

The idea of concentration, of socialization, of conviviality, the first stage of urbanization, the royal road to civilization, is essential. Yet we must be careful not to associate the word "reduction" with the idea of a camp—even though in a film we shall shortly be discussing the word is constantly rendered by that misplaced notion.

The reduction was thus a sort of collective crucible for the forging of civilized people; a workshop of socialization and conversion doing double duty as a fortress. The description we have given of San Ignacio Mini probably conveys this: Everything was designed, crafted, and built to foster communal living ordered by reason and illumined by faith in an only God.

Scholars have sought the origins of this grandiose design in the great European Utopianists of the period, Thomas More or Tommaso Campanella. That is why the Guaraní Republic has so often been discussed in this light—whereas it was in reality one of the most durable achievements, material as well as spiritual, of the Jesuit organizing spirit, anchored in sociological, agricultural, and military realities, and with highly utilitarian goals.

In fact, as Montoya's definition suggests, the dream of the reductions, maturing through divers experiments and abortive attempts, was inspired much less by foreign models than by Guaraní tradition. Admittedly, the idea of permanent settlement went against the semi-nomadic habits of these tribes; admittedly, the stress placed on community spirit did not reflect Guaraní individualism; and admittedly, the promotion of work as the community's code deeply disturbed a group given to a spontaneous heedlessness modified only as need arose. But the flexibility of the reductions' social organization, the balance struck between the authority of the cacique and the officials of the cabildo, egalitarianism, and protection of the nuclear family were all a response to the hopes and expectations of the Guaraní.

For a people so long ignorant of authority and discipline, such treatment was inevitably overwhelming. The "settled" (*reducido* in Spanish) Guaraní endured the constraints of four superimposed hierarchies:

- That of the Jesuit Father of the pueblo, himself owing obedience to the superior of the *misiones,* to the Provincial of the order, and to the Superior General in Rome—who himself owed obedience to the Pope, who himself . . .
- That of the Governor of the province of La Plata, subordinate to the Viceroy of Peru, appointed by Madrid;
- That of the secular clergy, the Bishop of Asunción, subordinate to the Archbishop of Buenos Aires: a parallel structure that greatly complicated things and was at the root of many clashes;
- and to the tribal authority of the cacique, backed by the cabildo, or council, a *corregidor* (or constable), an alcalde, and native *alguaciles,* all locked in a most complex relationship.[1]

To this impressive listing, we must add a fifth kind of authority, that of the shamans, wizards whom the Jesuits certainly tried to abolish but who here and there survived and who strove to exploit the Jesuits' mistakes. As Maurice Ezran observes, "The Indian who had left his tribe to enter the reduction was regimented and watched over. He had no option but to submit and adhere to this new system of values."[2]

What was a reduction like? Here we most often refer to the third-generation missions, those rebuilt at the end of the seventeenth century, like San Ignacio. The early ones looked very different: Toward 1650, when he arrived at San Francisco Xavier, Father Paucke, a solid German, was astonished to find nothing there

> that resembled a street or a square. The Indians' wooden huts, no more than eight or nine feet high, were separated by a stinking mud ooze: cows walked in it undisturbed and the Indians tossed the remains of slaughtered beasts there. The church and the Fathers' "dwellings" were made of untanned leather and looked like gypsy encampments. Yet the church had a straw roof: two small bells had been attached to a post nearby. The altar was of mud bricks dried in the sun; it was adorned with a crucifix and two cattle horns filled with sand in which to set candles.

And how many inhabitants could be found in a reduction? If from the seventeenth century onward its ground plan was uniform ("Who has seen one has seen them all," wrote a correspondent to Bougainville), and the dwellings standardized, the size and population of the community could vary from 300 to 1,000 families, that is, from around 2,000 to 7,000 or 8,000 souls.

There are many contemporary accounts of the daily life of a Guaraní reduction, particularly those that use the *Lettres édifiantes et curieuses* written by Jesuit fathers such as Florentin de Bourges. The bell rang at dawn. Mass for everyone, followed by the distribution of maize gruel. Compulsory school for children from the age of seven. The workshops of the *talleres* (craftsmen) began to open around the *colegio,* and the farmworkers needed for collective labor departed, singing and with pious banners flying, for the fields. An hour's rest for lunch, at about eleven in the morning. The afternoon hours, until about five, were devoted to caring for the family plot. The whole to the sound of ceremonial song.

The only comparable way of life was the monastic one. This became particularly clear during festivals, especially those of the patron saints of the reductions, Ignatius, Francis, Miguel, and Pedro. These displayed a tangled fusion of Jesuit theatrical religiosity and the wild baroque spirit of their neophytes, with an aftertaste of Spanish militarism and forest paganism. As Muratori wrote:

> They capture birds alive, the most striking by virtue of their appearance and the diversity of their colors, and attach them by their feet to triumphal arches with cords long enough to allow them to flutter . . . and set along the street small tigers and other fierce beasts tied up so as to harm nobody. . . . The feast is preceded by the playing of trumpets and drums drawn up around the officer bearing the royal standard . . . astride a richly caparisoned horse which sets off at the head of the procession toward the church.

Are we in San Ignacio, or Toledo, or Seville?

This Spanish-style *Gloria Dei,* this triumphant display of gold and incense and singing of psalms, this theophany in the service of theocracy, the Fathers had imposed on "their" savages only at terrible cost. No one has described better than Maxime Haubert the unbelievable effort implicit in what the exasperated Diderot called "the painful and unhappy function of the missionary."

Ruiz de Montoya reported that when he reached the first reduction, that of Loreto, he found Fathers Cataldino and Maceta

> very poor. . . . Their soutanes had been so often patched that the original fabric could scarce be seen; their shoes had themselves been patched up with pieces of soutane. Hut, furniture, and food would have well suited an anchorite. They had tasted neither bread nor salt for many years, and were reduced to sowing with their own hands the wheat necessary for the Host; half a jeroboam of wine [less than a gallon] lasted them nearly five years, for they used it only for the Consecration. To avoid having to beg from the Indians, the Fathers had their own little garden where they grew a few vegetables, sweet pota-

toes, and manioc, which made up their meals; as for meat, they set eyes on it but rarely, when their pupils were kind enough to bring them a small piece of game.

According to an account of 1628, for the greater part of the year the missionaries wear a cotton soutane crudely dyed black ("with mud and the juice of certain leaves"); they eat without seasoning, like the Indians; some years they have wine, and others not; they sleep in hammocks. . . . Father Falconer, who has no plate for eating the horsemeat he shares with them, uses instead his hat: This became so greasy that the dogs ate it while he slept; similarly, termites invaded the bed of Father Dobrizhoffer. . . . Leeches, bats, and toads infest the roads, the houses, clothing, utensils, the church itself; dormice, which travel in droves, destroy all in their path, gnawing cloth and hungry for beef . . . and biting sleeping people. Florian Paucke swears that he has identified forty-eight species of worm on his table. If the missionary does not wish to find his soup full of hairs and lice, he must prepare his food himself.

Did the missionaries—who had turned the prodigious miracle of the Iguazú Falls into a strategic weapon—find some esthetic consolation in contemplation of the somber beauty of the pampas or the Chaco? Apparently not, says Maxime Haubert. They found no such compensation for their strivings and suffering: "Among the savages, it is with God alone that the Jesuits live and work: It is only in His love that they find comfort, only in His glory that they situate their pride."

People talk of a Jesuit state, sometimes adding the qualifier "Socialist," and even "Communist." But a state? Why use a word which is both overambitious and inadequate? From 1609 onward, through countless incarnations, the Jesuits founded more than forty reductions on the river Paraná and its surroundings, grouping (depending on the period) anything from 30,000 to 150,000 Indians. Three of them lasted more than a century. They could therefore claim longevity. They also boasted two capitals, one political and religious in the north, Candelaria, the other economic and in the south, Yapeyu. But neither singly nor collectively could they be defined as states, even in comparison with the Italian and German principalities of the time.

As we have seen, each of these colonies was slotted into a hierarchical machinery managed from Madrid and Rome. That a degree of administrative—and later economic and military—autonomy was granted them does not imply a state structure. From the economic standpoint, the prosperity of the reductions was such that Pierre Chaunu entitled his book about them *L'Empire du Maté*. We have seen too that Montesquieu spoke in terms of a "republic" of the mind rather than of practical reality. Maurice Ezran speaks of a "proto-state," which perhaps comes closest to what they represented.

In fact the Guaraní Republic was a confederation of autonomous cooperativist theocracies, but so far from true independence that when they attempted to assert their right to existence in the face of an unjust treaty* that condemned them to disintegration, they were mercilessly broken and scattered.

What was Spain's underlying objective when it encouraged its representatives in America to support and legalize the Jesuit project? As we have seen, it was partly an attempt to revise a system of aggression that was dying of its very excesses, and that would have imploded in horror and revulsion if the political arts of the Jesuits had not restored order. But it was also a strategic project.

A century after the Borgia Pope imposed the Treaty of Tordesillas on Madrid and Lisbon, no one knew any longer where the frontiers he had drawn actually lay. But what was obvious was that two imperialist systems had locked horns— the Portuguese, based on unbridled exploitation of land and people, in ceaseless quest of mineral deposits and of slaves for its planters; and the Spanish, more rational, more organizing, with longer-term goals, and which, having destroyed real empires from Mexico to Lima, now realized that this continent could produce something other than manpower and precious metals.

Outstripped or overshadowed by Spanish power ever since 1492, the Portuguese sought to recapture lost ground through feverish energy and unbridled recklessness, which were further exacerbated when (to cap it all) the large neighboring empire delivered lessons of morality, prohibitions on slavery and servitude. It was too much: They would go weapons in hand to seize this labor force that the Spaniard claimed to have confiscated—and as a matter of Christian virtue to boot . . .

Madrid decided that it would be wise to arm itself with an extra shield, and one blessed by God, to counter these furious, vengeful, and occasionally bloody energies. The Jesuit-Guaraní Republic was thus called into being—or at least accepted—as a buffer state between the Spanish Habsburg empire and the unruly henchmen of Lisbon. And so, in 1649, Philip IV of Spain granted the Guaraní the right of vassalage as the "barrier of Paraguay against Brazil."[3]

However fascinating, ideological debate over the nature of the Jesuit "state" would be misleading if it failed to recognize a potent economic fact that to a certain extent buttressed the reductions—the Jesuit schools of Latin America. The Swedish historian Magnus Mörner has made a special study of these underpinnings of the "socialist" enterprise of the Paraná, which were to the reductions what the generosity of the Jewish diaspora would later be to Israeli kibbutzim.

*The so-called Treaty of Limits of 1750 between Spain and Portugal. See p. 247.

Base camp, training center, and command post combined, the influential Jesuit schools at Buenos Aires, Córdoba, Asunción and Santa Fé, financed by inheritances and bold land purchases, had become veritable latifundia, economic bastions in which, according to Mörner, the Jesuits had put African slaves to work in order to avoid enslaving Indians. Without in any way detracting from our admiration for the Utopia created in Guaraní territory, from the superb efficiency and economic success of this paradoxical endeavor, we are forced to acknowledge the dark part played by this substantial supplementary source, by these capitalist cradles of a happy "socialism."

The history of the Paraguay reductions is just as turbulent as that of the Ignatian Society. And even more tragic. Nothing was missing: not audacity, invention, generosity of vision, self-sacrifice; not enormous material success, the temptations of the age, the tricks of power (Jesuit or anti-Jesuit); not the martyr's crown or the glory of genius. Was it the finest hour in the Jesuits' 500-year history? It was in any case the one Jesuit episode guaranteed to fire the imagination of novelists and filmmakers.

We have already mentioned the Franciscan forerunners. They had been, however, too closely linked to the colonial power to be welcomed to Guaraní territory in the sixteenth century, as the Jesuits would be in the seventeenth. We have also indicated that officials like Hernandarias and Alfaro at the very least "went along" with Spain's humanizing policies. It must also be said that in Rome, at the outset, Loyola's fourth successor, Superior General Claudio Acquaviva, supported the "Paraná adventurers" with admirable foresight: On May 1, 1609, he addressed to the fathers of Asunción an "instruction on the behavior of our people in regard to the foundation and to the direction of the Indian missions, which is the same as the advice we sent to the Province of the Philippines in April 1604 and to New Spain in June 1608."

We already know this method: Despite the difference in customs and in familiarity with the subject, it was the same as that which Francis Xavier, Valignano, and Ricci had developed in Asia, based upon a profoundly original conception of Christianity. As the sociologist Girolamo Imbruglia wrote in his preface to Muratori's book, it implied "a very broad vision of divinity which made it possible to exchange ideas with other cultures, which the Jesuits placed upon the same scale as the Christian religion, with the latter merely representing the topmost rung."[4]

It was those principles that drove the five founding fathers, the pioneers: Diego de Torres-Bollo, Provincial of Asunción (who was in a way their begetter); Antonio Ruiz de Montoya, strategist of the great 1630 exodus; the two Italians, Simone Maceta and Giuseppe Cataldino, who founded the first reductions at Loreto and San Ignacio; and Roque González, a Creole from Paraguay who was the most hot-blooded of the movement's militants until he was murdered in a plot devised by a shaman.

The first reductions were born in the closing months of 1609 and the first months of 1610. They were founded by the two Italian fathers Cataldino and Maceta, who enjoyed the support of Diego de Torres-Bollo. The latter had been named Provincial of Paraguay one year earlier by Superior General Acquaviva in order to give him greater independence from the Church hierarchy in Lima and Buenos Aires. Torres was an expert: A few years earlier he had launched an experimental Indian community at Juni on the shores of Lake Titicaca, which drew inspiration both from Inca communal life and from a similar effort in Amazonia by Manuel de Nobrega, the forerunner of all Latin American Jesuits. Nobrega had drawn this vital conclusion from the failure of his experiment: that success was tied to two conditions, respect for native culture and isolation of the Indians from the colonial world.

It was with these lessons in mind that Father Diego sent Cataldino and Maceta to the Guairá country, which lay on the Río Paranapanema, a tributary of the Paraná. The inhabitants of the region were said to be friendly, and their lands ripe for agricultural development. Since the newcomers brought with them the promise that the encomiendas would be abolished, the first reduction, christened Loreto in memory of Loyola's fondness for our Lady of Loreto, was flooded with Guaraní volunteers. Indeed the idea seemed so good that a local cacique, Aticayani, suggested that a second mission be founded. This was San Ignacio, already familiar to us in its third (and last) incarnation.

Judging by the model on display at the Curitiba Museum, the mission in this first phase was a military-style encampment made of wooden barracks built on a low hill on the south bank of the Paranapanema. A hundred or so buildings, drawn up in rigorously geometric order around the lofty church (built first of giant Parana cedar and later of red sandstone), the *colegio,* and the *cabildo.* Water, a bell, a defensible position, land . . .

Of course, the Jesuits (two per reduction, a rector and his vicar) did not assume all official authority. The "political" or administrative leadership was indigenous, and dominated by the cacique, the legal owner of community property, and the corregidor, charged with enforcing the law.

But the fathers, by virtue of their skills, their dedication to community tasks, their religious influence, and the appropriateness of their administrative style to the community's rules, were the true animators, inspirers, organizers, and managers. Paternalism and theocracy started with them and came back to them.

We shall of course return to the day-to-day operation of these communities, the demarcation lines between the collective and private sectors, the kinds of things they produced to earn a living. But what must first of all be stressed is that these were limited communities—a few thousand members at the height of their prosperity—leading rigorously ordered lives according to strict schedules (although never more than six or seven hours' work) and ceremonies of monastic character.

It was along these lines that the first ten reductions developed in the Paraná region between 1609 and 1630. Torres attempted to push his men in the direction of the Chaco, into the area peopled by the Guaycurú. But the horse, imported by the Spanish, had given wings to the Guaycurú's nomad ferocity, and they turned out to be intractable. The future of the reductions thus lay to the south, where Roque González typified the muscular Jesuit missionary.

A powerful figure. Contemporary observers all speak with admiration of this son of Asunción dignitaries, the perfect embodiment of the conquistador turned sturdy apostle, builder, farmer, architect, orator, polemicist, a superb agitator of galvanizing charisma and thunderous speech, with the gaze and demeanor of a prophet—and perhaps too obviously a "white shaman" not to attract a special hatred from witch doctors discredited by the newcomers. Which led to his murder (and that of his companion Alonso Rodríguez) on the steps of his church by a shaman's henchmen.

It was this eminently dynamic man, according to Maurice Ezran, who inspired the Indians to sow and raise cereals, a decisive innovation in the cultural transformation wrought by the Jesuits. More than any other factor, it would contribute to the prosperity of the reductions—so much so that contemporaries even spoke of the reductions as an "empire."

Already, though, the venture was under threat.

We have already spoken of the rapacity of the Portuguese-Brazilian planters. Unlike their Spanish competitors, who were bound by Alfaro's laws and the influence of a priesthood alerted by Las Casas and Montesinos, they were unrestrained by any central state authority. To these predators, the reductions were a challenge flung in their teeth. To deprive them of their human cattle, the Guaraní, their precious raw material! And to make of these subhumans citizens who, through an annual tribute to the King of Spain, were protected from the encomienda system and promoted to the rank of producers, of competitors!

The Spanish had to bite the bullet, since Madrid had spoken. But for the Portuguese, Madrid's laws did not exist. They quickly noted that since these guileless Jesuits had concentrated several score thousand Indians into a few enclosed areas, they would no longer even be obliged to track them down through the forests. These *aldeas* were so many henhouses for the fox.

And what foxes! São Paulo, founded less than a century earlier by Father José de Anchieta, was now a lawless metropolis dominated by a handful of clans possessing militias made up of the Tupi-Portuguese mameloucos. With the Paraná only two or three hundred miles from São Paulo, these gangs very quickly made a specialty of organizing slave raids against the reductions. The missions were unarmed and prosperous; the raids were risk free.

From 1628 onward, the vulnerability of the reductions was exacerbated by the nomination to the governorship of Asunción of a certain Luis de Céspedes, firmly on the side of the Portuguese, and owner of a large sugar plantation in Brazil. The Paulistas were quickly given the word: Henceforth nothing and no one would come to the rescue of the Jesuits' charges, earmarked for annihilation, or at the very least for the role of slave-breeders for the Brazilian plantations. In 1629 came the first organized assault on the Encarnación reduction. There was only one solution for the Jesuits: to move their faithful out of range of the mameloucos, far south of the Guairá region.

The man destined to play the part of Moses proved more than equal to the dual challenge of persuading the Guaraní to leave their home and of leading them to the promised land. A huge canvas in the Curitiba Museum, powerful and primitive, depicts the great journey. Gigantic, arm outstretched over the flotilla of hundreds of boats and rafts extending out into the Río Paranapanema, looms the black silhouette of Father Antonio Ruiz de Montoya, who, in just six months, moved the Guaraní people 500 miles south. It is estimated that some 50,000 Indians had been settled on the reductions before the mamelouco raids, and that something like 30,000 undertook the exodus.

The Indians from Loreto, San Ignacio, and San Miguel took the forest paths—nearly a hundred days on foot. Reaching the Paranapanema, they crowded onto the 700 boats and rafts Ruiz de Montoya had built. Then nearly 200 miles by river to the gigantic obstacle of the Iguazú Falls. The leader of the expedition tried floating a few empty craft down the cataracts: They were smashed to pieces. The fugitives had to slip along the foot of the cliffs through rushing shallows and foam. Many died in these rapids, and most of the boats were lost. But when they reached the foot of the fifteen miles of cataracts, the survivors felt that a rampart now stood between them and the mameloucos.

We do not know how many survivors Montoya gathered together for the final leg of this journey to the Mesopotamia of Entre-Ríos. There were possibly some 10,000 of them, a fifth of the total population of the reductions before the Paulista raids began. Their anabasis had cost them dearly. But those who survived the ordeal would prove to be effective pioneers, and the venture had given the Guaraní a great leader.

Ruiz de Montoya knew that although he had wrested this people from the worst, they would not long be able to defend themselves without serious weapons. Whether through Uruguay or by sea, the mameloucos would be back. The Guaraní must fight. He therefore obtained permission from his superiors to plead his cause before the King of Spain, Philip IV. Not only did the Council in Castile grant him the right to arm and train the Guaraní, but Pope Urban VIII issued a bull proscribing every form of slavery on pain of excommunication.

It was a first rebuff to the manhunters. But it was in the field that the Guaraní and their protectors had to prove themselves. The mameloucos soon provided the opportunity. In 1641, ferried by a hundred river craft, they set off down the Uruguay and landed in Entre-Ríos, close to the reduction whose defenders were led by the cacique Abariu. The Indian militias, mustering several hundred guns and supported by armed boats, confronted the attackers and cut them to pieces on the Río Mborore.

The Guaraní had assured themselves a century of relative safety. Their militia had displayed such valor that they were henceforth regularly used by the Spanish authorities against various neighbors or unwelcome visitors, Charrúa or Abipone Indians, or the Dutch and English who were active along the coasts. Whence the royal "schedules" that granted the Guaraní the status of protected vassals in return for an annual payment of one peso per head.

The Jesuits seemed to have won. And the whole enterprise now basked in the bright light of a book published in Madrid in 1639 by Ruiz de Montoya, *La conquista espiritual de Paraguay.*

But the battle would resume on quite different territory in Europe. And the Company—which had seemed in so strong a position there and which for once had the support of the *philosophes* of enlightenment in Paris—was to suffer one of the cruelest and most humiliating defeats in its history. And this was the Company that had succeeded with the skimpiest of means in imposing its living Utopia, its too earthly Paradise, on the Americas.

To understand this tragedy we must first grasp its political and diplomatic lineaments. At the center of everything stood relations between Madrid and Lisbon, the hellish spouses of the Treaty of Tordesillas. The two countries had of course been united in 1580 by the marriage of Philip IV to a Spanish Infanta. But in 1640 the Portuguese had regained their independence, and colonial rivalry, barely blunted by the fusion of the two crowns, had revived. A century of costly conflicts finally persuaded the two powers to seek agreement, at least territorially, in America.

The so-called Treaty of Limits of 1750 delivered the first irreparable blow to the Guaraní Republic. In exchange for ceding to Spain the port of Sacramento, on the River Plate, Lisbon acquired rights to seven reductions located east of the new frontier. A decisive victory for the Paulistas, and an unbearable moral and material defeat for the Jesuits, now forced (as subjects of the King of Spain and as model subjects of the Pope) to hand over to the slavers people who had trusted them, whose protection they had assumed, and whose conversion to Christianity they had supposedly guaranteed.

If the Portuguese were able to bring off such a diplomatic and psychological victory over the Spanish, it was not simply because the power of Madrid had declined over the past century. It was also because the influence of the French Court at Madrid (which had been decisive under Philip V, the grandson of Louis XIV) was waning, while in Lisbon British influence was on the rise. For England was more and more active in South America, and determined to use its Portuguese allies to destroy the empire built by Charles V.*

Moreover, England's long-standing anti-Jesuit tradition now found support in the courts of Lisbon, Madrid, and Paris. There three men of the so-called Enlightenment had come to power: the Marquês of Pombal, the Count of Aranda, and the Duc de Choiseul. All were strongly prejudiced against the "Iñiguists," the first because of Paraguay, the second for dynastic reasons, and the third as an ally of Madame de Pompadour, of the Gallicans and the Jansenists.

The zeal of this aristocratic coalition was moreover fanned by a double legend: that of the "treasure" of the good fathers, who could never have brought their missions to such a pitch of prosperity without digging up gold nuggets with their bare hands in some hidden mine, revenues that they withheld from the powers in Madrid and (or) Lisbon. And the legend of the secession of the "Guaraní State," a fictitious entity that had apparently already proclaimed its own "Emperor"—an old Indian cacique named Nicolás Nengiru. This was a major theme of the violent pamphlet drawn up at the Marquês of Pombal's instructions (*Abridged Report on the Jesuit Missions*), which caused a great stir in Madrid.

Thus, considered to have acted feloniously toward the Spanish Crown and to be the possessors of hidden treasure, the Jesuits found themselves weathering an avalanche of vicious slander campaigns by Spanish settler interests outraged by the competition of the reductions. For example, a memorandum delivered to the Inquisitor of the Holy Office at Lima condemns the Jesuits not only as hoarders of wealth but as the propagators of polytheistically tainted doctrine intended to corrupt the unfortunate Indians.[5]

Nor should we forget France's contribution to the destruction of the Guaraní Republic, not as the result of deliberate effort but through state traditions imported from Paris by Madrid with the coronation of the Bourbon Philip V.

*Read the excellent article by Roger Lacombe, "La Fin des bons sauvages," *Revue de la Société d'Ethnographie de Paris*, 1989.

Spain had an imperial tradition: The Emperor Charles V was (only?) King among kings, which implied a kind of federalism, a division and delegation of powers. But with the advent of the Bourbons, French-style state centralization came to Madrid. It proved much more hostile to marginal or outlying powers of the kind the Jesuits had founded in America. It was in this sense that the Bourbons, no matter how well intentioned toward the Society of Jesus, helped in the destruction of its most glorious overseas enterprise.[6]

It took nearly eighteen years, from 1750 to 1768, for the Jesuits' enemies, Portuguese or Anglo-Portuguese and then Spanish, to annihilate the Guaraní Republic. It did not come about without political and then military resistance from the Indians, who were of course exhorted, preached to, and led by their men in black. Roger Lacombe has unearthed sublime letters of protest issued by the caciques in the name of their people—the most solemn and picturesque being addressed to the Governor of Buenos Aires by the famous "Nicolás I, King of Paraguay," who would later lead the armed revolt:

> The Indians of Paraguay are convinced that it cannot be the King's intention that they withdraw. . . . This land God alone has given us. . . . Neither the Portuguese nor even one Spaniard has given us anything: the magnificent church, the fine village, the stables for our livestock, the barn, the cotton depot, the farms and all their dependencies are our work alone; why is it then that they greedily seek to seize the goods that are ours? They seek to mock us. It shall not come to pass in this way. God our Lord does not wish it so. . . .
>
> Is it for this then that the "Father Commissioner" has come? Is it he who wishes our Fathers to be different from what they once were? He has deceived them. He has brushed aside our love and wants only to make us leave our villages and our lands, at once and swiftly, that is all; he wants to turn us loose in the mountains as if we were rabbits, or in the desert as if we were snails. . . .
>
> I have written to you, Lord, the true words of the Indians. We members of the cabildo no longer possess words enough to silence them, nor to oppose them when they are angered. Therefore we humble ourselves before you so that you, according to the King's word, will come to our aid. First of all, we are his vassals: make the King understand our wretchedness and our pain.[7]

What emerges from such texts (no matter what part the Jesuits may have played in their drafting) is that a kind of national self-awareness had been born of the theocratic and productivist adventure of the reductions. By forging men in order to lead them to Christianity, the fathers had helped turn a few dozen scattered tribes, linked only by a common language and customs, into a kind of nation. "We humble ourselves before you." Words expressing at once wounded pride and a collective spirit.

But the European masters were not to be put off by such trifles. Their mind was made up. The Jesuit republic was not wanted. In May 1754 two armies were sent out against the reductions: One was Portuguese, coming by sea from the north, the other Spanish, moving up the River Uruguay from the south. Well before it reached the region it was to "purge" of Jesuits, the Spanish column collided with militia from Yapeyu, the southern capital of the "Republic" (even though that particular reduction was not one of those whose liquidation was planned: a remarkable proof of Indian solidarity). The Spanish overcame the Guaraní forces but were forced by dwindling supplies to fall back on Buenos Aires.

The Portuguese, surrounded and trapped by Indian guerrillas, were forced to sign a truce with the Guaraní, who insisted that the text be in both Portuguese and their own language. We can imagine Pombal's fury as he accused his Spanish allies of allowing him to be led into a trap so as to humiliate him. Madrid reacted by sending reinforcements and agreeing to a combined operation. In February 1756 the Guaraní War ended with the total defeat of the Indians at Caybate. The Spanish-Portuguese had bled them white. Some historians speak of 10,000 Guaraní killed,* against a total of 150 taken prisoner, which gives an idea of the ferocity of the struggle and the cruelty of the ensuing repression.

The King of Spain, Charles III, finally realizing that by liquidating a buffer zone of his Empire and slaughtering his own subjects he had been working for his Lisbon rival, now reversed course. Abolishing the treaty of 1750, he authorized the Indians to return to the seven reductions handed over to the Portuguese. But the spring had broken: The almost childlike faith of the Guaraní in their Jesuit mentors was profoundly shaken. The French explorer Louis Antoine de Bougainville, whose ship the *Boudeuse* was lying in the River Plate at the time, and who conversed with the Spanish authorities, reported that according to the Governor of Montevideo, many Indians had begged to be taken away from the reductions. Why? In his *Voyage autour du monde* he suggests this judicious argument (but only after lavishly praising the Jesuit system of governance which "did mankind such honor"):

> Subject to a cruelly monotonous uniformity of work followed by rest, a monotony rightly called mortal, . . . they left life without regret and died without having lived; so much so that when the Spanish entered the mission this great multitude administered like a convent appeared willing to break down the walls.[8]

*Spanish archives acknowledge only 1,350.

A specious explanation? We should remember that Bougainville was close to Diderot, author of *The Nun*. What is certain is that this monotony would have seemed less "mortal" if the Guaraní had not been betrayed by the Roman superiors of the Company, and later vanquished in 1757 by the Spanish-Portuguese.

The truth is that the respite granted the reductions after the Guaraní War was not experienced as a resurrection. Everyone, from the fathers to the converts, seemed only to be awaiting the coup de grâce. It was duly delivered in 1767 by Madrid, when it expelled the Company of Jesus from Spain and its American holdings. "Holy obedience" prevailed over the real chances of armed resistance to the grenadiers and dragoons of Buenos Aires. In April 1768 the last Jesuits, herded like rebels, were deported to Europe—but not before the *cabildo* and the caciques of the San Luis reduction had sent the Viceroy in Buenos Aires a new petition in which innocence takes on the beguiling accents of insolence:

> Concerning the request of our King for the dispatch of parrots of divers species, we deeply regret that we are unable to send them to him, for these live only in the forests where God creates them, and they flee from us and that is why we have been unable to hunt them.
>
> Nevertheless, we remain the loyal vassals of our God and our King, ready at all times to fulfill whatsoever he may desire. . . . We implore God to send us the most beautiful bird of all, which is the Holy Spirit, to you and to our King, to fill your eyes with light and prompt the guardian angel to assist you.
>
> Ah, Lord Governor! We who are truly your sons, demeaning ourselves before you, we beseech you with tears in our eyes to allow the Priest Fathers to stay always with us. . . . We do not love monks, nor do priests please us. The Apostle Saint Thomas, Pa-I-Zume, God's holy minister, converted our ancestors on these lands; and these priests and monks have taken no interest in us. . . . Then the sons of Saint Ignatius came and took great care of our fathers, instructing them and raising them in obedience to God and the King of Spain. . . . The Fathers of the Company of Jesus support our feeble natures with compassion, and we live a happy life for God and for the King. We are ready, if you wish it, to pay a higher tribute in plantation maté.
>
> We wish furthermore to tell you that we are not any kind of slaves, any more than our ancestors were.[9]

To close this tragic chapter we could do no better than to quote the great ethnologist Alfred Métraux:

> In 1767, following a gigantic police operation, the Jesuit missionaries were arrested and deported from all Spanish lands in America. This

date is important in the history of the New World. Vast territories which had been conquered and pacified were returned to nature. Thousands of Indians living peacefully in missionary settlements were doomed to death or material and moral decline. Others disappeared forever into the unexplored solitudes of Amazonia and the Gran Chaco. The mass expulsion of the Jesuits destroyed an empire created by the "conquistadors," an empire of a new kind which had achieved glittering successes.[10]

"Conquered," "pacified," "empire," "conquistadors" . . . The colonial-era vocabulary Métraux instinctively chooses helps highlight the ambiguity underlying this great venture. It was an enterprise not adequately defined by the phrase Maurice Ezran chose as the title to his book ("*colonisation douce*" or gentle colonization), nor even by the "tutelary aristocracy" coined by the Argentine sociologist Oreste Popescu, and still less by "Communist Christian Republic of the Guaraní," the subtitle of Clovis Lugon's book.*

In these pages we have tried to cover each stage of a human adventure that Father Philip Caraman has called "Homeric." But we must also try to define its political and social character, and to assess what was achieved on both the religious and the cultural planes. Lugon's use of "Communist" to describe the Paraná reductions is perhaps not charitable to the Jesuits but does at least pinpoint the authoritarian and arbitrary character of the missions. We shall not push the parallel any further by comparing the church of San Ignacio Mini to the Party Residence in Novosibirsk, or equate the two fathers traditionally assigned to each reduction with the local Party secretary and the *kolkhoz* manager; but we must not forget the collective, or rather communal, character of the system imposed upon the Guaraní.

A first comment: The begetters of the reductions—Torres, González, Montoya—were careful to incorporate existing traditions and institutions, both South American and purely Guaraní. Whether or not they had read Thomas More or Campanella, the founders stressed Amerindian teachings: Torres's experience in Peru prompted him to seek inspiration in Inca collectivism; González's knowledge of local conditions, which he owed to his Creole origins, drove him to draw upon Guaraní custom. It was onto these fundamentals that they affixed, or grafted, their European productivist system—which was inspired, as we have said, by the great monasteries of the Middle Ages.

Beyond its religious and cultural goals, the venture was essentially agricultural. The reductions were therefore based on a system for sharing or using land more or less codified by Guaraní tradition—the *nandereka*, or ancestors' law. In

---

*Its title translates as *The Republic of the Guaraní, the Jesuits in Power*.

the case of these semi-nomadic hunter-gatherers, it was obviously out of the question to seek answers from the experience of rural European populations, long rooted in their lands and haunted by fear of losing them. With the Guaraní, it was all a question of relationships.

The Guaraní, changing their territory every three years or so, from burned-out clearing to burned-out clearing, knew property only as temporary and communal. But the act of settlement implicit in the reductions meant a kind of appropriation. Was it collective or individual? Bearing in mind both Guaraní traditions and Incan community organization, Torres and his founding fathers instituted a hybrid system: On the one hand, the *ama'mbae* (man's land) or privately owned family plot; on the other, the *tupa'mbae** (or God's land), in other words, collective. In 1743 the system was legalized by royal decree, which specified that each private plot must meet the basic needs of a family.

At Madrid's behest, the Spanish colonial authorities objected that the fathers were discouraging the Indians from private ownership. They were ignoring the facts. A Guaraní set little economic store by his private plot: He worked it in the traditional way to keep the family in vegetables, and was not tempted to enlarge it or increase its yield. Semi-collectivism, paternalistic and family-oriented, under the control of the cacique and the fathers, seemed best suited to his needs.

Since inheritance did not exist, the modest possessions of a reduction's citizens returned, after death, to the community. As for women's jewels and ornaments, which were limited to two ounces of gold per person, the fathers encouraged their parishioners to make a gift of them to the church, where they adorned saints' statues. It was thus the *tupa'mbae* or collective property—which included livestock and buildings—that tended to grow, while the *ama'mbae* remained static.

Compulsory work was a salient feature of the reductions. Without such a constraint there would have been no community and no production, since the Guaraní were motivated neither by money nor by a desire to increase a family's wealth with a view to passing it on. However, the total hours worked both on collective and private land were relatively few, and were interrupted by frequent ceremonies and services.

Distribution of the harvest was handled by the fathers and the cacique, less in function of the needs of each (socialist-style) than "by favoring the requests of those who worked hardest . . . in order to stimulate them."[11]

In fact, if the Jesuits exercised any kind of coercion, it tended to be in the direction of privatization. According to Oreste Popescu, "Freedom to choose one's place of work and employment, to decide on one's own garden plan, to

*Tupan was the original deity, whose name the Jesuits had appropriated for "God."

determine one's level of consumption or to exchange goods was neither . . . hampered nor controlled but on the contrary encouraged. . . . The primary objective, in the *ama'mbae,* tended not to destroy but to elicit motivation for freedom of behavior."[12]

It is as difficult to discern in all this any ideological principle beyond paternalistic theocracy as it is to pinpoint the motives and reasons for the extraordinary century-and-a-half-long success of the venture. Neither terror (the penal system was benign for the period, with no provision for the death penalty) nor greed nor imperialism nor spirit of competition nor ethic. And where comparisons with the Israeli kibbutz are tempting, there is no possible parallel between the formidable energies generated by the tragic history of the Jews and the fundamentally easygoing nature of the Paraná Indians. Perhaps, in fact, Guaraní success in the reductions lay simply in their respect and admiration for these men in black who wore themselves out, and sometimes met a martyr's end, for their benefit.

But it was the production of maté, the favorite drink of the meat-eating denizens of the Paraná and the Entre-Ríos, which built the wealth, and perhaps prepared the downfall, of the Guaraní Republic. More than anything else, it was profits from maté that excited the jealousy of the Spanish settlers, and probably gave birth to the legends of goldmines, which the rapacious authorities in Lisbon and Madrid could not bear to leave in the hands of Indians and Jesuits. The drink was produced in such prolific quantities that, as we have noted, the historian Pierre Chaunu even wrote a book called *L'Empire du Maté,* a title that reveals the widespread equation in people's minds of the economic power of the "Republic" and that of the Company of Jesus.

But had the Jesuits achieved their essential goal? Had they transformed the Indian, humanized him, "civilized" him? Certainly this easygoing and unacquisitive being had become productive. But as a member of a society, or of human history? Was he really a free contributor to, and a conscious builder of, this system in which he had been placed by a handful of foreign masters he believed to be "white shamans," the "civilizing heroes" foreseen in tribal myth?

Overall, conversion was carried forward by persuasion rather than coercion, even though the reductions never mustered more than 150,000 Indians at a time, out of a probable total Guaraní population of more than a million. But can we be sure about the freedom of these conversions? As Maxime Haubert has observed, "Adoption of the religious practices of conquerors is the best way of arming yourself against the evil effects of conquest."[13] But we must also note that such "evil effects" would have been far more virulent outside the reductions, where they also proved much less conducive to conversion.

As we have seen, the beliefs and mythology of the Guaraní may have predisposed them to accept the notion of an only God and an afterlife. They believed in Paï-Sumé, in the concept of a land free of evil, of a "civilizing hero": It was a vaguely messianic mindset, not at all unfavorable ground for Christian proselytizers, even though the Indians never grew inclined to distinguish the natural from the supernatural and remained unreceptive to the notion of sin. What tied them most closely to the fathers' teaching was Christian ritual, with its pomp, gold, incense, and, above all, music, which they loved.

A whole literary genre grew up around this theme of the Jesuit Orpheus charming the Indian serpent. From Muratori to Chateaubriand, there has been much ink spilled around this magic flute. It even inspired a scene in Roland Joffe's film *The Mission*. The idea has great beauty, but Roger Lacombe has asked the very pertinent question, "Who played the Pre-Columbian flute better, the European Jesuit or the Indian?"[14]

Contemporary ethnographers have confirmed this native gift. The Guaraní displayed their musical talents well before the arrival of Europeans. We shall later be discussing a film by Silvio Back that offers us heartrending music utterly unrelated to the sound studios of Paris or London. But there is no denying that music made for an authentic Jesuit-Guaraní exchange.

And it remains a fact that sacred music played an indispensable part in soothing the Guaraní breast. In his *Happy Christianity*, Muratori devoted many pages to this passion of the Indians, to their enthusiasm for chanted ritual and all forms of vocal worship. A great contemporary musician, Domenico Zipoli, a Jesuit and rival of Vivaldi, contributed more than anyone else to the process, composing a number of cantatas for the Guaraní. The Indians were enthralled by chanted mass, their voices filling listeners with wonder, and many missionaries owed their prestige among the Guaraní to their talents as flautist or violinist. (But we know of course that the flute and the harp were not the most effective instruments of Christian conversion among the Guaraní, coming a poor second to the iron implements and firearms purchased with the profits from maté.)

Thus conversion was apparently shaky in terms of lasting religious effect. Did it then have a more durable impact on morals? Did Indian women and men, in the space of a few decades, change behavior that European observers and travelers had described as "savage" and "barbarous"? Behavior still impregnated with primitive practices and, of course, marked by polygamy and cannibalism?

Banning polygamy was, of course, one of the fathers' first goals. But they quickly realized that the custom was limited mainly to the caciques, and that interference in this area might alienate those on whom they counted to buttress their authority. At San Ignacio Mini, they kept silent for two years on the subject of the Sixth Commandment, until their personal power was sufficiently established. Nevertheless, monogamy became law in 1646, entering into the Libre de Ordenes, the civil code of the reductions. Fifty years later the Provincial of Asunción tacked on very precise instructions for reforming the Guaraní way of life: Each family was to live "separately, with no communications between the houses, for otherwise the Indians risk too many occasions for the temptations of adultery and other offenses against Our Lord."

Young people married early—boys at sixteen, girls at fourteen—and the husband was warned against all commerce with other women. Fountains had separate premises for the two sexes. And if each reduction boasted a "house of widows" (the *cotiguazú*), it was not because Guaraní males died particularly young but because the ban on polygamy had led to the automatic repudiation of many wives—whom the community then had to take in. It is worth noting that the good fathers agreed that older-generation polygamists would not be required to return to their first wife, but could choose the latest in line—as long as she remained the only one.

And cannibalism? Even before the reductions, it had not been practiced on an everyday basis by the Guaraní. It was mainly war captives who suffered this fate, for reasons connected less with dietary needs (livestock was plentiful and hunting easy) than with sociocultural symbolism. Could a victory be complete unless accompanied by ingestion of the foe—and at the same time of his vital energies? Moreover, consumption of prisoners did not take place immediately. The captive first lived among his captors, reasonably well treated and fully aware of what awaited him. When the time came, he was informed of his imminent fate. Making no attempt to resist, he was killed with clubs and then consumed amid general festivity.

Prohibition of this ritual cannibalism came as a surprise to the Indians, for the Catholic priests made a grand show of consuming their own God in His various aspects. But they resigned themselves to the ban, all the more painlessly because the Jesuits—at least from 1641 onward—had brought peace among them. No more war, no more prisoners, no more human stew. But who could swear what might happen to a plump mamelouco falling into their hands?

Two stories passed on by Maxime Haubert suggest that the Guaraní did at least regret their cannibal days for a considerable time. One day the father-rector of a reduction came to visit an old Indian woman at the hour of death. Having administered last rites, he asked her if he might not ease her suffering in some other way. Some sweetmeat perhaps? "Ah, grandson of mine," she sighed, "I could not stomach anything of the kind, but if I had the hand of a good tender little Tapuya boy I would gladly gnaw the bones. But alas, there is no one to go and kill one for me."[15]

Moreover, the good fathers ran the risk of playing roles other than that of inculcators of virtue. Some shamans proclaimed that

> Jesuit meat was tastier than that of others. In Tayaoba province one cacique, inflamed against the Gospel by the magicians, promised his concubines "a savory morsel of Jesuit for the victory feast." Father Ruiz de Montoya managed to escape, but his sacristan was caught as he went to get an image of the Conception of the Virgin that had been left beneath a tree. A little later the father and his neophytes found jars full of meat and maize. They were hungry; they ate. It was the sacristan.[16]

That the elimination of cannibalism was a "civilizing" factor cannot be questioned. The suppression of polygamy probably belongs in the same category, if only as it concerned the dignity of women and the equality of the sexes. But the enshrining of work, the imposition of quasi-military order, the creation of the state, all these Jesuit contributions to Guaraní society—long accepted as signs of cultural progress—are nowadays questioned, particularly by Indian specialists, as intrusions into a civilization that had its own wisdom and its own reasons for being.

Favorable though he was to the founders of this "happy Christianity," Muratori recalls that the Jesuits had taken under their wing "peoples who never dreamed of inviting them" to do so. While their intrusion did not take the form of military violence, it was very much a part of a historical sequence that had started in 1492 and was accompanied by unspeakable cruelties. It is hard to imagine Montoya without Cortéz. And it stemmed from the internal violence inherent in states, which legalized and validated such violence, and from that other brand of violence implicit in all attempts to "re-form" or remodel people and things.

Such observations underlay the inquiry conducted by Girolamo Imbruglia, which throws a glowing light on the adventure of the "civilizing heroes" sent to the Paraná by Diego de Torres:

> How did the Jesuits manage to impose and validate their power? How could peoples who were not only ignorant of the State but rejected all notion of separate authority agree to become part of a system based specifically on a relationship of political dependence as well as on the alien notion of labor? It is a crucial question, which the Paraguay case obliges us to ask with all its implications. Here we have a State confronting a society without a State: It is an exceptional historical moment, and the beginning of modern anthropology. . . .
>
> The civilizing effort of the Jesuits, the heirs of Machiavelli . . . and upholders of the notion of reason of State . . . confront us with all the

problems of political anthropology: the nature of the so-called savage society and the nature of the State. . . . To men entrusted with bringing European order to them, the discovery of the Guaraní societies was the discovery of the passage from society without a State to the State. And it was by observing the conduct of the Jesuits among the Guaraní that eighteenth-century men* were able to formulate the problem of the origin of the State in a new form.[17]

We must not forget that the thinking that inspired Torres-Bollo and his cassocked conquistadors was almost of the same order as that professed by Montaigne (a great friend of the Jesuits), for whom "savages" were essentially "men of goodwill," and for whom a society without constraints could only be "happy." If the Jesuits were the first to make a benevolent effort to understand the institutions and customs of these forest dwellers, sometimes to the point of becoming "barbarians among barbarians," it was probably not as readers of Montaigne's *Essays*. And the conclusions they reached—taking into account Ruiz de Montoya's preliminary remark that the Indians of the Paraná "did not live without government"—were most assuredly very far from Montaigne's "libertarian" thinking.

The fathers thus stood somewhere between Montaigne and Montesquieu: One could choose worse company. On one side the author of the *Essays* and his good savages, his "men of goodwill" from the forest, men the Jesuits tried desperately to understand in order to transform them. And on the other hand the author of *L'Esprit des lois*, dazzled by this heady attempt to create the rational, Platonic state. Thus all the problems of life in society were present, from the sublime to the ridiculous, fiasco to martyrdom, absurdity to sacrifice—the sacrifice of the Indians in the "Guaraní wars," and often too the sacrifice of the fathers. Should we side with Montaigne and those who lamented the "reduction" of their "happy savages"? Or with Montesquieu, who approved the creation of a rational society even though it implied coercion and the abandonment of certain worthwhile values? Nature or nurture—or rather, "natural" nurture versus superimposed nurture? There is no older or more well worn argument, and none more novel.

Novel enough in any case to inspire two films during the 1980s. They offer conflicting interpretations of the problem, their directors emerging as prosecutor and defense counsel for the Guaraní Republic: the Englishman Roland Joffe and the Brazilian Silvio Back. It is hard to imagine two more refreshingly conflicting interpretations. *The Mission,* Joffe's film, though of great visual beauty and sub-

*Montesquieu in particular.

lime in tone, is arguable from the historical standpoint, if only because it concentrates events that took place over more than a century into a short time frame and because it cleaves very closely to the official Jesuit point of view. But it is not unworthy of the great human adventure it depicts.

Back appears to have made his *Guaraní Republic* in order to dispel the illusions and chimeras disseminated worldwide by Joffe's film, which Back likes to call an "aquatic Western." His own picture is a vigorous indictment of what he calls the "ideological occupation of the native," the consequence as he sees it of "the encounter between two forms of magic thought separated by an Atlantic of differences in seventeenth-century America, an encounter that produced one of the most astounding experiments in human history: the baroque Jesuit-Guaraní theocracy."

But Silvio Back's documentary is not just a scathing condemnation of the dispossession of the "savage" by the European "Other." Without masking his pro-Indian bias, he gives the floor to a score of Latin American and European experts of varying opinions, some of them very much in favor of the reductions. He evokes the Indian culture in particular with great sensitivity; and he makes a most telling artistic counterpoint between the music of Father Zipoli, the so-called Orpheus of these "barbarians," and the heartbreaking sounds of Guaraní song. But what is most gripping in the film is the pro-Indian brief of Father Bartolomeu Melia, summarized for us by Back:[18] "The reduction to a foreign culture of the Amerindians of the seventeenth century—or of today— substituting rational for mythic thinking, and the order of the State for a libertarian relationship, could only be considered progress from the standpoint of a purely arbitrary assessment of civilizations."

There is much to be said about that word "arbitrary." But it would be pedantic here, and moreover imprudent, to attempt a confrontation of the ideas of Claude Lévi-Strauss, Jacques de Soustelle, or Alfred Métraux with the theories of the radical "Indianists" such as Pierre Clastres,[19] or the more shaded opinions of Maxime Haubert.[20]

Ultimately, our decision also depends on the time frame in which we consider the question, on the historic caesura we choose: 1492, which implicates the enterprise of the reductions in the overall conquest of the continent by the Iberian empires, with Cortéz and Pizarro merging into Torres and Montoya; or 1610, the year Diego de Torres devised his ethnic-rescue strategy.

Should the historian consider the Paraná reductions as one chapter—a more or less corrective one—in the great colonial pirate enterprise, or as a unique (and perhaps futile) attempt to save a civilization and sublimate it, by integrating a handful of Guaraní myths within an alien spiritual order—the "Land Without Evil" to which the "civilizing heroes" were to lead them?

Whether or not we acknowledge the concept of a hierarchy among cultures—the implicit right of the Hellenistic world to "civilize" the "barbarians" of the Danube, Rhine, or Seine—it does after all represent a summary of human history. And since it is no more possible to isolate civilizations from one another than to prevent the transmission of light or heat, the basic question remains the ability of the more dynamic or "advanced" civilization to take the "Other" and his values into account. When Islam took root in Spain in the eighth century, it was not simply a force. It was a system of values, a vigorous cultural grafting; and from its marriage to native Spanish society, cemented by Jewish genius, the brilliant Andalusian civilization was born.

Despite the terrible shadow thrown across their efforts by the undying fury of the conquistadors, the Jesuits Torres and Montoya on the Paraná River acted as pioneers of a humanism defined by respect for the "Other." They were not doomed to the martyrdom of 1767 by their mistakes or excesses, by their inability to train a native priesthood, or even by their gloomy final submission, *perinde ac cadaver,** to European powers (over a matter concerning only the Company, and moreover involving the survival of a people they had taken under their care). They were doomed by the hateful example they provided to European monarchies of "another" way of treating different cultures.

*Condemned, as we have seen, by the Jesuit theologian Karl Rahner.

· IX ·

"expelled like dogs"

A Long-Brewing Storm • *Nation-State vs. Black International* •
The Unholy Three • *The Revenge of Gallican Jansenism* • *Madame
de Pompadour's Confessor* • *"Compulsus Feci!"* • *In the
Dungeons of the Vatican*

THE OBLITERATION OF the Guaraní experiment in the last third of
the eighteenth century was a dramatic, "exotic" instance of the Company's difficulties in its dealings with temporal powers. But it was by no
means an isolated or improbable instance. Indeed, as we have seen, the Jesuits
had faced opposition in their European homeland even before the Ignatian enterprise was properly launched. That opposition flourished as the power and influence of the Jesuits grew.

Throughout Catholic Europe, but perhaps most particularly in France.
There—in the raw—from the Company's initial campaign to establish itself on
the nation's educational stage in the sixteenth century right down to the advent
of the Fifth French Republic in mid-twentieth century, every possible contradiction and convulsion made itself manifest. From those convulsions, involving
relations between kings and parliaments, Calvinist revolution and Catholic reform, Gallicanism and Ultramontanism, public and private education, the
French nation-state as well as the Society of Jesus would emerge. From the beginning (even though they came initially as educators, not as crusaders for
Counter-Reformation) Jesuit attempts at penetration of France faced formidable national resistance. It was resistance led by teaching bodies such as the
Sorbonne as well as the parliamentary institutions, which thus confronted both

the Crown (at first favoring the Company) and the perceived Ultramontane threat, the thrust into France from the Roman side of the Alps. The Jesuits were seen as half-monks, two-thirds Spanish, and three-quarters foreign, who proposed nothing less than to compete with the national educational elite for prestige—not to mention the money that went with it.

French resistance was both an assertion of the ancient privileges of the country's educational bodies and a patriotic parliamentary reaction against Spanish-dominated papalists who were seen as "foreign agents," as a kind of Renaissance "fifth column." And although—after a long struggle—the Jesuits finally won the teaching status they sought in France, the sources of conflict endured. From the Company's struggle to achieve teaching status there emerged the first, and one of the most scurrilous, of a long line of French Jesuit-baiters, Étienne Pasquier (see Chapter XII).

A century later Blaise Pascal, a foe of quite another order, emerged to castigate the Company with his *Lettres Provinciales,* widely considered the masterpiece of anti-Jesuit literature. Pascal wrote the book on behalf of the Jansenists, an austere and initially reclusive group who held that God's grace was limited to a selected few, and for whom the Jesuits' influence as confessors to the kings of France (and the confessors' perceived willingness to compromise in order to retain that influence) was anathema. And although the Jansenists as a group were ultimately eliminated, with royal and papal approval, their spirit spilled over into France's increasingly nationalist and Gallican—and vengefully anti-Jesuit—parliamentary bodies. It was a cause enthusiastically embraced by the "philosophers" of Europe's eighteenth-century Enlightenment.

The extinction of the Company of Jesus at the hands of four European Catholic monarchs and the Pope is one of the most troubling events of the Enlightenment. It is proof of the far-reaching strategic effectiveness of the *philosophes* and their political disciples. And proof of the suicidal urge of these absolute rulers, who one after the other fell into a sacrificial act that, only twenty years later, would either sweep them away or forever weaken them.

It was on July 21, 1773—233 years after the Company's solemn investiture by Pope Paul III—that another Pope, Clement XIV, jostled, harassed, and threatened by the four Most Christian sovereigns of Lisbon, Paris, Madrid, and Naples—all shrines of Jesuitism—abolished Ignatius's Company.

In that year, Voltaire had published *The Laws of Minos,* d'Holbach his *Principes naturels de la morale et de la politique,* and Diderot wrote *Jacques le Fataliste.* Mozart had put on *Lucio Silla,* Goethe published *Goetz von Berlichingen.* And in Boston the colonists had started the tea party that would lead to the American Revolution.

It is tempting to make Clement XIV's gesture part of a vast sequence that might be entitled the "Triumph of Philosophy over the Church." For the disciples of the *philosophes* were in power in Lisbon as well as in Paris, Madrid, and Naples, and had played leading roles in the tragedy.

But this would be much too simple. For the Jesuits of the Enlightenment were already preaching a message much closer to that of the *philosophes* and the world of learning than their most implacable adversaries, the Jansenists of the French Parliament and the *argousins* of Lisbon. René Pillorget stresses the "deist" character of Jesuit teaching in the eighteenth century.[1] On the basis of research by his colleague Jean de Viguerie, he observes that most of the French *philosophes* had themselves been trained in Jesuit colleges, where the teachings of Malebranche and of Father Mersenne—who promulgated a "natural" religion owing little to Revelation—held sway.

Indeed the public controversies the Jesuits had been involved in—such as the "scandal" of the Guaraní Republic—had turned them into champions of a universalism in which Montesquieu, Buffon, and even Voltaire saw themselves reflected. Admittedly, the brand of education they offered had aged, and was only now opening itself to science. But it was still advanced enough for Frederick II of Prussia to hold it up as a model for his nation's youth.

It was certainly true that the leaders of the "philosophical party" execrated the Ignatian Company, beginning with d'Alembert, who devoted a vindictive article to them in his and Diderot's great *Encyclopédie*, and who had contributed to their pillorying in 1765 through the publication of a murderous little book. It was equally undeniable that the Portuguese Pombal, the Frenchman Choiseul, the Spaniard Aranda, and the Neapolitan Tanucci were aware that in harpooning their homegrown Jesuits they were gaining merit by paying homage to the spirit of Voltaire—even though the sage himself felt obliged to condemn a few of their assaults. But the Company's destruction must be sought elsewhere, in the structure of the modern nation-state.

The Company Loyola founded was born into a Europe dominated by the spirit of the Holy Roman (and German) Empire, in which the master of all worldly holdings and the master of men's minds (those "two halves of God") attempted for a time to maintain a joint hegemony that transcended frontiers . . . even though Francis I, Henry VIII, and the Protestant princes of Germany had hoisted their own national flags, which the Society of Jesus—internationalist to the bone—pretended not to see. Papalist? Certainly. But above all European. It is unlikely that Ignatius felt Spanish. In any case, he never behaved as if he were, not even with Philip II or the Infanta Joan. Laínez may have been a Castilian, but he never allowed it to influence his actions. And it was not French Huguenots but German Lutherans whom the Frenchman Pierre Favre strove to lure back to the Catholic fold.

But in the seventeenth century, in the hands of Cardinals Richelieu and Mazarin and Louis XIV, the centralized, bureaucratic national French state was born. The Sorbonne hugged its nationalism to itself. The Church of France loudly proclaimed its "Gallicanism." Everywhere, the Company of Jesus butted against national barriers. Naturally, it attempted, as always, to adapt. The archetypal court Jesuit, Père François de La Chaize, Louis XIV's confessor, turned Gallican for a while in 1682, just like his royal penitent, before Rome called him back to Roman order.

But such attempts to erase its external, transnational, ultramontane origins came permanently to grief at the end of Louis XIV's reign, when the Pope used the Company to promote dissemination in France of his bull *Unigenitus,* a document whose express aim was the rejection of Jansenism. This was the real breaking point. It branded the Society forever in French eyes as the instrument of an inquisitorial, oppressive procedure directed from abroad. It was in thus conducting themselves, as if they were under orders from a foreign power, at the very moment when France's sense of nationality was burgeoning, that the Jesuits signed their death warrant.

Under such circumstances, the so-called Jesuit International, whose makeup and universalist and multicultural vocation should have made it the natural ally of the *philosophes* and the table companion of every "enlightened despot," instead declared war on the *Encyclopédie* and all those for whom its rationalism and skepticism were gospel. Throughout Europe, the new kind of authoritarian state turned out to be highly allergic to any transnational undertaking, whether it clashed directly with its own interests, like the Jesuits in Spanish-Portuguese America, or simply impaired the smooth operation of the social and cultural machinery, as the Society did in France. The key was not "philosophical" but political.

Could the Ignatian order have survived by adapting to these new conditions, not only on the plane of ideas but in its very makeup, by melting into the various national structures, by repudiating its Papalism, by decentralizing, by granting autonomy to its Provinces (as several princes, including Henry IV of France, apparently urged it to do)? The fact is, it did not.

The Company that had so often given birth to inspired characters confronted this formidable obstacle without a leader to match, either in France or in Rome, where Father Lorenzo Ricci,* elected General in 1758, lacked the stature to fight back with the spirit so many of his predecessors had displayed.

Moreover, the ties between the Holy See and the "shock troops" created and deployed by Ignatius of Loyola had loosened. Clashes between Curia and Com-

*No relation of Li Mateou.

pany, epitomized by (but not confined to) the discord over the Paraguay missions, were signs of this estrangement. While in France, haunted until 1770 by the need to placate a hostile Parliament, Louis XV was more and more overtly distancing himself from religious authorities of all kinds, and seemed resigned to offering up the Jesuits in France to the vengeance of the Jansenists, the Gallicans, and the *philosophes.*

But the great combined offensive against the Company of Jesus began in Portugal, that same Portugal in which Loyola had found his first crowned sponsors, John III and Catherine, and from whose shores the most famous European missionaries had set sail for Asia in Francis Xavier's wake.

Of course, such a reversal could not be ascribed to the rise of just one man, even a man as remarkable as Sebastião de Carvalho, later Marquês de Pombal. Its old, deep-lying cause was the simmering conflict between the Jesuit founders of the Guaraní missions and the Portuguese colonies. In the beginning, and at first under the very open and direct protection of Madrid, the fathers had set up the reductions as bastions against slave hunters who were mostly Portuguese mameloucos or were operating from Portuguese territory. Thus relations between the Guaraní Republic and Lisbon were born of opposition.

They turned into outright hostility when, after the Treaty of Limits of 1750, seven of the reductions were detached from the Spanish orbit and passed into the hands of the Portuguese. As we have seen, the Portuguese at once set about dismantling them, not just to destroy a system they loathed but to seize the gold or silver mines they believed they would find in the reductions, whose prosperity could be explained in no other way. To the subsequent disappointment of the Portuguese Governor Gómez de Andrade was added his fury at being fiercely and stubbornly resisted by the Guaraní militia, armed beforehand by the Jesuits (with Spanish help).

Whatever the part played by the fathers in this Indian resistance (and we have seen that it was slight and even nugatory), Lisbon blamed the Company. And it would have taken less than this to kindle the anti-Jesuit anger of Joseph I's Chief Minister, known to history as the Marquês de Pombal.

By turns magistrate, officer, and diplomat, this gentleman of minor noble origin (some said he was a "New Christian") had been called to power by the Queen Mother. He very quickly displayed outstanding qualities as a leader, administrator, and reformer, leading some to compare him to Richelieu—although for brutality, cynicism, and ferocity he far outstripped the French Cardinal.

Was Sebastião de Carvalho filled with such radical hatred for the Jesuits because of his "philosophical" leanings, or because he had grown up in London?

Or did he become their executioner to punish their real or imagined attitude in Paraguay? The fact is that in 1757 he began a campaign against them in the form of scurrilous pamphlets entitled *Nouvelles intéressantes* (*Interesting News*; the French version was published in Amsterdam), concerning the "affairs of the Jesuits, principally in South America and the Kingdom of Portugal," written under Pombal's aegis by a defrocked Capuchin monk. They condemned the rapacity of the Jesuit missionaries, whose reductions lived solely on cynical exploitation of the hapless Indians; their wealth; their capacity for work; and their claims to be building an independent empire under the scepter of Nicolás I, the Company's straw man.*

After the military clashes with the Guaraní, the Portuguese minister published an *Abridged Relation of the Republic Which the Jesuit Priests Have Established in the Overseas Domains of the Two Monarchies, and of the War They Have Provoked Against the Spanish and Portuguese Armies*. But this time he had gone too far. Spain took umbrage at being thus placed in the same humiliating position as Portugal: to have all Europe believe that Spain too had suffered the misfortunes inflicted on its neighbor at the hands of these wretched tribesmen! The book was solemnly burned by Castile's public executioner.

But Pombal would be given another opportunity of crushing his cassocked foes. Let us examine the version of a fateful event as described in *Nouvelles intéressantes* of November 14, 1758:

> On September 3 toward midnight, the King, it is said, having just seen the young Marquise of Távora with Pedro Texeira, three men on horseback surrounded their carriage. One of them, armed with a blunderbuss, fired upon the coachman. By a miracle the spark did not ignite the pan, for otherwise he would have been killed and the King could not have escaped. The astonished coachman spurred his mules and fled. At the same moment, the two other assassins fired from behind the carriage. The King and Texeira were wounded, the King most perilously in arm and shoulder; but thanks be to Heaven, he had only to suffer to be healed—which blessing has not yet been vouchsafed him as his wound was dressed like a King's.† . . . The Court wished to hide this abominable act. The public learned of it two days later. . . . Nothing happened, and nobody had left Lisbon. . . . It cannot be held to have happened because of the King's too great love for the Marquise: A subject, whoever he may be, is patience itself when gold rains upon his house.‡ And that was the prac-

---

*See Chapter VIII.
†Admirable, utterly mysterious phrase!
‡A phrase worthy of Rabelais.

tice in all previous reigns, even among those Portuguese most punctilious about honor. Moreover, if one seeks revenge, is this how one
should set about it?[2]

This juicy story is not the final word, and suggests only the most romantic
theory. What is certain, however, is that the reprisals conducted by Pombal fell
on the family of the Marquise in question, the illustrious line of the Távoras.
While her husband was spared, her father-in-law, the old Marquês of Távora,
her mother-in-law, and their friend the Count of Atoguia were arrested and interrogated. They confessed that they had fomented a plot, at the instigation of
the Jesuits, to place the Duke of Aveiro on the throne. Although they several
times retracted their story once the torture stopped, one was burned at the
stake, one broken on the wheel, a third was hanged, and the dowager Marchio-
ness was beheaded, while the King's beloved was consigned to a nunnery (where
royal visits were of course permitted).

And the Jesuits (since the matter now principally concerned them)? To begin
with, Pombal had three of them arrested. They included the King's former confessor and the old Italian father Malagrida, a former missionary in Brazil, a famous preacher but at that point an old man of eighty-two who babbled
nonsense in his prison cell. When his babblings had been recorded, he was condemned to the stake, where he was burned for "heresy." Voltaire himself described the old Jesuit's hideous ordeal as an "infamy." The prosecution argued
that the old preacher's Italian origins were proof that the plot had indeed been
concocted in Rome—and therefore by the Jesuit General.

As *Nouvelles intéressantes* commented:

Lisbon, February 26, 1759.
. . . The Jesuits are on the brink of being driven from this kingdom.
Other Powers may well follow the example of Portugal. These Gentle-
men have carried their ambition and their dissembling spirit too far.
They wished to dominate all consciences and invade the empire of
the Universe.[3]

Six months later, on September 16, 1759, four hundred Jesuits of Portugal
were expelled from their country and deported to the Papal States, where they
were deposited on the riverbank at Civitavecchia. Indignant at their treatment,
but judging it above all as a personal insult, Pope Clement XIII at first refused to
greet them. Finally, though, he agreed to take the refugees in.

The Jesuit missionaries living in Portuguese-held territories in Brazil and
Argentina were even more harshly treated. Transported en masse to Portugal,
they were incarcerated there without trial in the filthiest cells of Belém and
Saint Julian, where they were met by the former confessors of the royal family
and all the other fathers who had once held public office.

Nouvelles intéressantes published this "Comment" on the sentence of the Lisbon court:

> It was the King of Portugal who set out to despoil the Jesuits of that sovereignty which they usurped in Paraguay and which was dearer to them than the apple of their eye. . . . That is why the Jesuits give lessons not only in revolt and sedition but also in murder and bloodshed. . . . These Fathers decide in all confidence that it is not even venial sin to kill the King. . . . What must be the excess of this malice when deliberation & resolve are directed not at the life of a private person but at that of the Sovereign; when it is a question of sacrificing that life not to a real or invented public interest, but to the private interest of those who pronounce the decision? Only the Jesuits would have been capable of such enormity.
>
> These Fathers are perhaps not the only ones to advance the theory that it is sometimes permissible to kill Kings; but they are the only ones never to have abandoned this hateful doctrine. They are the only ones to have adopted it as a body. They are the only ones who teach it, in an unbroken tradition of more than two hundred and fifty years. They are finally the only ones who have ever adopted it as a code of conduct and have applied it to their own interests.[4]

Thus the Marquês de Pombal's spokesman. How else could he have treated such scoundrels?*

Portugal had waited for the Guaraní tragedy and Pombal to grapple with the Jesuits. In France, the confrontation was a permanent fact of public life. Since its very first months in the country, the Company had faced bitter resistance from several great state institutions (particularly the educational establishment). It had suffered so many threats, so many proscriptions and challenges that France seemed to have become a vast training ground in which to exercise its muscles, its agility, its firmness, and the mental sharpness of its best officers—just as Germany had once been a proving ground for the Roman legions.

The basic quarrel between Gallicanism and ultramontanism had been hardened by the ossification of the centralizing nation-state. Onto these contradictions the battles of the Counter-Reformation and then of Jansenism had been superimposed. The harsh implementation of the bull *Unigenitus,* with its long

*Eighteen years later, at the death of the King, Pombal was removed from office, banished to his estates, and then condemned for abuse of power—and forced to restore the property of the Jesuits and the rehabilitated Távora and Aveiro families.

trail of persecution of the Jansenist "appellants,"* had given a tragic turn to these confrontations at the end of Louis XIV's reign.

The Jesuits were held responsible for *Unigenitus*. While they had played only a minor part on the drafting committee in Rome (where there had been one Jesuit among nine representatives), they were believed in France to be firm advocates of its implementation. The Jansenist party was no longer a few dozen loners encouraged and promoted by a handful of fashionable salons and a brigade of fine minds. It now constituted the hard core of France's parliamentary bodies, which, in their struggle against royal absolutism (and for many of them against the corruption of the court and the high officials of state), had chosen this Gallican form of Puritanism as their rallying cry. Whether or not it was infected by what Louis XIV held to be a republican itch, this new brand of "political Jansenism" fiercely opposed the King's spendthrift, scandal-plagued, and priest-ridden administration.

While the alliance of the new Jansenists with those who swam in the Gallican stream seemed natural, their alliance with the "philosophical party" was somewhat disconcerting. But although Voltaire—who disliked all sects—made no secret of his distaste for Jansenism, the tacticians of the *Encyclopédie* were most eager to score off the common enemy. Once clerical absolutism was seen as the target, any effective sniper made an acceptable ally.†

Nevertheless, the alliance of the *philosophes* and the group known as the Richerists was distinctly startling. The latter were disciples of Edmond Richer, a provincial priest who had begun a populist campaign against the loose morals and laxity of the higher clergy and the Jesuits. Vaguely colored by Jansenism, this "left-wing" movement tended toward puritanism of the Gallican brand. And on the other wing of the broad coalition that would expel the Jesuits from France stood three key figures: King Louis XV, Madame de Pompadour, and the Duc de Choiseul. Although Madame de Pompadour had effectively ceased to be his mistress in 1751, the King remained under her influence until her death in 1764 (by which time the fate of France's Jesuits was sealed). He was also influenced by the Chief Minister whom Madame de Pompadour—seduced by the social talents, easy manner, decisiveness, and wit of this gentleman from Lorraine—had persuaded him to appoint: Stainville, later elevated to the Dukedom of Choiseul.

---

*The name for those who, refusing to repudiate Jansenism, were therefore denied the sacraments.
†D'Alembert, for example, considered both Jesuits and Jansenists "wicked and pernicious." But he made this distinction: "If one were forced to choose (assuming that each enjoyed an equal degree of power), the Jesuits would be the less tyrannical. For they, accommodating people as long as one is not their declared enemy, are reasonably tolerant of people thinking as they wish. The Jansenists, as uncompromising as they are unenlightened, want one to think as they do; if they were the masters, they would inflict the harshest of inquisitions upon works, minds, speech, and customs."

Louis XV was not so kindly disposed to the Company as his ancestors Henry IV or Louis XIII, his grandfather Louis XIV, or his own son the Dauphin. But although his private life brought clashes with his two Jesuit confessors, he could not really be said to feel personal hostility toward the Company.

Why then did he let himself be drawn into the great hunt of the Jesuits between 1759 to 1773? First and foremost because he hated a fight, particularly with those closest to him—who happened to be Pompadour and Choiseul. Second, because he was modern enough—or, in the language of the day, a *philosophe*—to perceive (dimly enough) the overlapping of political and religious authority and to want (genuinely enough) to disentangle the two. And finally, because as always he needed to placate Parliament, which was up in arms against the Jesuits—and which handled the purse strings. The Seven Years' War was costing him dearly, and the legislators were balking at voting him further credits. What better way to win them over than by jettisoning the Company of Jesus? If Paris was worth a Mass, then funds for his military ventures certainly outweighed the loss of a troublesome institution (whose confessors, incidentally, raised an irritating amount of fuss over trifles).

Was Madame de Pompadour more viscerally hostile to the Jesuits? Like her friend Choiseul, she very soon became an ally of the Jansenists. But there is nothing to confirm that her "philosophism" predated her personal unpleasantnesses with her own or the King's Jesuit confessors. In fact, a remarkable document demonstrates that it was on the latter frivolous grounds that she would wage her war against the Company.

In late November 1757, when she was already what might be called "separated in body"* from the King but still the mistress of his decisions, Madame Lenormant d'Étioles, Marquise de Pompadour, sent the Pontiff a letter requesting that he exercise papal clemency and override the strict views of her Jesuit confessors. Observing that she was now linked to Louis "only by the most blameless of attachments" and that her conscience was therefore "untroubled," she suggested that it was now incumbent upon "persons of tact and with the welfare of His Majesty at heart [to] seek the means of appeasement" without "imposing unpleasant conditions"—such as Madame d'Étioles's return to the conjugal bed:

> The King, deeply mindful of the truths and obligations of Religion, wishes to use all the means in his possession to mark his obedience to the acts of religion set out by the Church, and above all His Majesty is desirous of lifting all obstacles before him in regard to the Sacra-

*She had ordered her door to the royal apartments walled over.

ments. The King is wounded by the difficulties his confessor has raised on this matter, and he is convinced that the Pope and those His Majesty earnestly wishes to consult in Rome, once informed of the facts, will by their counsel and their authority remove the obstacles that prevent the King from performing a duty sacred to him and edifying to the people . . . and will remedy the difficulties thus engendered, as much by the substance of the matter as by the intrigues that give birth to them.[5]

The Jesuits were thus blamed for their "intrigues," no longer in the cause of laxity but of excessive rigor. Such a tiny scandal . . . And such a pretty move . . . But the Roman Curia, although bountifully supplied with "persons of tact," could not easily take up the favorite's cudgels. So Madame de Pompadour's irritation injected an amorous piquancy into the campaign Louis XV now launched against the Company.

The Duc de Choiseul's motives for fighting were less personal. He had no confessor badgering him, no appearances to save. His mistresses, well bred and well born, encumbered him hardly at all. And he was too intelligent not to see that the destruction of the Company would open a breach in the walls of the French state, now in his care. But even more directly than the King, he was hounded by the need to extract war credits from Parliament. Behind his calculations there was the possibility of confiscating the Company's property, believed to be extremely valuable, and incorporating it into the royal exchequer. There was also the encouragement of *philosophes* like Voltaire, d'Alembert, and Diderot. And there was also, as we shall see, the chance of further cementing ties between the courts of Paris, Lisbon, and Madrid through a combined anti-Jesuit operation.

> According to the historian Sismonde de Sismondi, Madame de Pompadour aspired to earn a reputation for force of character, and believed that she had found an opportunity to do so by demonstrating that she could mount a *coup d'état*. . . . Like the Duc de Choiseul, she was most happy to distract public attention from the war, hoping to acquire popularity by flattering at one and the same time *philosophes* and Jansenists, and to cover the costs of war through the confiscation of the property of a most wealthy Order, instead of proceeding to reforms that might sadden the King.[6]

Many logs were thus piling up at the foot of the Jesuits' stake in France. And soon an attempted regicide, a financial scandal, a handful of pamphlets, and a Pope's death would send the flames leaping high.

* * *

The attempted regicide was Robert-François Damiens's murderous attack on Louis XV in 1757. As always in such cases, suspicion fell on, or was directed at, the Jesuits, with whom the assassin had been involved in his youth. Some noted, but in vain, that Damiens was much closer to the Jansenists than to the fathers. The rumor of Jesuit connections persisted, once again shedding sinister light on the Company, a light intensified by d'Alembert and the great lawyer Adrien Le Paige, the coordinator of the attack and the author in 1760 of a devastating *Histoire des Jésuites.*

The financial scandal had a name attached to it: Father Antoine de Lavalette. This Jesuit, scion of a great family of the Knights of Malta, was the Company's purchasing agent in Martinique. He had realized that the very prosperous trade of the West Indies—coffee, sugar, spices, indigo—could be channeled into financing good works: Did the Gospel itself not suggest that "the riches of iniquity" might help foster the cause of salvation? However, planting (which he himself practiced, with the help of slaves) was one thing. Trade was quite another. Nevertheless, with considerable initial success, he took the plunge, thus flouting the most obvious canonical prohibitions and the Company's own rule of poverty.

In 1753 de Lavalette was denounced to his superiors in Paris and Rome after a decade of fruitful dealings. When he received a stern warning, he asked his friend the "steward of the Windward Isles" to reply that his activities were "of infinite benefit" to the colony. He was summoned to Paris, where he justified himself with exceptional eloquence. His superiors were rash enough to give him another chance. When he returned to the islands two disasters struck him. An epidemic carried off "great numbers of his Negroes," and English pirates seized several of his ships. It meant ruin, which he attempted to circumvent through fraudulent dealings with the brothers Lancy, merchants of Marseille, and with the widow Grou and her son, of Nantes, who brought charges against him.

Meanwhile the Superior General of the order, Father Centurioni, had finally reacted, sending a visitor to the West Indies to put a stop to Lavalette's peculations (although it was too late to snuff out scandal). In 1759 his first emissary died at sea. A second envoy, the purchasing agent for the Canadian missions, broke his leg at Versailles on the eve of departure. A third was captured by pirates. Finally, early in 1762, the Superior General's fourth envoy landed in Fort-de-France. After a two-month inquiry, he issued this stern judgment: "By virtue of the authority vested in us, and the unanimous consent of our Fathers: first, we desire that Father Antoine de Lavalette be utterly removed from all administrative responsibility; second, we command that the said Father Antoine de Lavalette be sent back to Europe as soon as possible; third, we declare him ineligible for the Sacraments."

At once obedient to what might be called a pressing invitation, Lavalette protested his "repentance" and pleaded guilty—although, as he pointed out, it was from "lack of knowledge or forethought, or perhaps even from chance, that I engaged in this profane commerce, which I renounced as soon as I learned how deeply this commerce had disturbed the Company and Europe." He further declared that "among the first Superiors of the Company there was not one who authorized, or advised, or sanctioned the kind of commerce in which I engaged," and that his confession had been prompted "neither by force, nor threats, nor caresses or other tricks," and that he offered it "in full freedom."*[7]

But although the Company's action set the affair to rest as far as principles were concerned, it had already boomeranged into the legal and political arena. For two years the plaintiffs in the case had been demanding the repayment of the debts contracted by the Jesuit speculator. They were valued at three million livres, an enormous sum. The Marseille courts judged the Company jointly responsible for the losses, ordering it to pay not just that sum but an additional 50,000 livres in interest and damages. Was the Society of Jesus in a position to deal with the consequences of this disastrous judgment?

There were two ways in which it could escape its obligations: by invoking internal Society regulations forbidding the sharing of property among members of the Society, or by appealing. But that would have meant challenging the Paris Parliament—unless they sought to fall back on the right of *commitimus* granted several religious orders by Louis XIV, allowing them to plead before the King's Great Council rather than the parliamentary courts.

But Father de Nieuville, Superior of the Paris Jesuits, agreed to submit to Parliament's judgment, hoping thereby to prove his good faith and put a stop to the campaigns being waged against what were seen as the Company's lavish privileges. In the climate of the day, it was suicide.

The Paris Parliament was called upon to decide on a point of commercial law, a bankruptcy. Instead it seized the opportunity to turn it into a vast political-religious happening (exacerbated by the death of Pope Benedict XIV, which had convinced the Jansenists that the last hope of rescinding the bull *Unigenitus* was now lost), into a full-scale trial of the Company of Jesus and of its presence and activities in France.

The first decision of the parliamentary courts was eloquent: On April 17, 1761, it ordered the fathers to provide it with a copy of Loyola's *Constitutions*, believed to be a closely held secret (although every Jansenist lawyer had a copy). Father de Montigny, Provincial of the order in France, hastily complied. Three

---

*Taking refuge in England, Lavalette never recanted his confession, although pressed to implicate the Company.

clerk-counselors were named to examine the document. While the court awaited their report, it handed down a preliminary judgment on the decision of the Marseille court, ordering the Superior General of the Jesuits to pay the creditors the 50,000 livres—which through fines and penalties would eventually rise to five million. The Company was now in serious trouble.

Three months later the Abbé de Chauvelin, a man with strong ties to the authors of the *Encyclopédie* and duly briefed by the Jansenist lawyer Le Paige, who was the coordinator of the operation, presented his report on the Ignatian *Constitutions*. It was a pitiless indictment, presenting the Society of Jesus as a war machine, a cunning instrument of oppression, a tool in the hands of a foreign potentate. A fifth column . . .

The public applause that greeted these "revelations" was not merely a signal triumph for Parliament but a conspicuous humiliation of the "Most Christian" sovereign in Versailles and all his line. This was so obvious to Louis XV that he mustered enough courage to aim two counterblows at the operation launched by Choiseul and Pompadour: He appointed a committee to examine the Jesuit *Constitutions* in a less partisan spirit, and he ordered Parliament to suspend implementation of its decree for a year.

But although the royal commission delivered a much more moderate verdict on the *Constitutions,* it nevertheless managed to compromise the Company in the eyes of the King. For the modifications it suggested to the Jesuits with a view to integrating them into French society were so rigidly contested by the General and the Pope that Louis XV—a Gallican like his grandfather—was seriously offended. However, his Chancellor, the Dauphin, and the Archbishop of Paris persuaded him to make one last effort to save the Society of Jesus.

On August 6, 1761, Parliament went on the offensive again, ordering that the works of the most illustrious Jesuit theologians be burned. It also authorized the attorney general to summon the French Company's General for questioning on the numberless "abuses" committed in the country by his Society, and forbade the Company to recruit novices and administer vows. Finally, it banned Jesuit congregations and schools.

Only by pointing out to the King how dangerous this last measure would be to the Crown, and how offensive to the clergy, was the "Jesuit party" able to wring from him a suspension of the school closures. There followed a general assembly of the French clergy to consider the following four points:

> One. The potential usefulness of the Jesuits in France, and the advantages and the drawbacks that might flow from the different roles assigned them;
>
> Two. The Jesuit attitude, in their teaching and in conduct, toward opinions contrary to the safety of the person of sovereigns. . . .

Three. The conduct of the Jesuits on the subordination owing to
bishops and ecclesiastical superiors. . . .

Four. How, in France, the authority exercised by the General of the
Jesuits might be tempered.

Only the last point drew lively debate. The Bishop of Soissons made it his
pretext for demanding abolition of the Society. But the minutes of the meeting
reveal that forty-four of the fifty bishops present finally recommended that "no
change [be imposed upon] the General's authority."

Chancellor de Lamoignon, a great friend of the Jesuits, nevertheless decided,
in accordance with the King, that the Company could save itself only if it moved
in the direction of "Gallicanism"—in particular by placing the Provincial of
France under the authority of the national Church as "vicar-general," and submitting the fathers in every see to the sway of the bishops. In December 1761, the
Company's leaders in France published a declaration of more or less unconditional submission to this process of Gallicanization, declaring among other
things, "that if, which God forfend, we might be ordered by our General to do
something contrary to the present declaration, persuaded that we could not defer to the order without sin, we would consider the order as illegitimate, null
and void, and a matter on which we could and should not defer in virtue of the
rules of obedience to the General as they are set down in our Constitutions."

A total rejection of *perinde ac cadaver.*

A "Jesuit Munich"? It was the only solution for the Jesuits of France. But in
the security of Rome, the Pope and the General reacted with predictable anger,
rejecting any kind of accommodation with venomous disdain. To an envoy
from Versailles who had come to press for "an adaption [of the *Constitutions*] to
French custom," Clement XIII (and not Superior General Ricci, as legend has it)
retorted with superb hauteur: "Sint ut sunt, aut non sint" (Let them be what
they are, otherwise let them not be).

Thus all efforts to save the Jesuit order in France by Gallicanizing it were
thwarted. Learning of the conciliatory spirit of the Parisian Jesuits, which they
saw as an admission of weakness, and of the unbending opposition of the "Romans," the Parliamentarians boldly followed up on their advantage. In February
1762 they published a formidable pamphlet directed against the fathers, entitled
*Extracts of Dangerous and Pernicious Assertions of All Kinds, Which the So-called
Jesuits Have at All Times and Most Stubbornly Maintained and Taught and Published in Their Books with the Approval of Their Superiors and Generals.*

The pamphlet accused the Company of teaching every error and professing
every heresy—except Jansenism! The Jesuit historian Father Brucker maintains
that "more than nine hundred false quotations"[8] were listed in the *Assertions,* in
which the influence of Étienne Pasquier and Voltaire was plain to see. Neverthe-

less, the work enjoyed huge success and prepared the ground for the last step—the kill. Whence d'Alembert's somber note in his *Destruction des Jésuites:* "Until such time as the truth is known, this pamphlet will have furnished the benefit the nation asked of it—the annihilation of the Jesuits."

But the blows would continue to rain until the final fall of the blade. After the Rouen Parliament ordered the "dispersion" of the Company in its jurisdiction, its Paris counterpart closed the colleges in the capital in April 1761.

The French bishops at last realized that disaster was at hand. After voting war funds on March 28, it drew up and presented to the King a solemn warning against dissolution of the Company in France. It was a document of such eloquence that to the King and his cabinet it seemed to outweigh the vituperations of Parliament:

> Everything pleads before you, Sire, in favor of the Jesuits. Religion commends its defenders; the Church its ministers; Christian souls the repositories of the secrets of their conscience; a large number of your subjects the masters who raised them; all the youth of your kingdom those called to shape their minds and hearts. Sire, do not refuse so many united desires. Do not suffer that in your kingdom, contrary to the rules of justice, contrary to civil law, a whole Society should be undeservingly destroyed. The very interests of your authority demand it, and we declare ourselves just as jealous of it as we are of our own rights.[9]

Their eloquence fell on deaf ears. The King, who as we have seen had mounted a sketchy (and elastic) defense of the fathers, and had not wanted this outcome, was by now resigned to it. Moreover, like Choiseul himself, he was overburdened by the disasters into which the war against England and Prussia was leading them. Which prompted d'Alembert to write to Voltaire on May 4, 1762, in the following terms:

> The Jesuits could say to Saint Ignatius: "Father, forgive them, for they know what they do." What seems curious to me is that the destruction of these phantoms, whom we believed to be so fearsome, is being accomplished with so little clamor. The capture of the castle of Arensberg by the Hanoverians* cost them no more than the capture of Jesuit property did the Parliament. Most people are content to jest about it. They say that Jesus Christ is a poor captain on half-pay who has lost his company.

The Company indeed seemed to be drifting leaderless on an unfamiliar battlefield. Nothing could have been stranger than the behavior of this vigorous

---

*The "English party."

body of men who from its birth had battered at the unyielding doors of the Sorbonne, won over Henry IV, and stood up to Richelieu, and which was now reduced to the phantom role ascribed to them by d'Alembert, unable even to exploit the silver-tongued eloquence of the assembled bishops. Was the Company's behavior suicidal, masochistic? And all this at a time when great jurists like La Chalotais, Paul Dudon, and Monclar, in the name of provincial Parliaments such as Rennes and Bordeaux, continued to undermine and nibble away at the Jesuit *Constitutions*.

Finally, on August 6, 1762, the Paris Parliament delivered its decision, proclaiming that

> there is abuse in the said Institute of the said Society, calling itself of
> Jesus, bulls, briefs, apostolic letters, constitutions, statements on the
> said constitutions, claims, decrees by the Generals and the General
> Congregations of the said Society, etc. This being the case, we declare
> the Society inadmissible by its very nature, in every orderly State, as
> contrary to natural law, as deleterious to all spiritual and temporal
> authority, and tending to introduce into the Church and into the
> State, under the specious cloak of a religious body, not an Order
> which aspires truly and exclusively to evangelical perfection but
> rather a political body whose essence is continual activity aimed at attaining, by every kind of path, direct or indirect, hidden or public,
> first of all absolute independence and secondly the usurpation of all
> authority.*

As a result of this decree, the four thousand Jesuits of France were scattered, driven from their homes. Their property, churches, and libraries were despoiled. They were forbidden to follow their rule, to live in a community, to wear their habit. Not Pombal's murderous tactics, perhaps, but just as effective . . .

Not every Parliament followed this lead. Those of Artois and Franche-Comté and the sovereign courts of Alsace† resisted the prevailing mood and voted to keep their Jesuits.‡ The Aix Parliament sent its own message: It announced that it was conforming with the Paris decision even though its major-

---

*When the counselors of the Parliament of Toulouse examined the *Constitutions* of Saint Ignatius, they were angered to find that there were only two provisions for deposing the Superior General: "if he violated the vow of chastity through scandalous commerce with women"; or if he "seriously wounded anyone with a weapon." They concluded: "A General of Jesuits is well protected, both by age and by his calling, against the likelihood of committing these two excesses." They might not have been right about the first point: Several acceded to the Generalate in their forties. As for the second, there have been many robust old men . . .

†Where Choiseul would soon have them expelled.

‡Majorities were slender even in those Parliaments that voted against the Jesuits: in Rennes, 32 to 29; in Rouen, 20 to 13; in Toulouse, 41 to 39; in Perpignan, 5 to 4; in Bordeaux, 23 to 18.

ity (29 to 27) had been challenged by its most distinguished members. The opposition included the thunderous voice of Mirabeau's brother and of its president, Boyer d'Eguilles, who wrote an angry letter to the King on the subject of the "excesses committed by a whole body [but which are apparently] the fault of nobody."

Although turned out into the street, the Jesuits were not doomed to the beggary that their founder Iñigo had made a survival art. Most Parliaments allotted them twenty sous daily (perhaps $4 today). Grenoble raised the figure to thirty, while Toulouse cut it down to twelve.

But it was the Jesuits who had traditionally cared for—and fed, with the children of city dignitaries helping distribute the rations—the chained columns of convicts who frequently passed through Toulouse (often Huguenots from the southwest being herded to the hulks of Toulon). A few weeks after the August 6 decree, a convict chain gang again crossed the city. And the Jesuits, although banned, were called back into service. But the Toulouse magistrates had priced the convicts' rations at seventeen sous per head—five more than the daily payment to the fathers. Public feeling ran so high that the city's parliamentarians adjusted the figure to match that paid out in Lyon and Bordeaux.

The historian Charles-Alain Sarre offers this detail: "Jesuits expelled from their colleges had the right to take with them twelve shirts per person . . . as well as three pairs of sheets and a dozen towels, and to receive a payment 'for travel' of 250 livres if they were older than thirty-three and 150 if they were younger."[10]

The fathers were of course invited to embrace a bright future in the lay clergy if they publicly broke with the Company from which they were now legally sundered. Only five (plus a score of novices and brothers) did so, out of four thousand. Public opinion, long dominated by traditional Gallican distrust of this powerful, mysterious Company—too rich, too close to the great—at first remained remarkably indifferent.

Scattered, "secularized," lost in the crowd, the Jesuits regained in prohibition something of what they had lost in power. They suddenly seemed to be countless, teeming in their facelessness. D'Alembert, the great intellectual huntsman in this nationwide meet, was alarmed. In January 1763, he confided his fears to Voltaire. The old sage of Ferney, the author in 1763 of the *Traité sur la tolérance*, had kept much of his fondness for his former teachers and had taken little pleasure in the Jesuit hunt. On January 18, 1763, he answered tersely: "The Jesuits are not yet destroyed: They remain in Alsace; they are preaching in Dijon, Grenoble, and Besançon. There are twelve of them at Versailles, and one who says Mass for me."*

*Voltaire's Jesuit was named Adam. The philosopher acknowledged only one virtue in him—that of being banned.

The fathers found other, more "official," advocates. The Archbishop of Paris, Christophe de Beaumont, was not a subtle mind. But he was a man of character, and sensible enough to realize that the destruction of the Jesuits was merely the destruction of a vanguard—the prelude to a general offensive against the whole French Catholic system. In October 1763 he published a pastoral instruction condemning the enchroachment of civil authority upon the spiritual. Parliament responded by ordering the hangman to burn the book and by summoning the Archbishop to appear before it—whereupon the King, reluctant to take sides, piously banished Beaumont from his diocese.

The first president of the Paris Parliament, Molé, like Voltaire had remained fond of his former Jesuit teachers and would have liked to join the ranks of the mourners. Yet it was Molé who in February 1764, in the name of his Paris colleagues, proclaimed a further aggravation of the decree of August 6, 1762: the banishment of the fathers from the constituency of the Paris Parliament. Toulouse, Rouen, and Pau* at once followed suit. The Jesuits expelled from these dioceses were given refuge in Lorraine, which would continue for a few more years to be governed by Duke Stanislas Leczynski, father of the forgotten queen, in Switzerland (particularly in Fribourg) or among the English Jesuits at Louvain, themselves expelled from their homeland more than a century earlier. But the German and Belgian fathers were forbidden by their princes to shelter the exiles.

Even the last Jesuits kept on at Versailles in the bosom of the royal family (particularly Father Berthier, tutor to the Dauphin's children†) were forced to take flight. Choiseul was inflexible, despite the King's emotional reaction to a declaration of "unshakable" loyalty addressed to him by the leading figures of the Company in France.

One last refinement would be added to the treatment inflicted on France's Jesuits. In November 1764, shortly before the death of Mme de Pompadour, and at the height of the devastation inflicted on France by the Seven Years' War, Louis XV confirmed the abolition decree of 1762 but granted former Jesuits the right to remain where they were as secular priests, subject to the authority of the diocesan bishops. But the Paris Parliament refused to extend this measure of tolerance to its own archbishopric, and specified that the "former so-called Jesuits" must reside in the provinces of their birth, with the natural exception of Parisians.‡

*A graph of the comparative rigor of these measures would reflect three centuries of religious life in France, from the Reformation to Jansenism.

†The Dauphin died in December 1765, angered by the treatment of the Jesuits. In a letter from Paris a few days later, Horace Walpole describes the "joy" of the "philosophical party," which had feared that the future King might restore the Company.

‡The legislation was further tightened in 1767. And in May 1777 the pious Louis XVI made the restriction total by forbidding former Jesuits to "assemble" or to "live in community."

We know Louis XV's true feelings from a letter he addressed to Choiseul:

> I certainly have no great love for the Jesuits, but all heresies have always detested them, which is to their glory. I will say no more on the matter. Although I am banishing them, against my will and for the peace of my Kingdom, I do not wish it to be believed that I subscribe to everything the Parliaments have said and done against them.
>
> I persevere in my belief that in expelling them we must break all that Parliament has done against them.
>
> In deferring to the opinions of others on the tranquillity of my Kingdom, we must change what I propose, otherwise I will do nothing. Now I will keep silence, for otherwise I would say too much.[11]

Commenting on the expulsion a few years later, Cardinal de Bernis wrote in his memoirs: "When the affair began, neither Court nor Parliament nor public had dreamed that it might be carried so far; one step followed another, and the end of the road was reached almost unawares."[12]

The Holy See could not passively accept this blow to its authority and prestige from the "eldest daughter of the Church." The Portuguese operation had wounded the Pope. But the French proscription had amputated a limb. Moreover, Clement XIII was very much more favorable than his predecessor to the Jesuits. He had consistently proved it, from his intransigence toward Jansenism to the glorious stubbornness with which he had rejected the slightest "French-style" modification of the Society's rules, which had been drafted at a time when national sovereignty had been much less clear-cut than in this second half of the eighteenth century. Did he continue to support them because he was conscious of the ruin his inaction had brought in its wake? Because the bishops of France and of every continent were urging him to come to the defense of the threatened Company? Or simply out of personal loyalty, a sense of his obligations? At all events, Clement XIII responded on January 7, 1765, to this "grave injury to the Church" with the bull *Apostolicum* and declared that

> the Company of Jesus breathes piety and holiness of the highest degree, even though there are men who, after disfiguring it with their malicious interpretations, dared characterize it as irreligious and impious, thus insulting the Church of God in the most outrageous manner.

As for the French bishops, their inevitable reaction seemed less a brief for the Jesuits (whom they defended) than a striking reaffirmation of the autonomy of the spiritual. Alarmed at the prospect of a Church owing allegiance to the state—particularly to this parliamentary-minded state, contaminated by Jansenism and "philosophical" theory—the assembly of the clergy convened in August 1765 solemnly and pathetically and unanimously proclaimed the intangible supremacy of the spiritual, the autonomy of the Church of France, and what must be called its distrust of royal power.

A whole host of revisions, of changes of position, of strategic redeployments: Whether conquered or conquering, the Jesuits had not lost their incomparable ability to disturb.

In the abolition of the Company of Jesus in France, Emmanuel Le Roy Ladurie sees "a Revocation [of the Edict of Nantes] in reverse," an act of "harassment" (fine understatement!) which

> no longer affected chance minorities or the outer bark, but the very trunk of the Counter-Reformation Church: The tree of piety would remain cut to the quick. In 1682 royal Gallicanism sought to subordinate Church to State, even if it meant the eradication three years later of the marginal, minority community of the Huguenots. Parliamentary Gallicanism, which both monarch and ministers accepted in 1762, reshaped the Church at its very heart. Between 1762 and 1790 less than a generation would go by before the Civil Constitution of the clergy, itself an offspring of the Gallicanism of the legislature.

Overall, Louis XV's biographer calculated, "the disappearance of this very vital branch, the Company of Jesus, was swiftly followed by the uprooting of dead trunks." On a different level, Le Roy Ladurie notes that "the suppression of the Ignatian teachers . . . forced the royal State to intervene in secondary education, in which it had until then taken little interest; it was an intervention that explains the proliferation of state responsibilities, starting with the monarchy and prefiguring the Jacobinism of the Empire."[13]

Dominique Julia, a specialist in religious history, observes that the very energetic reaction of the assembly of the clergy to what they perceived as Parliament's abuse of temporal power paradoxically contributed—on the very eve of the Revolution—to "the development of the ultramontanism" apparently so grievously stricken by the Company's expulsion. Julia emphasizes that "in fact the expulsion of the Jesuits marked the point at which the religious quarrels of the century were finally transformed into political debates, at which the theory of the [royal and religious] union of the two powers collapsed, together with the theology of relations between the spiritual and the temporal."[14]

The proscription of 1762–64 did not simply open the road to the French Revolution of 1789–94. It foreshadowed the actual configuration of that long-drawn-out and dramatic episode—its twists and turns, its progression from Parliament to Estates-General to Convention, from Choiseul to Necker to Mirabeau, from the night of August 4 to August 10. The liquidation of the Jesuits greased the slope, the increasingly slippery slope, down which the monarchy would slide. Perhaps Louis XV sensed it coming. Nevertheless, he preferred to keep silent, as we have seen, lest he "say too much."*

Tucked between Belém and Versailles, between the Tagus and the Pyrenees, between Pombal and Choiseul, the sovereign in the Escorial seemed immune to these fevers. The order of Saint Ignatius was of Spanish origin. The Spanish King was pious, unlike his French cousin, and energetically so, unlike his cousin of Portugal. And nothing was less Castilian than imitating a Frenchman, unless it was copying a Portuguese. At the beginning of the 1760s the Company seemed secure in the lands of Spain's Bourbons.

Charles III, Carlos Tercero: Everything now depended on him. His Chief Minister, Count Aranda, might well have been a Spanish Choiseul, a child of the Enlightenment, a Voltairean, a philosopher, and a voice of moderation in the Guaraní controversy. How much would his "philosophism" have counted for if the Most Catholic monarch, Louis XIV's great grandson, had not suddenly thrown all his weight behind anti-Jesuit repression? For it was at the instigation of the sovereign himself that the Jesuit hunt was launched, and pursued so far, so hard, and so furiously that once the Spanish abolition was accomplished fact, no one was more passionately determined to see the Company of Jesus uprooted from all Christendom like a weed, like the root of evil.

Let us again quote the monarchist historian Crétineau-Joly. "Charles III reigned over Spain. A pious and capable prince, honest and enlightened, but impetuous and stubborn, he possessed most of the qualities needed for the happiness of subjects. His character harmonized perfectly with that of his people: Like them, he exalted the spirit of family and the honor of its name. In Naples† as in Madrid, Charles III had always been devoted to the Company of Jesus."‡

It was this same Charles III who had condemned the irksome "Treaty of Limits" of 1750, which had ignited the Guaraní war of the Jesuits with the Portuguese, and later, by slow degrees, with Most Catholic Spain. But until that unhappy episode, it can safely be said that the Spanish King resolutely avoided taking any action against the Company, no matter what his private feelings.

What then propelled the pious monarch into the front rank of Jesuit hunt-

---

*In France's 1762–64 Jesuit hunt, we must bear in mind a situation in which grudge and myth weighed less than reality. First, the state's determination to recover responsibility for education, left in religious hands for two centuries. Second, the lapse of most contracts for the financing of missions and pastoral duties entrusted to the Jesuits. Third, the transformation of property laws, which made the system of ecclesiastical livings anachronistic.

†Where he first came to the throne.

‡Not true. His correspondence reveals a long-standing mistrust of the Company, sustained perhaps by his membership in the Franciscan order, and sharpened by his belief that the Jesuits were responsible for the failure of his efforts to obtain the beatification of Juan de Palafox, Bishop of Puebla, Mexico, which would have been a triumph for Spain.

ers? Why did he become the prosecutor *par excellence* of the Company, more so than Choiseul or even Pombal, in the sense that his piety, his faith, and his devotion to Catholicism were above suspicion in Rome as everywhere else?

Several things contributed to his change of heart. First, the development in Spain of a very specific, nationalistic, and essentially puritan form of Jansenism had turned substantial numbers of the clergy against a Company they considered too powerful.

The second influence was English—in other words, fundamentally anti-Jesuit. At the cost of unending intrigues and a ruinous war, Louis XIV of France had succeeded in establishing direct French influence in Madrid in the person of his grandson Philip (fifth King of that name in Spain). But on the eve of Charles III's accession to the Spanish throne, the Anglophile Duke of Alba replaced the Francophile Marquis de la Ensenada, partly by circulating letters by Jesuits said to be preparing to raise "their" American Indians against the government. Since these letters had been supplied to the "English party" in Madrid by Pombal, King Charles III had refused even to consider them. But they slumbered in the files of his Chief Minister, Count Aranda.

Pombal's weapons were somewhat crude, too crude for the gentlemanly Charles III. Choiseul's had been subtler. By sealing a "family pact" among the various branches of the Bourbons in 1761, Louis XV's Chief Minister had undoubtedly strengthened France's hand in Madrid. And by abandoning Louis XIV's absurd insistence that France automatically took diplomatic precedence over Spain, he further reinforced that hand. But this return of French diplomacy—and of Choiseul—to a position of influence in Madrid would work against the Jesuits.

The final, and perhaps most important, factor in changing the King's attitude was his former minister in Naples, the famous jurist Bernardo Tanucci, who had remained in close touch with a King he had sought to turn into the model of an "enlightened despot." Tanucci, exploiting every opportunity to put the Jesuits in a bad light, constantly warned Charles against the men in black.

Before making Aranda his Chief Minister, Charles had appointed the Neapolitan Esquilacce to the post—an unfortunate choice. It was Esquilacce who had given him the strange idea of forbidding Spaniards to wear the *capa* and *sombrero*, on the pretext that the cloaks could be used to hide daggers, pistols, and other implements of conspiracy—while a good sombrero was ideal for covering sidelong glances and secret gestures.

We can imagine how such a slight was greeted by the people who would rise so fiercely against Napoleon a half century later! Madrid rumbled with anger. People gathered, muttered, plotted. A few of the King's Walloon guards (inherited from Charles V) were killed. The King's advisers suggested that he go to the citadel at Aranjuez for his safety. Humiliated by this retreat from the wrath of his people, the King suffered a further blow to his self-esteem on learning that the Jesuits (who were highly influential in Madrid, a fact of which the King had apparently been unaware) had swiftly put down the "sombrero revolt" and, with a few speeches, had reestablished order in his name. To flee was bad enough. To owe your return to Madrid to the eloquence of a handful of priests was much worse. Count Aranda (a distinguished, lucid, cultivated man fully equal to his high responsibilities) seized every opportunity to hammer home the Jesuits' role in the King's humiliation.

His task was made easier by the fact that the Duke of Alba, long the Spanish ambassador to England, and the staunchly pro-British (though Irish) General Walsh constantly told the King that the Jesuits were plotting against him in Latin America and Europe. It was a theme that Choiseul eagerly endorsed. Thus both parties with a claim to influence in Madrid—the English and the French— sought to inject the King with Jesuitphobia.

Independently of Spanish historians like Menéndez Pelayo, the best sources here are German: Theodor Ranke *(The History of the Papacy)*, Christoph von Murr *(The History of the French)*, and Schoell *(The History of the European States)*. They offer an antidote to the disinformation fed to Charles III to inflame him against the Company of Jesus. Ranke writes that the King was persuaded that the Jesuits had concocted a plan to replace him with his brother Don Luis. Murr adds that Charles III remained scarred by the insurrection of the sombreros, believing it to have been due to some foreign intrigue, probably the work of the Jesuits. Aranda apparently even persuaded the King that the Jesuits were a threat to the royal family's lives; Charles III was so disturbed at the news that he revealed his fears in two letters to his friend Tanucci in Naples.

But other historians, such as Menéndez Pelayo, Modesto Lafuente, Crétineau-Joly, and the Protestant Schoell probably reach deeper into the heart of the matter. According to Schoell: "People swear that the King was shown a letter purporting to be from Father Ricci, Superior General of the Jesuits, which the Duc de Choiseul is accused of having forged. In the letter the General was said to have told his correspondent that he had managed to gather documents proving irrefutably that King Charles III was a child of adultery."

Crétineau-Joly's comment adds still another dimension.

> A man of King Charles III's mettle did not change the opinions of a lifetime in a single day. Still a fervent Christian, he had no intention of breaking an institution that had spread to every corner of his empire and had won more peoples to his banner than Christopher Columbus, Cortéz, and Pizarro. It would need extraordinary motives to drive him

to an act of such unprecedented harshness. The most plausible, the only one that would truly infuriate him, was to violate the royal escutcheon with the stigma of bastardy. His character had been thoroughly analyzed; he was believed incapable of yielding to philosophical argument; and so he was struck at his most vulnerable point.[15]

Of course, the letter may not have been a forgery. But it is not absurd to suggest that it was. It has been questioned by the most illustrious historians of the Papacy, the German Ludwig von Pastor, and Father Paul Dudon, who wonders why Crétineau-Joly never came forward with the proofs of his assertion. But he acknowledges the possibility that the famous "Ricci letter" containing the scandalous inference was found in the baggage (into which it had been surreptitiously slipped) of two fathers leaving Spain for Rome. Such things have happened.

Although highly colored and unsupported, the theory explains the King's astonishing behavior better than any other.

Moreover, Crétineau-Joly adds that "as he was dying, the Duke of Alba handed the Grand Inquisitor Bertram, Bishop of Salamanca, an admission that he had helped foment the insurrection of the sombreros in order to ascribe it to the Jesuits, that he had helped write the letter purporting to be from the Jesuit General against the King of Spain, and that he had invented the fable of King Nicolás I, 'Emperor of the Guaraní.'"[16]

The fact is that the suggestion of illegitimacy was perhaps the only move capable of upsetting the pious Charles III to the point of transforming him into another Pombal, of turning this "enlightened despot" into a furious "Jesuiteater." Almost like an Othello manipulated by a Iago with three faces—Aranda's, Pombal's, and Choiseul's . . .

A secret and far-reaching inquiry—of the kind that could happen in the land of the Inquisition—was set in motion by the King's sudden fury; it was aimed above all at the Jesuits, but also at all those who in the course of the past decade had had relations with them. It gradually spread throughout the country. Within six months an enormous file had been assembled and was submitted on January 29, 1767, to an Extraordinary Council at which the attorney general of Castile, Ruiz de Campomanes, delivered an angry indictment. It was followed by his verdict—which was surprising in that it brought no charge against the Society of Jesus, mentioned no crime, and went straight to the sentence: "Given what has been said, the Extraordinary Council will now move to make known its feeling on the implementation of the banishment of the Jesuits, and on the other measures which flow therefrom, in order that it be wholly and fully accomplished in the proper order."

Even more remarkable was the ominous precision and secrecy of the whole affair, suggesting the strong possibility of personal vendetta, of injured family honor:

> His Majesty reserves for himself alone knowledge of the grave causes that have decided him to adopt this just administrative measure by using the powers of trusteeship vested in him. . . . His Majesty must impose silence upon his subjects too in this matter, so that no one may write, publish, or distribute works relative to the expulsion of the Jesuits, whether for or against, without special leave from the Government . . . everything touching upon it must remain entirely within the competence and under the direct authority of the President and Ministers of the Extraordinary Council.

The Most Catholic King's ambassador to the Holy See, charged with passing this indescribable verdict on to a Pope dear to the heart of Charles III, received the specific order not to offer any explanation when he delivered the royal missive.

There are few examples in history of such an enormous step being taken—the abolition of the Company in Loyola's homeland and throughout the vast Spanish Empire—that left so few traces. Apart from the King, only four men (Aranda, the diplomats Roda and Monino,* and the jurist Campomanes) were in the picture and had access to the files. A handful of pages and young secretaries, who were kept uninformed, served as scribes. All the orders relative to the proscription were sealed in envelopes addressed to the security officers in all Spanish overseas possessions, with the note, "Not to be opened, on pain of death, until the evening of April 2, 1767."

But the most astonishing aspect of all was the royal letter addressed to the governors and sealed in the same fashion:

> I invest in you all my authority and all my royal power that you may at once hasten under arms to the house of the Jesuits. You will seize all of the Religious, and you will convey them as prisoners to the port herein mentioned within twenty-four hours. There they will embark for the destinations indicated. At the very moment of execution of this order, you will seal the archives of the house and the papers of individuals, not allowing anyone to take with him any but his prayer books and the linen strictly necessary for the crossing. If, after their embarkation, a single Jesuit, even sick or dying, remains in your department, you will suffer death.
>
> Myself, the King.

---

*Who, as Spanish ambassador to Rome, would ensure delivery of the coup de grâce.

More implacable than Choiseul, more implacable even than Pombal (whose brutality had at least been masked by manners) . . . In the name of the King, Aranda carried his arbitrary authority beyond the limits of provocation, without the motives behind the devastating step ever being made public.

Guilty or not, but most assuredly condemned, more than 5,350 fathers from 240 houses and schools created by the Jesuits over the past two centuries, from Europe to Africa, from Asia to America, were arrested during the night of April 2, 1767, taken to ports and bundled onto all kinds of vessels that then set sail for the Papal States.

Outraged by these procedures—as he had been ten years earlier by Pombal's similar actions—Clement XIII at first forbade the Spanish ships from entering the port of Civitavecchia, sending them instead to Corsica (one year before Bonaparte's birth). Only after a time for reflection did the Pope welcome the Spanish exiles to his lands.

The manner of the expulsion* was so brutal that Clement XIII could neither keep silent, nor forget, nor be satisfied by the terse notification served on him by the Spanish ambassador. Nor could he convince himself that the Company, as a body, had committed crimes horrible enough to warrant this collective punishment. Was there not a single innocent Jesuit to stand on trial and be exonerated? None of the exiles he received in Rome could offer him the slightest explanation. He therefore sent a secret emissary to Madrid bearing a letter in his own hand to King Charles. He called upon the King, in the name of the Church, to furnish him with the reasons for an act that, he said, had wounded Christendom, and he promised him that stern justice would be meted out in the name of the Holy See if Jesuits could be proven guilty.

The King replied, also in his own hand, that "to spare the world great scandal, he would keep forever in his heart the abominable conspiracy that had necessitated his harsh actions . . . , that his life's safety demanded of him profound silence on this affair," and that he was henceforth implacably resolved to carry out, with all the means in his power, the abolition of an order that the world's sovereigns would be well advised to annihilate.

Thus was announced, in the most unmistakable terms, the final act of this four-stage sacrificial ceremony. It was an operation as mannered and as progressively deadly as the successive stages of a bullfight. In Portugal the picador had done his accustomed heavy-handed work; in France the banderillas had been driven home; Spain, naturally enough, had delivered the death blow. All that

---

*Which was soon extended to Naples (Kingdom of the Two Sicilies), Parma, and Florence. Since the Two Sicilies were a Spanish possession, Charles III had reigned there before turning the throne over to his son Ferdinand IV, whose Prime Minister Tanucci and ambassador to Rome (Cardinal Orsini) would play leading parts in the Vatican's abolition of the Company.

now remained was the mercy thrust, the coup de grâce, which was administered, as tradition demanded, in the place known as the *querencia*, the last refuge of the bull, where it feels safe. Which for the Company, of course, was in Rome.

Despite the Spanish King's iron determination to destroy the Society of Jesus (and the less passionate but equally firm decision by his cousins in Paris and Lisbon to sever all ties to the Jesuits forever), the operation still entailed many imponderables, at least for as long as Clement XIII sat on the papal throne: We have seen his reaction to the banning of the Company in France and then in Spain. The Pope's anger (and the fact that he was now surrounded by exiles from Castile and Paraguay, all of them protesting their innocence in the face of arbitrary royal action) had indeed buttressed his support of the Jesuits. No doctrinaire or disciplinary or even personal differences now stood between the Vatican's "White Pope" and the Jesuits' "Black Pope." In fact the man elected Superior General of the Company in 1758, Father Lorenzo Ricci, a Florentine nobleman, was a gentle, cultivated, broad-minded, and modest man who posed no competitive threat to Clement XIII.

When disaster struck, Lorenzo Ricci would behave with exemplary dignity, dying with a stoic's strength in his prison cell. Yet he had barely lifted a finger through the various stages of the dismantling of the Company—from the hideous ordeal of old Father Malagrida in Lisbon to the exile of the French fathers and finally, in Castile, to the persecution of priests held responsible, among other things, for a libelous letter. In the course of their history, the Jesuits had been accused of many things. But not of passivity. Had the Superior General counted on everlasting papal loyalty? Louis XV and Charles III had turned against the Society. But Clement XIII?

Yet, inevitably, what had to happen happened. This particular Pope died. And the ensuing conclave, under pressure from hostile courts, elected a Pontiff who (whether to secure his election or of his own free will) was to look quite differently upon the Company. It was clear that the principal monarchies of Europe, with the apparent exception of Austria, wished to crown their labors with the liquidation of Jesuitry at its very source, and that they were intent on creating a Pope submissive to their will and ready to carry out their plans.

Clement XIII died at the beginning of February 1769. The conclave was convened for February 14, its members assembling beneath the ponderous gaze of those monarchs whose power would play a more decisive role in the Cardinals' choice than the dictates of their conscience, or their intelligence. Within the Sacred College there was a traditional opposition between a group of "Crown" Cardinals, eager to do anything to please the monarchs, and the so-called *zelanti* who, while not without their own faults, believed that the Pope should not be "made" at Versailles or the Escorial but chosen (largely . . .) because of apostolic criteria.

The rough-hewn representatives of monarchy—the French General Marquis d'Aubeterre, who seemed intent on conducting the operation as if storming a fortress, the Spaniard Azpuru, the Portuguese Almeida—were under orders to secure the coronation of the Cardinal most hostile to the Jesuits. They bent all their energies to intimidation, division, and elimination of the zelanti. To this end they had two allies within the conclave, motivated as they were by purely political considerations: de Solís, Cardinal Archbishop of Seville, and the Cardinal Archbishop of Albi, François de Bernis.

But while the former accomplished his duties by conforming strictly to the orders of his (temporal) masters, de Bernis played a game worthy of a man who seemed to embody all the characteristics of the age. He was brilliant to the point of dazzling even himself, crackling with benevolent cynicism, but with a record of disturbing zeal in his Archbishopric of Albi (where Choiseul had hoped he would be forgotten), pleasure-loving, plump, vain, more interested in delivering a witty sally than in voting his conscience, and more concerned with securing appointment as French ambassador to Rome than with electing the best Cardinal to the papal throne. François-Joachim de Pierre de Bernis was not basically an enemy of the Jesuits, whose pupil he had been at the Lycée Louis-le-Grand. He was moreover disgusted by the brutal way in which they had been handled and by the crude militancy of the representatives of monarchy. He had no wish to be the Jesuits' executioner. But, caught between his own graceful maneuverings, stern calls to order from Choiseul, and the exhortations of his "allies," he let himself be circumvented by his Spanish adversaries.

The sessions of the 1769 Roman conclave, which carried the anti-Jesuit campaign to its bitter end, were the most open in the history of the papacy. Not just because of de Bernis's scintillating *Memoirs* and the Neapolitan Cardinal Filippo Pirelli's *Journal of a Conclavist,* but also because the mid-nineteenth-century Catholic historian Crétineau-Joly was able to gain access to every report addressed to Aubeterre and Choiseul by the French prelates at the conclave (in contempt of the strict rules governing the secrecy of their deliberations), and published them in his *Clément XIV et les Jésuites.*

We thus know all about the negotiations that led to the preliminary elimination of the four Cardinals believed to support the Jesuits, then to the withdrawal of Vienna's support for the Company (following a visit to the Vatican by the future Emperor Joseph II), and then to the sidelining of Cardinals Albani and Fantuzzi, apparently the most capable of the candidates, because they had been careless enough to say that they would vote "according to their consciences." As we read in de Bernis:

In the list of those who might be chosen, there were Jesuits as Jesuitical as any of my acquaintance: and to find true enemies of this Society here, one would have to be God and read men's hearts. We shall revert to silence, cultivating our creatures and if possible increasing their number. They have all been instructed, before committing their votes, to ask us whether there are no difficulties relative to the items* proposed.

And when the French Cardinal suggested that his constituents let it be known that schism would descend upon Europe if the courts of Paris and Madrid were not given satisfaction, Ambassador Aubeterre seized upon the idea. He then took it further, asserting that "any election without the agreement of the [royal] Courts would be held void." The threat was so brutal that de Bernis was alarmed, preferring to "come out of the conclave without firing off his weapons."

However, his rival from Seville had no such scruples. De Solís went straight to the target. Like his French colleague, but with a surer instinct for the jugular, de Solís singled out from among the mass of scarlet robes a man less brilliant than many others, less verbally hostile to the Jesuits, less impetuous, more prudent, and the only religious (a Franciscan) at the conclave: Cardinal Ganganelli. How could this prelate, a member of a somewhat proletarian and somewhat lax order, not entertain some resentment toward the high-profile Company of Jesus?

De Solís dared what de Bernis (who had previously buttonholed Ganganelli) had not been able to bring himself to do. Cornering the friar, he put all his cards on the table: No candidate would be acceptable to the Powers unless he committed himself to abolition of the Company. If Ganganelli would take the initiative in conveying such a commitment to the King of Spain he, de Solís, could guarantee Ganganelli's election. Such were the circumstances in which the Cardinal-friar apparently wrote the following letter: "I recognize the right of the Sovereign Pontiff to extinguish in good conscience the Company of Jesus, in accordance with canonical rule, and that it is to be desired that the future Pope deploy every effort to fulfil the wish of the Crowns."

On this point, as on the "bastardy" question, Crétineau-Joly is challenged by his successors Von Pastor and Dudon. Father Dudon expresses surprise that Crétineau-Joly never produced a facsimile (as he had done with other pieces of evidence) of the "Ganganelli note."† Yet the author of *Clément XIV et les Jésuites* swears to the heavens that he had seen this note. In any case, both Pastor and Dudon cite a note from Cardinal de Solís to Ambassador Azpuru, which is al-

*Or rather of course "the" item.
†To which the *Journal of a Conclavist* never refers, even though it supports the theory of collusion between Ganganelli and the Spanish.

most as explicit: "I offered the candidacy to Ganganelli because of my certainty (having previously and secretly conferred with him) that he would accomplish our monarch's ideas and would satisfy all the expectations his Court entertained toward the new Pope."

What is undeniable is that after Ganganelli's election the various Spanish emissaries in Rome referred constantly in their dealings with him to his "promise" to abolish the Company. One of them even mentioned a "written promise."

De Solís was careful not to keep his "ally" de Bernis informed of the maneuver. Questioned by Aubeterre, de Bernis nonchalantly said of Ganganelli (who was already bound hand and foot by the Spanish): "Of all the *papabili,* he is the one whose horoscope, if he is elected, I would be most reluctant to hazard."

But ultimately he would have to acknowledge the success of the intriguer from Seville, recognizing that "this Ganganelli is a Jesuit . . . who has wholly broken from them. . . . At least let us take care that Ganganelli remain obliged to us for his Papacy."

Too late, de Bernis, too late. The time for charming French compromise was over. The future lay with the Spanish garrote.

Giovanni Vincenzo Antonio Ganganelli, of Rimini, was thus elected Pope as Clement XIV. Most contemporary observers, ecclesiastical and lay, believed that he was fairly favorable to the Company until the 1769 Conclave. Clement XIII saw him as "a Jesuit in monk's habit," and Cardinal Orsini, one of the plotters against the Company, as "a Jesuit in disguise."

Of all observers, de Bernis alone (who did not like him and cannot therefore be suspected of certifying his eligibility) described him on the eve of the Conclave as "no friend of the Society of Jesus."

But here sat Ganganelli on the papal throne. A queer fish, this friar. His biographers, who stress the "purity of his ways," depict him as a mettlesome horseman who "liked to gallop in short white habit and red hat so fast that he left his squires far behind." A bowls player and musician, botanist and entomologist, an admirer of Louis Bourdaloue and a reader of the revolutionary *Mercure de France,* he spent long hours at the Villa Patrizi playing *trucio* and at Castel Gandolfo indulging in billiards. "His Holiness is master of his words but not of his face," said de Bernis.

And the face of this bold rider must have reflected constant cruel fears. For Clement XIV had scarcely mounted the throne before Madrid began to harass him, reminding him of his "promise," his written (?) commitment to Charles III. Whether written or verbal, the commitment extracted from the Cardinal-friar by the King, boiling to carry his vendetta against the Company to the limit, made the Pope the moral hostage of the Spanish court.

It is true that his promise to "extinguish" the Company (if we accept the text of the note quoted by Crétineau-Joly) carried one condition—respect for canonical rule, which implied complex procedures that Madrid would have preferred to see discarded. And Ganganelli, without actually specifying it in writing, had intimated to de Solís that if he handed the Jesuits over to the vengeance of Charles III there would have to be some compensation—the return to the Papacy not only of the Principality of Benevento, which was within the Spanish King's disposition, but also of Avignon—which was not.

No matter. The Cardinal had made a promise, and as Pope he had to honor it. Henceforth there would not be one exchange of views between Rome and Madrid that did not carry a threat or a reminder. And the King possessed a considerable weapon against the Pope, located in his own backyard: a printing shop in the Holy See itself. From this establishment came increasingly venomous pamphlets, culminating in the following, reportedly written by the Spanish ambassador himself, and published under the title *Reflections of the Courts of the House of Bourbon on Jesuitry:*

> If everyone believes naturally in the discretion and probity of the honest man, however commonplace his origins, how much the more must this apply to the Vicar of Jesus Christ, the source of all truth? Yet for more than three years the Pope has promised the most illustrious Catholic Sovereigns, in his own voice and on many occasions, the abolition of a Society contaminated by perverse maxims, an abolition generally desired by all good Christians. But the Holy Father, under frivolous and contrived pretexts, keeps postponing its execution.

Clement XIV felt himself unequal to responding to this challenge, thrown at him from the heart of his possessions. Frightened at these constant demands by a sovereign who had a deadly hold over him, and at the idea (in which de Bernis also believed) that he would be poisoned either by the Jesuits or else by their enemies, cut off from the cardinals who might have been able to put a protective screen around him, or at least to provide him with an avenue of escape from the demands of those to whom he had committed himself (an art in which the Roman Curia excelled), and defended only by a handful of friars from his own order, he resorted to delaying tactics. (Although he also drew up in secret a draft "brief" for abolition, which he sent for comment to the courts of Paris and Madrid: an act that one writer sees as the ultimate expression of his "servility."[17])

To spare himself this act of abolition, an action he had once said would be "as perilous as the destruction of the dome of Saint Peter's," and sensing its unpopularity in his states and among Catholic believers (who, while not unanimously favorable to the Jesuits, feared the irrevocable overthrow of Church structures), Pope Clement opted for Pilate's tactics and attempted to substitute a series of less sweeping sanctions for the death penalty. For example, he authorized Cardinal Malvizzi, who hated them, to expel the Jesuits from his Bologna diocese.

This seemed poor compensation to the impatient Spanish King. He bullied his ambassador in Rome, and Florida Blanca's energy swept the last obstacles aside. To gain time, perhaps even to save the Society of Jesus, Clement XIV had mentioned the possibility of a Vatican Council to decide the matter. Given the important role the Jesuits had played in the history of Christendom, such a move did not seem excessive. When Clement V, in collusion with Philip the Fair, was planning to destroy the Templars, had he not convened an assembly of three hundred prelates to judge the accused? Had the Catholic Church in the ensuing four centuries lost that sense of justice, which first and foremost recognized the right of the accused man to defend himself in public?

But the royal courts, led by Madrid, absolutely forbade such a procedure. What would happen if the bishops, temporarily emancipated from royal authority, were to give these Jesuit casuists the right to sway minds and impress their judges? The ambassador of Madrid became imperious and abrupt. He insisted that the promise be kept, he spoke of honor, he threatened, all in the name of the Spanish and Mexican episcopate. Besides, he had drafted an eighteen-point plan: Did the Pope wish to read it? To his credit, Clement XIV did not lower himself to the point of endorsing Florida Blanca's draft. But he hastily set about writing one of his own.

July 21, 1773, dawned. That morning, Clement XIV did not begin his day with a hearty gallop in his white tunic and red hat, or with a game of bowls: At first light, he signed the text of the brief entitled *Dominus ac Redemptor*, which decreed the dissolution of the Company of Jesus.

We have it from one of his successors, Gregory XVI, that Ganganelli signed the brief in the half light, and in pencil, resting the paper on a windowsill in the Quirinale, and that having done it he fell in a faint on the marble tiles. Cardinal de Simone, then the Pope's "auditor," tells the rest of the story in the following words:

> The Pontiff was almost naked on his bed; he complained, and from time to time we heard him say, "Oh God! I am doomed! Hell is my abode. There is no other remedy." Fra Francesco [Buentempo] asked me to approach the Pope and speak to him. I did so; but the Pope did not answer me, and went on saying, "Hell is my abode! Ah! I have signed the brief, there is no other remedy." I answered him that there was indeed a remedy, and that he could withdraw the decree. "That is no longer possible," he cried, "I have given it to Monino,* and by now

*The Spanish Ambassador, Count of Florida Blanca.

the horseman taking it to Spain has probably left.""But Holy Father,"
I said, "one brief can be revoked by another." "Oh God!" he continued, "it cannot be done! I am doomed."[18]

What exactly was in this decree, in which a Pope read his own damnation?
We should first note that in choosing the form of the brief rather than a bull,
which was much more solemn—and which his predecessor Clement XIII had
used nine years earlier in coming to the defense of the persecuted Jesuits—
Ganganelli had apparently sought to minimize the consequences of his act and
relieve it of all doctrinal meaning. But its language was no less eloquent—and
virulent—for all that:

> When still almost in its cradle, the Society witnessed the birth in its
> own bosom of divers germs of discord and jealousies, which not only
> divided its members but incited them to rise against the other reli-
> gious Orders, against the secular Clergy, the Academies, the Universi-
> ties, the Colleges, the public Schools, and against the Sovereigns
> themselves who had welcomed them and admitted them to their
> States.
>
> . . . There was almost no charge too serious to be leveled against
> this Society, and the peace and tranquility of Christendom were long
> troubled by it [so much so that] our most dear sons in Jesus Christ
> the Kings of France, of Spain, of Portugal, and of the Two Sicilies
> were obliged to send away and banish from their Kingdoms, States,
> and Provinces all the religious of this Order, convinced that this ex-
> treme measure was the only remedy for so many ills, and the only one
> that must be taken to prevent Christians from insulting one another,
> from provoking one another, and from rending one another in the
> very bosom of the Church, their mother. But these same Kings, our
> most dear sons in Jesus Christ, believed that this remedy could not
> have a lasting effect and be sufficient to establish tranquility in the
> Christian world unless the Society itself were wholly suppressed and
> abolished.
>
> . . . Acknowledging that the Company of Jesus could no longer pro-
> duce those abundant fruits and those considerable advantages for
> which it was constituted . . . , after ripe reflection, and in the fullness
> of our apostolic power, we suppress and we abolish the Society of Je-
> sus; we liquidate and abrogate each and every one of its offices, func-
> tions and administrations, houses, schools, colleges, retreats,
> hospices, and all the other places that belong to it under any title
> whatsoever, and in whichever province, kingdom, or state they may
> be.

... This is why we declare broken in perpetuity and utterly extinguished all kind of authority temporal or spiritual, of the General, the Provincials, the Visitors, and other superiors of this Society.

... We further call upon and prohibit, in the name of holy obedience, all and every regular and secular ecclesiastic, whatever his rank, dignity, quality, and condition, and particularly those who have until now been attached to the Society and who belonged to it, to oppose this suppression, attack it, write against it, and even to speak of it, as of its causes and motives.

The language is by itself astonishing, with its naïve admission of the political motives behind it and of the Pope's overriding concern to bow to the will of the Bourbon Kings. But the last paragraph goes beyond anything else. To the absence of any canonical debate within the bosom of the Church, this Pope adds a ban not only on any form of criticism but even of comment, of any question about the causes and the bases for his act. The arbitrariness of absolute power ... Had the Jesuit principle *perinde ac cadaver* ever been as rigid as in this text, which consigned its inventors to destruction?

Welcomed in Madrid and hailed in Paris by "philosophical" Jansenist and Parliamentarian circles (which came near calling for Clement XIV's canonization), this brief of July 21, 1773, was not only criticized—despite the Pope's warning—but rejected with unbelievable scorn by the Archbishop of Paris, Christophe de Beaumont. Recalling that Clement XIII's bull, emanating from virtually the whole Church, had ten years earlier declared the "odor of sanctity" of the Company of Jesus, the French prelate addressed the following words to Ganganelli:

This brief which destroys the Company of Jesus is nothing other than an isolated and particular judgment, pernicious, reflecting little honor on the Papal tiara and deleterious to the glory of the Church and to the glory and propagation of the orthodox faith. . . . Holy Father, it is not possible for me to commit the Clergy to acceptance of the said brief. I would not be heard on this point were I wretch enough to attempt to lend my ministry to it, which I should be dishonoring.

Even had the Pope-executioner been untroubled by his act, such a slap would have given him pause. Some contemporary observers indicate that Clement XIV's mental state was ever after deeply troubled. It is said that he wandered through his apartments sobbing, "Compulsus feci!" (I did it under duress). When he died less than two years after signing the brief, rumor naturally blamed the Jesuits, his victims, who were said to have poisoned him with "water of Tolfana." This time there was no mystery as to motive: De Bernis, who had meanwhile been appointed French ambassador to Rome, hints in two letters to his minister that the Pope's death might not have been "natural," and that the deceased had been "heard to utter cruel suspicions leading one to believe that [the suppression of the Jesuits] was just and necessary." We have seen Mme de Pompadour's friend in better form: Today not a single historian considers the question worth considering.

To d'Alembert, who had conveyed these rumors to him, Frederick II of Prussia retorted: "Nothing less true than the rumor of the Pope's poisoning. . . . When they opened him up they found not a trace of poison. But he had often reproached himself for the weakness that led him to sacrifice an order like the Jesuits. . . . In the last days of his life his mood was sorrowful and cantankerous, which helped to cut short his existence."[19]

The life of his victim, Lorenzo Ricci, former General of the former Jesuits, whom Clement XIV steadfastly refused to see, was cut short in a different manner. Six weeks after publication of the brief *Dominus ac Redemptor,* the seventy-year-old Father Ricci and the five fathers closest to him were taken to the Castel Sant'Angelo where they were imprisoned and sentenced by a tribunal named by the Pope. The hearing took place under the watchful eye of the Spanish ambassador. Meanwhile, more or less everywhere, confiscations, depredations, and scattering of the property, collections, and libraries of the Jesuits began.

The verdict preceded the trial. Would the next Pope, Pius VI, spare himself this lugubrious formality and release the fathers pent up in the famous dungeon? The court at Madrid would not hear of it. It insisted not only on the continued incarceration of Father Ricci and his companions but on the staging of the trial.

The tribunal that convened at the Castel Sant'Angelo consisted of five cardinals* and two prelates. It had before it the confiscated archives of the Company. What would better testify to the global iniquity of the institution? In fact, the hearings were reduced to a series of skirmishes aimed at demonstrating attempts by the Jesuits in recent years to obtain the protection of this or that sovereign (particularly Maria Theresa of Austria) or such and such a cardinal. The brief for the prosecution also mentioned the attempt to "raise the bishops against the Holy See."

But they were empty squabbles, sustained only at the insistence of Spain and the unbending Charles III. What was the purpose of the trial? To add to or detract from the authority of an act not judged but accomplished? It is difficult to imagine what the court's sentence might have been, for death intervened. In early November 1775, Lorenzo Ricci, long suffering from an illness aggravated

*One of whom, Marefoschi, though known for his hostility to the Jesuits, withdrew from the proceedings, sickened by the irregularities committed.

by his three years of confinement in a cell, was unable to rise from his bed. He requested the last rites and wrote a letter that stated the essentials. Before he died, on November 23, 1775, he read it to his companions and jailers:

> ... I declare and protest that I have given no cause, of even the slightest kind, for my imprisonment. .... I make this claim because it is necessary for the reputation of the defunct Company of Jesus, of which I was Superior General.

Perhaps Pius VI, who had lacked the courage to rescue the old Jesuit from his cell, felt he made amends by staging a solemn funeral and burying Ricci at the Gesù, beside the founders of the order. It was a less splendid funeral than the one organized a few years earlier by the Emperor of China for Father Castiglione, his favorite painter, after composing in his own hand an ode to the departed Jesuit ... Thus, from across the seas, Matteo Ricci's ghost shouted its condemnation of the suffering inflicted on Lorenzo Ricci's order by Catholic Europe.

Perhaps because the successive stages of the Company's demise had been ordered and carried out by "tyrants," the fledgling French Revolution at first attempted to render justice to the Company executed twenty years earlier.

At the session of the Constituent Assembly of February 19, 1790, the Duke Abbot of Montesquieu urged his colleagues to demonstrate their "generosity" toward "this famous Congregation, in which doubtless many among you began your studies, and to these unfortunate ones whose wrongs were perhaps a problem, but whose woes most certainly are not." The president of the Assembly, the Protestant Antoine Barnave, then raised his voice to declare that "the first act of newborn freedom must be to repair despotism's injustices: I therefore propose the drafting of a text in favor of the Jesuits."

But the most important speech was delivered by a man whose qualifications on the matter were beyond dispute. A man of known hostility to the Jesuits, a supporter of Gallican and Jansenist popularism, the Abbé Grégoire:

> Among the hundred thousand vexations of the former government which weighed so heavily on France, we have to number one inflicted upon a celebrated order, the Jesuits: You must now extend your justice to them.

The Revolution failed to act upon the urging of this honest man. But the call had gone forth.

WANDERING
IN THE DESERT

*Silence and Obedience • Providential Poland • Frederick, Savior of
the Company • In the Bosom of Catherine • "Approbo, Approbo,
Approbo" • Meanwhile in Parma • Growing Again*

CHARACTER EMERGES FROM ordeal, our Jesuit teachers used to tell
us. Nothing like earthquake, persecution, epidemic, and military disaster to bring forth and confirm outstanding men, organizations,
and nations. And what organization seemed sturdier than this Company of Jesus? What men tougher than Ignatius and the founders? What corporate rules
better shaped to survive calamity and the ordeal of diaspora after so many insults, proscriptions, and perils confronted and overcome, from Paris to Japan
and from China to Paraguay?

Yet the mean-spirited decree of abolition, issued in 1773 by Clement XIV, after the Portuguese (1759), French (1764), and Spanish (1767) bans, seemed to
shatter the Company. There was no underground movement, no Catacombs,
no resistance network to confront an illegal order extorted by coercion and
blackmail. With the hapless Lorenzo Ricci dying in his cell at the Castel
Sant'Angelo, the Company appeared simply to expire.

Where now were Jesuits like Laínez and Canisius, constantly hunted, persecuted, and proscribed, but always in the breach? Was this formidable body of
men, which had once made the Holy Office tremble and infuriated the gentlemen of the French Parliament, destroyed forever by a feeble Pope and a quartet
of spineless or deranged monarchs? No. As we shall see, it would be rescued
from the persecutions of its natural allies by its apparent enemies, but only after

its tame submission to the batterings of the storm. For the next quarter century we shall see stunned silence and fear among the successors of men who had once remained stoical under torture, persecution, and mockery.

There were of course instances of individual courage, of steadfastness and heroism among these men who were now expelled, dragged through the courts, persecuted, and murdered. (Between 1793 and 1794, twenty-three refractory former Jesuits were guillotined in France.) The French bishops were not the only ones to protest the brief of abolition or Superior General Ricci's incarceration: In Vienna, Warsaw, and Brabant other voices were raised. But not a sound came from within the Company. That great institution—which people had believed armored against the Inquisition, the hired assassins of the Holy Office, and the henchmen of the Bourbons—seemed suddenly prostrate, resigned to the worst outrages against justice, the worst excesses of arbitrary power. It took a truly curious kind of "obedience" to bow to such flagrant injustice.

Were the Ignatians so hungry for humiliation, so incapable of distinguishing right from wrong in papal pronouncements, or simply eager, after the Paraguay controversy, to demonstrate how far they were prepared to carry the notion of *perinde ac cadaver*—even when applied to a crime committed by a Pontiff working hand in glove with unscrupulous powers? "A staff in an old man's hand . . . " But what if the old man were mad, or manipulated by scoundrels?

The help and refuge that now materialized were so unlikely that some Catholic historians speak of "miracles"—even though these were wrought through the non-Catholic intercession of the most holy Frederick of Prussia and the most pious Catherine of Russia. "Anti-miracle" might be a more appropriate description of the spectacle of this famous fighting Company first tamely submitting and then being rescued by Machiavellian expediency.

In the events that lay ahead it was as if the Jesuits, fatally inclined to rub elbows with power, to join forces with the establishment and act through it, were now paying the price for a strategy repudiated and annihilated. It was punished where it had sinned: in its devotion to established power, its eagerness to pay court to the great. In their attempts to be "worldly," the fathers had been crushed by the "world," and were now apparently demoralized beyond recall by this stunning betrayal.

Outside the sanctuary offered them by a heretic Caesar and a schismatic Jezebel, it would take a quarter century for the first "resistance fighters" to emerge, Jesuits able to brave Republican or Napoleonic repression in France, the stings of Italian princelings, or the vindictiveness of Iberian Kings.

To a reader familiar with the work of earlier Jesuits in Asia or America, such passivity is amazing. The day after the Crucifixion, the Apostles were nowhere to be seen. Nor were the fathers any more visible after the "abolition." As d'Alembert noted, "The destruction of these ghosts we had considered so powerful took place in silence."

Even bodies as scattered and humiliated as the Prussian army after the battle of Jena, or the French forces after the defeat of 1940, managed to secrete a Clausewitz or a de Gaulle. Yet the Society of Jesus, faced with the illegalities, abuses of power, and state excesses that led up to the 1773 brief, submitted to its degradation and dispersion as if executing a decree from God on high. And when rebellion finally flared, it was largely political. For in the age of kings, the fathers had suffered the high-handedness of Versailles and Rome without a murmur.* Only when such arbitrariness became "Republican"—twenty years later—did Jesuit resignation give way to resistance.

In short, the Society of Jesus, founded in epic spirit by a band of fearless adventurers in the mid-sixteenth century and journeying out for the next two and a half centuries to conquer—or at least encounter—the world, allowed itself to be strangled in a silence broken only by Lorenzo Ricci's smothered protest. When it finally dared envisage a rebirth, its efforts were marked by timid circumspection and furtive groping, like a village community emerging from the cracked ground after an earthquake. You would have to be a historian of the Company (and a talented one) like Father Dudon to speak of "resurrection" or even of renaissance, terms much too ornate and lyrical to describe what in reality seems more like a resurgence, or quite simply a restoration.

Fabulous? Baroque? How can we describe the Company's itinerary from 1773 to 1796? The rescue of this most papalist of Companies, destroyed by the Pope, at the hands of the Lutheran Frederick? And then its welcome and revitalization at the hands of the schismatic Empress of Russia? Perhaps the answer lies first and foremost in the gloomy fact that the Catholic world had almost with one accord abandoned the Company of Jesus to its fate. Who, once the few murmurs of protest had died down, had not turned from the Company? When one reflects on the enormous services it had rendered the world in terms of education, of the intellectual prestige it had enjoyed, of its influence over both monarchs and masses, this sudden collapse has something terrifying, almost biblical, about it.

That the Company had been rejected like a leper was strikingly demonstrated at the conclave that met in 1774 to elect a successor to Clement XIV, who had survived the murder of the Company by only fourteen months.

Most of the assembled prelates retained the humiliating memory of their treatment at the conclave five years earlier, where the Bourbon monarchs and their agents had used naked pressure and dictated their conditions in order to

*Although, as we shall see, there were exceptions like Father de Clorivière. See below, page 317.

effect the election of a Pope who would do away with the Jesuits. The cardinals known as *zelanti*, religious, firm in their convictions—unlike the *politicanti*, who remained subservient to monarchic command—were determined not to be manipulated any longer by the royal courts and their red-robed henchmen. Particularly since the "Jesuit question" remained on every mind. Indeed, the process had been widely perceived as so illegal and so inadmissible that the charges brought against Lorenzo Ricci had ended in his posthumous acquittal. Should they now reexamine the notorious brief, amend it, annul it, augment it?

Even before the conclave began, Madrid, Paris, and Lisbon conveyed to the princes of the Church that the status quo must not be disturbed. Any candidate not specifically committed to the brief *Dominus ac Redemptor* would be eliminated. Cardinal de Solís quickly obtained from Cardinal Braschi the promise that, if elected, he would not open the Jesuit question. De Solís even passed on to Madrid what Braschi had told him: "In my opinion the Company should not be resurrected, even if all the Bourbons wished it." The ideal candidate, one prepared to go beyond what was asked of him![1]

Thus was elected, under the name of Pius VI, Gianangelo Braschi, a former pupil of the Jesuits. A man, as everyone knew, who had disapproved of the 1773 brief, to which he too was now tied. Like Ganganelli, he had paid in advance. Moreover, he had agreed to accept as secretary of state Cardinal Pallavicini, who was known to be Madrid's man. And like Ganganelli, he would learn what it cost to make such a bargain.

The Catholic world, abetted in its cowardice by the "corpselike" capitulation of the Jesuits, accepted the expulsion as an irreversible fact, along with the disappearance of seven hundred schools and the exile from their respective countries of twenty thousand religious, now crowded into the papal domains. To all appearances, most Christians of the day reserved for this liquidation a verdict as icy as that of the authors (L. J. Rogier and others) of the *Nouvelle Histoire de l'Église:* "It should not be presented as a scandal. Very real deficiencies had at that point irreversibly* undermined the Company's credit."[2]

But we should understand nothing of the tangled events to come if we did not bear in mind the bizarre procedure the Pope had pursued, decreeing that the proscription would not enter publicly into force until promulgated and passed along to the Jesuit communities. But the brief had not been posted in the traditional locations in Rome, such as the Campo dei Fiori. Did the Papacy fear reactions of Roman citizens? And the actual manner of promulgation remained ill-defined. Whence the fog of confusion in which the "former Jesuits" were able to scatter and seek refuge elsewhere, particularly in Prussian and Russian

*This word is, to put it mildly, an exaggeration. Not to mention the tranquil cynicism of the judgment: deficient, therefore liquidated . . .

Poland, and in countries where connivance between Catholic leadership and political power did not mandate immediate execution of the Roman decision.

One of the strangest of the many paradoxes of this story is that the Company owed its salvation to the eighteenth-century partition of Poland, a nation that the Jesuits had turned into one of their bastions. Since Augustus of Saxony, a convert to Catholicism, mounted the Polish throne at the end of the sixteenth century, the Society of Jesus had enjoyed a commanding position there. More than two thousand of its people (one tenth of its total numbers worldwide) exercised various ministries in Poland.

There as elsewhere, the Company was ready to bow before the fait accompli. But one year before its abolition, Maria Theresa of Austria, Frederick of Prussia, and Catherine of Russia had signed a treaty partitioning Poland "in the name of the Holy Trinity" (in a letter to his brother, the King of Prussia spoke glowingly of this "Communion in the single ecclesiastical body that is Poland"). The move abruptly swelled the number of Catholic subjects of the rulers of Berlin and Saint Petersburg. And while the pious Maria Theresa complied with the orders from Rome and abolished the Company in Austria, Frederick and Catherine, ignoring the Catholic Pontiff, acted in the exclusive interests of their states and dynasties.

Each faced a fundamental problem, different of course in each case: the maintenance of peace within the Catholic populations newly under their authority, which would have been needlessly disturbed by measures against the Jesuits; and the education of the young, essential to the fulfillment of their ambitious plans for reform. How could you build a modern state without well-trained officials? As a matter of basic interest, they could not afford to damage relations with the Jesuits' enemies, the Holy See, Spain, and France. But to these Machiavellian rulers, a manipulated Pope and a decadent Spain counted for little. As for France, it seemed quite simply to have forgotten the scattered Company.

There remained the reactions of the *philosophes,* who were friends and admirers of these two sovereigns they called the Solomon and Semiramis of the North. But neither the strategist in Potsdam nor the lady of Saint Petersburg were the kind to lose sleep over the question. Not that they discounted the glory that Voltaire, Grimm, d'Alembert, and Diderot had added to their laurels. But they had never set them on the scales of their most basic interests. As we shall see, in fact, they took pleasure in reminding the beacons of the Enlightenment of this reality.

Frederick II held Silesia not because of the Polish partition but because of his victories in the Seven Years' War: He had annexed it in 1763 (just as the Jesuit witch hunt was gathering momentum in France). He had found the Company both popular and effective there, so much so that he proposed to General Ricci that the exiles from Portugal (and soon from France and Spain) be redirected to Breslau. In 1770, a year after the Spanish ban and three years before Clement XIV's brief, he wrote to Voltaire: "This good monk in the Vatican is letting me keep my Jesuits, who are everywhere persecuted. I shall hoard the precious seed in order to redistribute it one day to those who may wish to cultivate this rare plant in their own land."

Yet Frederick did not want to cut himself off completely from the "philosophical party." Two years later he wrote to d'Alembert in language so pleasing to the editors of the *Encyclopédie* that they circulated a copy of the letter all over Europe:

> I have received an ambassador from the Ignatian General, who presses me openly to declare myself protector of that order. I answered that when Louis XV saw fit to abolish Fitzjames's regiment* I had not felt it incumbent on me to intercede in that body's favor; and that the Pope was sufficiently master in his own house to carry out whatever reforms he considered necessary without interference from heretics.

Yet no sooner had the Papacy issued its brief than the King of Prussia did indeed start to "interfere," observing that while the Pope might be "master in his own house" he had no authority on Prussian territory. He then decreed as follows:

> We, Frederick, by the grace of God King of Prussia, to each and every one of our loyal subjects, greeting. . . . We have resolved that this recently executed destruction of the Society of Jesus shall not be promulgated in our States. We graciously command you to take within your jurisdictions the steps necessary to render null and void the said bull† of the Pope; and to this end you will, on receipt of these presents and in our name, expressly forbid, on pain of stern punishment, all ecclesiastics of the Roman Catholic religion residing in your jurisdiction to publish the said papal bull doing away with the Society of Jesus; you will be most vigilant in ensuring that this prohibition be obeyed, and will at once notify us in the event that senior ecclesiastics from foreign nations attempt to insinuate bulls of this nature into this country.

And to drive his point home, the Prussian King handed his unofficial representative in Rome the following note, addressed to the Pope. It is at once the most insolent and gleeful lesson in virtue that a heretic can ever have had the pleasure of inflicting on the leader of the Roman Church:

*The Duke of Berwick, James Fitzjames, English noble and marshal of France, who led French forces in the wars of the early eighteenth century.
†In fact, as we know, it was a brief.

On the matter of the Jesuits, my mind is made up to preserve them in my States just as they have always been. In the Treaty of Breslau I guaranteed the status quo of the Catholic Religion, and I have never known better priests. You will add that, since I belong to the class of heretics, the Pope may not dispense me of my obligation to keep my word nor my duty as an honest man and a King.[3]

We do not know how the Holy Father reacted to this slap. But we do know that the *philosophes* were pained at this rescue of the "men in black" by a pillar of the Enlightenment. D'Alembert wrote indignantly that Philosophy had "taken fright," and warned Frederick II that he might have cause to "regret . . . giving asylum to the Jesuit Pretorian Guard . . . so clumsily repudiated by the Pope."

After his sermon on honor to the Pope, the King's reply to the philosopher, sent in January 1774, was a sermon in humanity:

I have nothing to fear from the Jesuits: The monk Ganganelli has trimmed their claws, drawn their teeth, and left them in a condition in which they can neither scratch nor bite but merely impart learning to the young, at which art they are better than all others. . . . And you philosophers must not reproach me for treating men with goodness and for exercising humanity toward all of my species, whatever their religion or rank. Believe me, practice philosophy and metaphysics less: Good actions are more beneficial to the public than the subtlest of philosophical systems.

Four months later he again took the *philosophes* to task, and in even more biting tones:

Can so much spleen enter the heart of a true wise man? the poor Jesuits would ask if they learned how, in your letter, you express your-self on their account. I did not protect them while they were power-ful; in their misfortunes, I see in them only men of letters who would be hard indeed to replace as teachers of the young. . . . Thus none will obtain of me a single Jesuit, being most interested in preserving them.

Preserver of the Jesuits: This theme would be most ferociously put forward in a letter he wrote to Voltaire, proving once again that people performing "good actions" can never resist the temptation of adding a touch of deviltry:

My brothers the Catholic, Most Faithful and Most Apostolic Kings, have expelled the Jesuits. And I, most heretical, am taking in as many as I can. Thus I keep this race alive. Soon these Catholic Kings will come to ask me whether I might have a Jesuit for them. And then I will sell him dear: not less than three hundred crowns for a single fa-ther-rector; and for a provincial father, at least six hundred.

And in a more serious vein this letter, also to Voltaire, dated November 18, 1773:

> In our domains there is no educated Catholic except among the Jesuits; we had no one capable of holding classes . . . other kinds of monks are of the crassest ignorance; we had therefore to preserve the Jesuits or allow our schools to die. . . . Moreover, it was in the Jesuit university that theologians destined to fill the parishes were trained. If the order had been suppressed the university would have ceased to exist, and we would have been obliged to send the Silesians to study theology in Bohemia. Which would have gone against the fundamental principles of the government.
>
> All these good reasons have made of me the Lancelot of this order.

And since no Prussian King (and Frederick was a strategist to boot) could remain on the defensive, he risked the following sortie: "Remember, I beg you, Father Tournemine who was your nursing-mother . . . and reconcile yourself with an order which last century provided France with men of the very highest merit."

Quoting this decisive letter, Father Dudon notes that while it was easier (however risky) for the powerful sovereign to make fun of the author of *Candide* than to maintain the Company in Silesia and the area of Poland he had seized, "the King of Prussia went about it energetically,"[4] while the Catholic clergy and the Jesuits, badgered by the agents of the Holy See, were divided as to what action to take: Should they comply with orders from Rome, circumvent them, seek an alternative?

Father Gleixner, Provincial of Silesia, considered becoming the leader of embryonic resistance to Rome by founding a Nordic Company of Jesus. It would consist of the fathers of Prussia, Poland, England, and Holland, and would be led, for want of better, by an elected vicar-general. Frederick would willingly have backed this venture if his bishops had not firmly blocked it and piled up obstacles before the officially tolerated Jesuits, threatening to refuse them ordination and forbid them the exercise of the priesthood.[5]

Negotiations with Rome began. Perhaps alerted to the danger of a Jesuit schism, the Vatican suddenly began to dump much ballast. In March 1774, the nuncio Garempi announced that the Pope authorized the Jesuits in Poland and Prussia to teach, preach, and administer the sacraments to the extent deemed necessary by higher authority. They could even live in community. It was a straightforward capitulation by the Sovereign Pontiff. Clement XIV's death seemed for a time to put this unhoped-for arrangement at risk. But his successor, Pius VI, approached in his turn by Potsdam, let Frederick know that if he could find a way of "saving the Jesuits," he would not oppose him.

Acting with uncharacteristic clumsiness, the Prussian King was so noisily triumphant that the Curia and the Bourbon courts took offense and cried scandal. Pius VI made a hasty clarification: He had condoned the status quo only for Jesuits reduced to the secular condition, in other words Jesuits scattered after the dissolution of their communities. In his turn Frederick, flanked by his cousin Karl von Hohenzollern, Bishop of Culm, and anxious to soothe the Holy See, retreated. He affected to find the Pope's retraction acceptable and, in an effort to mitigate the effects of the secularization he had insisted upon, created a Literary Institute and a Royal Schools Institute, which would keep the Jesuits in a communal group . . . and under his wing.

Thus, until the death in 1786 of the philosopher-king, the fathers of Silesia and Poland continued to live in community, remaining very active and influential, particularly at Breslau University. But when his successor, Frederick-William, deprived them of the income from their schools in the closing years of the century, they were obliged to disperse. Some, secularized, remained where they were. Others went to Russia, where an Empire-wide Jesuit rescue operation was under way.

After eleven years on the throne, Catherine II was at the peak of her fortunes. She had defeated the Turks and conquered the Crimea, and the partition of Poland had handed White Russia to her. Grigory Potemkin was about to enter her life and help her defeat the "false Peter III," Pugachev. Diderot traveled eagerly to Saint Petersburg. To Catherine—a German Lutheran who had become head of the Russian Orthodox Church—a brief issued by an exhausted Pope (whether or not manipulated by a few well-armed Kings) meant little. ·

Her position was at once like and unlike Frederick's. Less involved than the Prussian monarch in the power games of European courts, she believed that she enjoyed a greater freedom to maneuver. And White Russia was a less delicate administrative proposition than Silesia. But now that she was free of the Turkish threat, and about to break the Cossack rebellion, Catherine had to keep in mind the precedent of Peter the Great who in 1721 had "forever" expelled the Jesuits from the Empire.

For relations between the Roman Company and Russian Tsarism had already known many ups and downs since Ivan the Terrible had seized the reins of Muscovy. A diplomatic mission had been sent there under Antoine Possevin, one of the greatest negotiators the Company ever produced. But despite his wiles, the Jesuit was threatened by Ivan's iron-tipped staff and driven out by the terrible Tsar.

Relations did not improve under Boris Godunov, since the Jesuits—as we learn in Mussorgsky's opera—had taken sides with the pretender Dmitri and his Polish supporters. It was a misstep for which they would pay for a whole century, until Peter the Great decided that he needed educators for his project to Westernize Russia. But the excessively close links the Jesuits maintained with Vienna aroused the Tsar's suspicions, and Peter expelled them. (And not coincidentally, two Jesuits had been the extremely efficient experts on the Chinese side at negotiations twenty years earlier at Nerchinsk, where the Russian-Chinese frontiers in the Amur River region were fixed for two centuries.)

During the ensuing phase, the most important one in relations between the Russian Empire and the Company, "it was not the Jesuits who went to Russia, it was Catherine II's Russia that came to them."[6] The first partition of Poland, which gave White Russia to the Empress, placed 200 Jesuits under her rule in Mazovia. This was followed almost immediately by the Pope's dissolution order. Should Catherine carry it out or ignore it? It did not take her long to decide. Like Frederick, of course, she might have foreseen, and regretted, the indignation of the "philosophical" party or the distress of Diderot and his friend the German writer Friedrich Melchior de Grimm. But such storms raised more waves at Potsdam than at Saint Petersburg, not to mention Paris. The stout lady had known worse.

Indeed, thumbing her nose at Rome cost her little and gave her much satisfaction. Like her Prussian fellow-monarch, she readily lectured her philosopher friends on the virtues and wisdom of tolerance; on the importance of education in the construction of the "enlightened" state; and on the assurance that she would vigilantly oversee the content of the teaching dispensed under her aegis. In short, the Semiramis of the North would deploy all her talents in the victorious prosecution of this rescue operation, bringing into the fight "a very feminine flexibility and a very Tartar will."[7] Although the latter aspect would overshadow the former . . .

Moreover, she owed "her" Jesuits a debt. When she annexed White Russia, they had been the first to rally to her, pulling in their wake the clergy, the nobility, and the people. Perhaps the Empress was not above gratitude.

The pontifical brief was delivered to Saint Petersburg in October 1773. Catherine reacted promptly and decisively, declaring it null and void. Like Frederick, she made its publication and dissemination a matter for severe punishment. And the Roman clergy of the Empire, particularly in White Russia, was subjected to a discipline that not a single bishop dreamed of questioning. The Jesuits might be "abolished" in Rome, Madrid, Vienna, or Paris. Not in the Great Autocrat's Russia!

The only one to object to this sovereign decision was in fact a Jesuit, the most distinguished of them in the entire Empire, Father Czerniewicz, rector of the famous college of Polotsk, the Company's intellectual center in White Russia. He addressed the following plea to the Empress imploring her to submit to the Roman decree, *perinde ac cadaver*—and now it was truly a corpse whose fortune was at stake!

> Prostrating ourselves before your most august imperial throne, and by all that is most holy, we beg Your Majesty to permit us to render prompt and public obedience to our jurisdiction which resides in the person of the Sovereign Roman Pontiff. . . . By condescending to the dissemination of the brief of abolition, Your Majesty will exercise her royal authority; and we, obeying promptly, will show ourselves as loyal to Y.M., who has thus permitted its execution, as to the authority of the Sovereign Pontiff.[8]

So now the fathers were pleading to be allowed to die while the Empress ordered them to live. Her reply to Czerniewicz was uncompromising:

> You owe obedience to the Pope in the things touching on dogma; for the rest you must obey your sovereigns. I note that you are a man of scruple. I shall therefore instruct my ambassador in Warsaw to reach agreement with the Pope's nuncio and unburden you of your scruples.

It was not only from the nuncio but from the Pope himself that the Empress obtained exemption from the 1773 brief for the Jesuits in her Empire. But in what form? Written or spoken toleration, explicit or implicit? Both questions and answers are disputed. The debate is as lively as that surrounding Cardinal Ganganelli's promise, delivered to the Spanish court during the conclave of 1769, to abolish the Company.

Is there written evidence, perhaps a letter on the subject from Clement XIV to Catherine II—who several times referred to such a document and published an abridged (or forged or doctored) version of it? It has never been found in Saint Petersburg, and the leading historian of the Papacy, Ludwig von Pastor, challenges the authenticity of the various versions that have turned up in different places. It is much more likely that, in at least unofficial terms,* the Pope let the sovereign know that he would not oppose the survival of the Company, in discreet and noninstitutional form, in her Empire.

Anything could have been made of this tolerance on Russian soil: resurrection pure and simple, or the slow withering away of the Company. Everything depended on long-term relations between Pope and Empress and the prelates (Slav and Roman) who would serve as mediators, with almost all the Roman side being unfavorable to the cause of the Society of Jesus.

---

*J. Crétineau-Joly (*Histoire religieuse, politique et littéraire de la Compagnie de Jésus*, vol. V, p. 473) mentions a "rescript" from the Pope to the Empress, dated June 7, 1774, which "soothed the fathers' anxieties."

At this point a larger-than-life character strides onstage, breathing added life into an affair already remarkable for its liveliness. He was called Stanislas Siestrzenciewitz, and if the name is a tongue-twister, it is a mere diminutive compared to the tortuous extravagance of its bearer. He was Lithuanian. The people of that country were largely Catholic; he was a Protestant, and remained one until his thirtieth year; he had even studied Lutheran theology at Koenigsberg. Tiring of religion, he joined the Prussian Army and become a captain of hussars. Because he spoke seven languages, Prince Radziwill, the very model of a Polish nobleman, made this theologian-hussar his children's tutor—which brought about his meeting with a noble Catholic heiress. It was for her that he converted to Catholicism. In vain, for she rejected him.

Touched by this misfortune, the vicar of Vilna persuaded him to become a priest. Soon he was a canon, and his protector urged him to aim for a bishopric. Better still, he was shortly thereafter attached to the court, where Catherine noticed him. How far did her interest go? The fact is that a ukase of November 1773 made of this little bishop *in partibus* the holder of the See of Mohilev—and the head of the Roman Church in the whole Empire!

Although in principle deeply hostile to the Jesuits, Siestrzenciewitz, out of a courtier's servility, would become the instrument of their Russian resurrection, always one step ahead of the opposition with a move here, a promotion there, an anti-Roman provocation there, his courtier's extravagances coming close to upsetting the "feminine and Tartar" diplomacy of Catherine. To his Roman superiors, who expressed their disapproval of the Crown's support for the exiled fathers, he responded in tones even more cutting than the Great Autocrat's: "The most high will is unmovable in its decrees. . . . I have received the order to leave the Jesuits as they are. Her Majesty must be obeyed."[9]

Siestrzenciewitz's arrogance and duplicity reached their height in the question of the Polotsk novitiate. By the end of Clement XIV's pontificate it was obvious that the Jesuits (even where grouped into communities) were tolerated in the Russian Empire, whatever form Rome's acquiescence might have taken. But it was equally obvious that Rome did not want Russian novitiates turning themselves—under the wing of the all-powerful Empress—into breeding grounds for global redeployment of the Company.

The Empress was too attached to "her" Jesuits not to want them to multiply (if the term is acceptable). She indicated to her bishop-of-all-work that she had to have a novitiate in Polotsk, and ordered him to negotiate the question with the Roman hierarchy. The Bishop of Mohilev approached the Curia and suggested that if he were named "apostolic visitor" of the Jesuits in White Russia, he would be able to keep a closer eye on their activities. As soon as the mandate was conferred on him, Siestrzenciewitz announced *urbi et orbi* the opening of the Polotsk novitiate.

Consternation in Rome, fury in Madrid—whose liege man, Cardinal Pallavicini, the new Pope's secretary of state, had thus been tricked. Worse: The Empress, who seemed to take pleasure in infuriating and even humiliating the Papacy, now demanded Siestrzenciewitz's elevation to the Archbishopric of Mohilev as a reward for his services.

On October 27, 1781, Pius VI wrote Catherine that to his great regret he would be unable to satisfy her request: Siestrzenciewitz had so abused the extraordinary powers vested in him that he had "restored to the status of religious a group of men whom the Sovereign Pontiff had divested of that status, even daring in an order published on that occasion to attribute to him, Pius VI, an act that he knew full well he held in abhorrence." Nevertheless, the Pope declared his readiness—in consideration of the "so wise, so good, so human" Empress—to pardon Siestrzenciewitz, on condition that he acknowledge his error, request forgiveness, and make public amends.

An apology? The "so wise, so good, so human" Tsarina responded with a resounding rebuff to the Pope: On her orders Mohilev was elevated to an Archbishopric and Siestrzenciewitz, flanked by a "coadjutor," the former Jesuit Jan Benislawski, was named Archbishop. The Pope could not have been more cruelly mocked—and through him the monarchs urging him to deliver the death blow to the Jesuits.

Spanish fury ran so high that a Russian flotilla moored off Cádiz was seized. Then more moderate counsel prevailed, and the Empress was offered a most advantageous trade agreement if she would proclaim the abolition of the Jesuits in White Russia. Oranges for men in black . . . Whether she was irritated, amused, or angered, Catherine's reaction was energetic. Through the nuncio Archetti, in Warsaw, she informed the world that "the Autocrat has no intention of having her power in her Empire challenged."

This gleeful rejection of Rome and Madrid reached its apogee when (after a most solemn official visit to the novitiate in Polotsk) Catherine invited her neighbor the Emperor Joseph III, another friend of the *philosophes,* to the Mohilev school. Himself no friend of the Jesuits, the Austrian ruler later told his entourage that nothing—neither prelates nor soldiers nor crowns—would ever overcome the stubbornness of the Empress who was convinced, he told them, that by "maintaining the Jesuits in flourishing condition" she would be assuring their later redeployment throughout Europe.

Thus rebuffed, humiliated, even threatened with vigorous counterattack, Pope Pius VI decided to send his nuncio Archetti to Catherine, instructed to return from Saint Petersburg with at least a few shreds of satisfaction: closure of the Polotsk novitiate, for example, or the dismissal of Siestrzenciewitz, or guarantees of the right of Catholic worship in the Empire. For that was what it had come down to! Even before he left for Saint Petersburg, Archetti had received a letter from Catherine to the Pope, which he later described in his memoirs as a "thunderbolt."[10]

In the letter, the Empress made plain that she was ready to "abrogate her subjects' freedom to practice freely the Catholic religion, to forbid its rites and to abolish its institutions, unless the Holy Father gave immediate satisfaction to her demands concerning Siestrzenciewitz and Benislawski." She warned the Sovereign Pontiff that he "would very soon learn the fatal consequences to him and to the Catholic religion of his neglect of the just demands of Catherine II" and told him not to attempt "to seek the intercession of favor, friendship, or prayer from anyone whomsoever. . . . It would serve nothing."

It was indeed a thunderbolt for the Holy See. Now it was up to Archetti to play the lightning rod. Which he did, capitulating at Saint Petersburg along the whole papal line. Pope Pius VI would bow to the Thunderer's decisions—although he still attempted to save face with Madrid and Versailles by sending them a message declaring illegitimate everything done in contravention of the 1773 brief abolishing the Jesuits.

But the Autocrat (who had had the gall to ask Rome for a Cardinal's hat for Archetti, herald of the Pope's capitulation!) wanted still more: formal recognition by Pius VI of the survival of her Jesuit protégés in White Russia. And the messenger she chose to wring this final concession from the unhappy Pope was not the scandalous Siestrzenciewitz himself but—even more emblematically—his coadjutor Benislawski, the former Jesuit who made no secret of his wish to rejoin the Company.

As for Catherine's message, its simplicity spoke worlds:

> I know that Your Holiness is most disturbed, but fear ill suits
> him. . . . My motives in granting my protection to the Jesuits are
> founded on reason and justice, as also on the hope that they will be
> useful to my States. This band of peaceable and innocent men shall
> live in my Empire because, of all the Catholic Societies, theirs is best
> fitted to instruct my subjects and inspire in them feelings of human-
> ity and the true principles of the Christian Religion. I am resolved to
> support these priests against any power whatsoever; and in this I do
> but fulfill my duty, since I am their sovereign and consider them loyal,
> useful, and blameless subjects. Who knows whether Providence will
> not make of these men the instruments of union, so long desired, be-
> tween the Greek and the Roman Church?[11]

When he received this call to order (with its curious concluding bait) from the hands of ex-Jesuit Benislawski (whose sly glee can readily be imagined), Pius VI, pinioned though he was by his promises to Madrid, could only acknowledge once and for all the survival of the Society of Jesus in Russia. On March 12, 1783, he told the messenger from Saint Petersburg: "Approbo Societatem Jesu in Alba Russia degentem. Approbo, approbo . . . " (I approve the maintenance of the Society of Jesus in White Russia. I approve it, I approve it).

Madrid's man in the Curia, Secretary of State Pallavicini, was not present at the meeting; nevertheless he claimed that the famous triple "Approbo" was an invention by "that Jesuit" Benislawski. He was the only one to say so. The Pope himself did nothing to cast doubt on his approval. And when, a few months later, a Spanish nobleman asked his permission to travel to Russia and join the Company "if it exists there," Pius VI answered crisply: "Yes, it exists, and if it were possible I would extend it to the whole world."

Cardinal de Bernis, French ambassador to the Holy See, made this wry comment in a letter to a friend: "The Pope contents himself with stating his opinion without endowing it with the necessary force, being at great pains not to irritate a party with which he once had weighty relations." The Frenchman who had been instrumental in Clement XIV's election affected to see in this the defeat of only one "party." In fact, though, while Madrid had entered the lists with greater clamor, Versailles too had received its share of the avalanche of slaps inflicted on the Pope by the Empress and her "Tartars," led by Potemkin, "that warrior-statesman whose projects always had something of the sublime or the trivial about them [and who], having conceived a fondness for the fathers, nourished the idea of making Russia the seat of Saint Ignatius's order, regenerated by Catherine."[12]

The Company thus survived for long years in Russia under the formidable Orthodox Empress's wing—directly until her death in 1796, and then under her two successors, Paul I and Alexander I—and under five vicars-general recognized by Rome: Stanislas Czerniewicz (1782–85), Gabriel Lenkiewicz (1785–98), Xavier Karen (1799–1802), Gabriel Gruber (1802–5), and Tadeusz Brzozowski (1805–20).

Paul Dudon draws the typically Jesuit conclusion from the affair: "And thus did Providence, through a paradoxical turn of events, make use of the imperial caprices of the Semiramis of the North to preserve in Russia, as if beneath the ashes, the flame lit in Rome in 1540 by Ignatius of Loyola."[13]

"Caprices"? No, Reverend Father, no! This was no imperial caprice, merely a grand, absolutist, Pan-Russian strategy, operated both domestically ("I am sole mistress of my Empire and its plans for modernization") and abroad (impervious to foreign decisions, Russia did not hesitate to promote its influence and its interests as far afield as Western Europe and the heart of Catholic institutions). If she needed "her" Jesuits, she would preserve them; she would even use them, given the opportunity, as further instruments of imperial influence in the West.

It was a strategy that would make the next Tsar but one the arbiter of post-Napoleonic European policy at the Paris peace conference of 1814.

The advantages of this strategy to Russia and the Tsars were so obvious that when Paul I succeeded his mother in November 1796 he adopted it wholesale. His former tutor, Father Gabriel Gruber, was a famous member of the Company of Jesus. A brilliantly accomplished Viennese physicist, linguist, architect, musician and even occasionally physician, he was a Jesuit in the tradition of Clavius. The moment Pius VII was elected Pope, Gruber persuaded Tsar Paul I, a fervent admirer of Bonaparte and of his dual restoration strategy (of civil and religious authority), a monarch who called himself "Catholic in my heart," to demand of Rome, if not the pure and simple restoration of the Company, then at least the definitive recognition of its canonical existence.

As he wrote to the Pope:

My Most Holy Father,

The Reverend Father Gruber, Superior* of the religious of the Society of Jesus established in my States, having conveyed to me the desire of the members of this Society to be recognized by Your Holiness, I have decided that it would not be fitting for me to refuse to request for this order, in which I have a special interest, Your Holiness's formal approval, hoping that I shall not have wasted my efforts in taking this step.

The most affectionate friend

of Your Holiness, Paul.

In fact Pius I did want to reestablish the Society, which, as Bishop of Imola, he had sheltered in his own diocese. But he suffered the same pressures as his two predecessors. He named a committee of four Cardinals who, despite their reputed hostility to the dissolved Company, acceded to the Tsar's request (although they managed to curtail some of its effects). On March 7, 1801, Pius VII signed the brief *Catholicae fidei*, which restored the Society of Jesus, but only on Russian soil.

A few days later Paul I was assassinated: For once suspicion did not fall on the Jesuits, who had now lost a fiery protector. Paul's son Alexander I, not so deeply committed to the Company as his father, nevertheless shared his confidence in Gruber. He openly welcomed Gruber's election to head the Company, and in 1802 permitted the fathers to found a school for the nobility in Saint Petersburg. It would prove a most useful lever.

The alliance between Tsar and Jesuits lasted nearly twenty years despite the death of Gruber, who perished in a fire in March 1805. The Emperor had assigned

*The title of "Superior General" would not be reestablished until the reconstitution of the Society in 1814.

the Company a mission: the technical and moral supervision of the vast reclamation project in the Volga Basin launched by German settlers—one of the great initiatives of his reign. The fathers worked wonders, so much so that the rescue operation begun by Catherine II after the great Roman proscription of 1773 appeared to be leading to the Company's deep and lasting establishment in Russia. Perhaps Potemkin and Paul I had dreamed of making Russia not just the cradle of the new Society of Jesus but the springboard of an international redeployment that would have made Saint Petersburg (where the Knights of Malta had also resettled) the capital of Christendom. If they did indeed entertain such a vision, it was shattered on political and cultural realities, as well as religious ones.

The French invasion of 1812 poisoned the ties established between Russia and the West by Peter the Great, while Rome's restoration of the Company of Jesus in 1814 deprived Russia of its privileged role of asylum and gave the Company back its international power based on Western capitals. Everything changed. From being a trump card in Russia's hand, the Company now slid into the hands of the monarchs of Vienna and Paris. Whence the next crises it would undergo.*

Thus for twenty years, in western Europe and the world as a whole, the Company of Jesus truly had been the "cadaver" of the too famous precept. It is no accident that the most pious historiographers speak of a "resurrection." Submissive to the point of absurdity before Clement XIV's terrified "brief," it had sunk into prostration. Terrorized by the Bourbon monarchies, it seemed to regain its courage only when the strongest of those monarchies—the French—was liquidated in its turn. Having accepted its own execution without a murmur or a struggle, it did not begin to react until the execution of its most notorious killer, twenty years later.[14]

And yet a Catholic sovereign had already spoken out in the Society's favor: admittedly one of the smaller ones, the Duke of Parma, nephew of the archetypal anti-Jesuit Charles III of Spain.

This ruler had played his part in the "Enlightenment crusade" of 1759 to 1773, siding with the Madrid cousins to whom he owed his throne. But he was a conservative, deeply religious man, and he believed he saw a connection between the destruction of the Jesuits and the French Revolution. As early as 1787 he had attempted to make the point to his Spanish uncle—who brusquely rejected his arguments. The revolutionary developments in France and the trial and execution of Louis XVI dispelled his last doubts—and the "miracle" here is that he was the only one whose eyes were thus forced open.

*See Chapter XI.

It was Ferdinand of Parma who now took measures aimed at the restoration of the Company, in which he saw the surest bulwark against Revolution (although for the moment all he could restore was a Jesuit school in Parma). His efforts provoked the following response from Pius VI, dated February 15, 1795, a year after Louis XVI's execution:

> We have never said or thought that we did well in abolishing a Body, which for education and instruction was very useful in the Church, whose founder is praised in the public liturgy, and whose absence today has the disastrous consequences we discussed. . . . This notwithstanding, the law is in effect, and we must observe it, but we shall act as if we knew nothing, as we have done with those who have sought refuge in the North. And if certain great Catholic princes were to take your undertaking ill . . . under the influence of certain *Filosofanti* who set [this whole] machinery in motion, we shall be constrained to reprove Your Highness, whose actions we now content ourselves with ignoring even while knowing them well.[15]

Is this not the most toothsome caricature of what is popularly known as "Jesuitry"? Alongside his running battle with Catherine, the Pontiff was displaying a genius for counterthrust and camouflage that must have dazzled the Duke of Parma, who was himself no slouch at subterfuge: His own Parmesan Jesuits had to dress like lay people* while observing the same code of conduct as the dissolved order.

Ferdinand's Spanish uncle, Charles III, died in 1783. But his cousin Charles IV had inherited his father's obsessions, and quickly let Ferdinand know how angered he was at this "betrayal." Which led to a correspondence of delectable coarseness, in which the Pope and the Queen of Spain (whose lover, Manuel Godoy, was a badly camouflaged Jesuitophile) occasionally joined.

The King wrote to his cousin: "If Charles III were alive, he would act in no other manner today than he did. A good son must observe his wishes. If it is God's will that the Jesuits be restored, He will let it be known. Until then, the King of Spain must consider that the Jesuits are enemies of his kingdom."

The ruler of Parma replied by deploring the "stubbornness" of the King, who did not understand that "the present events are divine chastisement of Kings and peoples who have allowed evil doctrines to prevail! Those who set out to destroy the Company wanted nothing less than the destruction of religion."

As for Pius VI, he reminded Queen María Luisa of Spain of "the incalculable evils that have flowed from the abolition of the Jesuits," and addressed this plea to the somber virago immortalized by Goya: "If Spain does not want Jesuits, let

*Which was in any case their custom.

her at least make it clear that she has no objection to the Pope giving them back to those who do."[16]

Thus this Pope, believed to be a good man, who in his last hours revealed the courage and dignity he had been unable to invest in the Company's behalf, spent nearly twenty years letting himself be intimidated over the Jesuit question by a moribund Spanish court that would soon passively endure Napoleon's worst outrages.

His successor, elected in 1800 as Pius VII, after a conclave held under Austria's very obvious protection at Vienna, was Barnaba Chiaramonti. He was a Benedictine who had never hidden his sympathy for the Jesuits: When still in the shadow of Pius VI, as the modest bishop of the tiny See of Tivoli, he had declared himself in favor of the Society's worldwide reestablishment. Unlike his predecessors, he was elected by the *zelanti* cardinals rather than the *politicanti*, and was bound by no promise. The Bourbons—or what was left of them— could not oppose him. Nevertheless, it would take him fourteen years to realize his objective, through the storms of a pontificate that Napoleon would not be alone in shaking.

It is moreover surprising, in a story full of surprises, that the restoration of the Society felled by the Bourbons—yet considered the symbol of counterrevolution—was carried out by a Pope whom the twentieth century would call a "liberal." A Pope who, while still a Cardinal, had declared in the thick of Revolution (1797) that the democratic form of government in no way contradicted the teachings of the Church.

As this new Pope began the long campaign that would lead to the Company's restoration in August 1814, he held two good cards in his hand: He enjoyed the marginal but important support of Russia, and he had a minor but busy ally in the Duke of Parma. He had a vehement adversary, the Spanish court; an open sympathizer, King Ferdinand of Naples; and a benevolent but cautious partner, the Emperor Franz II of Austria. Portugal seemed to be uninterested. As for France, we shall see that the signature of the Concordat with the Vatican, on the one hand, and Napoleon's antipathy to the Jesuits, on the other, would make of her the great unknown quantity.

The story of the French Jesuits' crossing of the desert, from their expulsion in 1764 to the restoration of 1814, can be divided into three distinct phases. From Louis XV's edict until the Revolution: a period of resigned immersion by a community that seemed to accept as normal the disappearance of the powerful organization which had apparently governed it for two centuries. From 1789 to 1800, under the Revolution: a period during which little groups slowly emerged, societies or congregations of Jesuits "without being Jesuit," which seemed at once concerned with clinging in mind and body to the Ignatian trunk and with concealing all connection to the dissolved order. And finally under the Empire: a period when bodies visible enough to be proscribed and flexible enough to survive would pave the way for reconstruction.

Among those returning, some would stand out and make their mark—Pierre Picot de Clorivière, Éléonor de Tournély, Charles de Broglie, and Joseph Varin d'Ainvelle. These might be called the new French founders, all of them more or less involved with anti-Revolutionary movements and the émigrés, all persecuted by the Revolution and active in counterrevolution, all afire (however "charitable" in other ways) with the spirit of conspiracy and revenge. With the rarest of exceptions, the powers of Revolution and Empire could seem only Satanic to them. Shaped by their history, if not by temperament and conviction, they were destined to be the forerunners and harbingers of Restoration.

Standing against them, although not always as enemies, were four outstanding figures. Napoleon did not try to hide his dislike for the kind of clerical and ultramontane power the Jesuits willy-nilly embodied, while his minister of police, Joseph Fouché, bore them a vigilant hatred. But his minister of religion, Joseph Marie Portalis, never tried too energetically to implement the texts aimed at them, texts he would have preferred to be more ambiguous. As for the Emperor's uncle, Cardinal Fesch, he would carry his goodwill toward them so far that he attracted angry reprimands from Napoleon.

This refounding "resistance" movement had three branches in France: the Society of Fathers of the Sacred Heart of Jesus, the Society of the Heart of Jesus, the Fathers of Faith, and, parallel to them, the "Congregation."

Pierre Picot de Clorivière (born 1735), the Breton priest who took the first step, did it less as a persecuted Jesuit than as a rebel against the Revolution. Clorivière was from Saint-Malo, and tough as a pirate. His family—petty nobility engaged in trade—curiously enough sent him to study at an English Jesuit school at northern Douai in France. He was a teacher at the school in Compiègne in 1762 when proscription of the Jesuits overtook him. Clorivière was not a man to accept punishment passively. Soon he invited one of his friends to participate in a plot aimed at "evangelical vengeance," consisting of offering up prayer for those guilty of this "destruction"—starting with the Kings of France.[17] There was a chance that the network he might thus develop could serve as a seedbed for the rebirth of the order, or of a similar organization. In the meantime, Clorivière managed to stay in the Company by exiling himself to Liège in Belgium, where he took his last vows—at the very moment when Clement XIV was issuing his murderous verdict.

Clorivière the fervent royalist had rebelled against Louis XV's decision in

1762. But he received the Pope's edict submissively. Accepting the secularization decreed by Rome, he became a simple parish priest in Saint-Malo. A return to his roots.

He was taken in those days for a "man of the Enlightenment," concerned with the struggle against poverty, a believer in "progress."[18] He exchanged views with people initially favorable to the Civil Constitution of the Clergy—the "nationalization" of the Church of France by the Revolution—the most anti-Jesuit measure imaginable.

It was before the Pope condemned this measure, which Rome called the fruit of "the detestable philosophy of the rights of man," that the Breton priest decided to lead the fight. He entered into correspondence with Adélaïde de Cicé, the niece of Archbishop de Cicé, with a view to coordinating their efforts to revive the Jesuit congregations. He founded an Association of Poor Priests, she a Society of the Daughters of the Heart of Mary. What was remarkable in Clorivière, and would remain so, was his concern to work hand in hand, and without misplaced paternalism, with a female organization.

Did he really envisage a resurrection of the Company in the teeth of revolutionary anticlericalism? In a letter of 1794, at the height of the Terror, he said he was called "less to raise up the former Company of Jesus than to create a new one to be its offspring and extension."[19] But this man of action, of initiative, of resistance, of planning—of networks—was in these very things an authentic Jesuit. Through the terrible political ups and downs of 1789–1814, he recreated the image of the Jesuit man of action—political in his essence, conspiratorial by necessity. Above all, he represented the continuation of a certain Ignatian current (despite the general collapse of the Jesuits of the West), flowing still from the royal proscription of 1762 to Republican persecution and to the imperial domestication of the early nineteenth century.

Clorivière's Association of Poor Priests became the Society of the Fathers of the Heart of Jesus, which sank roots in Brittany and Provence. In 1800, on the eve of Napoleon's Concordat with the Vatican, he sent two emissaries to Rome to try to interest Pius VII—who favored the Company's restoration—in the new project. But the Supreme Pontiff would soon be focusing his energies on a much vaster enterprise: the Concordat, which would at one stroke restore the status of the Catholic clergy in France. And the Breton priest had all the faults that went with his prophetic and combative virtues: He was unable to remain aloof from conspiracies less pacific than his own. He was now implicated in an attempt to assassinate First Consul Bonaparte. Was it simply because he had heard the confession of one of the plotters? In any case, he was sought by the police and arrested in May 1804, just as the Empire saw the light of day. He spent five years in the Temple prison: wonderful for spiritual meditation, disastrous for purposes of organization or action. He emerged in 1809 to find that the Society of the Fathers of the Heart of Jesus had been dissolved in June 1804.

However, the similarly named Society of the Heart of Jesus was not just a provincial body: It was Parisian. Its guiding light was perhaps the celebrated M. Emery, parish priest of Saint-Sulpice Church. In any case, two of his parishioners were its founders: Éléonor de Tournély and Charles de Broglie, son of the Marshal,* who were soon joined in Germany by an émigré cavalry officer, Joseph Varin d'Ainvelle. When he placed himself under Tournély's orders, Varin said to him, "Make of me anything you wish, except a monk."

"Have no fear," said the founder, "you shall always be a soldier. Almost all your companions are leaving the army, and we firmly intend to serve God in military fashion."[20]

Did he believe he was being faithful to the Ignatian spirit? In any case, these pioneers—who appear not to have known Clorivière—regularly performed *The Spiritual Exercises* and, like the early Jesuits, bound themselves by a special vow to place themselves at the disposition of the Pope, to serve the Church wherever and however he decided. There were six of them. The conspirators of 1534 had been seven. Thus was founded the Society of the Heart of Jesus, in Bavaria, at the end of 1794.

Their concern to maintain continuity with the Company was such that the founders could at first think only of leaving for Russia, where it survived and prospered under the Tsarina's auspices. But the fortunes of war prevented them from getting farther than Vienna. It was at Haggenbrun, on the outskirts of the Habsburg capital, that they planted their flag. And it was there, on the death of Tournély—who had in the meantime founded the order of the Ladies of the Sacred Heart—that they elected Joseph Varin to succeed him. The founder had been a saintly man. His heir would display the qualities of a man of action worthy of the hussar he once had been.

The third wellspring of Jesuit rebirth in France was the group known as the Fathers of the Faith. In its first phase, however, it would to its great misfortune be associated with the name and person of Niccola Paccanari.

We know that the story of the Jesuits is too closely bound up with the wicked world to have the simple smoothness of a Carmelite's forehead. Adventurers swagger through it, frauds, hypocrites, and hired killers. "Cut your coat according to your cloth . . . " But although it inspired heroism, the arduous episode of the desert crossing, from one century and one Company to the next, threw the field open to adventurers who were equal to the risks involved and the means employed. Such as Siestrzenciewitz in Russia and Paccanari in Italy.

*Who had emigrated after remodeling the French Army in the wake of the Seven Years' War, turning it into one of the future Republic's greatest assets.

There was nothing ordinary about this native of Trieste. A seeker of danger thrown into a pious intrigue whose profane dimensions he mastered more readily than its spiritual ones. A simple tonsured cleric, uneducated but silver-tongued, he emerged from a retreat at Our Lady of Loreto to declare that the Lord had called him to resurrect the Company of Jesus. As inspired as ever, Pius VI granted his protection to the little community Paccanari gathered around him at Spoleto, and advised him to coordinate his efforts with those of Varin's disciples.

In April 1799 the two communities signed a pact. Elected Superior of the combined order, Paccanari rechristened it Fathers of the Faith.* His associates quickly realized that Paccanari talked more readily than he prayed, and that his sociable manner could not compensate for an obvious lack of spirituality. Was it wise to advance the cause of Jesuit restoration behind such a naïve caricature? Pius VI advised Varin, who called on him at Fontainebleau on the occasion of Napoleon's coronation, to break off ties. Varin's readiness to comply was reinforced when Paccanari was hauled before the Holy Office and sentenced† to incarceration in the Castel Sant'Angelo, where he remained until released by the occupying French forces in 1809. He then decided to lose himself in the crowd and disappeared from the eyes of history. But before his imprisonment he had recruited many people whose activities did not always reflect glory on the Company.

Freed of this encumbrance, and despite Fouché and Napoleon, Joseph Varin worked for the survival of the Fathers of the Faith. Fouché, the Emperor's minister of police, was violently opposed to Jesuits in any guise. His most important biographer, Louis Madelin, elaborates on the blend of hatred and sarcasm that fueled his behavior toward the Company and all religion.

The Emperor, on the other hand, was the man who had declared: "You do not govern people who do not believe in God; you cut them down!" But he loathed religious groupings, particularly the Company of Jesus, and forbade his newspapers to print even the word "Jesuit." The signing of the Concordat by the Holy See in July 1801 did nothing to change this: It affected only the secular clergy. Witness this statement to his minister of religion: "I want no ecclesiastical congregations: they are useless. Good vicars, good bishops, good priests, well-disciplined seminarians, that is all we need."‡

Moreover, his absolutist instincts rebelled at the existence of any power be-

---

*Although they were known to the man in the street as "Paccanarists."
†For some petty crime?
‡On page 1268 of Jean Tulard's *Dictionnaire Napoléon* (Paris: Fayard, 1987), he deftly summarizes the Emperor's policies toward religious congregations: "No to the Jesuits, yes to the Sisters of Charity" (because they were almost camp followers?).

sides his own—particularly since the Jesuits maintained links with a foreign entity, the Holy See. In this, Napoleon was as Gallican as Louis XIV. What exactly were these companies of men in black or brown, as well organized for plotting as for praying, for spying as for charity work? And were they not also partisans of the King? He would not tolerate the existence beyond his control of such collective entities.

Admittedly, the Concordat made no provision for the religious orders. But this was simply because a law passed in 1792 had abolished them all in one fell swoop, with the Dominicans and Franciscans consigned to the same fate that had befallen the Jesuits twenty-five years earlier. The Concordat left this state of affairs intact. Indeed, one of its articles stipulated that the only ecclesiastical establishments allowed would be cathedral chapters.

The imperial regime would base its religious policies on three principles: condemnation of "monastic idleness"; rejection of any interference from Rome; and rejection of all education competing with that offered by the state—which implied fundamental hostility to the Jesuits. Whence the rule stipulating that a religious association could not exist without the government's express permission. This was the theme of a ministerial circular of 1803 declaring "religious corporations . . . illicit for the simple fact that they are not authorized. Their religious aims are inadequate to justify the irregularity of their existence."[21]

Entrusted with implementing these texts inspired by Napoleon and Fouché were two men. Portalis, minister of religion, a devout Catholic and moderate disciple of Montesquieu, went about it in a liberal spirit. Cardinal Fesch, Napoleon's uncle and primate of the Gauls, openly sought to divert them from their objectives, thus becoming an accomplice in the resurrectionist strategy of Varin and his Fathers of the Faith.

How could this association not have awakened the regime's suspicions? In an 1803 report Portalis wrote: "The Fathers of the Faith are but Jesuits in disguise. They follow the Institutions of the former Jesuits; they even profess their maxims; their existence is therefore incompatible with the Gallican state and imperial law." These reflections inspired the far-reaching decree of January 22, 1804, which dissolved the Fathers of the Faith, the "Paccanarists" (with whom they were confused), and the "Worshippers of Jesus" (which did not exist), as well as all other religious congregations, with the exception of a few nursing communities. In fact, says Joseph Burnichon, the decree "was aimed at the Fathers of the Faith, who seemed to be either a Jesuit vanguard or true Jesuits under a false name."[22]

The Emperor appeared to summarize his feelings in a note addressed to Fouché in 1807: "My principal aim is to prevent the Jesuits establishing themselves in France. I want no Heart of Jesus nor Brotherhood of the Holy Sacrament, nor anything resembling an organized religious militia, and under no pretext do I intend to go one step further, nor to see any other ecclesiastics than secular priests."[23] And he wrote to Cardinal Fesch: "My secular clergy is besides too good for me to need these zealots whose principles are unknown to me."

In fact, though, Napoleon authorized Portalis to bend the rules in several ways, and it has been calculated that more than a thousand religious institutions were indeed authorized by imperial decree between 1804 and 1814.[24] But his dislike for the Jesuits, "disguised" or not, remained unshakable. This was clearly demonstrated by his angry reaction to Fesch's clandestine encouragement of the teaching activities of the Fathers of the Faith.

Under the Cardinal's protection, Father Varin had managed to open several schools, including one at Armentières, which Fesch wanted to make "France's most distinguished seminary," dismissing the "secular priests" who ran it and replacing them with the "former Fathers of the Faith."

But Joseph Fouché was on the alert. He presented the Emperor with a report that triggered the urgent convening on October 19, 1807, of a "limited cabinet meeting," which

> will examine the situation of the religious Congregations. . . . What are the Fathers of the Faith? H.M. has abolished them in Amiens, they have been banned in the diocese of Lyon, yet they exist; there is one in Clermont* which competes with public education, brings discredit to the schools, and lays hold of the minds of the young.
>
> It is asserted that they entertain relations with Rome and that they have a secret leader. Is this true? Where are they established? How many are they? What sets a Father of the Faith apart from a Father of the Company of Jesus? How may they be recognized? How many schools are in their hands? Finally, what measures must be taken to prevent associations that maintain foreign practices and correspondence in France?

The storm glared black. Twelve days later it burst. In the presence of the whole court, of the French ministers and foreign princes drawn up in front of the Chateau of Fontainebleau, Napoleon addressed Cardinal Fesch, angrily accusing him of deceiving him, or of letting himself be deceived by the Fathers of the Faith. The Emperor denounced the men who "plan to seize control of the education of France's youth" and "threaten the imperial university in its cradle." Ordering his uncle to proceed at once to the dissolution of colleges and seminaries, he declared that all priests who had not returned to their respective dioceses within two weeks would be deported to Guyana.

*Here Fouché was misinformed.

A few days later he sent these instructions to Fouché:

> You will work in conjunction with M. Portalis on measures for the
> dissolution of all congregations of the Fathers of the Faith, taking
> care to choose the gentlest but the most effective means. Extend these
> measures throughout the Empire. You will be at pains to ensure that
> these individuals shall not foregather, and I hold you responsible for
> the existence of any group of these religious. . . .
>
> You will begin with the Archbishop of Lyon. . . . With this prelate
> as with the others, you must speak only with proofs in hand and not
> engage in any discussion of theology. I do not want the "Fathers of
> the Faith," and still less do I wish to have them meddling in public in-
> struction to poison the young with their absurd Ultramontane pre-
> cepts. You will be able to obtain the information you need on the
> Fathers of the Faith from their Superior, Father Varin, who seems an
> adventurer.[25]

No matter that Napoleon had confused Varin with Paccanari, and the Fathers of the Sacred Heart with those of the Faith. The fact is that for the life of
the Empire this conspiracy-that-wasn't was strangled, reduced to a spectral existence, and its members, particularly Varin, scattered and harassed by the police. Fouché had tried to win him over, offering him the post of vicar-general in
Lyon or Paris. When he refused, he was placed under house arrest in his native
town, Besançon, with orders to the prefect to keep an eye on him. Despite all the
imperial huffing and puffing, however, Burnichon has estimated that the measures affected only forty priests and thirty coadjutor brothers in 1807, in charge
of just eight schools and small seminaries: Clearly the ghost of the Jesuits still
frightened the powerful.[26]

That ghost would assume even more mysterious form than the Fathers of the
Heart of Jesus, the Paccanarists, or the Fathers of the Faith—that of the so-
called Congregation. The name stands for so many phantasms, illusions, dis-
guises, and above all misunderstandings that venturing into this tangled forest
of hunted Jesuits is daunting. But we must try.

"Congregation": Here the name takes on very particular meaning, different
from the one attributed to it by the lawmakers of the Revolution—an organized
group of "regular" priests or nuns. The early nineteenth-century interpretation
of the word indicated a more or less secret organization of lay members led by
men of religion, with the initial aim of worship but assuming more or less consciously a political, and indeed oppositional, coloration—and capable of leading to activities of the same nature.

It was not necessarily a "Jesuit plot." A Protestant "Congregation" was
formed under the Consulate. And while the Catholic organization we are dis-

cussing here, founded at the same time, was created by a former Jesuit, other very similar groups took shape that were unconnected to the Company.

The most famous of these was founded in 1801 by the Abbé Bourdier-Delpuits, who had been a member of the Society of Jesus. It was to find an unexpected chronicler in the person of Charles de Gaulle who, as a seventeen-year-old pupil of the fathers in Antoing, Belgium, wrote an essay on the subject,[27] clearly inspired by the work of historians of the Company. He points out that associations of this kind had been created by the Jesuits of Rome since the end of the sixteenth century to promote the veneration of the Virgin Mary, that they had next flourished in Central Europe, where their numbers had included several Austrian sovereigns, while in France they had attracted people of the stature of the Vicomte de Turenne (although Louis XIV prohibited their spread to the royal armies). The step taken in 1801 was thus part of a long tradition of Jesuit action in lay circles.

De Gaulle's essay does not mention another Jesuit tradition, which partly inspired the founder of 1801. This was the one commonly called the "Aa," or "Assembly," created in 1630 by Father Bagot, a celebrated Jesuit of Richelieu's day.[28] This secret congregation, made up of both clerics and lay people, was often confused with that of the Holy Sacrament, and like it played a leading part in dispatching missions to Asia.

But why "secrecy" (which would have been understandable under Revolution or Empire, but is surprising in the days of the powerful Jesuit confessors of Kings)? Was it simply the Jesuits' incorrigible leanings toward the clandestine? One Jesuit offered this strange reply: "Without this strict secrecy, . . . 'persons of quality' could have demanded admission to the group without its being possible, or even conceivable, to refuse them. At that time, in fact, there was no such thing as a society that a 'well-born' man could not enter at will—and in which he could even demand the chairmanship or special honors. Clearly these small pious associations would have lost all meaning by undergoing such intrusions." Apart from this judicious Jesuit, writes Alain Guillermou, "the authorities of the Company of Jesus never ratified this tendency to secrecy, nor this taste for mystery so peculiar to members of the Aa."[29] Perhaps . . .

The congregation of the Abbé Bourdier-Delpuits, whose motto was "Cor unum et anima mea" and which boasted eminent members, particularly from scientific circles, obviously did not confine itself to religious or charitable activities. At first Napoleon refused to see in it anything but "a choirboys' cabal." But he changed his mind when one of the most famous "Congregationists," Mathieu de Montmorency, received by the Pope at Savona,* brought back with

---

*Where he had been exiled by Napoleon.

him (reportedly hidden in his boot) the bull of excommunication that Pius VII had hurled at the Emperor. A forbidden document if ever there was one.

Was the distribution of this text, lethal to the regime and instrumental in destroying the Emperor's prestige in Catholic circles, the work of the Congregation or of the Knights of the Faith (of which Montmorency, along with Alexis de Noailles and Bertier de Sauvigny, was a founder)? When Fouché ordered Noailles's arrest, the move was probably directed against the rabidly monarchist Knights rather than the Congregation as such.

The mutual involvement of these organizations was clear. And the semi-secret aura the disciples of Abbé Delpuits liked to cultivate was complicated by the mystery with which the pro-Bourbon Knights (for very understandable reasons) surrounded themselves. Earlier, Pierre de Clorivière's first moves had overlapped those of the violent antirevolutionary Breton movement known as the Chouans. This was the stuff on which the Black Legend fed. (Although we shall find the Company stupefied all over again by power after the Restoration.)

How could a ghost, even one animated by Loyola's spirit and Varin's energy, overcome the hostility of Napoleon and Fouché? The Empire in its heyday had let it live. The Empire at bay would not tolerate it. From the Pope's break with the Emperor, who called the Jesuits "Pope's Grenadiers," they had to run for shelter. In France, at least, the Company's resurrection would coincide with the Empire's fall.

However tight the Grand Army's hold on continental Europe, Jesuitry scrabbled here and there to lift the tombstone. First in Naples, where the proscription of the Company had been forced on King Ferdinand by his father and suzerain Charles III of Spain. It was clear, however, that Madrid no longer carried the same weight as in the time of Philip II. The stubborn anti-Jesuitry that poor Charles IV had inherited from his father lingered on in Castile; but the new man of influence, Manuel Godoy, made no bones of his opposition to it, and conveyed to Spain's Neapolitan vassal that Madrid did not care "one way or the other" about the reestablishment of the Company in Naples. The very pious Ferdinand IV saw this as an invitation: He at once summoned the good fathers to his domain, led by a distinguished man, José Pignatelli, a "Spanish grandee" and a man of great intelligence. And he invested the operation with a solemnity that all Europe noted.

Was it time for the return of the "men in black"? Paul Dudon quotes a dispatch from the French ambassador in Naples to his foreign minister, Talleyrand, in which the diplomat reports a conversation with one of the guiding lights of Jesuit restoration. Having congratulated him on this success (but adding that France would long remain closed to the Jesuits), the diplomat received this answer: "Let the Almighty do His work. France is a country where we count many friends. The servants of God and of the House of Bourbon are for us. Intelligent workers are there, secretly preparing our path."[30]

The old Jesuit pride. But before the French monarchy could be restored, that of Naples was extinguished. The next year, Napoleon set his brother Joseph (a declared Freemason) on the throne of the Two Sicilies. Once again the fathers had to scatter. But the Neapolitan operation had sounded the tocsin and reminded people that the "cadaver" lived on in the West. What Bourbons had unmade, other Bourbons could remake.

One of the puzzles of this desert crossing was the attitude of the most Catholic Viennese court. Admittedly, the "sacristan" Emperor Joseph II (who had been a leading supporter of Clement XIV at the conclave of 1769, and therefore a key figure in the suppression of the Jesuits) had since installed a kind of Austrian-style Gallicanism known as "Josephism." But his successor, Franz II, as pious and conservative as his cousin in Naples, burned to rescue the good fathers. Moreover, the Company's provisional General in Saint Petersburg, Father Gruber, was himself Austrian.

In 1804 the "Josephists" among his advisers submitted a plan for reconstituting the Company in Austria, controlled by Vienna and thus, as it were, "nationalized."* But the spokesman of the Ignatians, Angiolini, at that time involved in the Neapolitan restoration process, sent a "frank and pathetic"[31] note to Rome, protesting against any change in the Company's status ("Sint ut sunt, aut non sint")—and thus delayed by ten years the restoration of the Jesuits in the Habsburg Empire.

No matter. The process was under way. In Madrid, under Goya's pitiless gaze, Charles IV could wish the Company to the Devil. In Vienna, Franz II could sigh helplessly. In Naples, the French could flaunt their militant anticlericalism. In Paris, Fouché could hunt down the Fathers of the Faith. Even in Saint Petersburg, Tsar Alexander could cool toward Gabriel Gruber's successor. But the shattered Company was rebuilding.

Near Rome the Bishop of Orvieto, Monsignor Lambruschini, put his seminary (which would become a seedbed of the new Company) at the disposal of José Pignatelli and the refugees from the Two Sicilies. In Saint Petersburg General Tadeusz Bzrozowski, henceforward treated more like a hostage than a guest by the Tsar, was busily placing his "black" pawns on the world's chessboard. In France, Varin, Clorivière, and the "Congregation" were preparing the double

*A plan like that suggested by Guillaume de Lamoignon in an attempt in 1761 to save the Company in France.

restoration of Bourbons and Jesuits. The fall of the Empire, preceded by the return of the Supreme Pontiff to Rome, would be the signal.

Seeing the approach of Revolution thirty years earlier, the perspicacious Prince de Ligne wrote to Madame de Choisy: "I, who am a prophet neither in my own nor in others' countries, have long since told whoever wishes to listen that, if the Jesuits had not been expelled, we would not be seeing this accursed spirit of independence, of turbulence, of pedantry, this mania for politics spreading like a torrent that threatens all the thrones of Europe."

The day of thrones was back. And with it, the Jesuits.

·XI·

THE SECOND
COMPANY

Disaster in Saint Petersburg • Clorivière's Day • Paganized France?
• A Tolerant Regime • The Children of Saint-Acheul • Jesuit
Valhalla • Montlosier • The Cowardice of Charles X

"WE CAME IN *like lambs and we rule like wolves. We shall be expelled like dogs and return like eagles.*"

Did the third Jesuit General, Francesco Borgia, really utter these words, as legend claims? Did anyone speak them at all? One thing is certain: If the image of lambs and wolves and dogs is open to question, the evocation of eagles is hopelessly off the mark.

The Jesuits had celebrated many triumphs, sometimes of the headiest and most ostentatious kind. But in extent and importance, few matched the celebration of August 7, 1814. Some Jesuit historians have presented it as a "resurrection," while Paul Dudon has even invoked Christ's words to Lazarus—"Veni foras!" (Come forth!)—to describe the occasion.

On that day Pope Pius VII left the Quirinal Palace with much pomp for the Gesù, seat of the Jesuits in Rome. And there he read the bull *Sollicitudo omnium ecclesiarum,* which, after forty-one years of Roman ostracism, restored the Company of Jesus to its rights and privileges.

The amends could not have been more solemnly managed. The text, haggled over for months by the Curia's drafting experts, emphatically restored the active alliance of 1540 between the Holy See and the Ignatian order. Let the reader judge:

> With one voice the Catholic world demands the reestablishment of
> the Company of Jesus. We would believe ourselves guilty before God

of great error if, among these great dangers to the Christian Republic,* we neglected the help granted us by God's special providence,
and if, placed in Peter's boat, rocked and assailed by continual storms,
we refused to make use of vigorous and tested branches which offer
themselves up spontaneously to break the force of a sea that threatens
us at every moment with shipwreck and death. Resolved by so many
and such powerful motives, we have decided to do today what we
would have wished to do at the beginning of our Pontificate. . . .

We have therefore decreed, by virtue of our apostolic powers and
to be held valid for all time, that the concessions and facilities granted
by us only to the Empire of Russia and the Kingdom of the Two
Sicilies shall henceforth be extended to all of our ecclesiastical state,
and to all other states. . . . We take into our trusteeship, our immediate obedience and that of the Apostolic See, all the Colleges, all the
Houses, all the Provinces, and all the members of this order.

Finally, we earnestly recommend to the illustrious and noble temporal princes and lords, as to our venerable brothers the Archbishops
and Bishops . . . that they shall not suffer these Religious to be molested in any way, but that they shall be treated with goodness and
love, as is fitting.

Pius VII had endured and grown through his repeated ordeals. He could not
have taken a more resolute stand against the series of proscriptions and aboli-
tions decreed by, among others, his predecessor Clement XIV. Nor could he
have come forward more boldly as the protector of men only yesterday accursed. The links woven in 1540 and broken in 1773 were apparently mended.

Apparently. For the Pope's Jesuit partners of 1814 had little in common with
the ardent young squad of adventure-seekers who had offered themselves to
Paul III in 1538. What now emerged from the shadows to which most of them
had unprotestingly crept was a group of veterans resigned to death and unex-
pectedly saved, sometimes despite themselves, by the Machiavellian graces of
two non-Catholic monarchs.

One survivor stood out from the rest during the "resurrection ceremonies"
at the Gesù: Father Alberto de Montalto, who was said to be 126 years old. He
had entered the Company in 1716, ninety-eight years earlier.

"Getting up on the wrong side of bed" implies rising—or rising again—in such
a way as to ruin the day ahead. The expression suggests itself with compelling
force in the case of the Jesuit resurrection.

*Strange words from a recent victim of Jacobinism!

But do we have the right to disparage a state of mind shaped by harsh circumstance? For the emergence of what has often been called the "Second Company" took place within a constricting historical context and in an atmosphere of inevitable reaction against the fifty-year sweep of historical events—whose many illustrious victims had included Loyola's Society.

"Reaction" is the key word. Whatever ideological coloring it is given, it always denotes the pendulum movement called into being by every social acceleration, deviation, or tremor. In this case the French Revolution, from its "philosophical" beginnings to its Napoleonic culmination.

We cannot therefore be surprised that the Bourbon Restoration in France unfolded against the negative image of Revolution, that the returning *ancien régime* trampled its gravediggers as soon as it squeezed from under its tombstone, that the *émigrés* repaid the Jacobins blow for blow. Of course all this was in a relatively minor key: The White Terror never rivaled the scope of its predecessor; indeed the most surprising aspect of the matter was the brevity and half-heartedness of reprisals. By way of harsh comparison we have only to consider the death toll of the reprisals that followed the 1871 Paris Commune. The royalist reaction was of course harsh. It could not be otherwise, particularly after Waterloo.

But the factors at work in the French social and political debate, factors that have nothing to do with morality or love, cannot be applied in the same way to a group of men dedicated to spreading the Gospel. Was it really necessary for the Jesuits to make of themselves the chorus, the stagehands, of this preordained opera of conservative revenge?

For three centuries, from Kagoshima through their European schools to the River Plate, the fathers had made themselves the pioneers of Western humanism. In every latitude they had invented and reinvented egalitarian cultural exchange and respect for the Other's vision. Yet here they were transformed into bloodhounds of Bourbon and Roman conservatism, into militants for the alliance of Cross and Crown, into propagandists for the restoration of kings, into guardians of the European order established at the Congress of Vienna.

They had made an art of acting in harmony with their times, of making themselves not only "all things to all men" but of adapting their transformation to every season: humanists during the Renaissance, world-eaters in the age of discovery, and (almost) deists in the Enlightenment. Now, however, they sank into a less glorious kind of emulation, becoming extremists with the extremists and reactionaries alongside the upholders of counterrevolution. As one of their most fervent supporters, Jean-François Bellemare, has put it, they now became "the first seeds destined to reproduce the social order"[1] of pre-Revolutionary Europe.

In the next chapter we shall underline the baseless and frequently grotesque nature of such charges, which would be consistently leveled against the Company by writers and historians like Jules Michelet. We shall observe the Company's efforts to open itself to science and modernism and thus prepare the ground for its innovative work in the twentieth century. But what we cannot escape here is the astounding fact that—after a half century of mauling at the hands of four Bourbon dynasties, stubborn Gallican zealots, vengeful Jansenists, sneering *philosophes,* papal opportunists, and intriguing Habsburg agents—the only target the Jesuits chose for vengeance was Enlightenment thought.

Had the Company, like most of the returning *émigrés,* "forgotten nothing and learned nothing"? Was its memory so selective that it forgave only the Vatican—the institution that in betraying the Jesuits had also betrayed itself? Or the Bourbons, who had sacrificed them on the altar of their own perceived interests? Had it left Ignatian "discernment" so far behind that it was unable to perceive the things that glorified God in the heritage of the Enlightenment?

For more than a century, the Society of Jesus would pretend to be unaware that its death had been ordained not by Voltaire (although he paved the way), nor by the Revolution's Convention (although it spilled Jesuit blood), nor by the Italian *carbonari,* nor by Germany's *Sturm und Drang* movement, but by the politicians in Versailles and Madrid and by the Roman Curia. And it was with the latter group—and against the former—that it would now form an alliance. A most Holy Alliance . . .

The resurrection of the Company was everywhere hailed as a matter of state, of states. But what is striking is the furtive, arid, partial, and technical nature of the restoration. Only in the ceremonies at the Gesù was the event marked by the dramatic intensity that had accompanied dissolution a half century earlier. Outside Rome there were no public amends. Just a laborious reentry, improvised, sometimes painful, even shamefaced, closer to artificial respiration than resurrection. Cartoonists of the period showed a black legion flooding back into Europe. But in fact the fathers returned more or less everywhere on tiptoe and in a trickle.

Even Spain, with its love of flamboyant ritual and its burden of guilt for the Company's dissolution, was careful to offer no public consolation. The pitiful sovereigns manhandled by Napoleon (not to mention Goya), Charles IV and María Luisa, were in exile and happened to be passing through Rome at the time of the Gesù ceremony. They did not attend. Only later, in Spain, did they muster the courage to see the Jesuits, and then, according to Paul Dudon, "the Spanish fathers kissed their hands."[2] Such marks of affection and respect toward these ruthless persecutors were a measure of how low the order had fallen. For the fathers thus proved themselves more royalist and anti-revolutionary than Jesuit. There were similar marks of dynastic servility north of the Pyrenees.

Their heir, Ferdinand VI (who actually managed, with the help of his Paris cousins, to outdo his parents' ignoble conduct), urged the Council of Castile to raise the shield of the Company of Jesus between his throne and "liberalism," but it was nearly a year before the Spanish government would authorize the fathers to exercise their ministry in a Spain where, the Marquis de Custine observed, "the Middle Ages still stand." It was a difficult return, contested and tightly controlled by the dominant Franciscans, and opposed by a "liberal" faction whose actions took the form of outright persecution.

The grand Jesuit return was not much grander in Italy. From Naples to Turin, concordats between the Holy See and the monarchies of the Two Sicilies and of Piedmont opened the way for the Company (which would be expelled from Turin in 1848). But it could not avoid the disgrace of being universally seen as an accomplice of the power occupying much of Italian territory—Austria. The Jesuits' very conservative attitude on the question of Roman sovereignty finally soured their relations with the leaders of the *Risorgimento*. Modern Italy would build itself despite them.

In Vienna itself the old mistrust between the Habsburgs and the Company persisted. More or less permanent since Charles V, it had in a sense been contained by "Josephism," the strict control of religious activities by the state. Emperor Franz II, a bigot but a frightened one, wanted to forge an alliance with the fathers against the revolution incipient throughout the country. Metternich, at first reluctant, gradually relaxed his opposition to the plan under the influence of his third wife, the Countess Zichy, who was infatuated with the Jesuits. Thus, in 1836, the fathers were permitted to open schools in Innsbruck and Linz. But in Austria too the Company's revival was choppy, sporadic, and semiclandestine.

And now we shall return to the story (interrupted in the last chapter) of the Jesuits' Russian adventure. For just as the Company was climbing out of the grave, it was ejected from the Tsarist Empire by a power that had (not exclusively out of Christian charity) saved or at least preserved it.

Was it because the fathers had acquired excessive power, because of a status that outraged the Orthodox clergy, because of Russian pride? Because they had adopted an ambiguous posture during the Napoleonic invasion of 1812, a position much too French for the taste of those who had taken them in? All these reasons played a part, and after 1812 the Jesuit position was downright shaky. Pan-Slavists were disturbed at this Western influence, patriots cried collusion between the fathers and Napoleon's Grand Army, and Bible societies, supported by England, sprinkled salt on the wounds.

The King of Sardinia's ambassador to Saint Petersburg, Joseph de Maistre, a friend of the Jesuits and like them a staunch supporter of the Pope, observed that "the ground beneath the order's feet was sown with mines. Every conversion was noted, reported as disloyalty to the Motherland, as betrayal of the Sovereign, the absolute master of men's consciences."

As in Portugal in 1757 and France in 1764, it was the combined weight of a handful of public and private scandals that sealed the Company's fate in Russia. The Minister for Public Worship, Prince Alexander Golitsyn, a cousin of Marshal Kutuzov, Napoleon's conqueror, had a nephew who attended the Jesuit school in Saint Petersburg. In 1815 the boy announced that he intended to convert to Catholicism. It was claimed that his Jesuit teachers had violated the rules of neutrality they were supposed to observe. Feelings ran high, and Golitsyn asked the Tsar to eject the Company from the Empire.

Alexander, his hands full with deposing Napoleon and redrawing the European map at Vienna, merely ordered the fathers' expulsion from Saint Petersburg and Moscow. But his moderation gave way to vindictiveness when his Polish Catholic mistress, Princess Narychkin, was refused absolution by her Jesuit confessor, which promptly put an end to her assignations with the Tsar. A distant echo of the Pompadour affair sixty years earlier.

On March 13, 1820, reported Joseph de Maistre, "the Ukase left the palace like lightning from the clouds: All Jesuits active in the Empire were expelled and forbidden ever to return, 'in any form and any denomination whatsoever.' "*

A new disaster for the Company? Apparently so. First Potemkin, and then Paul I, struck by the pace of Jesuit expansion in their country,† had planned to make Saint Petersburg the center of the Company's worldwide redeployment. Since Rome had rejected it, Saint Petersburg would assume the role of the city of the Popes. So a grand design now foundered. But to this perspective we should add the following comment by a former student at the Polotsk novitiate, a man who would play a leading part in Company history. He was Jan Philip Roothaan, and he would one day be the Company's Superior General. "This expulsion," he said, "was the Company's salvation."

Why? Because following the resurrection decreed in 1814 by Pius VII, it supplied the renascent Company in Western Europe with leaders trained at Potolsk, who would otherwise have remained in Russia. A comment by Joseph Burnichon lends its full meaning to the Dutch Jesuit's remark: "Apparently paradoxical, it was in fact the simple truth. The Company's reconstruction was beset

---

*A similar ukase had been issued a century earlier by Peter the Great.
†In 1783 there were 28 Jesuit fathers, 38 brothers, and 16 novices in Russia. By 1805, there were already 280 members of the order there. By the time of their expulsion from Russia in 1820, their numbers had risen to 358. Zelenski, *Les Jésuites en Russie blanche* (Paris: Letouzey, 1874), vol. I, p. 483.

with difficulties, above all in Italy. At that period [1820], it was suffering what might be called growing pains, which reached their pitch during the General Congregation convened at the end of that year. The return of the upholders of tradition served as a brake on the activities of the innovators."[3]

Alas true. It was not so much the Society's "salvation" that was guaranteed by the return of the fathers trained in White Russia as the supremacy of those who had "upheld the tradition" in their Russian-Polish refuge, under autocratic regimes in a time and a place of counterrevolution.

Declared a "Province" in 1820, the reborn French Company received thirty-four Jesuits from Potolsk, including eighteen Frenchmen and nine Poles who gallicized their names. The whole history of the Society of Jesus in nineteenth-century France—with the Fathers straining against the "frenzy of the innovators"—is perhaps best summed up in the paradox of Father Roothaan and his commentator Father Burnichon. And it was, fatally, "tradition" that would prevail over "modernism."

Bled white by the Empire, saturated by revolution, France rallied more or less half-heartedly behind the Bourbons in 1814, once the charter proposed by Louis XVI's brother on June 4, 1814, appeared to guarantee that there would be no return to absolutism. The King's intentions were plainly moderate, as were those of his first two prime ministers—Armand-Emmanuel du Plessis, Duc de Richelieu, and Elie, Duc de Decazes. For a few years at least, neither the fury of the White Terror that followed Napoleon's Hundred Days nor the parliamentary squabbles of 1815 succeeded in tilting the system toward vengeful absolutism. However, the extremists within that system could not be forever contained.

If the "new Jesuits" had been given the choice, would they have opted for this flabby, well-intentioned regime? It seems unlikely. Their experiences under Revolution and Empire, their lives under cover or on the run, their friendships (with the likes of the Fathers of the Faith), the state of mind of the Congregation, their long protection under Russia's autocratic wing—everything incited them to espouse the extremists' cause against the democratizing Charter.

Joseph Burnichon, the Company's historian and a man not given to criticizing his colleagues, observes that

in the public's mind the causes of religion and of royalty were closely linked; both friends and foes would henceforth see them as one; their union would be expressed in the formula *throne and altar.* . . .

Inevitably the royal family favored religion, which in its turn guaranteed the respect and loyalty of the people. This [conviction] was unanimously held in the country in 1815. . . .

People quoted a remark Talleyrand reportedly made to Louis XVIII after Waterloo: "Sire, Your Majesty wishes to remain at the Tuileries; he must therefore take precautions. Only a wise and solid education can prepare future generations for that inner calm of which everyone proclaims the need. The most effective and painless means for achieving this end would be the legal reestablishment of the Company of Jesus."[4]

Shrewdly speculating on the authenticity of the remark, the Jesuit historian argues that the versatile Talleyrand had "too much feeling for what are called political possibilities to venture such a suggestion." Burnichon goes on: "It must be acknowledged that a measure like the official reestablishment of the Jesuit order so soon after the Restoration would have been wildly impolitic. The time was not yet ripe. All that could reasonably be expected from the benevolence of the monarch and his government in such difficult circumstances was freedom to live and to work."

But the "new Jesuits" of 1815 did not see it in that light. In an article on Pierre de Clorivière,[5] Father Pierre Vallin mentions the testimony of a nephew of the former Temple inmate, to whom the old priest wrote that the Hundred Days were a punishment inflicted upon the restored monarchy. In his view, the King forgave too much, God's justice had not been satisfied, and scandal was probably more widespread than during the Revolution! "The King forgave too much . . . " From the pen of a priest . . .

In another letter, written in 1815 to his friend the American bishop John Carroll, two months after Waterloo and the return of Louis XVIII to the throne, Pierre de Clorivière described his and his order's situation in gloomy tones: "I am left alone in the house with one other priest and three lay brothers. I have not been much molested there in the two months since the partial restoration of order. . . . Things are more or less on the same footing [as under Bonaparte] and we do not know when they will be adjusted for the Church's general good. . . . Our horizons are indeed still cloudy."[6]

A Jesuit historian, Jean-Claude Dhôtel, wrote in 1986 that the fathers called upon in 1814 to rebuild the Company "still lived with the memory of Louis XIII and Louis XIV; they believed that they enjoyed the same protections under the Bourbons, who had in fact betrayed them."

What emerges from Clorivière's correspondence of this period, according to Vallin, is a nostalgia for public recognition, in the old sense of the term, of the Company. Without "positive public sanction" for restoring the Jesuits and the clergy in general to their pre-1789 (or pre-1763) positions, the Bourbon monarchic state would continue in the eyes of these men to be tainted with "revolutionary atheism."

Thus, fifty years after the rejection of Roman political Jesuitism by the European monarchies, after twenty years of Revolution and of domestication under the Empire, and with all Europe falling prey to a fever of innovation, the saintly Clorivière was still dreaming of the restoration of the Company's ancient right of participation in public affairs. Not surprisingly, this urge to turn back history's clock led to clashes.

Poorly informed of Western European developments in his Russian confinement, the General of the restored Jesuits, Father Tadeusz Brzozowski, decided to recruit figures from the past in order to breathe new life into the Company (and it is true that few new figures had emerged). And however saintly, these men of yesterday burned with what can only be called the spirit of revenge. They would be faced with a terribly new world. From a past wiped out by gigantic upheavals, they were hurled into an unimaginable future. Unsurprisingly, their story now descended into incoherence, apparent sterility, and pain.

Decades of often misguided lip service to the "rights of man"; the emergence of a middle class created by the sale of national property often wrested from the clergy, and therefore earmarked for reclamation by the victims; the brutal disappearance of the two "orders" that before 1789 had enjoyed a virtual monopoly of public administration; a military epic that, whether in triumph or disaster, could not be laid at the door of any higher power; the advancement of a "constitutional" or state clergy with few attachments to the ancien régime—all these factors had stirred relations between the French people and its leaders (particularly religious ones) to the depths. And between the people and religion itself.

Perhaps Alexis de Tocqueville was thinking about these Jesuits, just back from exile or emerging from the ranks of the Fathers of the Sacred Heart, when he said that, having seen "the first use men had made of independence had been to attack religion, they feared their contemporaries and stood back in horror from the liberty the latter were cultivating. Lack of belief seeming to them a new phenomenon, they encompassed in the same hatred everything that was new."[7]

Was post-Empire France then paganized? The answers vary. We shall consider two, one affirmative, by the nuncio representing Rome in Paris, the other negative, and expressed by the anarchist Pierre-Joseph Proudhon.

According to the nuncio, Monsignor Macchi, writing in 1826: "More than half the nation wallowed in total ignorance of Christian duties and in indifference. In Paris, scarcely one eighth of the population was practicing, and it was doubtful whether ten thousand men in the capital attended church."[8]

Paradoxically, it was the doctrinaire Proudhon who called this diagnosis into question: "In France, despite eighteenth-century 'philosophy,' Catholicism survived well beyond the Revolution and did not receive its first shocks . . . , I am speaking here of the masses, until around 1830."

Successive readings of the legitimist, royalist Balzac and the republican

Stendhal will bear out both the nuncio and the anarchist. More often the latter, however, if we confine ourselves to the urban world and the well-to-do circles traditionally "worked" by the Jesuits—whose sphere of action would now suddenly expand to encompass *les misérables*. But rustic parsons, particularly in the east and west of France, would have disagreed with the nuncio.

On this uncertain foundation the monarchy handled the clergy in general and the Jesuits in particular, at least until 1822,* with the utmost caution. As Louis XVIII said, "Let the fathers resume neither the name nor the habit of the Company; let them go noiselessly about their affairs and they have nothing to fear."

He little knew the Jesuits. "Let them go noiselessly about their affairs?" But, sire, the Jesuits'"affairs"were by definition everyone's affairs. "Noiselessly?" Perhaps. But not without an effect on the course of events (no matter what their name or habit). However hard they might try, the Jesuits could not work without purpose, without encumbrances, without at least some commotion.

In this field as in many others (with the exception of love), Louis XVIII resembled his ancestor Louis XV. He lacked neither shrewdness nor goodwill nor tolerance, but rather information and decisiveness. He did not like "making scenes." And Jesuits by definition make scenes. Relations between this court-bred Voltairean and the fathers could never be cordial. And the situation was exacerbated by the working of two negative influences on the King: that of Louis XVI's daughter, the Duchesse d'Angoulême, the austere "Dauphine," which was rooted in the past; and that of the modernizing influence of his Prime Minister, Decazes.

The bigoted, backward-looking Duchess blamed the Jesuits for the assassination of her ancestor Henry IV, and worked hard to embitter her husband and her whole family toward the Company. Decazes was a Freemason. Inevitably, he tried to influence the King—who hung on his advice, although in this instance it was contradicted by the counsels of his brother, the Comte d'Artois, a roué turned believer—against them. Louis himself most willingly observed the principles and provisions underlying the 1814 Constitutional Charter, which had disappointed Jesuit expectations of the royal restoration. Article Six of the Charter recognized Catholicism as the state religion—but also freedom of conscience and of worship. The Napoleonic civil code had been extended,† and the speculators of the Revolutionary decades had been confirmed in their ownership of what had been national property. In short, the nation's institutional and legal framework was closer to the imperial system than to the *ancien régime*.

But there was one area of agreement between King and Jesuits: their shared

*Date of the appointment as Prime Minister Villèle, leader of the "ultra" or extremist faction.
†The abolition of divorce would come in 1816.

loathing of the 1801 Concordat, in which the Jesuits saw the instrument of the subjugation of religion to the French state, the triumph of neo-Gallicanism, while to the King it seemed like an act of homage by the Church to the Great Usurper. Monsignor de Pressigny, the man Louis XVIII sent to Rome to expunge from the Concordat everything whose elimination would not humiliate the Pope who had signed it, was a friend of the Company. But the joint efforts of the Prelate and the fathers resulted only in a vague rephrasing of the language of the text—to which Pius VII remained attached despite the humiliations heaped on him by the Emperor.

When it confronted the challenge of reconstruction in this climate of ambiguous tolerance and suspicion, the Company mustered only a few dozen men in France. Some were just emerging, still blinking in the light, from long proscription in France itself; others were returning from Russian exile or from protracted stays in England or the Low Countries. There was also an Ignatian militia, its roots in one or another of the societies created twenty-five years earlier and outlawed by Fouché, and in the Congregation, whose ranks were stiffened by powerful personalities like Clorivière, Ravin, Rozaven, Grivet, and Roger.

Even so, in 1815 their numbers did not exceed a hundred, of whom fifty were priests. A novitiate was soon founded in Montrouge, attracting many volunteers, so that by 1817 the strength of the Society (which was still only tolerated, its members simply enjoying the same rights of practicing and purveying religion as all citizens) had risen to 167, a hundred of them priests.

Pierre de Clorivière dominates this first period of new beginnings. The new French Company—and the "new Jesuit"—grew up and defined itself around this heroic old man. Was this restoration or counterrevolution? The latter in no way implies a radical return to the old order. For the "new Jesuit" turned out to have little in common with his predecessors.

The religious who had been dispersed by royal and then papal authority at the end of the century of Voltaire were on many counts Voltaireans themselves. Whether their teachings were now as "deistic" in metaphysical matters as their moral views were accommodating and their "colonization" gentle is debatable. But overall, their cultural and even their spiritual initiatives now faithfully reflected the "philosophical" spirit that impregnated the age, just as humanism had done two centuries earlier. Men of the Renaissance (although with reservations) at the time of Erasmus and of the Baroque (although not without flaws) in the century of Louis XIV, they were now in step with the most outspoken exponents of "natural" religion.

Nothing could have been less like these "philosophical" Jesuits than the ones who emerged from the rubble of Revolution and Empire. Expelled by some and persecuted by others, buffeted by "liberty," rescued by foreign autocrats, they had inevitably become the enemies and the avengers of recent history. Revenge is not too strong a word. As Élisabeth Antébi and François Lebrun observe in their *Les Jésuites et la Gloire de Dieu*, these reinstated priests "tended to cling, in Europe at least, to the values of the past, of defunct monarchies. Throughout the nineteenth century, and often with good reason, their name became synonymous with reaction, conservatism, and ultramontanism."

What was the Company's legal position in Restoration France? However amiable the official relations between the reinstated Bourbons and the Vatican, the kind of worldwide Jesuit resurrection Pius VII had announced obviously did not imply that the French state was obliged to conform to his declaration. The basic French constitutional document was of course the 1814 Charter, whose sixty-eighth article specified that "existing laws which are not contrary to the Charter remain in force until legally suspended." This in effect meant that Restoration France took on board the whole legal heritage of the *ancien régime* and the Revolution, a heritage uniformly negative toward the Jesuits. The very existence of the Jesuits (as of their Franciscan, Dominican, and Benedictine colleagues) could thus be legitimately considered illegal in Bourbon France: Indeed there was no matter on which pre-Revolution "tyrants," Directory, Consulate, and Empire had shown greater unanimity, or rather continuity.

It is true, of course, that Louis XVIII, unlike the late Emperor, wanted the Company to lead an active existence in his kingdom—to go "noiselessly" about its business. But the Jesuits had too many enemies (and too many embarrassing friends) for such a "tolerated" status to endure indefinitely. Whence the agitated, fluctuating, almost tragic course their history followed in this France where throne and altar were asserting their joint supremacy.

Through the fifteen years of the Restoration, the Jesuits' fundamental, constant, and implacable enemy would be the cluster of forces grouped under the heading of "liberalism." A "liberalism" that was virtually a synonym, a mirror image, of what Voltairean "philosophy" had been before the Revolution, and of what "anticlericalism"* would later stand for. Obviously, however, this kind of across-the-board rejection of religion and Church power would affect more than just the Jesuits. What singled the Company out for the thunderbolts of liberalism (which was ready to accept the ordinary clergy and a circumscribed religiosity), what kindled the inextinguishable fury of the liberals, was its organized, collective, disciplined, and associative character, whether in its original form or its later "Congregational" incarnation. As René Remond astutely points out,[9] liberal suspicion was directed essentially at "all organizations and groups,

---

*The word would not appear until midcentury.

at everything likely to stifle the initiative of the individual." Not surprisingly, therefore, coherent, disciplined Jesuitism was seen as the worst of enemies.

Thus the Jesuits found themselves allied with a disparate range of forces and viewpoints that supported the union of throne and altar—the Jesuits, the Congregation, the Knights of the Faith, and many others, including the "Priest party," which was legitimist and ultramontane. It was against this deeply reactionary backcloth that the story of the Jesuits during the Bourbon Restoration unfolded. It was in this light that an irritated Stendhal and Champollion and an astounded Balzac viewed them. It was in this climate that they earned the nickname of "turkeys," setting them aside from the generic term for the clergy, "crows." Both of them birds, of course, but in the case of the Jesuits pompous, clumsy, and vain. . . .

Popular opinion held their breeding ground to be the École Saint-Acheul on the outskirts of Amiens. It was principally at Saint-Acheul,* people felt, that future leaders were indoctrinated with the aim—through the agency of the Congregation—of sinking state and educational system under the weight of the clergy and the numbers of the extremists.† Although Saint-Acheul was described by friends of the Company as a "fashionable school," enemies denounced it as a kind of children's penal colony, a sadistic concentration camp, a factory for "ultras" (reactionary ultra-royalists). Here are the impressions of a former pupil of the Jesuits, author of *Coup d'oeil dans l'intérieur de Saint-Acheul* (A Glimpse Inside Saint-Acheul; Paris, 1826):

> Let us approach and push through the studded iron gates defending this gloomy place. What are those screams that assail our ears? Is it some ravenous beast rending a human victim and drinking his blood? No, it is a man a thousand times crueler than tigers and leopards joining his fury to the bitter cold and lacerating the hands of a six-year-old.
>
> Deeper inside a scene from the Middle Ages awaits us: The Almighty is being called upon (so to speak) to single out the guiltiest among the pupils: A wretch is picked by lottery to expiate the crimes of all the others [who] are routinely herded into rooms no one may enter . . . and where virtue is rarely found . . .
>
> The objective of the disciples of Loyola . . . is to acquire the highest offices of state for the men they have thus poisoned with their maxims. . . . Their happy protégés enjoy the right to inflict arbitrary punishment on their co-disciples, exercising absolute power over them.[10]

Most of these claims are, of course, absurd. But a glance at the rules govern-

---

*The Jesuits ran six other schools outside Paris.

†A by no means absurd scenario: While the first "ultra" head of state, Villèle, was simply a Knight of the Faith, his successor, Polignac, was a Congregation member.

ing the schools—both from the disciplinary and the curricular standpoint—makes it clear that the "good fathers" of Saint-Acheul, a school attended in 1825 by six hundred students, left themselves open to criticism.

Discipline? Corporal punishment was not unknown, even though the Jesuit Provincial, Father Simpson, who had spent twenty-four years of his life as a teacher at Stonyhurst School in England, had declared it "demeaning." But at Saint-Acheul the dominant disciplinary criterion could be summed up in the following formula: "The most effective penalties are those that humiliate most." One of its teachers went so far as to strap a sandwich-board complete with relevant inscription onto offenders' backs.

The curriculum? Latin, still used to inculcate philosophy, took precedence over rhetoric and declamation. Arithmetic was taught earlier than in the past, and history—of a kind—had regained pride of place. As for the "liberal arts," censorship was the rule. Apart from what might have a practical application (this applied mainly to drawing), "art was out of bounds." Music was so full of temptations that it was better for the majority to remain in complete ignorance of it. Most detestable of all was a "soft, effeminate, or passionate" demeanor. Fencing was viewed more kindly, since it promoted physical development and in any case had to be taught to "those who wished to enter the Army."

Even these skimpy "innovations" alarmed the Company's leaders in Rome, earning the rector of Saint-Acheul a stern reprimand: "Arithmetic if you must. But in the past one studied neither arithmetic nor geography nor history. . . . Prizes for Drawing and Music . . . Who is responsible for this innovation? Neither Drawing nor Music is part of the education the Jesuits offer."

Most of the teachers at Saint-Acheul had been "Fathers of the Faith" in the dark days of abolition. The spirit of the great emigration, of royalist reaction, of conspiracy still burned within them. In contemporary correspondence between the Jesuit survivors of the *ancien régime* and those who had entered the Company after being trained in the fighting organizations of Clorivière and Varin, disagreements and misunderstandings leap out. The older group deplored the toughness, overzealousness, and impatience of the newcomers. To them, the men whose vocation had been forged in the Terror or during Fouché's manhunts seemed better prepared for confrontation than for understanding.

This phenomenon is again observable in the second of the Company's Restoration "shrines," its novitiate at Montrouge. Here the myth took on crazed proportions. Through the pen of liberal publicists, Saint-Acheul had become a sort of breeding ground for little ultras. But Montrouge was what the GPU or KGB would be to twentieth-century anti-Communist writers, a gigantic cookhouse of subversion. Saint-Acheul shaped the oppressor classes, Montrouge turned out their teachers.

The myth of this Jesuit Valhalla crossed frontiers. Jean-François Bellemare tells the story of a Russian prince, a reader of the anti-Jesuit paper *Le Constitutionnel,* who having arrived in Paris asked to be taken to this famous Jesuit metropolis: He expected a black Potsdam, a fortified Versailles. All he found was a handful of villages, in one of which was a large building, an herb garden, a few cows, and some sixty young clerics out for a peaceful walk. If this was the headquarters of a black revolution, France's freedoms were not in such great danger as he had thought. His conclusion? "Damned irresponsible newspapers!"

A notable contributor to this legend was Abbé Marcet de la Roche-Arnaud, himself a former novice. His *Mémoires d'un jeune jésuite, ou la Configuration de Montrouge* (Memoirs of a Young Jesuit, or the Montrouge Conspiracy) depicts the suburban novitiate as another fortress of the Old Man of the Mountain, bending his drugged "hashishins" (or assassins) to his most ferocious whims:

> Obedient to the voice of their superior, novices have horribly mutilated and sacrificed themselves. Here is a man, weaponless, powerless, of no renown [whose] will, even whose glance, can set in motion a thousand hands armed with daggers to murder princes and destroy empires. For the last ten years the provinces have been filling up with these formidable slaves, and every day even more terrible ones emerge from his hands . . .

This Old Man of the Mountain, master of an assassin sect, this "tyrant of Montrouge," was Father Jean-Baptiste Gury, a former member of Clorivière's company, the Society of the Fathers of the Sacred Heart. Once again, the excesses of caricature are liable to make us overlook the real excesses of the character himself. His assistant Father Guidée (himself known to students as a fearsome guardian of order) says of him: "It must be admitted that Father Gury's manner was not the most appealing. Of lively and sanguine temperament, he was sometimes somewhat abrupt." Beneath this "rough exterior," however, as Father Guidée assures us, one glimpsed "true charity." But all the other things we know about Father Gury suggest that penetrating that rough exterior was an arduous undertaking. We judge the tree by its fruit, and tolerance was not one of those fruits. Montrouge was no more an academy for hired killers than Saint-Acheul was a child's penal colony, but what was taught there—apart from God's grace—did not really foster goodwill among men.

Clorivière's mandate from Superior General Brzozowski—to rebuild the Company in France—was short-lived. Because the former prisoner of the Temple was already old? Because they realized in Rome that the heroic age of counter-revolution was over—or that the age of real right-wing extremism had not yet dawned?

The Marquês of Pombal—Enlightenment enforcer.
Tombo Archives, Lisbon (photo Giraudon).

Chief Minister Choiseul: to the greater glory of his King.

Portrait by Van Loo. Giraudon Archives. Bibliothèque Nationale, Paris.

Madame de Pompadour,
by François Boucher.
Giraudon Archives. Louvre,
Paris.

Clement XIV: "Compulsus feci!"
Private collection.

The Company's unlikely rescuers: the Lutheran Frederick, to the greater glory of Prussia . . .

Roger Viollet collection, Bibliothèque Nationale, Paris.

. . . and the Orthodox Catherine—"a woman and a Tartar."
Catherine II of Russia by Chibanoff.

Pierre de Clorivière, France's last Jesuit in 1773, its first in 1814: architect of the Company's "Restoration."

Archives of the Province of France, Society of Jesus, Vanves.

Spearhead of the Jesuit-bashers at the Collège de France: Michelet (seated),
Quinet (standing). Behind them (perhaps), the young Renan.
Roger Viollet collection. The Sorbonne *by Flameng.*

Arrogant beetle-swarm of Jesuits, as seen by Honoré Daumier.
Le Crapouillot *magazine.*

P. J. de Smet, sturdy peacemaker of the Rockies.
Paul de Smet d'Olbecke collection.

De Smet observing Mass with the Dakota Sioux.
Paul de Smet d'Olbecke collection.

Two pillars of courage and light: Father Gaston Fessard . . .
"Les Fontaines" library, Society of Jesus, Chantilly.

. . . and the tireless Father Pierre Chaillet.
Teilhard de Chardin Foundation Archives.

Henri de Lubac, theologian on the firing line.

Father Karl Rahner, the theologian of reconciliation.

Pierre Teilhard de Chardin . . .

. . . the paleontologist and his implements . . .

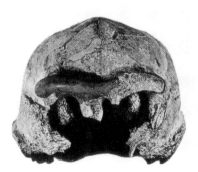

. . . and the skull of Sinanthropus.

Teilhard de Chardin Foundation Archives.

Vatican Council II. The Jesuits were tucked away in the wings . . .
Wilson. Dalmas/Sipa.

. . . all except for Cardinal Bea.

Peter Hans Kolvenbach, twenty-ninth Superior General, with his cosmopolitan general staff.

Gamma. Photo Brissaud.

"General" Arrupe kneels to John Paul II: a lesson in "holy obedience."

Notre Histoire.

After three years the Company's first "resistance fighter" was asked to step down in favor of Father Simpson. The real name of the Jesuits' new master in France was Sionnet; but he had lived in England for twenty-three years, teaching mathematics at Stonyhurst, and had chosen to anglicize his name (shades of Li Mateou in China). Everything we know of this priest places him in the moderate wing of his order as a man who stressed the need for modernization and a "paternal" guiding spirit in Jesuit teaching.

If Father Simpson had lived another ten years, perhaps the Company would have moderated the combative line promulgated by Clorivière and moved toward compromise and understanding. It seems unlikely, though. It was not Simpson's death alone that led to the hardening of Jesuit attitudes: After the assassination of the Duc de Berry,* the whole of French society moved into a reactionary mood.

Ever since the Charter of 1814, the "ultras" had been establishing and reinforcing their position. The liberals responded with the only weapons at their disposal—newspapers, pamphlets, and songs. And since it was out of the question for them to attack the monarchy, the Jesuits became the prime target for their sometimes ribald offensives. Editions of the works of the eighteenth-century *philosophes* poured from the presses (seven editions of Voltaire's complete works in twelve years). Also republished was a crude opus written in the seventeenth century by a former Jesuit, the Pole Hieronymus Zahorowski, entitled *Monita Secreta* (Secret Instructions): It purported to contain orders issued by the Company's superiors with the aim of laying hold of souls (and inheritances). It was a ludicrous document, which has drawn the scorn of historians of all schools of thought, but between 1825 and 1828 it went through a dozen reprints.† Other popular publications bore titles like *Redskins at Montrouge: Take Cover!; The Jesuits Through Their Own Eyes, or Jesuitry Naked and in Action;* and *France Wrestles the Jesuit Hydra. . . .*

In all these publications, noted the liberal historian of the Restoration, Viel-Castel, "the terms 'Jesuit' and 'Congregationist' were applied without distinction to anyone professing religious sentiments. The dramatic impact of those words was enhanced by the fact that nobody had a clear idea of what the Congregation was, and that the still-unofficial existence of the Jesuits had an aura of mystery that opened vast fields for the imagination."[11]

Anti-Jesuit campaigns sometimes took less public form. In his *Annales* of Montrouge, Father Gury published a threatening letter he received in 1826:

Tremble, satellites of Loyola: Your final hour is at hand! Vile scoundrels, infamous perverters of youth, monsters of treachery, tremble!

*The second son of the Comte d'Artois (the future Charles X of France), he was assassinated in 1820.
†See Chapter XII.

France rejects you as the scum of the human species. Hypocrites, villains, the colossus of your power will crumble and crush you beneath its ruins. Cursed race, enemies of the Nation, you will perish. Laden with your crimes, your name will be held in execration by future generations: Forty thousand defenders of our liberties have sworn your downfall. . . . Another forty days and Montrouge will be no more . . .

Signed: Geoffroy, friend of the Constitution; Jouvillier, friend of Liberty; Trouvel, friend of Equality; Gardeau, friend of the Republic; Tournilly, enemy of Traitors.[12]

It was a hatred that fed upon its own hallucinations. And it could take more direct form. When the *Monita Secreta* were first reprinted, Father Debrosse, superior of the small seminary in Bordeaux, was attacked with a sickle by a neighborhood laborer who had to be dragged from his Jesuit victim.

Naturally such attacks, taken in conjunction with hostile articles in *Le Constitutionnel,* or the popular songs that portrayed the fathers as flagellators and corrupters of youth, hardened Jesuit attitudes and discredited members of the Society who favored accommodation. Once Charles X—"Charles the Pious" —was on the throne, the Comte de Villèle's "ultra" party in office, and religious conservatives in key positions, militant Jesuitism seemed unconquerable.

The man who embodied all the nation's combined grievances against the Jesuits, the man who would deliver the death blow, was neither a Republican nor a liberal nor a "socialist." He was an aristocrat, a product of the aristocratic emigration, ardently royalist, unimpeachably religious. It was not Jansenism but Gallicanism that fed his hatred of the Jesuits. Not to mention a most aristocratic disdain for the fathers: Where on earth had all these awful people, Pierre Ronsin, Gury, Jean Nicolas Loriquet, come from, manipulated by Rome and in turn manipulating the government ministries, the archbishops, the court, even the aristocracy? What a ghastly crew!

In 1826 he published the work that would assure him a prominent position in the gallery of the most illustrious Jesuit-eaters, after the likes of Pasquier, Pascal, d'Alembert, and Béranger, and before Michelet. Its title was bizarre: *Mémoire à consulter sur un système politique et religieux tendant à renverser la religion, la société et le trône* (Memorandum on a Political and Religious System Designed to Overthrow Religion, Society, and the Throne). Its opening broadside was thunderous: "A vast system—no, let us not mince words, a vast conspiracy—has arisen against Religion, King, and Society. I saw it in its first stirrings, I have followed its progress, I see it now as it prepares to crush us beneath its ruins. This situation being known to me, by my conscience I must fight it, and by our laws I must reveal it."

The "conspiracy" the Catholic and royalist Comte de Montlosier felt compelled to lay bare for his contemporaries resulted from an alliance of four forces: the Jesuits, the Congregation, ultramontanism, and the pervasive intrusions of the priesthood. The combination of these four "calamities," he believed, threatened society, throne, and religion. His indictment was not worthy of Pascal's, nor even Pasquier's or d'Alembert's. Of the Company's long history, he noted only its regicide obsession: According to him, all the fathers' teachings over the past three centuries could be boiled down to instruction in the art of assassinating kings. . . . And perhaps fearing that the charge might seem somewhat dated, he insisted: "Perhaps it will be said that today's Jesuits are not like yesterday's: They are harmless. Yes, but they are only beginning. Young wolfcubs play with you, they lick you. But let them grow, Kings of Europe: Today's Jesuits play with you and lick you; they have the innocence of childhood. But wait until they attain puberty."

Not an exalted level of argument. But the fact that it was patent nonsense did not deter the *Journal des Débats* from hailing Montlosier as "France's beacon" and saluting his "chivalrous dedication to the public weal." *Le Constitutionnel*, comparing him to Pascal, called him a "gladiator in the cause of truth." Thus encouraged, the noble Count decided to follow up his *Mémoire* with further indictments, embodied most particularly in his *Pétition à la Chambre des pairs, précédée de quelques observations sur les calamités objets de la Pétition, pour faire suite au Mémoire à consulter* (Petition to the Chamber of Lords, Preceded by Some Observations on the Calamities Leading to the Petition). This time Montlosier shifted his sights somewhat, arguing that there were now three parties in France: the monarchical, the liberal, and the "priest party." To the latter group he proceeded to add a few finishing touches, ascribing the following "missions" to the Jesuits and the Congregation: "Platoons of missionaries, escorted by platoons of gendarmes, impervious to the disgust of the whole nation, seek through the terrors of hellfire to acquire the domination only yesterday claimed by another reign of Terror."

The *Petition* itself was a request addressed to France's Upper (and nobly born) House of Parliament: "That Your Lordships, taking into account the imminent danger presented by these establishments and the urgent need to dissolve them, at once consider the swiftest measures to bring about their dissolution."

The question was duly raised in the Upper House. It ultimately provoked furious debate in both houses, in the course of which the conservative Archbishop Frayssinous—thinking to protect the Jesuits by stressing the fragility of their position—agreed that they purveyed their teachings in seven institutions. And when the opposition leapt upon this admission, the Archbishop, who was also a government minister, appealed for "tolerance" toward them. But the liberals, led by Casimir Périer, said that it was unworthy of France that public order should be left to the whim of a system that tolerated such violations of the law.

Nevertheless, the accuser might have emerged defeated from the conflict, and the accused speedily granted a status associating them freely with the university system, if the Villèle government had not fallen at the end of 1827, and with it the Jesuits' sturdiest advocate, Archbishop Frayssinous. A liberal-leaning cabinet took office. Its minister of justice was Portalis, the son of Napoleon's minister. He was unable to secure their outright abolition. But he obtained from the King, the very pious King, the most devoted King Charles X, the removal of the Jesuits from all forms of education. A betrayal in the finest Bourbon tradition.

It is worth reading the monarchist historian Joseph Burnichon on this royal capitulation. Although scarcely able to hide his anger, Burnichon cannot quite bring himself to unmask Charles X's hypocrisy, in which spinelessness cowered behind a façade of respect for the public welfare. The memory of Pope Ganganelli in 1773 springs to mind: the same fearfulness, the same whining prevarications. A monument to crowned cowardice.

Portalis's bill proclaiming the eviction of the Jesuits had actually been presented to the King, who was making ready to countersign it, when Monsignor Feutrier, Frayssinous's successor as minister of religion, urged him not to condone what he considered an unworthy act. The King, Burnichon reports, took the bishop's hands, his eyes brimming with tears: "Bishop of Beauvais, will you then abandon me?"

Frayssinous, who was also present, insisted in his turn that from the Catholic standpoint the proposed measure was indeed unworthy.

"That is true," agreed the King, "but you told me that if I deemed it truly necessary, no one would have the right to condemn me."

"Yes, sire, but that is something of which I am not the judge."

"Well then," said the King, "I have reflected, I have pondered, I have prayed to God to the best of my ability to enlighten me, and I remain convinced that were I not to take this step I should place the fate of the clergy and perhaps that of the state in jeopardy."

And thus the Jesuits were thrown to the wolves by a King who flattered himself that he had restored the spirit of chivalry. On June 16, 1828, the law banning the fathers from teaching went into effect. By the end of the year, not a single Jesuit was teaching in the whole of France.

When Rome reacted, as it had to, Charles X's government sought to buy its silence by assuring the Vatican that "the overwhelming majority of the nation" had cried out for the move (although most historians agree that the French as a whole were ignorant of Jesuit activities: If Monsignor Frayssinous's "revelation" of the existence of seven Jesuit schools had caused a sensation, it was because even in parliamentary circles the "conspiracy" had gone largely unnoticed).

His own recent family history should have taught Charles X (whose adversaries were scarcely of Revolutionary caliber) the dangers of step-by-step capitulation. But he failed to read the lesson. So, alas, did France's Jesuits, called to revive the Company founded in Montmartre in 1534. So much so that their restoration seems a mere caricature of the Crown's.

· XII ·

The Black Legend

Power-Mad, Devious, Prudish • Pascal and Pasquier • Michelet Furioso • Hugo at the Heights • Black Robes, American Tragedy • The Wrong Century

THE AVERSION THAT the Company of Jesus arouses in so many people (including the most pious and the most devout) is hard to explain on rational grounds, for it feeds on fantasies anchored most tenuously in reality.

We are here in the area of social myth. We are speaking of a phobia. The Jesuit is not so much evaluated as "felt." His case in Christian society is unique. It stems less from doctrinal or political controversy than from popular imagination.

Let us first examine external forms—language and appearances—starting with the very word "Jesuit" and its accompanying connotations of cold, negative, sinister intent. It was the Company's adversaries, particularly Germany's Lutherans, who coined the name. They used it against Canisius, known to his supporters as "the hammer of the heretics" and to his foes as "that dog of a monk."* But the name assumed more official coloration at the Council of Trent, where Loyola's successor, Diego Laínez, was introduced as *generalis jesuitarum.* Explicit scorn had given place to implicit mistrust, and the tone remained negative.

But irrational aversion to the Jesuits lay beyond semantics. The Jesuits' capacity to disturb lay in what a famous adversary, Étienne Pasquier, called the "hermaphroditic" character of "this Monster which, being neither Secular nor Regular, was both things together, thereby introducing into our Church a Hermaphrodite Order." Pasquier meant the ambiguous nature of an organization

*Canisius was the Latinized form of his real name, Hondt (meaning "dog" in Dutch).

structured along traditional monastic lines but whose members took a most active part in public affairs. In other words, were they or weren't they? What was this blend of rigorous discipline and worldly activity? Monastic rule indoors, everyday life outdoors? This dual nature—this double game—disturbed and irritated.

All the more so because it represented not just a duality of means but a duplicity of goals: on earth as in heaven. Monastic but mobile, regimented but free-ranging, eyes gazing heavenward but hands on the wheel, everything for God but all things to all men . . . Where did they stop? Where would they meddle next?

Ordinary common sense, Gallican tradition, Cartesian reason all prefer clearly defined categories, clear-cut distinctions—priest or pikeman, sacred or profane, Cross or Crown . . . But the Jesuit stood in the middle, or on both sides, too much a priest for public affairs, too worldly for a priest: unclassifiable, elusive, and therefore hateful.

But popular imagination did not see the Jesuit only as "hermaphroditic." It believed—or it felt—him to be secret, subterranean. Did this legend of the "underground" Jesuit spring from the fact that the Company, unlike its Dominican or Franciscan predecessors, initially rejected honors or positions in the Church hierarchy—although it soon had its Cardinals, if not Popes*—and its members never wore anything but the humble soutane of regular priests?

We might, of course, suggest that the Jesuit was not hated for his "underground" image, but on the contrary was perceived as "underground" because he was hated—and leave it at that. But clearly more is at play in this popular perception of Jesuit ambiguity and subterranean maneuvering.

Dominique Bertrand, in his masterly *Politique de saint Ignace* (Politics of Saint Ignatius),[1] addresses this contradiction (widely seen as hypocrisy) between the Jesuits' rejection of "worldly honors" and their strikingly "worldly" actions—spurning no "means" and no alliances in order to arrive at ends whose spiritual and temporary dimensions were not always distinct from one another. According to Father Bertrand: "What disconcerts observers of the Ignatian venture is also what fascinates them: the conjunction of a radical refusal of honor (even religious life, even the Church and its hierarchy were a means, in other words grace for achieving the end) and of extreme realism in their conception of success. If one is not a part of this game, which is not without subtlety, how can one fail to see 'duplicity' in it?"

Ignatius of Loyola, says Father Bertrand, made himself the "opponent of all worldly honor" in order to further "the greater glory of God, which is the real

*There has never been a Jesuit Pope . . . so far . . .

furtherance of all sorts of men." Whence the "covert or open resistance" brought into being by this "lucidity," the "nervous reflex" of a society that felt "slapped in the face." It was here, Bertrand concludes, that the "misunderstanding" between the world and the Company lay.

Let us not challenge the word. But we are forced to note that this "misunderstanding" was constantly nourished by a "game"—with its alternating humility and arrogance, spotlight and shadow, sacrifice and pomp—whose "subtlety" had more than the mere appearance of "duplicity."

And public opinion across the social spectrum, at least as "disconcerted" as it was "fascinated," attributed tortuous designs and endless intrigue to these mysterious men who so long claimed to reject crook and miter, bishoprics and red hats, preferring to serve as confessors, tutors, and teachers. For who would be satisfied to walk in the shadows—unless in stealthy search of powers that lay beyond the regular channels of advancement? They were too distanced from honors not to be hiding something up their sleeves, too close to kings not to seek to sway them (unless, for the salvation of the order or the Pope or the faith, it became necessary to do away with them).

Much has already been said about French Gallicanism. But it is worth repeating that despite its strong and even overwhelmingly Catholic traditions, French society was deeply hostile to Roman authority, to papalism, to anything that smacked of ultramontanism. And beyond religion, there was a political dimension to Gallicanism. The French had always been wary of the Jesuits' Spanish origins; the Company had been founded at a time when the Spanish, Dutch, and Austrian Habsburgs were harassing the French crown in its slow evolution toward a blend of "patriotism" and absolutism. However "non-Spanish" Ignatius's global strategy, however uneasy his relations with the Spanish Emperor Charles V, many saw the Jesuits, if not as outright French-haters, at least as objective agents of a foreign power (and the most dangerous of them). Whereas, only three centuries earlier, no one would have dreamed of reproaching Saint Bruno for his German origins, Saint Francis for being born in Umbria, or Saint Dominic for his Castilian roots.

How did people *see* these men in black? The stock caricature is born of centuries-old fantasies. The Jesuit was thin, sallow, and smooth-skinned, tonsured to the bone. No Capuchin potbelly, no Friar Tuck jolliness. Lowered lids, high-pitched voice, niggardly gestures. His soutane spotless and well cut, his biretta brushed and shiny, he could hold his own at table, tell jokes, quote Tacitus, and even Voltaire. But no boozing or guzzling—that he left to the regular clergy and to corpulent prelates.

Devious in manner, modest in demeanor, but sly and vain of his appearance, he went his way, from confessional to bedchamber, stage left, stage right—a stiletto concealed between the pages of his prayerbook or between soutane and velvet hairshirt, all *ad majorem Dei gloriam*. . . .

And the supreme defect in this swarm of imagined flaws? The French Jesuit was not highly sexed. You had to journey to Italy to hear penitents' complaints of inflamed confessors,* and to Munich to be told that Peter Canisius (that "dog of a monk"!) dallied with an Abbess from Mainz. Not in France! The men in black could slaughter kings and make the Pope's bed, but they would never wallow in carnal sin.

However, a persistent tradition attributed a love of flagellation to these great teachers. To each his pleasures according to his means. . . . As Béranger's song went:

> *Swish, swish, swish, the boys are howling,*
> *Their pretty little bottoms pink and warm . . .*

Thus were Loyola's disciples typecast, lampooned, lent a thousand doubtful faces. And as such they became a leitmotif of literary history. But although preponderantly anti-Jesuit, the chorus was not uniformly hostile. Rabelais's sneers would eventually be balanced by praise from Montaigne, who considered the educational program at the Jesuit school in Rome one of the wonders of the world. And while Pascal became their most illustrious denigrator, Descartes remained loyal. Similarly, Racine was too much the Jansenist not to revile the fathers, but Corneille publicly defended their ideas.

Voltaire, although widely seen as a scourge of the Company, had imbibed Jesuit teaching and was a great admirer of the Paraguay missions. Rousseau was moved by the hardships they endured. Stendhal quite simply hated them. Balzac saw them as monuments of genius and virtue. Lamartine sang the praises of the "Fathers of the Faith." Victor Hugo, who at first looked with favor on these champions of legitimate monarchy, would turn into their most eloquent prosecutor in the course of the long campaign that led to their expulsion from France at the end of the nineteenth century.

Even the larger Catholic world was deeply divided over the Jesuits, some seeing them as providential deliverers, others as messengers of doom. The mark of contradiction sat heavily upon them. It was said of them—as it had been said of Christ Himself—that they preached not peace but war. "Ite et inflammate," Loyola had told his missionaries. Mission accomplished.

Jesuitphobia was born with the Jesuits. It existed even in uterine form. Loyola had not yet become "Master Ignatius" when Rabelais portrayed him as "Fray

---

*Although certain biographers suggest that Père de La Chaize led a turbulent life, and Father Coton was accused of handling his penitent Henry IV with kid gloves.

Iñigo" in *Pantagruel*. And scarcely had the doctors of Montmartre secured the decisive approval for their new order from Pope Paul III than the Augustinian Mainardi was bellowing at them from his pulpit. Less noisy but more effective was Cardinal Giudiccioni, who warned the Pope against these disturbing adventurers.

Inevitably, the existing orders looked warily upon these reformers who disdained ritual and promoted a strangely personal religion. Even before the Council of Trent, the great Dominican Melchor Cano set himself up as their most ferocious censor, seeing them as "Pelagians" who despised the power of grace. In Rome, meanwhile, Franciscans were condemning their conduct in the confessional as well as their friendliness toward women of easy virtue, while in Germany they were held to be heretic burners. But it was in Paris—in the heart of the university world where they had first met one another—that the "Iñiguists" would attract the most vicious assaults. Even before Étienne Pasquier, Paris had become the world capital of elegant Jesuit bashing by clerics and the untonsured alike.

But the only true begetter of Jesuitphobia, the man who raised the phenomenon to the level of a literary genre (and export product), was Étienne Pasquier. As the university's advocate in 1565 against the Jesuit "petitioners" seeking university affiliation for their schools, this eminent jurist had suffered defeat: Although he succeeded in blocking integration of the Jesuits into the Paris university establishment, he was unable to persuade the court to bar them altogether from teaching—which had been his chief goal. But his plea (and his invention of the fertile myth of the "secretive Jesuit") was translated into seven languages. It became the matrix of every subsequent anti-Jesuit campaign, the quarry from which all future Jesuit haters would mine their raw material.

This success, allied to his talent and his sincere convictions, impelled him further along the same road, from prosecutor to prophet. Appointed advocate general of the King's revenue court, he published in 1594 (sandwiched between two volumes of love poetry) *La Cathéchisme des jésuites, ou le Mystère d'iniquité révélé par ses supports par l'examen de leur doctrine même, selon la croyance de l'Église romaine* (The Jesuit Catechism, or the Mystery of Iniquity Revealed by Its Initiates Through an Examination of Their Very Doctrine, According to the Beliefs of the Roman Church). Its tone is playful. Pasquier, fierce in matters of substance, nevertheless favored the light approach. He put forward his thesis in the form of a story that from its opening words has the feel of an eighteenth-century tale: "Leaving Paris some two years ago, we chanced to fall in with six companions, some of us wending our way to Rome, others to Venice . . . " A promising beginning.

Nor is the rest of the story disappointing. Along their way, the companions are taken in by a local gentleman at whose home they meet "a Jesuit wearing disguise" ("My Order permits me this travesty in order that I may the more easily know men's hearts") and a "lawyer highly versed in the Bulls, Constitutions, and Ordinances of this order of Jesuits." Thus the stage is deftly set, with our author assuming the discreet role of recorder.

Despite his "disguise" (which he readily admits), the Jesuit presented by Étienne Pasquier is a poor illustration of the guile and hypocrisy attributed to his colleagues, for he bristles with effrontery, conceit, and bravado. "We hold our Company superior to all others," he boasts. He adds that its members swear two different kinds of vow, and that unlike the "solemn" orders, they are permitted to amass wealth or to take a wife, and refuse to separate matters of state from matters of religion.

Then, throwing caution to the winds, Pasquier's Jesuit begins to claim credit for the assassination ("for the greater glory of God") of various "evil-living" princes, whose killers, confessed beforehand, were thus assured of Paradise. "But," cries the lawyer, "Jesus objected when Saint Peter cut off the soldier's ear!" Not at all, says this curious messenger of religion: Jesus did not tell Peter not to take up his sword; He merely told him, after the blow was struck, to sheathe it again. "If your superiors told you to kill a sovereign," replies the lawyer, "would you then do it? And would you kill the Pope?" "Ah, for that I would have to counsel with myself for a whole day before replying."

The disguised Jesuit then launches into increasingly foolish and provocative utterances, declaring that one day of prayer in a Company house gave absolution for any crime; that the Company's General was fully empowered in every country to bestow all "Bachelor's, Master's, and Doctor's" degrees; or to practice medicine "if our Superiors consider us fit to do so," to censure and burn any book whatsoever "if we find therein the smallest hint of heresy"—and even burn the Pope himself "were we to find him straying from his ancient duties."

Étienne Pasquier does not tell us how this Jesuit was "disguised." But we may surmise that he was got up as some worldly gallant, some swaggering Renaissance bullyboy. Was the famous lawyer Pasquier unaware that making his adversary so foolish inevitably blunted his own satirical bite, and that his blows would have been shrewder if he had respected the laws of probability? Having thus depicted his foe as a bold and bloodthirsty humbug, he ends the chapter with the wish that the Jesuits be "exterminated from our France without hope of return."

The rest of the *Catechism* is a kind of chronicle of the unctuousness and ambiguity of the Ignatians, beginning with the founder himself, whom he calls "Ignoramus of Olé." But the strangest passage, and the least flattering one for the illustrious lawyer, is the one in which he attempts to equate Jesuits with Jews, the better to direct his barbs at both. The author imagines a debate in the bosom of a Christian gathering between Saint Peter and Ignatius of Loyola. When the Apostle rebukes the founder for usurping Jesus' name to designate his order, the General answers that it is from humility that he has given his people the Christian name of Jesus, "very common among Jews." Which provokes an "uproar" among their listeners, and draws this comment from the author: "They must be exterminated from our Church, for this remark shows clearly that there is much Jewry in Jesuitry: For here, just as the Jews of old put Our Lord Jesus Christ on trial, so did these new Jews accuse the Apostles. The which Apostles had known the virtue, strength, and incomparable greatness of this Holy Name, unknown to all Jews."*

Such was the indictment proposed by Étienne Pasquier,[2] a man who has been seen as the model of great French jurists, one of the pioneering spirits of Parliament under the *ancien régime.* The great lawyer's talent is not in dispute. But his *Catechism* makes embarrassing reading today, particularly when we consider the sway it so long exercised over the public mind. A century later, French Jesuitphobia would give the world Pascal's anti-Jesuit masterpiece, *The Provincial Letters.* But in the primitive hues lent it by Pasquier, Jesuitphobia looks more like a libelous and sterile tantrum—particularly in light of the fact that Father Coton, alongside Henry IV, was at that very time working toward the model of enlightened Christianity embodied in the tolerant Edict of Nantes.

And what part did Pasquier's pamphlet play in generating the rumor that, after ascribing the murder of Henry III (actually committed by a Dominican) to the Company, blamed it for the various attempts on Henry IV's life? It was Pasquier's friend the jurist Antoine Arnauld (father of the famous Jansenist) who most violently condemned these "agents of Spain . . . their hands bloody with the King's death, planned and undertaken in their schools."

The historian Robert Mousnier has examined the bases for this inference, which he finds absurd. He too points to its symbolic character, the Jesuits' enemies having forged a "myth of duplicity, of tortuous intrigue, of deceit, of vindictiveness."[3]

A hundred years later it must have seemed to many that Pasquier's bogeyman was already on its deathbed. Writing in the nineteenth century, the historian Charles-Augustin Sainte-Beuve observed of the seventeenth-century Company: "Brought into the world in 1540, it received its death wound in 1656. . . . It has been inwardly dying ever since. . . . The Jesuits come, go, come back again, intrigue, sow dissension, even attempt to do good, but they are not alive. . . . *Ed era morto.*"[4]

*Clearly Pasquier was not aware of the ethnic origins of the Apostles!

The year of that "death blow," 1656, also saw the publication of Blaise Pascal's *Lettres Provinciales*. Subtle, witty, and wide-ranging, the letters—the acknowledged masterpiece of anti-Jesuit literature—have been widely and exhaustively commented upon. Of all the shafts unloosed over the course of four centuries at the Company of Jesus, from Pasquier to Pombal to Pope Clement XIV, the *Provinciales* were the most devastating, calling into question Jesuit honor as well as the celebrated Jesuit "discernment," to the delight of the Company's enemies and the greater glory of the French language.

But the question here is not so much whether the Jesuits survived Pascal's onslaught intact or weakened or mutilated, but why this great order, dedicated a century earlier by a small group of noble adventurers to the service of Christ, reformation of the Church, and a heroic worldwide apostolate, should have been nailed to the pillory for doctrinal perversion and corruption by one of the greatest writers Christianity ever produced.

Many causes were here involved, moral and theological, social, diplomatic, political, and esthetic. French nationalism—and not just in its narrowly Gallican form—was a major factor, not so much in Pascal's strategy as in the minds of his readers, in the minds of those who sought to turn his cry of anger into a death sentence on the Jesuits. Gallicanism too was a major factor, as was anti-Spanish feeling (the Jesuits were after all known as "the Spanish" in their Latin Quarter days) in a country where the memory of the French-Spanish wars still rankled.

That a Company embodying the Roman Church's ascendancy over the Most Christian French King should be boldly attacked by a group of men—Pascal and the Jansenists—who simultaneously condemned contemporary mores (whose most flagrant example was the private life of the monarch) and the official theology underpinning both King and University, was clearly a threat to the State. The King (to whom the Jansenists were the equivalent of Oliver Cromwell's Puritans) saw only rebellion and refusal in the "reheated Calvinism" of the Jansenists of Port-Royal. "I will see to the destruction of the Jansenists," he confided to his *Memoirs*. And he did, giving the Company short-lived respite and revenge.

But why had this Company, which we have followed from Paris to Beijing and Yamaguchi, become the target of Pascal's charges of immorality, of the prostitution of faith and morals, and of insidious acquisition of all powers of Church and State—not to mention money? And what made so many ordinary French people happy to witness a psychodrama in which the Jesuits represented vice and the Jansenists virtue?

By the time Pascal wrote *The Provincial Letters*, the Company was seen in a dazzling variety of lights. First as a monument of baroque splendor, all organ blasts, trumpets, and triumphal song. As the defenders of free will in questions of the human soul. As the proponents of a casuistry and opportunism that made of them (at least from a Jansenist perspective) a school for theological laxism. As the upholders of a mystic rigor, the incarnation of activism and reform.

And what of the Jansenists? Clearly, the doctrine in whose name Pascal entered the lists was not simply a system of extreme Puritan morality, of belief in a harsh divine dispensation that reserved grace—and therefore salvation—to a chosen and predestined few. Nevertheless, Pascal was haunted by the universal corruption of a human nature irreversibly inclined to evil. At the heart of this sea of defilement, he felt called upon to wage a battle with no quarter asked or given, convinced, as François Mauriac has expressed it, that he lived among "lepers unaware of their leprosy." Pascal was the man who dared write: "We understand nothing of the works of God unless we accept the principle that He decided to blind some and open the eyes of others. There is enough brightness to enlighten the elect, and enough darkness to humble them. There is enough darkness to blind the outcasts and enough brightness to condemn them and set them beyond forgiveness."

It was this fundamental pessimism that bound Pascal to the certainty of a predestination that made him one of the elect but doomed Sodom, Gomorrha, and the rest of humankind to the fires of hell. As Mauriac has said, Pascal was not a desperate man, and that is because he believed himself a "member of the small group . . . of those preferred of God."[5] Mauriac adds the impious but inescapable question: "Did belief in the small number of elect reinforce his joy at being one of that number?" Not unlike people in a nuclear bomb shelter gloating over their escape? . . .

Hand in hand with this pessimism went the extraordinary courage of the Jansenists, their determination to "resist," which emboldened them to challenge all the powers of Church and State—and which won the cloistered group a wide and influential circle of supporters. So much so that Pascal's *Provinciales* were considered to have won the day against strong Jesuit counterblasts, at least in the eyes of all who did not actively execrate Port-Royal.

But the Jesuits had other weapons: Their credit at the Louvre, the Archbishopric of Paris, and the Vatican was immense. After Pascal's barbs had found their target and the storm had died down, the Assembly of the French clergy ordered all priests, religious, and nuns to sign a "formula" expressly condemning the theses of the Jansenists. Port-Royal and its innumerable supporters found themselves set before the wrenching dilemma either of breaking with the Church—which in October 1656, from Rome, delivered the most rigorous of condemnations, the bull *Ad Sacram*—or to recognize the heretical nature of the doctrine of predestination maintained by the Jansenists and Pascal.

As a layman, Blaise Pascal was not subject to the terrible decree. Indomitable to the end, he opposed signing the "formula." After the King, the Church of France, and the Vatican had condemned *The Provincial Letters*, placing it on the Index, he continued in his recalcitrance. A few months before his death, he had this to say about the condemned "letters":

"I have been asked whether I regret writing the *Provinciales*. I answer that, far from regretting them, if I had to do them now, I would make them even stronger."

We will not dwell further on *The Provincial Letters*, that miracle of biased argument, the apotheosis of deception illuminated (if not redeemed) by conviction, the masterpiece of anti-Jesuit literature. We would willingly concede it this honor, at least from a literary standpoint, if Saint-Évremond had not just previously (in 1669) published *La Conversation de M. d'Hocquincourt avec le père Canaye*. Saint-Évremond was no more concerned than Pascal with justice. His monk, sitting at the table of the Maréchal d'Hocquincourt,* is even more stupid, spineless, and conniving than the Jesuits who bicker over "sufficient grace" and deteriorating morals in *The Provincial Letters*.

When Father Canaye (who may once have been Saint-Évremond's teacher) speaks of war, security, horsemanship, or the Jansenists, he is depicted as incorrigibly frivolous and accommodating—exactly as the austere Jansenists must have seen the Jesuits. Under one heading at least, the author even falls into premeditated deception: He puts a highly improbable panegyric of war into the mouth of the Marshal's Jesuit table companion. In fact, though, one historian, René Ternois, quotes words actually spoken by Father Canaye, words that violently condemn war: "The world makes of this brutality its idol and honors nothing so much as the force of an arm that gives no quarter. So much so that it is today almost a maxim of nobility that he who spills another's blood ennobles his own. . . . I cannot accept that an insatiable yearning to harm others, which commonly styles itself valor, should lay claim to an honorable fame that it deserves not."

And can we give the smallest credit to these words put into Canaye's mouth in response to the author's question about "the great animosity between the Jansenists and your fathers . . . on the doctrine of grace":

"What madness," Canaye replied, "what madness to believe that we
hate each other for not having the same view of grace! It is neither
grace nor the five propositions that have stirred bad blood between us.
Envy of the right to rule consciences is the only culprit. The Jansenists
found us in possession of the government, and they wished to dislodge

*Originally in Cardinal Mazarin's service, and famous for his dalliances with Madame de Montbazon, this soldier ended his life in the service of Spain, killed by a Swiss bullet.

us. To attain their ends, they have employed means contrary to ours. We use gentleness and indulgence, they affect austerity and rigor. We comfort souls with the example of God's compassion. They affright them with examples of His retribution. They bring fear where we bring hope, and seek to make servants of those we would attract to us.

"It is not that one or the other does not purport to save men; but each seeks credit by saving them; and to speak frankly to you, the interests of the director almost always outweigh the salvation of the one he directs. I address you in different terms than those I used with the Marshal. With him I was purely Jesuit, and with you I have the frankness of a man of war."

But Saint-Évremond would laugh at our objections. Honesty has no place in such exercises. The important thing is the well-aimed dart. And *The Conversation Between M. d'Hocquincourt and Father Canaye* is itself a masterpiece, a comic opera opposing the gold-braided lout and the cassocked manipulator in an outpouring of cutting remarks and slapstick gestures. Indeed, it makes Saint-Évremond a precursor of Voltaire rather than Pascal.

But the fathers did not always inspire genius in their detractors. For every Pascal or Saint-Évremond there was a swarm of hysterical scribes and gutter falsifiers. A model of the species, a notch down the scale from Pasquier, was a certain Hieronymus Zahorowski, a Polish Jesuit expelled from the Company who became priest of a parish in Silesia. Drawing very freely upon the letters sent (under the title *Monita Generalia*, or General Instructions) to members of the Company by its Superior General Mutius Vitelleschi, Zahorowski wrote the *Monita Secreta* (Secret Instructions), in which he claimed to expose how the Society of Jesus built its power—by laying hands upon inheritances as well as consciences.

Like Pasquier's *Catechism*, the *Monita Secreta* was long considered to be the definitive revelation of Jesuit strategy. It was first published in Cracow, then in Prague and Padua. A trilingual version (with a French translation) appeared in Paris in 1661, its publisher asserting that the sensational document had come to light during the sack of Paderborn (where the Jesuits had a school) by the Duke of Brunswick. Although the *Monita Secreta* was immediately denounced as a forgery by Church authorities, including the Archbishop of Cracow, a new French edition appeared in 1761: Within the context of the Parliamentary struggle which was to lead a year later to the Company's expulsion, it was an enormous success.

It is surprising that this laborious forgery, heavily caricatural, as stupid as Pasquier's Jesuit portrait, should so long have been believed.

But because of the book's legendary aura, and because it was a mine of inspiration for what might be called run-of-the-mill Jesuitphobia, we must give it at least passing due. Here, in 1612, are the seeds of the next three centuries of libel and slander and gossip—which would later find their way into works of higher quality.

From Chapter One:

> You must give to the poor for the edification of those who do not yet know the Company and to encourage them to be so much the more generous to us. . . .

> If our people engage in investment, let it be under names borrowed from loyal friends who will keep it secret, in order that our poverty appear the greater. . . .

> Let only the Provincial of each province know exactly what our revenues are; but let what is in the treasury in Rome remain a holy mystery.

And Chapter Two:

> We must make every effort to win everywhere the ears and minds of princes and of the most considerable persons, in order that no one whatsoever dare rise against us; but on the contrary that everyone should be obliged to depend upon us.

> . . . Experience teaches us that princes and great lords are fondest of people of the Church who hide their odious actions, and that they interpret such actions in a favorable light; as we may note in the marriages they contract with their relatives or allies, or in similar matters. We must encourage those who so do, giving them reason to hope that they may through our intercession earn the dispensation of the Pope . . . on the pretext of the common weal and the greater glory of God, which is the Society's goal.

> Above all we must win over the favorites and servants of princes, that they may faithfully report to us on mood and inclinations of princes and the great.

> Princesses are readily to be won over through the ladies of their chamber, for which purpose their friendship must be courted, since we shall thus everywhere be made party to even the most secret of family matters.

Chapter Five is entitled "How We Must Conduct Ourselves Toward the Religious Performing the Same Duties in Church as Ourselves."

> We must steadfastly suffer this sort of person, at the same time letting princes and all persons of authority who may be bound to us know that our Society represents the perfection of all other Orders combined.

. . . Let the faults of other religious be spied out and noted, and discreetly revealed and imparted, as if in dismay, to our loyal friends . . .

Nor was this the height of the stupidities scaled by the *Monita Secreta*. Chapter Six, "How to Ensnare Rich Widows," goes to the heart of the matter:

For this, choose fathers advanced in years, of lively appearance and pleasant discourse; let them visit such widows. . . . Let these be provided with confessors by whom they will be properly directed with a view to maintaining them in widowed condition, even by . . . telling them that they will thereby earn eternal and most effective merit and spare themselves the pain of Purgatory. . . . As much money as possible must be extorted from widows. . . . Let them be permitted, moderately and discreetly, what they ask to satisfy their sensual urges. . . . Let them be permitted to consort and disport themselves with whomsoever they prefer. . . . And suffer this kind of widow to see no other sort of priest on any pretext whatsoever.

Chapter Eighteen is perhaps the most repulsive of all. In it Zahorowski, in the guise of General of his order, holds forth on the way in which children of widows are to be led toward the monastic condition in order to secure their inheritances for the Company. "Mothers must be taught to imbue their infants with sorrow from their tenderest years . . . " Here, however, the Polish priest appears to have caught himself in his own trap, and his murderous assault falters. He began with parody, but now finds himself floundering over the meaning of the Sixth Commandment: "If two of our own have sinned carnally, let him who first confesses be permitted to remain in the Society and the other be banished. But let the one who is kept be so harshly mortified and ill-treated that from remorse and impatience he gives reason for being himself expelled."

And even more shocking: "We must . . . incite all princes . . . to wage bloody war on one another so that our succor is constantly implored. And finally, the Society . . . shall strive at least to be feared by those that do not love it."

We are tempted to imagine Zahorowski, as he wrote that final line, smiling to himself and thinking that this time he had really overstepped the line beyond which he could expect to be taken seriously.

But no. And what is surprising in this tissue of vulgar rubbish (which the Protestant historian Gabriel Monod calls an "unsustainable fable") is not that someone ejected from the Company (for an offense apparently unconnected with the one mentioned above) should have devoted long hours to revenge. It is that the *Monita Secreta* was considered by intelligent people, during the Enlightenment and deep into the nineteenth century, to be a faithful reflection of the methods and procedure of the Company Loyola had founded and Francis

Xavier glorified. It is the fact that a Paris court accepted this libel as evidence during the trial that culminated in the Company's expulsion from France in 1762. That is the true cause for wonder. As we have said, we would not have bothered to quote such drivel had the *Monita* not served as perennial fodder in anti-Jesuit campaigns, its role in every respect comparable to that played by *The Protocols of the Elders of Zion* in anti-Semitic propaganda.

Nor is the parallel with the *Protocols* merely casual: Both are forgeries, with the same crude manner, the same unremitting underhandedness, the same concern to cloak a perceived manipulation in the mantle of secrecy and power, the same across-the-board denunciation of a mysterious group, the same charges of inciting the powers to war.

The Belgian Jesuit Pierre Charles dedicated much of his life to proving that the *Protocols* were a Tsarist police forgery dating from the first years of the twentieth century. Could those expert Jew-baiters have had the *Monita* in mind? Anti-Semitism is of course a far cry from Jesuit-baiting, just as being a Jew is a far cry from being a Jesuit. Yet the *Protocols of the Elders of Zion* extends the following curiously collegial compliment to the Company of Jesus: "Only the Jesuits could rival us in political manipulation; but we have succeeded in discrediting them in the eyes of the unthinking mob because they were a visible body, whereas we remain in the shadows with our secret organization."

In *Mythes et mythologies politiques*,[6] Raoul Girardet powerfully equates the obsessions of anti-Semitism with those that drive hostility to the Jesuits and Freemasons. He points out that perhaps the most violent of the countless caricatures of the Jesuits is that of Father Rodin in Eugène Sue's notorious *Wandering Jew*. Rodin brings to mind the fictitious Grand Rabbi of Prague of the *Protocols*, who speaks of crushing the States of Europe in the "vise" of Judaism. The same relentless obsessions, the same bogeymen.

The *Monita* did not become famous overnight. Long ignored, or overshadowed by Pascal's masterpiece, Zahorowski's malicious squib did not take on the dimensions of a social phenomenon until the second half of the eighteenth century, when the Company of Jesus had become the target of wholesale campaigns as a result of its intervention in the second so-called Jansenist crisis in France, the one that stirred up so much fury over the papal bull *Unigenitus*. That monument of spiritual oppression ordered confessors to deny absolution to any penitent unable to furnish proof of his opposition to Jansenist tenets.

The Company (supplying only one out of nine consultants in the process) apparently played only a minor role in the drafting of the infamous bull. But if the Jesuits did not dream up this inquisitorial text, they were active in its practical implementation—which drew down on them a richly deserved oppro-brium. It is thus not surprising that the Jansenists, who were well represented in legal and Parliamentary circles and were tactical allies of the "philosophers," pressed their counterattacks home without quarter.

Witness this indictment by the famous Jansenist lawyer Le Paige, who as-serted that Ignatius's Company, "the enemy of all orders, all rules, of all disci-plined society . . . seeks only to set itself up as a universal despotism and to bring about in the Catholic world all the evils that have seen the light of day in the last two centuries."[7]

And d'Alembert, despite his coolness toward the Jansenists (he even consid-ered the Jesuits to be "less fanatical" than their enemies), did not hesitate to turn the Company's entry in his *Encyclopédie* into a compendium of hoary anti-Jesuit myth, particularly on the subject of regicide:

> Subject to the most excessive despotism within their house, the
> Jesuits are its most shameless propagators within the State. . . . They
> ascribe infallibility and universal domination to the Pope so that, be-
> ing masters of one man alone, they may be masters of all. . . .
>
> In 1593, Barrière was armed with a dagger against the best of Kings
> [Henry III] by the Jesuit Varade. . . . In 1594, the Jesuits were driven
> from France as accomplices in the parricide of Jean Châtel. . . . In
> 1610, Ravaillac assassinated Henry IV. The Jesuits remain under suspi-
> cion of guiding his hand. . . .
>
> In 1757, a parricidal attempt was made upon our Monarch Louis
> XV, and this by a man [Damiens] who had dwelt in the halls of the
> Society of Jesus, a man these fathers protected and placed in various
> of their houses. And in the same year they published an edition by
> one of their classic authors [Father Marianna] which teaches the doc-
> trine of the murder of Kings, as they did immediately after the assas-
> sination of Henry IV. Same circumstances, same comportment . . .
>
> In the span of two hundred years there is no order of villainy this
> race of men has not committed.

D'Alembert of course knew that the "Jesuit theory" of tyrannicide was shared by the majority of Catholic thinkers. Nor could he have been unaware that the Company had neither inspired nor armed Ravaillac or Damiens, and that in the cases of Barrière and Châtel, King Henry himself had personally ex-onerated his Jesuit friends. But to the great thinker and encylopedist the inter-ests of "philosophy" outweighed the dictates of truth.

Even if d'Alembert had been inclined to more moderate views, Denis Diderot would have brought him back on course, directing as he did all his brilliant fury at these folk "abandoned to commerce, to intrigue, to politics, and to occupations alien to their condition and unworthy of their profession,"* and in consequence fallen "into the contempt which followed and which will always follow, at all times and in all religious houses, the decline of study and the corruption of morals." The latter shaft is open to debate; not the former, for Jesuit teaching† was not at its apogee at the time of the *Encyclopédie*. Nevertheless, it was good enough in comparison to other educational offerings for Frederick II to refuse to prohibit it in his country.

We have seen‡ the great Parliamentary offensive against a Company discredited by its crusade in defense of the bull *Unigenitus*, tainted by the scandals surrounding Father de Lavalette's financial dealings in Martinique, harassed by the concerted attacks of the Jansenists and *philosophes*. We have read various indictments pronounced against it by Parliamentary jurists assigned to examine the Society's *Constitutions*. But it was a good Christian and a decent man, Counselor de La Chalotais, royal prosecutor of the Rennes Parliament, who delivered the most crippling blows. He was, he said, "alarmed at the ease with which a General of the Jesuits could intrigue, spin alliances, and let us be frank, plot. A man with twenty thousand Subjects devoted to his orders, ready to shed their blood for the Society . . . , accustomed to the yoke of the most absolute obedience, to considering their General as God, as Jesus Christ . . . ; a despot whose slightest gesture is law, whose written letter is a decree, an ordinance, who holds in his hands the profits of the Society's commerce, is informed 177 times a year of events in every Kingdom: What can he not undertake?"

This time the indictment rings true. Here the old Gallican argument is productive of more than bombast. Although the surprise manifested at the time by most censors was feigned, since the founding texts of the Society had long since been published and disseminated, nevertheless, the potential threat denounced by La Chalotais was cause for alarm to any lawmaker at a time when the French monarchy, anticipating Revolution, had officially founded the nation-state.

By proclaiming the doctrine implicit in the Company's *Constitutions* "seditious, detrimental to the Royal power, likely to stir up the greatest disturbances in his states," the Paris Parliament made itself the precursor of the Revolutionary Assemblies, of the Civil Constitution of the Clergy, and the Concordat of 1801: political Gallicanism emerging from under its religious and legal variants. Here we have fleetingly "decoupled" ourselves from social myth and the fantasies it

*A profession for which he had little respect!
†Of which Diderot, like Voltaire, was a product.
‡In Chapter IX.

spawned to return to realities (even if the condemnation of the Jesuits at Rennes and Paris took on the hyperbolic form inherited from Pasquier and Pascal).

Curiously, the years of Revolution were no golden age for Jesuitphobia. The "men in black" were not the targets of the sansculottes. Was this because the Company had been banished from France for thirty years? Not at all! Jesuit-hunters were in no more need of real targets than Jew-baiters. But it would take Napoleon's dramatic and visionary genius for the Jesuit to return to the historical stage.

The Emperor was not the man to deprive his grand opera of such a fellow player. The "Fathers of the Sacred Heart," the "Paccanarists," and the "Fathers of the Faith" were small fry only to small minds, to "lawyers" and "ideologues." Napoleon, however, saw right through them—and ruthlessly pursued "this Society dominant by nature and in consequence the irreconcilable foe of everything that constitutes power."

Thus did the eagle's gaze resurrect the fathers from oblivion. And in the eagle's fall the Jesuits would find resurgence. What an enthralling sequence of major historical events—Pius VII's flight from Fontainebleau at the outset of the Hundred Days,* the Emperor's abdication in that same Fontainebleau, and the solemn restoration of the Company! As if the world were too small to hold Napoleon and Loyola at one and the same time . . .

The Roman ceremony of August 7, 1814, which seemed to have set the stage for a glorious resurrection of the Company, in fact ushered in the golden age of literary Jesuitphobia. It is true that nothing was published between 1814 and 1860 to rival the writings of Pascal and Saint-Évremond. But those five decades saw an outpouring of verse, lampoon, and song that would fatten the world's anti-Jesuit arsenal from Saint Petersburg to Paris and Rome to Luxembourg. And all this at a time when the fathers numbered sometimes only in the hundreds, had few schools, and in fact were concentrating their pressure on the Papacy rather than on lay princes and civil societies.

It was at this low point, with the intellectual reach of the Jesuits as enfeebled as their financial or economic reserves, that Jesuit-baiting assumed its purest form, its essence, its "water," as we say of a diamond, its ideal guise, resonant and rampaging—while a few wondered about the reality of this monster. The perfect bogeyman, a schoolboy nightmare, a chimera whose very formlessness made it more dreadful. The Jesuits . . .

Here they stood, these few hundred (later to be a few thousand) Jesuits, admittedly readopted and exalted anew by the Pope (what, though, was a Pope in this restless nineteenth century?) but shorn of their old influence over the sov-

*Napoleon's return from Elba on March 1, 1815, to his abdication on June 22, 1815, after Waterloo.

ereigns of Europe. Handled most gingerly by Louis XVIII, betrayed by Charles X, disdained by Louis-Philippe, eclipsed by the Dominicans, and equated by the victorious bourgeoisie with the unlamented symbols of the *ancien régime,* they would now face the assault of political, intellectual, and literary forces that found an enduring scapegoat for its frustrations in this shrunken, withered Company with its desperate hold on the past.

As before, the Jesuits were characterized as "half-foxes, half-wolves," fawning and slinking in manner, ruthless and insatiable in action. But if the outward image was relatively harmless popular lore, other attacks took more serious form.

On April 23, 1843, the lecture on history and morality at the Collège de France was heckled by a dozen or so young people who applauded every time the illustrious anticlericalist on the podium made any kind of reference to Christianity. The lecturer was Jules Michelet, revered as the author of the monumental *Histoire de France.* Every time he mentioned the word "Providence" the applause burst forth. Breathless, outraged, he stopped speaking, while his friends seized hold of one or two of the hecklers and threw them out. The noisy claque attempted to repeat its performance when Michelet resumed the lecture series on May 4, but this time their victims were ready. The renowned historian, acclaimed by almost all sectors of the press, had triumphed over the Jesuits—for no one doubted that (whether or not they had been put up to it by the Company's superiors) the handful of hecklers was objecting to the violent indictment* of the Jesuits they perceived Michelet's latest series of lectures to be.

Three months later Michelet's four lectures on the Jesuits were published, to be reissued a few years later in a collection entitled *Les Jésuites,* with this note by the publisher, Flammarion: "There was never a more successful book. When it first appeared six printings were sold out in eight months despite foreign forgeries. The work was translated into all languages."

The publisher went on to assure readers that this was "the actual text of the lectures that raised such a tempest." *Les Jésuites* opens with a magisterial Introduction by the crusading teacher, a broadside that pulverizes the whole length of the enemy's beam:

> God only knows what the future holds for us! . . . Only I beseech Him,
> if He should strike us again, to strike us with the sword. Wounds in-
> flicted by the sword are clean visible wounds, which bleed and which
> heal. But what of those shameful sores we hide, which persist, and
> which implacably worsen? Those wounds, the ones we fear most, come
> from the insinuation into the things of God of a police mentality, of a
> spirit of pious intrigue, of holy betrayal—the spirit of the Jesuits.

*Both "violent" and "indictment," as readers will see, are a drastic understatement.

God give us ten times over political and military tyranny, every kind of tyranny, rather than that such a police mentality ever sully our France . . . ! At least tyranny sometimes has the merit of kindling national spirit: We break it or it breaks of itself. . . . But once feeling is extinguished and the gangrene well advanced in your flesh and your bones, how will you expunge it . . . ? Death kills only the body, but what remains when the soul dies? Death when it kills you allows you to live on in your sons. Here you lose both your sons and the future.

Jesuitry, the police and informer mentality, the low habits of the tattletale schoolboy, once transported from school and convent into open society, what a hideous prospect . . . ! A whole people living like a house of Jesuits, in other words occupied from top to bottom with informing on one another. Betrayal in the very home, wife informing on husband, child on mother. . . . Be assured that this is no imagined picture. From where I stand I see peoples daily thrust deeper by the fathers into this hell of eternal mire. . . . While we were wondering whether there actually were any Jesuits, they deftly stole our thirty or forty thousand priests out from under our noses and took them God knows where!

"Are there Jesuits?" Such a question, when already they rule your wife through her confessor—your wife, house, table, hearth, bed. . . . Tomorrow they will have your child.[8]

But let us return to Michelet's incendiary lectures of 1843.

"Take the first passerby and ask him, 'What are the Jesuits?' He will at once reply: 'Counterrevolution.' "

Here the historian had hit on at least part of the truth—of the journalistic kind. For such a statement, once made, can hardly be denied, and the fathers themselves would willingly have owned it. But Michelet follows this straightforward statement with outright low-grade provocation: "Study the Jesuits' books, and all you will find is one message, *the death of freedom.*"

For Michelet, there were "but two parties in France: *the spirit of life and the spirit of death.*" He modestly adds that perhaps thanks to himself "the progress of the men of death will be arrested. . . . Light has flickered within the tomb. . . . We know and we shall know still better how these returning ghosts have stolen in through the night. . . . How, as we slept, they crept in on wolf's paws and surprised defenseless people, priests and women, religious houses . . . "

But how had this "progress of the men of death" found a footing in a country like France, in which public opinion was so lively, where history moved so inexorably toward freedom?

No matter how high one's opinion of Jesuit skill, it would not suffice

to explain such a result. There is a mysterious hand in all this. . . .
The hand which, well directed, has since the world's first day gently
worked miracles of guile. A weak hand which nothing can with-
stand—the hand of woman. The Jesuits have used the instrument of
which Saint Jerome spoke: "Poor little women, all covered in sin!"[9]

Are these the same people the seething historian calls "the Jesuitesses, delicate and sweet-mannered, clever and charming, who, eternally walking ahead
of the Jesuits, have everywhere spread oil and honey, softening the path"—and
the more dangerously so since, under their name of Ladies of the Sacred Heart,
they have "enjoyed the same Constitutions since 1823"?

With all the respect due this giant of French history, we have to observe that
here he is scraping the bottom of the barrel. It had seemed that from Pasquier to
Pascal and d'Alembert to Montlosier we had established a full inventory of the
various forms of Jesuitphobia—the Gallican, the Jansenist, the strategic, the
Bourbon, the devout—and counted up every kind of bogeyman or phantom in
this haunted domain. But how moderate Pascal appears, and how punctilious
about the truth, and how self-controlled, when we compare his *Provincial
Letters* to such frenzied pomposities! The Jesuit enemy facing the great defender
of the Jansenists had been powerful. He held on to power, confessed the King,
distributed livings, supervised the schools. He could hunt and strike, and did.
But the Jesuits of Michelet's day?

The author of the *Histoire de France* had this answer for the people who inevitably questioned him about the numbers and real strength of his enemies:

According to one who believes himself well informed,* it seems that
there are now in France more than 490; when the Revolution began
there were 423. At that time they were concentrated in a handful of
houses; today they are scattered throughout every diocese. At this
moment they are spreading everywhere. They obtain papal requests
for their services from Mexico and New Granada. Already masters of
the Valais, they have just seized Lucerne and the smaller Cantons.[10]

And at the end of his series of lectures, Michelet picked up an old parallel,
Pasquier's invention, one sure to arouse anger and fear: Faced with this Jesuit
invasion, "dear old France appeared to slumber. They wrote to one another, like
the Jews of old Portugal: 'Come quickly, the land is good, the people are fools, it
will all belong to us.'"

Nine hundred and sixty Jesuits and their dozen fake-student hecklers—it
was enough to terrify this great historian as he spoke of history and morality

*Scarcely the language of a historian! The writer who had accounted for the smallest pike section in
the army of 1793 could not make a personal tally of these Jesuits? Did he fail to do so in order to
deepen the desired impression of mystery?

from his lofty podium, a historian acclaimed throughout Europe, surrounded by his disciples and supporters, supported almost without a dissenting voice by the press, a seer whose books were best-sellers.

But blinded by rage though he was, Michelet was aware how pathetic the enemy must seem when painted in such colors. He therefore exposed him in his sphere of influence, in the sway he exercised over parishes and the clergy:

> You have forty thousand pulpits which you urge or you force to speak out; you have a hundred thousand confessionals from which you stir up dissension in the family; you hold in your hands what is the basis of the family (of the world!); you hold the *mother* (the child is merely an accessory). So what will a husband do when he returns to his home and she falls in his arms and cries, "I am doomed!" You can be sure that he will deliver his son to you the very next day. . . . Twenty thousand children in your little seminaries! And soon one hundred thousand in the schools you rule! Millions of women who act only through you.

And in *Le Prêtre, la Femme, la Famille* (Priest, Woman, and Family), Michelet violently sums up his perception of the Society of Jesus: "Having taken the family by surprise, hypnotized the mother and won the child, having through devilish artifice raised the *man-machine*, we realized we had created a monster, whose only idea, life, or act is *murder*, as simple as that."[11]

There are two powerful leitmotifs in the avalanche of criminal denunciation Michelet rained down from his place of eminence. The first was based on the fundamental nature of Jesuitry: According to Michelet, this was the substitution of the *mechanical* for the *organic*, of the "spirit of death" for that of life. It could take the form of mind control, lethally rigorous discipline, or an educational technique aimed only at taming and destroying the spirit of freedom—that peculiarly Jesuit education which for the professor-prosecutor of the Collège de France was "a machine for shrinking heads and flattening minds." (We are entitled at this point, however, to wonder about the illustrious pupils and famous disciples raised by the fathers.)

The historian draws a further conclusion from this sterile mechanization of the "spirit of death," notably that the Jesuits created nothing, invented nothing, left nothing to posterity. Seeing them only as "flavorless writers, ponderous pedants, grotesque posturers," he states:

> The most potent satire on the Jesuits is one they themselves have created—their art, the paintings and sculpture they have inspired, all dimpled decrepit coquetry, simpering where it seeks to smile, those ridiculous sidelong glances, those expiring gazes, and all the cluttered rest . . .

As with art so with men. It is difficult, I admit it, to augur well for the souls of those who beget such art, who call forth such pictures, strew their churches with them, distribute them by the thousand and the million. Such taste is a serious sign. Many immoral people retain some sense of elegance. But willingly to opt for the false and the ugly, the soul must be at its lowest point.

Michelet sees "not a single man of genius" in the Company's history. Even in its accomplishments he sees "nothing fertile," not even in its missions—a blanket denial that would have astonished Montesquieu and Voltaire. And, concluding his scorched-earth campaign, he finds the strength to charge Ignatius, Francis Xavier, and Matteo Ricci with indulging in "more police than policy." Basically, he says, "you have only one achievement to your credit: a code" (which he graciously refrains from calling "penal").

But our frothing French nationalist reserves his harshest salvo for last:
Where have you come from? What paths did you take to come here? The French sentinel must have been slumbering at the frontier that night, for he did not see you pass. But I saw you coming by the light of day, O men who see in the dark; I remember it only too well, and I remember those who brought you. Your name is . . . *foreigner.*

The cry of alarm has gone up . . . And who dare say it is too soon? And we, what are we in the face of these great forces? One voice, that is all; one voice to warn France. . . . Now she has been warned; let her do as she will. She sees and feels the net in which the enemy hoped to snare her as she slept.[12]

This is where Michelet truly reveals himself—the prophet of nationalism, Cassandra facing the Roman horse, political Gallican. His Jesuit is not Pascal's, d'Alembert's, or Stendhal's. He is the Jesuit of Pasquier and the Jansenists. He is the agent of foreign powers, the expatriate fifth column, the enemy of the patriot. And, alas, it was with this chimera that he drew his strongest support.

It is perhaps worth adding that Michelet's fellow teacher and historian Edgar Quinet, a colleague at the Collège de France, and a man reputed to be more moderate than Michelet in his anti-Jesuit campaigns, drew a tart rebuff from the Protestant historian Gabriel Monod. In his 1909 lectures on the evangelization of China, Monod harked back to a story told by Quinet about Monsignor de Tournon, a French prelate sent to investigate Church matters in Beijing, arrested at the instigation of the Jesuits, and left to die in prison. There Monod halted: "As many mistakes as there are words. Tournon was Italian. He was not arrested by the Jesuits. He did not die in prison. Arrested in 1705, he was quickly released, returned to Europe, was made a Cardinal, and died peacefully in 1710."

* * *

Thus by the mid-nineteenth century Jesuitphobia had sunk to truly low levels. Where were Saint-Évremond, Pascal, and Diderot? Would anti-Ignatian passion now have to be whipped up by the spluttering rage of a great historian blinded by his hatred, or a demagogic pamphleteer with a swashbuckling pen? It is tempting to turn instead to the cheerful imaginings of Alexandre Dumas who (in the *Le Vicomte de Bragelonne*) makes his beloved Aramis a Jesuit General capable of replacing Louis XIV (too recalcitrant for the Company's liking) with his more amenable twin brother.

But let us eschew Dumas's delectable vision and look at two addresses delivered to Parliament by the great poet-politician Victor Hugo, in which the sounds of the Gallicanism of the grand old school once again ring out. The occasion was a Parliamentary debate in January 1850 over a draft law aimed at restoring the Church's right to teach and run French schools. They represent Hugo's most vitriolic indictment of the "Jesuitization" of French education and of the "clerical party" he believed to be inspired by the fathers.

> This bill . . . proposes a privileged status for this wretched Ultramontane clique to whose tender cares public education is to be abandoned [*Cries of "Yes! Yes!"*]. . . . As for our Jesuit adversaries, as for these zealots of the Inquisition,* as for these terrorists of the Church [*Applause*] . . . I say this to them:
> Stop throwing in our faces the Terror and the days when people shouted, "Divine heart of Marat! divine heart of Jesus!"† We no more confuse Christ with Marat than we confuse Him with you! We no more confuse Liberty with the Terror than we confuse Christianity with Loyola's Society; we do not confuse the cross of God-the-Lamb and God-the-Dove with the cross of Saint Dominic; we do not confuse the martyr of Golgotha with the executioners of Saint Bartholomew's. . . . Nor do we confuse our religion, our religion of peace and love, with this loathsome sect, everywhere disguised and everywhere unmasked, which, having preached the killing of kings, now preaches the oppression of nations [*"Hear! Hear!"*]; which suits its sins to the ages it lives through, doing today with calumny what it once did with the stake, murdering reputations because it can no longer roast human beings, blackening the century because it can no longer butcher the people, odious school for despots, den of sacrilege and hypocrisy, which innocently utters unspeakable things, which

*As we have seen, on this score Hugo was misinformed . . .

†A counterrevolutionary Jesuit theme had indeed been that the new French Constitution had "Christified" Marat.

stirs maxims of death into the Gospel message and poisons the holy water! [*Sustained applause*]

As for the Jesuit party [*Commotion on the right*] which is today the heart of the reactionary movement although even the reactionaries are unaware of it; this party in whose eyes thought is a misdemeanor, reading a felony, writing a felony, and publishing an act of murder [*Commotion*]; as for this party, which understands nothing of this century to which it does not belong; which today calls for taxation of the press, censorship for our theaters, anathema on our books, condemnation of our ideas, suppression of our progress, and which in another age would have called down proscription upon our heads (*"Hear! Hear! Bravo!"*); this party of absolutism, of immobility, of silence, of darkness, of monkish obscurantism; this party which dreams of giving France not France's future but Spain's past. . . . It invokes in vain its ancient glories; in vain it dusts off its musty doctrines, dark with human blood; in vain it sets every kind of ambuscade and trap for all that is justice and law; in vain does it accomplish every underhanded chore and assume in every century and on every scaffold the part of hangman; in vain does it insinuate itself into our government, our diplomacy, our schools, our electoral booths, our laws, all our laws, in particular the one we are considering today; in vain does it pursue and achieve all this. . . . But let it be aware (and I am surprised to reflect that I once thought the contrary*); yes, let it know this—the days when it represented a danger to the public weal are over! [*"Yes! Yes!"*]

Yes, it is now distraught, reduced to exploiting small men, to the indignity of small means, obliged in order to attack us to wield the freedom of the press which it once sought to kill and which is now killing it [*Applause*], itself heretical in its methods, doomed to seek the support of Voltaireans in public life and in the counting houses of the Jews whom it would like to burn at the stake [*Applause, explosions of mirth*], mumbling its odious praises of the Inquisition in the heart of the nineteenth century. . . . The Jesuit party can now be nothing to us but an object of astonishment, an aberration, a phenomenon, a freak [*Laughter*], a miracle, if the word pleases them [*General laughter*], something as strange and hideous as an owl† aloft in broad

*The young Victor Hugo had been a loyalist and clericalist.
†Even in the heat of parliamentary debate, Hugo could not resist reaching into his vast ornithological baggage.

daylight [*Sharp intake of breath*], nothing more. . . . It disgusts us, yes; but it no longer frightens us! Let it be aware of this, and be modest! No, it does not frighten us! No, this Jesuit party will not slaughter us: the sun is too bright for that. [*Prolonged applause*][13]

This Jovian drumroll, of the kind that had once drowned the voices of men going to the guillotine, offers almost as many absurdities as Michelet's history courses. But the poet here has three advantages over the historian: Pulsating eloquence was expected of him, not truth; and he was speaking in a place—the hall of Parliament—where moderation and fairness most decidedly were not the rule.

France had thus been for centuries the promised land of Jesuitphobia, both as a political rallying cry and as a literary genre. From Pascal to Hugo at the crests, from Pasquier to Eugène Sue in the troughs, it flourished and prospered without ever suffering commensurate counterattack. But, no matter how powerful the Gallican dimension of Jesuitphobia, it flourished of course beyond France's frontiers. Once an international organization attracts hatred, that hatred becomes universal too, encompassing Pombal in Lisbon and Charles III in Madrid just as it had encompassed the Jansenists in eighteenth-century Paris.

And "hatred" is not too strong a word to characterize Anglo-Saxon attitudes to the Company. In England fears of a Popish Plot had long haunted decent minds. But from Bloody Mary to James II, from the "Invincible Armada" to the Gunpowder Plot, from Titus Oates to Queen Elizabeth's foreign confessor Father Colombière (beatified in 1992), we are not really talking of the kind of collective psychosis that drove the paranoid fantasies of a Michelet or a Hugo. For in the British case the plot did take solid shape, no matter how absurd its methods sometimes were. From Madrid to Versailles, the Jesuit network was shamelessly deployed against Anglicanism, fomenting Mary Stuart's Scottish revolt and uprisings in Ireland. Here, hatred of the Company was not a figment of vaporous obsessions, of "Black Legend" nightmares. It was founded on harsh realities—no matter how adroitly they were manipulated by the powers behind the English throne.

Nor were the anti-Jesuit campaigns that flourished in the Italy of the *Risorgimento* baseless witch hunts. For the Company of Jesus had been so hostile to Italian unity, to the establishment of Rome as the national capital, to the birth of the secular state, that the diatribes of Mazzini and Garibaldi seem models of reason beside the flights of French poets and historians of the same period. The Company's Italian strategy was plain, and it rightly suffered the consequences.

In Russia too, so long a refuge of the Jesuits, the Company's growing influence at the courts of Catherine, then of Paul, then of Alexander (culminating in their expulsion from the Empire in 1820), inevitably stirred rancor. No need to be a Pan-Slav to condemn the fathers' influence over the aristocracy of Saint Petersburg or to fume over the conversion to Catholicism of a prince of the blood.

In the century following its restoration, the "Second Company" continued to adapt, with varying success, to change. From its first footholds in Asia and the Americas, the Company was now represented around the world. We have space here to glance at just one nineteenth-century Jesuit missionary, Pierre-Jean De Smet, who with indomitable energy followed in the footsteps of the Company's North American pioneers—Jean de Brébeuf, Jacques Marquette, Father Charlevoix.

The eighth son of a Belgian shipbuilder reputed to have sired twenty-two offspring, the stocky, powerfully built De Smet ("Samson" was his nickname) had the bright blue eyes and rosy complexion of a Flemish peasant. In his long career as trailblazer on the Upper Missouri and the Rocky Mountains, he carried the Gospel to the Tetes Plates, Nez Percé, Blackfoot, and Gros Ventres, and helped pacify the Sioux. He was the Indian's permanent advocate in Washington; he conferred with President Abraham Lincoln and Sitting Bull and was the friend of paramount chief Pananiapappi—but also of General William S. Harney, of the "father of Oregon," John McLoughlin, and of John James Audubon. He wrote a half dozen classic works on Indian customs and culture. He was a botanist, a trapper, and one of the giants of Western lore, giving his name to two North American cities, one in Idaho, the other in South Dakota.

By the time De Smet, then in his early twenties, reached North America, the Indian nation was already being pushed steadily westward in the path of white settlement, with each successive move leaving the tribes more dislocated, more distanced from their traditional ways, and—even when not herded onto "reservations"—doomed to perpetual hunger, dependence, and begging. Nor is there any indication that the Jesuits strove to counter this predatory policy in Washington. But De Smet and the "Black Robes," as the Indians called them, were to accompany this great exodus, from river to river and mountain to mountain, from distress to famine and despair, and finally to the bloody uprisings of the Sioux people in 1862 and 1876. Along this painful road, De Smet dreamed of recreating the Jesuit settlements of Paraguay—as much to preserve the language and customs of the Indians as to evangelize—complete with churches, workshops, education, and music. It was a dream never to be realized.

From his superiors in Rome, De Smet (a man they held to be of spotty education, and "excessively sensitive" to the doleful events he witnessed) received disapproving sniffs. Superior General Jan Philipp Roothaan let him know that he was suspected of possessing scant respect for his vow of poverty, of acting "as if his funds were for him to use as he saw fit," and of making impossible promises to the Indians.

But to the authorities in Washington, well aware of the tragedies piling up ahead, De Smet appeared in a totally different light. In 1851, Colonel Donald Mitchell, federal Superintendent of Indian Affairs, called a meeting of the major tribes east of the Rockies to discuss the opening of trails through Indian teritory, the construction of forts to defend them, and an annual indemnity to be paid to the tribes. For the meeting, held at Fort Laramie in Cheyenne country in southeast Wyoming, Mitchell needed an Indian expert. He chose De Smet. Trusting in the good faith of the U.S. government, the Flemish Jesuit firmly advocated Mitchell's proposals, which were accepted by the Dakota Sioux and Cheyenne after twelve days of palaver. "This council is the beginning of a new era for the red men," De Smet commented. "Henceforth, travelers will be able to cross the wilderness unmolested, and the Indians will have nothing more to fear from ill-disposed white men." History does not tell us what the expression was on Mitchell's face as the Jesuit spoke nor what the commander of the army detachment present was thinking. But the report that went back to Washington made it clear that in their eyes De Smet's mediation was worth more than that of any army.[14]

It was the first of many such efforts, undertaken with progressively increasing mental and spiritual reservations, by De Smet. A few years after the Fort Laramie meeting, he would become known as the "pacifier of Oregon." But in 1862, with the Civil War raging and Washington's attention briefly distracted, the Sioux nation exploded, killing more than a thousand settlers in the space of three days, burning harvests, sowing destruction. After a costly military campaign the Secretary of the Interior and the Commissioner for Indian Affairs called De Smet to Washington, where President Lincoln asked him to go to the Sioux with the U.S. peace proposals.

"I fear I shall altogether lose my reputation in the eyes of the Indians," De Smet wrote his superior. "Until now thay have regarded me as the envoy of the Great Spirit, and have always heard me benevolently and attentively. If I were now to go among them as the representative of the 'Long Knife Leader' [Lincoln] in Washington, who was once their 'Great Father' but is now their deadly enemy, it would put me in a very bad position."

But he went and his mission was a failure. Sioux willingness to talk peace was neutralized by a local army commander's insistence that "exemplary punishment" be inflicted on the rebels before talks began. The Sioux insurgency spread: By 1867 the Cheyenne and Blackfoot had joined it. Once again De Smet found himself on the banks of the Yellowstone River, flanked this time by commanding officers who had undertaken not to hamper his mission (and who had received a letter from General William Tecumseh Sherman, victor of Atlanta, requesting that "unreserved assistance be given this Catholic priest as renowned for his loyalty to the United States government as for his tireless devotion to and enthusiastic love of the Indians."*

That love was well known to the tribes. But Native American anger ran high. It took all the eloquence of the Jesuit—now well past sixty, his once fair hair snow-white—to overcome their mistrust of the white men. "How," one of his biographers has asked, "could he defend a cause that was in so many ways unjust?"[15] Why indeed, Father De Smet? But he was not the first man to stand guarantor for powerful countrymen in an attempt to help friends he knew to be under mortal threat.

At all events, standing before the leaders of the invading army, Satanka, the old chief of the Minnecoujou (on whose head several governors had set a price), urged his people to accept peace: "We have fought the white man out of necessity. You have heard our complaints. We have given our hearts. Henceforth peace shall be our common heritage. I am old. Farewell. Perhaps you will never see me again. But remember Satanka as the friend of the white man."[16]

Satanka died before the promises made to him and to the twenty thousand warriors who laid down their weapons had been trampled underfoot. The Flemish Jesuit wrote to the Superintendent of Indian Affairs: "If the government takes the Indians' just demands into account, if the annuities are paid to them regularly, if they are given the promised construction materials, the tribes of the Upper Missouri will remain in peace, and the hostile bands will cease their depradations."

Altogether too many ifs . . .

As we have seen (in Chapter XII), one truth at least emerged from the flood of half-truths and calumny poured forth by Jules Michelet during his diatribes against the Jesuits in 1843—the observation that to most people the Company represented simply "counterrevolution." Indeed, one French Jesuit historian, F. Jullien, has made the rueful assertion that "the Jesuits just didn't 'get' the nineteenth century."

In France itself, nineteenth-century Catholicism was deeply divided. The spontaneous offspring of counterrevolutionary and anti-"philosophic" reaction, the French Church was at the same time the heir of the Republic and Empire, or at least of the spirit enshrined in the notion of the rights of man. It remained too the prey of the opposing forces of old-style Gallicanism and of

---

*A major volte-face for Sherman. In 1864 he had written: "We must act vigorously against the Sioux, even exterminate them: men, women, and children . . . "

"ultramontane" champions of papal authority. And the Company in all this? It would be simplest to say that it stood throughout the century on the political right, among monarchists, fundamentalists, and ultramontane militants.

In short, it rejected "liberalism," "movement," the "spirit of the century"—everything that might be called progress—in Italian and Southern European Catholicism as in the French variety. And it sought its support and its energy from the sources of political power, the law, papal hegemony, from everything that made nineteenth-century Rome the headquarters of European conservatism, of anti-modernism, of the rejection of democracy and of human freedoms. Inevitably, it stood shoulder to shoulder with Rome and autocracy in the wave of democratic and anticlerical revolution that convulsed Europe in the 1830s and 1840s.

The man under whose colors the Company would give battle for almost a third of the century (from 1846 to 1878) was Pope Pius IX. His predecessor, Gregory XVI, had been the archetype of authoritarian conservatism, the denigrator of all forms of "liberalism" and "modernism," the unconditional supporter of Austria in its struggle with the Italian Risorgimento (which also threatened his own political power). When he died he was so unpopular that his disappearance took on the somewhat indecent overtones of liberation, heightened by the election to the papacy of Pius IX, in whom Rome saw a herald of liberalism and modernity.

But the new Pope quickly disappointed such expectations. Six months after his election he published his first encyclical which, under the title *Qui pluribus*, denounced the fundamental principles of religious liberalism—"that frightful system of indifference, which abolishes all distinction between virtue and vice, truth and error"—and attributed to Catholicism itself the theory of humankind's absolute progress, "as if that religion were the work of men and not of God."[17]

As with the "liberal" Pope, so with the "patriotic" Pope. On April 29, 1848, Pius IX uttered the words that were forever to separate him from the Italian cause. "True to the obligations of Our supreme apostolate," he said, "we embrace all countries, all peoples, all nations, in an equal sentiment of fatherly love." "All nations . . . " In other words, Austria! Italian patriots received the words as a slap in the face, and the "Roman question" would henceforth be a conflict between Italian nationalism and the power of the Holy See.

And to an even greater extent with the Company of Jesus. For no Italian patriot doubted that the Pope's perceived support for Austria was the work of the Jesuits. Here, Michelet's "counterrevolution" was "counter-Risorgimento." Cardinal Manning, who visited Rome at this time, considered that the Jesuits formed the aristocratic and conservative wing of the clergy. Thus, seen as sworn enemies of liberalism, as the lackeys of imperial and Catholic Austria, the fathers could only be the Pope's evil geniuses, the instigators of papal betrayal. Justly or unjustly, from the violence of the Italian Risorgimento, through the rage provoked by the publication in 1864 of the so-called *Syllabus* of "modern errors," the bitterness of the turn-of-the-century Dreyfus Affair in France, all the way through to the rise of Marxist socialism and the beginnings of anticolonialism, the Company was the perennial enemy. As a certain Canon Morel observed in 1876: "In the whole wide world, apart from two or three muleheaded Belgians, a liberal Jesuit is a phenomenon no longer to be encountered."

· XIII ·

INCIDENTS AT VICHY

Dare, Dare Again, Forever Dare! • *"Established" or "Legitimate"*
Authority? • *Phalange and Fasces* • *Doncoeur's Cadets* • *Jesuits*
Underground • *"France, Beware of Losing Your Soul!"* • *Yellow*
Star as Guiding Light • *The Inhuman Condition* •
The Execution of a Jesuit

O NE DAY IN April 1941 the renowned Jesuit preacher Paul Panici mounted the pulpit of Notre-Dame Cathedral to deliver a Lenten sermon, carefully drafted to avoid giving offense to Marshal Pétain, enthroned in glory at Vichy. Not far from there, on the Left Bank of the Seine, the little Church of Saint-Séverin was welcoming another of the Company's Fathers, a priest whose name was then less well known than that of Notre-Dame's visitor. He would deliver a quite different message: "My brothers, if you want to know what conduct to adopt during these dark times, go and read the words on the plinth of the statue of Danton at Saint-Germain-des-Prés. Here they are: 'To overcome the enemies of the fatherland, you must dare, dare again, and forever dare' . . . "

Daring it was, with soldiers in gray-green uniforms combing the surrounding neighborhood and capable at any moment of pushing through the church door; with Admiral Jean-Louis-Xavier François Darlan installed just the day before as head of the Vichy government; with the recent addition of Greece to Hitler's swelling empire; and with a first roundup being planned in Paris for Jews who would be herded (temporarily) to Beaune-la-Rolande.

As a young priest, Father Michel Riquet had worked on various missions of welcome and support for anti-Fascist refugees from Austria, Spain, and other parts of Europe. He was now the director of the Laennec Conference, an association of Catholic students and doctors working in liaison with solidarity groups in which François Mauriac, Louis Massignon, and Claude Bourdet were active. "From 1938 on, I was a resolute anti-Fascist. My meetings with a group of Israeli pathfinders led by Simon Bouli and two young Zionist rabbis had also helped open my eyes. When disaster came in 1940, I was ready to resist."

Very soon, in fact, he transformed the Laennec Conference into a turntable of the struggle against the German occupation authorities. On November 11, 1940, he called his students together to read them passages from Clemenceau's memoirs condemning Pétain's recurrent defeatism of 1918. By the end of the year his friend André Noël (who would be beheaded two years later by the Nazis in Cologne) had put him in touch with men like Captain Guédon and Claude Bourdet, who would put together the *Combat* resistance group in northern France. Later Riquet met Henri Frenay, the movement's founder.

Father Riquet also made contact with a group of Belgian figures—De Staerke, De Jongh—who had created the Comète network, which helped evacuate downed Allied airmen seeking to return to the fight. He inspired the struggle of French students against the wartime system of compulsory labor in Nazi Germany: His letter of February 1943 to Marshal Pétain, setting out this refusal in terms of moral principle, served as a manifesto to those who had chosen disobedience, and who would soon swell the ranks of the Resistance.

So much rash activity could not fail to attract the Gestapo's attention. On January 18, 1944, two Nazi policemen entered the premises of the Laennec Conference at 12 Rue d'Assas. "No more hiding your Resistance friends under your cassock, Monsieur!" Interrogation sessions at Gestapo headquarters on the Rue des Saussaies followed. Then came the holding camp at Compiègne, the death train, and finally Mauthausen extermination camp, where he would greet his liberators fifteen months later.[1]

Father Riquet's story is not a nutshell version of the French Company's reactions to Nazism and war, not even of those Jesuits who actively fought the occupying power. Henri Chambre, for example, and Jacques Sommet, battled Nazism in a very diffferent way, as did Pierre Chaillet and Gaston Fessard. Different again were the struggles of Victor Dillard, Louis de Jabrun, and Antoine Dieuzayde. Not to speak of those who made a quite different choice. And choice is the right word for those who confronted the Nazification of most of Catholic Europe by adopting positions that if not exactly "passive" or "wait-and-see" were distinctly ambiguous. Their numbers included the Roman hierarchy—the "Black Pope" of Borgo Santo Spirito as well as the White Pope at the Vatican . . .

When a Jesuit preacher paid homage to the Marshal in Vichy, was he being more or less faithful to the Ignatian spirit of "holy obedience" than the likes of Father Riquet? A difficult question, particularly when you reflect that high-level

Jesuit directives did not even speak of obedience to "legitimate" authority but to "established" authority. Of course there were the occasional reminders from the Vatican of the incompatibility of race hatred and Christian doctrine: The Israeli historian Pinhas Lapide counted six of them.[2]

The fact is that the Jesuit order, despite its vaunted "military" discipline, was as vacillating and uncertain as France itself in the face of this major historical challenge. Whence the wide variations in French Jesuit behavior. We must seek the reasons and try to establish limits for this: For in the final analysis, despite much drifting and many serious missteps, Fascism met a worthy enemy in the Company of Jesus.

In March 1937, on the eve of the Second World War, two encyclicals by Pope Pius XI set out Catholic doctrine toward the two forms of atheistic totalitarianism whose violence and mass appeal had been shaking Europe since 1918.

The first, *Mit Brennender Sorge* (With Burning Concern), deliberately written in German, condemned Nazi race doctrine as anti-Christian pagan aggresion. The second, *Humani Generis,* stamped Marxism as "intrinsically perverse."

The latter encyclical presented few problems. By definition, "Godless Communism" lay ideologically, politically, and geographically beyond the Catholic pale. Even in its later "progressive" guise it had made few inroads in Western Christian society. Thus the Company, so attentive and alive to the events of the century, seemed not to have placed Communism at the head of its list of concerns. Only after the Second World War would the Society's leaders assign some of their best minds to the methodical study of Marxism and its concrete manifestations. But even this step was weighed down with reservations. The former Maquisard* Henri Chambre, assigned to explore Marxism after spending three years studying Russian, became one of the world's leading experts on the subject and published an influential book, *Le Marxisme en Union soviétique.*[3] But when he decided to flesh out and verify his knowledge on the spot, at his own bodily risk, the Company three times refused him permission to journey east. What had happened to the old Jesuit spirit of discovery?

Right up to the 1940s, apparently, the Jesuit intelligentsia paid little attention to the Soviet phenomenon,† doubtless relegating it to the third or fourth circle of Hell; and as we know, the Society of Jesus had never made a special study of the phenomenon of Evil. So when Pius XI called Communism "intrinsically perverse," his statement made little impact on the Company's theologians and strategists: All was as it should be.

*Member of the Resistance.
†Although we should remember that Abbé Boulet, one of the priests closest to the French Communist Party, was originally a Jesuit.

The papal malediction against the Nazis was a quite different matter. Written as it was in their own language, it seemed to address most imperatively those German Catholics who were spellbound by Nazism or on the point of joining hands with it—such as Franz von Papen, leader of the Catholic Center Party and Adolf Hitler's vice chancellor.

Not that the venom of Nazism had penetrated the Company of Jesus. The instances of accommodation in France, after the defeat of 1940, arose more from the classic religious attachment to "law and order" and stability than from any powerful attraction. But the marriage between Nazism and other European varieties of Fascism was blindingly clear: In 1936 it even assumed solemn official form with the signing of the Hitler-Mussolini "Pact of Steel." And in the 1930s Fascism was a partner, a confidant, and a temptation for the Catholic world, particularly in Italy and Spain.

In France, however, a line had been drawn between the Church and Fascism by the Pope's condemnation of the right-wing Action Française movement in December 1926.* By denouncing as "pagan" the positivism and Machiavellianism of Charles Maurras—the eulogist if not the begetter of Italian Fascism—Pius XI had not merely irritated Mussolini and shaken a large section of Mediterranean and Latin Catholic society, on whom Maurras's *Enquête sur la monarchie* (Inquiry into Monarchy) had exercised true intellectual sway. He had also stirred up the Company of Jesus, where the newspaper of "fundamental nationalism," Maurras's publication, boasted numerous subscribers, and where his theories had won him open support.†

Indeed, even after the condemnation of Action Française by Pius XI, Italian Fascism retained a degree of prestige and remained a political temptation. The Lateran Agreement signed in 1929 by Mussolini and Pius XI had been hailed by a Jesuit as unimpeachably antitotalitarian as Gaston Fessard as a "masterstroke of Christian politics." As the Pope's partner, the Italian dictator squeezed as many advantages from the treaty as Bonaparte had from the Concordat of 1801.

Neither Mussolini's attack on Ethiopia nor the conclusion of the Pact of Steel between Rome and Berlin nor even their armed support of Franco (blessed by the Spanish clergy as a crusade against the "Reds") seem to have cast a very heavy shadow over Il Duce in right-wing Catholic circles. And when, after Hitler occupied Austria in 1938, Mussolini marked his disapproval by sending two motorized divisions to the Brenner Pass (his new frontier with Greater Germany), right-thinking people praised the Italian dictator to the skies. Even his complicity in Hitler's Munich coup was applauded by the bulk of the French right wing. And there were Jesuit preachers, advocates of "order" and "author-

*While most of Charles Maurras's works were placed on the Index.
†Support that came from, among others, Michel Riquet.

ity" in the name of "anti-Bolshevism," who came close to advocating a Mussolini-style regime. Was Fascism just a theory—or an option?

But already a counter-fire had been lit in the very heart of the Company. In 1935, Father Fessard's *Pax nostra*[4] made its appearance. It is one of the key works of the period to express the opposition of the Christian conscience to Fascism and its dark methods. In this "international examination of conscience," the theology professor at the Jesuit school in Fourvière recalled that politics and the management of a civilization's collective patrimony were "ultimately a moral responsibility," and that "all political behavior is rooted in a spiritual posture."

During the 1930s, Fessard's solemn warnings attested to the presence in the bosom of the Company (where he was surrounded by an impressive cohort of followers) of a most lucid awareness of the essentially aggressive nature of Fascism and of the deadly danger it then posed to the world. There was nothing otherworldly in Gaston Fessard's political moralism. He spoke to "men of flesh and blood, organized into families and nations, conscious of the links binding them"—not to "angels adrift in human bodies"; and he was convinced that "life maintains itself solely through struggle." For him the pacifist's stand was just as infantile as the nationalist's,[5] and he mercilessly condemned those who had turned nation, people, and race into their gods.

Fessard later followed up this lucid anti-Fascist indictment with *Épreuve de force* (Test of Force),[6] a minute-by-minute commentary on the Munich crisis of September 1938. In it he went even deeper into his subject and into the controversies uncorked by that open-ended tragedy. Stressing "that primitive social fact of human history which is opposition and disagreement between groups," Fessard saw pacifism as the enemy of peace, just as he saw nationalism as the enemy of the nation. His little book is as much an indictment of naïveté as of passivity. In 1939 such words counted for a lot.

This turnaround of the Jesuit conscience was not the work of one man or even a group of men. It was the fruit of a slow and collective maturing of Christian society during the 1930s, in which Protestants played a considerable part. Amid the fever and turbulence brought about by the Depression, the 1930s would witness the emergence of a spirit attesting on the very eve of cataclysm to the fertility of a religion that Nazism had sworn to destroy.

Perhaps this spirit had emerged from the vast social and spiritual intermingling which took place in the trenches of the First World War, reimmersing the French clergy in an everyday life from which it had been separated by its own aristocratic traditions and by the exclusionary strategy of an anticlerical state. Perhaps too because men at the head of the French episcopate, such as Monsignor Verdier and Cardinal Liénart, had insisted on the need to set the clergy squarely back among the people. Perhaps because religious youth groups like the Jeunesse Ouvrière Catholique (JOC, Young Catholic Worker), Jeunesse Agricole Catholique (JAC, Young Catholic Farmer), and Jeunesse Étudiante Catholique (JEC, Young Catholic Student) worked to forge links with the whole of society.

Whatever the reason, the 1930s marked a revival of the Company of Jesus, which to observers like Ernest Renan, Léon Gambetta, Émile Zola, Jules Ferry, and Georges Clemenceau had seemed irrevocably stamped by imbecility. The magazines that began to appear—*Esprit, La Vie intellectuelle*, then *Sept* and *Temps présent*—speak of a new demand for answers, of an intrepid freedom of spirit. They were nourished by the contributions of several of the outstanding French writers of the day, boldly committed to the struggles for the freedom of German, Russian, or Spaniard: François Mauriac, Georges Bernanos, Jacques Maritain, Henri Guillemin . . .

These magazines were of the utmost importance in the history of relationships between Catholicism and Fascism. Less prestigious than *Esprit, Études,* or *La Vie intellectuelle*, the papers put out by the youth organizations, whose chaplains were frequently Jesuits, were also alive to the threat from the neighboring totalitarian regimes. *Les Annales,* organ of the French Catholic Youth Association, was less militant than *Messages* or *Chantier,* which expressed the basic mistrust of the French Student Youth Association for either Maurrassianism or Fascism—but welcomed Wladimir d'Ormesson's clearsighted book on *La Révolution allemande*[7] and the pamphlet by Abbé Delmasure on *Hitler et l'Église catholique.*

In this rebirth of the critical Catholic intelligence, the Jesuits naturally played their part. Thus, a dozen years after the First World War, and a quarter century after their expulsion from France in 1904, Jesuit thinking had reconstituted itself. In its English retreats on Jersey and in Hastings, the young men who would restore some of the glitter the Company had lost in the nineteenth century had found their bearings; Victor Fontoynont, Henri de Lubac, Teilhard de Chardin, Gaston Fessard, Yves Montcheuil, and Jean Daniélou . . .

But it was not so much the renewal of theological research that gave the Jesuit thinking of the day its originality. It was rather its methodical study of the origins of Christianity—origins that these young researchers readily sought in Judaism. The foundation of the Sources Chrétiennes publishing imprint, largely the work of Fontoynont and de Lubac, was a decisive gesture toward rapprochement between Christian culture and the Jewish world, the solemn affirmation of Pius XI's assertion that "spiritually, we are all semites."

To this acknowledgment of Judeo-Christian kinship, Father Joseph Bonsirven made an unparalleled contribution. Attending the Biblical Institute of Jerusalem in 1910, he had there written a thesis on "L'Eschatologie rabinique et les Éléments communs avec le Nouveau Testament," which his superiors had rejected. He entered the Company of Jesus in 1919 and continued his study of Judaism and its relations with Christianity. *Les Juifs et Jésus,* published in 1937, was a fearless challenge to recurrent Christian anti-Semitism. How better to shield yourself from racist thinking and Nazi neopaganism than by emphasizing the crucial Judeo-Christian family tie?

However, Christianity is an offshoot not only of Judaism but of Hellenism as well. And it was because he contributed more than anyone else to the rediscovery of this obvious truth (while also acknowledging Christianity's sources) that Victor Fontoynont now stands as one of the Company's twentieth-century reinventors—and one of its protectors against Fascist totalitarianism.

His *Vocabulaire grec,* published in 1930, exerted incalculable influence on the thinking of his day. The cherished instructor of Henri de Lubac and François Varillon, among many others, Fontoynont was a true teacher of humanism. If the Company was put on its guard against the temptations of "law-and- order" totalitarianism, it was as much through the teachings of this Hellenist lover of human freedom as through those of the rediscoverers of Christianity's Jewish sources.*

But neither Fessard's informed and militant conscience nor Fontoynont's reminder of the spirit of freedom inherited from Hellenism were enough to dispel—within the Company as within the French Catholic Church—the temptations of an authoritarianism based on contempt for democracy, on a kind of anti-Bolshevism seen as an end in itself, and on the urge to "remake Christianity" in militant guise. The man embodying this trend was the Jesuit Paul Doncoeur, a man of great energy and blessed with the physical and rhetorical gifts of the born leader. A highly regarded combat veteran of the First World War, Father Doncoeur had created a youth group in 1924, the "Cadets," who posed as emblems of a renascent chivalry based on risk, effort, and stoicism. There was no talk among them of "fasces" (as in Fascist Italy) or of "phalanges" (as there soon would be in Franco's Phalangist Spain). They drew their inspiration rather from the Scout movement, and talked a lot about "Christian disci-

---

*Although of course it would be equally wrong to see Hellenism as the perfect antidote to totalitarianism. Plato affords us little in the way of practical democracy. Renan maintained that Athens lived in a state of permanent terror. Pierre Vidal-Naquet states that in 1933 the majority of German Hellenists welcomed Nazism, and that when writing (during the German occupation) his *Histoire de l'éducation dans l'Antiquité,* Henri Marrou compared Sparta to the Third Reich, as did many Nazi academics. Nevertheless, "the Greek city as the place of collective decision" and "democracy properly speaking" are of "transformations of huge import." And "every time the debate over institutional democracy resurfaces . . . it is after all to Athens that we all turn." (Pierre Vidal-Naquet, in the publication *Citoyenneté et Urbanité,* Paris, 1991, p. 62, and "An Invention of Democracy," *Quaderni di Storia,* no. 35, p. 25.)

pline." But in the group's manifesto, Doncoeur listed among its goals not only a "country to be remade" but a "race to be reinvigorated."

The word "race" had not yet taken on the horrible connotation that Nazism was to confer on it. No "scientific" validity was ascribed to it. But examining these texts and documents fifty years later, we are seized with profound unease. And the historical sequel proved that the worm in this particular apple was truly virulent. It would not turn Doncoeur into a traitor when the time came: The Jesuit was strongly anti-German and, at the time he founded his Cadets,* had published a critical essay entitled "Dieu ou Wotan?" (God or Wotan?).

Meanwhile, Italian Fascism and its German variant continued to spill over national borders. In 1934 the assassination of Austria's Catholic Chancellor, Engelbert Dollfuss, confirmed the odious nature of Nazism. In the following year, Mussolini's invasion of Ethiopia revealed the naked bellicosity of Italian Fascism. The double lesson was driven home by the behavior of both nations in the Spanish Civil War.

Information on the Company's attitude to the latter conflict is hard to find. While evidence of Vatican reservations on Italy's support of Franco is available (if cautiously framed), the position of the Jesuit organ *Civiltà cattolica* is somewhat shrouded. For France, there are a few firsthand recollections. A Jesuit who was young at the time, François Varillon, reports[8] that a senior would call out in the refectory: "Things are going better for us in Spain!", and receive the response, "Who is us?" And Father Pontet, quoted by Renée Bédarida in her biography of Pierre Chaillet: "We sided with the Republicans because a lot of us were Basque. . . . Guernica too had been a brutal shock."[9] And Gaston Fessard, reporting in *Études* on an essay published by an anti-Franco Spanish jurist, vigorously attacked the notion of "holy war" invoked by Franco to justify his anti-Boleshevik "crusade."

Growing persecution in Germany (first of Jews, later of Christians) and the formal alliance between Berlin and Rome dispelled the illusions of those people—so numerous among the Catholic middle classes—who might have wanted to join forces with Fascist Italy against Nazi Germany. Everything now conspired to convince the alert of the essentially aggressive nature of both regimes.

On this score, and amid more or less general blindness, we shall see that the Company had yet again secreted the appropriate antidote. *L'Autriche souffrante* (Suffering Austria) was published[10] in 1939 by Father Chaillet, who had been an eyewitness as Hitler's Third Reich gobbled up the small state that had emerged

---

*Which mustered men who fought bravely against Nazism.

from the Versailles Treaty. We shall be returning to this all-important work. (However, Chaillet's cry of alarm was no more effective than Gaston Fessard's two books in mobilizing French minds against Nazi aggression.)

Independently of the Jesuits, a handful of specialists in German affairs, such as Edmond Vermeil and Albert Rivaud, were stripping away the Hitlerian façade. More pugnacious still was Robert d'Harcourt, whose *L'Évangile de force* (Gospel of Force) appeared in 1936, to be followed in 1938 by *Catholique d'Allemagne*[11] (Germany's Catholics)—books widely reported and commented on by youth publications such as those of the JEC and the JOC, already fired by the energetic language of the encyclical *Mit Brennender Sorge*. Thus the "doctrinal body" of French anti-Fascism was already in place by the eve of the outbreak of war, and with the active participation of the Company of Jesus.

The vanguard role of the Jesuits was due to a number of factors: its far-reaching international antennae; its diversified sources of information; and the extensive German contacts of many of its theologians.

Every European war has driven deep fissures through the international body of the Company. The death of Pius XI had handed the papacy to Cardinal Pacelli, a Germanophile who had shown no particular firmness toward Fascism. The crystal-clear positions of Pius XI (nicknamed Isaac Ratiche* by French anti-Semitic writers such as Louis-Ferdinand Céline) now became blurred. For the Jesuits, this uncertainty was compounded by the death of their Superior General, the Polish Wladimir Ledochowski. It left a vacuum at the top, with "administrative" responsibilities temporarily entrusted to a Norman Jesuit, Norbert de Boynes, Assistant for France. His attitude toward totalitarianism would fluctuate as wildly as the new Pope's.

Indeed, Pius XII's "Catholic" prevarication was to be matched by the "Jesuit" vacillation of Father de Boynes, both within the Company and in the Church as a whole, resulting in an ambiguity emphatically unequal to the catastrophe ahead, to the unprecedented challenge about to be hurled at the whole of Judeo-Christian civilization.

The high dignitaries of Church and Company, apparently more concerned with safeguarding their institutions than defending the basic tenets of their religion, behaved when calamity struck as Pope Benedict XV had done during the First World War, caught in a power struggle it was beyond his capacity to solve. Kaiser Wilhelm or "Tiger" Clemenceau? Bavarians or Bretons? A most understandable dilemma. But this time the clash was no longer between empires but between two visions of the world. In 1914 everyone could shout "Gott mitt uns!" or "Dieu est français!" But in 1940 one camp howled out against God. The Pope was one war behind the times—more so even than the French general staff.

*His name was Achille Ratti.

There were a few chinks in Rome's silence. On January 21, 1940, Vatican Radio condemned the suffering inflicted on Catholic Poland by the Nazis and the Red Army as "one more insolent offense against human morality." Vatican Radio was run by the Jesuits. But, as Xavier de Montclos notes, although the Fathers were "in principle responsible for the content of their broadcasts, those broadcasts clearly committed the authority of Rome as well." Feeling altogether too "committed," Pius XII asked Vatican Radio to stop talking about the Nazi occupation of Poland.*

Pius XII's many acts of "caution" are well known.[12] Those of Father de Boynes call out just as loudly for a comment, infuriating as they did many Jesuit fathers and sundering them once and for all from the duty of "holy obedience." In August 1941, eight months after Vichy had promulgated its "Jewish statutes," Father de Boynes took it upon himself to issue a long memorandum—to be read publicly in every Jesuit community—to the Jesuits of France. This distressing text was a response to an admirable appeal by Father de Lubac, urging his superiors to help him and his colleagues to "save their souls" and "prevent people from thinking that Catholicism has given up the struggle in the face of this terrible upheaval." Father de Boynes replied to those poignant words in the following terms, in their own way just as poignant:

> Here are the directives I feel duty-bound to give you to help you confront the difficulties [sic] we now face. There is in defeated France a legitimate government whose leader, universally respected by honest folk [sic] for his patriotism, dedication, and disinterestedness, is Marshal Pétain. Outside this government there is no other French government. . . . Alongside the established government, there is the fact of dissidence, which works to destroy French unity. What should our attitude, as members of the Company, be? We must first of all accept the established government† and obey it in all that is not contrary to the law of God, whatever our own political preferences. In no case may we oppose it, whether within our communities or outside. We must even use our influence . . . to guide souls toward the practice of that obedience which everyone, and above all Catholics, owes to the Head of State. . . . It is clear that for the same supernatural [sic] reasons, we must in no way help foster dissidence. . . . It has too often been said that the Jesuits were opposed to Marshal Pétain's government. . . . You know that all too often the mistakes and carelessness of a few or even of one man alone can fall upon the whole body. . . . You may easily imagine the influence such rumors exert on the govern-

*But on August 1, 1941, Vatican Radio condemned "this scandal . . . the treatment of the Jews."
†Then led by Pierre Laval.

ment at the very moment when it is turning its attention to the most serious question of the statute of the religious.*[13]

According to Jesuit rule, it was the "study monitor's" duty to read the text to the assembled community: At Fourvière this was Father Fontoynont. When he saw this "call to order," the founder of Sources Chrétiennes simply refused to read it, and asked his superiors to relieve him of the task. Visiting Lyon a few months later, Father de Boynes refused to meet Fathers de Lubac and Fontoynont (Father Fessard had returned to Paris).

From then on, the split between the two camps was open: those called "dissidents" by the authority entrenched in Rome, and those who, "for supernatural reasons" and/or the greater glory of the "statute of the religious," followed the Vichy line.

Of course, Norbert de Boynes's message cannot be fairly assessed independently of the mental context of the Roman Curia and the French bishops and clergy. A context neatly summed up by Cardinal Liénart: "For the English, we have de Gaulle; for the Germans, [Marcel] Déat†; for France, Pétain." More telling still is this warning in 1942 by Monsignor Marmottin, Archbishop of Reims: "A French Catholic is committing a sin if he sides with the rebels!"[14] Whence the condemnation by Canon Aubert of those prelates for whom "the Church's interests outweigh the Christian conscience."[14]

Overall, it could be claimed that apart from a notorious handful, the French Catholic hierarchy upheld the Vichy regime but rejected collaboration—if indeed it was possible to distinguish one from the other after Pierre Laval rejoined the government in April 1941. In a book published in 1947, Monsignor Guerry, who had taken an active part in the conflict, argued that the French Church had succeeded in maintaining its core values—a claim that the Catholic historian André Latreille has called a "model of apologetic dishonesty."

Compared to the French bishops, the Company of Jesus (like the Dominicans) distanced itself from collaboration, and firmly rejected any kind of collusion with the occupying power (although we must bear in mind that the mass of the priesthood experienced daily constraints and unavoidable contacts in the exercise of their ministry).

What must also be underlined is that the upper echelons of the priesthood complied more readily than the lower ranks with the enemy's orders: Ordinary Jesuits and diocesan priests generally displayed greater courage than bishops or

*It is worth reading Norbert de Boynes's biographical note in the *Dictionnaire du monde religieux en France contemporaine* (p. x), vol. I, *Les Jésuites:* " . . . difficult years of the Occupation, when his directives to young Jesuits caused many problems of conscience among them." That is all. . . . When one thinks what people like de Lubac and Fontoynont, Dillard, Fessard and Chambre, Sommet and Chaillet suffered through, the torments they endured . . .
†A notorious collaborator.

the superiors of religious orders. It was a courage that brought tragic results: Between 1940 and 1944, more than two hundred of the religious were deported to Germany, while 143 were shot, guillotined, or slaughtered by the occupying forces or their French accomplices.

Other members of the Company were no less zealous than de Boynes in their support of Vichy. Such as Father Paul Coulet, who kindled terror in the hearts of wavering Bordeaux parishioners as he thunderously consigned them to the fires of hell. Masochism? The leitmotif of "national repentance" hammered into the French by the old Marshal in Vichy fitted this Jesuit inquisitor like a glove (an iron glove). For Coulet, democracy and permissiveness had led France to ruin; God in His mercy had entrusted the annihilation of that whole wicked world to the Marshal, staunch guarantor of the moral order. And woe betide any who dared stand in his way.

Of a different order was the Vichy experience of the seventy-one-year-old Father Gustave Desbuquois. For him, life in the Marshal's capital offered a chance to carry out his social self-help plans free of the harassment of Marxist agitators. Placing his trust in the Marshal and his labor minister, the union leader Belin, he founded two magazines, *Renouveau* (Renewal) and *Cité nouvelle* (New City)—titles both eloquent and pregnant with silence. Questioned later about his behavior during the occupation years, Father Desbuquois summed it up in the following terms: "[At Vichy] I found the opportunity to obtain something for the Church of France, and I seized that opportunity."[15] We need not waste too much irony on that word "opportunity," so often exploited to justify so many much more baneful actions (the "opportunity" to break and remake a state, its army, its judges, its police, its youth . . .).

Can Father Victor Dillard be ranked among Vichy's dupes? Of course not, since the last line of his obituary reads "Died at Dachau, January 12, 1945." But in its early days Pétain's cabinet named this renowned political economist and monetary expert to be the resident preacher at Vichy's official Church of Saint-Louis. Having accepted this forbidding assignment, Father Dillard resolutely turned his back on servility. A few weeks after his own maiden sermon, he called on his friend Gaston Fessard (whose opinions he well knew) to substitute for him in the pulpit. The first sermon delivered by the author of *Pax nostra*, on December 15, 1940, jarred so gratingly on Vichy ears that Mme Pierre-Étienne Flandin, whose husband had just replaced Pierre Laval at the head of the government, saw fit to complain. Nor did Dillard's own sermons conform very closely to the ideas then reigning at Vichy; indeed they won him the dangerous honor of being called "the bravest man in Vichy" in French radio broadcasts from London.

A few months later, Father Dillard went to visit the prisoners in the Château de Bourrassol where the Vichy regime—on purely arbitrary grounds—was holding figures of the discredited Third Republic and French Army, such as Blum, Daladier, and General Gamelin. The visit was a hanging offense, and Dillard's case would have been even darker had the Nazis got wind of the letter he wrote in December 1941 to Henri de Lubac:

"If we could obtain an official statement from the Cardinal [Gerlier, Archbishop of Lyon] on the Jewish question, I believe it could get past [the censors] while there's still time. . . . The whole thing is made more painful by the fact that a year ago I begged Father Desbuquois and others to take a stand in *Cité nouvelle* or *Renouveau*. It seemed to me that it was there that our duty lay. Now it's too late."

Soon Victor Dillard was on the run. He was hiding in Paris in 1943 when the creation of the Service de Travail Obligatoire (the compulsory labor service system whereby all young Frenchmen were conscripted to do war work in Nazi Germany) confronted French priests with a wrenching problem: whether to accompany the deported workers or to stay behind and preach disobedience. As we have seen, Michel Riquet and others chose the latter path. Victor Dillard chose the former, but in its most dangerous form: Taken on as an electrician at Wuppertal, he became clandestine chaplain to the deportees—an activity formally prohibited by the Gestapo on Himmler's personal orders. Uncovered in April 1944, he was transported to Dachau where he soon died, with his friend Jacques Sommet at his side.

The man emblematic of the Company's wartime aberrations, more so even than Fathers de Boynes, Panici, or Coulet, was of course the haughty Paul Doncoeur—orator, inspirational figure, "leader." We have already noted his prewar creation of the Cadets, a movement that aimed to "remake" the French race. In a sense, a man prefabricated to become the figurehead of Vichy's "National Revolution." Indeed, how could he have failed to fall into the Vichy trap?

Was the foundation of the Vichy "French State" in July 1940 really a "divine surprise" for the French, as it was for the royalist writer Charles Maurras? It is impossible at this remove to judge. But what is certain is that Doncoeur himself enthusiastically and even passionately endorsed it, becoming its poet and its ideologist.* And not satisfied with this role as director of the nation's conscience, Doncoeur set about galvanizing the masses. On August 15, 1942, he organized a mammoth Catholic youth pilgrimage to Puy-en-Velay. Taking part were Cardinal Gerlier, the apostolic nuncio, as well as many bishops and leading Vichy figures from the army and the Veterans Legion. As Renée Bédarida noted, it was the "apotheosis of the union of power and religion." While a Carmelite named Edith Stein was dying at Auschwitz, while Pierre Laval in his nearby cha-

---

*The *Dictionnaire des jésuites* modestly notes that "he did not hide his sympathy for the Marshal." Nothing more.

teau of Châteldon was studying police reports on the roundup of French Jews just one month before at the Paris cycling stadium known as the Vélodrome d'Hiver, while in Strasbourg the local *Gauleiter* made ready to conscript young Alsatians into the *Wehrmacht,* the Francisque* and the aspergillum, blessed by Father Doncoeur, were celebrating their holy union. (But at the very same time—and to the glory of the Company of Jesus—the third *Cahier du Témoignage chrétien* made its appearance.)

Paul Doncoeur could not know all this. But what he should have known, or respected, was a certain attitude of the soul in the face of evil, crime, and suffering. "He was a man of great nobility," people who had chosen the other camp now insist. And yet, two months before his triumph at Puy, at the peak of his Vichy career, he sent a then-persecuted writer named François Mauriac a letter which the writer described to his wife on June 4, 1942: "Received a letter from Father Doncoeur in response to my article 'Les Écrivains du néant' (Writers of Nothingness)† which has plunged me into an abyss of sadness and despair. He holds me responsible for all the woes of a whole generation, and condemns me to the Court of God who will avenge 'my victims.' Luckily God is not a Jesuit, but to receive such a letter from a man of God is horrible to me."‡

It is time now to talk of other Jesuits.

Who was the Company's first "resistance fighter," at least in France? The honor probably goes to Victor Fontoynont. In the summer of 1940, as a prostrate nation sought answers from the old Marshal, François Varillon came to the Jesuit school in Lyon. "Do you think Pétain can get us out of this mess?" he asked. Fontoynont, then in charge of course assignments at Fourvière, replied: "Not a chance. He's a spineless old coward. Even in 1918 all he thought about was surrender." Without this Spartan hoplite, this reminder of the heroic days of Christianity, would the Jesuits at Fourvière been tempted to follow Paul Doncoeur? No. For the best mind in the school, its leading intellectual light, Henri de Lubac, already famous as the author of *Catholicisme* (published in 1938), in which Christianity's indebtedness to Judaism is explicitly recalled, was equally firm in his convictions. Witness his two lectures delivered from the pulpit at the Theology Faculty in Lyon, in January 1941, against Hitlerian purveyors of race hatred.

---

*A double-headed axe, supposedly of remote Gaulish origin, resurrected by Vichy to serve both as a decoration for merit and to ape the Nazi swastika.

†Published clandestinely and targeting in particular the collaborationist writer Pierre Drieu La Rochelle (*Oeuvres complètes,* vol. XI, p. 316).

‡A Jesuit who fought the enemy made this comment about Doncoeur: "He believed in man's 'honor,' not in his rights. After the war he changed radically. He felt condemned and excluded. Profoundly sad . . . "

But it was Father Fontoynont who pronounced the following words, which rang for his young fellow Jesuits like a call to action: "The theologian should not meddle in politics except perhaps four or five times in his life. This is one of them!" As 1940 waned, he wrote a commentary on the Epistle to the Romans, dedicated to the Jewish people, concluding with these words: "Their belonging to Christ, their very tribulations . . . oblige us to speak of them only with respect. According to Saint Bernard, if you harm them you harm the apple of the Lord's eye."[16]

Yet the two central figures of Jesuit resistance were Gaston Fessard and Pierre Chaillet. For it was around their publication, *Témoignage chrétien*, that the essence of Jesuit resistance was distilled.

We have already encountered Father Fessard. Even before the war he had fiercely attacked totalitarianism (thus establishing himself, as his friend Raymond Aron put it, as France's director of conscience). And toward the end of 1939, while so many others were indecisive and vacillating, he published an article entitled "Pourquoi nous combattons" (Why We Fight), a compendium of his indictments of the Third Reich.

As we know, some of those Frenchmen who had foreseen and condemned the perversions and crimes of Nazism were briefly halted in their tracks in June 1940, as if stunned by the cataclysm of national defeat. Not Gaston Fessard. True, he was badly shaken by the disaster, writing on July 16, 1940, to Father de Lubac: "We are only at the start of our suffering . . . This period of demobilization is atrocious." And his first public address in the wake of defeat—his sermon at the Church of Saint-Louis in Vichy on December 20, 1940—was a cry of pain, a condemnation of "present darkness" and of race hatred, rather than a call to resistance. But how daring to evoke the "present darkness" before Vichy's smug congregation of admirals shorn of their fleets, defeated-but-satisfied generals, and beret-wearing zealots of Pétain's "National Revolution"! People now began to quote his remark about several of his Jesuit associates in Lyon (starting with Doncoeur), who, he said, were afflicted with "Pétainitis."

Gaston Fessard happened to be in Lyon (which was in the unoccupied zone) because his superiors knew that the Nazis had him in their sights: His prewar books *Pax nostra* and *L'Épreuve de force* were at the head of the "Otto List" of works banned by the occupying power. Which did not deter Fessard from making several trips to Paris as 1941 drew to a close. This was the period that saw him move from "dissidence" to resistance—even before *Témoignage chrétien*, created by Father Chaillet (himself linked to Henri Frenay's Resistance group Combat), loudly proclaimed the "Christian dimension" of Resistance. But it was a different path that led Father Fessard to fire the opening shot.

Renée Bédarida, drawing on the personal histories of those involved, has written what seems the definitive "prehistory" of *Témoignage chrétien*. Early in 1941 a Catholic student in Lyon, Jean Neyra (who would later enter the Company), called on Father François Varillon at the Jesuit Collège de Mongré at Villefranche-sur-Saône. Neyra wanted help in countering the pro-collaboration propaganda with which he and his classmates were saturated. Together with his fellow student Jean Daniélou, Varillon decided that the antidote should be an appeal written by an unchallengeable authority. He at once thought of Father Fessard. In Lyon, the author of *Pax nostra* warmly welcomed the two young Jesuits. "Action at last! It's high time! Everyone in this city is flat on his face!" His visitors wanted a text a few pages long? They would have it.

Fessard threw himself into the task. When Varillon came the following week to pick up the promised text, he was handed a fifty-page essay. He and Neyra had had the distribution of a leaflet in mind, not the publication of a treatise. How to print and distribute something so long? Fessard thought of Vatican Radio's printer in Marseille. Others suggested entrusting the job to an anti-collaborationist printer in Salon.

But a swifter solution was at hand: Fessard knew that his friend Pierre Chaillet was "up to something," something that would fuse and galvanize his multiple Resistance activities. He therefore turned to Chaillet (already organized and by now acquiring a considerable printing and distribution capacity). The appeal would appear as the first issue of *Cahier du Témoignage chrétien*, under the title "France, Beware of Losing Your Soul!"*

Right from the start, like the good Jesuit he was, Fessard identified his points:

One. The fundamentally anti-Christian nature of the Nazi mystique.

Two. The insidiousness of Hitlerian penetration and persecution.

Three. Its implementation in France, and the results so far achieved.

One of Fessard's key arguments in the appeal revolved around a syllogism that later became famous: "Collaboration with the Marshal's government = collaboration with the 'New Order' = collaboration in the triumph of Nazi principles." Fessard then apostrophized devout Pétain supporters: "The Marshal has accepted the principle of collaboration [which] in fact is merely the enslavement of vanquished by victor [and] an acknowledgment of the conception . . . of the National Socialist world [based on] domination by Germany."

Before ending with the exhortation that titled the indictment, Fessard had kinder words to say of the Jesuits of Vatican Radio, which had once upon a time urged Christians "not to sit down with the enemies of Jesus in order to save themselves"—since "charity without justice is a weakness unworthy of the Christian."

*The closing words of Fessard's appeal, which Chaillet used for the title.

By the time his appeal was published, Gaston Fessard was back on Rue Monsieur in Paris, right under the enemy's nose in one of the most closely watched "Jesuitries" in the French capital. There he learned of a leaflet written and published in late 1941 by a certain Abbé Lesaunier, with the imprimatur of the Archbishopric of Paris. Not content with urging "unreserved" obedience to the Marshal, Lesaunier added: "I submit myself without recrimination to the occupying authorities," for "whoever refuses obedience to legitimate authority [*sic*] refuses obedience to God Himself and merits retribution"—a precept the complaisant ecclesiastic aimed at supporters of General de Gaulle.

Furious, Fessard made a hurried call on Cardinal Suhard, who admitted that he himself was in some doubt over the rights and wrongs of resistance. By rising against the occupying forces, he asked Fessard, was he not helping the Bolshevik cause? Did he not fear Bolshevism? "Yes, Excellency, but first we must fight Nazism ... " "Do you believe it threatens us?" And so on. Finally, the Cardinal asked Fessard to draw up "a brief report" on the question.

With the help of his teacher Jules Lebreton, editor of the periodical *Recherches de science religieuse*, Fessard wrote a hundred-page report, *La Conscience catholique devant la défaite et la révolution* (The Catholic Conscience Faced with Defeat and Revolution)—better known under the title *Le Prince-Esclave* (The Slave-Prince). He submitted it to Cardinal Suhard* at the end of August 1942, together with a leaflet by Father Lebreton excoriating the "spiritual vassalage" that had put "our Christian faith" at risk.

The Slave-Prince is a key wartime text. It expresses the refusal of a handful of Frenchmen (long in the minority) to countenance direct or indirect collaboration with the enemy. It was of course far from being a call to arms. Very Jesuit in its coupling of fact and abstract principle, it acknowledges, for example, that "faced with the will of the unjust master, one can say 'yes' with the head ... while resisting in all one's limbs." Basically, though, Fessard argues that the Christian may not obey any order unless it conforms to the dictates of his conscience. If it is legitimate to obey a prince, it is not legitimate to accept enslavement—or to accept the prince's enslavement.

Like the Hegelian he was, Fessard moved from freedom to legitimacy to slavery in these dialectical maneuverings. His language, and the level of his thinking, do not make easy reading of this austere and sometimes ambiguous text.†
In his Rome lecture on Gaston Fessard in 1983, Raymond Aron recalled that when he first saw this anonymous text in wartime London he said to friends:

---

*Whose attitude toward the invader would gradually grow bolder: Six months later, the Prelate finally protested against the deportation of Jews.

†There are insistent reports that the text was invoked by Bastien-Thiry's Benedictine confessor during preparations for the attempt to assassinate President de Gaulle at Petit-Clamart in the 1960s.

"There's only one Frenchman* capable of writing this—and that's Father Fessard . . . "

But *The Slave-Prince* manifesto was not widely read at the time—since, unlike its predecessor, it did not draw upon the resonance of *Témoignage chrétien*.†
But the last of Gaston Fessard's great war writings is the powerful culmination of the endless struggle this gentle-eyed theologian waged against Nazism and collaboration.

Pierre Chaillet we have already met. Quicker to action than Fessard, he was built like a bull, with an intense stare behind thick glasses, a lantern jaw, a rough voice. Jesuit for Jesuit, he was a Riquet rather than a de Lubac. When he entered the Fourvière novitiate, Chaillet was among the eminent teachers who influenced him. He taught literature at Dole, at Notre-Dame d'Afrique, and in Algeria, before going on to Austria—which inspired an excellent book—and where he found his way. The assassination there of Chancellor Engelbert Dollfuss, Hitlerism's first international crime, left him forever angry, forever rebellious.

But this encounter with the Germanic world was not just a preparation for wartime resistance. It also cemented Chaillet's ties to the Tübingen School, the group of Catholic priests who (a century earlier, around Drey and Möhler at Württemberg) had drafted a plan for the reunification of the Christian churches. A little later on, a study session in Rome confirmed him in his horror of Fascism. As a professor of theology at Fourvière, he displayed his breadth of mind by taking up the cudgels for Robert Simon, a contemporary and rival who had endeavored to apply historical critical methods to the sacred texts and had seen his works consigned to the flames by the Bishop of Meaux.

The Anschluss, Hitler's (largely welcomed) seizure of Austria, brought Chaillet back to Vienna where his old connections helped him amass documentation for a book he published in 1939, *L'Autriche souffrante* (Suffering Austria),[17] a kind of premonition of the struggles ahead. Did he know Malraux's earlier book of the same title when he chose to call one of his chapters "Le temps du mépris" (The Time of Contempt)? His own inquiry is no less an indictment than Malraux's novel. No holds barred, he attacks "political and racial hatred and religious persecution," as well as the "absolute power of the Gestapo" and the "numbing epidemic of fear which paralyzes all thought of opposition ahead of time."

---

*Did he think "except me"?

†At a 1984 symposium, participants expressed regret that so few people ("a few dozen," suggested Germaine Ribière, Pierre Chaillet's closest collaborator) had read *The Slave-Prince*. After conducting a discussion on the subject, Jacques Prévotat wryly concluded that "he robbed Cardinal Suhard of a few nights' sleep: that in itself is something . . . "

He directs his fiercest anger at race persecution. His visit to the Nazi exhibition *Der ewige Jude* (The Eternal Jew) horrified him. Raising the specter of the "pitiless extermination" of those delivered up defenseless to the rage of "passionate" anti-Semitism, that "shameful manhunt in which man is tracked down like some unclean creature," he concludes with this warning: "It is enough to have witnessed it in Vienna to be incapable of resigning oneself to a complaisant or complicit silence."[18] The Nazis had been warned. Here was one man, at least, they would be unable to circumvent, a man ready to fight.

When war broke out on September 3, 1939, Father Chaillet was not satisfied to be a chaplain or medical orderly: Instead he offered his services to the War Ministry, and more specifically to its counter-espionage branch, the Deuxième Bureau. A true Jesuit: To beat the Devil, we must use maximum force. He was sent into the German sphere of influence, to Hungary, which he found leaning toward the Third Reich. The intelligence information that Renée Bédarida publishes in her biography of Chaillet shows him to have been highly gifted for the trade of clandestine informer, shielded by his soutane.

Recalled to France by his superiors immediately after France's defeat in 1940, Chaillet now transformed himself into a militant, burrowing ever deeper underground. Lyon was becoming an anthill of resistance activity. At Fourvière he found the determined spirit he sought, embodied in Fontoynont, de Lubac, and Pierre Ganne. Constantly standing out as the most intransigent and anti-Vichy of his companions, he made contact with Stanislas Fumet (who considered the Jesuits "readier to fight than the other religious orders"[19]); with Emmanuel Mounier; with the creators of the *Chronique sociale,* such as the Lyonnais Marius Gonin, with union leaders like Paul Vignaux—and finally, in early May 1941, with Henri Frenay, cofounder with Bertie Albrecht of what was to become the *Combat* group. (At the time Frenay was busy publishing a newspaper called *Petites Ailes,* followed a year later by *Vérités;* Chaillet wrote its "religious" column under the pseudonym Testis.)

Strangely, when the arch-Catholic François de Menthon merged his own movement with Frenay's, thus replacing *Vérités* with *Combat,* the Jesuit's column was dropped. To influence events and shake up opinion, Chaillet needed a forum. The idea of an underground newspaper steadily took shape that summer, with the energetic encouragement of the Fathers at Fourvière, the support of Alexandre Marc, a veteran militant of the European Christian Left, and the help of Louis Cruvillier. It received its long-awaited kick start when Gaston Fessard handed Chaillet the appeal written at the request of Varillon and Daniélou, which would become "France, Beware of Losing Your Soul!"

The title Chaillet originally gave the paper was *Cahier du Témoignage catholique* (Journal of Catholic Witness). But at the last minute, as *Combat's* regular printer (lent to him by Frenay) completed his task, "the Jesuit decided to associate Protestants with the endeavor* . . . and to make it an expression of the Christian conscience. So they changed the title by sticking a piece of paper with the word 'Christian' over the word 'Catholic.'"[20]

One month later, in December 1941, the second *Cahier* appeared. Entitled *Notre Combat* (Our Struggle), it gathered together well-known anti-Nazi writings, Protestant and Catholic, from the great Basel theologian Karl Barth to the intrepid Bishop of Münster, von Galen. The latter's homilies so infuriated Heinrich Himmler that the head of the Gestapo arrested him with the intention of shooting him; when that step threatened to inflame the whole of Catholic Westphalia, however, Hitler ordered the prelate's release.

Perhaps the most remarkable of the *Cahiers* were published in February and April of 1942, under the titles *Les Racistes peints par eux-mêmes* (The Racists Through Their Own Eyes) and *Antisémites*. They included some frightening texts, such as the Nazi theoretician Alfred Rosenberg's description of the God of the Bible as a "typical old Jew, everyman's Hebrew," of Hitler as a being "clinically free of all Christian contagion," of Christ as "a superman fighting at the head of disciples whose triumphant symbol is the Twisted Cross, the Swastika," and of the kingdom of God as a "Jewish pipedream."

The *Cahiers du Témoignage chrétien* did not simply strip the mask from what Charles Péguy had called "the villainy and stupidity of anti-Semitism." They also condemned the specifically anti-Christian nature and judicial inadmissibility of Vichy's anti-Jewish laws: Following a profound examination of the historical problem of France's Jewish community ("emancipated by the French Revolution"), they declared that "Christians, Catholic and Protestant alike, who themselves belong to spiritual communities at once national and supranational, have no difficulty accepting the legitimacy of this spiritual bond linking the Jews but not preventing their loyal and wholehearted integration into their nation; it is simply a recognition that the idea of a 'people,' often applied to the Jews at the risk of serious misunderstanding, has a spiritual and a ritual meaning which is no impediment [to their] adhesion to a specific national community."[21]

Publishing *Témoignage chrétien* was probably the heart of Pierre Chaillet's activities. But by no means their sum. He continued his work to support Jews and secure their clandestine passage to Switzerland and Spain. He ran a workshop that produced false identity papers and kept in close touch with Colonel Descour, head of the French Forces of the Interior for the Alpes-Rhône region. Among other testimonies to his many-headed concerns is this one by Max

*Chaillet was a veteran fighter for ecumenism and worked with the Protestants in the "Christian Friendship" movement.

Heilbronn (Resistance name: "Harrel"), which suggests that the Jesuit exercised an active and selective influence on Henri Frenay: "Father Chaillet had a kind of power [over] Frenay... While people talk a lot about Frenay and others, Chaillet, who is rarely mentioned, gave me the impression of being a sort of 'clandestine orchestra conductor.' "[22]

At all events, he ceased to be a soloist at the head of *Témoignage chrétien*. Contributors besieged him. After the historians Joseph Hours and Henri Marrou came the philosophers Joseph Vialatoux, André Mandouze, and Jean Lacroix, the German expert Robert d'Harcourt, the Alsatian priest Pierre Bockel (who ran the issue of *Cahiers* devoted to his own Reich-annexed province), and the Protestant minister Roland de Pury. But there were also of course the Jesuits Henri de Lubac, Pierre Ganne, Henri Chambre, and Yves de Montcheuil, not to mention Georges Bernanos, from whom Chaillet obtained the famous "Lettre aux Anglais" (Letter to the English), published in Brazil in 1942, which would become *Cahiers* XVIII to XIX under the title *Où allons-nous?* (Where Are We Going?).

In its wake, Father Chaillet broadened the formula in 1943 to launch *Courriers du Témoignage chrétien*, tripling his publication's circulation and handing its management over to André Mandouze. It was *Courriers* (Mail) that bore the brunt of the fight against the German-imposed Compulsory Labor System, publishing crucial writings by Henri de Lubac on the duty of disobedience. It was a major challenge and perceived as such by the authorities. This was the period when an irritated French Assembly of Bishops condemned "theologians without a mandate"—theologians whom Monsignor Salièges would later call "the glory of Christian thinking in France." And Monsignor Fontenelle, attached to the Roman Curia, would say that "we passed the *Cahiers du Témoignage chrétien* around as if they were the Epistles of Saint Paul."

The Prefect of Lyon, Angeli, had already consigned Pierre Chaillet to house arrest at Privas, then forced him into hiding at Saint-Julien-du-Retz in the Isère, when the Jesuit decided in September 1943 that it would be wiser for him to go underground in Paris (where he was unknown) with the *nom de guerre* Prosper Charlier. There he lived in the apartment at 13 Rue Jacob of his friends the Bédaridas, giving up none of his activities and assuming the leadership of the Resistance Social Services Committee. It was in this capacity that, in the weeks immediately following the Liberation, the Jesuit was appointed virtual Minister for Social Welfare in liberated France's provisional Health Ministry.

Would *Témoignage chrétien* outlive the Occupation? Most of its sponsors—de Lubac, Fontoynont, Fessard, Lebreton—were in favor, as well as the man who had become Chaillet's right arm, André Mandouze. It was therefore planned to continue publication around a few key postwar themes: Communism's double game, European union, decolonization.

But a crisis now shook the editorial team and provoked the departure of its leading lay contributor. In the early summer of 1945, Father Fessard drew on his past pioneering achievements to submit a new manifesto to the editors: "France, Beware of Losing Your Freedom!" A pendant to his wartime anti-Nazi indictments, it was an attack on Communism and the penetration of French society by Marxism and its agents. The same Fessard who had once so spiritedly risen against Vichy's "Anti-Bolshevik Crusade" now asserted that, with Hitler overcome, it was time to condemn what had become the principal enemy—just as his friend Raymond Aron and André Malraux were doing.

But the article caused deep divisions. Some, like Mandouze, took offense at this linking of the two doctrines and their respective histories. Others argued that its publication would cut *Témoignage chrétien* adrift from the world of the worker. But despite reservations from de Lubac and sharper criticism by Daniélou, Jean Baboulène and the new management agreed with Chaillet to publish. Which led to the break with André Mandouze.

Ten years later, Chaillet would be ordered by his superiors to resign from the weekly, whose "partisan spirit and tendency to national self-criticism"* were being condemned in high places. The Algerian war was raging and *Témoignage chrétien* was unbending in its condemnation of French interrogation techniques and tactics of repression. Now that peace had come, the man who had contributed so much to rescuing France's priesthood from shame between 1940 and 1944—ignoring orders from Rome and from Father de Boynes—was no longer able to snap his fingers at the constraints of "holy obedience."

The following year, Chaillet was invited by B'nai Brith to take part in a New York tribute to Europeans who had risked their lives to save persecuted Jews, but Rome refused him permission to attend. Renée Bédarida suggests that the presence of this fearless Jesuit in New York would have drawn attention to the silence others had observed during the war.[23]

And thus, from Grenoble to Dijon to his final sojourn at the Martel-de-Janville sanatorium, removed from the leadership of his last remaining activity, the Resistance Social Services Committee, and in growing isolation, Pierre Chaillet ended his days a hero disavowed. At his funeral on April 29, 1972, the eulogies were delivered by Jean-Pierre Lévy, founder of the Franc-Tireur Resistance group, and Father Jacques Sommet, the survivor of Dachau.

Sommet was a true brother. He was born on the eve of the First World War into

---

*Was this impious?

a family of small Lyon craftsmen in the neighborhood of the silk district, of a Catholic father and atheist mother. But Jacques Sommet did not discover Christianity until the approach of his twentieth year, through the chaplains of the Young Catholic Worker movement (JOC) and of the Scouts. He entered the Company of Jesus in the depths of the Great Depression, which had condemned multitudes to hopeless and ineradicable unemployment, because he saw in the Jesuits a particular ardor for action and a venturesome spirit.

His attachment to the Company was further cemented by Fessard's *Pax nostra*, Henri de Lubac's *Catholicisme*, and by studies shared with fellow pupils like Varillon amid a spiritual and intellectual ferment inspired by Lebreton, Fontoynont, and Pierre Teilhard de Chardin. He knew he had found his way. When war and occupation came, all seemed clear. Had they seemed perplexing, the sight of a yellow star on the breast of an old Jewish man would have dispelled all doubt: "Could I say that that star became my guiding light?" Through Gaston Fessard, he joined the *Témoignage chrétien* group. Was that why the Provincial of France, Father Marcel Bith, now called him in? Or was it just for the annual "inventory of conscience" every Jesuit owes his superior?

Bith was a large man of no special charm, his voice heavy and a little weary. He looked at the young Jesuit: "Hmm, I see you're busy with certain matters . . . Hmm . . . Well, I have no instructions for you there, nor even advice . . . Hmm . . . But let me ask this of you: Choose someone at your own discretion, and let him know all about what you're doing . . . Hmm . . . Now, let's get to this 'inventory of conscience.' Are you happy in the Company? And do you still pray to God?"

Yes, Jacques Sommet was "happy" in the Company. Yes, he "still" prayed to God . . . But he would soon have to call upon all his happiness and all his faith to surmount the ordeals ahead. In 1943 he slipped through a Gestapo dragnet in Paris. But in March 1944, on his way home from an examination, he was stopped by two men who told him he was being "arrested in the name of the German police." (His first reaction: "I was glad it wasn't the French police!")

Fresnes, Compiègne, "the train of lost hope," Dachau—"the inhuman condition." At the camp he encountered a radiant personality, Edmond Michelet, and an organization (Jesuit though he was) which impressed him, that of the Communist Party. At Dachau he also found that curious outer edge of individual freedom that resists the worst captivity, independently of any hope of liberation. And "evil in its purest state," the mystery of evil.

Jacques Sommet, reflecting a half century later on that "central focus of crystallization" between the "*nada*" of Saint John of the Cross and the "God-in-all-things" of Ignatius, acknowledges that "this historical failure of everything, of Christianity, society, history . . . hid the light of God." But he concludes that

"Faith in an incomprehensible and brotherly God . . . cannot but lead to a new faith, the faith of the charnel house."

When, at the end of April 1945, the exhausted survivor of Dachau knocked on the door of the "Jesuitry" on the Rue de Grenelle in Paris, he at once began to list those of his friends who had died there. He was interrupted: "You'll have to add another name—Father de Montcheuil, shot in Grenoble . . . "

"A Breton rock," in Sommet's words. Yves Moreau de Montcheuil was born at Paimpol in 1900. He entered the Company at seventeen, obviously a theologian and a philosopher of freedom if ever there was one, flesh-and-blood, of a piece with his historical context, a man for whom the vocation of man was to fulfill himself in action[24] "here and now." An action that was "transformative and still to be transformed" and that, borne by "a limitless hope," impels us "to take on new perspectives opened up by the action itself."[25] This, Jacques Sommet believes, was "philosophical anthropology . . . obsessed by the prospect of synthesizing love of God and love of man."[26]

As a professor of theology at the Catholic Institute in Paris, where his teaching evolved in close contact with that of the Fourvière group, Yves de Montcheuil exercised vigorous sway over the student world, an influence that turned into unalloyed ascendancy when the German occupation began. His intellectual prestige was henceforth buttressed by admiration for his behavior, particularly among members of the Catholic Student Movement (JEC).

As early as July 30, 1940, de Montcheuil was writing to de Lubac: "We will perhaps (?) have the chance to know what it means to run risks to ensure the freedom of the Word of Jesus. It will be a time to prove that what we said before the war was something other than sterile chat."

Had Yves de Montcheuil consulted his superiors before delivering these words in November 1940 to a gathering of his students at the Church of Saint-Séverin,* a few days after publication of the "Jewish statutes"?

> A Frenchman who remained unmoved by a Jewish countryman
> suffering under present conditions would not be a Christian. A French
> Catholic may not leave one of his Jewish countrymen in the isolation
> into which he is likely to find himself cast if the current anti-Semitic
> fever makes further strides. He may not agree to treat him thus as a pa-
> riah because others wish to impose this conduct on him. Let us tell
> ourselves that this will be the "test" of our charity, of Christian charity:
> At the moment when the Jews are most persecuted, at the moment
> when they can give nothing in return, will we abandon them?

*Where, as we have seen, Father Riquet would soon quote Danton.

It seems extraordinary that Yves de Montcheuil (like Pierre Chaillet) was not arrested until the spring of 1944. In that year the French bishops, who until then had stubbornly refused to send chaplains to serve Resistance members, decided at the insistence of several Maquis leaders to change its policy. (Although men like the Abbé Grouès and the Jesuit Father Lucien Fraisse were one jump ahead of the Episcopate in the matter. And the Jesuit fathers on the faculty of Fourvière, inspired by de Lubac, had come up with an ingenious suggestion: The Resistance fighters, the *maquisards,* were to be considered as being "on the point of death,"* and as such might be given the sacraments by any priest.)

And so Father de Montcheuil was sent on mission to the Resistance stronghold on the Vercors plateau in southern France. However, it was not as a fighter but as chaplain to the nursing services of the secret army that he was greeted in the Vercors. There, ever since the Allied D-Day landings on June 6, the group's fighting strength had risen from five hundred to five times that number, but without the requisite administrative arrangements to accommodate them. Moreover, their numbers were now seen as a threat by the German general staff: On July 20 two *Wehrmacht* divisions from Grenoble and Valence were dispatched to attack the Maquis groups in the Drôme and Isère regions.

The second-in-command of the Free French Forces in the Drôme, Father Lucien Fraisse (who like his colleague Father Henri Chambre, engineer officer, had been conscripted as a combatant by Colonel Descour), was surprised to find Father de Montcheuil, whom he liked and admired, at his command post. On July 20, just as the German offensive began, Montcheuil had been redirected to the Vercors hospital, which had just been evacuated and relocated to the Luire cavern.

Struggling up steep slopes to reach the cave, Yves de Montcheuil met Juliette Lesage,† a nurse who had been wounded during a previous German assault and who was now rejoining her unit. The climb was very hard, a spotter plane was hovering, and the priest and nurse were constantly forced to hide under the trees to avoid guiding the aircraft to the cave-hospital.

When they reached the cavern, they found terrible tension, intense anxiety, and—toward the Jesuit—a level of hostility that, according to Lesage, "must have hurt him terribly." De Montcheuil was kept to one side, isolated from the young wounded he wanted to help, allowed to say Mass only once, in the open air and on a large stone altar. Was it the mistrust of veteran maquisards toward this eleventh-hour worker? Rejection by militant Communists of this "parson" come to claim souls *ad majorem Dei gloriam?* However, the medical staff—Drs.

*Which one of their leaders, André Malraux, later recalled to them.
†Her account, which she gave at a symposium in 1984, is the chief source for this section.

Ullmann, Ferrier, and Ganimède—had time to make friends with him before they met their common fate.

When the attackers burst in "like madmen," according to Juliette Lesage ("Don't shoot!" the doctors shouted. "There are only wounded here!"), they shoved the unwounded and the women against a rock face. "We're going to be shot," she thought. But they were dragged off out of earshot of the volleys putting an end to the sick on their straw mattresses in the cavern. Not one escaped. Doctors, nurses, and chaplain were bundled down to the roadway below and loaded into a truck. In Harbouilly Forest a German officer stopped the column. Would they be executed here? No: The officer whacked the hood with his swagger stick and bellowed, "Bandits, you're all going to be shot!" A French officer rose: "I am not with these bandits, I am their prisoner." De Montcheuil silenced him.

During a halt at Villard-sur-Lans, the chaplain whispered to Lesage: "My name is Father de Montcheuil. You have a chance of getting out of this. Tell my people on the Rue Voltaire and my father that I have no regrets."

Interned with his companions at a military headquarters in Bonne whose doors and windows had recently been blown in by a Resistance bomb, Yves de Montcheuil underwent two interrogations in Grenoble prison. To the officer who asked him whether he was indeed the group's chaplain he replied, "I came from Paris for that exact purpose." From July 20 to August 8 he was incarcerated in a cell with some thirty people, almost all of them destined for the firing squad, including the doctors from the Luire cavern and Colonel de Chivre. He marveled at the fact that Dr. Ullmann, who was Jewish, knew *The Imitation of Christ*.

On the evening of August 8, Montcheuil and Drs. Ullmann and Ferrier were taken to a secluded prison center. There they were again interrogated. During the night of August 10–11, 1944, Yves de Montcheuil and the doctors were executed. In August 1942 he had written to his family: "There is a greater intensity and quality of existence in the act of dying through faithfulness to duty than in a long, contented life preserved through cowardice."

·XIV·

OBEDIENCE
AND TEILHARD

Fools and Ignoramuses • *War as Intellectual Honeymoon* •
Discovery of the "Feminine" . . . • *Banished to China* •
Catholicism or Pantheism? • *Death in Exile*

O N MARCH 15, 1946, the name of Pierre Teilhard de Chardin suddenly rang out in the French National Assembly. The man who had
uttered it, during a parliamentary debate on religious education,
was himself a scientist, founder of the Musée de l'Homme, and once a founding
spirit of the Socialist National Front, which ruled France in the late 1930s—the
living embodiment of revolutionary democracy in France: "Despite the respect
I had and still have for that great priest and scientist, Father Teilhard,* I would
not again vote for him if he were a candidate for public office, for I cannot stomach a man of science obeying orders handed down by fools and ignoramuses."

Had the speaker himself always dealt only with competent and intelligent
people? In any case, if Paul Rivet now condemned the "fools and ignoramuses"
forcing their will upon the author of *Le Coeur de la matière* (The Heart of the
Matter), it was not his own words he used. Teilhard himself had spoken them
twenty years earlier in a conversation with the fiery old Socialist to describe the
people who had just expelled him from the Catholic Institute of Paris, foremost
among them its rector, Monsignor Baudrillart.†

We know that Pierre Teilhard de Chardin was deeply wounded by this expulsion, the first of countless rebuffs inflicted by the Catholic Church (and by his

---

*Then preparing to return from China to France.
†Who would become a celebrator of wartime collaboration with the Nazis.

own order) on the twentieth century's most illustrious Jesuit, the man in whom the pioneer spirit of the founding fathers seemed to live again.

In a letter to the man who long remained his closest confidant, Father Auguste Valensin, he wrote these words in 1925, words that seem to drip blood:

> I put on a brave front; but within me it was more like death throes or a storm. . . . Which is the more sacred of my two callings? The one [religious] I received as a kid at eighteen? Or the one [scientific] that showed itself to be my true spouse in the fullness of my life as a man? I tell myself that there is no contradiction. . . . Oh! my friend, tell me I am not disloyal to my ideal in obeying . . . [1]

Prophets are rarely destined for a peaceful life, for gently purring careers, for red hats and soft honors. Teilhard had already taken the prophetic function upon himself on that mid-March day in 1916 when he wrote from the muddy bottom of a front-line trench to his friend and fellow student Victor Fontoynont:

> Cannot the *Object,* the very *Matter,* of our human passions be transfigured, transmuted, into the definitive and the divine? I think it can. The intoxication of antique paganism I would convert to Christian use, acknowledging God's work of creation in all caresses and in all clashes, in all unavoidable and insurmountable acts of passivity. The lofty passion of the struggle for knowledge, for domination, for control, I would unleash upon its natural objectives, but with the afterthought and ultimate goal of pursuing God's work of creation, begun for example in the unconscious processes of the human brain but fated to generate souls of new or subtler shadings thanks to the influences and structures of a higher civilization. The naïve or questioning love of the Earth Mother I would make divine, telling myself that from this mysterious All which is Matter something must pass, through the Resurrection, into the Heavenly world—my own efforts for human Progress being perhaps the necessary condition for the building of the new World.

"Pursue God's work of creation . . . " These are the words of a demiurge. A spark of madness flickered within Teilhard, a fever of pride later stilled by humility—equally balanced components of a larger-than-life character.

At the memorial service held in Paris after the death* of the author of *Le Phénomène humain* (The Phenomenon of Man)—a book throbbing with "rashness," if not "irreverence"—his faithful and affectionate counselor Father René d'Ouince saluted him fearlessly. "The order to which [Teilhard] be-

---

*In exile in New York, April 10, 1955.

longed," he said in his eulogy, "maintained a protective watch on him and demanded heavy sacrifices," which Teilhard accepted "with total loyalty." On the subject of those "sacrifices" and that "loyalty," d'Ouince speaks with impeccable authority, since none had tried harder or stronger to soften the blows showered on the prophet by Roman bureaucrats of both the Vatican and the Gesù.

As for the order's "protective watch," no doubt you had to have sworn the vow of obedience and to have relished the bitter virtues of discipline to give the words the positive ring Father d'Ouince piously gives them. "Protective . . . " Just like those long-sleeved jackets they use in places called "asylums."

If Jesuit education tends to turn out diligent executives of a corporation in harmony with the world and under the gaze of a satisfied God, then the education Pierre Teilhard de Chardin received was close to a masterpiece, a model. In him the fathers could boast of having shaped, for the greater glory of God, a trouble-free product, smooth and submissive, the kid raised in the traditions of an impeccably Christian family and a cautiously conservative background.

Voltaire's great-grandnephew on his mother's side,* and something of a cousin to Blaise Pascal (by way of the building blocks of Clermont-Ferrand),† the infant Teilhard doubtless inherited a dose of rebelliousness. But born as he was into a family of impoverished Auvergnat noblemen, fourth of the eleven children of Emmanuel (Chartist, naturalist, huntsman) and of Berthe, *née* Dompierre d'Hornoy and militantly pious, he turned out to be what his rhetoric professor in high school called "hopelessly well behaved."

Was his meek behavior really "hopeless"? It did at least promise a future rich in honors, office, and power. For the young Teilhard led his class in everything. When he entered the Company before his twentieth year, on the eve of the new century (and of yet another expulsion of the Jesuits from France), he seemed destined to follow in the footsteps of heroic predecessors whose efforts had for centuries transformed the misfortunes of the Company into triumphant restorations.

Without a doubt, though, it was Pierre Teilhard de Chardin's own genius, his smoldering inner fire, that saved him from the destiny of model pupil and well-behaved child that seemed his as he progressed from the novitiate at Laval to the "junior college" in Aix-en-Provence. A fire combining Voltaire's irreverence and Pascal's rigor. And fanned to fierce heat by his encounters in Jersey and Hastings during his years of final training, and by the cataclysm, which for him was defining, of the Great War.

At the dawn of the century young Jesuits had to pursue their studies outside France. For Teilhard, this meant the Isle of Jersey (literature and philosophy)

---

*She was the great-granddaughter of Voltaire's sister, Catherine Arouet.
†The family lived in a house once frequented by Pascal.

and Hastings (for theology), a stint interrupted by the two years he spent teaching physics at the Jesuit College in Cairo—where, inevitably, he fell under the spell of the civilization of the Nile. In Jersey, and above all in Hastings, he took his place in a galaxy of eager young minds whose appetite for renewal was whetted by the pains of exile. Here, under the aegis of Father Léonce de Grandmaison, there emerged a whole new generation of Jesuits who would have horrified Pius X and the Roman Curia (and would have their successors shaking in their slippers): Victor Fontoynont, Pierre Rousselot, Auguste and Albert Valensin, Christian Burdo, Pierre Charles, Joseph Huby, and—although he would "turn out badly"—Paul Doncoeur.

From Jersey to Hastings, between the 1901 expulsion and the First World War—the time of the great quarrel over "modernism," which saw Pius X's Rome crush the stirrings of learning and innovation—a phalanx of bold, inventive Jesuits was formed, avid for knowledge and freedom of expression, profoundly aware of the impotence and blindness of the Church whose energies they longed to release.

The well-behaved child, the kid Teilhard, now mutated so swiftly and boldly that his brilliant Hastings companions would remain forever open to his "Pan-Christism," if perhaps not his "Pantheism of Union." All the seeds were already germinating in Teilhard as he devoured philosophers like Henri Bergson (whose *L'Évolution créatrice* was published in 1907) and Édouard Le Roy—but also the works of geologists and prehistorians like Pierre Termier, Marcellin Boule, and the Abbé Breuil. And in 1912, he embarked on the study of paleontology, in which he at once displayed striking gifts.

War came to a mind at full boil, and heated it to melting point. For four years Stretcher-bearer (later Stretcher-bearer Corporal) Teilhard, who had stubbornly refused a commission and promotion to Chaplain, served alongside Moroccan riflemen and Zouaves, the first units to be thrown into battle in order to man the most waterlogged of front-line positions. There he displayed a coolness and fearlessness that won him a glittering cascade of honors, including the Legion of Honor. What he called his "baptism into the real" another writer called the "awakening of his genius." And Teilhard himself had the strange courage to call it (such words, applied to such hellish circumstances!) his "intellectual honeymoon." His *Écrits du temps de guerre*,[2] in which the strange canticle-manifesto quoted at the beginning of this chapter appears, are like a mine, a quarry, from which he would extract the ore of forty years' work.

An achievement pronounced "staggering" by Father d'Ouince, who adds:
I myself lived through that war. I learned the mind-numbing effects
of constant vigilance and constant physical effort—and I was twenty.*

*Teilhard was thirty-five when he wrote his "manifesto."

To me Teilhard's case seems a psychological miracle. Out on the front line, he thought all day long, and often at night. . . . He would make for the nearest wood and pace up and down for hours, consigning it all to notes at first light. At his next rest break, in some parish church or rundown sacristy, he would write . . . twenty or thirty pages in a meticulously neat hand.[3]

It was the shock of reality in its rawest, most aggressive form, the perception of that absolute which was the firing line he daily lived in, and which inspired in him pages pregnant with fascination. The war he was to remember with "nostalgia" was the midwife of his inner revolution. After that ordeal, what rashness would be beyond his scope? What challenge? From that furnace, in which both his thinking and his style had been tempered, he emerged a free man ("How can one be the most Christian of all men yet at the same time the most human of all men?"): "I write these lines out of love for life and the need to love: to enunciate a passionate vision of the Earth. . . . Because I love the Universe, its energies, its secrets, and its hopes, and because I have at the same time dedicated myself to God—sole Entrance, sole Exit, sole End . . . "[4]

Thus did Stretcher-bearer Corporal Teilhard emerge from war, shrugging off the teaching of the Jesuit fathers, wrenched from his youthful docility, freed from the "closed-off spaces of normal life," putting to rout "the slavery of the everyday." He was instilled with the lessons and exchanges of Jersey and Hastings, rich too from his encounters with the hoary old universe, henceforth knowing an Earth no longer abstract but in all its terrifying mud, flame, and fire, having borne in his arms life in its final throes and death in its first approaches, and having become familiar with death and closer to life, living fully through surviving, and worthy of declaring himself in love with the Universe.

Because he had just reconciled within himself the abstract and the concrete, lessons and life, the obedient child and the man braving fire, he believed he was also called to reconcile the spiritual and the temporal, the Church and his century. As he wrote, with magnificent candor, in *Mon Univers:* "Fate has set me down at a privileged crossroads in the world where, in my dual role as priest and man of Science, it has been given to me—under particularly exhilarating and varied conditions—to feel the double tide of human and divine powers surging through me."[5]

The complete man thus returning in 1918 almost from beyond the grave had also drawn near, in the full sweaty savagery of combat, to what he would always call "the feminine." Most of his war writings were intended for his cousin Marguerite Teilhard-Chambon, the confidante of his youth in Auvergne. He had run across her again at Clermont as he was leaving for the war. She was now a professor of philosophy and principal of a religious school in Paris, the Institut Notre-Dame des Champs.

She too was warm, generous, highly educated, and fearless in her convictions. Did Teilhard love her as an adolescent, or on the eve of war, when he was thirty? Jean Guitton, who knew them both well, calls the dark, Spanish-looking, pensive Marguerite "his Beatrice." In any case, there is nothing to confirm that Father Émile Rideau was referring to Marguerite when he wrote: "1913: discovery of the 'feminine' and of the importance of the sex problem. Why attempt to hide it? At this period Teilhard's chastity was tested. The temptation would return during his stay in Paris from 1927 to 1928."[6] Beatrice?

Would it be too much to maintain, as Jacques Madaule has done, that "it was first and foremost through his encounter with the feminine that Teilhard perceived the particularly unique and irreplaceable essence of the human person"? In any case, we should keep in mind this admission by the author of *The Heart of the Matter:* "Nothing ever grew in me except beneath the gaze and under the influence of a woman."

There is no doubt, though, that the wartime blooming of Teilhard's genius took place under the gaze of Marguerite Teilhard-Chambon, the recipient not only of the letters in which he exposed his soul but also of the twenty essays he wrote at the time. For a man as given to dialogue and exchange as Teilhard, it was a real and twofold creative experience. At the end of the war he made this decisive confession to his cousin: "You have meant much to me these last four years, more perhaps than you can imagine."

Intellectual friendships in the bosom of a fertile group of fellow students at the dawn of the century, first steps in biology and paleontology, the exhilarating flights of the war, proximity to the "feminine": When peace arrived, Pierre Teilhard de Chardin was approaching his forties and ripe for the great intellectual adventures ahead—adventures that would put his faith sorely to the test.

He himself acknowledged it: Only "after twenty years of groping and of inner experimentation" (in other words, even during his "well-behaved" childhood) was he able to harmonize "the love of Creation with that of the Creator." As René d'Ouince puts it: "A pantheist and pagan temperament, more fitting in a son of the earth than in a child of heaven? No doubt, and he unequivocally acknowledged it. In order to give himself without reserve to the revealed God, he needed nothing less than conversion."

It is a bold claim. But d'Ouince knew his subject. And he went on to say: "The fundamental duality that [his masters] maintained between man's natural efforts and the supernatural work of salvation tore him in two. . . . The lure of worldly goods was presented as a snare . . . [given that] the whole world lay in the power of the Evil One." But soon "his mind was made up, there was a holy face to the World, a commitment to the World desired by the Creator. . . . A communion with God through the Earth." Father d'Ouince's conclusion: "Here we are at the heart of Teilhardian thinking."[7]

Certainly. That is, at the heart of a ruthless debate that would leave the Verdun stretcher-bearer battered and bruised. And worse—immured in silence because he had dared to say, write, and proclaim that Man was the lord of creation once he was set free, once he was borne on a multimillennial concept of evolution, once his action "harmonized with the fulfillment of all cosmic perfection."[8]

A certainty that his friend Henri de Lubac would express differently, but with the same boldness: "Modern man has begun to understand that in the immensity of things he is not and cannot be just a spectator. . . . He knows that this World as such has a future, and that it is he who builds that future."[9]

When Teilhard emerged from the war brandishing these dangerous notions— "a Jesuit, and excessively so, in every fiber," writes the loyal d'Ouince, "resolute and revolutionary" enough to dazzle young emulators who thought they had found in him one of the legendary Jesuit giants, a Ricci or a Xavier—setting off for uncharted continents, he was fully aware of the risks he ran.

He wrote to Marguerite that his superiors feared he would "sink into pantheism," and he asked her to pray that it would always be the "*good* Spirit that inspired [him]." He reminded Valensin of the dangers he faced: "Enlarging the Universe to the point of eclipsing or 'materializing' God. . . . Using the natural resources and affections of life to the point of . . . taking pagan pleasure in them." Whereupon he decides: "Avoiding [these risks] is a question of Catholic sense and of Christian prudence."[10]

Unfortunately for Teilhard, and even more unhappily for the Roman Church, the latter never stopped interrogating itself about this "Catholic sense" and "Christian prudence."

The "Teilhard problem" can thus be summed up in one word: evolution. Since around 1911, when he first began his geological, prehistoric, and paleontological studies with the Abbé Henri Breuil and Marcellin Boule, Lamarck's and Darwin's theories had spilled all their riches before him. Yet the Roman theologians condemned the notion of evolution outright, even in its most timorous forms. And one of them had discovered a "new" argument against evolution, a decisive one: that the theory—among its many other inconveniences—allotted man an inferior role to woman's! For although Eve had most assuredly emerged from Adam's rib, the first man had apparently been born out of the animal kingdom! No need to be a student of bigotry to recognize in this a regrettable demotion of the dominant sex.

At the time Pierre Teilhard de Chardin began his great career in scientific research and teaching* (which to his mind was not without apostolic relevance), the Catholic Church still saw itself as a besieged citadel. The zealots of the Holy Office had launched a full-fledged witch hunt to cleanse the Roman Church. To see a Jesuit uphold the heresy of evolution appalled them. Worse, the scandal was quietly brewing in the very heart of Paris, at the hallowed Catholic Institute on the Rue d'Assas where Teilhard held the Chair of Geology.† Matters grew even worse when the author of *The Heart of the Matter* spectacularly and publicly defeated the Catholic scientist Vuilleton, a stubborn denouncer of evolutionary theory. Teilhard was indeed a decidedly pestilential Jesuit.

But he was also generous in word and deed; he was eloquent and knowledgeable (and bold); he charmed his listeners; and many Catholic and non-Catholic institutions were asking him to lecture, particularly on the origins of man. Not content with a fearless exposition of his Darwinist notions, he would invite an outpouring of questions and then unhesitatingly answer them—with a sincerity seized upon by the adversaries who packed the lecture halls. On the question of the Garden of Eden and (especially) Original Sin, the sometimes careless or sarcastic freedom of his speech generated still greater alarm. Reports went off to Rome. The Jesuit General, Ledochowski, was alerted.

One day in 1925 Teilhard de Chardin was invited to speak in the main amphitheater of the Sorbonne. His friend Abbé Gaudefroy was in the audience beside the rector of the Catholic Institute, Monsignor Baudrillart, who told him after the lecture: "Your friend Teilhard is going to leave us. He has become suspect." And to inject venom into his menacing words, Baudrillart added that the Superior General had received a warning from Cardinal Merry del Val, considered the most powerful figure in Rome. "The Jesuits will stand up to a cardinal!" retorted Gaudefroy. "You don't know this one!" said Baudrillart. "He's more likely to ban the Company!"

Thus, writes René d'Ouince,[11] "Teilhard was now on the list of suspects." The core of his accusers' case against him was a "note on Original Sin," which obviously questioned the concept of a Garden of Eden (as well as Catholic "concordism," which attempted to reconcile the Genesis story with scientific findings). And indeed if he did not actually reject the concept of "Original Sin," Teilhard did refuse to give it a historic form incompatible with his own vision— informed by science—of the world.

*In 1922 he presented his paleontology thesis on "The Lower Eocene Mammals in France."
†For two years, before his first stay in China.

Cardinal Merry del Val did not immediately use this note on Original Sin to drag the Jesuit to the now metaphorical stake. Superior General Ledochowski was ordered to obtain from Teilhard a written acknowledgment of the doctrine of Original Sin. The teacher bowed to the demand. But henceforth he remained outcast, contagious. A growing burden of suspicion would now weigh on him, in the upper reaches of the Company as in the bosom of the Roman Curia.

And so, at the close of the first quarter of the twentieth century, in the age of Einstein, one of the greatest Christian thinkers of modern times was reduced to silence by his Church. Simply because he questioned the Genesis fable, which situates the origins of the world and of humankind's tragedy in a flowered enclosure, where a tree conceals a serpent of indeterminate species but possessing a hand deft enough to hold out a fruit to the scantily clad lady, herself earlier extracted from the sleeping body of Adam, who would sire upon her two sons, one at least of whom would father the human race. Exiled, Teilhard was condemned to specialize thousands of miles from home in the hunt for Peking Man (*Sinanthropus pekinesis*). Who, as it happened . . .

Whence the cry of revolt we have already heard from Pierre Teilhard de Chardin, the "death throes" and the "storm" he spoke of to Auguste Valensin; whence too his biting mention of "fools" and "ignoramuses," later picked up in the French National Assembly by Paul Rivet. From that time too dates Rivet's urgent plea to the Jesuit: Leave this Company that bullies and stifles you, leave this Catholicism that turned itself into the enemy of the World and of Science! And finally, it was then that the Jesuit firmly turned down this logical advice.

Yet despite his acquiescence in the orders from above, Teilhard was bitterly aware that his banishment was absurd and harmful. "Paris is where my roots lie," he rumbled. "Never have I felt so well settled and ready to act, in my own milieu—and now they ask me to leave again."

When his friend Valensin suggested that this removal from Paris intellectual circles meant that God would now offer him the things dearest (or too dear?) to his mind and heart, Teilhard retorted: "Can I be sure I won't be 'deserting'? Yes, I believe I would take Communion with joy from that small chalice, but at least let me be sure that it is Christ's blood."

There lay the question. A doubt: "I would take Communion" is not future but conditional. "At least let me be sure . . . "Yet he had already decided on obedience. *Perinde ac cadaver?* No. A free choice between the revolt proposed by Rivet and a loyalty he considered reasonable, since he saw a break with the Company as a "biological blunder" ("blunder," not scandal; "biological," not spiritual).

All of which led up to the tormented conclusion he framed in a letter to Valensin:

I think I see that if I rebelled in any way whatsoever (humanly speaking, it would be so simple and so "nice") I would be disloyal to my belief that all things are the work of Our Lord. . . . Moreover, I would be compromising the religious worth of my ideas in the eyes of our own people (and perhaps of others). It would be seen as deserting the Church, as pride, as what you will. . . . It is essential for me to show by my example that if my ideas appear innovative, they leave me just as faithful as anyone imbued with the old viewpoint.

His refusal to countenance the "unimaginable"—a break with the Company and the Church—was undoubtedly an act of submission. But we must have no illusions that it extended to inward acceptance, or that it modified the attitude of the Church establishment that had reduced him to obedience. Submission erased nothing for either party. As Father d'Ouince says of Rome's and the Company's attitude: "The matter did not end there. It had many consequences that went beyond the Far Eastern exile of the Paris teacher. Merely by having been denounced in Rome, Teilhard was suspect. His position in his order and the Church was fundamentally changed. Although he did not realize it, his disgrace in 1924 was the first stage in a misunderstanding between the father and his Roman superiors, a stubborn misunderstanding that would only increase."[12]

And it was indeed a "disgrace," d'Ouince stresses. Henceforth, Pierre Teilhard de Chardin had a "record" in Rome. The trial would come later, and would continue to hound him even after his death.

As for the man returning to China in May 1926, he had no doubt that he was going into exile. "I am being sent away because of my ideas," he wrote. "They have demolished my whole research structure." Indeed, he never used any word but *exile* to describe his position.

But China was not Saint Helena. It was a magnificent research laboratory, as Pierre Teilhard de Chardin well knew, for he had already wandered there between 1922 and 1924 with a man he liked and admired, Father Émile Licent. And once returned, he swiftly regained a kind of serenity, or at least a research worker's exaltation, a scientist's sublimation.

We may well wonder at the curious choice his superiors had made in encouraging the specialist and paleontologist in him to the detriment of the humanist and the Christian apologist—thus shackling him to Matter (which is what China chiefly represented for Teilhard) at the expense of the spirituality of which he had given such striking evidence. We may also note that Church and Company (we shall distinguish later on between the attitudes of the two institutions) had once again opted for caution over creativity, for silence rather than the scandalous Truth, and for a prudent dichotomy between laboratory analysis and creative synthesis. The treatment of an aged confessor "shielding" genius against its "excesses," Church against the winds of freedom, dogma against life?

And now Teilhard was back in China.

What might be called his "Chinese cycle," of such great importance in his growth and the maturing of his scientific genius, consisted of ten Chinese sojourns of varying duration and significance. The last of them, which occupied nearly seven years (from 1939 to 1946), was extended beyond its intended duration by war. Of course our purpose here is not to record the life of the author of *The Phenomenon of Man*, still less to assess his achievements in paleontology, but to examine his relations with the Church and with his order. However, if we were to downplay the importance of Teilhard's voyage into the heart of China we should simply be playing Rome's game, that is, promoting the dichotomy between research—authorized, but as far away as possible—and religion—isolated, untouchable, immutable. For in China Teilhard pursued the task of explaining the universe which would help revitalize the challenge to the Stone Age Catholicism entrenched by the Vatican and by Pius X. That task long condemned the great lantern-bearer to work in semisecrecy.

First, two or three rather naïve questions. Why pack a paleontologist off to China in the mid-1920s? What were his material resources? And what of his priestly calling?

From the Jesuit standpoint, China was, and had been for three centuries, the ultimate arena of grand ventures (the latest of them being the Museum of Natural History founded at Tianjin by Father Licent). Moreover, since North China had not been shaken by tectonic quakes for millions of years, living beings had evolved there undisturbed. The study of their transformation over the millennia thus took on an exceptional fascination and importance. Only toward the end of his life would Teilhard place Africa in the first rank of paleontological research zones.

And resources? Whether or not we believe in a hypothetical Jesuit "treasure chest," it is a fact that from the first *maravédis* begged by Ignatius on the streets of Barcelona, the Company never seems to have lacked funds. In Teilhard's case, subsidies came from Paris museums and institutes and American foundations. He was one of those men who cross worlds without ever seeming worried by the problems that so sorely try other mortals.

As for the priestly function, it was part of the Jesuit genius to turn every act into a component and an emanation of priestcraft. No order had ever so boldly freed itself of ritual formalities—to the point of arousing charges of anti-sacramental heresy. Nor has anyone ever denied that Teilhard de Chardin was a priest most attentive to the fulfillment of his duties, with or (more often) without a soutane.

The secular aspects of his activities never overspilled the traditional boundaries of his order. Although paleontology, unlike astronomy, mathematics, or cartography, was not a Jesuit specialty, he was neither more nor less "detached" on the scientists' planet than Christophorus Clavius, Athanasius Kircher, or Ràder Boscovitch. In short, Teilhard the priest was "Jesuitissimus."

We cannot dwell here on the fresh tribulations of a Jesuit in Asia—no matter how flavorful, picturesque, or fruitful—as we did with Matteo Ricci. We can merely recall a few high points, grouped* in four highly differentiated sequences: his research work from 1922 to 1924 with Father Émile Licent; the Zhoukoudian digs of 1929 to 1930; the Gobi crossing of 1931; and the creation of the Geobiological Institute with Pierre Leroy.

It was Father Licent, founder of the Tianjin Natural History Museum, who had asked his superiors in the Company for a coworker. The new professor at the Catholic Institute seemed the logical choice. Forty years old, complete with his brand-new doctorate, Teilhard was ripe for such an adventure. For eighteen months, Licent and his assistant rode their mules the length and breadth of the Ordos uplands west of Beijing, the deep Shara Ousso-Gol Valley, then eastern Mongolia and Manchuria, making a rich harvest of discoveries linked to Paleolithic man in the northern Himalayas and to the Quaternary geology of the Far East. Far indeed from Genesis and the Garden of Eden so dear to the gentlemen in Rome. . . . In fact, too far.

Rich though their harvest was (or perhaps because their finds were immediately ushered into Father Licent's museum), he returned to France in the autumn of 1924 with eyes, mind, and heart brimming with an Asia where millions of centuries and millions of square miles conspired to force upon him the obsessive notion of a Cosmos in the process of limitless, endless change. As on the firing line in 1916, he had been given a foretaste of the Absolute toward which he had aspired since childhood. So when the excited scientist landed at Marseille in November 1924 he was in no mood to bow meekly before Parisian interrogators or Roman censors. With predictable results.

So, in November 1926, back again he went to China. This time battered by hostility and ostracism, but drawing strength from his ordeals, Pierre Teilhard de Chardin began his second adventure in the Chinese Far East. It is summed up in three Chinese syllables—Zhoukoudian—or in English as *Sinanthropus: Peking Man.*

Zhoukoudian is in the Western Hills some thirty miles west of Peking. The site had been discovered back in 1921 by the Swedish geologist Johan Gunnar Andersson, shortly followed by two colleagues, the Canadian Davidson Black

*As was skillfully done by Pierre Louis-Martin, president of the Teilhard de Chardin study group in Bordeaux, in an article in the newsletter of the Jesuit School at Tivoli.

and the Scot George Barbour. From the discovery of the first fossil fragments, of quartz blocks foreign to the area, and of mammal teeth, they were soon convinced that a creature of the Paleolithic era, *Sinanthropus*, Darwin's missing link, was about to be exhumed.

In October 1927, Davidson Black unearthed two teeth that seemed to herald victory: According to Black, they belonged to *Sinanthropus pekinensis*. One year later they dug up a human jaw. At the end of December 1929, having taken part in the last phase of the dig led by the Chinese Bei Wengzhong, Black, and Barbour, the Jesuit paleontologist sent this cable to Marcellin Boule in Paris: "Discovered Zhoukoudian uncrushed skull adult *Sinanthropus*, intact except face. Letter follows. Teilhard."

Less a revolution than a confirmation of the elaborators and defenders of the evolutionary theory, the discovery of Peking Man, overlapping that of Java Man, proved the existence on this high Asian flatland—perhaps 100,000 and more probably 400,000 years ago*—of a *homo faber* group which had mastered fire (as traces of man-made hearths attested). Teilhard could justly hail this "discovery of a pre-Neanderthal phase of human life" as a "major scientific conquest."

What can the formidable Cardinal Merry del Val, ensconced in his spacious Vatican office, have thought of these goings-on? What would he have said if he had read this note in *Lettre au voyage (Letter from a Traveler)* sent by the errant Jesuit, his sandals crusted with the mud of the Western Hills: "The fundamental discovery has been made: We are borne on a walking wave of awareness"?

Who had the idea of calling on Teilhard to be the geologist on the Gobi crossing, the motorized caravan sent out over the face of Asia in 1931 by André Citroën to find the old Silk Road and test his newfangled caterpillar equipment? There was no clear connection between Peking Man and the caravan. But Jesuits were long familiar with the endless roads of Asia: Had not the sixteenth-century Portuguese Bento de Goes been the first European to retrace Marco Polo's tracks? Whatever the explanation, in the spring of 1931 Teilhard found himself embarked on this adventure, whose scientific possibilities may have somewhat compensated in his eyes for its commercial undertones. Would a Carthusian have undertaken the journey? But he was a Jesuit—the most Jesuit Jesuit in centuries ("Excessively so," suggests Father d'Ouince).

One column, led by Georges-Marie Haardt, manager of Citroën, left Beirut for China. Another, under a naval officer named Victor Point, headed for Beijing from the West, with Teilhard aboard. They arranged to meet at Aksou, in the northern Himalayas. Driving five half-tracks, Teilhard and his compan-

---

*Toward the end of his life, Teilhard would raise this figure further.

ions crossed a Xinjiang aflame with civil war into Turkestan. They were taken prisoner at Urunchi, but managed to meet the Haardt squad, as arranged, at Aksou. Then they crossed the Gobi Desert (where the thermometer fell to twenty-five below zero), reaching Beijing in May 1932.

The expedition's historian, Georges LeFevre, has left us this hurried sketch of the long-legged geologist: "His alert eyes spied the smallest reddish carved stone standing out against the gray bare windswept ground. He would stop the vehicle, hop nimbly down, pick up first one pebble and then another, and off we would go again. Could this be a true center of Middle Paleolithic culture? No . . . But of an apparently Mousterian center of the quartzite industry."[13]

The commander in chief of the enterprise, Haardt, wrote that "this prince of the Church was [as animated] as was possible with the spirit of the expedition."[14] As for Teilhard himself, he wrote from Beijing to Marguerite Teilhard-Chambon that the adventure had "increased [his] knowledge of Asia twofold."

It is no less certain that between *Sinanthropus* and the Gobi crossing, the "prince" whom the Church had attempted to bury in those remote vastnesses had emerged as a figure of international fame. For better or for worse? Teilhard's strength was that he was no more ruffled by this rather clamorous glory than he had been by the shower of darts from the Vatican. Soon every conceivable kind of large-scale geological or anthropological expedition—whether the Oxford and Cambridge team in India or the Harvard-Carnegie group in Burma—was calling on him to join.

One of his biographers, Georges-Henri Baudry, maintains that his China exile was "providential," the "chance of a lifetime"; and that, "confined in the laboratories of Paris or adrift in social circles," he would never have attained "such stature" or such a "worldwide hearing."[15] Untrue. Teilhard's influence would have extended no matter where he found himself, in the laboratories as in the trenches. But the "terrain"—not only in China but in Abyssinia or the Malay Archipelago—gave him constant nourishment and helped root him in his evolutionist convictions. Every blow of the pickaxe moved the Zhoukoudian paleontologist a little farther from the Roman vulgate.

Pierre Teilhard de Chardin's last stop in China was expected to be brief. On his return from a third voyage to the United States, followed by a stay in France, he had planned to spend a few months in Beijing in order to reorganize the university's geological department there with his friend Bei. It was August 1939.

But the turning wheels of history immobilized him for six years in China—mostly in Beijing, since the Japanese occupying forces temporarily banned movement. It gave him the opportunity to discover the Chinese people and to forge a deep friendship there with his junior, Pierre Leroy, with whom he helped found the Beijing Geological Institute.

You can be a great biologist and paleontologist and prehistorian without being a good sociologist. Like Teilhard. His perception of this China—and above all of the Chinese—as it neared the end of the millennium lacked the subtlety of his great forerunners Ricci, Joseph-Marie Amyot, and Father Lecomte. Was this because he did not speak Chinese and had taken little interest in China's ancient culture? Diplomat-poets with the same drawbacks—Alexis Léger and Paul Claudel—have looked with greater perspicacity upon the Far East. But we must attend to the following penetrating observations, even though they fail to reflect the greater Teilhard, who is here caught in a spirit of rare but flagrant pessimism:

> Submerged in the mass of the Chinese people, an enormous, inert, earthbound mass, instinctively* hostile to strangers proposing changes it does not need. . . . An ocean of primitive beings, doubtless good and affectionate, but inquisitive, clinging, as lacking in tact as savages. . . . Poor, well-meaning, and defenseless creatures whose life is hard. . . . Between Chinese and Europeans it is always the formal and the approximate that predominate.[16]

In fact, the focus of Teilhard's gaze was elsewhere. His duties recalled him to the practice of geology, and he was drawn to biology by his young friend Pierre Leroy—who had just arrived in China, and who, in the second half of Teilhard's life, would fill the role of confidant that Auguste Valensin had played in the first half. And above all, he was now feverishly and strenuously writing and rewriting his major work, *The Phenomenon of Man*.

He also made new women friends: the American sculptor Lucille Swan, an enthusiastic paleontologist who dedicated years to reconstructing male and female *sinanthropuses;* and Claude Rivière, a professor of literature turned self-taught journalist and then navigator, who was managing Shanghai's French radio station when Teilhard and Leroy stopped there in 1942.†

This time, however, his "China exile" assumed its literal meaning. For someone of Teilhard's stature and international reputation, to remain cut off from the gigantic game being played from London to Tokyo and from San Francisco to Stalingrad to Singapore, reduced to a blind half-captive spectator's role in the conflict in which his friends Lebreton, Fontoynont, or Fessard (and, on the other side, Doncoeur) were taking an active part, a conflict to which he felt deeply committed, was nothing short of mutilation.

What part would Pierre Teilhard de Chardin have played had he remained in France? We shall later attempt to reply in terms of his "politics." Let us for a moment look for clues. In a letter of December 9, 1933, he had written to fellow

*How many comments this word begs!
†In 1966 she published *En Chine avec Teilhard* (Paris, Grasset).

Jesuit Henri de Lubac: "The different brands of Fascism seem (to the extent that they are race-hating and nationalistic) an abnormal, sterile, regressive reaction."[17] (In the Teilhardian vocabulary, the last word is truly the most damning.) And we have it from Father Leroy that Teilhard caused a scandal during a dinner at the home of the (Vichy) French ambassador in Beijing by supporting the cause of the defenders of Stalingrad.

Everything—his close ties to his Jesuit friends at home, his spontaneous (and scientific) horror of race-motivated thinking, and his disinclination for Vatican-style conservative opportunism—inclines us to think that Teilhard de Chardin would have been on the side of angels like Lubac and Gaston Fessard, rather than opportunistic devils like Paul Doncoeur and Norbert de Boynes.* But the fact is that during his four years of confinement in Beijing he never seized the chance to convey his sympathy and understanding to those who fought Vichy's collaboration with the occupying enemy. There is just a "Teilhard silence," hovering like a black mark over this great and exalted life.

It was not on taking final leave of China in 1945, but at the time of the Gobi crossing, that he wrote the following words. They serve as the epitaph to his "China phase" and his first exile—and they show no sign of his wanting to return to the bosom of Catholic orthodoxy: "I wanted to emerge from the fog to see things for themselves. . . . What I saw first of all was that Man alone can help Man decipher the world." Man alone . . .

Such was the Teilhard who returned to France early in May 1946, at sixty-five, tired, frustrated by his long Chinese exile, irritated by the disciplinary harassments of a sour-tempered superior at the quarters made available to him and Leroy—but also master of his learning, of his thinking, haloed in a glory attested to by the universities of North America, and bearing in his baggage what he considered his masterwork, *The Phenomenon of Man.*

We have already caught a glimpse of his style, his vibrato, his tempo. We must pause here for a clearer understanding of his fame, the spell he cast on ancient canons and young students, on so many free-spirited women and so many recalcitrant priests, so many touchy scientists and men of action. Indeed no one failed to be seduced by this Jesuit condemned to "death throes" by Church busybodies. He was set on a pedestal and hailed as a prophet by numberless Christians thirsting for intellectual freedom, but also by unbelievers seeking understanding of the world.

In truth, the man was irresistible. Not just his friends—de Lubac or Chenu, Pierre Leroy who lived so long by his side in China, Paul Flamand who pub-

*See Chapter XIII.

lished him—but his agnostic fellow workers and his audience across the world spoke of the unaffected charm of a luminous personality almost recklessly offered, open to the point of innocence (more Franciscan than Jesuit in this regard?). What struck people about the author of *The Phenomenon of Man* was his perpetual alacrity, pulsing with joyful vitality and optimism.

Teilhard walked through life with long strides, from continent to continent, from millennium to millennium, from the Gobi Desert to Harar in Abyssinia, a beret on his head, or a sun helmet, or a turban, a cape slung across his shoulders, in shorts and bush-jacket, wearing boots or rope soles—something of Marco Polo, something of Claudel, something of Rimbaud—tough, laughing, pick or hammer in hand and a parable on his lips, twenty stories in his head, a too human human at once riveted to the priestly fetters he had accepted and in permanent violation of Church law, a prophet constantly struck down and constantly reborn.

Writers and scientists, priests and miscreants, the devout and the skeptical, all have attempted to capture (in a few lines or in hundreds of pages) this great prophetic bird with its albatross wings. One—Marcel Brion—speaks of his Oxonian demeanor, evocative of great British scholars in the Darwin and Newman tradition. Another claims to have seen in him a kind of Liszt, "so musical [were] his hands, as if he were fingering piano keys, sometimes holding a *Pithecanthropus* or hominid tooth with the tips of his fingers, like the Host, to let us assay the human phenomenon through these relics."[18]

And this shrewd note by Jean Guitton on his last visit to Teilhard: "I was struck more than ever by a sort of casualness, of indifference.* I saw in him not a master but a pioneer. Pioneers tear their hands on thorns, they grope. Pioneers go before the masters who will build roads for vehicles, who will, as Péguy put it, set up signposts."[19]

Teilhard a cultivated man? Teilhard a "politician"? Here we are in the dark. René d'Ouince and Pierre Leroy mention some of his reading: curiously, André Gide rather than Claudel, Pierre Termier, René Grousset, Emmanuel Mounier, Jacques Maritain. In his penetrating article about Teilhard in the *Dictionnaire de spiritualité*, Father Pierre Noir tells us that on his return to France in 1946 "he attentively read Sartre, Camus, and Bouchard, and reread Nietzsche and Freud."

Was he a great devourer of books outside his own fields of paleontology and geology? His letters show him to have been rather conservative: When he mentions Descartes, Hegel, and Marx, they are adversaries rather than partners. He was a passionate reader of Bergson, whose *L'Evolution créatrice* might have

*The great Jesuit virtue . . .

served as a cover-all title for the whole of his writings:* Both the convergences and the differences between priest and philosopher were remarkably well laid out by Madeleine Barthélemy-Madaule in the very first university thesis devoted to Teilhard.

His friendship for Édouard Le Roy, whose work was placed on the Index by the Holy Office, probably contributed to his own disgrace. But Maurice Blondel was probably his closest intellectual kin, unless it was Julian Huxley, the great English biologist and first director-general of UNESCO, who attempted to invent a kind of religion without God.

Politically speaking, Teilhard is beyond classification—even though, from the *Osservatore romano* to *La France catholique,* his work was denounced as a breeding ground of "progressive" subversion, and he was never afraid to meet with such figures as the French Communist leader Paul Vaillant-Couturier. He was an impoverished landowner from the Massif Central, born into a conservative background and committed by solemn religious vows to an order no less conservative, scarred by the crisis of the separation of church and state, and his letters show him to have been little concerned at the possibility of breaking with his own people on this point—with what he himself called the "establishment."

It would be ridiculous to assign excessive meaning to this note of March 1, 1948, which appears in his correspondence with Pierre Leroy: "Who can say whether, in the very interests of God's reign, a man immersed in Marxism is not the one meant to save us?" A fleeting thought, no doubt. But in any case, Teilhard so favored the "long term"—and in his case of course the words are an understatement!—that he can justifiably be accused of neglecting the short term, which other great minds have also similarly underrated.

Did he consider himself a prophet? His letters show that he saw a surprising parallel between his own role and that of John the Baptist. And Father d'Ouince, his spiritual director (who knew both what he was talking about and what his illustrious "pupil" was saying), entitled his excellent book about Father Teilhard *Un prophète en procès* (A Prophet on Trial). We have the tragic expression of the prophet's condition, with all the risks and suffering it implies, in one of Teilhard's very last texts, written a few weeks before his death: "How is it, as I look about me still intoxicated by what has appeared to me, that I find myself more or less alone of my species? Alone in having *seen?*" Is not the last temptation of the prophet first to feel himself alone, and then feel deserted by everyone?

"We should give him freedom to wander," wrote Jean Guitton, a man not associated with rash progressivism. But that point had not yet been reached. In

*So could *Le Chant du monde,* but Jean Giono chose that one.

those years immediately after the end of the Second World War, the Church was trying to forget its resonant silences—not only over Jewish genocide but also over the martyrdom of Poland's Catholics in 1941, on which the Jesuits of Vatican Radio were ordered to keep silence.

This Church, whose self-serving performance could not be redeemed by the sacrifices of Maximilien Kolbe or Alfred Delp or Yves de Montcheuil, did not see its mistakes as grounds for reform. While lay collaborators almost everywhere were paying the price for their games with the defeated Fascist enemy, the Holy See and its dignitaries kept in power figures whose authority was forever after discredited. The old "signposts" remained the same.

No one felt this more painfully than Pierre Teilhard de Chardin when, back from an exile that had cut much deeper than geographic and cultural distance, he was burning to speak out, break out, and publish. While a heart infection put him at death's door in June 1947, while the Republic hailed him as "a glory of French science," while the Collège de France was proposing that he succeed Abbé Breuil at its head, while the Institute was fêting him—Rome was enjoining silence on everything that lay outside his scientific sphere. Peking Man, yes. Christ, no.

The bans of 1952 fell upon an academic at the height of his career who suddenly found himself back on treacherous, mine-strewn terrain—Original Sin. His adversaries of 1947, and of the years to come, aimed at and struck an illustrious scholar intent on showing the world that a Christian speaking of his faith was not necessarily an imbecile in a biretta.

Thus in August 1947 the Jesuit Superior General, Father Jean-Baptiste Janssens, conveyed to the Superiors of the Company in France that Teilhard had been denied the right to express himself on anything but his own discipline. As we know, Teilhard was not the man to rebel. But still less the man to yield without setting forth his arguments. In September 1947, he wrote to Superior General Janssens:

> You may count on me. . . . I hope only that the Lord will help me to find my way unfalteringly through a psychologically difficult situation. Luckily I have around me here in the Company great and trusted friends whom you know, and who will help me along my path.
>
> Allow me to add, in all filial simplicity and confidence, that as I see things there is a measure of contempt or misunderstanding in the conditions imposed on me, which I believe will finally be dissipated by loyalty. Since 1939 (all my incriminated papers date, I believe, from before then) I have (according to the authorized theologians who follow my steps) made great strides toward the correct explication of a point of view which—given my experience among the "Gentiles"— truly seems to have a chance of serving the Kingdom of God. Do you

not think it might be a pity to discard without examining it a fruit that is perhaps on the verge of ripening . . . ?[20]

That message was sent at the height of a campaign of personal harassment: While silence shrouded *The Phenomenon of Man*, submitted a year earlier to his superiors, the latter had forbidden him to apply for a teaching post at the Collège de France in 1946, and then in 1948 renewed their veto over a second university chair.

At that point he decided to go and plead his cause in Rome—for the Collège de France and above all for *The Phenomenon of Man*. His plan was approved: He would see the General. Full of confidence, he wrote to his friend George Barbour: "If they give the green light for publication, there's every chance that I'll be allowed to stand for the Collège de France." And he confided to his friend d'Ouince, "I'm glad to be seeing the boss. I'll tell him what's in my heart."

Here was Teilhard in Rome: Teilhard of the clear gaze, naïve Teilhard, wandering into the den of theologians. These "holy places I never dared think I might ever approach," this "frightening display of Church pomp,"[21] failed to seduce him. But the Church of the Gesù, with its "teeming statues and moldings," found an echo in his Jesuit upbringing and reawakened "family recollections" ("and don't think I'm turning all syrupy and deliquescent!"). He found this whole world "very nice" and the Boss (this time capitalized) "frank, direct, and human"[22] (exactly the reaction of a dazzled captain, invited to headquarters behind the lines by a four-star general . . . ah, these Jesuits!).

In vain did Janssens try to "win him over" and assure him of his support: Nothing came of the long-awaited interview. His "watchful" colleagues spoke to him of necessary "revisions" of his book, and of the "need for patience." But even the Collège de France was now out of the question. It all came about as if the "frank and direct" General Janssens had "put him to sleep." In his letters to Leroy he pretends to laugh about it, and says he is "most philosophical." But he was less disappointed for himself than humiliated—not *by* but *for* those who treated him in this fashion.

And because there was always greater explosive power within him than slip-inducing ploys outside him, he was able to write to Pierre Leroy, in an apparently innocent postscript, the following words about the "frustrations of modern Christians": "Religion explicitly and officially presents us with the God we need. That is why it seems to me so all-important, so utterly fundamental, to rethink Christology and reveal to the world what I call the Universal Christ."[23] And on his return to France he was very soon speaking of "giving birth to a new faith," to a "religion of tomorrow" springing from the "Roman trunk" (here he was hewing faithfully to the line drawn four centuries earlier by Loyola and his fellow workers).

The more he was pilloried, the more energetically Teilhard reacted; the more the gentlemen of Rome felt they had sanitized and fettered him, the harder and more explosively he fought. All of it, of course, "from within." René d'Ouince describes him at this period as shocked by the offer from a defrocked cleric to join his "Old Catholic Church" (as though Teilhard ever thought of anything but the future!). The same writer has him quoting Antoine de Saint-Exupéry's line: "To act upon his house, one must be of his house." Or else responding to a questioner: "Do you think me mad enough to create a second religion? Or to believe myself a second Jesus Christ?"[24]

His Roman excursion had been a fiasco. The world of the Holy See (and even that of the Jesuit general staff) was then impervious to such thinking. Half-amused, half-angry, he concluded that in Rome—twenty years after the discovery of Peking Man—evolution was still considered a mere theory. (A certain Cardinal Ruffini even published a book to disprove it yet again: "The cardinal is still bogged down in the idea of God breathing a soul into a monkey.")

Could there be divorce without physical separation? Clearly Teilhard had submitted to the rule, but what about the mind? He saw himself as an exile, no longer in remoteness, as he had between 1925 and 1945, but in internal exile. He had once and for all acknowledged that the Church from which he would never sunder himself had in a sense sundered itself from him—or in any case from that irrefutable scientific truth on which, sooner or later, the "new religion," reconciled with science, would have to be reinvented from the Roman "trunk," the Roman "phylum."*

Did he differentiate here between Church and Company? Yes and no. He saw with gratitude and joy that his companions at the Rue Monsieur offices of the Jesuit magazine *Études*—who could be startled and sometimes even frightened by his boldness ("new faith," "religion in need of reinvention"), and were then constrained to see him, according to Father d'Ouince, as less "defensible" than "forgivable"—created a protective cocoon around him, a brotherly "first circle" proud of his genius.

But he had also seen that he disturbed and worried the people at the Borgo Santo Spirito, the Company's Roman seat. He admitted that he had been received "extremely pleasantly" there, but both Father Gorostarzu,† Jesuit Assistant for France, and Superior General Janssens were less alive to his fame and his genius than to the risks he represented. And the review *Civiltà cattolica* made it clear that when the occasion arose the "Black Pope" knew how to put some distance between Teilhard and the Company—or at the very least serve as the "trusted arm" of the Holy See's prohibitions.

*A typically Teilhardian term, evoking species, lineage . . .
†See Chapter XV.

In fact, though, the distance was shorter between the two institutions, Papacy and Company, than between the two cities, Rome and Paris. Teilhard felt closer to many French Dominicans than to the upper Roman tiers of his own order. Closer as well to laymen, Christian and non-Christian alike.

We have dwelt at some length on the Vatican institution and its Jesuit neighbor. In 1925, as in 1948, they were more concerned with stifling the Teilhard "scandal" than distilling nectar from the wealth of his ideas, of his contribution, of the new graft he prophetically held out to Catholicism. We should well wonder at the "admissibility" of this message sent out by the Catholic Church in the very middle of the twentieth century. It is not enough to condemn the grotesque shortsightedness of these princes of the Church. We must also, in all innocence, ask ourselves just how reckless Pierre Teilhard de Chardin's ideas were. In fact, are we still even talking about Catholic thinking?

Teilhard's integration of evolution into Catholicism (unless it was the other way around) was bound to shake, if not anger, the supporters of dogma based on a revelation that twenty centuries of heated debate (conciliar or otherwise) had left untouched. To proclaim God "in a state of becoming," God "in evolution," was to go much further than many of the heretics—consigned in former times to the stake—had dared venture.

Teilhard never claimed to make Lamarck or Darwin fathers of the Church. But he was the man for whom "God never stops being born," for whom God "happens" in the history of the world, this world of which men are "co-creators." And the man who wrote to his confidante Jeanne Mortier that "there are two ways of comprehending both the 'heart' and Jesus' 'Cross.' Here a 'heart,' simply suffering and in need of 'consolation.' There a center of creative energy that sets the world in motion."[25] From a grieving Christianity to one of creator energy: The tall Jesuit was indeed taking immense strides.

To understand something of the alarm felt by the aged prelates, we must read *L'Hymne à la matière* (Hymn to Matter) ("Blessings unto Thee, dangerous Matter, violent sea, untamable passion. Blessings unto Thee, powerful Matter, irresistible Evolution, ever reborn Reality . . . "). And these lines from *The Heart of the Matter:* "Let us admit it: If the various neo-humanisms of the twentieth century dehumanize us under their excessively low skies, then the still-living forms of theism (beginning with Christianity) tend to sub-humanize us in the rarefied atmosphere of their too lofty skies."[26]

Should we ascribe to the present author's theological ignorance the fact that he believed he detected so many dissonances between his own vision and what he believed he knew of Christian doctrine? Or at least of the doctrine frozen by a couple of councils and ossified by Pius IX and Pius X?

Given that a theologian of Henri de Lubac's stature saw in his friend more blank spaces and gaps than errors, and that Teilhard was never, properly speaking, condemned by the Holy Office, it would be odd to aspire to be more Roman than Rome and more conservative than Pius XII.

Let us then assume that, of the eleven kinds of pantheism the meticulous Claude Cuénot attempted to differentiate in the author of *The Heart of the Matter,* the only one that can truly be attributed to Teilhard is his "pantheism of Union," a schema derived from the so-called pantheism of convergence. The doctrine that God is all in all, the Me seeking to reach a real and transcendent Center of Evolution.

Let us also consider that if the ever meticulous Cuénot considered it unnecessary to pause at and define the word "sin" among the hundred-odd words making up the Teilhardian vocabulary,[27] it was not because Teilhard failed to incorporate concepts related to evil or error into his universe*—but because the word in fact occurs very rarely in his reasoning (indeed he had been wary of the word ever since his bitter experience of 1925 on the question of Original Sin).

On Teilhard's relationship to "sin," Jacques Laberge, a Quebec Jesuit and psychologist, has written some penetrating lines in *Pierre Teilhard de Chardin et Ignace de Loyola,* based on notes Teilhard put together while on retreat. He ascribes Teilhard's apparent indifference to sin to the fact that he wrote above all for the "Gentiles," for "contemporaries who had lost the sense of sin as a violation of the law of God and who found no God to worship around them. To them, Teilhard felt close. Had he not written, discussing the incoherent nature of his doctrine of sin, that he led 'an outlaw life'? And here he also reveals an important aspect of his psychological makeup: he 'escaped the law.' "

Here are some jottings by Teilhard in retreat, as quoted by Jacques Laberge:
Sin affects me little:
One, because I always manage to *justify* what I do . . .
Two, because in the "Via Tertia" in which I blindly grope, the "code" has not yet been fixed—so that errors, not being classified, are less obvious.
—What makes me unreceptive to the Meditation of Triple Sin is the fact that the current *(deposed)* "Laborious Universe" seems *more beautiful* to me than the World of Paradise. . . . A further obstacle to my perception of sin is that I discern intensely the "dynamism" of Evil.[28]

The " 'dynamism' of Evil." These words were not written for publication. But it was wise beyond a shadow of a doubt to keep them from the eyes of Cardinal Ottaviani, Prefect of the Holy Office.

---

*De Lubac demonstrates the opposite, at great length.

As for the fundamentally and almost exclusively Christlike nature of his Catholicism, it is obviously tempting to see in it a questioning of the Trinity, particularly in its determination to "humanize" (or, to use a word of the author's) to "hominize" Christianity by merging it with the one Ernest Renan called "the sublimest of men." But here too, good theologians exonerate Teilhard, placing him somewhere along the path taken by Saint John and Saint Paul.

The reader will understand that these few badly expressed and inarticulate questions are not intended to pick fundamentalist holes in the great Jesuit from Clermont. Everything about this man compels the author's admiration, not least his heroic attempt to bring together modern science and Christian belief, the profound humanism underpinning that effort, the optimism that drove him. Nothing could be less wide-eyed or less comfortable than that quest, linked to a crisis of tension in which Teilhard, wrestling to keep the ship on course, ceaselessly sought new bearings.

There are few visions more extraordinary than that of the author of *The Phenomenon of Man*—of a universe evolving through millions of centuries toward *homo faber* and beyond him, to this final recapitulation, this *omega* placed under the sign of Christ and of love. Clearly a vision likelier to fascinate poets and astrophysicists than the old gents of the Roman Curia.

Until 1949 Pierre Teilhard de Chardin received from the Vatican only warnings by omission, or tacit, tactful signals transmitted and filtered through his superiors and his friends. "It was" hoped that . . . "It was" regrettable that . . . "It was" suggested that . . . But on January 30, 1949, the *Osservatore romano*, the semi-official organ of the Vatican, published this poisonous little squib about a report on a conference on modern humanism, in the course of which a newspaper had described Teilhard as an "eminent theologian" (an honor he had never claimed): "We are duty-bound to emphasize that (without denying the Father his special paleontological skills) . . . many of his observations of a doctrinal nature must be held subject to serious reservations, given that his system, from the philosophical and theological standpoint, is not uncontaminated by a dangerous obscurity and ambiguity."

The blade, hanging over him since June 1926, had dropped.

It should therefore not be surprising that Pius XII's encyclical *Humani Generis*,* published eighteen months later, should initially have been read as a condemnation of Teilhardism. But in fact, the text included a small concession to the Jesuit's views when it authorized Catholic scientists to accept as "probable" the creation of the first man from "preexisting, living matter." Oho,

---

*Commented one eminent Jesuit: "Every time an encyclical begins with the word 'human,' you can be sure it will be merciless."

what have we here! But the rest of the pontifical document was such a bloodless warning against all innovation (which it called "temerity") that it was recognized as an indictment of the pioneer—who had just been elected to the French Academy of Sciences and was writing his autobiography, *The Heart of the Matter.*

Teilhard reacted angrily:

> For ten days I have been delivering oral and written replies to SOS calls from every quarter. In fact . . . the notorious document leaves me undisturbed. Shouting won't make the earth stop turning. . . . Overall, there's a strong whiff of fundamentalism in the air, particularly marked in condemnation of "irenism." As if adjusting and enlarging Christology to the quantitative and organic dimensions of the new world were making "concessions"! I even wonder whether, in the two Roman acts of this year, a good psychoanalyst would not detect clear traces of a specific religious perversion: the sado-masochism of orthodoxy; taking pleasure in swallowing or making others swallow the truth in its crudest and stupidest shapes. . . . And yet the world is in a flap, is lost, simply because the Church, repository of modern Monotheism, refuses to let it worship the God it awaits. . . . The question is not whether the Church has more or less held on to its inner cohesion, but whether—given this wretchedly lukewarm approach to worship—it is equal to its specific vocation of setting the world ablaze!
>
> I am as untouched by bitterness and as optimistic as I can be. But I know full well that from now on nothing will make me change by a single line my conviction that we now stand in need—because the human mind changes—of a richer figuration of God.[29]

If "setting the world ablaze" was what was required, his only possible course was to take once more to his travels. China had already been forced upon him. This time it would be America, in New York, where the Wenner-Gren Foundation for Anthropological Research extended an invitation to Teilhard. Objectively, notes Father d'Ouince, his position was "much harder even than in 1926." He was now spied on and harassed, as the article from the *Osservatore romano* attests. But henceforth he was freed of all "temptation to rebel," ensconced as he was in a peace "at times serene, at times painful," and marked by this prayer he sent to many of his correspondents: "Lord, give us the grace to end well." In other words, in tranquil submission.

We shall consider only briefly the last (and chiefly American) stages of the life of the great Jesuit, welcomed by his New York colleagues not as an outcast but as a friend. Nevertheless, the *cordon sanitaire* around him remained impenetrable. The Company carried its "protection" very far: Father d'Ouince reports that during the 1950s Jesuit General Janssens agreed (and then very rarely) to receive journalists only on condition that Teilhard's name not be mentioned in the interview.[30]

The "Black Pope" was on his guard. In December 1951, he had received from the author of *The Heart of the Matter* a very out-of-the-ordinary message, conveying at once the untamable independence and the obedient spirit of the most famous of his "charges":

> Before anything else, I think that you must resign yourself to taking me just as I am—in other words, with the congenital virtues (or weaknesses) which have decreed ever since my youth that my spiritual life should be ceaselessly dominated by a kind of profound "sense" of the organic reality of the World. . . .
>
> I have found [in it] an extraordinary and inexhaustible source of inner clarity and strength, and an atmosphere outside which it has become physically impossible to breathe, to worship, to *believe*. And what people may have seen in my attitude over the past thirty years as obstinacy or impertinence, is quite simply the result of my inability to let my wonder explode from within me. That, psychologically, is the bottom state of affairs from which all else derives, and which I can no more change than my age or the color of my eyes.
>
> . . . I feel today more inextricably tied to the hierarchical Church and to the Christ of the Gospels than I have ever been. Never has Christ seemed to me more real, more personal, more immense. How can I believe that the path I tread is the wrong one . . . ?
>
> Nonetheless, as I fully acknowledge, Rome may have its reasons for judging that in its present form my vision of Christianity is premature, or incomplete, and could not at this time be disseminated without causing problems.
>
> It is on this important point of outer fidelity and obedience that I am particularly anxious (indeed it is the essential object of this letter) to assure you that—despite certain appearances—I am resolved to remain a "child of obedience."
>
> Clearly I cannot (at the risk of inner catastrophe and of disloyalty to my dearest calling) stop seeking for myself.[31]

Father Teilhard had brought things into the open. Here was his personal reading of *perinde ac cadaver*. And the man to whom—by reason of his election—he owed that obedience knew both the limits of that reading and the price Teilhard had freely paid. The rules regulating both sides were known and henceforth clear. But as a scientist Teilhard was too conscious of his contribution, and as a priest too passionately convinced of the need for his message, not to seek to turn his death (which after two heart attacks he knew to be imminent) into an intellectual liberation.

On July 2, 1951, Jeanne Mortier, Teilhard's secretary and friend, called on him at the offices of the magazine *Études,* where he lived whenever he was in Paris. There she received a curious proposal from Father Raymond Jouve, assistant to Father d'Ouince: "Father Teilhard is leaving for the Transvaal. The journey could aggravate his heart condition. Ask him to bequeathe his writings to you, because we, as Jesuits, will never be allowed to publish them." No sooner said than done. Teilhard at once drew up a will in which he "gives exclusively" to his beneficiary "all my writings, published or dictated, in your possession"* and "all rights to the best use thereof depending on circumstance (preservation, publication, distribution) in the event of my demise."

Legally speaking, what mathematicians call an "elegant solution"[32] had been found to the problem. René d'Ouince adds that in his last conversations, Teilhard acknowledged the Company's right either to "disavow" his work, or to associate itself with its publication, or to maintain its distance by leaving the responsibility with Teilhard's beneficiary. Did he suspect that the latter option—the Pilate option—would be chosen?

Mid-1950s America was not the China of the 1930s: His exile there was spacious, fruitful, rich in encounters, travel, lectures, and conferences. From New York's Wenner-Gren Foundation to Washington and from Harvard to Berkeley, the Jesuit paleontologist was at home. Resigned as a Christian to working in outer darkness, as a scientist he experienced discreet fame, in permanent touch with what he described as "the cream of American scientists," everywhere received with the respectful warmth the United States so spontaneously extends.

But how could he, with his intimate everyday experience of the schizophrenic situation, ever find consolation for the enduring schism between science and Christianity, between the Church and the world? His letters to Leroy, d'Ouince, and Jeanne Mortier constantly return to his frustration: "The dangerous thing about Rome's silence on . . . myself and many others is [that] under the disciplinary lid they have slammed down, ideas ferment and are deformed or even corrupted in the public mind." And: "People can't be blamed for calling me 'pagan,' since Rome will not allow me to publish what I think of God."

To his last day he continued to utter such melancholy appeals, sometimes referred to as his "posthumous" utterances. Even a final visit to Paris in June and July of 1954—with a detour via Lascaux and his birthplace in the Auvergne—was marred by petty irritations. As he went "heroically" (d'Ouince) downhill,

---

*In other words, the bulk of his work.

amid countless requests for articles, lectures, conference appearances, interviews, and biographical sketches, he was refused the right to translate his early articles into German, or to attend a conference (on paleontology!) in Paris. He was even forbidden to write the foreword to a collection of his late sister's correspondence (God might have entered the picture . . .). And he was kept under unrelenting pressure, from the highest circles, to return to his American retreat.

He died in New York on Easter Sunday (April 10), 1955, gasping out, "Oh, this time it's terrible!" as he was struck down by his third heart attack. Only a dozen people attended his exile's funeral two days later. Four days before, he had written to a friend that he did not want to die before publicly confessing his faith in the "Crucified One, hominization's most powerful spiritual motor." A wish unfulfilled. Yet another.

René d'Ouince, for once a better Jesuit than historian, offers us this comment: "Thus, through the instances of its highest representatives, the Company remained to the end both brutal and motherly. To the end, Teilhard's Roman superiors obeyed their injunction to silence, while his immediate superiors, who faithfully helped him to obey, encouraged him in his silent research and shared his hope."[33]

A flawless separation of Roman denial (including the Company's) and the support of his friends (including the Jesuits). But the fact is that the latter's support was weightier than Rome's negation. And it is no less a fact that from 1951, banished to America, the old man no longer enjoyed the brotherly climate of *Études* and of all those—d'Ouince, Jouve,* de Lubac, Fessard, Ravier, Leroy— who had "shared his hope."

In the final analysis more "brutal" than "motherly," the Company had consigned to distant, mute, and lonely death this priest who, preferring to be "stifled" within it rather than "asphyxiated" outside it, had refused to leave. He had chosen to live stoically through what Hans Küng, evoking the fate of Galileo, called his "Calvary" and the "ignominious exploitation of his obedience . . . , a revolting testimony to the antimodernist mentality of a Roman system that smells heresy in every corner."[34]

Teilhard had passed the test of obedience "in exemplary manner,"[35] insists the man who was his immediate superior, André Ravier, Provincial for Lyon. But his "trial" had scarcely begun. Galileo experienced his in the flesh; the Jesuit would be condemned by contumely. And as so often happens, this manner of proceeding would, at least for a time, add further weight to the sentence.

Inevitably, the disappearance of so silent a figure echoed deafeningly. It also

*Who had died in 1952.

started to unlock doors. On April 13, *Le Monde* published an enthusiastic article by Étienne Borne: "It can now be said, with the tranquility of certainty, that he was a religious genius and one of this century's greatest thinkers." Whereas Henri Marrou in *Témoignage chrétien*—after hailing this "personal thinker of unheard-of courage"—justified the censorship imposed on him, "as on Origen and all the great religious thinkers": which amounted to justifying the practices of the hypersensitive present by evoking those of the distant past. It also amounted to a bizarre note of encouragement to the Roman Curia to go on assailing and mutilating the dead Teilhard as obsessively as they had hounded the living man.

As soon as the author was dead, Jeanne Mortier busied herself carrying out the provisions of the July 1951 will by getting in touch with the Paris publishing house of Le Seuil, where she was joyfully welcomed by Paul Flamand, an old friend of Teilhard's.

Two upper-echelon priests were dispatched to confront Flamand: "As a Catholic, you must know that Rome disapproves of this work." "Yes, but this book does Christianity great honor and may reach and move many non-Christians."* "You intend to go ahead?" "Yes." The two fathers beat an orderly retreat. Hardly had the door closed behind them when it opened again. The face of one of the visitors reappeared. "It's a wonderful book!" he said.†

Publication of *The Phenomenon of Man,* an instant public success, rekindled the dispute over Teilhard all the more fiercely because *Civiltà cattolica* had had the good taste to write shortly after his death that it would have been better "had the controversies sparked by the Father's writings been buried with their author." And without a doubt, the French Jesuits spurred their Italian colleagues on to greater bitterness. After a good article by Father Russo, published the day after Teilhard's death, *Études* seized the occasion of the publication of *The Phenomenon of Man* to stress the "questionable" aspects of the book. "It amounted," wrote René d'Ouince,‡ "to a guilty plea" (I no longer know this man). And for the next seven years not a single French Jesuit spoke up for Teilhard.**

The first (and the greatest) to dare pumped the anti-Teilhard reaction to paroxysm level. Henri de Lubac had first sought the green light from Superior General Janssens (himself aware of the change of heart of several notables in Pope John XXIII's entourage) before tackling the challenge of a (critical) apologia for Teilhard. *La Pensée réligieuse du père Teilhard de Chardin* appeared in April 1962.††

*The publisher's editorial staff, made up of Catholics, non-Christians, and agnostics, had at once voted for publication.
†Paul Flamand denies that the man who said this was Jean Daniélou.
‡Who had by then left the management of the magazine.
**Except, once again, Father Russo in *Études,* reviewing three books about him.
††Two months after a penetrating article by Jean Daniélou in *Études.*

Its author was not considered a Teilhardian; indeed, he had sometimes publicly aired a few disagreements with his celebrated colleague. His tribute, accompanied by very firm reservations, is all the more striking:

No true thinker is ever completely "at peace." Yet taken overall, Teilhard's boldness was nonetheless the "joyful boldness of faith." At the very hour when "humankind becomes aware of its collective destiny and can receive that destiny only terrestrially or else transcendentally," it was given to him . . . to point out the only valid direction. Taking account, of course, of the inevitable imperfections of human nature, the Catholic Church . . . to which it would be an understatement to say that he remained always and in all circumstances unshakably loyal, may itself acknowledge that in Pierre Teilhard de Chardin it had given birth—as our century needed—to an authentic witness of Jesus Christ.[36]

It was too much for the old Roman guard. A clandestine Teilhard had been irritating. A Teilhard in glory was unbearable. The Holy Office contemplated putting the book on the Index. But Pope John* put his foot down, and the Holy Office was constrained to vent its spleen through the lesser medium of a *monitum,* or warning, which appeared on June 30, 1962, in the *Osservatore romano:*

Some works by Father Pierre Teilhard de Chardin are in circulation, scoring a lively success in what they have to say about the positive sciences. It is very clear, on the philosophical and theological plane, that these works are replete with such ambiguities, and even grave errors, as to offend Catholic doctrine. . . .

For this reason the most Eminent and most Reverend Fathers of the Supreme Sacred Congregation of the Holy Office invite all Ordinaries, as well as the Superiors of religious institutes, the Superiors of seminaries, and university Rectors to alert minds, particularly young minds, to the dangers presented by the works of Father Teilhard de Chardin and his disciples.

This sharp crack of the miter was accompanied by an article that oozed venom. It accused Teilhard of opposing the Christian religion on five capital points of dogma, and Father de Lubac of reinforcing this attempt to "naturalize the supernatural."

Father Janssens, previously not in much of a hurry to rescue his endangered companions, had felt the wind of change at Saint Peter's. Rightly stirred by this double attack against a dead and a living man, he wrote to Henri de Lubac that he understood that the two articles in the *Osservatore romano* must have been

*Alerted by President Léopold Sédar Senghor of Senegal, a fervent Teilhardian.

"painful" to him, but that "for the moment" his own intervention would be "untimely." "The cause of truth," the Superior General continued, would be better served by "our silent suffering" than by "impassioned interventions." He added that a "change" might be expected in the "months to come." Father Janssens did not resist the temptation to remind the Lyon theologian that he himself had favored publication of the book—although he did attempt a dialectical tour de force by assuring Lubac that his book constituted a "warning in the very spirit of the *monitum*" against the temptation to extrapolate from the Father's thinking.

Still more tortuous reasoning was to come. The Vatican Council, although imbued with John XXIII's spirit of opening and renewal, and even though one or two of its concepts were inspired by Teilhard's galvanizing imagination, had not explicitly made amends to the great Jesuit. It took another sixteen years before a high Church dignitary paid the tribute to Teilhard that countless Catholics (and sardonic "Gentiles") were expecting.

In 1981, on the centenary of Teilhard's birth, the most important man in the Vatican after the Pope, Monsignor Casaroli, secretary of state, sent the rector of the Paris Institute a message* which amounted to absolution (from whom? to whom?), and which appeared to signal the desire to erase Rome's long hostility to Teilhard:

> . . . The astonishing echo of his research work together with the radiance of his personality and the wealth of his thinking have indelibly marked our era.
>
> A powerful poetic intuition of the profound value of nature, an acute perception of the dynamics of creation, and a vast vision of the world's future were wedded in him with an undeniable religious fervor.
>
> Similarly, his tireless desire for exchange with the science of his time and his fearless optimism faced with the evolution of the world have given his intuitions, through the radiance of words and the magic of images, a great resonance.
>
> Turned entirely to the future, this synthesis, often lyrical and shot through with the passion for the universal, has helped restore the taste of hope to men in prey to doubt. But at the same time, the complexity of the problems he tackled, like the great variety of approaches he essayed, inevitably raised difficulties, which is precisely why a critical and serene study of this out-of-the-ordinary work is required, as much on the scientific as on the philosophical planes. . . .
>
> No doubt, beyond the difficulties of conception and the deficiencies

---

*Which specified that it was written "in the name of the Holy Father."

of language of this audacious attempt at synthesis, our era will retain the testimony of the unified life of a man seized by Christ in the very depths of his being, and who struggled to honor at once faith and reason.[37]

Fine words, which might suggest that the Roman Curia had really changed. But a few weeks later, *Le Monde* (May 22, 1981) ran an approving article by Henri Fesquet on the modifications in the Vatican's view of Teilhard since the monitum of June 1962. A "press release" from the Holy See took upon itself the ridiculous (or odious?) task of assuring the faithful that Cardinal Casaroli's letter was "far from being a revision of the Holy See's previous positions"—particularly given that it, like the monitum, expressed "reservations." It was like comparing a maiden speech at the French Academy, received with good-natured collegial jeers, to a death sentence with attenuating circumstances attached.

But what of the Company, the "brutal" and "motherly" Company of Jesus? Did it intend to restrict itself to a few lofty-sounding articles by theologians? Should it not counter so many injuries, so much maneuvering, so many snares and denials by affirming its corporate solidarity with the most original of its contemporary spirits? With the man who had expressed the very essence of Jesuitism more strikingly than anyone since the founders, a Jesuitism that was the antithesis of Jansenism—the conviction that Man is the active bearer of a fundamental hope under God's gaze in all the Universe? Optimism, humanism, the belief that rebirth is no longer resurrection of the past but invention of the future.

Did not this Jesuit, who revived the spirit that had sent the founders in quest of multiple worlds and cultures, deserve that those who spoke in the name of his order should take a few risks for his sake? Dare to compromise themselves for him?

Which is what, at long last, the Reverend Father Pedro Arrupe did. Sixteen years after his election as Superior General of the Company, in a letter to Father Henri Madelin, then Jesuit Provincial in France, he hailed Teilhard, enfolded him in the Company's embrace, praised him to the skies. Paying homage to "the stubborn search for a better knowledge of fully realized faith" and the "missionary concern to proclaim this faith to those who had strayed from it," Father Arrupe recalled that in daring to say

> that only Christianity, the Church, can bring to the world the light without which it is doomed to ruin . . . thus wrenching so many frightened Christians from their narrowness of mind . . . , Father Teilhard heralded the opening to the world and the concern for inculturation which characterized the Council's teaching. . . . His shining love for Christ, at the center of his passion for a world transformed and fulfilled in Christianity . . . said it and proclaimed it, as much for unbelievers as believers.

Finally, Father Arrupe underlined Teilhard's unbreakable attachment to the Church: "And that he obeyed through deep faith in the Church and through love of it, we know from the weight of the suffering it cost him."

May we take that last sentence as "honorable amends"? It was after all Pedro Arrupe's predecessor who had taken all those disciplinary measures against the author of *The Phenomenon of Man*. Pedro Arrupe assuredly did not seek to disavow that predecessor. But his words ring with the sounds of painful regret, of remorse—of the kind Rome finally expressed for Galileo.

It was a Jesuit who drew the parallel between Teilhard and Galileo. Father Russo, an excellent exegete of his friend Pierre Teilhard de Chardin, had this to say:

> How can we not compare the two great figures of Teilhard and Galileo? Doubtless the two cases are in many ways different. But both arose at a critical moment in which a major transmutation of science appeared to be injuring Faith. Both, insisting on their determination to remain inextricably linked to their faith and to the Church, had to struggle to make Christian thinking receptive to these new views, convinced that it could draw enormous benefit from them, convinced that it had here a providential opportunity to cleanse itself, to become more authentic.
>
> And both were exposed, their whole life long, to the denial by the Church magisterium of their thinking. . . . Only long after their deaths did that magisterium acknowledge that they had been right on many of the points they had contested."[38]

Had Teilhard's "trial" ended in acquittal? The hundreds of works devoted to him over the past half century, and the dozens of conferences that had him as their theme, would lead us to believe it did. Particularly the one organized by UNESCO in Paris in September 1981, when Pierre Emmanuel ranked him as a poet with the likes of Saint-John Perse and Paul Claudel; while French President François Mitterrand noted that "there was nothing naïve about Teilhard's method . . . for the wager is not won in advance. The epic that began millions of years ago may still abort. With progress eternally dogged by the Promethean temptation, Teilhard's enthusiasm at scientific and technical conquests went hand in hand with sharp vigilance."

Prometheus? Teilhard is that herald of apocalypse who wrote, in *Mon Univers:* "In the bosom of an ocean made calm, but in which every drop will be aware of remaining itself, the extraordinary adventure of the world will be over. The dream of every mystic, the eternal pantheist dream, will have found its full and legitimate satisfaction."[39]

Does this song find an echo as our century draws to an end? After the long silence, partly compensated for by a *samizdat*-style circulation, the almost clandestine glory that contributed to the prestige of the great and clumsily gagged Jesuit, and then after the explosion of fervor ("a fad," they would say) of the 1960s, after the arrows and the acknowledgment of Rome—at the end of this Galilean pilgrimage, what is Pierre Teilhard de Chardin's status today, forty years after his death?

His fame, it would seem, is on a "back burner." In a faint odor of sulphur, votive candles admittedly flicker about "Teilhard's thought," while "Teilhard Associations" are born and endure. But as the echo of his hard-fought battles dies down, does the power of his message also wane? There are young Jesuits (and some not so young) who, while admiring his greatness and deploring his trials, find him less "inspiring" than in the past. Because less rebellious?

But if we judge by the noises coming out of Rome, the Catholic Church is in great need of the abrasive, energizing breath of a new Teilhard. Or in the interim (why not?) a return to Teilhard? Or, quite simply, a welcome for Teilhard?

· XV ·

THE EXORCIST
AND THE VATICAN

From Loyola to Dreyfus • Golan and "Deicide" • Augustin Bea,
Confessor to the Pope • John XXIII on Good Friday

FOR NEARLY FOUR centuries the Company of Jesus lived through the long and cruel story of Christian hostility to Judaism. And in the beginning, as we have seen,* its voice in that story was sometimes a dissident and even a revolutionary one.

Although the pure product of an Iberian culture most recently marked by the expulsion of Jews who refused to convert to Christianity, Ignatius of Loyola consistently struggled against the national thinking that had inspired that barbaric decree. His repeated reminders of Christianity's Judaic roots, and the welcome he extended to Jewish converts, had led his companions, as the most natural thing in the world, to elect as his successor a son of Jewish converts, Diego Laínez. This "scandal" prevented the later election to the Generalship of Ignatius's second secretary, Juan de Polanco, himself descended from a family of *conversos*.

More significantly, the founder vetoed Jesuit participation in the Inquisition established in Rome by Paul IV, the most anti-Semitic of the Italian Popes—and the only one of the four Popes Ignatius dealt with to have hostile relations with him.

And when, at the close of the century, with the founder dead and passions running high, the Spanish fathers in Toledo adopted a rule which (like that pre-

*See Chapter VI.

vailing in other religious orders) excluded from the Company those whose "pure blood" was in question, old Pedro de Ribadeneira, sole survivor of Ignatius's intimate associates, protested vehemently against this violation of the principles that had guided his master.

Nevertheless, whatever improbable alliances may later have emerged, not between Jews and Jesuits but between anti-Semites and Jesuit-haters (from Pasquier's assimilation of "Jewry" to "Jesuitry" to the Dreyfus-era "You start with a Jew and you end up with a Jesuit"), the Society of Jesus had aligned itself over the centuries with the anti-Semitism chronic in Catholic society.

As the twentieth century dawned, shortly after the Dreyfus affair—in which the Jesuits had not been models of courage—Albert and Auguste Valensin elected to enter the Company, where they became close friends of Pierre Teilhard de Chardin. The inquiry mandatory for every postulant revealed to them that—without knowing it—they were of Jewish descent. It required no less than a papal dispensation for them to join the Society of Jesus.

In other words, the Ignatian order was not wholly innocent as it prepared to face the great challenge to the Christian conscience flung down by the Nazi crusade, which became official in 1933 when the National Socialist Party wrested control of the German state.

We know that, despite regrettable exceptions, the Company's French branch essentially stood up to the tidal wave of Nazi racism, as did the German fathers on their side (Rupert Mayer, Alfred Delp), and the Poles (such as Josef Warszawski,* almoner to the French Resistance), and their Jesuit colleagues on Vatican Radio before they were "brought to their senses" by the Holy See.

But it was not enough that some Jesuits (like other religious or ordinary Catholics) implemented the Gospel teachings in relation to persecuted Jews, rescued children, sheltered fugitives, and contributed to the redemption of a Christian conscience confronted with Nazism. In certain cases, such as that of Yves de Montcheuil, they even gave their lives side by side with Jewish Resistance fighters. But Catholic anti-Judaism remained deep-rooted, not only as living tradition but also in liturgical texts that expressed a fanatical refusal to acknowledge the Abrahamic origins of Christianity, texts that spoke of a "deicide" and "perfidious" Jewish people.

Were the English, French, or Russian peoples ever called "regicides"? Can the history of the papacy be encapsulated in the hideous death of Giordano Bruno? That of the people of Baghdad reduced to the martyrdom of Al-Hallaj? How, on the basis of the fleeting hysteria of a mob manipulated by this or that power, can a people, and its history, and its "nature" be characterized?

*According to French Resistance historian Georges Mond, many Polish Jesuits fell victim to the Nazis during the Occupation.

It is unlikely that the idea of purging the Catholic liturgy of its most inflammatory anti-Jewish excesses was first born in the minds of militant Zionists. Inevitably, Christians like Jacques Maritain had given it thought. Among the Jewish intelligentsia, men like the historian Jules Isaac had long discussed the project with Christian friends. And Jewish-Christian friendship associations were patiently examining the chances of reforming or eliminating the most perverse wording when the episode described below took place.

Was it a mere episode? Perhaps. But it led to a decisive turning point in the centuries-long debate between Judaism and Christianity.

It was not until 1957, with Christians still fretting over how best to rectify the most glaring of the liturgical excesses, that a group of Jews sufficiently aware of their right to the truth (and sufficiently respectful of the Christian faith to believe it capable of self-correction) launched an operation that made a crucial contribution to the decisions taken at the 1965 Vatican Council. Thanks in large part to the effective cooperation of various leaders of the Company of Jesus.

The story that follows was told to me on a summer day in 1991, in Provence, by Joe Golan, an Israeli friend. Golan had long been assistant and adviser for Arab affairs to Nahum Goldmann, chairman of the Jewish Agency for Israel–World Zionist Organization and president of the World Jewish Congress, organizations involved with the Jews of the Diaspora, in association with the State of Israel but independently of it.*

I first met this former Israeli officer during preparations for an important meeting in Florence of various supporters of peace in the Middle East and North Africa. Joe Golan was a man incapable of turning his back on any contact likely to lead to negotiation.† He boasted a peerless network of connections from Rome to Paris, and from Africa to the United States.

The son of a famous Russian-born Zionist pioneer in Syria, Joe Gouldin, whose name was "Israelized" to Golan, he had made friends both in Italian Christian Democrat circles (Giorgio La Pira, Amintore Fanfani, Enrico Mattei) and in the French Catholic world. It was in their company that he dreamed up the project he now described to me.

His plan went straight to the heart of the matter, cutting across the blindness of "liberal" Catholics who had so far achieved little to purge their liturgy of its poisons. For unless one believed that racism, anti-Semitism, and more precisely anti-Judaism are innate poisons, written into the human gene, it was clear that to turn pious Christians into Jew-haters nothing could have been more effective than the intoned repetition of phrases condemning (in Christ's name) the "per-

*Those who knew Dr. Goldmann knew just how far he could carry the spirit of independence.
†Which drew down Golda Meir's wrath on Golan's head.

fidy" and the murderous nature of the Hebrews. Thus are generations of oafish "patriots" and all kinds of reflexive racists of every stripe mass-produced—with myth and chant, with ritual references to "wops" and "Japs."

The anti-Jewish language adorning the Catholic liturgy, particularly its Easter prayers, sweeping pulpit pronouncements upon "the Jews," the proclamation of "Jewish perfidy" (embodied by Caiaphas or Judas)—all this was so obviously at the root of the twisted thinking that had just driven so many human beings to the death camps. Surely anyone wanting to set Jewish-Christian relations on a footing of friendship and respect would naturally think of expurgating the Catholic liturgy of such vestiges of an age-old intolerance recently fanned to incandescence by the Holocaust.

Yet the idea of defusing these most explosive components of Christian anti-Semitism did not come to Joe Golan in conversation with his Christian friends. It struck him during an exchange of views about Jewish shortcomings with Nahum Goldmann.

That evening, the old president, a friend of Chaim Weizmann, of Martin Buber, and (though not without periods of hostility) of David Ben-Gurion, told Golan that he was haunted by the passivity of the Jewish diaspora, which during the late war had succumbed almost without a whimper to the implacable onset of the *shoah.* Joe Golan asked him if such horrors were still possible.

"Yes," Goldmann replied. "After all, the Germans were no more racially fanatical than others: The monster had arisen from the Christian world, and that world has not changed all that much. Christianity is still moved by hostile feelings toward the Jews, fueled by traditions and by texts . . . "

"Well, couldn't we get the Catholics to correct those texts? I have many contacts in Paris and Rome. Send me to take care of it!"

Goldmann at once gave him the green light, adding: "Above all, don't forget to make contact with Christian leaders who compromised themselves in Nazi eyes in favor of persecuted Jews. Particularly Cardinal Roncalli,* the Patriarch of Venice. As papal nuncio in Istanbul during the war, he rescued many Jews and persuaded King Boris of Bulgaria to protect others. And use your French friends . . . "

And so, with a mandate from the World Jewish Congress, Golan (a former student at the famous École des Sciences Politiques in Paris) arrived in the French capital early in February 1957 to shape his Roman strategy. How should he begin his campaign? There were many Jewish converts in French society, including a few priests—the Abbé Glasberg, tireless protector of refugees, the Dominican Father Jean de Menasce, long an intimate collaborator of Chaim

*The future Pope John XXIII.

Weizmann, first President of Israel, and a friend of Golan's. But Menasce had been warned to stay clear of Golan's "networking" efforts, which, he had been told, threatened to open more wounds than it could heal.

Golan decided it would be better to approach people linked simultaneously to the wartime Resistance, the present government, and the Catholic world, such as Governor Roland Pré and Colonel Claude Arnoux, a former military-academy classmate of General de Gaulle and, with Father Michel Riquet, the organizer of a wartime network for helping Jews. Both men ardently supported his plans, and gave him two "prospects": Cardinal Eugène Tisserant, Dean of the Holy College, and the Borgo Santo Spirito—the Jesuit residence in Rome.

Was the old French prelate a friend of the Jews? Whatever else, he was a veteran anti-Nazi and an expert guide through the Roman labyrinth. As for the Jesuits, Pré and Arnoux swore by them: As a body, they would be his best and most effective friends.

Cardinal Tisserant received the emissary of the Jewish Congress in Paris. His greeting was discreet, diplomatic. He said he was unsurprised by the Congress's move, and astonished that it had not come earlier. For all that, the old churchman considered it a most delicate business, and warned his guest that "not only friends" awaited him and his cause in Rome. . . . Everything, or almost everything, would hinge on the way he went about it and on the allies who joined him. Tisserant too gave names: Cardinal Lercaro, Archbishop of Bologna, a courageous man but too openly hostile to Pius XII, and Roncalli, a sympathizer but not one of the Vatican's rising stars.

According to Tisserant, the "Jewish case" could be usefully stated and argued only by one or several of the Pope's closest associates, men with influence over him, who could act with discretion. Trumpeting his aims would merely reawaken a humiliated past; the operation must not be known until it was in its final stages. And (still according to the Cardinal) everything would hang on the decision of the Pope, that same Pius XII for whom every reminder of the war years was cruel—and who was not a man willing to risk the appearance of seeking "redemption."

Clearly well disposed, Cardinal Tisserant asked Golan for time to prepare the trail. Meanwhile, he believed that the best door to knock at in Rome was that of the Jesuits—the Borgo. There Colonel Arnoux, whom Tisserant knew well, had a friend, Father Bernard de Gorostarzu, the Superior General's assistant for Jesuit affairs in France.

Golan squeezed two extra stops into his Roman trip. At Fribourg in Switzerland he called on the Abbé Journet,* Superior of the seminary there, a famous

---

*A future cardinal, and one of the guiding spirits of Vatican II.

Judeophile and guiding spirit of a wartime escape network through Switzerland. This model priest was at once skeptical and encouraging. He stressed the virulence of the anti-Semitism that still infested Roman circles, but also suggested several trails to follow—though Lercaro and Roncalli, and two Jesuit confessors of the Pope.

Since Cardinal Lercaro's name had several times arisen during his exploratory talks, the emissary of the World Jewish Congress requested an audience of him in Bologna. Golan saw the Archbishop before Sunday High Mass, perched on a stool as he was slowly being dressed in his priestly raiment. "The Jewish question? It's shameful that we've delayed considering it for so long. You know that it is a painful subject for Pius XII. . . . You will find many anti-Semites in your path. The Vatican is teeming with them. . . . But you'll find allies too. We'll help you!"

On February 18, 1957, Golan rang the doorbell of Jesuit headquarters at 5, Borgo Santo Spirito. He was at once admitted by a small red-faced man wearing a biretta, talkative and friendly. This was Bernard de Gorostarzu, described by Golan's French advisers as his most likely ally. The little Jesuit was breathless. Had he just put away the bicycle he used to travel through Rome?

Golan's host was clearly very much aware of his plans, and plainly very well disposed: "We have very often studied Judeo-Christian relations since the war, the Holocaust, and the creation of Israel. The Company's position has evolved, not just in relation to other religious communities but above all in relation to the government of the Church. For a long time now, we have abandoned the belief that the Jews must pay for Christ's death."

"Yet in your colleges you still speak of the collective responsibility of the 'deicide' people."

Without replying, Gorostarzu moved hurriedly on: "In the complex world of Rome you will have to choose your allies well. We'll help you. You're going to see our Superior General."

Father Janssens received Golan politely but without apparent interest. This slender high priest in white skullcap, his face pale and lined, cursed with an energy-sapping asthmatic condition, made little more than conventional remarks. According to him, the diaspora of the Jewish people and its age-old exile were the consequences of its refusal to acknowledge Christ's divinity. But he believed that Israel's resurrection as a state signified a fundamental change in the Divine Will as it related to the Jews. If God had permitted the creation of the State of Israel, said the old Jesuit, it was because he had "forgiven." Joe Golan could get no more from his host, who said he could "take things no further."

Yet the conversation would turn out to be decisive. Two days later, the emissary of the World Jewish Congress learned from Bernard de Gorostarzu that the

General had "authorized him to guide Mr. Golan" through the Vatican. Which meant that the Jesuits saw themselves as his allies, and that the visitor would be led right to the heart of the citadel. He would be taken to meet those Company members with the strongest claim to having the ear of Pius XII—the Pope's Jesuit confessors, Fathers Robert Leiber (who had previously been Pius XII's secretary) and Augustin Bea, both of them German.

Golan needed no further urging. He called the number Gorostarzu gave him. "Bea here." The Pope's confessor clearly knew all about Golan's business. He invited the Israeli to have tea with him the next day at the Gregorian University.

Like all Pius XII's close associates, Augustin Bea was German. He was born in 1881* in a village in Baden on the fringes of the Black Forest. His father, the local carpenter, had to seek the help of his family and neighbors to pay for the young man's studies, first at Constance and then at Rastatt. He entered the Company of Jesus in 1902—at a time when, expelled from Germany by Bismarck, it was sending its recruits abroad. Bea received his training at Valkenburg in the Netherlands, at Innsbruck in Austria, and finally in Berlin, where he specialized in biblical exegesis.

Appointed Jesuit Provincial for southern Germany in 1921, he became rector of the celebrated Biblical Institute in Rome in 1930, where he ruled for nearly twenty years over Catholic exegesis of the Old Testament: a good initiation into Jewish spirituality. Although raised in the illustrious German school of Gunkel and Bultmann, Augustin Bea was not primarily a great scholar. He was not appointed head of the university to promote research or blaze new trails but to maintain discipline in a field where, for more than a century, overinquisitive Jesuit students had rocked the boat by asking questions worthy of true historians about the connections between Moses and the Pentateuch and the uniqueness or plurality of Isaiah.

It was the task of Augustin Bea, who was well aware of the risks, to grasp this Pandora's box firmly, not to punish but to contain the damage. And there was no one better able than Bea to issue a gentle warning to rash spirits. He is reported to have told one of his charges: "Never forget, Father, that if you possess the knowledge, we possess the power." Did that "we" refer to the Company, to the Holy Office? The fact is that under Bea's aegis the Biblical Institute worked steadily but unspectacularly: In 1943 the encyclical *Divino Afflante Spiritu*, of which the German Jesuit was at least the coauthor, had recalled that the underpinnings of Christian dogma were not subject to experimentation or question. "They put a live grenade in his hand," one of his students told us, "and he prevented it from exploding." And it was also thanks to his caution that the Biblical

*The same year as Pierre Teilhard de Chardin.

Institute survived the storm raised by the publication of Alonso Schökel's *New Exegesis.*

But although cautious in matters of dogma, Father Bea proved his courage elsewhere: His Biblical Institute had spacious underground areas where he sheltered many members of Rome's Jewish community during the war—barring its doors in October 1943 to an SS (or perhaps Gestapo) officer.[1] Legend even has it that he converted Grand Rabbi Zolli to Catholicism there, but in fact it was another Jesuit, Father Paolo Dezza,* who accomplished that feat. Bea merely invited Zolli to lecture at the Institute after the war, and sought to deepen his own understanding of Jewish culture at that expert's side.

In 1945 he was called to assume the formidable role of confessor to Pope Pius XII (he met the three conditions: He was a German; a Jesuit; and he had conducted himself impeccably in his dealings with Nazism). First as assistant to his colleague Father Leiber, then alone, Augustin Bea four years later became consultant to the Holy Office, and in that function was entrusted with all matters concerning Christian unity and relations with non-Christian religions.

By the close of the 1950s he was considered a central figure of the Church. So much so that in November 1959, soon after his election to the papal throne, Pope John XXIII made Bea a cardinal. Pope John (the former Cardinal Roncalli of Venice) thus fulfilled a promise his predecessor Pius XII had made to Bea, but which had long been blocked by the "Black Pope," Father Janssens, on the grounds that Jesuit tradition† frowned on such promotions.

When Golan introduced himself to Bea, Roncalli was not yet Pope and the village carpenter's son did not yet wear the red hat. But he was becoming a key Catholic figure, the Pope's closest collaborator, the guardian of doctrine, the agent for all contacts with non-Catholics (and non-Christians), and moreover a man who was widely liked. Which, in a high Roman dignitary, was a miracle.

Everything then inclined this old-school Jesuit, symbol of the unity of the "peoples of the Book," steeped in biblical knowledge, and therefore disposed to admire Israel (he urged associates and friends to visit the Jewish state), to take Joe Golan under his wing. And his familiarity with Pius XII gave reason to hope that Golan's visit to the Gregorian University would open the way to further progress.

Entering the reception rooms of the university, the emissary of the Jewish Congress saw two aged clerics rise and approach him. The slimmer and sprier of the two turned out to be Bea, who told him that Father Leiber had asked if he might join their discussion. In fact it was Leiber who first broached the question

---

*We shall meet him again as Paul VI's confessor and John Paul II's "personal delegate" at the head of the Company.
†Which had allowed many exceptions since Roberto Bellarmino.

of the necessary peace with Jerusalem. He questioned Golan about his family background, his youth in Palestine, his contacts at Saint Joseph's University in Beirut: not for nothing was he the Pope's former confessor and a former university professor.

Golan plunged straight in, pointing to the "dangerous" ideas kept alive by the Catholic liturgy and reminding them that it was no accident that the Holocaust had taken place on Christian ground. But he added that neither he nor his organization had any remedy to propose: They were merely convinced that an initiative originating from Rome would have fruitful results.

It was obvious that Bea had long pondered the problem. He offered no precise proposal, but he took in everything his visitor said. He concluded the discussion by saying: "It's a serious problem which must be solved. If we can contribute, we will . . . "

Nahum Goldmann's envoy hurried to report to Cardinal Tisserant: Did the Dean of the Sacred College think he was on the right track? The Cardinal had no doubt that he was. The operation, he said, was off to a good start—and with the best of contacts, since they were not only Jesuits but Pope's confessors into the bargain—the surest guarantees of effectiveness and discretion. According to Tisserant, Joe Golan should see the two fathers again as often as possible, accustom them to his presence.

Leiber, of course, because before becoming confessor to Pius XII he had introduced him (in Munich, where the future Pope had been papal nuncio) to German culture, and remained his most erudite librarian. But especially Bea, for he had become (although only since 1945, alas . . .) Pope Pius's conscience and deeply influential adviser. Bea, said Tisserant, was Golan's trump card. He possessed the information and the power to decide.

At Borgo Santo Spirito, Father Gorostarzu was delighted, and full of encouragement. "It was the Superior General who persuaded Fathers Leiber and Bea to help you," he said. "Now it's not a question of whether they'll do it, but when they'll be able to raise the matter with His Holiness."

Next morning Golan was back at the Gregorian University. This time he and Father Bea were alone together. The Pope's confessor was obviously convinced of the worth of his visitor's mission, and made no attempt to hide it. He was now Golan's secret ally. But by the nature of his duties he was also a negotiator. And what negotiator worthy of the name could fail to try to score points?

Bea's first words to Golan seemed to indicate that his illustrious penitent, Pius XII, had urged him to counterattack: He spoke of being "hurt" and even "wounded" by the "campaigns" he said were directed against the Pope for his ambiguous stance during the Nazi era. He even asked whether, in those tragic circumstances, Pius XII could possibly have "acted otherwise."

But Golan was determined not to allow his hold over the old Jesuit to be nibbled away. Feeling that he was on firm ground, he recalled that the Holy See had been aware of Nazi actions and even (well before Jewish organizations) of the Nazis' extermination plans. Did that not make Pius XII and his associates witnesses of the Holocaust? As a friend of the Germans, on intimate terms with the German people and its culture, Pius XII had been the man best positioned to intervene and to raise the alarm in the name of charity or in the name of humankind.

Golan's deliberately pitiless attack told on the Jesuit. His pale eyes fixed on the Israeli, Bea was clearly moved. He admitted the strength of his visitor's arguments, but tried to object that the Pope had been responsible for the care of Christian communities and the salvation of the Church "in the storm," that he had nonetheless spoken out—and that not everything he had done during the war was yet "in the public domain." Golan was eager to remain on this converging track, and was moved in his turn by his host's sincerity. He recalled that the only object of his mission was "harmony." To which Bea warmly responded that he hoped to have good news soon.

The year 1958 also witnessed a major event—the death of Pius XII, whose name had become a symbol and his past a distinct obstacle* to the quest of the envoy of the World Jewish Congress.

That quest had now been extended and made official, for Nahum Goldmann had come to Rome to throw his personal support behind Golan—but without substantial returns, since his meeting with the Superior General had achieved no more than Golan had managed; and the planned "private" visit with Pius XII had been turned into a public audience. Golan's Jesuit associates and friends felt it made little sense: Had the President of the World Jewish Congress come to Rome merely to receive a collective blessing?

But with Pius dead, would his successor be able or inclined to speed the process Joe Golan's maneuvers had set in motion? The experts were predicting that if the conservative Cardinal Siri were elected Pope, the process would be held up. If it were Cardinal Lercaro, it would gain speed. But as we know, it was Roncalli who was elected by the conclave. (An election apparently engineered by Jesuits determined to prevent Siri's elevation and equally determined to open the way—after what they thought would be the short-lived interim pontificate of the aging Roncalli—to the throne for Giovanni Montini of Milan. For to his dying day, Pius XII had refused to make Montini, his secretary of state, a Cardinal, thus blocking his path to the conclave.)

*Although, in fact, Pius XII in his late years favored Bea's efforts.

Giovanni Roncalli's election, at first coolly received by "progressives" in the Vatican, soon revealed its happy results: A few months after his election, John XXIII declared his intention of holding a Council, the second in Vatican history and the first since 1870. It was a rare opportunity to bring the planned reform—along with so many others—to fruition.

During the deliberations known as the "Pre-Council" held at San Giovanni Fuori Muri in late January 1959, Golan had a long talk with Bernard de Gorostarzu and a colleague. The two fathers were confident. Not only was the file on Church relations with the Jews classified as "urgent Vatican business" that would automatically be carried over from Pius XII's to John XXIII's administration, but Monsignor Montini was about to be made Cardinal. John XXIII had moved him into an apartment of the papal palace, on the same floor as his own. They often took their meals together. Rumor had it that Pius XII's former secretary of state ruled the Church by proxy while waiting to take over directly. Which was quite wrong, but which was a good omen for Judeo-Christian relations, said those (foremost among them the Jesuits*) who knew Montini well.

And indeed a decisive step forward was taken a few weeks later, confirming that the efforts of the past two years had not been in vain: During Good Friday Mass at Saint Peter's in Rome, in April 1959, John XXIII interrupted the prayer and gave orders to erase the words "perfidious Jews" from the text.

Henceforth it could be said that an essential battle had been won, and that the campaign waged by Joe Golan, with the increasingly overt support of the Jesuit fathers, had scored a first success. It only remained for Augustin Bea to exploit his promotion to Cardinal (in December 1959) and his key position as secretary general of one of the most important committees of the coming Council, for the Catholic liturgy to be solemnly purged of its anti-Jewish poisons.

Two years before the Council began, the initiatives launched by the Jewish side in 1957 were to receive illustrious support. The old historian Jules Isaac, joint author of a famous volume of history that shaped the civic sense of two generations of Frenchmen, was received on June 13, 1960, by John XXIII. Isaac implored the Pontiff to set up a Council body specifically charged with reducing anti-Jewish prejudice. Touched by the request, the Pope asked Cardinal Bea to meet the historian with a view to cleansing relations between Christians and Jews. Isaac's talks with Bea led to the decision, on December 18, 1960, to draw up a Council statement in favor of the Jews. The Jesuit Cardinal was officially entrusted with preparing it.

John XXIII was not a man to rush blindly into unknown territory. "I am the executive," he told one of his intimates, "but I insist on being consulted."[2] How-

*But as we shall see, relations between the two would sour.

ever praiseworthy, this modus operandi could prove embarrassing. The year before, after causing a sensation on Good Friday by announcing the deletion of the words "perfidious Jews," the new Supreme Pontiff had decided to canvas the views of the world's bishops on his policy of reconciliation with the Jews as well as on all other subjects likely to arise at the Council.

The views of 2,594 bishops were thus duly gathered. In the *Bulletin des Soeurs de Sion*,[3] T. F. Stransky mentions that in condensing the seven volumes of responses sent in by the prelates of five continents he encountered only one explicit answer on the Church's relations with the Jews; the best that could be said of it was that it did not exactly encourage John XXIII to move forward.

It came from a bishop of Latin America, a continent apparently scarcely touched by anti-Jewish sentiment. The bishop favored "condemnation of all persecution of Jews for religious or ethnic reasons," but added that the Council should not forget "historical facts and the unmistakable claims of international Jewry. For centuries the leaders of this Jewry have conspired methodically and with relentless hatred against the Catholic name; they are making ready the destruction of Catholic order and the elevation of imperialist global Judaism. Should we too hate? No! But vigilance, charity, and systematic struggle against the systematic struggle of this 'Enemy of Man' whose secret weapon is the yeast of the Pharisee, in other words hypocrisy." Echoes of French Catholicism at the time of the Dreyfus affair . . .

Bitterly disappointed by the response of the episcopate, John XXIII in the following year received stronger encouragement from Catholic universities and religious research institutes. The Biblical Institute in Rome, in particular, sent a communication entitled *De Antisemitismo vivando*, setting out the arguments against notions of "malediction," of "retribution," or of "collective Jewish responsibility" in Christ's death, and against any idea of divine punishment in consequence.

Shortly after that, Monsignor Dougherty of the Darlington Seminary in the United States sent an urgent request to Rome for improved Jewish-Catholic relations. Then, in August 1960, priests and laymen convinced of the need to act on the matter met at Apeldoorn in the Netherlands. They sent their conclusions to Rome, shortly followed by the Institute of Judeo-Christian Studies of South Orange in the United States.

By the end of 1960, John XXIII and Cardinal Bea thus possessed a file that more or less addressed the urgings of the World Jewish Congress and scholars like Jules Isaac. But within the Church the "revisionist" party, which the Pope had openly taken under his wing by entrusting its leadership to the Jesuit Cardinal Bea, and which numbered the residents of Borgo Santo Spirito as well as cardinals like Tisserant and Lercaro, was the butt of criticism and attacks by extremely powerful conservatives. These were mustered around such princes of the Church as Tardini and Ottaviani and dignitaries of the Eastern Churches, who were more or less influenced by Arab nationalism, at that time intransigent on the question of Israel and the Jews. Their objections were everywhere echoed by statements in the spirit of the Latin American prelate quoted above.

"If I had foreseen all the difficulties we would encounter," said Cardinal Bea to his friend and biographer Stepan Schmidt,[4] "I don't know whether I would have had the courage to tackle the task." And indeed the peaceable, elderly, fragile Jesuit Cardinal* did not seem made for this kind of battle.

Closely following these pre-Council maneuverings, T. F. Stransky draws a beguiling picture of this former Pope's confessor turned herald of peace with the Jews: "I first met Cardinal Bea in September 1960, after being asked to be one of three staff members of the new Secretariat for Christian Unity. I saw in this stoop-shouldered eighty-two-year-old man† someone who had spent long years hunched over his desk, almost fused with it, his bony back like a frail tree constantly exposed to the high winds of knowledge."[5]

"The high winds of knowledge." We have seen that Augustin Bea, as rector of the Biblical Institute, had done his best to prevent those winds from blowing up a gale. But while confining exegesis to "prudent" limits, the old Jesuit had nonetheless absorbed and become intimately familiar with Jewish history and hopes.

In meetings with Protestants and (more rarely) Jews, he had learned to consider the Bible not as a great dead text but as the expression of a living reality. Familiar with the world and the spirit of the Bible, he lived in concrete contact with the God of the Old Testament and in harmony with the "signs of the times." God's adventure with His people was his own adventure. How could he fail to be scandalized by the demonization of the Chosen People of the Bible?

There was moreover the influence exerted on this dignitary of the Company of Jesus by the work of his colleagues, the founders and guiding spirits of the French Jesuit publication *Sources chrétiennes*—Fontoynont, de Lubac, and Daniélou—and by Joseph Bonsirven's research. No matter how independent of the Company he wished to be, he was and remained a Jesuit, imbued with the traditions and the initiatives of "his own kind"—and above all else, by the rediscovery and acknowledgment of Christianity's Jewish roots.

Neither winds nor tides could obscure the Promised Land from the old captain's gaze. On January 14, 1962, in an address at Rome's Pro Deo University to an audience of experts representing forty-three nations and eighteen religions (including Judaism), Augustin Bea offered a first hint of the spirit of the forthcoming Council declaration. If he made no explicit reference to Judaism (or any

*Stricken with tuberculosis at the age of fourteen, he had suffered a heart attack in 1942.
†Eighty, in fact.

other people or faith), his Jewish listeners and everyone else present understood that the Cardinal had opened the way for a new Church attitude toward other beliefs. And on several other occasions before the Council convened, Bea gave reason to hope that the Council declaration on relations with Judaism would be new and positive.

After more than two years' preparation, negotiation, consultation, and internal and external debate, the Second Vatican Council finally convened on October 11, 1962, at Saint Peter's in Rome. The central nave of the basilica had been laid out as a conference chamber. Twenty-five hundred and six "Conciliary Fathers" were gathered—bishops, heads of orders and congregations, authorized to intervene and to vote—in the presence of the diplomatic corps, consultants, observers, and the press. As always, the bulk of the work was delegated to committees. But the public exchanges were sometimes lively.

The first session, from October 11 to December 8, 1962, called to order under the aegis of the Council's "inventor," old Pope John, was marked by the first battle "for the Jews," and by the initial failure of Cardinal Bea, who had swiftly circulated among the conferees a preliminary text pleading Judeo-Christian reconciliation.

At one of their final meetings, Golan had asked the Jesuit that the words "Jewish people" replace the term "Jews." Bea had been against it: Although he personally preferred it, the old biblical scholar told the emissary of the World Jewish Congress that it would give a too political ring to the campaign and could only kindle resistance, particularly among the Near Eastern clergy.

Nevertheless, the document Bea circulated at once raised passionate—and swelling—objections in the assembly. One group of prelates requested, even demanded, that the words "deicide people" be specifically retained. During the debate, Monsignor Luigi Carli of the Roman Curia slipped a handwritten note to Bea reminding him "that the Jewish people at the time of Christ were collectively responsible for the crime of deicide, a responsibility which, objectively, it still bears."

It took no less than the intervention of the Pope to calm the debate. And at the price of a major concession: withdrawal of the "Schema on the Jews" drawn up by the aged German prelate; his biographer Stepan Schmidt marvels at his patience. A personal setback for the Cardinal, but an infinitely more terrible one for a Church still poisoned by racial bigotry.

Hearing the news, Golan hurried to see the venerable Cardinal Tisserant, who was unable to hide his irritation. He felt that Bea had "maneuvered clumsily," underestimating the power of conservative resistance. According to Tisserant, it would be possible, but difficult from the very first, to erase the anti-

Semitic features of Catholic ritual. But to insist that the Church's leaders condemn the persecutions, hatred, and racial prejudice of the past—in short, to make honorable amends—was to aim too high too quickly.

How could one forget, Tisserant reminded Golan, that the Inquisition Paul IV set up in Rome in 1555 had reigned supreme and sent Jews to the stake, that Jewish rights in Rome had not been reestablished until 1846? All that, sighed Tisserant, "was yesterday—and for some people today."

In short, the old Cardinal was disappointed at the Jesuit's naïveté. Bea, he said, should have known that the Council would have countenanced such a proposal only if it came from the Pope himself, no matter how high the esteem in which Bea's name was held. To make good the "blunder," Tisserant concluded, would require the intervention of the very highest authorities of the Company, working hand in hand with John XXIII.[6]

We do not know the results of this request for help from the Jesuits, called in as reinforcements under duress, and after a temporary defeat. But what is clear is that their colleague Bea, although "penitent," and under orders from the Pope to defer his campaign, had sent his "Schema" back to the drawing board and was consulting the Jews and various Jewish-Christian associations in different countries. His ear constantly to the ground, he received a flood of memos and suggestions from Jewish organizations, which, well aware of the stakes, were now besieging as fiercely as Goldmann and Golan had been doing for five years.

The death of John XXIII in June 1963 at first seemed a fatal blow to the Council and to similar ventures—so obviously had the old Pope, despite all his caution, been the driving force and protector of everything that promised to rid the Catholic Church of its flaws (foremost among them racial hatred). But the speedy election of Giovanni Battista Montini as his successor was a sign of the irreversibility of the movement, for Pius XII's former secretary of state had unreservedly plunged into the Council adventure by the side and in the spirit of the late John XXIII.

In any event the Jesuits, and Bea in particular, took heart from this passing of the flame. The Cardinal's secretary prepared a new text, released on September 25, 1964, which stressed even more strongly than its (retired) predecessor "the close association between the Church, the Chosen People of the New Testament, and the Chosen People of the Old Testament."

Stepping up the pace of his public pronouncements, the old Jesuit zealously assumed all responsibility for putting the case for his schema on the Church's attitude toward the Jews. He did so, addressing the Council on November 19, 1963, September 25, 1964, November 20, 1964, and October 14, 1965. Why this insistence on acting alone? One of his lieutenants says that "he was very clear on this score: Secretariat members and advisers knew it, and were convinced that he would do it. . . . When Cardinal Bea spoke in the Council Hall, everyone listened. They knew something important would be said."

According to one of those close to him, Lukas Vischer: "There was always something moving in his addresses, something that went out ahead to confront the future. I began to read the Cardinal's writings on unity only after hearing him during the first Council session, and I must say that reading them surprised me. I had the impression that Cardinal Bea's Council pronouncements went much further than his carefully prepared texts."

The organ of the Judeo-Christian Friendship Associations described the efforts he exerted throughout the third Council session, the one held in 1965: "Cardinal Bea proved a model of clarity, perseverance, and flexibility. . . . To save the substance, the essential, he was prepared to yield on more or less secondary points. [But] his prophetic figure truly ushered in a new era in relations between the Church and Judaism."[7]

The final text of the Council declaration on the non-Christian religions was adopted by 1,763 votes to 250 and issued on October 28, 1965. We quote here, verbatim, the eight paragraphs relating to the Jewish faith. That it had taken centuries, mighty efforts, and untold horrors for the highest reaches of the Catholic Church to proclaim such obvious things (just as there were 250 "Christian" dignitaries still to reject them in 1965) is enough to make the world weep. But the fact is that they had now been said, in the solemnest possible terms, and that, while they repaired nothing, they opened the way to a new vision.

The *Nostra Aetate* declaration on the non-Christian faiths, October 28, 1965:

As this sacred Synod searches into the mystery of the Church, it recalls the spiritual bond linking the people of the New Covenant with Abraham's stock.

For the Church of God acknowledges that, according to the mystery of God's saving design, the beginnings of her faith and her election are already found among the patriarchs, Moses, and the prophets. She professes that all who believe in Christ, Abraham's sons according to faith [Gal. 3:7], are included in the same patriarch's call, and likewise that the salvation of the Church was mystically foreshadowed by the chosen people's exodus from the land of bondage.

The Church, therefore, cannot forget that she received the revelation of the Old Testament through the people with whom God in his inexpressible mercy deigned to establish the Ancient Covenant. Nor can she forget that she draws sustenance from the root of that good olive tree onto which have been grafted the wild olive branches of the Gentiles [Rom. 11:17–24]. Indeed, the Church believes that by His

Cross Christ, our Peace, reconciled Jew and Gentile, making them both one in Himself [Eph. 2:14–16].

Also, the Church ever keeps in mind the words of the Apostle about his kinsmen, "who have the adoption as sons, and the glory and the covenant and the legislation and the worship and the promises; who have the fathers, and from whom is Christ according to the flesh" [Rom. 9:4–5], the son of the Virgin Mary. The Church recalls too that from the Jewish people sprang the apostles, her foundation stones and pillars, as well as most of the early disciples who proclaimed Christ to the world.

As holy Scripture testifies, Jerusalem did not recognize the time of her visitation [Luke 19:44], nor did the Jews in large number accept the gospel; indeed, not a few opposed the spreading of it [Rom. 11:28]. Nevertheless, according to the Apostle, the Jews still remain most dear to God because of their fathers, for He does not repent of the gifts He makes nor of the calls He issues [Rom. 11:28–29]. In company with the prophets and the same Apostle, the Church awaits that day, known to God alone, on which all peoples will address the Lord in a single voice and "serve Him with one accord" [Soph. 3:9; Isa. 66:23; Ps. 65:4; Rom. 11:11–32].

Since the spiritual patrimony common to Christians and Jews is thus so great, this sacred Synod wishes to foster and recommend that mutual understanding and respect which is the fruit above all of biblical and theological studies, and of brotherly dialogues.

True, authorities of the Jews and those who followed their lead pressed for the death of Christ [John 19:6]; still, what happened in His passion cannot be blamed on all the Jews then living, without distinction, nor upon the Jews of today. Although the Church is the new people of God, the Jews should not be presented as repudiated or cursed by God, as if such views followed from the holy Scriptures. All should take pains, then, lest in catechetical instruction and in the preaching of God's Word they teach anything out of harmony with the truth of the gospel and the spirit of Christ.

The Church repudiates all persecutions against any man. Moreover, mindful of her common patrimony with the Jews, and motivated by the gospel's spiritual love and by no political consideration, she deplores* hatred, persecutions, and displays of anti-Semitism directed against the Jews at any time and from any source.[8]

*The Austrian prelate Monsignor Osterreicher publicly expressed his regret that the word "deplores" had replaced "condemns," the verb used in his original version.

t. An abscess lanced? No. Monsignor Rijk,
ιe Vatican Office for Catholic-Jewish Rela-
uncil, notes that many Jews, particularly the
lly very reserved about what they might ex-
ιt believe that the Church could radically
The publication of *Nostra Aetate* seemed to
ι though the final version had disappointed
the attitude proclaimed by the Council was
ιane this time—of assimilating them into

'line" was incorporated into the framework
ιr Christian Unity was indeed disturbing to
ι persuaded the Vatican to create the Office
h put the dialogue in a new light.
ncil text was merely a beginning: "Two years
of thinking forged over two thousand
we must labor to disseminate both its spirit
liscover concrete structures for improving
e a long struggle demanding patience and
to produce lasting fruit."9

epticism reigning in many Jewish circles af-
 been directed at the person and the efforts
 w that he was exerting tireless pressure for an
increase of Catholic-Jewish contacts, for the establishment of Judeo-Christian
associations, for encouragement of ecumenical activities of orders like the Sisters of Our Lady of Zion. But they chafed at the tortoise pace of change, particularly in Catholic thinking.

When he died in 1968 at the age of eighty-seven, the carpenter's son from Riedböhringen had won the respect not only of Protestants but of his Jewish partners. He had become the symbol of détente, no matter how meager, slow, and disappointing its progress. Monsignor Rijk reports that in the course of some twenty interviews during the last two years of the Cardinal's life, the old man was usually in the company of Jews who had come to thank him for his efforts, Jews touched by his sincerity, his eagerness to persuade or understand—no matter how strongly they disagreed with his theological reading of the links between the Old and the New Testaments!

It is indeed remarkable that this tired old man—in whom only the pale, almost joyful gaze seemed alive as he dutifully accomplished his multifarious assignments from the Curia and his own Order—never let his need for rest, for continued life, come between him and his labors for Judeo-Christian reconciliation.

That one man, a Council, Jesuit clear-sightedness,* the dedication of countless organizations, and the history of the *Shoah* had not been enough to wipe out twenty centuries of contempt or blindness, the so-called Carmelite scandal at Auschwitz offered spectacular proof (one proof among many).

Whatever one might initially have thought of the desire of the Carmelite Sisters "to preserve a place of prayer on the site of the most terrible of the Nazi death camps" (in which Christians too had perished), the sense of rejection that the project inspired in the Jewish world—which could rightfully claim a painful priority there—should immediately have cut the project short. It should have led to immediate renunciation on the part of every Catholic aware of the sufferings endured a half century ago by Europe's Jewish communities, and of the part played in that torment by the Christian world.

But we know that, moving from blindness to failure of understanding, the Sisters (supported by Cardinal Archhbishop Marcharski of Cracow, and despite pitiable exhortations and warnings from many Catholic leaders), stubbornly persisted, to the point of total rupture with the representatives of the various Jewish communities, wounded by what they saw as an attempt by Christians to reclaim a space, a symbol, a memory that were eminently Jewish. Nor did the eventual solution of the dispute conceal the emergence of tell-tale tensions.

On that occasion, words of truth and lucidity were uttered by (among others) a French priest. In the daily *Libération,* Paul Valadier adopted positions "askew" of official Catholic thinking and was rewarded by dismissal in 1989 from his post as editor of the Catholic publication *Études.*† As it turned out, his position was hailed not only by his Company superiors but by the Cardinal Archbishop of Paris, Jean-Marie Lustiger, a recognized authority on Jewish-Christian relations.

Once the "grief" expressed by many Catholics at the obstinacy of the Carmelites and Monsignor Marcharski had been aired, Valadier—refusing to be satisfied by this convenient proclamation of indignation—recalled that, in the course of periodic debate in which the rights of one side and the errors of the other were clearly stated, "relations between Judaism and Christianity . . . are in conflict." To acknowledge this, said Valadier, was not to "rekindle differences" but to be realistic, for "they can always spring back to life." Why? Because "relations between Jews and Christians are founded on a common ground . . . which separates them."

Who can question the fact that the Scriptures handed down by Israel are the very texts in and upon which Christians too read God's will,

*While the Jesuits were particularly diligent at the Council, they were not alone: Father Dujardin, a leading spirit of the Jewish-Christian Friendship Associations, was an Oratorian.
†See Chapter XVII.

His redemptive design, His desire, and His Covenant with Man? There could be no more powerful indentification and continuity. On the other hand, it is unquestionable that these same Scriptures are read differently by the one and the other; Christians hold that it is not the Law but Christ the Lord which saves, and that thus the Old Covenant is but the foreshadowing of the New, that Grace has replaced the Law. Therein lies the difference, and no discontinuity could be more powerful.

There is thus between Christians and Jews an inheritance struggle, as between older and younger siblings, which finds so many (prophetic?) precursors in the Bible. And thus, as Saint Paul might have said, a kind of insurmountable jealousy, of unremitting rivalry, festers permanently between them.

It is precisely because of this fundamental rivalry or "jealousy" that every effort must be deployed, on both sides, to ensure that prejudices, passions, and excess not be allowed to inflame a complex dispute, which, we repeat, will always remain so (until—to quote Saint Paul—the end of time?). This rivalry demands a particular concern, discretion, and intelligence in relations between Jews and Christians. As between twins, mimetic rivalry is latent, and explosive. One more reason for keeping one's head, for digging down to the roots of the shared heritage and finding what unites and what, in all honesty, separates. For his part, the Catholic Christian must more than anyone else (in holy rivalry?) work vigilantly to eliminate everything in his Church that appears to be and is hostile to the Jew's memory and perception of self: not as a tactic or to placate, but in the name of what binds him to the Jew.

. . . It is precisely in his reading of the Scriptures and dogma, of his traditions, that the Christian must allow anti-Semitism no foothold. For that phenomenon so profoundly contradicts the essence of Christianity (since "salvation cometh from the Jews") that its vestiges within us (always, alas, potential) would be the surest sign of our idolatry, and thus of our faithlessness toward the faith.

If this analysis is right, we must at once deplore the Catholic deafness that is at the bottom of the Carmelite affair—and not imagine a rosy future between Jews and Christians once the storm has blown over. Our extreme proximity within our spiritual heritage will always lead to misunderstandings. One more reason for tirelessly seeking to surmount rivalries of the kind that spring from missteps, from the absence of contact and exchange—and that we can avoid through

mutual knowledge, through shared efforts and commitments in
which we prize ourselves exactly as we are: close, and different.[10]

What could possibly be added to those magnificent words? They express the
very best of Jesuit tradition, born with Loyola, revived here by *Sources chrétiennes* after endless betrayals, and courageously reinstated by Cardinal Bea.

·XVI·

JUSTICE AND
PEDRO ARRUPE

The Great Dawning • The Jesuits and the Spirit of the Times •
A Basque in Hiroshima • "Staunch Conservative" • Paul VI Puts
on the Brakes • Medellín and Liberation Theology • Decree Four •
"Who Are You? Where Are You Going?" The Anger of John Paul II •
Pope Against Constitutions *• Don Pedro's Calvary*

I N 1965 THE Company of Jesus entered a period of storms that was to last more than twenty years, a period some have seen as "movement" and others as protracted death throes. Clearly no single event, however crucial, could have brought this about. Nor could one man, Ignatius's twenty-seventh successor at the head of the Company, be credited with lighting the fires that burned through those two turbulent decades.

For the Company of Jesus is not an island cut off from the Catholic mainland. It is at most a peninsula—and one designed to protect the mainland from storms. The connective isthmus could be severed only by the will of Rome—or, as in 1773,* as a result of papal submission to external pressures. Of course, the history of the Jesuits has a life of its own, independent of the Church. We have seen the Company both leading and lagging, racing ahead then putting on the brakes. But the rule of obedience established when Loyola placed himself and his nine companions at the disposition and discretion of the Supreme Pontiff had never been questioned.

Indeed, the boldest of the Company's advances had always been met with

---

*See Chapter IX.

radical "adjustment" by Rome. The greater the Jesuits' reforming zeal the harsher the resultant papal curb, all the way from Paul III to John Paul II.

The great Jesuit adventure of the twentieth century, necessitated in part by the Company's spinelessness throughout the nineteenth, found specific expression in the great *aggiornamento*, the opening up, the bringing up to date, of the Catholic Church proclaimed during the Second Vatican Council of 1962 to 1965. If the Jesuits of the twentieth century were as a body (and some out of deep personal conviction) very different from their recent predecessors, it was partly because the whole Catholic Church was being nudged into profound mutation by the good-natured man elected in 1958 under the name of John XXIII.

Jesuits like Augustin Bea, Karl Rahner, John Courtney Murray, Henri de Lubac, and Jean Daniélou* played a vital part in the preparation and general course of the Council. But it was the new Pope's awareness of the anemic state in which the Church languished as a result of its confinement, its isolation from the real world, that planted the seed of aggiornamento. It was Pope John's decision, taken in 1959, to convene a Council, that brought the forces of Catholic renewal out into the light. The decision unbolted locked doors for the vegetating Church, and within the Company of Jesus itself.

First assembled in 1962, Pope John's Council was fed by so many expectations and galvanized by so many frustrations that its agenda survived its creator's death in June 1963 and extended past the election of Cardinal Giovanni Battista Montini, who became Pope Paul VI. The new Pope, while equally aware of the need for reform and renewal, was more timid than his predecessor, and still influenced by Pius XII, whose secretary of state he had been.

Vatican II could only be the revolutionary antithesis of the previous, ferociously "antimodernist" Council of 1869, Vatican I: its predecessor's repudiation, an act of amends. Vatican I had declared and shouted to the rooftops the Church's rejection of the modern world, of democracy, even of humanism. A century later, it was inevitable that its successor be dedicated to freeing the great trussed body.

The world condemned as perverse by the reactionary prelates of Vatican I was now welcomed with open arms, particularly in documents like the constitution *Gaudium et Spes*, a virtual hymn of reconciliation with "the whole human family," with the "world as the theater of human history, bearing the marks of its travail, its triumphs and failures."

It was from such conciliatory impulses (and from other Council formulae, such as the recognition of people's consciousness "of being deprived of the world's goods through injustice and unfair distribution") that Superior General

*Alongside Hans Küng and the Dominicans Edward Schillebeekx, Chenu, and Congar.

Pedro Arrupe's battle as head of the Society of Jesus sprang, a battle naturally stamped with the energies peculiar to the impetuous Ignatian fellowship. (Yet what was surprising—and what made the Jesuits of the 1970s and 1980s seem far ahead of the rest of the Church—was not so much their boldness as their fidelity, their "papalism." More than all other religious, they took literally the decisions, constitutions, and recommendations of Vatican II.) And all this was largely at the urging of an inspired man, Pedro Arrupe, whose election to the Generalate coincided too closely with the ferment of the Council not to be interpreted as a sign.

Arrupe was elected Superior General on May 22, 1965. He was fifty-eight, and spoke eight languages, including Japanese, which he had learned during wartime internment in Japan. He was a Basque from Loyola's homeland—the second Basque General in the Company's history—and physically almost Ignatius's double. A little taller than the founder, not quite so haggard or ethereal, slender rather than emaciated. But with the same almond-shaped face, the same bony forehead, backward-sloping and hairless, his skull like an ivory helmet, his nose an eagle's beak, his eye-sockets like vaults, a nimble gait allied to a curiously heavy manner. A typically Basque head and body, shaped by rocky terrain, hard marches and climbs, by stalking—and with a smuggler's eyes.

But not Ignatius's gaze. According to surviving portraits, the founder's eyes were as black as China ink, as dense and as heavy as mountain lakes. Arrupe's eyes were gray, lively, piercing, matching his gestures—more Mediterranean than his predecessor's—and his softer speech. He differed from Loyola too in his extrovert gaiety of manner.

Was he then a joyous version of the founder, a General who substituted the gift of laughter for Ignatius's "gift of tears"? Everyone who knew Don Pedro, even when he was the powerful "Black Pope" at grips with the conflicts that studded his Generalate, was struck by his cheerfulness, his accessibility, and his adaptability to communal living. Like the founder, he possessed a most intense capacity for listening and taking note, as well as great "presence." He had only to make an appearance for changes to happen. Small stature, great radiance—in other words, charisma.

That the Jesuits under Arrupe embraced the letter of the Council's conclusions was of course a matter of obedience. But it was also because the great aggiornamento pointed in a direction many of them had long recommended, planned, hoped for, and perhaps anticipated. But to understand the interaction between the Vatican Council and Arrupe's Generalate we must remember that the Company had itself been a vigorous driving force in the preparatory stages of the Council. Thus, causes and effects dovetailed neatly: no Arrupe without the Council—but no Council without Arrupe's precursors and electors. Hardly surprising, then, that the Council found its champion among its first and most enthusiastic promoters. Pedro Arrupe set his own luminous stamp on the Council, less as pioneer than as executor and interpreter of a global strategy. Indeed the Basque General is now seen as the bravest and loyalest disciple of Pope John.

At the age of thirty, the fledgling Jesuit and former medical student Pedro Arrupe never read the newspapers. On the rare occasions when he asked his companions for political news, someone would observe, "So, Don Pedro's pulled his head out of the clouds, has he?"

He pulled his head out of the clouds for good on August 6, 1945. On that day he was master of novices at the Jesuit seminary at Yamatsuka in Japan, three miles from Hiroshima. What he witnessed there marked him forever. Racing from hospital to hospital, listening to horrifying stories from victims, watching the appalling deterioration of their wounds, he was now deeply and inescapably involved in the vast tragedy of the twentieth century.

Even before Arrupe became Superior General, the Congregation gathered to elect him was faced with an unprecedented problem—the duration of the General's mandate. Something like a consensus had emerged for a revision of the Generalate-for-life principle established by Loyola and accepted by his companions. The fathers of the second half of the twentieth century were well aware of the system's defects. Generals were younger at election than Popes—whence some excessively long Generalates that committed the Company to periods of senile management. Six Generals per century . . .

The new Jesuits were therefore eager to establish provisions for retirement, for incitement to retirement if not to an actual provision for American-style impeachment. And curiously the Company, which had been forced to fight the Pope four centuries earlier to uphold the principle of a lifelong Generalate, now had to fight the Holy See to modify it. Arrupe himself was elected within the framework of the existing Jesuit Constitutions. But with his consent, the Congregation established the so-called ejector seat arrangement, which gave the Superior General the option of resigning (although he still lacked the right to refuse election). On the other hand, the Congregation strengthened his authority by granting him the right to nominate the four "Principal Assistants" heretofore elected by the Congregation to support and advise the leader. (As things turned out, Pedro Arrupe did not take advantage of the Superior General's newly acquired power.)

It was perhaps inevitable that the strong-willed sovereign of the Vatican should clash with the ebullient commander of his imperial guard. The contradictions between Black and White Pope could not remain forever hidden behind the privacy of their monthly face-to-face meetings (not to mention the almost daily meetings between the Pope and his Jesuit confessor, Paolo Dezza). Did those differences have to be aired? Paul VI thought they did.

Giambattista Montini was not hostile to the Jesuits. On the contrary, he had very largely been educated by them, admired their diligence and efficiency, and sometimes even their intellectual boldness. But this emotional Pope could tolerate neither the secularizing trend within this most papalist of orders, nor any relaxation of discipline, nor the slightest reform that might make the Company more independent of him. The Congregation was barely over when he summoned General Arrupe and two hundred of his companions to the Sistine Chapel to ask menacing questions about the new directions the Company was "rumored" to be considering. Like many fragile beings, Paul VI could go to the utmost limits of violence, and he would prove it.

But the Company was on the move, with or without Paul VI or Arrupe. Yet it was the Basque General who, as a follow-up to the 1965 Jesuit Congregation (soon nicknamed the "Black Council"), which elected him, decided to send a "sociological" questionnaire to the 33,000 Jesuits then registered throughout the world. Each community was asked to give its views on the Company's place and prospects in contemporary society. The specific goal, said Arrupe, was to seek out and define "the kind of service that the Company must render the Church in this period of rapid change in the world, and thus confront the challenge the world has issued to us. . . . The world and the Church, and therefore the Company as well, have undergone such profound and rapid change that I believe we must submit the current situation to a deep, objective, wide-open scrutiny."

Three years later, Don Pedro and his staff had some 400 responses in hand, sent in from all over the planet. From them emerged the sense of a worldwide demand among Jesuits for social justice, for a break between the Church and the world of the rich and powerful.

This was only a beginning. In 1967, two years after the Watts riots in Los Angeles, Arrupe wrote to the "Jesuit fathers in the United States" to criticize the inadequacy of the Company's response to the "black question." According to Arrupe, the American Jesuits had not led the struggle against racial discrimination and had "increasingly tended to identify with a section of the middle class. . . . Too many Jesuits are cut off from the world of the poor, and therefore from the majority of blacks. . . . We have too readily forgotten that the Company is at the service of humankind, and most especially of the poor, of those who are shunned, such as Christ."

The following year the Latin American bishops met at Medellín in Colombia. The assembly claimed to speak for the wretched, for outsiders, for victims of persecution. The impact of the bishops' stand was enormous: Less than two years after the death in Bolivia of Ernesto "Che" Guevara—which to so many of the disadvantaged had seemed like the death of hope (no matter how illusory that hope might have been)—the Church and its leaders were now seen as ready to take up the "cause of the people." That expression, politically charged, even revolutionary, was no accident of phrasing.

From the time of the Medellín conference, a violent wind (and a wind of violence) swept over Catholicism from Latin America. There, Cuba's failure and Che's death had seen the torch of "liberation" fall into the hands of the priests, from Dom Helder Camara to Monsignor Oscar Romero. And Pedro Arrupe was more involved than most with this cresting wave. The new wind blew into every corner. At the congress of German Jesuits at Trier in September 1970, Arrupe declared that "for hundreds of thousands of Catholics in the world, the real crisis of faith stems neither from materialism as such, nor from an inadequate grasp of theology, but from brutal poverty. . . . For the people of the Third World, it is difficult to take a message of 'Good Tidings' seriously when it has not succeeded in making them happy."

While it is easy to imagine the horror and amazement that greeted such words in Rome, we must not forget that Catholic bishops everywhere—not just the Jesuits—were now promoting (exactly as if they were labor leaders) the "struggle for justice" and the radical "transformation of the world." Their audacious theories found a name when in 1972 a Peruvian priest, Gustavo Gutiérrez, published *A Theology of Liberation,* the gospel of all those who called for justice under the sign of the Cross and sought to strengthen—if not physically arm—the forces struggling for the justice invoked by the Vatican.

Paul VI, apparently alarmed by these movements, which claimed to be carrying out his own will, attempted to condemn the "ambiguity" of the word "liberation," in which some could confuse spiritual message with social struggle. But some words are hard to tame, and this one was already in exultant flight. And the "men in black" were sharp-eyed, surefooted, and keen of hearing.

Preparing for the Company's own great aggiornamento, which is how he saw the next General Congregation, planned for 1974, Arrupe formed a committee headed by Father Jean-Yves Calvez, whose purpose was to give sharper focus to the two major items on the congregation's agenda: the democratization of Jesuit society, and reaffirmation of its social calling. The "staunch conservative" many Jesuits thought they were electing in 1965 was henceforth the symbol of a liberalization both internal (a time frame for the Superior General's mandate, equal status for the various components of the Company) and external (for Arrupe had not flinched from visiting Father Daniel Berrigan, incarcerated in the United States for his opposition to the Vietnam War).

When the Congregation opened in Rome in 1974, the reports of its preparatory committees reflected a worldwide desire for deep-seated change. Indian Jesuits, condemning the "abject and unjust conditions in which large portions of humankind exist," proclaimed that it was "impossible for a Jesuit today not to make it his constant preoccupation." They demanded that the Company distance itself from "the forces and structures that perpetuate sin in our society." Their Brazilian colleagues insisted on "liberation from all forms of slavery, including the slavery that coexists with excessive wealth," as well as "a general mobilization of our forces in support of the most disinherited . . . so that we may recover our image as the Church's flying column [whereas] today the majority of Jesuits are at the service of the minority, which needs them least."[1]

But these calls to justice met with vehement opposition. Father Calvez reports that "a not negligible minority criticized these proposals as 'likely to deform our apostolate in the direction of humanism and social activism,' finding in them 'a whiff of rabble-rousing and Marxism.' " It was against this contentious background that the Thirty-second General Congregation of the Society of Jesus began its deliberations in December 1974.

In all its 433 years of existence, the Company had met in Congregation only four times for any other purpose than to elect a Superior General. Two hundred and thirty-seven Jesuit fathers, representing ninety Provinces on five continents, gathered for the Company's Hundred Days.

The texts adopted by Jesuit Congregations are known as "Decrees." At the 1974 Congregation all eyes were at once focused on "Decree Four," a resolution of such importance, and one which so swiftly passed into legend, that one observer called it the "new Jesuit Gospel."

Everyone in attendance knew that—quite independently of questions of discipline or hierarchy—the leitmotif of the Congregation would be social justice. And Decree Four was concerned with precisely that. Its impact would be enormous.

"Impact" is not too strong a word. By declaring that solidarity with all victims of "injustice in all its forms" was a "duty," by recalling that certain members of the Company were often the beneficiaries of social inequalities, at least on the plane of culture and physical security ("Often our social origins, as well as our education and our membership in this community, shield us from true poverty. . . . We have access to power that others do not share"), the assembled fathers squarely endorsed the views already expressed by their Asian and Latin American colleagues.

Decree Four was amended to conciliate Spanish fathers who had threatened to create a separate Province, not geographic but ideological, and grouping all those Jesuits of Mediterranean Europe opposing this "progressive" reordering of the Company's priorities. It was also amended to avoid disappointing American and Dutch Jesuits who demanded even more radical departures. Nevertheless, it remains a text of great clarity, standing as the core document of the Society's future directions.

Of course it bears the stamp of a time when everything seemed possible, when from Berkeley to Amsterdam and Warsaw to Guernica ideas flared, oppressors stumbled, and hopes grew. Like its framers, it has aged. But it expresses a very high point in the history of the Company of Jesus, a time of strong winds, of bellying sails, of intense human solidarity. How then could we be surprised at the alarm that swept the Vatican even before the end of the Congregation's deliberations? Paul VI's criticisms of the "Jesuit Council" are well known and have been abundantly commented on. But perhaps not always appropriately. For the battle was not fought out over the Company's "swing to the left."

"Apparently the Pope did not see the argument in favor of justice as a danger in itself," says Father Calvez (that linkage of "justice" and "danger" speaks worlds for the state of the Catholic Church!). What infuriated the Pope was something unrelated to such concerns.

Many young Jesuits opposed what they saw as the growing "sacerdotalization" of the Company, which (they said) tended to turn out priests who gave the sacraments and preached to the already converted rather than apostles who faced the dangers of preaching "in the open" and to the "outside world." They sought heroism, not the humdrum. Was this a challenge to the Pope?

"Paul VI's real fear," wrote Father Calvez, "centered on the Company's loss of identity [through] reforms that might make it abandon its presbyterial role."[2] Indeed the information (or the veiled denunciations?) reaching the Vatican throughout 1973 all led the Pope to believe that the Society was laicizing itself, turning into a humanitarian agency, a social solidarity league, a sort of labor union. Did not some Jesuits praise Marxism? Had not others questioned the celibacy of priests?

In a letter to Pedro Arrupe written in September 1973, Paul VI denounced "certain tendencies of an intellectual and disciplinary order which, if encouraged, would usher in serious and perhaps irredeemable changes . . . in the very structure of your order"—by which the Pope meant "certain ruinous interpretations of Ignatian obedience, even of chastity."[3]

So much so that, on the opening day of the 1974 Congregation, Paul VI moved to warn the assembled fathers against such errors. "Where have you come from?" he apostrophized the two hundred and eighty-four delegates. "Who are you? Where are you going?" He went on to condemn in the Jesuits "a profound uncertainty . . . a fundamental questioning of their identity," and to insist that "the spirit of service can degenerate into relativism . . . into secularism, into fusion with the profane." And in an emotional evocation of Isaiah, the Supreme Pontiff added: "May you never be tempted, we implore you, by the *spiritus vertiginis!*" The spirit of vertigo? Of the abyss?

With this sermon from the head of the Catholic Church still ringing in their ears, the fathers went to work—and imperturbably opted to give absolute priority to the order's commitment to justice. Once again, it was not this orientation that angered the Pope. What must have looked like defiance of his orders was that question of *priority* within a context more secular than priestly.

And once again, it was another subject of dissension that rekindled the quarrel. The young Jesuits were not simply eager to promote "justice": They also sought a relative equality within the bosom of the Company. It was not just papal absolutism they questioned. They wanted to lessen the differences in the organization between priests and nonpriests,* to give the latter a larger role in the Company, and even to soften disciplinary standards by extending the Jesuit's right to object to certain commands—not just from immediate superiors but from the Pope himself. It was a demand that Paul VI found absurd, and irritating.

It has been suggested by an American author and former Jesuit, Malachi Martin, that relations between Pope and Company reached such heights of tension that the Supreme Pontiff was thinking a short time before his death of dissolving the Company a second time. This has been dismissed as "novelistic" and "pure forgery" by Father Bartolomeo Sorge and Superior General Kolvenbach in separate interviews. But although a very relative tranquility may have crept into relations between Black and White Pope, tensions within the Company itself only worsened. There, many leading figures saw Father Arrupe and his "henchmen"—the American Vincent O'Keefe, the Indians Divarkar and Alamendros, and the Frenchman Calvez—as "Red commandoes."

Calvez quotes letters received by the Superior General from Jesuits who could scarcely be suspected of opposition to the Company's social reorientation (to which they were long since committed). These were their reactions to Decree Four:

> The document is very weak on the "content" of a program in favor of justice, and may therefore be open to much ambiguity in its interpretation. . . . The concept of justice, as presented in this document . . . seems to identify itself with that of "socialism": the equality of ownership among men. . . . There is much talk in the document of changing those structures that are unjust. But this is not possible without at least an overall conception of possible alternatives. . . . Unless a substitute model is proposed, our activities risk being impelled to adopt

*Average age on entering the Company: twenty-three. Average age at ordination into the priesthood: thirty-two. It was thus a question of revolt by the young.

the "Marxist" (or rather "Leninist") model, characterized by one-party dictatorship, with all the defects of such a model and the new forms of injustice flowing from it.

Thus Pedro Arrupe, twenty-seventh in line from Ignatius of Loyola, was suspected by some of his own people of turning the Company into a Communist (not to say Leninist) war machine—at the very same time as Paul VI, his superior, was publicly accusing him of "selling out" the venerable Society, of turning it into a charitable association undermined by secularization, rejecting tradition and its priestly mission.

But neither as a Jesuit nor even as a Basque was the promoter of Decree Four a man to take risks for risk's sake, or try to perpetuate a tension-fraught situation. Arrupe now traveled the world to proclaim to his followers that the cause of justice was not that of revolution, but a natural component of the apostolic function. His secondary mission was to cool the ardor of those who (to use his own bizarre turn of phrase) "interpret our mission in too 'horizontal' and politicized fashion."

In the field, in the thick of things, he also strove to ensure that the fathers' labors in the cause of justice (which could take militant form in Latin America or India) were redirected toward causes such as refugee assistance, even creating a special corps of "Jesuits for Refugees": This was a time of massive population shifts in Africa and Asia, of the boat people's flight from the suffocating Hanoi regime.

Yet contradictions between the Vatican and the Borgo Santo Spirito remained so strong and tenacious that they even surfaced during the fleeting pontificate of John Paul I, who died less than five weeks after donning the papal tiara. The unfortunate Luciani had scarcely been elected before he summoned a delegation of the Company's "Procurators" to the Vatican (although he died a day before the audience was scheduled to take place). It is easy to imagine the innuendo and whisperings such a sequence of events would have raised a couple of centuries earlier—yet another Pope poisoned by the Jesuits! Particularly since the address the Pope proposed to deliver was apparently "rather severe." It included these words: "Learn to distinguish the tasks of the religious from those appropriate for the lay. . . . Priests must not substitute themselves for the latter and neglect their own duties."

Inevitably, such dissensions were rekindled by the accession to the papal throne of Karol Wojtyla, Cardinal Archbishop of Cracow, the product of a Polish clergy that combined a long-standing conservative tradition with a very natural antipathy to any display of benevolence or "understanding" toward Communism. Once elected as Pope John Paul II, Wojtyla possessed the means of imposing his views on any and every Jesuit, American, Indian, or Basque—and with an authority justified by a fair knowledge of Communism and of Leninist might, as well as by the acknowledged courage with which he had pursued a lifelong social apostolate.

John Paul II's attitude to Pedro Arrupe and to the Company in general has been summed up by the late British ex-Jesuit Peter Hebblethwaite as one of "coldness" and "hostility." He adds that the Pope seemed to have made the Company "the scapegoat for the crisis of Catholicism."

Pedro Arrupe would certainly never have admitted that the new Pope was "hostile" to the Company. But he could not help seeing that the 1980s would represent the trial by ordeal of his Decree Four strategy, and that the new Pope's character, his swiftness to act, and his experience of political relations with Marxism would further inflame the issues. Which did not deter Arrupe from vigorous promotion of forms of action that had long since branded him a "progressive" within the Society of Jesus.

The pressures from Latin America remained powerful. The conference of Latin American bishops, held in Puebla, Mexico, in January 1979, with Don Pedro in attendance, was their most powerful expression since Medellín. Bartolomeo Sorge asserts that this meeting was "the most impressive experience" of his life, the "cry of the suffering people," a reminder of the "pressing need to proclaim the gospel of the poor."[4] Arrupe did not return from the meeting any more kindly disposed to heeding pontifical calls to prudence.

It was about that continent in ferment that he now began to deliver militant utterances, reminding his listeners that "the gospel was written in the language of the oppressed, of society's outcasts," declaring that "if the oppressed are not given help in their liberation, their faith might be affected," and quoting some of the terrible complaints he had heard from Latin American Jesuits—"Father Arrupe, we are tired of knowing that many candles are lit in our churches and that the dead receive a Christian burial. We must take care of the living!"

A year later he convened the leading representatives of the Jesuit worker mission in Europe—an organization under constant suspicion from the Holy See and subject to a thousand petty harassments. What he told them was not calculated to calm troubled waters:

> In Latin America the cause of justice, of the defense of the poorest, of
> respect for human rights, calls for shared effort. Decisions to be made
> demand profound analysis and great discernment. . . . To adopt
> Marxist analysis itself, and not just a few of its components or meth-
> odological positions, is not our way. At the same time, let us be frater-
> nally ready for dialogue with the Marxists. And in the spirit of
> *Gaudium et Spes* let us not refuse specific practical collaboration re-

quired for the common good. But let us bear in mind our proper role as priests and religious, let us never act as freelancers separated from the Christian community and its leaders, and let us be certain that such collaboration encompasses only action acceptable to Christians. . . .

We must also resolutely oppose the inclination on anyone's part to use our reservations about Marxist analysis as a pretext for condemning as Marxist or Communist, or for deprecating, the commitment to justice and the cause of the poor, to the defense of their rights by the exploited, to their just claims. Have we not often seen forms of anti-Communism that are but ways of masking injustice? From this standpoint too, let us remain true to ourselves, let us refuse to allow our critical judgment of Marxism and of Marxist analysis to be abused.

Such words could only add to the Polish Pope's misgivings. By the end of 1980 the contradictions between White and Black Pope had reached such a pitch that the Superior General of the Company decided to hand his mandate over to those who had elected him fifteen years before. After all, his campaign of renewal and revival within the Company had been long and fruitful. He had set the Company squarely back in the center of the world's affairs, at the crest of the wave that was sweeping contemporary Catholicism—finally wrested from generalized inertia by Pope John and Vatican II—forward into the future.

Don Pedro had earned retirement. His mission seemed over. He had turned the Company irreversibly in a new direction and restored it to its original function of yeast within the dough of the Catholic Church. And since he seemed to be the cause of persistent problems . . . He therefore let it be known that he would relinquish his mandate at the end of 1980 and convene a new General Congregation—the third in fifteen years—to choose his successor.

Everything suggested that the Pope would accept this gesture at its face value. But Wojtyla gave a startling example of his rigidity by stubbornly refusing the solution Arrupe proposed. He was firmly against this unilateral abdication. How dare this Jesuit, on his own initiative, alter one of the articles—the permanence of the Generalate—of the Ignatian *Constitutions* of which the Supreme Pontiff was the guarantor, almost the co-contracting party? Moreover, John Paul II was aware of the wholesale transformation of the Society of Jesus within the bosom of the Catholic Church, and he feared that it was evolving in a democratic, "parliamentary" direction. He did not believe that the 1980s would produce a more malleable, or more conservative, successor than the man already in place. He preferred to wait for quieter times and a cooling of the blood before he allowed a Company freed of its rash enthusiasms to elect a leader less impulsive and more adaptable to the prelates of Rome.

Thus, as 1980 came to a close, Arrupe's attempt to pass on the torch came to grief. Finally aware of the unhealthy nature of his relations with his powerful adversary, and exhausted by the terrible tension of constant travel, conferences, and decision making, he now saw himself caught in the vise of apparently insurmountable contradictions.

But let us give the floor to one of the Company's sages, whose liberal temperament and profound knowledge of his colleagues did not always shield him from surprises during those fevered years:

Father Arrupe was too good, too naïvely optimistic to channel the torrent he had helped set in motion. Like Teilhard before him, he literally did not see evil. Indeed he was more a mystic than an activist, trusting everyone, insufficiently vigilant in overseeing the implementation of what he had so magnificently engendered. He had allowed an excessive permissiveness to gain ground in the Company. We had cases of fathers entrusted with important and very conspicuous missions suddenly deciding to elope with their secretaries. . . .

And bear in mind that the Superior General was of fragile constitution: His mission totally exhausted him. Shuttling from Rome to Santiago, Vienna to Paris, Madrid to Manila, racing to lend support to an idea, to cool tempers, to persuade spiritual "dissidents" . . . You can imagine what storms there were among Spanish—or Latin American or Polish—conservatives, and the signs of impatience that flared sporadically in northern Europe, India, and France! Arbitrating, appeasing, pleading, forever climbing or descending aircraft gangways: The risks were enormous! But what goodness, what radiance shone from this man! Spellbinding, and utterly without artifice. . . .

Arrupe liked to say that one saint was worth more than ten thousand Jesuits: He could have applied the words to himself. Perhaps he was indeed a saint; and perhaps it was precisely this saintliness, this disarmed trust that caused the hemorrhage the Company suffered during these years, when, between 1965 and 1990, the ranks of the Jesuits shrank from 35,000 to 25,000.

From the moment John Paul II refused to let Arrupe resign and make way for a successor, relations between the two powers seem to have reached a breaking point. Both men attempted to stave off the worst through public assertions of their shared ground. In the spring of 1981, as the Pope was preparing his encyclical *Dives in Misericordia* (a reminder to Christians of their duty to fuse charity and justice), Arrupe was delivering and distributing a lecture entitled "Rooted in Charity," a plea for justice founded in love, which recalls with elegant cruelty that "there is an apparent charity that is a disguised injustice, whereby we give to a human being out of 'benevolence' what is his due in justice. Then almsgiving becomes but a subterfuge." The Jesuit here seems sharper than the political Pontiff. But each had taken a step toward the other.

And it was in the Pope's absence that the high Church authorities in Rome pronounced what we might consider Arrupe's banishment from any kind of power. Cardinal Baggio, chairman of the Latin American Bishops' Conference meeting in June 1981, virtually ordered Father Arrupe to disavow the Jesuits of Nicaragua, who had been denounced as "Marxists" by several of the Cardinal's informers. Don Pedro replied that he stood by his Jesuits and that to incriminate them would be to incriminate himself. He remained loyal to his own people. But he had now made permanent enemies of the Vatican's masters.

On May 13, 1981, what might have been his last chance of dialogue with the Pope himself had been shattered when a Turk named Mehmet Ali Agca shot and seriously wounded John Paul II on Saint Peter's Square. A few months later, a melancholy Arrupe spoke to a small group of Jesuit fathers:

> The Company is feared everywhere. . . . People say, "These Jesuits are wily! And so powerful!" As I told a group the other day, we are neither so powerful as some people think nor so good as others think! No! We are ordinary people—ordinary in the sense that we are not geniuses. Perhaps we have geniuses in the Company, but precious few! A long time ago it was said that the Company's strength lay in its well-trained mediocrity. . . . In Saint Ignatius's thinking, excellence is not of an intellectual order. It may of course be of that order. But true excellence lies in our gift of ourselves.[5]

He concluded by saying, "I was particularly anxious to tell you these things, for I feel that this is perhaps my swansong in the Company." The idea of withdrawing had taken root, and he knew that his physical strength was betraying him. He had no idea how much, however, and with what consequences.

On August 7, 1981, in his sixteenth year as Ignatius of Loyola's twenty-seventh successor, Arrupe had just stepped from his plane at Fiumicino airport in Rome when he was struck down by a cerebral thrombosis, the classic retributive affliction of men who take on too much and live under constant strain.

The little man of fire and ivory survived this terrible ordeal. But he was so diminished that the solution he had proposed to the Pope before being struck down—retirement—was now mandatory. Hemiplegic, and virtually deprived of the power of speech,* bound to a couch in the infirmary of the Borgo Santo Spirito, Don Pedro Arrupe was no longer equal to the backbreaking mission entrusted to him by his companions in 1965, a mission his fearless, generous spirit had made even more onerous.

*Although he would soon recover the ability to speak—in Spanish only.

Lying on his sickbed, his small general staff of principal assistants at his side, Arrupe at once (and in accordance with the rules and traditions of the Company) began the work of setting up provisional arrangements for his succession. From his four lieutenants he selected the American Vincent O'Keefe, who had grown accustomed to making major decisions during Arrupe's frequent absences from Rome (even though the fact that he was a citizen of a great power did not sit particularly well with the fathers), to serve as "vicar general"* until a General Congregation could elect a successor.

Everything thus seemed in order, or at least sufficiently so to ensure that the Company could continue to function within its legal norms, when the inconceivable happened. Something as improbable as the Pope's attempted assassination (and much more surprising than the thrombosis that had struck down the master of the Jesuits): what could only be called a pontifical coup d'état.

Wojtyla decided to block the Superior General's arrangements—which had all the appearance of a last will and testament—with arrangements of his own. Renewing the veto he had imposed on Arrupe's move to seek retirement, he elected to maintain in office a man no longer capable of opposing him.

Vincent O'Keefe's designation as vicar general dated from August 10, 1981. It was in that capacity that the American Jesuit had presided over the "consultations" of the Society of Jesus, made up of the four principal assistants, with a view to convening the Congregation to elect a new Superior General. On October 6 Father O'Keefe was informed that Secretary of State Cardinal Casaroli (the Pope's "Prime Minister") would be arriving at noon to see Father Arrupe.

Were the high officials of the Holy Office unaware that the titular General was no longer able to conduct a conversation? Was it honorable to discuss a weighty matter with a seriously ill man when he had an entirely legal replacement? Father O'Keefe therefore went to meet the Cardinal at the door—and was told that Casaroli had been ordered to see the sick man alone. Casaroli asked the vicar general to leave the infirmary.

Here let us leave the floor to the historian Alain Woodrow, whose excellent account is obviously based on sound sources: "The visit lasted several minutes. Without saying a word, the Cardinal asked to be led to the front door. When he returned to Father Arrupe's bedside, Vincent O'Keefe found the Pope's letter, placed on a small table. The General was weeping."[6]

In a letter to the author dated June 2, 1992, Vincent O'Keefe offered a slightly more detailed account: "After reading the Pope's letter to Father Arrupe, the Cardinal had me called in because he could not understand him. I entered and spoke with Father Arrupe, who asked me to lead the Cardinal to another room

*The last man to bear this title had been the Frenchman Father Norbert de Boynes during the Second World War.

where he would meet with Father Dezza.* . . . After that, I returned to Arrupe and read the letter to him. Given the contents of the letter, he was very moved—and so was I."

If Don Pedro wept, it was not just because the Pontiff's letter had inflicted the most stinging of disavowals by refusing to recognize Father O'Keefe's appointment and replacing him with a "personal delegate" of the Pope. It was also because this gesture represented a humiliating contempt for the institution founded so long ago by Ignatius of Loyola.

The aged General—sick, unable to frame the slightest protest, to make the merest reference to legal norms—was thus faced with a fait accompli, forced to acknowledge his total powerlessness, and reduced to the most painful speculation. Could such contempt for legality mean that the Supreme Pontiff was no longer content with the *perinde ac cadaver* requirement once imposed on a man like Teilhard, that he was now questioning the essence, the management, and conduct of the Company? Was this move also a blanket condemnation of every Company initiative taken during his Generalate, of Decree Four and the Thirty-Second Congregation, of the conception of "justice" framed and practiced by him and his companions since 1974? Such were the thoughts that must have run through the mind of the captive and virtually speechless hemiplegic of the Borgo Santo Spirito . . .

An Italian journalist has called this final period of meditation "Father Arrupe's Calvary."[7] And Don Pedro's former assistant, the Indian Father Divarkar, wrote in the American Jesuit review *America* that for the old Jesuit walled inside his silence it was a true "crucifixion."

As his "personal delegate" at the head of the Company, John Paul II chose a Jesuit (at least!†), Father Paolo Dezza, Paul VI's former confessor, assisted by Father Giuseppe Pittau, once the Provincial of Japan (as Arrupe had been). Two Italians considered to be "moderates," in no way involved with the rash moves of the "Arrupe era." Even a man targeted by the pontifical ukase, Father Calvez, said that Dezza was invariably circumspect and conciliatory, refusing to make a rule of the abuse of power to which he owed his promotion. But a power play is a power play, no matter how delicately handled. And feelings ran very high both within the Company and elsewhere.

Father Henri Madelin, Provincial of France, sent the leaders of the Company a message that breathes real pain:

This is a test of our faith. . . . What has happened to us is outside the

---

*Named in the Pope's letter as his "personal delegate" at the head of the Company.

†The Italian press reported that the Pope had originally thought of appointing Cardinal Paolo Bertolli but that the (Jesuit) Cardinal of Milan, Monsignor Martini, had persuaded him that confiding the post to a non-Jesuit would have a disastrous moral effect on his companions.

normal course of the law that governs us. . . . We are entering a delicate period. With all the defects and qualities peculiar to it, the Company must not seek self-justification. . . . It must resist the
suggestions of those who would set it up as a rival Church to the true
Church. . . . It will be judged on the quality of its "discretion" in the
face of what is happening to it, . . . on the strength of the unity of
which it is capable.

But this French show of abnegation, this uncharacteristic "discretion," was
not observed by every Province. While the reaction of the Jesuits of France was
particularly moderate (considering that most of them had supported Arrupe's
direction, and that their Gallican tradition might well have encouraged them to
stress the illegality of the papal operation), Jesuits elsewhere were astounded,
angry, and sometimes outspoken in ways that had little to do with the famous
perinde ac cadaver principle.

In England, where spokesmen for Catholicism still display a "Britishness" that
puts its own particular insular spin on the Gallicanism flourishing across the
Channel, the excellent journal *The Tablet* condemned the "insult" delivered by
John Paul II to one of the "most respected and admired Company Generals since
Loyola." In Germany, a score of priests—including the illustrious Karl Rahner—
let it be known that it failed to see "the finger of God" in the Pope's action.

As for the Jesuits of Canada, they called a press conference at which they
more or less declared that Karol Wojtyla, the native of a country of the East,
shaped by the regimes under whose shadows he had exercised his priestly actions, was not very familiar with the democratic procedures that were the Company norm.[8] They did not quite accuse the Pope of Stalinism, however.

The brutality of Wojtyla's action, inflicted upon a physically diminished man
and a Company made vulnerable by the speed and multiplicity of the muta-
tions triggered by Vatican II, naturally raises problems that go deeper than John
Paul's character, his political background and culture, and his Polish origins.
What such a step called into question was both the nature of relations between
the Holy See and the Company, and the limits of obedience.

On February 27, 1982, the Pope received the Provincials of the Company at
the Vatican. He paid tribute to the fathers for weathering the "ordeal" (*prova*) in
"authentically Ignatian spirit." His natural authoritarianism clearly reinforced
by their docility, the Pope went on to tell his visitors that they must extend the
"fourth vow" (obedience) which they had sworn to the head of the Roman
Church (as Ignatius's *Constitutions* stipulated) to the leaders of every branch of
the Catholic Church.

The Supreme Pontiff was thus not content with humiliating the Society dedicated more rigidly than any other to his service. He intended henceforth to put

it at the disposition of the bishops and of bodies that had never held any sway over it. The Vatican operation was beginning to look like bullying. From one turn of the screw to the next, the deeply revolutionary nature of the venture launched in 1534 on Montmartre by Loyola and his six companions seemed doomed to slow extinction.

The hemorrhage the Company suffered in the 1960s has often been ascribed to the "laxism" of the Arrupe Generalate. Why remain a Jesuit if it no longer meant being a priest but some kind of militant social worker? Why not join Doctors Without Borders or Amnesty International? And why become a Jesuit if such adherence no longer implied fidelity to a very special brand of inventiveness, freedom, and creative energy?

The Pope had imposed his own "personal delegate," vested with full powers, on a Company decapitated by its leader's illness. He did not intend to prolong indefinitely the situation created by this abuse of power. He simply intended to purge the Ignatian Company of its "progressivist" fever, put it through a disciplinary cure, tighten the links between the Jesuits and the Church's common leadership, even if it meant the loss of their particular stamp—the stamp of Xavier, Ricci, and Teilhard.

Indeed the "cure" could not safely be prolonged beyond eighteen months. It was essential to return to Ignatian legality. Thus, in 1983, the Thirty-third General Congregation of Jesuits was convened to elect a successor to Pedro Arrupe—confined to his room in the infirmary in Borgo Santo Spirito, where he was gradually regaining the power of speech, but neither the power nor the inclination to intervene.

And meanwhile, there was no letup in the series of insults and calls to order—or rather to papal order. It could be the case of Father Robert Drinan of Massachusetts, the only Catholic priest ever elected to the United States Congress. Rome ordered Drinan not to campaign for renewal of a mandate in whose course he had veered from the establishment line (particularly during the Vietnam War): Only in such cases of confrontation with established authority, apparently, are Jesuits accused of "dabbling in politics."

Or else it would be the angry public reproof delivered by Pope John Paul II to Father Fernando Cardenal, Minister of Culture in the Sandinista government of Nicaragua, during a papal visit to Latin America. Although Cardenal had left the Company of Jesus, he was considered the archetypal "Red Jesuit." The papal reproof was also directed at Cardenal's brother Ernesto, a non-Jesuit priest serving as Nicaraguan Foreign Minister. These were two further displays of the authoritarian change of course which dispelled the last doubts about the Pope's "Jesuit policy."

But relations between the Pope and "his" Jesuits (for that is what they seemed to have become) suddenly grew sweeter after the Thirty-third Congregation, which in September 1983 elected Father Peter Hans Kolvenbach as the (legal) successor to Arrupe. The choice of this sagacious, moderate man at a time of turbulence was in itself significant. But even more significant than this clearly judicious choice were the texts that emerged from the Congregation. They set the tone for what would be the Company "line" in the 1990s.

Of themselves these conclusions were modifications rather than amendments of the orientation Arrupe had sought for the Company. There was no absolute break, no shamefaced repudiation. But just as relations between Black and White Pope had been changed by the brutal takeover of 1981, forcing the Company into more constricting dependence on the papacy, the statements made at the Thirty-third Congregation resolutely soft-pedaled the militancy of the past two decades.

Their general tone breathes contrition. They speak "with humility" of "failings," "deficiencies," and "difficulties":

> The interpretation of "Decree Four" of the Thirty-second General Congregation was possibly sometimes "truncated, partial, or ill-balanced."* We did not always keep before our eyes that truth which ordains that we must seek social justice in the light of the "justice of the Gospel," which is as it were the sacrament of God's love and compassion. We imperfectly understood that we should wholly dedicate ourselves to a mission that is not a ministry like any other but "the integrating element which unites all ministries." Or else we failed to see the way in which the Church had of late been urging us to change the structures of society, and the manner in which we should behave when we worked alongside the laity in this process of transformation. Deficiencies then in many areas, yet essentially linked to the tendency to reduce the concept of justice to too-human dimensions.

But why should there not have been tensions within the Company? Particularly since "some have occasionally and unilaterally laid undue stress upon one aspect of this mission to the detriment of the other. And yet neither a disembodied spiritualism nor a purely secularized militancy really serve the general proclamation of the Gospel in today's world. The experience of these last years daily makes it clearer: The more a Jesuit commits himself to situations and structures foreign to faith, the more he is forced to renounce his own identity as a religious."

*Incidentally, Arrupe's own words.

Examining this series of texts, Jean-Yves Calvez concludes that after so much controversy, so many tensions, internal struggles, and papal interventions (which he is careful not to characterize), "Decree Four endures." Later, he qualified the assertion by adding: "Serving the faith and the cause of justice in *integrated* fashion." In other words, restoring that service to a wider context in which its rough corners, its "social edge," would be less obtrusive. It was still a question of a "profound renewal of humankind according to the Second Vatican Council," and therefore of a humanist message. But everything that had smacked of innovation in 1974, of significant militancy, was now "integrated," herded back into the fold. No more avant-garde, the Pope had ruled.

What of the silent man sunk deep in his hemiplegic's wheelchair in the Borgo Santo Spirito for ten long years, daily becoming more ethereal, mumbling the occasional indistinct Spanish sentences? How did the General, so long exiled from power, view the touches being added to his work?

We left him in tears after reading the Holy Father's fatal letter, undoing his choice and imposing his own "personal delegate" on the Company. According to people who called on him, he lived in physical pain and spiritual anguish. How did he receive the comment by his successor, who acknowledged that in the 1970s (the time of Decree Four), the Company had been too "worldly," too secularized, and that the Pope's intervention in 1981 had administered "healthy therapy?"[9]

Don Pedro Arrupe had long since overcome the temptations of melancholy or resentment. When the Pope visited him in early 1991 to congratulate him on the model docility of the Company's submission to the ferule of authority, he asked Arrupe to support him "with his prayers and his sufferings." To which the sick man replied, as best he could, with a protestation of "total obedience."

Beyond bitterness, which perhaps never assailed this best of men, he had the leisure and the right to take preliminary stock of the Generalate now known as "the Arrupe years." Apart from a few diehard fundamentalists (they also exist in the Company of Jesus), a couple of radio personalities, and a handful of Spanish theologians and Roman canonists, who can deny that between 1965 and 1981 the Company of Jesus rediscovered the Fountain of Youth?

But should the Company thus launch itself "without charts or general staff" toward an unknown future? Having asked himself the question, Karl Rahner answers in the affirmative. That the Jesuit Society was amputated (unburdened?) of a quarter of its members in twenty years by the contradictions between its temporal and spiritual missions, between a distinct acceptance of faith and a specific vision of justice, between what remained of its disciplinary corset and the impulses set free by the creativity and permissiveness of the period, could only rekindle its vocation and liberate its capacity for movement.*

Pedro Arrupe was the man who dared declare that "injustice is atheism in action." Never perhaps had anyone made a stronger connection between the most respectable of human aspirations—the struggle for greater justice—to an even greater religious exigency. What more did he have to say? The concerns of power and hierarchy no longer concerned him in the slightest. He had pronounced those words.

The Reverend Father Pedro Arrupe, S.J., twenty-eighth Superior General of the Society of Jesus, died in the infirmary at Jesuit headquarters in Rome on February 5, 1991, at the age of eighty-four.

---

*To a journalist who bewailed the departure of a thousand Jesuits from the Company François Mauriac retorted shortly before his death: "At this point in its history, the Church has less to fear from those who leave it than from some who stay."

·XVII·

the thiRO coMPANY?

The Great Generation • Karl Rahner and "Nameless Christians" •
"We Hold These Truths" • In Danbury Prison with Daniel
Berrigan • A Massachusetts Politician • Salvadoran
Holocaust • The Linguistics of Discernment

VERY NATION, EVERY society, every national or international organization have gone through periods of dull stagnation between days of
expansion and hours of defeat, between falling and rebounding.

In the early years of this century, a hundred years after Pius VII restored it to
its prerogatives, the Society of Jesus seemed adrift between memories of past
glory and fears of future worldwide repudiation: not a crushing 1773-style official proscription this time, but a forced recourse to dodging and parrying, expulsion in this place, close surveillance in another, unpopularity where officially
sanctioned, and apparently bereft of the energy to rebuild—not with a bang but
a whimper.

The nineteenth century had not been propitious for Loyola's Society. Romanticism did not suit its taste for reason, belief in science its obsession with
faith, the cult of nationalities its basic internationalism. Hugo, Darwin, and
Mazzini had thrust it into an embittered twilight that belied its expansionist
traditions. And the great proponents of state education, like Bismarck in Germany and Jules Ferry in France, had shorn it of its most conspicuous mission,
the education of a ruling class.

Worse, its inventiveness seemed to have dried up. It had produced no doctor,
preacher, astronomer, or teacher to rival the great figures of the heroic past.
Writing in the 1980s, Jesuit historian Émile Rideau presents a self-critical picture that shows us a Company floundering in this period of uneasy vacillation,

480

between the ferocious antimodernism of Pius X and hopes of a renewal that seemed impossibly remote.

> The Company suffered from a blind spot to the modern world: Disloyal in this regard to its founder's spirit, it was unable or unwilling to recognize the signs of the times. Its realism lacked clear-sightedness and prophetic discernment. Shackled like a handmaiden to the Church, it endured the ponderous slowness of a Christianity largely detached from the world.
>
> In a sense it would be accurate to say that the Company was underemployed, which considerably diminished its productivity. Yet it possessed all the tools for influencing the course of history and introducing the dialogue of Church and humankind two centuries in advance.[1]

This "blind spot" of yesterday's Jesuits to the "signs of the times"* cannot be ascribed only to their reaction to persecution suffered at the hands of the heirs of the French Revolution and militant secularism or to their slavish acquiescence in the antimodernism of Pius X. It also stemmed from the loss, or perhaps the suffocation, of the spirit of inquiry and research its founders had stamped on the Company.

The mummy's bands were now tight-swaddled, and the very institution was ossifying, falling back on rigid, lifeless structures to act as a brake on mobility; on the immutability of dogma to still the world's storms. In 1923, during the austere Generalate of Wladimir Ledochowski, the Company's Twenty-seventh General Congregation was exploited by this Polish monk (not distinguished by his flair for the "signs of the times") to enhance the immutable character of the order's *Constitutions*.

To forestall once and for all every possibility of "change," the Twenty-seventh Congregation identified a list of "untouchable" points. It further distinguished between "substantial points of the first rank" and those of the "second rank." As Father Maurice Giuliani observed, "the life of the Company was now fixed within a rigorously legal framework, a framework which assumed such importance that it tended to impose itself upon succeeding General Congregations."[2]

Rarely in history had a corporation so tightly mortgaged its past and future.† Yet it was from the bottom of this abyss of educational restriction and mindless discipline that what might be called the "third Company" now sprang and flourished. Not a "restored" Company, as in 1814, but one resuscitated by the generation forged at the time of the Jesuits' expulsions from France in 1901 and 1904, of the crusade launched by Rome against "modernism"—in other words

---

*Title of a Dominican magazine.
†Meanwhile in Moscow, at that very same hour . . .

against the application of historical and scientific criticism to the study of the Scriptures, and consequently of Christian dogma.

On the eve of the First World War—as the Company's fundamentalists rushed to fend off the century with philosophical prohibitions and imprecations—within the Company, in its most peaceful circles, and tended by its most "reassuring" figures, a spring was bubbling forth and swelling. It would eventually grow into the four or five revolutions whence the Company would emerge transformed, and reconciled with a world in search of knowledge, freedom, and justice: Teilhard's revolution, which located Christianity within the timeless evolution of the cosmos; Karl Rahner's revolution, which freed the Catholic Church of its monopoly on salvation (Charon on the banks of the Styx!) and substituted a helping, participatory, more human role; John Courtney Murray's revolution of 1965, which raised on high the principles of pluralism and religious freedom; and the role of the most recent General but one, the Basque Pedro Arrupe, who embodied the principle of charity in justice.

Thus the still-numb body of the Company was—or would shortly become—ready for the real battles of modern times. A series of historically interlinked phenomena brought it to this point and restored it to its full-blooded calling, phenomena that acted upon it like revulsants, and along different but converging paths. There was the Great Depression; the emergence of Nazism as a state structure in Germany; and the long process of decolonization set in motion in the early 1930s by Gandhi's liberation movement in India.

It might seem surprising that the economic and financial crisis that gripped the world after the Wall Street crash of 1929 should have served as a spur to a Company hitherto more closely associated with the wealthy than the poor (and this in spite of the missionary work we have dwelt on in the course of this book). But we possess the testimony of several Jesuits who entered the Company during the Depression decade. Jacques Sommet, for example, was horrified by the increasingly palpable misery around him in Lyon at the beginning of the 1930s. He went into the Company the way others join a union or a political party, out of solidarity (although of course motives other than the sudden pauperization of his neighbors were at play).

The Jesuits were not resuscitated by poverty alone, but this general misery was one of the warning signs that led them back (through what was called "popular action" and through awareness of the world of the worker) to their reason for being—as they very soon came to see it. So intensely, in fact, that when the worker-priest movement was banned some twenty years later, the Company took it as an insult and a major injury.

* * *

We have already seen the extent to which the Company's history was linked to that of colonialism. Inevitably, then, the fissures that began to gape across the world political map in the 1930s affected and disturbed the Company. (Not that the Jesuits at once espoused the cause of overseas liberation movements. Indeed in 1942 the French Jesuit magazine *Études* voiced concern at the fact that "innovators like Gandhi have slowed the conversion rate in India.")[3]

But the old empires—the British and above all the French—were starting to disintegrate after the Second World War. The American Empire was being vigorously challenged south of the Rio Grande. The Russian colossus looked as if it might endure for several decades (but there were already rumblings in Berlin and Warsaw). And China's resurgence put the whole world balance of powers in question. In short, an international organization like that of the "men in black"—so long and so incautiously associated with the imperial powers—was inevitably forced into a deep-seated revision of its planetary implantation. Gone were the days when all the Company needed to influence events was a handful of royal or imperial confessors in Madrid, Lisbon, Paris, or Vienna. Henceforth a hundred sovereign states could claim some small power of decision, of control, of prohibition. Henceforth the faithful prayed not just in Latin but in more than thirty languages. Henceforth human rights on five continents were no longer "granted" (where they were not actually denied or trampled) but claimed and taken. Jesuit "discernment" was sorely tested. But it survived its first stumblings. It devised a whole new concept of mission. From 1945 onward it espoused the cause of national liberation and decolonization. A doleful yet inspiring turning point for the Company of Jesus.

But in the final analysis, the decisive reanimating factor was the rise of National Socialism in Germany. Of course Leninism in Russia and Latin Fascism in Italy and Spain had already warned Christian Europe of the dangers of totalitarianism. But as we have seen, the former operated in a sphere that was peripheral from the Church standpoint; and with Italian Fascism (which affected a degree of respect for the Vatican and promoted neither militant paganism nor racial exclusion), the Papacy—and the Company—had already established polite relations.

But Nazism encroached directly upon Catholic domains: Bavaria, the Rhineland, eventually Austria. Its hostility was palpable, often framed in the terms of a very eloquent anti-Christianity. We have earlier noted some Jesuit reactions to the approach of the barbarian, and seen that most of the Company's leaders, whether German or not, perceived the frenzied hatred of humanism that towered behind Nazi calls for "order" and "efficiency" and behind anti-Bolshevik rhetoric.

Even more unmistakably than the wave of misery set in motion by the 1929 crash or the decolonization movement, the Nazi eruption signaled a new dawn of the Company's conscience. Countless compromises and burdensome ambiguities were swept away. The Society that had failed to see what promoted the cause of man and of justice in the broad-based program of the French Revolution, the Society that had abetted the obscurantism of Pius IX's Vatican and the intrigues that sent Dreyfus to Devil's Island, perceived Nazism as an affront. To turn Adolf Hitler into the midwife of the "third Company" would be excessive. But in picking up the Nazi gauntlet, the Company of the 1930s and 1940s reached back to its fighting origins, to its vocation at the very heart of things.

We have already mentioned Teilhard and Arrupe; the first tried to integrate the Christian tragedy into a vast movement of cosmic optimism; the second reminded people that material and spiritual justice are inseparable. They were not alone. Once fossilized in its role as guardian of the past, the Company now offered freedom and renewal to the aging Catholic Church. While in France Henri de Lubac reintroduced into life a "spiritual" element somewhat etiolated by its isolation from nature, John Courtney Murray secured Vatican II's acknowledgment of the fundamental doctrine of freedom of conscience, and Karl Rahner fearlessly extended the promise of salvation to embrace the whole universe.

And we would be doing such pioneers an injustice if we did not note that their achievements took place within the framework of a Society that was still arthritic, and led between 1914 and 1965 by two figures timorously wrapped in an overriding concern for order and discipline. We have already mentioned Superior General Ledochowski. In *America,*[4] the most influential Jesuit organ in the United States, Peter Hebblethwaite likened Superior General Jean-Baptiste Janssens to an old dry stick in need of watering, ridiculed for his advice to young Jesuits about the cinema (*bis sex in anno*), a man apparently content to "sit in Rome and there transmit the Holy Office's prohibitions to John Courtney Murray and Karl Rahner."*

Janssens was a canonist, in other words chiefly a guardian of the rules. Even though his illustrious predecessors in Pascal's day had shown that the legal mind could be injected with imagination, this austere watchdog did not consider himself intended for innovation or even interpretation. One of his rare impulses toward liberalism, during Joe Golan's campaign to purge the Catholic liturgy of its anti-Semitic overtones, was founded in a decree of the Lord: Since God had permitted the Jews to reach the Holy Land, and thus set a limit on their "punishment," why continue to persecute the "deicide" people!

* * *

*Teilhard and de Lubac were of course even more severely treated.

Karl Rahner, short, stocky, radiating energy and boldness, his gaze intense behind thick glasses, did more than anyone else, with his *Fundamental Treatise on Faith*, to destroy the barbed-wire fences and watchtowers both inside and outside the Catholic world. Of his vast achievements, we have space here to note only the concept that did more than anything else to guide Catholicism out of its ghetto: the notion of the "anonymous Christian." We have already seen the progressive fading of the concept of "no salvation outside the Church" in the Company's mission activities. More recently, though, Vatican Council II, particularly its constitutions *Lumen Gentium* and *Gaudium et Spes*, had thrust back to the Middle Ages (or perhaps merely to the nineteenth century) the exclusionary principles to which the Jesuits had contributed, but which were now replaced by the following more reasonable considerations:

> Those who, through no fault of their own, do not know the Gospel of
> Christ or his Church, but who nevertheless seek God with a sincere
> heart, and, moved by grace, try in their actions to do his will as they
> know it through the dictates of their conscience—those too may
> achieve eternal salvation. Nor shall divine providence deny the assis-
> tance necessary for salvation to those who, without any fault of theirs,
> have not yet arrived at an explicit knowledge of God, and who, not
> without grace, strive to lead a good life.

It is hard not to discern the influence of Rahner's writings about "anonymous Christians" in Vatican II texts. Since the 1950s the Jesuit theologian had tirelessly developed this concept of man justified outside Catholic preaching. But it was in his *Foundations of Christian Faith*, his masterwork, that he formulates it with greatest strength:

> Many have encountered Jesus without knowing that they
> grasped . . . the one whom Christians rightly call Jesus of
> Nazareth. . . . Are not God and Christ's grace given as the secret es-
> sence of any reality we might choose? Whoever . . . then assumes his
> existence, and therefore his humanity, in silent patience (or better: in
> faith, hope, and love), who assumes it as the mystery hiding in the
> mystery of eternal love, that man—whether he knows it or not—says
> Yes to Christ. . . . Whoever assumes fully his being-human . . . has
> welcomed the Son of Man. And if we find in the Scripture, accom-
> plished by the law, the man who loves his neighbor, that is the ulti-
> mate truth, because God himself has become that neighbor and
> because in every neighbor it is always this unique near and distant be-
> ing that is at once welcomed and loved.[5]

Rahner did not remain in the realm of theory. Calm in the liberation storm, he took his stand on all the most exposed heights, alongside Arrupe under attack by his companions, with the worker-priests. No one had ever directed a freer gaze on the Church's evolution and on that of the Company of Jesus than this Jesuit theologian when he foresaw for both organizations in the 1960s a coming "diaspora."

As for the future of the Company, the theologian from Freiburg believed that the democratic practices inaugurated by the Council (and developed in Jesuit circles by Pedro Arrupe) meant that the "monolithic army" of yore could never be reconstituted. But one has to read the pages he devotes to obedience in his *Discourse of Ignatius of Loyola to Today's Jesuits* to gauge the boldness of his thinking. Not only does he call the *perinde ac cadaver* formula "foolish"; he deplores the fact that the Company had been too "submissive" to secular authority; and that, to defend their reductions in Paraguay, the fathers had been unable to fight injustice with force. He further recommends that certain "orders" from above be met with "a modest and unequivocal refusal dictated by conscience." Recalling the many historical clashes between Papacy and Company, from Pius X and Sixtus V to Clement XIV ("a case for investigation by Amnesty International"), Rahner exhorts his colleagues to feel no "shame" for the fact that Paul VI was "not precisely satisfied by our Thirty-second General Congregation." Not surprisingly, conservative Catholics, religious or secular, have painted Rahner in the Devil's colors.

In fact, though, the author of the *Discourse of Ignatius of Loyola* rose above and beyond antagonism toward the Church hierarchy. He posed the giant problem of the presence or the awareness of God in the bosom of evolving humankind: "Will there one day be people who . . . no longer ask themselves the question of the Unsayable? . . . If such a thing were possible, what would happen? . . . The history of humanity, stamped by freedom, responsibility, guilt, and forgiveness, would then be over, and all that would change would be the manner of the end which we as Christians await. Men worthy of the name would all the same have found eternal life."[6]

"Men worthy of the name": Are not those the same men who fight for Father Arrupe's justice? This time, the opening is limitless. Whether or not we assimilate such men into the plurimillenary movement described by Teilhard, we have to admit that—among others—today's Jesuits have thrown the doors of the Church wide open.

Theology has never been considered the strong point of American Jesuitry, generally more distinguished by its educational methods and university system. But there have been notable exceptions, such as Josef Fuchs, Richard McCormick, and above all John Courtney Murray. From his chair at Woodstock College in Maryland, Murray opened the way to recognition by the Catholic Church of the doctrine of freedom of conscience, which it formally acknowledged in Rome in 1965.

Everyone who ever met John Courtney Murray has retained the memory above all of great style. And everyone who has read his major work, *We Hold These Truths,*[7] considers him a peerless advocate of pluralism.

Initially, no one could have been less rash, less agitated, less "controversial" than Father Murray. A liberal scholar in the great New England tradition, he was a perennial contributor to journals like *America, Modern Age,* and *The Critic,* and dedicated much of his labor to demonstrating not that Catholicism was compatible with American democracy ("The question is invalid as well as impertinent"), but that "American democracy is compatible with Catholicism." That, he said, is "one of the truths I hold."[8]

John Courtney Murray endlessly reiterated that the American Catholic, faithful to an ancient and universal religion, experienced particular difficulties in reconciling his membership in the Church with respect for a Constitution that involves the "advice and consent" of all citizens. Clearly, then, the American system posed a problem for the Church, but that problem must be resolved in the sense of adhesion to freedom of conscience and religious pluralism.

By the time Father Murray's major essay was published, his ideas were already widely known, opposed by conservatives, and studied by the preparatory committees of Vatican II. The American Jesuit traveled to Rome to try to have them placed on the Council agenda: He knew that John XXIII looked with favor on his theories. But he stumbled up against Cardinal Ottaviani, head of the Holy Office, who shot back at him: "You hope to align the Catholic Church with the doctrine of a State founded by Protestants and which reflects Freemason ideology! You will find me blocking your way. Don't forget that I am the rifleman of the Vatican!"

For John Courtney Murray to be able to defend his ideas before the Council he needed the help of another "rifleman"—the hired gun of the American Empire, the redoubtable Cardinal Francis Spellman, who was to become the advocate and preacher of the crusade in Vietnam. For once the American "arrogance of power"* was beneficial. Appointed assessor of the Roman sessions ("ad majorem Americae gloriam") by the grace of the Archbishop of New York, Father Murray was able, with impressive authority and learning, to plead the cause of religious freedom and the separation of church and state, stressing like a good American (and good Jesuit) the benefits accruing to Catholicism from such an attitude.

They were all words that, a century earlier, under Pius X's intolerant Pontifi-

*Senator J. William Fulbright's term for U.S. involvement in Vietnam.

cate, would have led him not to the stake but to the ignominy of the Index. John Courtney Murray's plea for freedom of conscience and every man's "right to respect," even if he was in error, rested on formidable ecclesiastical scholarship: his ability at the fiery heart of Council debate to quote the monk Gelasius's arguments of 494 B.C. against the Emperor Athanasius's claims to reign both as Caesar and Pope equipped him to stop Cardinal Ottaviani in his tracks.

Thus this American Jesuit, impregnated with the ideas of John Adams and Abraham Lincoln (and who recalled that another American Jesuit, Monsignor John Carroll, had been close to the Founding Fathers of 1787), succeeded in grafting onto Catholicism a spirit directly inherited from New England Puritanism, if not from Scottish Freemasonry. A spirit that led a younger Jesuit, Charles Graham, to liken Murray to "a knight on the firing line."

And thus the Society of Jesus, once dedicated to the unequivocal preservation of the ferociously antimodern and antidemocratic religion of Pius IX and Pius X, of the temporal power of the Papacy, once again played its healing part. Like Teilhard and Rahner before him, and Arrupe after, Murray contributed to the flowering of religious freedom, to the reconciliation of his century with faith, to the Church's emergence from the fortress-like temple* where it had barricaded itself, inside a Vatican beyond whose walls no salvation was possible.

Not all American Jesuits assumed the majestic style or followed the Council paths of John Courtney Murray. All those, American or not, academics, politicians, journalists, and students, embroiled in opposition to the Vietnam War, still recall a dazzling name that from the close of the 1960s symbolized the most radical forms of antiwar activism: Father Daniel Berrigan, S.J., hero of a pacifist guerrilla campaign that landed him in jail, and then of a film that shook university campuses and a play enthusiastically received by New Yorkers—not to mention the many biographies he has inspired.

In early April 1971, several American publications, including *Newsweek,* and four leading Christian reviews, two Protestant and two Catholic, published "We Accuse," a violent indictment of President Nixon and the ten men chiefly responsible for the conduct of military operations in Vietnam, culminating in these words by Father Berrigan: "Peace will not triumph without action undertaken . . . by great numbers of honest men and women."

But Dan Berrigan was not one who spoke in order to spur others to action. On October 9, 1968, he was sentenced to three years in prison for an act committed five months before: the incineration by napalm of draft cards stolen from the Catonsville, Maryland, recruiting office. A few months before that his

---

*See below, the Italian Jesuit Bartolomeo Sorge's *Uscire dal Tempio,* "Leaving the Temple."

younger brother, Philip, also a priest though not a Jesuit, had blazed the trail by spraying pig's blood on military documents at a Baltimore recruiting center, which had earned him a six-year jail sentence.

Daniel Berrigan, a professor at Cornell University, a well-known poet nearing his fifties, was no irresponsible hippie, but he chose to disappear before he could be locked away. He lived for six months on the run like a sort of pacifist Robin Hood, appearing in a church to deliver a brief sermon, vanishing again, uttering a few fiery words at a public meeting, before he was finally caught.

From his cell in Danbury prison, in Connecticut, where he spent twenty months, Berrigan consistently presented his imprisonment at once as a purely voluntary matter and a "Christian duty," a testimony and a symbol, a contribution to the "poetic liberation of the American conscience." There he wrote the books *No Bars to Manhood* and *The Trial of the Catonsville Nine*. At that time too a film of his life, *Holy Outlaw: Father Daniel Berrigan*, was made, while a leading Jesuit review, *The Holy Cross Quarterly*, published what amounted to his absolution in an article by Father Edward Duff. Superior General Father Arrupe himself (who had told a press conference that if the defense of freedom meant incarceration, a Jesuit had to take that risk) visited him in his cell—"not to condone his action," Don Pedro explained, "but because I must give myself to all our Company."

At the end of 1970 the "Berrigan affair" suddenly looked much grimmer: The rebellious brothers, still in jail, were charged by FBI director J. Edgar Hoover with planning to blow up the heating system in the White House basement, with calling for armed resistance against the draft, and . . . with plotting to kidnap Henry Kissinger, President Nixon's closest foreign policy adviser! But although they were arraigned before a federal grand jury in Harrisburg, Pennsylvania, the charges were dropped.

Released in 1972, Daniel Berrigan resumed his antiwar campaign in the United States and abroad. In May of that year, in Paris, he even said that "the American bishops are more responsible for this war than the German bishops under Hitler." The words raised a storm, as well as the bitterest complaints from Cardinal Spellman to the highest authorities of the Company.

But what of the holy outlaw today, twenty years down the road? According to a response from his superiors in July 1992, "Father Berrigan is very well. He lives in New York. He is continuing his work for peace and against all wars of aggression."

A third American Jesuit chose yet another path to reach his compatriots: Elected by a constituency in the suburbs of Boston, Father Robert Patrick Drinan entered the House of Representatives in 1971, the first Catholic priest ever to do so—but preceded there by ninety-six ministers of various Protestant denominations. He spent ten years as a congressman, until Pope John Paul II insisted in 1980 that he not seek re-election.

An eminent jurist, the author of several works on international law, a professor on the faculty of Georgetown University, Father Drinan was a very visible and active Democrat, whose constituents were not just Irish Catholics but also Protestants and Jews. Which led him to emerge as a particularly prominent advocate of Israeli policy, so much so in fact that the Vatican was alarmed.

But if Father Drinan drew down the Holy Office's wrath, it was on much more dangerous ground: his consistent votes in favor of legalizing abortion. When an English Catholic visitor, Peter Rawlinson, expressed his astonishment, Drinan responded in a manner that might have stimulated Pascal: "As a Catholic priest I disapprove of abortion. But as a member of Congress elected by a pluralistic society, I am not entitled to impose the views of my coreligionists in such a way."[9]

His declared opposition to the Vietnam War, to his country's "imperialist" strategy in Latin America (particularly in Chile and Nicaragua), and to nuclear weapons, pitted him against many of his fellow Democrats. And so, when the Sovereign Pontiff (intervening illicitly in American public affairs) demanded his withdrawal from Congress, Robert F. Drinan, S.J., was left with only his voters to encourage him to fight. Which was not enough.

In mid-November 1989 the Salvadoran regime seemed on the verge of collapse: The guerrillas of FMLN (Farabundo Martí de Liberación Nacional), who had surrounded the national capital, San Salvador, were pressing home the attack. In that fear-filled national climate, El Salvador's state radio broadcast death threats—some of them by the country's vice-president—against the political and religious "accomplices" of the attackers, in particular Father Ignacio Ellacuria, rector of the Central American University. Ellacuria was a man already under constant threat. And fresh in every mind was the recent assassination of Father Rutilio Grande, another Jesuit who had taken up the cause of the poor.

At first light on November 16, the bullet-riddled and mutilated corpses of Father Ellacuria, five other Jesuits, their housekeeper, and her daughter were found in the garden shared by the Jesuit University and the Monsignor Romero Pastoral Center.* Jesuit headquarters and records had been ransacked, and on the university gate hung a poster saying that the FMLN had "executed these informers."

*Named after Archbishop Oscar Romero of San Salvador, assassinated by rightwingers in 1980.

The reaction of San Salvador's Archbishop Rivera was stinging. "This is the work of the same people* who murdered Monsignor Romero and who are not satisfied with seventy thousand deaths!" The Jesuit Provincial, Father Tojeira, echoed his charges, speaking of "absolute proofs" of the army's guilt. Right-wing President Alfredo Cristiani declared himself prepared to "punish the guilty, whoever they are." A woman who worked in the Jesuits' quarters told the Archbishop that on the night of the crime she had seen soldiers entering the building.

Who were the victims? Father Ignacio Ellacuria, a Spanish Basque and naturalized Salvadoran, a respected sociologist and director of the journal *Estudios Centroamericanos,* was considered a moderate critic of the government: A personal friend of President Cristiani, he was seen as the ideal mediator. Indeed, since he had contacts among the guerrillas (many of his former students had taken to the hills and jungle), he had recently had several interviews with the president. By killing him, the army sought to kill any chances of a political settlement. Ellacuria was eliminated, and Cristiani terrified.

The other victims, all Jesuits, were Fathers Martín Baro, university vice rector; Segundo Montes, director of the Institute for Human Rights; Armando López, former rector of the University of Managua in Nicaragua; Ramón Moreno, director of the journal *Diaconia*; and Joaquin López, known as "Father Lolo," the only native Salvadoran among them, founder of the Fe y Alegría (Faith and Joy) adult education association. Jon Sobrino, the most celebrated member of the Jesuit community, was teaching a course in Asia and escaped the killing. His teachings had contributed to "liberation theology"—the army's most hated enemy.

In the weeks following the massacre, clues and tips piled up. Roberto d'Aubuisson, leader of the extreme-right Arena party, and generally considered the man really responsible for the assassination of Monsignor Romero, denied any part in the crime. The Salvadoran defense minister, Colonel Rene Emilio Ponce, swore that the assassins had no ties to the army "as an institution." But the United States House of Representatives (where links between the Salvadoran and U.S. armed forces stirred a scandal) appointed a commission of inquiry headed by the Democrat Joe Moakley. By the end of 1989 it was clear, first, that the tiny nation's army was implicated to the hilt, and second, that for once Washington would not hush up the affair.

In fact, on January 2, 1990, Major Buckland, an American "adviser" of the local forces, passed along to his superiors a revelation by one of his Salvadoran contacts: The commander of the Salvadoran military academy, Colonel

*In other words, the Salvadoran army.

Guillermo Benavides, was compromised in the November 16 "operation." The American major was at once stripped of his functions and shipped back hastily to the United States. But the news had leaked out, and the truth soon emerged: On January 7, President Cristiani announced over the radio that "elements of the army" were implicated in the crime. Which ones? The head of state went on to specify them: the elite Atlacatl battalion, trained in torture and repression by American advisers.

Two events would now bring the army down in flames: While American Secretary of State James Baker declared that "this matter is a defining moment in El Salvador's history," even adding that continued American aid would be tied to punishment of the guilty, a well-known Salvadoran army firebrand, Colonel Ochoa, interviewed on the CBS program *60 Minutes*, acknowledged that the killing of the Jesuits had obviously been "planned" by the general staff, and that Colonel Benavides* was either merely a participant or was obeying orders.

Sooner or later the affair had to come to trial. Colonel Benavides, three junior officers, and four soldiers of the Atlacatl battalion appeared before the court. "Overlooked" were the leaders most consistently implicated in acts of repression, such as Colonels Zepeda, Ponce, Cerna Flores, and Linares, who had repeatedly accused one another before the investigating magistrate without anyone daring to indict them.

After the U.S. Congress had voted a 50 percent reduction in military aid to El Salvador and threatened a total cutoff if the "Jesuit affair" was not cleared up, the trial finally started on December 26, 1991. The Salvadoran military had decided to deliver up a few cronies in order to avoid desertion by Washington.

Curiously enough, given the rigid structures of Salvadoran society, it was the highest-ranking officers, Colonel Benavides and Lieutenant Mendoza, who were sentenced,† while the others (members of the Atlacatl battalion, all found guilty of the massacre) were acquitted. Given the nature of the evidence produced, this verdict was an open act of defiance: The only ones condemned were those whose guilt was in doubt. But most observers considered that the army had sustained an unprecedented, and irreparable, reversal. It was no longer— for the time being—able to oppose a ceasefire.

The killers of November 16, 1989, had beheaded the Salvadoran intelligentsia. But they had also triggered a mechanism that led to the political solution preached by the most famous of their victims, Father Ignacio Ellacuria. The cease-fire between guerrillas and government was signed on December 31, 1991.

---

*Since Benavides had not so far been heavily involved in terror activities, the Jesuits questioned his direct involvement in the crime. It is possible that the army decided to hand over a "lukewarm" element, a scapegoat, either to punish his moderation or else to destabilize the prosecution.
†To thirty years' imprisonment.

The sacrifice of the Jesuits of San Salvador had moved Central America in the direction of respect for the law and human rights.

During the celebrations in the Basque region of the 500th anniversary of Ignatius of Loyola's birth, Jesuit Superior General Kolvenbach told the Spanish press: "Our insistence on bringing the authors of the crime to justice was intended to procure a final guarantee of human rights in El Salvador, where thousands of innocent civilians have been murdered without recourse to justice."

The killing of Father Ellacuria and other equally horrifying episodes turned the Jesuits into "nerve centers" in the "northern cone" of Latin America. There, the debate was not just between powers drunk on violence and wretched masses more or less supported by political and religious organizations, but also between two conflicting currents of Catholicism.

On one side stood an "institutional" episcopate, inspired by the Colombian Cardinal López Trujillo, for whom the Church was the disciplinary structure of societies that would otherwise be doomed to anarchy or revolution. On the other, an "evangelical" clergy inspired by Cardinal Arns of São Paulo, who assigned to the religious a boldly apostolic mission among the poor, to the point of being condemned as a "Marxist"—and, like Ellacuria, of suffering the consequences.

Were "liberation theology" and the documents that emerged from the Medellín and Puebla conferences still at the core of that debate? To an observer as keen-eyed as Charles Antoine, the contradiction between the two currents now lay rather in the "evangelicals' " emphasis on biblical teaching among the poor. To its defenders, this was the most radical way of giving the poor what Father Vincent Sentuc* called "knowledge of their wretchedness." To its detractors (most of the upper ranks of the clergy), it was an almost subversive program tending to the de facto creation of a "people's Church."

While it is obvious that the Vatican welcomes the stand taken by Cardinal López Trujillo, it is equally obvious that the Society of Jesus looks favorably on the "evangelical" current. Which is why Central America remains the site of the most painful contradictions between the Holy See and the Company of Jesus. The more so because Arrupe's successor—while not questioning the Pope's high-handed decisions on the governance of the Company—has not retreated an inch on matters of substance.

The Borgo Santo Spirito is at once fortress, convent, university, and government ministry. There a visitor does not feel lapped in esthetic wonders (as one does in most of the buildings adjacent to the Vatican) nor does one feel part of a

---

*Sentuc fought on two fronts in Peru—against exploitation of the peasants but also against the terrorist Shining Path movement.

celebration of the spirit. The atmosphere is one of work, of meditation of course, and, for those who practice it, of prayer. Performed here, *The Spiritual Exercises* would most certainly be exercise.

The man who emerges to greet the visitor from a long, dark fourth-floor corridor is one of the few Jesuits still to wear a soutane (crossed on the chest, Eastern style). Nonetheless, he resembles a scientist rather than a man of religion. The sharpest of eyes behind spectacles, beard trimmed to a point, hair graying, complexion crimson, the busy appearance of those who shut themselves in laboratories only to burst forth full of ideas shortly afterward, he has the look of an experimenter about him, a research worker, an analyst . . . Charcot, Marconi, Jung . . .

This is the archetypal Jesuit, the Black Pope himself, the General of the Jesuits—someone as legend-shrouded as the chief of British Intelligence or the Dalai Lama. His silences are dense, heavy-laden, exotic, shifting, a mirror game. Only the unspoken really matters—and the concern not to say anything that will help reveal what should be hidden.

And yet conversation with the Reverend Father Peter Hans Kolvenbach flows easily.* A swift impression of cordiality and openness, an astonishing ability to listen and retain. According to legend, Kolvenbach is as taciturn as his predecessor was talkative, and niggardly with his confidences. But the guests of the Borgo can testify to the contrary.

He was born at Druten near Nijmegen in Holland in 1928, of Germanic descent through his father and Latin through his mother ("I feel Italian one day and German the next"), but there is nevertheless more of the Mediterranean than the North Sea in him: He spent the greater part of his life among the Armenians of Beirut before completing his linguistic studies in Paris—and then, a dozen years ago, coming to Rome to succeed Don Pedro Arrupe. Nothing mysterious in all that. Unlike his only Dutch predecessor as General, Jan Philip Roothaan, he feels at home in the heat of Rome—where what "cold" there is comes from the Vatican next door.

Cold? No, no, he says. Relations with the Polish Pope are now utterly serene, even though (or because?) the two men see little of one another. But Father Kolvenbach is eager to dwell on the recent history of relations between Company and Papacy.

According to him, the tensions between the Supreme Pontiff and Father Arrupe (which were in fact much graver in Paul VI's time) stemmed from faulty communication, from differences of viewpoint. The Pope saw only the reversals, the General only the leaps forward. Father Arrupe's favorite saying

*Apart from one or two isolated sections, I have put our exchange in indirect form. As author, I did not want to reopen unhealed wounds. Was this "discernment" on my part?

(Basque? Japanese?) was, "The falling tree makes a noise, growing grass does not." The fact is that on the eve of the Jesuits' 1974–75 Thirty-second General Congregation (which gave birth to Decree Four), there were countless complaints about the direction the Company was taking. Paul VI, of whom a powerful Spanish Jesuit faction was demanding the creation of a new Company opposed to "secularization," hoped that Father Arrupe would take things in hand, would rebuild. Instead the General, oblivious to these preoccupations, was proclaiming: "We are living a new Pentecost, let us allow the Holy Spirit to speak. Let the congregation decide."

What Father Kolvenbach wanted to make clear was that rejection of the so-called Arrupe line originated within the Company itself, and that the Vatican was urged to act by many Jesuits who were disturbed or angered by steps that, they claimed, were leading them to substitute social for apostolic activism. When Paul VI asked the Jesuits, for example, "Are you still, and will you remain, priests?" he was expressing a fear emanating from a minority within the Company itself.

There was also the problem of the Pope's authority over the Society. When the question of the right of "representation" (that is, of framing objection to authority) arose at the Thirty-second Congregation, and its extension to the 30 percent or so who had not taken the "fourth vow" or become priests, the Supreme Pontiff had visions, beyond secularization, of liberalization, of a democratization that challenged the powers the Ignatian *Constitutions* accorded the head of the Catholic Church.

As for Pope John Paul II, one of the difficulties he experienced with the Company stemmed from his ignorance of the life of religious orders. Unlike his predecessor, the Archbishop of Cracow was without experience in this field, never having had contact with any but secular clergy and the vibrant parish structures of Poland. Whence the false notes that quickly sounded—particularly in relations with the order most intimately bound to the Papacy.

To demonstrate that the ordeals recently endured by the Company were more often caused by internal problems than outside interventions, pontifical or not, the General points to what might be called the "Teilhard affair." While asserting that rejections of such magnitude are unlikely to recur, he points out that the author of *The Phenomenon of Man* had been exalted by no less a prelate than Cardinal Casaroli.

Asked whether cases like Teilhard's might not reveal a touch of Jesuitphobia at the *Osservatore romano* or a dash of Francophobia at the journal *Civiltà cattolica*, for example, Peter Hans Kolvenbach retorts with a half-smile, "Don't forget the part played by good French Jesuits. They were the most ferocious of all."

And if Father Kolvenbach is asked why not a single Frenchman has ever been elected to lead the Company of Jesus in more than four centuries of existence, the Dutch General cannot resist—if only for a few seconds—falling into the role of the "stage Jesuit." The brows rise. "No Frenchman? I had never noticed!" A courtesy gesture, perhaps. Better a lapse than a surfeit of memory—Pascal, Pasquier, Choiseul, Charles X, Michelet, and all their Jesuit-hating kind . . . how many sharp stones in the fathers' black shoes!

Peter Hans Kolvenbach, his beard looking more ironic by the second, his delivery more rapid-fire, his eyes more sparkling, knows very well that sooner or later we shall be broaching the key question—pluralism.

How aware is this Society (founded as an "order") that it can only revive and reinvent itself "in disorder"? Up to what point can his own authority tolerate polymorphism and polycentrism? Given (for example) the power, wealth, cohesion, and organizational sense of the Jesuits of the United States,* does Father Kolvenbach feel he is also the General of the American Jesuits?

"For my part, dear sir, I 'feel' nothing. But I can assure you that they feel it!"

"Good. But what about representatives of less powerful societies, of less confident cultures—are they free to express themselves, to speak up and be heard?"

"To that I have only one answer: Our Company, the one our founder called the 'little Company,' now numbers twenty-five thousand religious. I am certain that I do not exaggerate when I tell you that that means twenty-five thousand opinions."

"Are they heard, recorded, instrumental in opening new paths?"

"Yes. And the more so because the government of this Company is a government by correspondence: We receive twelve thousand letters a year here, not all of which sing our praises. . . . I can guarantee that nothing is done here anymore which is not the product of teamwork, of exchange, of collective and even collegial effort."

Clearly Father Kolvenbach will never go so far as to acknowledge that the Society of Jesus can only forestall explosion by the boldest kind of pluralism, protect itself from explosion by the subtlest of implosions. But he knows his Rahner well, and the multiform prospects dreamed up by the German theologian. Moreover his own life, from Saint Joseph's in Beirut, from the shores of Lebanon, the alleyways of the Armenian quarters of Aleppo and of Damascus, from this African village or that Brazilian settlement, has shown him how exotic the directives from Rome can appear in certain surroundings.

He recalls arriving in Rome in 1974 as Provincial of the Near East and being disturbed by the debates over Decree Four at the Thirty-second Jesuit Congregation. Why, he had wondered, should "justice" generate such an orgy of self-

---

*Five thousand of the world's 25,000 Jesuit fathers.

examination? Seen from Beirut, the urgent need for justice was so obvious, and so indissociable from everything the nations expected from Christianity.

After all, the Jesuit who is today entrusted with the Company's future is a Dutchman born to a German father and Italian mother, deeply Roman by habit, impregnated with French culture, and moreover (from the religious standpoint) a product of the Armenian rite* and (from the intellectual one) a linguist in command of a dozen languages and idioms. A good first step along the road to that fundamental pluralism that, from Francis Xavier and Matteo Ricci onward, has always tended to reinvent the Ignatian universe on truly pluralist bases.

But is the very intelligent, very judicious, very "political" Father Kolvenbach ready to open the perspectives sketched by the likes of Karl Rahner onto a limitless diversification, making of the Society the crossroads of a constellation of communities without borders and without exceptions of any kind, sexual, religious, denominational?

We must always remember first that Ignatius of Loyola was an "outsider" in his day, and second that the Society of Jesus prided itself on the ordeals undergone in the name of pluralism and of its respect for difference. From the invention of the Paraguay reductions to the recognition of *Sinanthropus,* the Jesuit has eternally spurned frontiers of time and place and exulted in otherness.

In considering the term "discernment" (Jesuit to its marrow), it is tempting to conclude by giving the floor to a Jesuit, Louis Bernaert, who has taken concern for "discernment" further than most:

> The Jesuits are workers, nurses, sociologists, scientists, even psychoanalysts. But, in a break from what transpired in earlier centuries (and this is a radical departure), they no longer do these things as they did them in the nineteenth century, for some other sake, for example in order to win a renown that would help them preach or harvest new believers for the Church. They do them now as tasks they share with other men, no matter what their relationship to religion.
>
> And in carrying their experience through to its conclusion, should they not deduce that the order has had its day, that the Jesuit as such had merely been a transitional form between the religious of yesteryear and the layman of today? Some of them have indeed reached just such a conclusion, and have detached themselves from a group whose historical weight seemed to them to be an obstacle to the very thing they had nevertheless discovered in the Company.

*Which is distinguished not only by the length of its services but also by the non-requirement of priestly celibacy.

Others stay. . . . In doing so, they ratify their membership in the Company and their wish to live in one of those little communities in which we find today, although in different forms, the things that characterized the first band of companions.[10]

But there remains suspended, and unanswered, one vital and overriding question which hundreds of readers have put to me. Why have so many men of such diverse genius chosen to add to the yoke the Church imposes on its ordinary priests the even more tyrannical yoke of the Company?

To seek there a more mysterious fulfillment? To conquer a deeper freedom in the bonds of submission? Like the classical poet bowing to his rigid rule?

After this long and exhaustive inquiry, the author would be happy to be able to answer this decisive question. But once again, research has led only to a reframing of the question. I hope, though, that I have perhaps formulated it a little more clearly.

Roussillon, France, August 1992

CHRONOLOGY

JESUITS

1492 Iñigo of Loyola born.

1505 Pierre Favre born.
1506 Francis Xavier born.
1507 Iñigo at the court of Castile.

1512 Diego Laínez born.

1521 Loyola wounded at Pamplona.
1523 Loyola in the Holy Land.

1528 Loyola arrives in Paris.

1532 "Ignatius" of Loyola made Master of
Arts, Paris.

WORLD

Founding of Collège de Montaigu, Paris.
Columbus's New World landfall.
Expulsion of Jews and Moors from Spain.
1493 Treaty of Tordesillas between the
Pope, Spain, and Portugal.
1497 Vasco da Gama opens the sea route
to India.
1500 Cabral lands in Brazil.

1509 Henry VIII King of England.
Erasmus, *In Praise of Folly*.
1510 Albuquerque conquers Goa.
Sultan Selim I, master of the
Mediterranean.
1515 Francis I King of France.
1517 Luther nails his protest to the door.
1519 Charles V Emperor of Germany.
1520 Suleyman the Magnificent, Sultan.
Hernán Cortéz takes Mexico City.

1525 Defeat and capture of Francis I at
Pavia.

1529 The Turks lay siege to Vienna.
1530 Founding of the Collège de France.
1531 Pizarro conquers Peru.

1533 Henry VIII excommunicated.
Paul III Pope.

1534 The Montmartre vow.

1536 Jacques Cartier on the Saint
Lawrence.
In Geneva, Calvin writes *Institutes of the
Christian Religion*.

1538 Ignatius and his companions settle
in Rome.
1540 Paul III approves the Company of
Jesus.
Francis Xavier leaves for India.

1542 A Portuguese vessel lands in Japan.
1545 Council of Trent.

1546 Death of Pierre Favre in Rome.
1547 Bull excluding women from the
Company.

Charles V crushes the Protestants at
Mühlberg.
Coronation of Ivan the Terrible.

1549 Francis Xavier reaches Japan.
1551 Founding of the Roman school, forerunner of the Gregorian University.
1552 Death of Francis Xavier.
1554 Joan of Spain, a Jesuit but . . .

1555 Abdication of Charles V.

1556 Death of Ignatius of Loyola in Rome.
Laínez succeeds him.
1557 Oviedo's mission to Ethiopia.

1558 Elizabeth I Queen of England.
1559 Franco-Spanish treaty of Cateau-
Cambrésis.

1565 Francesco Borgia succeeds Laínez.
University of Paris tolerates Jesuit teaching.

1571 Lepanto: the "Christian" fleet
crushes the Turks.
Saint Bartholomew's Day Massacre.

1572 Mercurian: fourth General.
1579 Valignano in Japan.
1581 Claudio Acquaviva, first Italian
General.
1562 Matteo Ricci admitted to China.

1588 Spanish Armada.
1589 Assassination of Henry III. Henry
IV King of France.

1593 Fifth Jesuit Congregation (anti-
Semitic resolution).

1595 Ricci a mandarin.
1598 Acquaviva's *Ratio studiorum*.
1600 Death of Luis de Molina.
1601 Ricci in Beijing.
1603 Edict of Rouen: The Jesuits granted official status in France.

1606 Roberto de Nobili in India.

1609 First Paraguay reduction.
1610 Death of Ricci.
1612 Death of Clavius, father of the Jesuit scientific school.

1614 Sacchini's first *History of the Jesuits*.

1622 Canonization of Ignatius and Francis.

1627 Alexander of Rhodes in Tonkin.

1631 The Paraní reductions move south.

1634 Jean de Brébeuf among the Huron.

1645 Rome warns the Jesuits against "worship" of Confucius.

1594 Henry IV in Paris.
A Midsummer Night's Dream.
Edict of Nantes.

1605 *Don Quixote*.

1608 Quebec founded.

Assassination of Henry IV.

1613 Russia: the first Romanov.

1616 Copernicus on the *Index*.
Death of Shakespeare.
1618 Thirty Years' War begins.
1620 *Mayflower* lands.

1623 Velázquez in Madrid.
Richelieu in power in Paris, Olivares in Madrid.

1628 Defeat of the Protestants at La Rochelle.
1629 Charles I dissolves Parliament.
1630 Death of Kepler.
Urban VIII approves of long-term loans.
1632 Queen-elect Christina of Sweden.
1633 Galileo condemned.

1635 New Franco-Spanish war.
1636 Corneille's *Le Cid*.
1637 Descartes's *Discours de la méthode*.
1640 Revolution in England.
1641 Rembrandt: *The Night Watch*.
1642 Richelieu dies.
Pascal invents calculator.
1643 Louis XIV King.
Mazarin Prime Minister.
Cromwell victorious at Naseby.

1648 Thirty Years' War ends. Unrest in France.
Charles I executed.

1649 Martyrdom of Brébeuf and Lallemant.

1651 Cromwell crushes Charles II at Worcester.

1653 Antonio Vieyra condemns slavery in Brazil.

1654 Colbert succeeds Fouquet.
1665 Poussin dies.
1666 Newton works on integral calculus.
1672 William of Orange Protector of the Low Countries.

1673 Marquette descends the Mississippi.

1677 Racine's *Phèdre.*
1679 Peace of Nijnmegen.
Declaration in France of the "Four Articles" of Gallicanism.

1680 Death of Athanasius Kircher.
1682 Collège de Clermont becomes "Louis-le-Grand."

1683 Vienna under siege by the Turks.
1685 Edict of Nantes revoked.
1686 Leibnitz discovers kinetic energy.
1689 William of Orange King of England.

1692 Emperor Kang-Xi's edict of tolerance of Christians.

1696 Peter the Great.

1705 Tournon's China mission: forbidding ancestor worship among Christians.

1709 Louis XIV defeated at Malplaquet.
1710 Jansenist monastery of Port-Royal demolished.
1713 Bull *Unigenitus* condemns Jansenism.
Louis XIV dies.

1715 Castiglione in China.
Rome orders the Jesuits to break with Confucianism.

1717 Voltaire in the Bastille.

1720 Father Charlevoix in the American West.

1721 Montesquieu: *Les lettres persanes.*
1722 Peter the Great proclaims sovereignty in Northern Europe.

1724 Emperor Yongzheng orders persecution of the Jesuits.

1725 Peter the Great dies.
1740 Frederick II of Prussia.

1742 Rome officially condemns Jesuit links
to Confucianism.
1743 Muratori's *Cristianesimo Felice.*

1745 Battle of Fontenoy.
Madame de Pompadour becomes the
King's "favorite."
Frederick II conquers Silesia.

1750 Spanish-Portuguese "Treaty of
Limits" in Latin America: Guaraní War.

1751 The *Encyclopédie* published and condemned.

1754 The Jesuits expelled from Brazil.

1758 Foreign Minister Choiseul.

1759 The Jesuits expelled from Portugal.
1761 Father de Lavalette condemned.

1762 Catherine the Great.
1763 Treaty of Paris: France loses Canada
and cedes Louisiana to Spain.

1764 The Company banned in France.

1765 Emperor Joseph II of Austria.
1766 Bougainville's circumnavigation
begins.

1767 The Jesuits expelled from Spain and
from the American missions.
End of the reductions.
1768 Jesuits expelled from Parma.

1769 Napoleon born.
1770 Beethoven born.
1772 Prussia, Austria, and Russia partition Poland.
Mozart's *Lucio Silla.*

1773 The brief *Dominus ac Redemptor*
abolishes the Society of Jesus in Rome.
Frederick the Great refuses to abolish
Prussia's Jesuits. Catherine the Great
follows suit.
1774 Death of Clement XIV, the "executioner" Pope.

Louis XVI succeeds Louis XV.

1776 American Declaration of
Independence.

1779 Serfdom abolished in France.
1780 Maria Theresa of Austria dies.
1781 Kant: *Critique of Pure Reason.*

1781 General Congregation of Russia's Jesuits.

1783 Versailles Treaty: England recognizes American independence.
1784 Joseph II subjugates the Austrian Church.
1786 Mozart's *Marriage of Figaro.* Frederick the Great dies.
1787 Legal recognition of Protestants in France.
1789 Estates-General meet at Versailles.

1790 Pierre de Clorivière founds the Society of the Fathers of the Heart of Jesus and the Society of the Daughters of the Heart of Mary.

1793 The Jesuits officially readmitted to Parma.

Louis XVI executed.

1794 Fathers Varin and Tournély found the Fathers of the Faith.

Terror; execution of Robespierre.
1796 Catherine the Great dies.

1799 Paccanari becomes superior of the Fathers of the Faith.

Bonapartist coup. Pope Pius VII.

1800 Madeleine-Sophie Barat founds Ladies of the Sacred Heart.
1801 Abbe Bourdier founds the "Congregation."

Concordat between Pius VII and Napoleon.

1802 Father Gruber, interim General.

1804 Emperor Napoleon I.

1805 Gruber dies.

Beethoven's *Fidelio.*
1807 Peace of Tilsit.
1808 Spain resists Napoleon.

1809 Napoleon dissolves the "Congregation."

1812 Tension between the Jesuits and Tsar Alexander

Napoleon's retreat from Moscow.

1814 Pius VII restores the Company. Father Clorivière entrusted with its leadership in France.

Napoleon abdicates: Louis XVIII and the First Restoration.

1815 Waterloo. Second Restoration. Napoleon to Saint Helena.

1817 Father Simpson (Sionnet) replaces Clorivière.
1820 Jesuits expelled from Russia by Alexander I.
Luigi Fortis, General.
1823 Pierre-Jean De Smet leaves for the United States.

1824 Charles X succeeds Louis XVIII.

1826 Fresh anti-Jesuit campaigns in France.
1829 Jan-Philip Roothaan, General.

1829 Pius VIII succeeds Leo XII.
Creation of the first trade union (textile workers) in England.
1830 Revolution in Paris; Belgian independence.
1831 Gregory XVI succeeds Pius VIII.
1833 Carlist war in Spain.

1835 New expulsion from Spain.

1837 Dickens's *The Pickwick Papers*.
Victoria, Queen of England
1838 The Preaching Fathers restored in France.
1839 Stendhal's *The Charterhouse of Parma*.

1840 The Saint Francis Xavier Society.

1841 First railway line in France.

1843 Michelet publishes *Les Jésuites*.
1845 Guizot attempts to disperse the Jesuits of France.

Mérimée's *Carmen*.

1846 Pope Pius IX.
Wuthering Heights.

1847 The *Sonderbund* war: the Jesuits expelled from Switzerland.

1848 Revolution in Europe. Louis Napoleon President.

1850 *Civiltà cattolica* founded in Naples.

1852 Bonapartist coup: Napoleon III.

1853 Pierre Beckz succeeds Father Roothaan.

1857 *Madame Bovary*.

1858 Father Ravignan dies.

1859 Darwin's *Origin of Species*.
War of Italian independence.
1860 Piedmont annexes all papal territories but Rome.

1862 The Jesuits in Ecuador.
Bismarck Prime Minister of Prussia.

1863 Father De Smet mediates between Washington and the Indians.

American Civil War: Gettysburg.
Renan's *Life of Jesus.*
1865 Lincoln assassinated.
1866 Prussia crushes Austria.
Crime and Punishment.
1869 Napoleon III abandons Maximilian in Mexico.
First Vatican Council proclaims Pope's infallibility.
1870 France defeated by Prussia.
The Pope expelled from Rome.

1871 Six Jesuits shot by the Commune.
1872 The Jesuits expelled from Germany.
1873 Death of Father De Smet.

The Paris Commune.
Nietzsche's *Birth of Tragedy.*

1875 By a single vote, France adopts a republican constitution.
Anna Karenina.
1878 Pope Leo XIII.

1880 "Ferry" decree aimed at the Jesuits and most other congregations in France.
1881 Pierre Teilhard de Chardin and Augustin Bea born.

Tsar Alexander II assassinated.

1885 National mourning for Victor Hugo.
Death of Gordon in Khartoum.
1890 Van Gogh's suicide.
1891 Encyclical *Rerum Novarum* on the condition of workers.

1892 The Jesuits in the Belgian Congo.

Leo XIII calls on French Catholics to support the Republic.
1894 Dreyfus condemned.
1899 Second Dreyfus trial. Despite Zola, new guilty verdict.
1901 Waldeck-Rousseau law against religious congregations.
King Edward VII.
1902 Debussy's *Pelléas et Mélisande.*
Dreyfus cleared in retrial.

1904 Jesuits expelled from France.
Karl Rahner born.

1905 Kaiser Wilhelm in Tangiers.
Anti-"modernism" encyclical of Pius X.

1907 Pedro Arrupe born.
1909 George Tyrell: *Christianity at the Crossroads.*

1912 Father de Grandmaison attacks anti-modernist fundamentalism.
1913 Pierre Teilhard de Chardin takes up paleontology.

French protectorate established in Morocco.

1914 First World War.
Benedict XV succeeds Pius X.
Italy joins the Allies.

1915 Father Rousselot killed in action.
1916 Teilhard writes in the trenches.
1917 Henri de Lubac seriously wounded.

Revolution in Russia.
The United States enters the war.
1918 Allied victory.
1919 Treaty of Versailles.
Proust's *Within a Budding Grove.*

1920 Wladimir Ledochowski General.
1923 Teilhard banished to China.

1924 Lenin dies.
Left cartel in France.
1926 Rome condemns Action Française.

1927 Father de Grandmaison dies.
1929 Teilhard participates in the discovery of *Sinanthropus.*
1931 Teilhard on the Gobi Crossing.

Concordat between Rome and Mussolini.
Wall Street crash.

1932 Bergson: *The Two Sources of Morality and Religion.*
Céline's *Journey to the End of Night.*
1933 Hitler in power.
1935 Mussolini invades Ethiopia.
Popular Front in France.
Civil war in Spain.
1937 Anti-Nazi encyclical *Mit Brennender Sorge.*

1936 Father Gaston Fessard's *Pax nostra.*

1938 Henri de Lubac's *Catholicisme.*
1939 Karl Rahner's *Spirit in the World.*

Munich agreements.
Second World War.
Poland occupied.
Pius XII succeeds Pius XI.
Invasion of France.
The Soviet Union and United States enter the war.
1942 Hitler defeated at Stalingrad.

1940 Teilhard's *Phenomenon of Man.*
1941 First *Cahier du Témoignage chrétien.*

1944 Father Delp executed in Germany.
Yves de Montcheuil executed in Grenoble.

1945 Roosevelt dies.
Europe liberated.

Hiroshima and Nagasaki.

1946 Father Janssens succeeds Ledochowski.

1947 Marshall Plan proposed.
Cold War begins.

1948 Teilhard rebuffed in Rome.

Birth of Israel.

1949 Meeting of French worker-priests.

Mao Zedong master of China.

1950 De Lubac and four other Jesuits forbidden to teach.

Encyclical *Humani Generis* directed against "innovators."
Korean War.

1952 Eisenhower President-elect of the United States.

1953 Condemnation of worker-priests, including Jesuits.

Stalin dies.

1954 Socialist government in France.
End of "first" Indochina war. Start of Algerian war.

1955 Teilhard de Chardin dies.

1956 Suez Incident.

1957 Rome Treaty creates European Common Market.

1958 Daniélou's *Théologie du Judeo-Christianisme.*

De Gaulle returns to power.

1960 John F. Kennedy President-elect.

1961 Jesuits help lay ground for Second Vatican Council.

Encyclical of John XXIII: *Mater et Magistra.*

1962 Vatican II.
End of Algerian war.
Cuban missile crisis.

1963 Encyclical *Pacem in terris.*
Paul VI succeeds John XXIII.
Kennedy assassinated.

1964 Father Janssens dies.

1965 Pedro Arrupe elected General.

Vatican II ends.
Paul VI in Jerusalem.
Vietnam War escalates.

1966 Crisis begins between Paul VI and the Company.

1967 The Company launches global self-examination.

Six-Day War. Israel controls the Holy Places.

1968 Arrupe espouses the causes of "the poor."

Worldwide student agitation.
Richard Nixon President-elect.
Bishops' Assembly at Medellín.

1969 Many defections from the Company.

De Gaulle resigns.

1973 Vatican-Company tensions worsen.

Watergate inquiries.

1975 Thirty-Second Jesuit Congregation: Decree Four: *Faith and Justice.*

Franco dies.
Saigon falls.
1976 Jimmy Carter President-elect.
Paul VI dies.
Election of John Paul I and then of John Paul II.
1979 Latin American Bishops' conference, Puebla.

1980 Creation of the Jesuit Refugee Service.

Bishop Oscar Romero assassinated.
Ronald Reagan President-elect.
Attempt on John Paul II's life.

1981 Pedro Arrupe struck down.

Mitterrand President of France.

1983 Election of Peter Hans Kolvenbach.
1984 Karl Rahner dies.

Reagan reelected.
1988 George Bush President-elect.

1989 Six Jesuits murdered in San Salvador.

1990 Persian Gulf crisis; John Paul II against military intervention.

1991 Loyola's 500th anniversary.
Pedro Arrupe and Henri de Lubac die.

War in Iraq.

1992 Yugoslavia dissolves in war.

NOTES

I. THE VAGABOND AND THE INQUISITOR

1. Ignatius of Loyola, *A Pilgrim's Journey: The Autobiography of Ignatius of Loyola*, trans. Joseph N. Tylenda (Collegeville, Minn.: The Liturgical Press, 1991); hereafter, *Autobiography*. P. 7.

2. Ibid., p. 13.

3. Father Benedetto Palmio, quoted in Candido de Dalmases, *Le Fondateur des jésuites* (Paris: Le Centurion, 1984), p. 42.

4. *Autobiography*, p. 7

5. Ibid., pp. 7–9.

6. Ibid., p. 9.

7. Ibid., pp. 9–10.

8. Ibid., p. 10.

9. Ibid., pp. 17–18.

10. Ibid., pp. 14–15.

11. Ibid., p. 16.

12. Ibid.

13. Quoted in Baltasar Gracian, *La Pointe ou l'art du génie* (Paris: L'Age d'Homme, 1983), p. 123.

14. *Autobiography*, pp. 36–38.

15. Ibid., pp. 38–39.

16. *Ignace de Loyola, le dictateur des âmes* (Paris: Payot, 1936).

17. *Autobiography*, pp. 50–51.

18. Ibid., p. 59.

19. Marcel Bataillon, *Erasme et l'Espagne* (Paris: Droz, 1937).

20. *Au coeur réligieux du XVIème siècle* (Paris: Livre du Poche, 1983), p. 126.

21. Bataillon, *Erasme et l'Espagne*, p. 128.

22. Ibid.

23. *Autobiography*, p. 83.

II. THE SCHOLARS FROM MONTMARTRE

1. Michel de Certeau, Preface to *Mémorial*, by Pierre Favre (Paris: Desclée de Brouwer, 1959), p. 14. Hereafter, *Memoirs*.

2. Emmanuel Le Roy Ladurie, *Histoire de la France urbaine* (Paris: Le Seuil, 1980), p. 7.

3. *Autobiography*, p. 131.

4. Thurot, *De l'organisation de l'université au Moyen Age*, pp. 39–40.

5. Jules Quicherat, *Histoire de Sainte-Barbe, collège et institution* (Paris: Hachette, 1864), p. 151.

6. Du Boulay, *Histoire de l'université de Paris*, vol. V, p. 572.

7. Quicherat, *Histoire de Saint-Barbe*, pp. 88–89.

8. Du Boulay, *Histoire de l'université de Paris*, vol. VI, p. 378.

9. Pierre Imbart de la Tour, *Les Origines de la Réforme en France* (Melun: Librairie d'Argences, 1948), vol. III, p. 213.

10. *Autobiography*, p. 86.

11. Ibid., p. 134.

12. Quicherat, *Histoire de Saint-Barbe*, pp. 191–92.

13. *Autobiography*, p. 89.

14. Ibid.

15. Ibid.

16. Hercule Rasiel da Silva, *Histoire de l'admirable Dom Iñigo de Guipúzcoa* (The Hague: Le Vier, 1736), pp. 92–96.

17. Quicherat, *Histoire de Saint-Barbe*, p. 194.

18. *Memoirs*, p. 61.

19. Georg Schurhammer, S.J., *Francis Xavier: His Life, His Times* (Rome, 1982), pp. 106–7.

20. Rasiel, *Histoire de l'admirable Dom Iñigo de Guipúzcoa*, p. 98.

21. Quoted by Father André Ravier, *Ignace de Loyola fonde la Compagnie de Jésus* (Paris: Desclée de Brouwer, 1973), p. 64.

22. Schurhammer, *Francis Xavier: His Life, His Times*, p. 187.

23. Rasiel, *Histoire de l'admirable Dom Iñigo de Guipúzcoa*, p. 108.

24. *Mémorial*, Michel de Certeau Preface, p. 20.

25. Ibid., p. 116.

26. Ravier, *Ignace de Loyola fonde la Compagnie de Jésus*, p. 70.

27. Henri Fouqueray, S.J., *Histoire de la Compagnie de Jésus en France* (Paris: Picard, 1910–25), vol. I, appendix.

28. Recollections of Diego Laínez, in *Monumenta Historici S.J.*, vol. II, p. 133.

29. Pedro de Leturia, in *Civiltà cattolica*.

30. Quoted by Ravier in *Ignace de Loyola fonde la Compagnie de Jésus*, pp. 35–37.

31. Conversation in Rome, April 27, 1990.

32. Hugo Rahner, *Ignace de Loyola et les femmes de son temps* (Paris: Desclée de Brouwer, 1964), vol. I, p. 37.

33. In the version given in Ravier, *Ignace de Loyola fonde la Compagnie de Jésus,* pp. 82–99.

34. Ibid.

35. James Brodrick, *Origines et expansion des jésuites* (Paris: Éditions Spelt, 1950), vol. I, pp. 85–87; Schurhammer, *Francis Xavier: His Life, His Times,* vol. I, p. 593.

36. Rasiel, *Histoire de l'admirable Dom Iñigo de Guipúzcoa,* p. 140.

III. "*PERINDE AC CADAVER*"

1. *Epistolae et Instructiones,* vol. I, pp. 179–180.

2. *Monumenta Fabri,* quoted by Certeau, *Memoirs,* p. 67.

3. *Monumenta Fabri,* quoted by Brodrick, *Origines et expansion des jésuites,* p. 173.

4. Brodrick, *Origines et expansion des jésuites,* vol. I, p. 183.

5. Karl Rahner, *Discours d'Ignace de Loyola aux jésuites d'aujourd'hui* (Paris: Le Centurion, 1978), p. 56.

6. Quoted in Brodrick, *Origines et expansion des jésuites,* vol. I, p. 94.

7. Gaéton Benroville, *Les Jésuites* (Paris, 1934), p. 104.

8. Ravier, *Ignace de Loyola fonde la Compagnie de Jésus,* pp. 408–9.

9. Rasiel, *Histoire de l'admirable Dom Iñigo de Guipúzcoa,* p. 149.

10. Roland Barthes, *Sade, Fourier, Loyola* (Paris: Le Seuil, 1971), p. 49; (New York: Hill and Wang, 1976; trans. R. Howard).

11. Ignatius of Loyola, *Lettres* (Paris: Desclée de Brouwer, 1959), p. 511.

12. *Autobiography,* pp. 163–64.

13. Léon Marcuse, *Ignace de Loyola, le dictateur des âmes* (Paris: Payot, 1936), p. 247.

14. André Suarès, *Portraits sans modèles* (Paris: Grasset, 1935), pp. 243–44.

IV. FRANCIS XAVIER, ORIENTALIST

1. Francis Xavier, *Correspondance (1535–1552),* (Paris: Desclée de Brouwer, 1987), p. 263.

2. Ibid., pp. 207–8.

3. A. Brou, *Saint François Xavier* (Paris: Beauchesne, 1922), vol. I, pp. 433–34.

4. *Correspondance,* p. 248.

5. Edwin O. Reischauer, *Histoire du Japon et des Japonais* (Paris: Le Seuil, 1973), vol. I, p. 86.

6. Ibid., p. 94.

7. Schurhammer, *Francis Xavier: His Life, His Times,* p. 281.

8. Dominique Bouhours, *Vie de Saint François-Xavier* (Lyon: Périssi Frères, 1842), vol. II, p. 145.

9. Schurhammer, *Francis Xavier: His Life, His Times*, p. 281.

10. *Correspondance*, pp. 324–32.

11. Ibid.

12. Ibid., p. 347.

13. Ibid., p. 331.

14. Ibid., p. 365.

15. Ibid., p. 367.

16. Bouhours, *Vie de Saint François-Xavier*, p. 21.

17. *Fontes narrativi*, vol. III, pp. 278–79.

18. Bouhours, *Vie de Saint François-Xavier*, p. 28.

19. *Correspondance*, pp. 368–72.

20. *Encyclopaedia Britannica*, vol. 15, pp. 225–26.

21. *Correspondance*, p. 374.

22. Bouhours, *Vie de Saint François-Xavier*, p. 33.

23. Ibid., p. 57.

V. NO WOMEN NEED APPLY

1. Hugo Rahner, *Ignace de Loyola et les femmes de son temps* (Paris: Desclée de Brouwer, 1964), 2 vols.

2. *El Gentilhombre Iñigo López en su patria y su siglo* (Montevideo, 1938).

3. See Rahner, *Ignace de Loyola et les femmes de son temps*, vol. I, p. 139.

4. *Autobiography*, chapter I, p. 46.

5. Ibid., p. 49.

6. Ibid., p. 78.

7. Ibid.

8. Ibid., pp. 148–49.

9. Ibid., p. 160.

10. H. Rahner, *Ignace de Loyola et les femmes de son temps*, vol. I, p. 33.

11. Ibid., p. 37.

12. Ibid., p. 40.

13. Ibid., p. 90.

14. Ibid., pp. 231–34.

15. Ibid., vol. II, p. 49.

16. Ibid., p. 50.

17. Ibid., p. 104.

18. Ibid., vol. I, p. 109.

19. E. Antébi and F. Lebrun, *Les Jésuites et la Gloire de Dieu* (Paris: Stock-Antébi, 1990).

VI. THE JEWS AND THE JESUITS

1. Eusebio Rey, in *Razón y Fe* (Madrid), no. 696, February 1956.

2. Lucien Febvre, *Au coeur religieux du XVIème siècle* (Paris: Livre du poche, 1983), p. 116.

3. Ibid.

4. Pey Ordeix, *Historia Crítica de San Ignacio* (Madrid, 1916).

5. Ribadeneira Papers, vol. II, pp. 375–76.

6. Feliciano Cereceda, *Diego Laínez en la Europa y la religión de su tiempo (1512–1565)*, (Madrid, 1943), vol. III, p. 591.

7. *Laínii monumenta*, vol. VIII, p. 831.

8. Cereceda, quoted in Gabriel Maura, *La Vida y reinado de Carlos II* (Madrid, 1942), p. 191.

9. Ibid.

10. Rey, in *Razón y Fe*, p. 191.

11. J. H. Fichter, *Laynez, Jesuit* (Saint Louis, Miss., 1944), p. 3.

VII. LI MATEOU, THE CLOCK, AND THE MASTER OF HEAVEN

1. Francis Xavier, *Correspondance (1535–1552)*, p. 423.

2. Matteo Ricci, *Histoire de l'expédition chrétienne au royaume de la Chine* (Paris: Desclée de Brouwer, 1978).

3. Henri Bernard-Maître, *Aux Portes de la Chine* (Shanghai, 1936), pp. 110–15.

4. Henri Bernard-Maître, *Matteo Ricci et la Société chinoise de son temps* (Tinajin, 1937), vol. I, p. 55.

5. Ricci, *Histoire de l'expédition chrétienne au royaume de la Chine*, p. 201.

6. Bernard-Maître, *Aux Portes de la Chine*, p. 148.

7. Bernard-Maître, *Matteo Ricci et la Société chinoise de son temps*, vol. I, p. 89.

8. Ibid., p. 65.

9. Ibid., pp. 70–75.

10. Ibid., p. 72.

11. Ibid., pp. 73–74.

12. Ricci, *Histoire de l'expédition chrétienne au royaume de la Chine*, p. 216.

13. Ibid., p. 230.

14. Ibid., p. 227.

15. Ibid., p. 229.

16. Ibid., p. 240.

17. Ibid.

18. Ibid., p. 307.

19. Ibid., p. 308.

20. Ibid., p. 310.

21. Bernard-Maître, *Matteo Ricci et la Société chinoise de son temps*, vol. I, p. 200.

22. Ibid., p. 202.
23. René Étiemble, *L'Europe chinoise* (Paris: Gallimard, 1988), vol. I, p. 187.
24. Ibid., p. 198.
25. Bernard-Maître, *Matteo Ricci et la Société chinoise de son temps,* vol. I, p. 221.
26. Jacques Gernet, *La Chine et Christianisme* (Paris: Gallimard, 1982), p. 198.
27. Étiemble, *L'Europe chinoise.*
28. Bernard-Maître, *Matteo Ricci et la Société chinoise de son temps,* vol. I, p. 334.
29. Étiemble, *L'Europe chinoise,* vol. I, p. 257.
30. Gernet, *La Chine et Christianisme,* pp. 263–69.
31. Ibid., p. 53.
32. Vincent Cronin, *The Wise Man from the West* (London: Rupert Hart-Davis, 1955), p. 33.
33. Ricci, *Histoire de l'expédition chrétienne au royaume de la Chine,* p. 390.
34. Ibid., p. 392.
35. Quoted and translated by Gernet, *La Chine et christianisme,* pp. 29–30.
36. Ricci, *Histoire de l'expedition chrétienne au royaume de la Chine,* p. 408.
37. Ibid., p. 451.
38. Ibid., p. 486.
39. Bernard-Maître, *Matteo Ricci et la Société chinoise de son temps,* vol. II, pp. 31–32.
40. Étiemble, *L'Europe chinoise,* vol. I, p. 246.
41. Jonathan Spence, *Le Palais de mémoire de Matteo Ricci* (Paris: Payot, 1986), pp. 150–52. (Originally published in English in New York as *The Memory Palace of Matteo Ricci* by Viking in 1984 and Penguin in 1985.)
42. Ibid., p. 9 of Penguin edition.
43. Gernet, *La Chine et Christianisme,* p. 147.
44. Ibid., p. 217.
45. Ricci, *Histoire de l'Expedition chrétienne au royaume de la Chine,* pp. 659–60.
46. Ibid., pp. 682–85.

VIII. UTOPIA AND THE GUARANÍ REPUBLIC
1. See Louis Baudin, *Une théocratie socialiste: l'État jésuite du Paraguay* (Paris: Genin, 1975).
2. Maurice Ezran, *Une Colonisation douce: la mission du Paraguay* (Paris: L'Harmattan, 1989).
3. Ibid., p. 99.
4. Girolamo Imbruglia in Muratori, *Relation des missions du Paraguay* (Paris: Maspero-La Découverte, reprint, 1983), p. xiii.
5. Montevideo, Uruguay Archives.
6. Alfred Métraux, in *Revue de Paris,* June 1952.

7. Quoted by Roger Lacombe in *Revue d'histoire économique et sociale*, 1964.

8. Louis Antoine de Bougainville, *Voyage autour du monde* (Paris: La Découverte, 1980), p. 65.

9. Roger Lacombe, "La Fin des bons sauvages," *Revue de la Société d'Ethnographie de Paris*, 1989, p. 119.

10. Métraux, in *Revue de Paris*.

11. L. Baudin, *Une théocratie socialiste*, pp. 32–33.

12. Oreste Popescu, *El Sistema económico en las misiónes jesuíticas* (Buenos Aires, 1952).

13. Maxime Haubert, "L'Oeuvre missionnaire des jésuites au Paraguay," doctoral thesis, 1966, p. 89.

14. Roger Lacombe, *Revue française d'ethnographie*, 1989, p. 113.

15. Maxime Haubert, *La Vie quotidienne chez les jésuites et les Guaranís* (Paris: Hachette, 1986), p. 108.

16. Ibid., p. 136.

17. Imbruglia in Muratori, *Relation des missions du Paraguay*, p. xv.

18. Quoted in Rio de Janeiro, Oct. 14 1990.

19. Pierre Clastres, *L'Esprit des lois sauvages* (Paris: Le Seuil, 1990).

20. Haubert, *La Vie quotidienne chez les jésuites et les Guaranís*.

IX. "EXPELLED LIKE DOGS"

1. René Pillorget in *Histoire de France*, edited by Georges Duby (Paris: Larousse, 1971), vol. II, pp. 208–9.

2. *Nouvelles intéressantes*, Nov. 14, 1758.

3. Ibid., Feb. 26, 1759.

4. Ibid., vol. III, p. 477.

5. Jacques Crétineau-Joly, *Histoire religieuse, politique et littéraire de la Compagnie de Jésus* (Paris-Lyon, 1844–46), vol. V, p. 266.

6. *Histoire de France*, vol. XXIX, p. 233.

7. Crétineau-Joly, *Histoire religieuse, politique et littéraire de la Compagnie de Jésus*, p. 246.

8. Joseph Brucker, S.J., *La Compagnie de Jésus* (Paris, 1919), vol. V, p. 266.

9. Ibid., p. 816.

10. In his master's thesis "Les jésuites au collège de Bourbon d'Aix-en-Provence" (Aix, 1990).

11. Crétineau-Joly, *Histoire religieuse, politique et littéraire de la Compagnie de Jésus*, p. 284 fn.

12. Ibid., vol. II, p. 104.

13. Emmanuel Le Roy Ladurie, *L'Histoire de France*, vol. III (Paris: Hachette, 1991), chapter X.

14. Dominique Julia, "Le Catholicisme, religion du royaume, 1759–1789," in *Histoire de la France religieuse* (Paris: Le Seuil, 1991), vol. III, pp. 39–47.

15. Crétineau-Joly, *Histoire religieuse, politique et littéraire de la Compagnie de Jésus*, p. 293.

16. Ibid.

17. L. G. Rogier, *Nouvelle Histoire de l'Église* (Paris: Le Seuil, 1966), vol. IV, p. 118.

18. Crétineau-Joly, *Histoire religieuse, politique et littéraire de la Compagnie de Jésus*, p. 314.

19. Ibid., p. 305.

X. WANDERING IN THE DESERT

1. Paul Dudon, "La Résurrection de la Compagnie de Jésus," in *Revue des questions historiques* (1932), p. 2.

2. L. J. Rogier *et al. Nouvelle Histoire de l'Église* (Paris: Le Seuil, 1986), vol. IV, p. 122.

3. J. Crétineau-Joly, *Histoire religieuse, politique et littéraire de la Compagnie de Jésus*, vol. V, p. 465.

4. Dudon, "La Résurrection de la Compagnie de Jésus," p. 25.

5. Ibid.

6. Constatin Simon, "Les Jésuites et la Russie," *Plamia*, no. 81 (June 1991), p. 9.

7. Dudon, "La Résurrection de la Compagnie de Jésus," p. 27.

8. Ibid., p. 29.

9. Ibid., p. 30.

10. Ibid., p. 33.

11. Crétineau-Joly, *Histoire religieuse, politique et littéraire de la Compagnie de Jésus*, vol. V, p. 490.

12. Ibid., p. 485.

13. Dudon, "La Résurrection de la Compagnie de Jésus," p. 37.

14. Joseph Burnichon, S.J., *La Compagnie de Jésus en France: histoire d'un siècle*, (Paris, 1916–1920), vol. I, p. 12.

15. Dudon, "La Résurrection de la Compagnie de Jésus," pp. 37–38.

16. Ibid., p. 41.

17. B. Plongeron, "Histoire et méthode: à propos de la correspondance du R.P. de Clorivière," *Christus*, no. 131, p. 67.

18. R. P. Vallin, "Clorivière et son temps," *Christus*, no, 131, p. 15.

19. *Christus*, no. 131, p. 67.

20. Burnichon, *La Compagnie de Jésus en France: histoire d'un siècle*, vol. I, p. 10.

21. Ibid., p. 18.

22. Ibid., p. 19.

23. Ibid., p. 23.

24. Dudon, "Le Concordat et les conjurations," *Études,* vol. XI, chapter VI, pp. 23–43.

25. J. Flourens, *Napoléon et les jésuites,* p. 39.

26. Burnichon, *La Compagnie de Jésus en France: histoire d'un siècle,* vol. I, p. 30.

27. Published in Charles de Gaulle, *Articles et Documents* (Paris: Plon, 1975), pp. 28–37.

28. A. Guillermou, *Les Jésuites* (Paris: Presses universitaires de France, 1968), p. 106.

29. Ibid., p. 107.

30. *Études,* July 5, 1902.

31. Dudon, "La Résurrection de la Compagnie de Jésus," p. 54.

XI. THE SECOND COMPANY

1. Jean-François Bellemare, *Le Siècle de fer des Jésuites* (Paris: J. G. Dentur, 1828), p. 68.

2. Dudon, "La Résurrection de la Compagnie de Jésus," p. 43.

3. Burnichon, *La Compagnie de Jésus en France: histoire d'un siècle,* vol. I, p. 63.

4. Ibid., pp. 66–67.

5. Vallin, "Clorivière et son temps," *Christus,* no. 131, pp. 12–21.

6. Letter kindly made available to the author by M. Le Bastart de Villeneuve.

7. L. J. Rogier *et al. Histoire nouvelle de l'Église* (Paris: Le Seuil, 1986), vol. IV, p. 315.

8. Ibid., p. 320.

9. René Rémond, *Introduction à l'Histoire de notre temps* (1974), vol. II, p. 27.

10. Quoted in René Rémond, *L'Anticléricalisme en France de 1815 à nos jours* (Paris: Fayard, 1976), pp. 93–94.

11. Viel-Castel, *Histoire de la Restauration* (Paris, 1860–78), vol. V, p. 355.

12. *Annales de Montrouge,* p. 340.

XII. THE BLACK LEGEND

1. Dominique Bertrand, *Politique de saint Ignace* (Paris: Le Cerf, 1985), pp. 636–37.

2. Étienne Pasquier, *Oeuvres,* vol. II, pp. 77–78.

3. Robert Mousnier, *L'Assassinat d'Henri IV* (Paris: Gallimard, 1964), p. 212.

4. Sainte-Beuve, *Port-Royal* (Paris: Hachette, 1901), vol. III, p. 218.

5. François Mauriac, *Blaise Pascal et sa Soeur Jacqueline* (Paris: Hachette, 1931).

6. Raoul Girardet, *Mythes et mythologies politiques* (Paris: Le Seuil, 1986), p. 36.

7. Quoted by Cathérine-Laurence Maure, "La Légende noire des jésuites," *L'Histoire,* no. 84, Dec. 1985.

8. Jules Michelet, *Les Jésuites* (Paris, 1843), pp. 291–93.

9. Ibid., pp. 298–300.

10. Ibid., p. 299 note.

11. Michelet, *Le Prêtre, la Femme, la Famille* (Paris: Flammarion, 1882), p. 81.

12. Michelet, *Les Jésuites,* pp. 372–73.

13. Parliamentary debate, Jan. 15, 1850.

14. H. M. Chittenden and A. T. Richardson, *Life, Letters and Travels of Father Pierre-Jean De Smet, S.J.* (New York, 1905), vol. I, p. 57.

15. Eugène Laveille, S.J., *Le Père De Smet* (Liège, 1913), p. 389.

16. Ibid., p. 484.

17. R. Aubert, "Le Pontificat de Pie IX" in Fiche and Martin, *Histoire de l'Église* (Paris: Bloud et Gay, 1952), p. 23.

XIII. INCIDENTS AT VICHY

1. Michel Riquet, *Chrétiens de France dans l'Europe enchaînée* (Paris: SOS, 1972), p. 18.

2. Pinhas Lapide, *Rome et les juifs* (Paris: Le Seuil, 1967).

3. Henri Chambre, *Le Marxisme en Union soviétique* (Paris: Le Seuil, 1960).

4. Gaston Fessard, *Pax nostra* (Paris: Grasset, 1935).

5. Jacques Prévotat, *Spiritualité, théologie et résistance* (Presses Universitaires de Grenoble, 1984), p. 102.

6. Fessard, *Épreuve de force* (Paris: Bloud et Gay, 1939).

7. Wladimir D'Ormesson, *La Révolution allemande* (Paris, 1934).

8. In Varillon, *Beauté du monde at souffrance des hommes* (Paris: Centurion, 1980).

9. Rénée Bédarida, *Pierre Chaillet, témoin de résistance* (Paris: Fayard, 1988), p. 62 fn.

10. Pierre Chaillet, S.J., *L'Autriche souffrante* (Paris: Grasset, n.d.).

11. Both books published by Plon, Paris.

12. Paul Duclos, *Le Vatican et la Seconde Guerre Mondiale* (Paris: Pédoni, 1955); Jacques Nobécourt, *Le "Vicaire" et l'Histoire* (Paris: Le Seuil, 1964); Saul Friedlander, *Pius XII and the IIIème Reich* (Paris, Le Seuil, 1964).

13. Quoted by R. Bédarida, *Vichy et les Français* (Paris: Fayard, n.d.).

14. Ibid., pp. 462, 465.

15. Jacques Prévotat, *Le Père Desbuquois et l'Action Populaire* (Paris: Éditions Ouvrières, 1981), p. 352.

16. Quoted in Bédarida's *Pierre Chaillet, témoin de résistance.*

17. Chaillet, *L'Autriche souffrante.*

18. Ibid., pp. 104–5.

19. Bédarida, *Pierre Chaillet, témoin de résistance,* p. 110.

20. Ibid., p. 146.

21. *Témoignage chrétien, Cahiers et Courriers,* unabridged text, 1980, p. 147.

22. Bédarida, *Pierre Chaillet, témoin de résistance,* p. 187.

23. Ibid., pp. 278–8.

24. *Problèmes de la vie sprituelle* (Paris: 1943), pp. 100–3.

25. Ibid., pp. 278–88.

26. Prévotat, *Spiritualité, théologie et résistance,* p. 217.

XIV. OBEDIENCE AND TEILHARD

1. René d'Ouince, *Un prophète en procès: Pierre Teilhard de Chardin dans l'Église de son temps* (Paris: Aubier, 1970), p. 129.

2. *Écrits du temps de guerre* (Paris: Grasset, 1965).

3. D'Ouince, *Un prophète en procès,* p. 67.

4. "La Vie cosmique," in *Écrits du temps de guerre,* p. 7.

5. In *Écrits du temps de guerre.*

6. Émile Rideau, *La Pensée du père Teilhard de Chardin* (Paris: Le Seuil, 1965).

7. D'Ouince, *Un prophète en procès,* p. 75.

8. Rideau, *La Pensée du père Teilhard de Chardin.*

9. Henri de Lubac, *La Pensée religieuse du père Teilhard de Chardin* (Paris: Aubier-Montaigne 1962), p. 29.

10. "Mon univers," *Écrits du temps de guerre,* p. 279.

11. D'Ouince, *Un prophète en procès,* pp. 108–16.

12. Ibid.

13. In Jeanne Mortier and M.-L. Audoux, *Pierre Teilhard de Chardin, images et paroles* (Paris: Le Seuil, 1966), pp. 114–19.

14. Ibid.

15. G. H. Baudry, *Qui était Teilhard de Chardin?* (Lille, 1972).

16. Teilhard de Chardin, *Lettres de voyage* (Paris: Grasset, 1956), p. 60 (*Letters from a Traveler;* New York: Harper, 1962).

17. Mortier and Audoux, *Pierre Teilhard de Chardin, images et paroles,* p. 120.

18. *Les Cahiers du rocher,* no. 4: *Pierre Teilhard de Chardin, naissance et avenir de l'homme* (Paris, 1987), p. 45.

19. Ibid., p. 51.

20. D'Ouince, *Un prophète en procès,* p. 34.

21. Mortier and Audoux, *Pierre Teilhard de Chardin, images et paroles,* p. 181.

22. Teilhard de Chardin, *Lettres familières du R. P. Leroy* (Paris: Le Centurion, 1976), pp. 38–39.

23. Ibid., p. 34.

24. D'Ouince, *Un prophète en procès,* p. 133.

25. Mortier and Audoux, *Pierre Teilhard de Chardin, images et paroles,* p. 193.

26. *La Coeur de la matière* (Paris: Le Seuil, n.d.), p. 113.

27. Cuénot, *Pierre Teilhard de Chardin* (Paris: Le Seuil, 1962).

28. Laberge, *Pierre Teilhard de Chardin et Ignace de Loyola* (Paris: Desclée-Brouwer, 1983), p. 88.

29. Teilhard, *Lettres familières,* pp. 76–78.

30. D'Ouince, *Un prophète en procès,* p. 187.

31. Teilhard, *Lettres familières,* pp. 114–15.

32. "Approved by a great canonist," Father Ravier confided to the author.

33. D'Ouince, *Un prophète en procès,* p. 187.

34. Hans Küng, *Dieu existe-t-il?* (Paris: Le Seuil, 1981), p. 209.

35. Letter to the author, April 1992. In an earlier conversation, Father Ravier spelled out the conditions of the "contract" between Teilhard and himself. It simply requested that his friend not publish anything before showing it to him. Which was done, except for one occasion, three days before the scientist's death.

36. Lubac, *La Pensée religieuse du père Teilhard de Chardin,* p. 295.

37. Quoted by François Russo, "Rome et Teilhard," *Recherches de science religieuse,* vol. LXIX (1981), p. 495.

38. *Revue des questions scientifiques,* no. 154 (1983), pp. 506–7.

39. *Mon univers* (Paris: Le Seuil, 1965), p. 125.

XV. THE EXORCIST AND THE VATICAN

1. Stepan Schmidt, *Augustin Bea* (Graz-Vienna: Styria, 1989).

2. *Bulletin du SIDIC,* no. 3 (1968), p. 12

3. 1968, p. 3.

4. Schmidt, *Augustin Bea,* p. 527.

5. *Bulletin du SIDIC,* no. 3 (1968), p. 2.

6. July 1991 conversation with Joe Golan.

7. *Bulletin du SIDIC,* no. 3 (1968), p. 15.

8. *Vatican Council II: The Conciliar and Post-Conciliar Documents* (Northport, N.Y.: Costello, n.d.).

9. Statement before Jewish group, New York, 1963.

10. *Libération,* Aug. 22, 1989.

XVI. JUSTICE AND PEDRO ARRUPE

1. Jean-Yves Calvez, S.J., *Foi et justice* (Paris: Desclée de Brouwer, 1985), p. 35.

2. Ibid., p. 46.

3. Ibid., p. 47.

4. Bartolomeo Sorge, *Uscire dal tempio* (Gênes, 1989), p. 54.

5. Alain Woodrow, *Les jésuites, histoire des pouvoirs* (Paris: J.-C. Lattes, 1984), p. 267.

6. Ibid., p. 268.

7. In Hans Peter Kolvenbach, *Fedeli a Dio ed all'Uomo* (Rome, 1990).

8. Woodrow, *Les jésuites, histoire des pouvoirs*, p. 279.

9. Peter Rawlinson, *The Jesuit Factor* (London: Weidenfeld and Nicholson, 1990).

XVII. THE THIRD COMPANY?

1. *Les ordres religieux actifs, la Société de Jésus* (Paris: Flammarion, 1980), p. 680.

2. Jean-Yves Calvez, S.J., *Vivre devant Dieu notre présence au monde* (L'Arbalétière, 1985), p. 7.

3. In *Sur les frontières de l'église* (Paris: Albin-Michel, 1942), p. 4.

4. Feb. 1991, p. 152.

5. Karl Rahner, *Traité fondamental de la foi* (Paris: Le Centurion, 1983), pp. 257–58.

6. K. Rahner, *Discours d'Ignace de Loyola aux jésuites d'aujourd'hui* (Paris: Le Centurion, 1978), p. 72.

7. John Courtney Murray, *We Hold These Truths* (New York: Sheed and Ward, 1985).

8. Ibid., p. ix.

9. Peter Rawlinson, *The Jesuit Factor* (London: Weidenfeld and Nicholson, 1990), p. 127.

10. Louis Beirnaert, *Aux frontières de l'acte analytique* (Paris: Le Seuil, 1987), p. 242.

ELEMENTS OF A BIBLIOGRAPHY*

Antébi, Élisabeth, and Lebrun, François. *Les Jésuites et la Gloire de Dieu.* Paris: Stock-Antébi, 1990.

Arrupe, Pedro, S.J. *Écrits pour évangéliser.* Paris: Desclée de Brouwer, 1985.

———. *Itinéraire d'un jésuite* (with J.-C. Dietsch). Paris: Le Centurion, 1982.

Arsac, Jacques, *et al. Le Savant et la Foi.* Paris: Flammarion, 1989.

Astrain, Antonio. *Histoire de la Compagnie de Jésus en Espagne.* Vol. III, Madrid.

Aubert, Roger. *Le Pontificat de Pie IX,* in Fiche et Martin, *Histoire de l'Église,* Vol. XXX. Paris, Bloud et Gay, 1952.

———. *Vatican I.* Paris: L'Orante, 1964.

Back, Silvio. *Republica Guaraní* (screenplay). Rio de Janeiro: Puz y Terra, 1982.

Bangert, William, S.J. *A History of the Society of Jesus.* Saint Louis: Institute of Jesuit Sources, 1986.

Barthes, Roland. *Sade, Fourier, Loyola.* New York: Hill and Wang, 1976.

Bataillon, Marcel. *Érasme et l'Espagne.* Paris: Droz, 1937.

Baudin, Louis. *Une théocratie socialiste, l'État jésuite du Paraguay.* Paris: Genin, 1962.

Bédarida, Renée. *Pierre Chaillet, témoin de la résistance spirituelle.* Paris: Fayard, 1988.

Beirnaert, Louis, S.J. *Aux frontières de l'acte analytique.* Paris: Le Seuil, 1987.

Bellemare, J.-F. *Le Siècle de fer des jésuites.* Paris: J. G. Dentu, 1828.

Benichou, Paul. *Morales du Grand Siècle.* Paris: Gallimard, 1948.

Bernard-Maître, Henri, S.J. *Aux portes de la Chine.* Shanghai, 1936.

———. *Matteo Ricci et la Société chinoise de son temps.* Tien-Tsin, 1937.

Bertrand, Dominique, S.J. *La Politique de saint Ignace de Loyola.* Preface by Pierre Chaunu. Paris: Le Cerf, 1985.

Bordet, Gaston. *La Pologne, Lamennais et ses amis.* Paris: Éd. du Dialogue, 1985.

Bougainville, Louis-Antoine de. *Voyage autour du monde.* Paris: Maspero–La Découverte, 1980.

Bouhours, Dominique, S.J. *Vie de saint François Xavier.* Lyon: Perissi Frères, 1842.

Brémond, Henri. *Histoire littéraire du sentiment religieux en France.* Vols. IV and V. Paris: Armand Colin, 1967.

Brodrick, James, S.J. *Origins of the Jesuits.* Chicago: Loyola University Press, 1986.

Brou, Alexandre, S.J. *Les Jésuites de la légende.* Paris: 1906, 2 vols.

*Only works mentioned several times in the text are cited here.

————. *Saint François Xavier*. Paris: Beauchesne, 1922.

————. *Cent Ans de missions, 1815–1934*. Paris: Spes, 1935.

Brucker, Joseph, S.J. *La Compagnie de Jésus. Esquisse de son institut et de son histoire, 1521–1773*. Paris, 1919.

Burnichon, Joseph, S.J. *La Compagnie de Jésus en France, Histoire d'un siècle*, 59 vols., Paris: Beauchesne, 1916–20.

Calvez, Jean-Yves, S.J. *La Pensée de Karl Marx*. Paris: Le Seuil, 1956.

————. *Foi et Justice*. Paris: Desclée de Brouwer, 1985.

Capéran, Louis. *Le Salut des infidèles*. Toulouse, 1934.

Casalis, George. *Luther et l'Église confessante*. Paris: Le Seuil, 1962.

Certeau, Michel de. *La Possession de Loudun*. Paris: Julliard-Gallimard, coll. "Archives," 1970.

————. *Le Christianisme éclaté* (with J.-M. Domenach). Paris: Le Seuil, 1974.

————. *L'Écriture et l'Histoire*. Paris: Gallimard, 1975

————. *La Faiblesse de croire*. Paris: Le Seuil, 1987.

Chaillet, Pierre, S.J. *L'Autriche souffrante*. Paris: Bloud et Gay, 1939.

Charles, Pierre, S.J. *Église, sacrement du monde*. Paris: Desclée de Brouwer, 1960.

Charmot, François, S.J. *La Pédagogie des jésuites. Principes et actualité*. Paris: Spes, 1943.

Chatellier, Louis. *L'Europe des dévots*. Paris: Flammarion, 1987.

Chittenden, H. M., and Richardson, A.T. *Life, Letters and Travels of P.-J. De Smet*. 4 vols., New York, 1905.

Cholvy, Gérard, and Hilaire, Yves H. *Histoire religieuse de la France contemporaine*, 3 vol. Toulouse: Privat, 1989–92.

Clair, Charles. *Le R. P. Olivaint, prêtre de la Compagnie de Jésus*. Paris, 1878.

Clastres, Pierre. *Le Grand Parler. Mythes et chants sacrés des Indiens Guaranís*. Paris: Le Seuil, 1974.

Courtney Murray, John, S.J. *We Hold These Truths*. London and New York: Sheed and Ward, 1961.

Crétineau-Joly, Jacques. *Histoire religieuse, politique et littéraire de la Compagnie de Jésus*. Paris-Lyon, 1844–46, 6 vols.

————. *Clement XIV et les Jésuites*. Paris: 1847.

Cronin, Vincent. *The Wise Man from the West*. London: Rupert Hart-Davis, 1955.

Cuénot, Claude. *Pierre Teilhard de Chardin*. Baltimore, 1969.

Dainville, François de, S.J. *La Naissance de l'humanisme moderne*. Paris: Éditions de Paris, 1940.

————. *L'Éducation des jésuites aux XVIIème et XVIIIème siècles*. Paris: INRP, 1978.

————. *La Géographie des humanistes*. Paris: Beauchesne, 1940.

Dalmasès, Candido de, S.J. *Ignace de Loyola, le fondateur des jésuites*. Paris: Le Centurion, 1984.

Dansette, Adrien. *Histoire religieuse de la France contemporaine*, vol. II. Paris: Flammarion, 1951.

Delumeau, Jean. *La Civilisation de la Renaissance*. Paris: Arthaud, 1967.

Derville, André, S.J. *et al*. *Les Jésuites, spiritualité et activités*. Paris: Beauchesne, 1974.

De Smet, Pierre-Jean, S.J. *Voyages aux montagnes Rocheuses*. Brussels: Devaux, 1873.

————. *Lettres choisies*. Brussels: Closson, 1878.

Dhôtel, Jean-Claude, S.J. *Les Jésuites de France*. Paris: Desclée de Brouwer, 1986.

Duchêne, Roger. *L'Imposture littéraire dans les Provinciales de Pascal*. Université d'Aix-Marseille, 1985.

Duclos, Paul, S.J., in *Dictionnaire du monde religieux dans la France contemporaine*, Vol. I, *Les Jésuites*. Paris: Beauchesne, 1985.

Dudon, Paul, S.J. *Saint Ignace de Loyola*. Paris: Beauchesne, 1934.

Duquesne, Jacques. *Les Catholiques français sous l'Occupation*. Paris: Grasset, 1986.

Durkheim, Émile. *Education and Sociology*. Trans. S. Fox. New York: Free Press, 1956.

Étiemble, René. *La Querelle des rites*. Paris: Julliard, 1966.

————. *L'Europe chinoise*. Paris: Gallimard, 1988, 2 vols.

Ezran, Maurice. *Une colonisation douce: les missions du Paraguay*. Paris: L'Harmattan, 1989.

Febvre, Lucien. *Au Coeur religieux du XVIème siècle*, EPHESS. Paris: Le Livre de Poche, 1983.

Fessard, Gaston, S.J., *Pax nostra*. Paris: Grasset, 1935.

————. *Épreuve de force*. Paris: Bloud et Gay, 1939.

Foulon, Louis. *Histoire de Mgr Darboy*. Paris, 1889.

Fouqueray, Henri, S.J. *Histoire de la Compagnie de Jésus en France*. Paris: Picard, 1910–25, 5 vols.

François Xavier. *Correspondance (1535–1552)*. Paris: Desclée de Brouwer, 1987.

Friedländer, Saül. *Pie XII et le IIIᵉ Reich*. Paris: Le Seuil, 1964.

Fülop-Miller, René. *Les Jésuites et le Secret de leur puissance*. Paris: Plon, 1933, 2 vols.

Fumaroli, Marc. *L'Âge de l'éloquence. Rhétorique et "res literaria" au seuil de l'époque classique*, EPHE. Geneva: Droz, 1980.

Gagarin, Ivan, S.J. *Un nonce du pape à la cour de Catherine II*. Paris, 1872.

Garragan, Gilbert, S.J. *The Jesuits of Middle America, 1840–1910*. New York: America Press, 1938.

Garrisson, Janine. *L'Édit de Nantes et sa révocation*. Paris: Le Seuil, 1985.

Gauthier, Robert. *Dreyfusard!* Paris: Julliard, 1974.

Gernet, Jacques. *Chine et Christianisme. Action et réaction*. Paris: Gallimard, 1982.

Girardet, Raoul. *Mythes et Mythologies politiques*. Paris: Le Seuil, 1896.

Giuliani, Maurice, S.J. "L'expérience des Exercices spirituels dans la vie," *Christus*. Paris: DDB, 1990.

Godwin, Joscelyn. *Athanasius Kircher*. London and New York: Thames and Hudson, 1979.

Gonçalves da Câmara, Luis. *Mémorial*. Paris: Desclée de Brouwer, 1966.

Gracian y Moralès, Baltasar, S.J. *La Pointe ou l'Art du génie*. Paris: L'Âge d'homme, 1983.

Grœthuysen, Bernard. *Origines de l'esprit bourgeois en France*. Paris: Gallimard, 1927.

Guibert, Joseph de, S.J. *La Spiritualité de la Compagnie de Jésus*. Rome: IHSI, 1953.

Guichard, Alain. *Les Jésuites*. Paris: Grasset, 1974.

Guillermou, Alain. *La Vie de saint Ignace de Loyola*. Paris: Le Seuil, 1956

————. *Saint Ignace de Loyola et la Compagnie de Jésus*. Paris: Le Seuil, 1960.

————. *Les Jésuites*. Paris: Presses universitaires de France. 1961.

Guillet, Jacques, S.J. *La Théologie catholique en France, 1914–1960.* Média-Sèvres, 1988.

Guitton, Georges, S.J. *Le R. P. de La Chaize, confesseur de Louis XIV.* Paris: Beauchesne, 1959.

Haubert, Maxime. *La Vie quotidienne des Indiens et des jésuites au Paraguay.* Paris: Hachette, 1986.

Ignatius Loyola. *A Pilgrim's Journey: The Autobiography.* Trans. Joseph Tylenda. Collegeville, Minn.: Liturgical Press, 1991.

———. *Lettres.* Paris: Desclée de Brouwer, 1959.

———. *Journal spirituel.* Paris: Desclée de Brouwer, 1959.

———. *The Spiritual Exercises.* Trans. Anthony Mottola. Garden City, N.Y.: Image, 1964.

Imbart de La Tour, Pierre. *Les Origines de la Réforme en France.* Melun: Librairie d'Argences, 1948.

Jacquin, Robert. *Tapparelli.* Paris, 1943.

Julia, Dominique. "Le catholicisme, religion du royaume, 1715–1789," in *Histoire de la France religieuse* (coll.). Paris: Le Seuil, 1991, vol. III.

Kolvenbach, Peter Hans, S.J. *Vous avez dit jésuite* (entretiens), trans. from the Italian. Paris, 1991.

Küng, Hans. *Does God Exist?* Trans. E. Quinn. New York: Doubleday, 1980.

Laberge, Jacques, S.J. *Pierre Teilhard de Chardin et Ignace de Loyola.* Paris: Desclée de Brouwer, 1983.

Lac, Stanislas du, S.J. *Jésuites.* Paris: Plon, 1901.

Lapide, Pinhas. *Rome et les Juifs.* Paris: Le Seuil, 1967.

Laveille, Eugène, S.J. *Le Père De Smet.* Liège, 1913.

Leclerc, Joseph, S.J. *Histoire de la tolérance au siècle de la Réforme.* Paris: Aubier, 1955.

Lécrivain, Philippe, S.J. *Les Missions jésuites.* Paris: Gallimard, 1991.

Le Goff, Jacques, and Rémond, René. *Histoire de la France religieuse.* Vol. III. Paris: Le Seuil, 1992.

Léon-Dufour, Xavier, S.J. *Saint François Xavier. Itinéraire mystique de l'apôtre.* Paris: La Colombe, 1953.

Le Roy Ladurie, Emmanuel. *L'Histoire de France,* vol. III, *L'Ancien Régime, 1610–1774.* Paris: Hachette, 1991.

Leturia, Pedro de, S.J. *El Gentilhombre Iñigo Lopez de Loyola en su patria y en su siglo.* Montevideo, 1938.

Ligthart, Cornelius, S.J. *Le Retour des jésuites au XIXème siècle:* le R. P. Roothaan. Namur: Culture et Vérité, 1991.

Longchamp, Albert, S.J. *Petite Vie de Ignace de Loyola.* Paris: Desclée de Brouwer, 1989.

Lubac, Henri de, S.J. *Catholicisme.* Paris, 1938.

———. *La Pensée religieuse de Pierre Teilhard de Chardin.* Paris: Aubier-Montaigne, 1962.

Lugon, Clovis. *La République des Guaranís, les jésuites au pouvoir.* Paris: Édition Économie et Humanisme, 1970.

MacNaspy, Clement, S.J. *Lost Cities of Paraguay.* Chicago, 1982.

Madelin, Henri, S.J. *La Menace idiologique.* Paris: Éditions du Cerf, 1988.

Marcuse, Léon. *Ignace de Loyola, le dictateur des âmes.* Paris: Payot, 1936.

Margolin, Jean-Claude. *Érasme.* Paris: Le Seuil, 1967.

Marrou, Henri-Irénée. *Saint Augustin et l'Augustinisme.* Paris: Le Seuil, 1978.

Maupied, Mgr. *Le Syllabus.* Paris, 1872.

Mauriac, François, *Blaise Pascal et sa soeur Jacqueline.* Paris: Hachette, 1931.

———. *Men I Hold Great.* Trans. Elsie Pell. New York: Philosophica Press, 1951.

Métraux, Alfred. *La Civilisation matérielle des Tupi-Guaranis.* Paris, 1928.

Michelet, Jules, and Quinet, Edgar. *Les Jésuites.* Paris, 1843.

———. *Le Prêtre, la Femme, la Famille,* in *Oeuvres complètes.* Paris: Flammarion, 1882.

Minois, George. *Le Confesseur du roi: les directeurs de conscience sous la monarchie française.* Paris: Fayard, 1988.

———. *L'Église et la Science.* Paris: Fayard, 1990.

Moisy, Pierre. *Les Églises des jésuites de l'ancienne Assistance de France.* Rome, 1958.

Mörner, Magnus. *The Political and Economic Activities of Jesuits in the Plata Region.* Stockholm, 1953.

Morlot, François. *Pierre de Clorivière.* Paris: Desclée de Brouwer, 1990.

Mortier, Jeanne, and Auboux, M.-L. *Teilhard de Chardin, images et paroles.* Paris: Le Seuil, 1966.

Muratori, Antonio. *Relation des missions du Paraguay.* Paris: Maspero-La Découverte, 1983.

Mus, Paul. *Hô Chi Minh, le Vietnam, l'Asie.* Paris: Le Seuil, 1971.

Namer, Émile. *L'Affaire Galilée.* Paris: Julliard, 1975

Nobécourt, Jacques. *"Le Vicaire" et l'Histoire.* Paris: Le Seuil, 1964.

Orcibal, Jean. *Saint-Cyran et le Jansénisme.* Paris: Le Seuil, 1961.

Ouince, René d', S.J. *Un prophète en procès: Pierre Teilhard de Chardin dans l'Église de son temps.* Paris: Aubier, 1970.

Padberg, John W. *Colleges in Controversy.* Cambridge, Mass.: Harvard University Press, 1969.

Pascal, Blaise. *The Provincial Letters.* Trans. A. J. Krailshammer. New York: Penguin, 1967.

Pastor, Ludwig von. *Histoire des papes,* vol. XVI. Paris: Plon, 1962.

Peyrefitte, Alain. *Le Choc des cultures.* Paris: Fayard, 1991.

Pierre Favre, *Mémorial.* Paris: Desclée de Brouwer, 1959.

Philibert, Anne. "Problèmes religieux du monde contemporain dans *Études*" (thesis). Paris, 1986.

Pierrard, Pierre. *Les Papes et la France.* Paris: Fayard, 1982.

Prat, J.-M., S.J. *Histoire de la Compagnie de Jésus au temps du père Coton.* Paris, 1831.

Quicherat, Jules. *Histoire de Sainte-Barbe, collège et institution.* Paris: Hachette, 1864.

Rahner, Hugo, S.J. *Ignace de Loyola et les femmes de son temps.* Paris: Desclée de Brouwer, 1964, 2 vols.

Rahner, Karl, S.J. *Discours d'Ignace de Loyola aux jésuites d'aujourd'hui.* Paris: Le Centurion, 1978.

———. *Foundations of Christian Faith.* New York: Crossroad, 1978.

Rasiel da Silva, Hercule. *Histoire de l'admirable Dom Inigo de Guipuzcoa.* The Hague: Le Vier, 1736.

Ravier, André, S.J. *Ignace de Loyola fonde la Compagnie de Jésus.* Paris: Desclée de Brouwer, 1973.

———. *Les Chroniques de saint Ignace.* Paris: Desclée de Brouwer, 1973

Ravignan, Xavier de, S.J. *De l'existence et de l'Institut des jésuites.* Paris: Poussielgue, 1844.

Rawlinson, Lord Peter. *The Jesuit Factor.* London: Weidenfeld and Nicholson, 1990.

Rébérioux, Madeleine. *La République radicale.* Paris: Le Seuil, 1975.

Redondi, Pietro. *Galilée hérétique.* Paris: Gallimard, 1985.

Reischauer, Edwin O. *Japan.* New York: Knopf, 1990.

Rhodes, Alexandre de, S.J. *Voyages et Missions.* Paris, 1864.

———. *Histoire du royaume de Tonkin.* Paris, 1864.

Ricci, Matteo. *China in the 16th Century.* Trans. Louis Gallagher. New York: Random House, 1953.

Rideau, Émile, S.J. *La Pensée du père Pierre Teilhard de Chardin.* Paris: Le Seuil, 1965.

Riquet, Michel, S.J. *Chrétiens de France dans l'Europe enchaînée.* Paris: SOS, 1972.

———. *Augustin de Barruel, un jésuite face aux jacobins francs-maçons.* Paris: Beauchesne, 1989.

Rochemonteix, P. de, S.J. *Nicolas Caussin et le Cardinal de Richelieu.* Paris, 1911.

Rogier, L. J., *et al. Nouvelle Histoire de l'Église.* Vols. IV and V. Paris: Le Seuil, 1986.

Sainte-Beuve, Charles-Augustin. *Port-Royal.* Paris, 1902. 5 vols.

Sallentin, Xavier. *Le monde n'est pas malade, il enfante.* Édition S.O.E.I.L., Fondation Bena, 1989.

Schmidt, Albert-Marie. *Jean Calvin et la Tradition calviniste.* Paris: Le Seuil, 1957.

Schurhammer, Georg, S.J. *Francis Xavier, His Life, His Time.* Rome, 1982. 4 vols.

Skinner, Quentin. *Machiavelli.* New York: Hill and Wang, 1981.

Sommet, Jacques, S.J. *L'Honneur de la liberté* (avec C. Ehlinger). Paris: Le Centurion, 1987.

Sorge, Bartolomeo. *Uscire dal Tempio.* Gênes, 1989.

Spence, Jonathan. *The Memory Palace of Matteo Ricci.* New York: Viking, 1985.

Teilhard de Chardin, Pierre, S.J. *Écrits du temps de guerre.* Paris: Grasset, 1965.

———. *The Phenomenon of Man.* Trans. Julian Huxley. New York: Harper, 1965.

———. *The Divine Milieu.* New York: Harper, 1965.

———. *Lettres familières au R. P. Leroy.* Paris: Le Centurion, 1986.

Tellechea Idigoras, Ignacio, S.J. *Ignace de Loyola pèlerin de l'absolu.* Paris: Nouvelle Cité, 1990.

Valadier, Paul, S.J. *L'Église en procès.* Paris: Calmann-Lévy, 1987.

———. *Inévitable Morale.* Paris: Le Seuil, 1990.

Valignano, Alessandro. *Les Jésuites au Japon: relation missionnaire (1583).* Paris: Desclée de Brouwer, 1990.

Vallin, Pierre, S.J. "Pierre de Clorivière en son temps," in *Christus,* no. 131.

———. "Un projet de société à travers l'éducation," in *Politique et Mystique chez les jésuites.* Centre Sèvres, 1989.

Varillon, François, S.J. (with C. Ehlinger). *Beauté du monde et Souffrance des hommes*. Paris: Le Centurion, 1980.

Vaux (de) et Riondel, S.J. *Le R. P. Roothaan*. Paris, 1935.

Viel-Castel. *Histoire de la Restauration*. Paris: Levy, 1860–78.

Wachtel, Nathan. *La Vision des vaincus*. Paris: Gallimard, 1971.

Woodrow, Alain. *Les Jésuites, Histoire de pouvoirs*. Paris: Jean-Claude Lattès, 1990.

Zelenski, Stanislas, S.J. *Les Jésuites en Russie blanche*. Paris: Letouzey, 1874.

INDEX

Boulet, Abbé, 380
Bouli, Simon, 379
Bourdet, Claude, 379
Bourdier-Delpuits, Abbé, 324, 325
Bourges, Florentin de, 240
Boynes, Norbert de, 386, 387–90, 473n
Bradina, Lucretia de, 152
Brasanelli, Giuseppe, 228–29
Braschi, Gianangelo, see Pius VI
Brébeuf, Jean de, 373
Breuil, Henri, 407, 410, 422
Brion, Marcel, 420
Broët, Paschase (Pasquier), 52, 72, 77
Broglie, Charles de, 317, 319
Bruno, Giordano, 439
Brzozowski, Tadeusz, 312, 326, 336, 342
Buber, Martin, 441
Buchanan, George, 52
Buddhism, 200–201, 222
Budé, Guillaume, 4, 106
Buentempo, Francesco, 293
Buffon, Georges Leclerc de, 231, 263
Burdo, Christian, 407
Burnichon, Joseph, 321, 323, 334–35, 346

Cabral, João, 124
Cáceres, Lope de, 26, 45
Cahiers du Témoignage chrétien, 392–93,
    396–99, 400, 432
Calixto de Sá, 26, 31, 32, 45
Calvez, Jean-Yves, 464, 465, 467, 474, 478
Calvin, John, 36, 85
Calvinism, 53, 78
Campanella, Tommaso, 238, 252
Campomanes, Ruiz de, 285, 286
Canaye, Father, 357
Canisius, Peter, 79, 80, 348, 351
Cano, Melchor, 81–82, 143, 352
Caraman, Philip, 252
Cardenal, Fernando, 476
Cardoner revelation, 19–20
Carli, Luigi, 451
Carmelite Sisters, 456–57
Carroll, John, 488
Cartier, Jacques, 106
Carvalho, Sebastião de, Marquês de
    Pombal, 248, 263, 265–67, 277, 283, 285,
    287, 372

Casaroli, Cardinal, 434–35, 473, 495
Casas, Bartolomé de las, 231–33, 236, 245
Cassiano, Matteo di, 143
Castile, see Spain
Castro, Americo, 162–63
Castro, Juan de, 44
Cataldino, Giuseppe, 227–28, 240, 243–44
Catalina (Catherine), Princess, 9, 138–39,
    145–46, 265
Catherine II (Catherine the Great), em-
    press of Russia, 299, 302, 306–14, 315
Catholicae fidei (papal brief), 313
Catholic Church:
    and aggiornamento, 460, 461
    and anti-Semitism, 439–55
    Armenian rite of, 311, 497
    and Council of Trent, 80
    and democracy, 487–88
    and evolution, 410–11, 424, 425, 430; see
        also Teilhard de Chardin, Pierre
    and Fascism, 381–83
    in France, 37, 279, 280–81, 318–19, 337,
        339, 355, 375–76, 381
    and Germany, 380, 381
    Greek and Roman, 311, 497
    Jesuits as scapegoats for, 469
    and Laínez, 168
    in Latin America, see Latin America
    legitimacy of, 53
    and Marxism, 380
    and pluralism, 487–88, 496
    reforms in, 62–63, 65, 80, 448, 460,
        484–85
    revisionist party in, 449
    and sack of Rome, 62
    and salvation, 482, 485
    and social justice, 464
    in Spain, 6
    and worker-priests, 469–70, 482, 486
    and World War II, 380–81, 387–88
Cattaneo, Father, 209, 230
Céline, Louis-Ferdinand, 386
Central America, see Latin America
Cereceda, Feliciano, 168, 169, 172
Céspedes, Luis de, 246
Chaillet, Pierre, 379, 385, 392–93, 395–99
Chamberlain, Houston Stewart, 172
Chambre, Henri, 379, 380, 398, 402

Nicolás I, king of Paraguay, 249, 266, 285
Nieuville, Father de, 273
Ninjitsu (Ninxit), 117–18, 119
Noailles, Alexis de, 325
Nobili, Roberto de, 104, 124
Nobrega, Manuel de, 232
Nobunaga Oda, 108
Noël, André, 379
North America:
 Indians in, 373–75
 Jesuits active in, 373–75, 486–90
 religious freedom in, 488
 Revolution in, 262
 social justice in, 463
 Teilhard in, 428, 430, 431

O'Keefe, Vincent, 467, 473–74
Oñaz, clan of, 7, 10
O'Neill, Charles, 65
Ordeix, Pey, 164
Orlandini, Father, 170
Ormesson, Wladimir d', 383
Orsini, Cardinal, 291
Ortiz, Pedro, 44, 45, 65, 67
Ory, Mathieu, 45, 55, 59, 67
Ottaviani, Cardinal, 487–88
Ouince, René d', 405–6, 407–8, 409–10,
 411, 413, 421, 424, 428, 430, 431

Paccanari, Niccola, 319–20, 323, 364
Palafox, Juan de, 282n
Pallavicini, Cardinal, 301, 310, 312
Pananiapappi, Chief, 373
Panici, Paul, 378, 390
Pantoja, Diego de, 211, 218, 224
Papal States, see Rome
Papen, Franz von, 381
Paragressa, Angelo, 228
Paraguay:
 Guaraní territory in, 233–34
 Jesuits in, 83, 84–85, 227–60
 reductions in, 237–47
 see also Guaraní Republic
Paris:
 Catholicism in, 37
 humanism in, 35, 36
 Inquisitor in, 45

as intellectual center, 35–39
 journey to, 33–34, 37
 Loyola in, 37–59
 and modus parisiensis, 34, 160
 University of, 38, 39–44, 53–55
 see also France
Pascal, Blaise, 372, 484
 and Jansenists, 262, 355, 356
 Lettres of, 262, 344, 345, 351, 354, 355, 356,
 357, 361, 367
 and Teilhard, 406
Pascual, Inès, 22, 26, 140
Pasio, Francesco, 183
Pasquier, Étienne, 262, 275, 344, 348,
 352–54, 364, 369, 372, 439
Pastor, Ludwig von, 285, 290, 308
Paul I, emperor of Russia, 312, 313, 314, 333
Paul III, Pope, 6, 329, 352
 and converted Jews, 89
 and Council of Trent, 80
 and reforms, 62–63, 65, 80
 and Society, 66–67, 69, 71–72, 76–77
 and women, 71, 137, 149, 152, 153–54
Paul IV, Pope, 95, 97, 165, 438, 452, 486,
 494–95
Paul VI, Pope, 452, 460, 462–64, 466–68
Paulistas, 229, 238
Paulo de Santa Fé, see Anjiro
Pax nostra (Fessard), 382, 392–93, 400
Péguy, Charles, 397
Peking Man, 415–16, 424
Pelayo, Menéndez, 284
Pelletier, Jean, 88
Peña, Juan de la, 47, 49
Peralta, Miguel, 44
Perez, Francisco, 180–81
Périer, Casimir, 346
Pétain, Marshal Philippe, 378, 379, 387,
 388–89, 391–93
Peter I (Peter the Great), tsar of Russia,
 306, 307, 314
Phénomène humain, Le (Teilhard), 405,
 418, 419–20, 423, 432, 436, 495
Philip II, king of Spain, 91, 150, 155, 170,
 172, 179, 263, 325
Philip IV, king of Spain, 242, 247
Philip V, king of Spain, 248, 283

in World War II, 387
Russo, Father, 436

Sá, Calixto de, 26, 31, 32, 45
Sacchini, Paolo, 170–73
Sainsaulieu, Jean, 202, 223, 225
Sainte-Beuve, Charles-Augustin, 354
Saint-Évremond, Charles de, 357–58, 364
Saint-Exupéry, Antoine de, 424
Sakyamuni, 200
Salamanca, Loyola in, 31–33
Salièges, Monsignor, 398
Salmerón, Alfonso, 51–52
  and Council of Trent, 80
  mission to Ireland, 77
  and Society's foundation, 57, 59, 72
Salvador, 490–93
Sánchez, Alonso, 174, 181
Sánchez, Matteo (pseud.), 155–58
Sanda, Duarte de, 197
San Estéban, Dominicans in, 31–33
Santa Maria della Strada, 75, 76
Sarre, Charles-Alain, 278
Sarte, Pedro de, 164
Satanka, Chief, 375
Sauvigny, Bertier de, 325
Savonarola, Girolamo, 4, 62, 85
Schillebeekx, Edward, 102, 460n
Schmidt, Stepan, 450, 451
Schoell, historian, 284
Schurhammer, Georg, 51
Seneca, 201, 203
Senghor, Léopold Sédar, 433n
Sept, 383
Sherman, Gen. William Tecumseh, 375
Siestrzenciewitz, Stanislas, 309–11
Siliceo, Martínez, 163, 166, 172
Silva, Pedro da, 110, 113, 116
Silva, Ruy Gómez da, 166
Simon, Robert, 395
Simpson (Sionnet), Father, 341, 343
Siri, Cardinal, 447
Sismondi, Sismonde de, 271
Sisters of Saint Joseph, 159
Sisters of the Sacred Heart, 159–60
Sitting Bull, 373
Si Ye, 205

Skarza, 173
Sobrino, Jon, 491
Society of Fathers of the Sacred Heart of
  Jesus, 317–19, 342, 364
Society of Jesus:
  accomplished works of, 87–90
  and acculturation, 135, 185–86
  action vs. predestination in, 87
  anthropological approach of, 104, 108
  anti-Jesuit campaigns, 261–97, 348–77
  caricature of, 350–51
  communal prayer renounced by, 70
  concertation of, 126n
  as confessors of kings and popes, 264,
    271, 444, 463
  Congregations of, 464–66, 476–77, 481,
    486, 495, 496
  Constitutions of, 70, 76, 82, 83–84, 85, 92,
    93, 94, 136, 273–74, 277, 363, 470
  debates on organization of, 68–71
  Decree Four, 465–69, 477–78, 495, 496
  democratization of, 464–66, 470, 487–88
  and direct reference to Jesus, 69
  Dominicans vs., 81
  dual nature of, 348–50
  education as task of, 46, 68–69, 76, 88,
    104, 263, 274–75, 281, 302, 304–5, 307,
    313, 340–41, 346, 351, 352, 368, 480, 486
  "ejector seat" arrangement, 462
  and exclusion principle, 102, 103
  "First Formula" of, 69–71
  first Superior General of, 72–74
  foundation of, 56–59, 68–71
  Generalate-for-life, 70, 462
  government by correspondence in, 496
  help and refuge to, 299–327
  initials of, 69
  inventory of conscience of, 400
  and John Paul II, 469–78
  in Latin America, *see* Guaraní Republic;
    Latin America
  and law of possibilities, 58
  and lay circles, 324
  and liberalism, 339–43, 376–77, 495
  and local authority, 187, 204, 211
  Loyola's instructions to, 77–78
  military myth of, 35, 64, 79

Society of Jesus (cont.)